SPEECH & POWER

The African-American Essay and Its Cultural Content, from Polemics to Pulpit
VOLUME 2

Edited by

GERALD EARLY

THE ECCO PRESS

The Ecco Press
100 West Broad Street
Hopewell, NJ 08525
Published simultaneously in Canada by
Penguin Books Canada Ltd., Ontario
Printed in the United States of America

Designed by Richard Oriolo

First Edition

Library of Congress Cataloging-in-Publication Data
(Revised for vol. 2)

Speech and power : the African-American essay and its
cultural content from polemics to pulpit.

(Dark tower series)
Vol. 2 has title : Speech and power.
Includes bibliographical references and indexes.
1. American essays—Afro–American authors.
2. Afro-Americans—Civilization.   I. Early, Gerald Lyn.
II. Speech & power.   III. Series.
PS683.A35S64   1990   814′.5080896073   90-49746
ISBN 0-88001-264-1
ISBN 0-88001-333-8 (v. 2)

The text of this book is set in Electra.

The editor would like to thank
Adele Tuchler, Raye Riggins, Catherine Rankovic,
Ida Early, and Ellen Rabin
for proofreading.

To Lenora and Rosalind,
with Brotherly Affection and
Sincerest Gratitude

CONTENTS

PART III: CULTURAL AND POLITICAL ESSAYS

PART IV: AFRICA AND THE AMERICAN BLACK

PART V: WASHINGTON'S COLORED ARISTOCRACY

PART VI: AUTOBIOGRAPHY

DISPERSION, DILATION, DELATION*

The editor wishes to direct readers to the introduction of the first
volume of *Speech and Power* for a fuller explanation of the African-
American essay and the occasion for these two collections.

That *Speech and Power* began as a considerably more modest project than
its final product will attest is attributable not so much to the editor's
laziness in the beginning or to an arrogance that would have him produce
a book that would be so large that no one would ever refer to it, as to his sheer
inability to resist falling in love with his work. At first there were to be 25 or so
essays by 25 or so black writers—the most famous, I might add. But the project
grew, dilated, not because I began to add more and more essays but because I felt
the need to categorize the essays, to disperse them as, say, Wordsworth or Robert
Frost their poetry, under headings. Having headings, categories, conferred, I felt,
an added weight to the essays. Perhaps they seemed a bit thin and lonely in one
long table-of-contents column of 25 or so, a bit too insubstantial to constitute a
book that ought to be taken seriously. This all may very well be the inferiority
complex of the essay writer, which I am. But dispersing the essays meant more had
to be added to any given section to make it truly a category of thought, of classifica-
tion, of legitimate notice.

As I continued to work on this project, I grew to love essays—that is to say, I
grew to love reading them and preferred like heck not to have to write them. I do
not think I loved essays before, when I was confined to merely writing them. In
fact, I was beginning to find doing essays a bit of chore, a labor for which there was
little enough reward, because, after all, doing essays told readers not that in the end
few subjects are worthy of the dilation of a full-length book, but simply that you,
poor little essayist, were incapable of writing one. Collecting essays made me feel
a great deal less inadequate as a writer. This seemed close to a public service,
especially in this day and age, when putting out any kind of collection of black
writing is bound, if not to make money (I can certainly bear witness to that), clearly
to be seen as a restoration of the lost voices of the race or some such business as

that. These days Black writing is a great deal like sex: No one can get enough of it—enough, that is, of Negroes talking about being Negroes. Or perhaps a more apt analogy is, as my daughter says, that it's a great deal like eating potato chips, which, as she tells me, is much like eating the hollow bones of birds. In either case, one hopes that this might become—pleasant as this turn of events is for even an absolutely unknown black writer like myself—something more of a fad than either sex or potato chips, since eventually blacks may wish to talk about more than themselves at some point, or be permitted, like white folks, to mis-know any number of subjects as well as they mis-know themselves. In any event, I even began to wonder if I could not after all make a living collecting other people's essays, asking other people to write essays for volumes, and the like.

But after going through the process of putting together *Speech and Power*, I returned to writing essays with a greater understanding of what the art was about, a certain deepening of the consciousness or should I say a kind of expansion of my unconsciousness, which seems a very 1960s assertion, but is, nonetheless, true. I understood that implied in virtually every essay I read by a black writer was the act of delation, an act of accusation (not necessarily against whites or against racism, which of course is always there for a black writer as his "natural endowment," so to speak, but against the absurdity of the necessity of the task at hand) balanced by an act of reporting (the importance of putting down an idea, an event, aright because there is always this sense as a black in this society that one is being misreported as well as misinterpreted). Black essay-writing can be considered a sort of standing-behind-the-arras work, being "a spy in the enemy camp," as the grandfather said in Ralph Ellison's *Invisible Man*. An essay is, in an odd yet compelling way, a revelation, an uncovering of something that is hidden that may have been obtained while in hiding. Yet there is something about an essay that remains intractably covert, a discourse of misdirection. After reading an essay on performance magic, one of my auditors said the essay itself was one of the greatest feats of legerdemain she had ever witnessed.

But an essay must be both covert and revealing because of the enormous risk involved. Ultimately the essayist brings to the essay only himself. In fact, that is both the essay's trick and its test, how well one can penetrate using only one's own immediately reachable resources to perfect, to bring off, a piece of writing whose tendency is to announce its own ephemeral nature as a contradiction of the strenuous demands of the effort. Writing an essay, especially a good personal essay, is much like trying to write a very good letter while in a very narrow confinement. This is the discipline of the essay. This volume contains a number of impressive personal essays, including an entire autobiographical section, as well as a range of essays on black aesthetic issues, including a healthy section on the black writer. Nearly all the significant black writers are here and some of my favorites by them, such as Langston Hughes on the black bourgeoisie in Washington, Ken McClane on his brother's death, Zora Neale Hurston on "Begging Joints," Bert Williams on black (pun intended) comedy, and especially William Melvin Kelly's "The Ivy League Negro" (more than slightly autobiographical for the editor himself).

Scott Russell Sanders put it best when he said about his own personal essays: "I meant to preserve and record and help give voice to a reality that existed independently of me. I meant to pay my respects to a minor passage of history in an out-of-the-way place. I felt responsible to the truth as known by other people. I wanted to speak directly out of my own life into the lives of others."**

So here, dispersed across these two volumes, is the black essayist as dilator and delator, speaking in many voices of realities and truths and failures and mis-sightings, some of which, I am sure, will only more poignantly remind all of us, black and white, of how much we are all extracting from the same small and precarious resources.

NOTES

* The title for this introduction was inspired by a talk given by Professor Patricia Parker, a Renaissance scholar at Stanford University whose talk was on Othello and Hamlet. I cannot in any way say that I use her terms in the way she used them or nearly as deftly. But as I heard the talk, almost instantly they seemed to me extremely useful to my attempt to get a handle on a very slippery subject indeed.

** Scott Russell Sanders, "The Singular First Person," in Alexander J. Butrym (ed.), *Essays on the Essay: Redefining The Genre*, Athens: The University of Georgia Press, 1989, p. 41.

I

The Arts,
Blacks in the Arts,
the Black American
Artist and His or
Her Audience

This group of essays generally deals with blacks and their connection to or interest in the arts other than literature, including music and the plastic arts. Subjects range from Alfred Stieglitz to the distortion of the black experience as presented in the film *Gone with the Wind*, the most popular American film in the history of cinema.

THE COMIC SIDE
OF TROUBLE

BERT WILLIAMS (1874 or 1875–1922) was one of the
most successful black comedians of his day. He and his partner, George
Walker, toured the United States and Europe and became a leading
vaudeville act. "The Comic Side of Trouble" is the only such essay that
Williams is known to have written. Combining autobiography,
Williams's protest against racism, and an account of his theory of
comedy, it is an insightful and important work. It appeared in the
American Magazine, January 1918.

O ne of the funniest sights in the world is a man whose hat has been
knocked in or ruined by being blown off—provided, of course, it be the
other fellow's hat! All the jokes in the world are based on a few elemental
ideas, and this is one of them. The sight of other people in trouble is nearly always
funny. This is human nature. If you will observe your own conduct whenever you
see a friend falling down on the street, you will find that nine times out of ten your
first impulse is to laugh and your second is to run and help him get up. To be polite
you will dust off his clothes and ask him if he has hurt himself. But when it is all
over you cannot resist telling him how funny he looked when he was falling. The
man with the real sense of humor is the man who can put himself in the spectator's
place and laugh at his own misfortunes.

That is what I am called upon to do every day. Nearly all of my successful
songs have been based on the idea that I am getting the worst of it. I am the "Jonah
Man," the man who, even if it rained soup, would be found with a fork in his hand
and no spoon in sight, the man whose fighting relatives come to visit him and
whose head is always dented by the furniture they throw at each other. There are
endless variations of this idea, fortunately; but if you sift them, you will find the
principle of human nature at the bottom of them all. The song of the "Slippery

Ellum Tree" at first sight seems to be different. It starts as a parody, if you remember, on George P. Morris's "Woodman, Spare That Tree." But the tree resolves itself into a peg on which I hang my troubles. It is the tree I climb when I am running away from my wife, my refuge whenever there is a ruction, a hiding place from my wife's relations, my creditors, the police and the dog next door.

Troubles are funny only when you pin them to one particular individual. And that individual, the fellow who is the goat, must be the man who is singing the song or telling the story. Then the audience can picture him in their mind's eye and see him in the thick of his misfortunes, fielding flatirons with his head, carrying large bulldogs by the seat of his pants, and picking the bare bones of the chicken while his wife's relations eat the breast, and so forth.

It was not until I was able to see myself as another person that my sense of humor developed. For I do not believe there is any such thing as innate humor. It has to be developed by hard work and study, just as every other human quality. I have studied it all my life, unconsciously during my floundering years, and consciously as soon as I began to get next to myself. It is a study that I shall never get to the end of, and a work that never stops, except when I am asleep. There are no union hours to it and no let-up. It is only by being constantly on the lookout for fresh material, funny incidents, funny speeches, funny traits in human nature that a comedian can hope to keep step with his public.

I find much material by knocking around in out of the way places and just listening. For among the American colored men and negroes there is the greatest source of simple amusement you can find anywhere in the world. The London 'bus-drivers, in the days before motor 'buses, were famous for their funny repartees. But Americans for the most part know little about the unconscious humor of the colored people and negroes, because they do not come in contact with them. A short while ago I heard an argument between two men. One of them was pretty cocky and tried to bulldoze the other, who was trying his best to be peaceable, and kept saying, "I don't want no trouble with you now." Presently it got too warm for him, and the peaceable man turned to the other and said, "Looka hyah, nigga, you better get away fum me, 'cause I'm jes' going to take this bottle an' bathe your head with it." Of course I put that line into the Follies the next day.

Many of the best lines I have used came to me by that sort of eavesdropping. For, as I have pointed out, eavesdropping on human nature is one of the most important parts of a comedian's work. Sometimes one hears and sees things too funny to be used. For instance, during the mobilization of the Fifteenth Regiment of the New York National Guard, a husky colored private was standing in the crowded armory eating a fried chicken. The rest of his company had had to be content with regular army fare, perfectly good, healthful food, the sort that stays with a man, as the soldiers say, but few of them had sweethearts to bring them such delicacies as chicken. A couple of men strolled past him quietly, and without any warning, one of them rapped him sharply on the wrist so that the chicken fell out of his hand, and the other caught it neatly, and off they both ran like hares, dodging in and out among the groups that were busily sorting out equipment.

The victim stood and gasped for a moment, then reached down into his boot and pulled out the grandfather of all the razors in the world and lit out like a cyclone after the robbers. He was caught and disarmed before he could do any damage and rebuked by his company commander, who threatened him with all sorts of punishments. But all the man could say in answer to the rebuke was: "Doggone! Stole my chickun! Stole my chickun!"

"You can do all the damage you want with your fists if you've any private quarrels," said the captain, "but a razor's no weapon for a soldier."

That gave the officers the idea of searching all the rank and file, and they filled a large-sized barrel full with razors taken off that regiment, which had to be confiscated temporarily for fear they might be used for social instead of tonsorial purposes.

Now I suppose Oscar Wilde would have said that episode was an example of how nature exaggerates art. The joke of a negro's fondness for a razor as a weapon has been done to death in the theater. It has become so hackneyed that even in burlesque they hardly dare to use it any longer. If a scene like that were put on the stage everybody would say it was an absurd, stale and moldy joke.

Most of the successful songs I have had were written by Alexander Rogers. He was the author of the words of "Nobody," "Jonah Man," "I May Be Crazy but I Ain't No Fool," and many others. The tunes to several of them I wrote myself, or perhaps it would be more correct to say that I assembled them. For the tunes to popular songs are mostly made up of standard parts, like a motor car. The copyright law allows anybody to take not more than four bars of any existing melody. As a machinist assembles a motor car then, I assembled the tunes to "Nobody," "Crazy," "Believe Me," and one or two others. It would be wrong for me to say that I composed those tunes, because as a composer I am a one-finger artist. I did study harmony and thorough bass, but that is as far as I went.

Before I got through with "Nobody" I could have wished that both the author of the words and the assembler of the tune had been strangled or drowned or talked to death. For seven whole years I had to sing it. Month after month I tried to drop it and sing something new, but I could get nothing to replace it, and the audiences seemed to want nothing else. Every comedian at some time in his life learns to curse the particular stunt of his that was most popular. "Nobody" was a particularly hard song to replace. Song writers say that I am a particularly hard man to write songs for. Whenever they have a song a man can use they seem to want a portion of his life before they will sell it to him. They want war prices for their songs, but I have not observed any war salaries being paid to artists. The way some of them deal with me is to calculate what my income ought to be for the next ten years, and then ask ten per cent of that.

Not that I grudge paying for a song; in fact, one is only too glad to pay for a really good song. My ambition is not that of Mr. Lauder. I don't want people to say of me when I am dead, "How much did he leave?" but rather—if they say anything at all—"How much did he enjoy?"

At one time it seemed to me that almost everybody in the United States was writing a song "just like 'Nobody.'" It never occurred to any of them that to be "just like 'Nobody' " a song would need to have the same human appeal as "Nobody" mixed in with its humor, the human appeal of the friendless man. Most of these imitations were called "Somebody," and that was the only single solitary idea they had, just a feeble paraphrase of "Nobody," with the refrain switched around to "Somebody." The majority of writers apparently think that one idea spread over three or four verses and the refrain is enough to carry a song. A really good song must be fairly packed with ideas. There should be at least two in every stanza and two more in the refrain. Take, for example, a number of songs I am singing, or rather talking, in the Follies now, by Ring Lardner: "Home, Home, Sweet Home— that's Where the Real War Is." Every line carries an amusing picture, and each verse is built up so that it leads to a fresh laugh in the refrain.

In picking a song I always consider the words. The tune will take care of itself. I should feel sorry for a song that depended on its tune if I had to sing it! When I was a lad I thought I had a voice, but I learned differently in later years. I did not take proper care of it, and now I have to talk all my numbers. And even what little voice I have left has to be nursed and petted like a prize cat. I study carefully the acoustics of each theater I appear in. There is always one particular spot on the stage from which the voice carries better, more clearly and easily than from any other. I make it my business to find that spot before the first performance, and once I find it I stick to it like a postage stamp. People have sometimes observed that I practice unusual economy of motion and do not move about as much as other singers do. It is to spare my voice and not my legs that I stand still while delivering a song. If my voice were stronger I would be as active as anybody, because it is much easier to put a song over if you can move about.

I hope nothing I have said will be mistaken to mean that I think I have found a recipe for making people laugh, or anything of that sort. The man who could find that recipe would be bigger than Klaw and Erlanger and the Shuberts put together. Humor is the one thing in the world that it is impossible to argue about, because it is all a matter of taste. If I could turn myself into a human boomerang: if I could jump from the stage, fly out over the audience, turn a couple of somersaults in the air, snatch the toupee from the head of the bald man in the front row of the balcony, and light back on the stage in the spot I jumped from, I could have the world at my feet—for a while. But even then I would always have to be finding something new. Look at Fred Stone: he can do anything the human body can be trained to do, but he is always learning something new and always just about six months ahead of his imitators.

People sometimes ask me if I would not give anything to be white. I answer, in the words of the song, most emphatically, "No." How do I know what I might be if I were a white man? I might be a sand-hog, burrowing away and losing my health for eight dollars a day. I might be a street-car conductor at twelve or fifteen dollars a week. There is many a white man less fortunate and less well equipped than I am. In truth, I have never been able to discover that there was anything disgraceful in being a colored man. But I have often found it inconvenient—in America.

My father was a Dane. He left Copenhagen some years ago and became Danish consul in Nassau. There he married my mother, who was half Spanish and half African. Her mother was brought over from Africa and destined for the Spanish Main, but thanks to an English frigate that intercepted the vessel she was brought in, she never reached her destination. She went to the British West Indies instead, where she married a Spanish cooper.

Williams, of course, is obviously not a Danish name. Nobody in America knows my real name and, if I can prevent it, nobody ever will. That was the only promise I made to my father. I left the West Indies when I was a youngster and came with my parents by way of Panama to San Pedro, California, now Los Angeles Harbor.

I had not the slightest idea of going on the stage at first, nor any very definite ambition except to get an education. I went through high school in southern California and was going to Leland Stanford University. A bunch of us, three white boys and myself, thought it would be nice and easy to make spending money by touring through the small towns on the coast in a 'bus and giving entertainments. That 'bus tour was the beginning of several disastrous years. We got back to San Francisco without a stitch of clothing, literally without a stitch, as the few rags I wore to spare the hostility of the police had to be burned for reasons that everybody will understand who has read of the experiences of the soldiers in the trenches. It was then that I first ran up against the humiliations and persecution that have to be faced by every person of colored blood, no matter what his brains, education, or the integrity of his conduct. How many times have hotel keepers said to me, "I know you, Williams, and I like you, and I would like nothing better than to have you stay here, but you see we have Southern gentlemen in the house and they would object."

Frankly, I can't understand what it is all about. I breathe like other people, eat like them—if you put me at a dinner table you can be reasonably sure that I won't use the ice cream fork for my salad; I think like other people. I guess the whole trouble must be that I don't look like them. They say it is a matter of race prejudice. But if it were prejudice a baby would have it, and you will never find it in a baby. It has to be inculcated on people. For one thing, I have noticed that this "race prejudice" is not to be found in people who are sure enough of their position to be able to defy it. For example, the kindest, most courteous, most democratic man I ever met was the King of England, the late King Edward VII. I shall never forget how frightened I was before the first time I sang for him. I kept thinking of his position, his dignity, his titles: King of Great Britain and Ireland, Emperor of India, and half a page more of them, and my knees knocked together and the sweat stood out on my forehead. And I found—the easiest, most responsive, most appreciative audience any artist could wish. I was lucky in that he liked my stories, and he used to send for me to come to the palace once or twice a week to tell some story over that he had taken a liking to, and found he couldn't tell correctly.

He was not the only man in England in whom I found courtesy and kindness. For example, whenever I go over, my manager comes to Liverpool to meet the boat and insists on taking me to his home at Maidenhead to stay for a few days before I go to London to begin work. Can you imagine an American manager doing that? Yes, I can—and I can imagine the German emperor of his own accord giving up Belgium!

To get back to my crazy 'bus tours. I floundered around in that way for several years. I was all for parodies in those days. I would get hold of popular song books and write parodies on anything. They must have been pretty sad. At any rate, they never got me anything but experience. Then, one day at Moore's Wonderland in Detroit, just for a lark I blacked my face and tried the song, "Oh, I don't know, you're not so warm." Nobody was more surprised than I when it went like a house on fire. Then I began to find myself. By that time I had met George Walker, and we used to travel around the country together. I took to studying the dialect of the American negro, which to me was just as much a foreign dialect as that of the Italian.

Shortly after that I met Thomas Canary, of Canary and Lederer. He promised to put us in a piece called "The Passing Show." But before that came off we got a telegram from him saying that "if we could get to New York" by September 14th we could have an engagement in "The Gold Bug." If we could get there! As if we wouldn't have crawled there on our knees! Unfortunately, "The Gold Bug" lasted only a week. Then we were with Sandow's troupe for a while, after which we went to Boston to join Pete Dailey's company.

Then came our first big success in New York. We were given a trial at Koster & Bial's and we stayed there for thirty-six weeks. It was Mr. Bial who first sent me to Europe. I was at the Empire in London and went on immediately after the ballet, and promptly died. That taught me to know better than to try to follow a ballet.

After that I went to Europe frequently, not only because I found kinder treatment there but in order to learn my trade. I used to go over every summer for a while and study pantomime from Pietro, the great pantomimist. He is the one artist from whom I can truthfully say that I learned. He taught me gesture, facial expression—without which I would never have been able to do the poker game stunt that was so popular. And above all he taught me the value of poise, repose and pauses. He taught me that the pause after a gesture or a movement is frequently more important than the gesture itself, because it emphasizes the gesture. The same thing is true in singing a song. The pause at the end of a line is often more important than the inflection you give the line. For instance, in Ring Lardner's song which begins this way:

My wife claims that all her folks
Come from good fighting stock
And now they're paying us an endless visit (*pause*)
At our apartment in the Mecca block.
There's three brother-in-laws (*pause*),
One sister-in-law (*pause*), one mother-in-law,
That's five (*pause*)
And any one of the quintet can jes' eat
Jess Willard alive.

It was Pietro who taught me that the entire aim and object of art is to achieve naturalness. The more simple and real the manner of your walking or talking the more effective, and that is the purpose of art. I played a good deal of pantomime in Europe. I did the Toreador in the pantomime version of Carmen, and many other parts.

Each time I come back to America this thing they call race prejudice follows me wherever I go. When Mr. Ziegfeld first proposed to engage me for the Follies there was a tremendous storm in a teacup. Everybody threatened to leave; they proposed to get up a boycott if he persisted; they said all sorts of things against my personal character. But Mr. Ziegfeld stuck to his guns and was quite undisturbed by everything that was said. Which is one reason why I am with him now, although I could make twice the salary in vaudeville. There never has been any contract between us, just a gentlemen's agreement. I always get on perfectly with everybody in the company by being polite and friendly but keeping my distance. Meanwhile I am lucky enough to have real friends, people who are sure enough of themselves not to need to care what their brainless and envious rivals will say if they happen to be seen walking along the street with me. And I have acquired enough philosophy to protect me against the things which would cause me humiliation and grief if I had not learned independence.

It was not people in the company, I since discovered, but outsiders who were making use of that line of talk for petty personal purposes.

Meanwhile, I have no grievance whatsoever against the world or the people in it: I'm having a grand time. I am what I am, not because of what I am but in spite of it.

THE NEGRO ARTIST AND MODERN ART

ROMARE BEARDEN's "The Negro Artist and Modern Art" is a very famous and not terribly sympathetic assessment of blacks in the fine arts in the 1920s. Bearden was later to repudiate or at least distance himself from this piece. Nonetheless, his criticism here remains both valid and vivid. This essay appeared in *Opportunity* in December 1934.

Born in Charlotte, North Carolina, on September 2, 1914, Bearden joined Charles Alston, Aaron Douglas, and Jacob Lawrence as one of the leading black painters of his generation.

For the moment, let us look back into the beginnings of modern art. It is really nothing new, merely an expression projected through new forms, more akin to the spirit of the times. Fundamentally the artist is influenced by the age in which he lives. Then for the artist to express an age that is characterized by machinery, skyscrapers, radios, and the generally quickened cadences of modern life, it follows naturally that he will break from many of the outmoded academic practices of the past. In fact every great movement that has changed the ideals and customs of life, has occasioned a change in the accepted expression of that age.

Modern art has passed through many different stages. There have been the periods of the Impressionists, the Post Impressionists, the Cubists, the Futurists, and hosts of other movements of lesser importance. Even though the use of these forms is on the decline, the impression they made in art circles is still evident. They are commendable in the fact that they substituted for mere photographic realism, a search for inner truths.

Modern art has borrowed heavily from Negro sculpture. This form of African art had been done hundreds of years ago by primitive people. It was unearthed by archaeologists and brought to the continent. During the past twenty-five years it has enjoyed a deserved recognition among art lovers. Artists have been amazed at the fine surface qualities of the sculpture, the vitality of the work, and the unsurpassed ability of the artists to create such significant forms. Of great importance has been the fact that the African would distort his figures, if by so doing he could achieve a more expressive form. This is one of the cardinal principles of the modern artist.

It is interesting to contrast the bold way in which the African sculptor approached his work, with the timidity of the Negro artist of today. His work is at best hackneyed and uninspired, and only mere rehashings from the work of any artist that might have influenced him. They have looked at nothing with their own eyes—seemingly content to use borrowed forms. They have evolved nothing original or native like the spiritual, or jazz music.

Many of the Negro artists argue that it is almost impossible for them to evolve such a sculpture. They say that since the Negro is becoming so amalgamated with the white race, and has accepted the white man's civilization he must progress along those lines. Even if this is true, they are certainly not taking advantage of the Negro scene. The Negro in his various environments in America, holds a great variety of rich experiences for the genuine artists. One can imagine what men like Daumier, Grosz, and Cruickshank might have done with a locale like Harlem, with all its vitality and tempo. Instead, the Negro artist will proudly exhibit his "Scandinavian Landscape," a locale that is entirely alien to him. This will of course impress the uninitiated, who through some feeling of inferiority toward their own subject matter, only require that a work of art have some sort of foreign stamp to make it acceptable.

I admit that at the present time it is almost impossible for the Negro artist not to be influenced by the work of other men. Practically all the great artists have accepted the influence of others. But the difference lies in the fact that the artist with vision, sees his material, chooses, changes, and by integrating what he has learned with his own experiences, finally molds something distinctly personal. Two of the foremost artists of today are the Mexicans, Rivera and Orozco. If we study the work of these two men, it is evident that they were influenced by the continental masters. Nevertheless their art is highly original, and steeped in the tradition and environment of Mexico. It might be noted here that the best work of these men was done in Mexico, of Mexican subject matter. It is not necessary for the artist to go to foreign surroundings in order to secure material for his artistic expression. Rembrandt painted the ordinary Dutch people about him, but he presented human emotions in such a way that their appeal was universal.

Several other factors hinder the development of the Negro artist. First, we have no valid standard of criticism; secondly, foundations and societies which supposedly encourage Negro artists really hinder them; thirdly, the Negro artist has no definite ideology or social philosophy.

Art should be understood and loved by the people. It should arouse and stimulate their creative impulses. Such is the role of art, and this in itself constitutes one of the Negro artist's chief problems. The best art has been produced in those countries where the public most loved and cherished it. In the days of the Renaissance the townsfolk would often hold huge parades to celebrate an artist's successful completion of a painting. We need some standard of criticism then, not only to stimulate the artist, but also to raise the cultural level of the people. It is well known that the critical writings of men like Herder, Schlegel, Taine, and the system of Marxian dialectics, were as important to the development of literature as any writer.

I am not sure just what form this system of criticism will take, but I am sure that the Negro artist will have to revise his conception of art. No one can doubt that the Negro is possessed of remarkable gifts of imagination and intuition. When he has learned to harness his great gifts of rhythm and pours it into his art—his chance of creating something individual will be heightened. At present it seems that by a slow study of rules and formulas the Negro artist is attempting to do something with his intellect, which he has not felt emotionally. In consequence he has given us poor echoes of the work of white artists—and nothing of himself.

It is gratifying to note that many of the white critics have realized the deficiencies of the Negro artists. I quote from a review of the last Harmon exhibition, by Malcolm Vaughan, in the New York *American*: "But in the field of painting and sculpture, they appear peculiarly backward, indeed so inept as to suggest that painting and sculpture are to them alien channels of expression." I quote from another review of the same exhibition, that appeared in the *New York Times*:

"Such racial aspects as may once have figured have virtually disappeared, so far as some of the work is concerned. Some of the artists, accomplished technicians, are seen to have slipped into grooves of one sort or another. There is the painter of the Cezannesque still life, there is the painter of the Gauginesque nudes, and there are those who have learned various 'dated' modernist tricks."

There are quite a few foundations that sponsor exhibitions of the work of Negro artists. However praiseworthy may have been the spirit of the founders the effect upon the Negro artist has been disastrous. Take for instance the Harmon Foundation. Its attitude from the beginning has been of a coddling and patronizing nature. It has encouraged the artist to exhibit long before he has mastered the technical equipment of his medium. By its choice of the type of work it favors, it has allowed the Negro artist to accept standards that are both artificial and corrupt.

It is time for the Negro artist to stop making excuses for his work. If he must exhibit let it be in exhibitions of the caliber of "The Carnegie Exposition." Here among the best artists of the world his work will stand or fall according to its merits. A concrete example of the accepted attitude towards the Negro artist recently occurred in California where an exhibition coupled the work of Negro artists with that of the blind. It is obvious that in this case there is definitely created a dual standard of appraisal.

The other day I ran into a fellow with whom I had studied under George Grosz, at the "Art Students' League." I asked him how his work was coming. He told me that he had done no real work for about six months.

"You know, Howard," he said, "I sort of ran into a blind alley with my work; I felt that it definitely lacked something. This is because I didn't have anything worthwhile to say. So I stopped drawing. Now I go down to the meetings of The Marine and Industrial Workers' Union. I have entered whole-heartedly in their movement."

We talked about Orozco, who had lost his arm in the revolutionary struggle in Mexico. No wonder he depicted the persecution of the underclass Mexicans so vividly— it had all been a harrowing reality for him.

So it must be with the Negro artist—he must not be content with merely recording a scene as a machine. He must enter wholeheartedly into the situation which he wishes to convey. The artist must be the medium through which humanity expresses itself. In this sense the greatest artists have faced the realities of life, and have been profoundly social.

I don't mean by this that the Negro artist should confine himself only to such scenes as lynchings, or policemen clubbing workers. From an ordinary still life painting by such a master as Chardin we can get as penetrating an insight into eighteenth century life, as from a drawing by Hogarth of a street-walker. If it is the race question, the social struggle, or whatever else that needs expression, it is to that the artist must surrender himself. An intense, eager devotion to present day life, to study it, to help relieve it, this is the calling of the Negro artist.

CITY PLOWMAN

JEAN TOOMER (1894–1967) was one of the most important and enigmatic figures of the Harlem Renaissance. A combination mystic, intellectual, poet, and ne'er do well, his literary gifts were considerable. He was very light-skinned, and his public demanded that he identify himself as black or white but he refused to do so, enjoying the tension of his ambiguity. His novel, *Cane,* is not only the most highly regarded book of that era, it is among the most impressive novels produced by a twentieth-century American. The following essay on American photographer Alfred Stieglitz (1864–1946), who was married to the famous American painter Georgia O'Keeffe and who edited several important photographic magazines, including the extraordinary *Camera Work,* appeared in *America and Alfred Stieglitz: A Collective Portrait* (1934), among whose editors were Waldo Frank, a good friend and booster of Toomer.

I. THE HILL

They tell me that what is now called The Hill was once a farmer's place. On this place were pigs. Pig stench drifted down to the big house of the Stieglitz family on the shore of Lake George. To get rid of this stench the family bought the farm. Thus they acquired the house and grounds which later, when financial reverses set in, they themselves occupied. Thus the place was linked with the life of Alfred Stieglitz. Once this happened, the linkings became so many and various that the old farm must have felt that the world had come to settle within its borders.

I wonder what the old house felt when rooms and baths were added, when furnishings which it had never seen the like of were moved in, when the complexities of the Stieglitz family began weaving in and out of the rooms and into the simple old wood and farmer's plaster. Surely it knew that an unexpected fate had overtaken it. Surely it gazed with amazement at Alfred Stieglitz and his camera, at Georgia O'Keeffe and her paints and canvases. And it affirmed the transformation and felt satisfied because the photographer and the painter, like the farmers before them, were producers, producers of things for America.

One may guess, too, at the surprise of the flowers when they saw O'Keeffe first paint them. At the surprise of the trees and weeds when they became important before Stieglitz's camera. Something new had come to pass in this Lake George place. The farm had become The Hill.

At The Hill the windows are uncurtained. Each window is all window. The outside can look in, the Lake George landscape, near-by trees, an old red barn, floating clouds. The house rests upon its earth, inviting this part of the American countryside to enter. And the countryside does enter, and something of the great earth, and something, I feel, of the great world.

What is of equal importance, the inside can look out—and this, particularly, is Stieglitz. The inside looking out unhindered, the human spirit being, with a permanent intensity to perceive, feel, and know the world which it inhabits, to give a sheer record of experiences.

I always see his eyes, those ever alert instruments of a consciousness whose genius is to register both the details and the vastnesses of life, of this part of the universe where now we happen to be dwelling—all with an extraordinary sense of significance, a feeling of relatedness.

Nothing for him is unrelated; even twigs and pebbles fit in as constituents of the universe. Even human stupidity, for he can see its function in relation to intelligence. An accepter, an affirmer, a rich nature with a generous interest in all that exists

One of my pictures of him is Stieglitz in a deep chair, people around him, his body relaxed, hands unoccupied, gray hair in whatever way it happens to be, but his head poised as if it were the prototype of all cameras, recording with uncanny sensitiveness all that is visible and much that is not.

There are deep chairs at The Hill, deep chairs in his rooms at the Shelton, one deep chair in his room at An American Place, and I see him in them. This actual or apparent physical immobility is an instructive feature of the man who has *done* more for modern art in America than any other single person, who has established a standard of truth.

Obviously his way of doing is not that which we ordinarily advertise and idealize. No one would mistake him for one of our publicized men of action. No, he has the dynamics of *being*—hence he can do. In this he is in striking contrast to those who believe they can do without being, and who are, therefore, under the awful delusion that is wrecking Western civilization.

Wherever he is, *he is*. I cannot picture him elsewhere. I cannot envisage him going anywhere. In the midst of people, many of whom bustle and scamper about nothing, he is with something. So surely does the center of him proclaim, "I am," that it is difficult for me to think of him in terms of growth, change, becoming— though I know he has grown.

Quite early he must have found the places on this earth which belonged to him; and he must have recognized that he belonged to them. Or, for all I know, he may have felt he was an essential stranger on this planet; hence, that all regions were, on the one hand, equally alien, and, on the other, equally meaningful as locales where one could see the cosmos in epitome. In any case, within what some might call a circumscribed habitat (mainly Lake George and New York City) he has remained, relaxed from the urge to go elsewhere, yet never resting.

Never resting. Always doing. Carrying on his own individual life and work, helping carry on the individual life and work of others, always initiating, always pressing against whatever tends to hinder his aim of sensitizing the world, deeply powered by a sense of what is beyond, the great potentiality.

He will sometimes tell you that he feels uprooted. From one point of view this is true. He has not had a fixed establishment. What is more to the point, he is not a tree. The human nostalgia to revert to vegetable may occasionally move him, but with him as with so many of us, it has come to nothing. Yet I do not feel he is suspended or unplaced. Always I feel he is rooted *in himself* and to the *spirit* of the place. Not rooted to things; rooted to spirit. Not rooted to earth; rooted to air.

If he is at The Hill at Lake George, I do not have the feeling that he has come from New York or that he may be going there. No, here he is, capable of sustaining and fulfilling himself with what is present. Now and again he may walk to the village, but even this short going seems foreign to him, and he usually does it with an air which makes one feel he is walking with an illusion of Stieglitz in a black cloak.

He lives in his house, the house with uncurtained windows, bare gray-white walls, deep chairs, tables, uncovered blue-white lights, and in this house he creates an atmosphere. A delicacy, a sensuousness, an austerity.

No ornaments anywhere, nothing that isn't used. No "oughts" or "ought nots" governing the running of the house except those which relate to the work of O'Keeffe, of himself, of whoever may be his guests at the time, his fellow experiencers. No ought even in relation to work. No ought in relation to life—providing you do not hinder someone else. Just life.

My first visit to The Hill I was soon struck by a feeling that came from him constantly and filled the house. I particularly remember one morning.

We were having fruit, Zwieback, and coffee in the kitchen. O'Keeffe and Paul Rosenfeld were there. Stieglitz was at the table, silent, his head lowered, eyes pensive on something not in sight, absently dipping Zwieback in coffee before eating it.

Outside, snow was on the hills, a cold hidden landscape; and to my eyes it seemed that we were four people far away from everything, practically lost in a remote frosty region of the earth, unconnected with wide living. But I *felt* warmth and a most amazing sense that life was coming into us, that the wide world was immediate out there, that we were in the midst of happenings in America, that Stieglitz had an interior connectedness with life, that through him I also felt connected.

Feeling, I believe, is the center of his life. Whatever he does, he does through feeling—and he won't do anything unless feeling is in it. Whatever he thinks, he thinks with feeling—and he won't think anything unless feeling is in it. His words convey it, his miraculously clear photographs, his silences, his sitting relaxed in a deep chair.

Feeling is being. Stieglitz can evoke the one and therefore the other; and this is why he can help people find and be what they are, why he can move people both into and out of themselves, why we value him, we who are younger than he but old enough to realize that thought and action are nothing unless they issue from and return to being.

I wondered when he would begin photographing. O'Keeffe was painting. Paul and myself were writing. Stieglitz was simply in the house. I wondered how he would be when working. In due time he began.

A natural happening. His working tempo was but a quickening (though what a quickening!) of his usual tempo. All he did was but an intensification of what had been in The Hill all the while. Work and life were the same thing, and life and art. No casual observer would have thought that anything "great" was going on. His camera was in evidence. Out he would go with it. In he would come. And soon the large table in the front room was filled with his materials and prints. It was that simple—and that real.

Only it wasn't simple at all. The search for truth and reality is a complex search, the attempt to extend consciousness is a difficult attempt, the effort to determine and demonstrate by experiments the possibilities of a comparatively new instrument and medium is intricate and it must be sustained—and all of these he was doing with and through the camera while I looked on at the apparent simplicity of it.

Though at various times to various people he has told, so to speak, the partial history of this or that photograph, the full genesis of his pictures is unknown, and perhaps it is just as well. Like himself, his photographs are explicit in themselves, direct communicants with one's feelings.

A genius of what is—this is Stieglitz, and this is why he uses a camera, and this is why he will never use a *moving*-picture camera.

The *treeness* of a tree . . . what bark is . . . what a leaf is . . . the *woodness* of wood . . . a telephone pole . . . the *stoneness* of stone . . . a city building . . . a New York skyscraper . . . a horse . . . a wagon . . . an old man . . . a cloud, the sun, unending space beyond . . . the *fleshness* of human flesh . . . what a face is . . . what a hand, an arm, a limb is . . . the amazing beauty of a human being . . . the equally amazing revelation of the gargoyle that hides in all of us but which he and his camera devastatingly see . . .

Here in these prints our earth is as it *is*, our dwellings as they *are*, ourselves, we humans, as we *are*.

If I were commissioned to travel through space and inform the beings of some other planet on the nature of this earth-part of the universe, I would take Stieglitz's camera works along, and I would feel confident that those beings would get, not subjective picturings and interpretations, but objective records, and I'd feel confident too that if, later on, they paid a visit to this planet, they would recognize it.

From Lake George to New York City is not far. But from the house that rests upon its earth to the 17th and 29th floors of the skyscrapers in which Stieglitz lives in New York, there is a great distance, a difference of a century. By means of the continuity and singleness of his life he connects them. The Hill, his rooms at the Shelton, An American Place on Madison Avenue, are but variations of the same thing—the world he has built and is building.

The beginning-structures of this world: 291 and *Camera Work*, those manifest crystallizations of his deep resources which had such vital functions in the life of their time, which have carried forward like good blood into the living body and spirit of today. I did not experience them; I do sense them now as they exist in the present in him, as they and their effects exist in present-day America which owes to them an important part of its cultural being.

The past is a solid life behind him. The future is a solid life before him. He is solid in today.

If he is in his rooms at the Shelton, there he is. From these uncurtained windows of a skyscraper he can see the weather before it reaches the city pavements—and when I think of him looking out I remember the artists he has seen and recognized before they became known to most of us, before they were solid figures on the horizontal earth. He saw them, he recognized them, he did something so that they were aided in becoming such figures.

Here in these personal rooms of his one can sense the richness of his private life, his friendships and devotions, affirmations of this one, lashings against that one, his warmth, his clean kindliness, his humor—in fine, his dimensions in human experience.

If he is at the gallery, there he is. Behind him are other galleries. Before him, maybe more. But here, now, in this one, he is; carrying it on from day to day, from year to year through personal, economic, and spiritual vicissitudes.

Here the world comes to meet and experience his world. Here life comes to meet life. Here he meets what comes in.

There is, let us say, a show of Marins. One day I go up and many people are about. Stieglitz is himself. He talks and makes things happen or says nothing and lets things happen, according to how he feels. Another day I go up and the place is vacant. Stieglitz is himself, relaxed in his deep chair, neither more nor less himself because of what others do or don't do.

Yet no one has such a profound (and, sometimes, such an anguished) sense of what is involved—the entire life work of an extraordinary human being. Here on these walls is *Marin*. We can understand what Stieglitz feels—and feel with him—when he sees the place vacant, or, what is worse, when he sees some candidate for humanity come in, glance around for ten minutes, and go out, feeling that he has seen everything and knows it all.

And no one cares so deeply. Ever since he discovered himself, Stieglitz has been working for truth and people, to demonstrate certain things about life, to make for art a substantial place in America, to aid certain people [to] bring forth the best from themselves, and of course he is concerned if what happens is less than what is possible.

And he tries to do something about it, and if he can't—he accepts, with the knowledge that there is an inevitability in life and events, that what must be must be, that because it happens (or fails to happen) there is a certain rightness in it. Then he tries again. It is rare to find anyone in whom the two attitudes—"I will," "Thy will be done"—are so balanced.

As a creator, the "I will" is stronger. "I will" and the opposite, "I won't." By affirming he has done what he had to do. By denying he has kept himself unimpeded.

This man who is living in the spirit of today will have nothing to do with the things of today that distract from this spirit. Sometimes it is a fiery rejection. Sometimes it is a natural unconcern, as if in past lives he had experienced and become disillusioned with the vanities of the world, as if now in this life they simply do not exist for him.

In these days of "great personalities," of small souls and swollen egos, he is a simple man, a sincere man, uncompromising, a quiet man who comes into the house and you hardly know he has come in, who has come into this ambitious world of ours, who exists and has his being in it, unmindful of its scurryings, its advertisements and publicities.

He has no place for what is unrelated. Others may be interested, the thing may be valuable, the person may be promising, but he seems to know by intuition what is his and what is not, how far he can go, how far he can't , and he keeps to what is related to him, and he remains faithful to the high task of building his world with the materials and the people who belong to this world—all the while knowing, of course, that what he does carries beyond the boundary of his immediate aims and reaches people near and far.

A man in his world. A world which he has made, not found already made. No one, no group, no race, no nation could have built it for him. His function in life was not to fit into something that already existed but to create a new form by the force of his growth. Now he calls this form, "An American Place"—which it is, authentically. Whoever goes to room 1710 of 509 Madison Avenue or to The Hill at Lake George will find certain American essences in the paintings, in the photographs, in the very life and atmosphere too. Yet deeper than the national reality is the human reality. He himself and his form are of the great body and spirit of mankind.

An *individual* who is himself, who is for those of the wide world that claim him by similarity of spirit and of values.

GONE WITH THE WIND IS MORE DANGEROUS THAN BIRTH OF A NATION

MELVIN B. TOLSON (1898–1966) was a poet, educator, columnist, and critic. He is most famous for his volume of poetry, *Harlem Gallery*. A political radical and a Christian, Tolson, displaying both uncompromising vehemence and an occasional unreal optimism, wrote a column entitled "Caviar and Cabbage" that ran in the *Washington Tribune* from 1937 to 1944. The column featured here on the 1939 film *Gone with the Wind* was published on March 23, 1940. Most of Tolson's columns can be found in *Caviar and Cabbage: Selected Columns of Melvin B. Tolson*, edited by Robert M. Farnsworth (1982).

The acting in *Gone with the Wind* is excellent. The photography is marvelous. Miss Hattie McDaniel registered the nuances of emotion, from tragedy to comedy, with the sincerity and artistry of a great actor. Some of my friends declare that the picture is fine entertainment. So were the tricks of Houdini. So is a circus for children.

But *Gone with the Wind* was announced in the movie magazines, in billboard advertisements, and in the film itself as more than entertainment. It was billed as the story of the Old South—not a story of the Old South. That difference is important for us truthseekers. Remember—the novel is a historical picture. Both the novelist and the producer say that.

Therefore, the first question is this: Does *Gone with the Wind* falsify history?

Take other historical pictures that came out of Hollywood. *A Tale of Two Cities, Zola, Abe Lincoln in Illinois, Juarez, Henry VIII, The Life of Louis Pasteur*. Historians were consulted and libraries ransacked to get the *historical* truth for these pictures. A *historical* picture is more than entertainment. Let us get that straight.

THE POINT OF VIEW IN A PICTURE

The Birth of a Nation was such a barefaced lie that a moron could see through it. *Gone with the Wind* is such a subtle lie that it will be swallowed as the truth by millions of whites and blacks alike. Dr. Stephenson Smith calls the moving picture the greatest molder of public opinion. And the Chinese say a picture is worth a thousand words. I believe it after listening to the comments of some of my friends on this movie, *Gone with the Wind*.

The fact that this movie caused a red-letter day in the South should have warned Negroes. The fact that it was acclaimed by Confederate veterans who fought to keep Negroes enslaved should have warned us. From Key West, Florida, to El Paso, Texas, the White South rejoiced. Margaret Mitchell, who wrote the novel, is the Joan of Arc of Dixie.

Why? Why? Because she told the story from the viewpoint of the South. The picture was praised extravagantly in Darkest Mississippi where Negro children are not permitted to read the Constitution in school. The commendation of the White South means the condemnation of the Negro.

The story of the Old South can be told from the viewpoint of the poor whites, the Negro slaves, the Yankees, or the white masters. Miss Mitchell took the viewpoint of the white masters. That's the reason the White South rejoices over the picture. Be not deceived, if you love your race. I am sure you would not ask an enemy to recommend you for a position.

WHAT FOOLED NEGRO MOVIEGOERS

If you put poison in certain kinds of foods, you can't tell it. If you beat a man long enough with your fists, you can slap him and he'll appreciate the slap.

The poor Negro has been kicked so often that he considers a slap a bit of white courtesy. Since *Gone with the Wind* didn't have a big black brute raping a white virgin in a flowing white gown, most Negroes went into ecstasies. Poor Sambo!

Negroes are like the poor husband who caught his wife in the bedroom necking the iceman and sighed, "Well, it might've been worse!"

I must give that Southern novelist and the white producer credit for one thing: they certainly fooled the Negro and at the same time put over their anti-Negro, anti-Yankee, KKK propaganda.

The tragedy is this: Negroes went to see one thing; whites went to see another. Negroes asked: "Were there any direct insults to the race?" The white folk wanted to know: "Was the North justified in freeing black men?"

Both questions were answered in this picture. Negroes were not directly insulted. The North was wrong in freeing the Negroes. For seventy years Negro-hating white men have tried to prove with arguments and lynchings that the North was wrong in freeing the Negroes. And some Negro fools have agreed with the white Negro-haters. If the North was wrong, then old Frederick Douglass and the Abolitionists were idiots.

LIES IN THE PICTURE

Gone with the Wind pretends to show historically the Old South. It fails to do this. It falsifies by leaving out important facts. *Gone with the Wind* is what a description of Washington would be like without the Capitol, the White House, the Federal buildings, Howard University, and other landmarks.

Half of the picture deals with the Civil War. But the Civil War comes like a spontaneous combustion. It appears like a rabbit out of a magician's hat. Every critic in America will tell you that a truthful work of art must have motivation—causation. *Gone with the Wind* shows not a single economic or social or political cause that led to the Civil War. How could a civilization be "gone with the wind" unless there was something to MAKE it go?

According to the picture, slavery was a blessed institution. (Stick to the picture.) The Negroes were well fed and happy. Last summer I stood in the slave market of Charleston. In the picture there were no slave markets tearing husbands and wives, mothers and children apart. As a young man, Abe Lincoln saw a slave market and cried: "If the chance comes, I'll hit this thing a hard blow."

Read Tourgée's historical accounts of his trips through the South. Read Dr. Frank's historical documents on the Old South. See Dr. Reddick's documents on slavery in the famous Schomburg Collection. Read what Thomas Jefferson said about the South. The Civil War was the inevitable culmination of economic, social, political, and psychological events spreading over a period of two hundred years.

It was like water piled up behind a dam finally breaking through. In dealing with history, leave the "if's" out.

The picture, then, lacked the motivation of historical truth, although it was supposed to be a historical picture. The Civil War was inevitable. It had to come because of definite economic causes. Slavery was a bloody institution. Of course, there were good masters. But the institution was built on the rape of Negro women, the hellish exploitation of black men, the brutalities of overseers, and bloodhounds that tore human beings to pieces. Read the documents of Dr. Frank, a white Southerner, in his book, *Americans*.

These are the reasons why the Old South is "gone with the wind." The picture does not show that. Therefore, millions of white men, women, and children will believe that the North was wrong in freeing the Negro.

PROPAGANDISTIC TRICKS IN THE PICTURE

The picture aims to create sympathy for the white South. We see thousands of dying and dead Confederate soldiers. The only Yankee who dies (in the picture) is a blue-coated soldier trying to rob and rape a Southern white woman. Yet General Sherman ordered the Yankees to protect women and children! When they didn't he had them shot. Atlanta burns. But the picture does not tell us that the Confederates set it afire! We get the impression that the damned Yankees did it.

We see a Union shell crash through a window of a church containing a painting of Christ; wounded Confederate soldiers are in the church. We are not told that white churches defended slavery in the South. These tricks will hoodwink millions of people.

Even the Ku Klux Klan is idolized. We see white gentlemen of the KKK returning home at night, while a big burly Yankee officer questions the innocent white ladies. Nothing is said about the brutalities of the KKK that stank to high heaven. Hitler's persecution of the Jews is nothing compared to the KKK's hellish treatment of our black forefathers!

The happy Negroes (in the picture, of course) go out to dig trenches for the Confederates, to keep themselves and their wives and children in slavery! The historical truth is this: When the Yankees marched through Georgia, the slaves, like sensible people, deserted the plantations by the tens of thousands. Some fell upon their knees and kissed the feet of their Yankee deliverers. General Sherman had to make thousands of them go back to their good (?) masters.

When old Abe Lincoln entered Savannah, he had to chastise the mammy slaves for kissing his boots.

"You should bow to no one but God," said the Great Emancipator.

The picture did not show the poor crackers, who outnumbered the white masters ten to one. These poor white men were degraded by pellagra, illiteracy, and the opium of poverty. That was a lie of omission in the picture.

Plato said 2,000 years ago that aristocracy is built on either chattel slavery or wage slavery. *Gone with the Wind* did not show that southern aristocracy was built on both. I sat for four long hours waiting for that gigantic historical truth to appear— and all I saw was the heartless action of Scarlett O'Hara.

THE SOUTH WON THE CIVIL WAR!

I am not bothered much with what Negroes think about *Gone with the Wind*. Most of them won't think. They have bridge, and the Strutters' Ball, and the fraternity powwow, and church politics, and fornications to think about.

What, then, will be the effect on millions and millions of whites from the Atlantic to the Pacific? What will be the effect when the picture is shown in South America, France, England, Germany, and the islands of the sea?

It will be this: The North was wrong in fighting to free black men. The grand old Abolitionists were lunatics. Negroes didn't want to be free anyway. Slaves were happy. The greatest pleasure of the slave was to serve massa.

Southern whites understand Negroes; that's the reason they treat them as they do. You need the Ku Klux Klan to keep Negroes in their place. All slaves were black; no white men had any mulatto children. There were no slave markets. Yankee soldiers went through Georgia raping white virgins. Negroes loved (with an undying love) the white masters, and hated the poor whites because they didn't own Negroes. Dixie was a heaven on earth until the damned Yankees and carpetbaggers came.

The Negroes were so dumb that they hated the very Yankees who wanted to free them. All masters were gentlemen—without high-yellah mistresses. Southern gentlemen were so honorable that they didn't yield to temptation when hussies, like Scarlett, threw their passionate bodies at them.

These are the untruthful things white people, all over the world, will believe when they see *Gone with the Wind*. Yes, some Negroes will believe these lies also.

And now, dear readers, to see what I have seen, you will have to put yourself in the place of a white man. Can you do that? I hope you can.

ART AND LIFE

N. ELIZABETH PROPHET (1890–1960) was a
sculptor. She graduated from the Rhode Island School of Design and
lived in Paris for 13 years. Along with sculptor Augusta Savage
(1882–1962), painter Palmer Hayden (1890–1973), painter Aaron
Douglas (1899–1979), sculptor Meta Vaux Warrick Fuller (1877–1968),
and painter William Henry Johnson (1901–1970), Prophet would have to
be considered one of important black artists of the Harlem Renaissance.
"Art and Life" appeared in *Phylon*, Fourth Quarter, 1940.

B y all evidence the prehistoric savage drew or painted his pictures on the
walls of his cave for the pleasure which he derived thereby in his leisure
time, but later as he became more practiced in his art, he turned his attention
to the decoration of his tools and articles of utility. This desire for such decoration
of his tools most likely spread through the community and a rivalry for better design
and execution led to real works of art.

As we look back through the historical ages, it is impossible to find at any time
during the history of man a people who have ever completely ignored art. There
are periods of low quality of expression, epochs when, because of some crisis,
political, economic, psychological, or otherwise, æsthetic expression reached a low
level in quality, but even in the so-called dark ages the desire for artistic expression
was not completely dead, for had this been so, it could not have revived itself and
produced the great art of the Renaissance. It was through this great desire and effort
on the part of the people of the dark ages that they were able to tear from themselves
the cloak of ignorance and clothe themselves in the garment of enlightenment and
creative expression.

All through the history of mankind, art has meant something more than just
pictures to hang on the wall to be forgotten or music to pass an hour's pleasure, or

sculpture to fill up a corner. There are abstract qualities which have had and still have a tremendous influence in the education and civilization of the people.

There is the art of the prehistoric savage, which so definitely represents his ability to correlate his actual living with his artistic expression. The bread and butter idea of the backward-thinking sociologist and economist of today, might easily be refuted through the artistic expression of the prehistoric cave man. For he, too, had to toil for his sustenance, which meant the hunting and killing of animals. Indeed, this was such an important part of his life, this providing of sustenance, that he carried it over into his leisure hours of thinking and dreaming, and thus for his joy and the enlightenment of archeologists, scientists, historians, and the peoples of all civilized nations of today, he drew on the walls of his cave during these leisure hours the animals which he hunted for food, the fish which he hoped to trap. Food, the great necessity of life, became his inspiration for creative expression. It is interesting, also, to note that unlike the Assyrians in their splendid bas-reliefs of feasting—banquets where they plainly show us their pleasure in feasting—the prehistoric man, in contrast, gives us the deer on the run, the fish swimming in the stream, as he hoped to catch them. He presents himself to us through his works of art as realistic in his thinking and thoroughly appreciative of movement and life.

Certainly the prehistoric savage can teach us who have not so many years ago emerged, that if in truth we are only capable of being taught to earn our bread and butter, we might add something to our interest as a people, if we could record some of our experiences while gaining that sustenance.

The progress of the human race has been traced by science, through the arts, monuments and written words. First the desire must be developed to crawl out of the cave and build a house. Here is the work of the architect. Then to live in it; here is a whole institution to be developed: how to live in the house, and how a home must be developed in the house. Next comes the family to be built up in the home of the house, and because of this family comes the development of all the arts and sciences. For the family in the home of the house becomes the embryo of the nation.

Each of the arts, if the fundamental principles would apply to your daily living, can be of some use. There are cosmic values which can be attained through the realm of art. It can enlarge your vision, your comprehension, and lessen the poverty of universal interest.

Music can develop a finer sensibility for sound. Sculpture, which is plastic form, makes us more sensitive to form. The Greek ideal for the perfect human body, developed through the Olympian games by the athletes, was co-ordinated with the plastic ideal of sculpture.

The concentration which is necessary for the execution of sculpture through constant practice can become a habit and thus develop balance, poise, harmony. A sculptor, through the constant tap of hammer and chisel, develops a super-sense for rhythm and harmony of movement and sound. The painter, draughtsman and sculptor develop a keen sense of observation through their constant search for character, line and form.

Touch, which music gives, might, I should say, be taught to many of our citizens who cannot pass through a door without shaking the very foundations of the building by their habit of banging doors, tearing off locks and hinges. A person must have a sense of proportion that he may know when to begin and when to stop in his conduct of life, his manners and occupation. Many people laugh too loud and too long and don't know when to stop through a lack of this proportional sense.

The principles of the arts which are form, rhythm, harmony; and the abstract qualities, some of which are poise and courage; are factors which no civilized man who aspires to be educated can live successfully without attaining.

In our approach to art, the broader our vision and understanding, the richer will be the results and experience from our efforts and interests in the field of the Fine Arts. Too frequently in thinking of art we carry it no farther than the walls of the gallery or the pleasure which we experience in its practice. It is true that this pleasure is of great importance, for it can lead to greater development, but there should be some thought given to its effect upon the public and society.

Our housing projects are examples. We do not need to visit the slums to find examples of stunted sensibilities, poverty of interests and appreciation, for it is too characteristic of the people in general.

If, in the current effort to rehouse the people of our slum areas, the idea had simply been to rehouse, I am sure that we would have built houses of some rugged material and placed them on a bed of cement which is durable. With heat, light and conveniences, certainly the lives of the people would be improved. But the Federal Housing Authority does not stop there; convenience and comfort are not sufficient. There must be something to uplift these people spiritually, and this is given in the landscaping of the gardens, through the addition of flowers and trees. Faculties which have been stunted through contact with nothing but degradation and squalor can be stimulated to an appreciation of something beautiful.

If the purpose of art is to give æsthetic pleasure, that objective has not been fulfilled until some higher æsthetic quality has been reflected in the lives, habits, and manners of the people. The artist has always had a strong educational influence, and the obligation of the modern artist is no less today than it was in the Golden Age of Greece or the Renaissance of Italy. Intelligent America and her educators are well aware of this and are attempting to give some cultural education to the people, for this can no longer be neglected if America is to take her place in the civilized world.

America has come to the sad realization that the education of her people has been sadly neglected and she has wisely decided to give the people some cultural training through the schools, colleges, and universities. Educators, psychologists, scientists have agreed that many of the faults in the American civilization come through this lack of cultural background.

A change of temperament is to be brought about in America through the realm of the Fine Arts. There are already established courses in most of the colleges and universities in America. Some of the Negro schools are being given an opportunity to raise the status of their people in the social system by benefiting from a broader education.

Negroes are sadly in need of this. It is surprising to hear so much talk of art in our group in America today and yet to see so little effort to put it where it belongs, that is, in our daily living. For example, poor articulation in speech is one of the Negro's greatest handicaps in a civilized society. The drama can certainly aid him there. The voice should be something of concern to each man or woman and, like the picture that is relegated to the walls of the gallery alone, if the voice is only thought of on the concert stage, we will continue forever to hear this mumbling, whining and grunting; we shall continue to be repulsive to cultured people and continue not to know why.

It is to be remembered that we are living in a civilized society; that our greatest aim should be to become a respected part of that civilization in which we should play a greater rôle in future generations than that which we play today. It should be our desire to emulate the best which that society has to offer, not the poorest. Many of the indignities inflicted by whites on Negroes are due to the former's lack of the finer sensibilities. They resent the limitations of the Negro, and pay it back in crude brutality.

It would be regrettable if, as a group, we should insist upon clinging to the early ignorance of the pioneer Americans in regard to art and the artists, for there is no country at present making a more eager effort to develop its artistic expression than here in America. Americans, like other civilized peoples, have come to realize that there must be some æsthetic expression for their people, that the artists' place in the community is not only that of the useless dreamer—dreaming may precede thinking. The great dreamer may become a great thinker and from there a great man of action.

There are many practical fields for the practice of artistic expression, once we are awakened to its need or usefulness in life or business. Take a walk down Fifth Avenue in New York City and take notice of the competition which one shop finds it absolutely necessary to carry on with its neighbor shop in the decoration of its windows. Through these well-decorated shop windows comes a psychological appeal to the passerby in the street to come in and spend his money. And each shop is compelled to outrival his neighbor in this appeal for attraction. This also means the development of highly paid window decorators who are college-bred and have had thorough training in draughtsmanship and painting.

If it is true that in our social and economic thought our development has gone little beyond eating, this condition need not endure forever and it should be our duty and desire to prepare for a different future. There is many a butcher who knows how to make an æsthetic appeal to his customers through the artistic arrangement of his goods in the window. The dentist wins his high-priced clientele through his ability to do an artistic job which defies the detection of artificiality as well as a good mechanical job.

It is unwise to discourage the artistic development of a people through slurring remarks about the artist's imagination and laziness. No man ever invented a success-ful plow, no statesman ever built a successful state, no man a great business, without imaginative ability; after which comes the hard thinking and technical development to make the imagined idea a reality. As for the laziness of the artist, he is like the men of all other professions: if he is lazy, he never reaches any degree of success.

All artists, present and past, who contribute something of value, are hard workers, working day and night.

As for the idea that the artists have been effeminate—Leonardo da Vinci was a giant of more than six feet who took pleasure when shaking a man's hand to crush it and send him down on his knees; Michelangelo could cut stone twenty-four hours at a stretch, sometimes forgetting to eat; and he could take a hammer and knock off five inches of stone at a blow; Picasso, the modern, is a powerful man physically; Titian, at the age of eighty, had the virility of a man of twenty-one.

If one does not care to think of the arts as a profession, there are the hours of leisure which can be filled with development and pleasure. Leisure as mere idleness is of no benefit nor pleasure to any man of intelligence and vigor. Enrich these boresome hours of which you complain after the day's work is done, through some intellectual pursuit, and life and yourself will take on a new and more interesting aspect and a more hopeful evolution.

WHERE ARE THE FILMS ABOUT REAL BLACK MEN AND WOMEN?

ELLEN HOLLY is an actress and writer. She was born in Queens, New York in 1931 and graduated from Hunter College in 1952. She has appeared in many stage productions and had a recurring role on the ABC soap opera "One Life to Live." "Where Are the films About Real Black Men and Women?" appeared in *Freedomways*, Third Quarter, 1974, at the time when Hollywood was making a number of films featuring blacks (the so-called blaxploitation films) in stereotypical roles of street hustlers and the like; it asks whether Hollywood has any interest in portraying blacks as anything other than white stereotypes.

Unlike "white" films which range at will over the full spectrum of human possibility from *Deep Throat* to the six-hour, hundred-million-dollar Soviet production of *War and Peace*, most "Black" films have been mired in the rut of a single formula—the so-called action film which deals with marginal antisocial elements in the Northern urban ghetto. These films have been subjected to a tremendous amount of criticism.

Law-abiding, tax-paying Black citizens who are not gunslingers, dope-pushers, pimps or prostitutes have been rightly and understandably enraged that the prevailing Black image in most films has been one that is so grossly at odds with their own.

In a healthier circumstance in which the full spectrum of Black life in all its remarkable variety could be seen on film, action films would be taken more calmly in stride as the equivalent of the cheaply made, Grade B gangster movies which shared the bottom slot of a double bill in the thirties and forties. In a healthier circumstance it would not be necessary to heap upon these films more blame (and, therefore, more significance) than they deserve, or to so hunger for alternatives that films such as *Five on the Black Hand Side* and the recently released *Claudine* are heaped with more praise than *they* deserve and heralded as events that would pale the Second Coming.

To that film critic who enthusiastically described *Claudine* as a landmark film, I would suggest that, rather, it is a charming, modest step in the right direction. A pleasant, upbeat film that has some nice things going for it. Above all, Diahann Carroll. Her beauty and skill, intelligence and plain old gumption, function as the keystone that holds the whole thing in place. Another plus is a delightful bunch of kids who are delightful precisely because they don't *behave* like a bunch—each one manages to leave his own quirky, individual imprint on the proceedings at hand.

Claudine is about a welfare mother with six kids—the ins and outs of her struggle to bring them up, and the ups and downs of her courtship with an engaging garbage man called Roop. It is a film with a lot of humor, but on the serious side, it has some very pertinent things to say about the Catch-22 maze of the welfare system, the tremendous energy required to pull oneself up by one's bootstraps, and the special inter-connectedness that Black people in a ghetto can feel for each other because, lacking money or power, the one certain thing they've got going for them is each other. Then there is the music. As a matter of fact, the one consistent star to emerge from "Black" movies in general is Black Music. Again and again, from one film to the next, by the beat, funk, and vitality of their music the Marvin Gayes, Isaac Hayeses and Curtis Mayfields have pumped life-blood into what would otherwise be thoroughly mediocre footage.

As for James Earl Jones, he plays Roop, the garbage man, as a big, warm-hearted, comic teddy bear. He is ingratiating, picturesque, and non-threatening. As a Black woman, I myself have problems with Black male portrayals that are so scrupulously de-fused of any masculine authority. For those who do not, this performance, too, is a skilled one that can be enjoyed as one of *Claudine's* assets.

More than a hundred "Black" films have come and gone in recent years. In the avalanche of buffoons and superstuds that can't be taken any more seriously than Batman and Captain Marvel, plain honest-to-goodness Black men of human stature who *can* be taken seriously are as scarce as hen's teeth. I suspect it's because the white-controlled film industry still has tremendous difficulty dealing with Black men as peers.

There have been many real Black heroes. *Spookwaffe*, an excellent film script by Paul Leaf dealing with the brilliant exploits of the all-Black 99th Fighter Squadron in World War II, remains undone. This group shot down more German planes over Anzio than any other fighter squadron in the history of the war. The record of the Spookwaffe (the name they facetiously gave themselves) has been as closely guarded as a military secret. Fantasy Shafts go down easily. Real Black performance does *not*.

One of the penalties of being Black and having limited money is that we seldom control our own image. We seldom appear in media as who *we* say we are, but rather as who *whites* say we are.

Entirely too many "Black" films have been Black in name only. The visible tip of the iceberg, the actors whose images flash on screen, have been Black, but they have been no more than hired hands . . . shills employed as window dressing to lure the Black public to the box office. Below the waterline, hidden from public view, lies the other seven-eighths of the iceberg, the writers who create the material, the directors who shape it, and the producers and distributors who put up the money, specify and control the content, and pocket the profits.

All too often this invisible seven-eighths of the iceberg has been solid, solid white. Black creative input behind the scenes has been virtually nil. Serious writers attempting to market scripts that deal with any kind of Black reality get nowhere while company hacks, free of any burdensome sense of racial responsibility, cheerily grind out the mindless *Hell Up in Harlem*'s that actually get on.

Half the time, the material not only isn't Black it isn't even original, as white material ready for the boneyard is given a hasty blackwash and sent on one last creaking go-round. *Cool Breeze* was a remake of *Asphalt Jungle*, *Blacula* and the upcoming *Blaxorcist* proclaim their origins in their titles. In the March 14 issue of *Jet* magazine, Clarence Brown listed, in dismay, still others which will shortly be coming our way. *Blackenstein*, *The Black Frankenstein*, *Werewolf from Watts*, *Billy Black*, and *Black the Ripper*. Are these films Black? I don't know the answer, but I think it's time somebody asked the question.

The problem will begin to be solved when Blacks gain more control over the making of their own films. Some rays of hope have begun to appear on the horizon. One of the national black sororities, Delta Sigma Theta (500 chapters cross-county, 75,000 members)—repelled by the constant presentation of the Black woman as Superslut and energized by the phenomenal organizational abilities of its national president, Lillian Benbow, and its Arts and Letters commission chairman, Dr. Jeanne Noble—has moved, through its media arm, DST Telecommunications, Inc., to finance, in association with a consortium of Black African businessmen a film called *Countdown at Kusini* that calls upon the talents of such responsible Black artists as Ossie Davis, Ruby Dee, and Al Freeman, Jr.

A truly decent solution to the problem, however, will require something more complex than a mere sorting out along racial lines. Being Black is no guarantee that you will make a decent film and being white is no guarantee that you will make a rip-off. I have seen Black directors turn in jobs that, in my opinion, constituted a gross betrayal of Black people and I have seen white producers like Michael Tolan (co-producer with Brock Peters of *Five on the Black Hand Side*) involve themselves out of sheer love and a deep sense of personal commitment. It is also worth remembering that whites were significantly involved with two of the most loving Black films that have yet been made, *Sounder* and *Nothing But a Man*.

While I fervently hope that more Black films will be made and controlled by Black people, I suspect that it is a lot closer to the point to hope that more black films will be made and controlled by people of any color whatsoever who *care* about Black people. That, in the final analysis, is really the point.

BILLIE HOLIDAY'S "STRANGE FRUIT": MUSIC AND SOCIAL CONSCIOUSNESS

ANGELA Y. DAVIS became a name in the news in the early 1970s when George Jackson and two other men tried to escape from prison. Jackson was a friend of Davis's and she was accused of aiding him in his aborted escape attempt, which resulted in the deaths of the escapees and a judge whom they were holding hostage. Davis was eventually acquitted of all charges but her case became a celebrated one. She is a communist and a professor of philosophy. Her books include *Angela Davis: An Autobiography* (1974), *Women, Culture and Politics* (1989) and *Women, Race, and Class* (1981). "Billie Holiday's 'Strange Fruit': Music and Social Consciousness" first appeared in *Political Affairs* magazine in February 1988.

Southern trees bear a strange fruit
Blood on the leaves, blood at the root
Black bodies swinging in the Southern breeze
Strange fruit hanging from the poplar trees
Pastoral scene of the gallant South
The bulging eyes and the twisted mouth
Scent of magnolia sweet and fresh
Then the sudden smell of burning flesh
Here is a fruit for the crows to pluck
For the rain to gather, for the wind to suck
For the sun to rot, for the tree to drop
Here is a strange and bitter crop.

This song, which Billie Holiday called her "personal protest" against the death-bringing ravages of racism, was destined to radically transform her status in American popular culture. If she had been previously acknowledged by the giants in her field as a brilliant innovator in jazz vocals, "Strange Fruit" would establish her as an unsurpassed aesthetic cultivator of social consciousness. Although she was only twenty-four years old when she recorded this song and integrated it into her performance repertoire, she had been striving for some time to reach beyond the circles of musicians and jazz cognoscenti who had faithfully and generously praised her work, in order to offer her art to the public at large. Yet, she staunchly refused to mar her art with tinges of commerciality which might have brought her the popular success for which she longed. She seemed to instinctively recognize that her musical genius was destined to serve a profound social purpose, for when she became aware of the impact of "Strange Fruit," she reconceptualized her role as a popular singer.

Prior to "Strange Fruit," the overwhelming majority of her music consisted of contemporary popular tunes, most of whose lyrics tended to be mediocre, if not downright trite. It was her unique phrasing, her striking transformations of original melodies and the timbre of her voice which elevated these songs to the status of art. She forged new content for these tunes by working wonders on the levels of form and technique. Now here was a song whose content had urgent and far-reaching implications—a song about hate, indignities and eruptions of violence which threatened every Afro-American in the country. Here was a song which could potentially awaken vast numbers of people—Black and white alike—from their apolitical slumber.

> I worked like the devil on it because I was never sure I could put it across or that I could get across to a plush nightclub audience the things that it meant to me.[1]

As long as her work appeared to be without manifest social content (and indeed, it only appeared to be so), she was lavishly praised by critics, whose belief in the "universality" of art presumptuously excluded themes relating to the collective struggles of Black people. Since "Strange Fruit" was unambiguously designed to prick the consciences of those who preferred to remain oblivious to the racist malevolence afflicting this land, it was inevitable that many critics would dismiss it as blatant propaganda, undeserving of the rubric of art. However, Billie Holiday needed no complicated aesthetic theories to grasp the artistic greatness of this work and to instinctively understand that "Strange Fruit" would render explicit the social function of her music in general.

Great art never achieves its greatness through an act of absolute transcendence of socio-historical reality. On the contrary, even as it transcends specific circumstances, it is deeply rooted in social realities. Its function precisely is to fashion new perspectives on the human condition—in its specificity and in its generality. "Strange Fruit" contained very specific references to the horrors of lynching at a time when Afro-Americans were still passionately calling for allies to assist in the campaign to eradicate this murderous manifestation of racism. At the same time, Billie Holiday's rendition expressed a universal condemnation of all assaults on the rights and lives of human beings.

*   *   *

During the 1930s, apologists for what was so cavalierly referred to as "American Democracy" attempted to pretend that the institution of lynching was merely a blemish on the country's past. While it was true that the lives of Afro-Americans were no longer systematically consumed by mob-violence in numbers that mounted into the thousands, as had been the case during the decades following emancipation, this did not mean that the hundreds of contemporary lynch victims could be brushed aside as insignificant. During the four years following the Stock Market crash in 1929, 150 Black people were lynched.[2] In the fall of 1934, a mere five years before Lady Day's encounter with the poem "Strange Fruit," a lynching occurred in Florida which should remain indelibly impressed on the memories of all who presume to understand the history of the United States. According to a newspaper account of the time,

> An eye-witness to the lynching . . . said that [Claude] Neal had been forced to mutilate himself before he died. The eye-witnesses gave the following account of the event which took place in a swamp beside the Chattahoochee River:
>
> ". . . first they cut off his penis. He was made to eat it. Then they cut off his testicles and made him eat them and say he liked it.
>
> "Then they sliced his sides and stomach with knives and every now and then somebody would cut off a finger or a toe. Red hot irons were used on the n————[deletion by Ed.] to burn him from top to bottom. From time to time during the torture, a rope would be tied around Neal's neck and he was pulled over a limb and held there until he almost choked to death, when he would be let down and the torture begun all over again. After several hours of this punishment, they decided to kill him.
>
> "Neal's body was tied to a rope on the rear of an automobile and dragged over the highway to the Cannidy home. Here a mob estimated to number somewhere between 3,000 to 7,000 people from eleven southern states was excitedly awaiting his arrival. . . .
>
> "A woman came out of the Cannidy house and drove a butcher knife into his heart. Then the crowd came by and some kicked him and some drove their cars over him."
>
> What remained of the body was brought by the mob to Marianna where it is now hanging from a tree on the northeast corner of the courthouse square.
>
> Photographers say they will soon have pictures of the body for sale at fifty cents each. Fingers and toes from Neal's body are freely exhibited on streetcorners here.[3]

Billie Holiday may never have witnessed such abominations firsthand, but she certainly grasped the connections between lynching, which constitutes one extreme of the spectrum of racism, and the daily routines of biases and prejudices which affect in some way every member of the Afro-American population. She apprehended in her own way a dynamic described by Franz Fanon when he wrote:

> One can not say that a given country is racist but that lynchings or extermina- tion camps are not to be found there. The truth is that all that and still other

things exist on the horizon. These virtualities, these latent tendencies circulate, carried by the life-stream of psycho-affective, economic relations.[4]

If the spectre of lynchings irrevocably conjured up other forms of racism, the lyrics of "Strange Fruit" immediately led Billie Holiday to reflect upon the circumstances of her father's death. When Lewis Allen showed her the poem he had written with the idea in mind of setting it to music, she said, "I dug it right off. It seemed to spell out all the things that had killed Pop."[5] Her father, jazz guitarist Clarence Holiday, had inhaled poison gas, during a battle in World War I, which caused him to have chronic lung problems. In March of 1937, while on tour in Texas with Don Redman's band, he developed a chest cold for which he received no treatment because of the segregation practices of the hospitals in that state. By the time the band reached Dallas, where he was able to seek medical attention, he had already contracted pneumonia and he died of a hemorrhage in the Jim Crow ward of the Veterans Hospital.[6] From Billie Holiday's perspective, to sing "Strange Fruit" was to release a passionate cry of protest against the racism which had killed her father.

Of course, Billie Holiday's gift of aesthetic communication did not simply consist in her ability to render in song the profound emotions underlying her own private woes. However skilfull she may have been in musically transmitting her own state of mind, this could never have served as the foundation for her greatness as an artist. While eloquently incorporating the emotions occasioned by her own personal tragedies in her songs, her particular condition functioned as a conduit permitting others to acquire insights about the emotional and social circumstances of their own lives. For Black people and their politically conscious white allies, "Strange Fruit" affirmed not only the existence of lynching and the web of racist institutions within which the abomination of lynching resided. It also signified the possibility and necessity of challenging and eventually eradicating this age-old oppression. For those who had not grasped the meaning of American racism, "Strange Fruit" functioned as a compelling statement of fact. As Bert Korall said of Billie Holiday in general, she

> . . . so illuminated human situations as to give the listener a rare, if frightening, glimpse into the realities of experience. Where others fear to tread, she reached out and touched, where others mask their eyes, she defiantly kept hers open.[7]

Invariably, some people had been so hardened by racism as to be impervious to her message. In a Los Angeles club, a woman requested that Billie sing "Strange Fruit" by saying, ". . . why don't you sing that sexy song you're famous for? You know, the one about naked bodies swinging in the trees?"[8] Needless to say, in such situations, for the sake of preserving the song's dignity, she refused to sing it.

In general, however, "Strange Fruit" rose out of socio-historical circumstances which provided the best backdrop, since the brief period of Radical Reconstruction, for the reception of such an impassioned plea for racial justice. If the 1920s had allowed for an expanding awareness of Afro-American art and culture in the wider population (even though this awareness was marred by racist notions of Black culture as "primitive" and "exotic"), the 1930s saw the emergence of important political and multi-racial alliances.

Organized challenges to lynching dated back to the turn-of-the-century efforts of Ida B. Wells. However, the ideological climate of the period, as well as through World War I and well into the 1920s, was so poisoned by racism that substantial numbers of white people could not be drawn into the anti-lynching campaigns. Billie Holiday's "Strange Fruit" echoed through circles of people who had been sensitized both by the trans-racial economic and social tragedies of the Great Depression and by the multi-racial mass movements seeking to redress the myriad grievances of Black and white alike.

Before the great movements of the 1930s and the consequent radicalization of large sectors of the population, "Strange Fruit" as a phenomenon would have been inconceivable. Indeed, an interracial night club like Cafe Society, where the song was born, would not have been viable at any other time. Barney Josephson, who opened this club at a time when even in Harlem Black and white people could not listen to jazz under the same roof, told Billie that " . . . this was to be one club where there was going to be no segregation, no racial prejudice."[9] And, in fact, according to Holiday's biographer, John Chilton:

> The liberal atmosphere of the club, with its clientele of "New Dealers," and the humanitarian principles of its owner made it a receptive setting for the presentation of the song's dramatic anti-lynching lyrics.[10]

If white people had developed a greater sensitivity to the plight of Afro-Americans, it was perhaps because enormous numbers of them had experienced in one form or another the devastation of the Great Depression. Workers' wages were cut almost in half and, by the last crisis year, seventeen million people were unemployed. Even more essential to the development of this sensitivity were the great mass movements which emerged during the 1930s—the campaign against unemployment and the extensive organizing of industrial unions associated with the CIO. The Communist Party, the Young Communist League and the Trade Union Unity League joined forces to establish the National Unemployed Councils, which were responsible for spectacular demonstrations throughout the country. On March 6, 1930, well over a million people participated in hunger marches in major urban centers—110,000 in New York, 100,000 in Detroit, for example. In December of 1931 and 1932, national hunger marches to Washington dramatized demands for unemployment insurance and other means of bringing relief to the unemployed.[11]

Such mass opposition to the anti-worker policies of the Hoover Administration played a pivotal role in the election of Franklin D. Roosevelt and the subsequent inauguration of the New Deal. Far from pacifying those who suffered the effects of the Great Depression, the New Deal served as a further catalyst for the organization of multi-racial mass movements. Black people, in particular, were hardly satisfied with the sedatives offered them by the New Deal Legislation. One of the most consequential of the mass organizations initiated during the Roosevelt years was the

American Youth Congress (AYC), founded in 1934. Although the government was responsible for the inception of the AYC, the more than four and a half million young people who joined it before the outbreak of the war in 1939 could not be contained by the policies of the government. Young Afro-Americans, especially in the South, played an indispensable part in developing the strategic direction of this organization. The Southern Negro Youth Congress, according to William Z. Foster, was "the most important movement ever conducted by Negro youth"[12] before the era of the Civil Rights Movement.

> It pioneered many of the constructive developments . . . in the South—including the right-to-vote movement, the unionization of Southern industry, the fight for the right of education and the general struggle against lynching and all forms of Jim Crow.[13]

As a result of the work of the American Youth Congress, the issue of federal anti-lynching legislation was placed on the national political agenda for the first time in the twentieth century since the thwarted efforts of the NAACP to secure the passage of an anti-lynching bill in 1921. Consequently, when Billie Holiday sang "Strange Fruit" in 1939, her message fell upon many ears that had long since been rendered receptive by the AYC's demand that the Roosevelt Administration support the enactment of a law against lynching.

This is not to say that Billie Holiday herself was necessarily aware of the political developments of the thirties which served as the backdrop for her own cultural contributions. She was not the only artist swept into the stream of political radicalization who was incognizant of all the political ramifications of her own work. The Thirties, according to Phillip Bonosky, constituted a "watershed in the American democratic tradition."

> It is a period which will continue to serve both the present and the future as a reminder and as an example of how an aroused people, led and spurred by the working class, can change the entire complexion of the culture of a nation.[14]

Bonosky continues,

> This period, for the first time in American history, saw the fundamental placing of the Negro and Jewish questions, which brought them out of the murky realm of private and personal ethics to their real roots in a class society. . . . [It] saw a dramatic change in every aspect of culture—its most characteristic feature being the discovery of the organic relationship between the intellectual and the people—the workers first of all.[15]

Although Billie Holiday was not directly associated with the artists' and cultural workers' movements related to the Works Progress Administration (WPA), she was clearly conscious of the need for radical change in the status of Black people in U.S. society. On countless occasions, she was herself the target of vitriolic expressions of racism. As a Black vocalist with Artie Shaw's all-white band, she encountered the crassness of Jim Crow on a daily basis when the band toured the Southern states. In Kentucky, for example, a small-town sheriff who tried his best to prevent her from performing, finally came up to the bandstand and asked Shaw, "What's Blackie going to sing?"[16] In St. Louis, the man who had hired the band to play in one of the city's largest ballrooms confronted Billie by saying, "What's that n----- [deletion by Ed.] doing there? I don't have n-----s [deletion by Ed.] to clean up around here."[17] Needless to say, there were numerous incidents surrounding her hotel rooms and the eating establishments where she attempted to buy meals. "I got to the point where I hardly ever ate, slept or went to the bathroom without having a major NAACP-type production."[18]

> Sometimes we'd make a six-hundred-mile jump and stop only once. Then it would be a place where I couldn't get served, let alone crash the toilet without causing a scene. At first I used to be ashamed. Then finally I just said to hell with it. When I had to go, I'd just ask the bus driver to stop and let me off at the side of the road. I'd rather go into the bushes than take a chance in the restaurants and towns.[19]

Billie Holiday's social consciousness was deeply rooted in her own experiences—and she had indeed experienced more than her share of racism. While she was not one to engage in any extended political analyses, she never attempted to conceal where her loyalties were. "I'm a race woman,"[20] she proclaimed on numerous occasions. According to Josh White, who developed a friendship with her after an initial collision surrounding his performance of "Strange Fruit," "she had more thought for humanity and was more race-conscious than people thought."[21]

Billie Holiday's unique ability to imbue her music with authentic human feelings and thus to touch the hearts of all who had the privilege of hearing her was more evident in her singing of "Strange Fruit" than any other song. And this song posed a number of serious problems with respect to its rendering. With its forceful metaphors, an overly dramatic rendering might have transformed its powerful emotional content into histrionics. The intent behind this song—both Allen's and Holiday's—was to invoke the emotions of solidarity with its auditors. Unfortunately sometimes, art with this intent misses the aim and instead occasions feelings of pity. If those who were touched by "Strange Fruit" exited from the experience of feeling pity for Afro-American victims of racism, instead of solidarity and compassion, the underlying dynamics of racism would have been reduplicated instead of challenged. For white people thus moved by the song, the superiority of the white race would have been implicitly affirmed. But unless one is an incurable racist, it is difficult to listen to Billie Holiday's rendering of "Strange Fruit" without sensing the plea for human solidarity—equality even in the process of challenging racist horrors and indignities. One is able to identify with the "Black bodies swinging in the southern breeze" as human beings who deserve the right to live and love. " The lyric is stark and moving," as John Chilton put it,

> and Billie wrings every ounce of emotion from the terrifying description of Black bodies hanging from the trees. Billie's supreme artistry ensures that there is no melodrama.[22]

Glenn Coulter writes about

[the] uncanny expression of horror which transcends its willful lyric when Billie sings it, and becomes a frozen lament, a paralysis of feeling truer to psychology than any conventional emotionalism could be.[23]

If Billie Holiday ushered into popular music culture a new and original approach to singing, her decision to feature "Strange Fruit" as the centerpiece of her work established the basis for a tradition that was taken up later by musicians such as Nina Simone, whose "Mississippi Goddam" became an anthem of the Civil Rights era. "Strange Fruit" was a frontal challenge not only to lynching and racism, but to the policies of a government which implicitly condoned such actions, especially in its refusal thus far to secure the passage of laws against lynching. It was an undisguised rallying cry against the state. "The message of Lewis Allen's poem," in the words of jazz critic Leonard Feather,

had a meaning more vital than any of the soufflé-songs she had been handed by record producers. This was the first significant protest in words and music, the first unmuted cry against racism. It was radical and defiant at a time when Blacks and whites alike found it dangerous to make waves, to speak out against a deeply entrenched status quo.[24]

Joachim Berendt called it

the most emphatic and most impassioned musical testimony against racism to become known before Abbey Lincoln's interpretation of Max Roach's "Freedom Now Suite" of 1960.[25]

"Strange Fruit" became a permanent piece in Billie Holiday's repertoire and, of more than 350 songs she sang, this one remains inextricably connected to the prevailing image of Lady Day. However, at the time, she was unable to convince Columbia, the recording company with which she was under contract, to permit her to record it. "They won't buy it in the South," was the company's response. "We'll be boycotted. . . . It's too inflammatory."[26] Billie persisted, however, and eventually John Hammond released her for one recording date with Commodore, whose head, Milt Gabler agreed to record it.

Billie Holiday's recording of "Strange Fruit" achieved something far greater than permanent preservation of her most important song, the aesthetic centerpiece of her career. Eventually millions would hear her sing this haunting anti-lynching appeal, and few not feel edified. People of many races, cultures and nations would be moved and simultaneously educated—thus fulfilling the artist's goal of lifting her listeners' consciousness. Yet, many others would be more deeply touched by Lady Day's musical protest than she could ever imagine. Would she have predicted that "Strange Fruit" would impel people to discover within themselves a previously unawakened calling to political activism? Or could she have understood how artists with incorruptible aesthetic principles would be inspired by this song to realize how passionately political their work could be without compromising an ounce of their aesthetic integrity? And could she have even sensed that catalytic role her song would play in rejuvenating a tradition of anti-lynching and anti-racist literature which had been initiated in the nineteenth century by such great abolitionists as Frances E. W. Harper. No, Lady Day could not have begun to fathom the vast influence and imperishable prestige of her courageous song of protest. Indeed, the literary continuum extending from "Strange Fruit" consists of works that would amount to volumes of poems, songs, novels and short stories about racist violence visited upon Black people. Occupying a prominent position on that continuum is a poem entitled "Lynchsong" whose author, Lorraine Hansberry, was linked by race and gender to the creator of the ancestral song. As an Afro-American woman who was far more knowledgeable of her people's culture than most of her contemporaries, Lorraine Hansberry was certainly conscious of the literary kinship between "Lynchsong" and "Strange Fruit."

Laurel:
Name sweet like the breath of peace

Blood and blood
Hatred there
White robes and
Black robes
And a burning
Burning cross

      cross in Laurel
      cross in Jackson
      cross in Chicago

And a
Cross in front of the
City Hall
In:
New York City

Lord
Burning cross
Lord
Burning man
Lord
Murder cross

Laurel:
Name bitter like the rhyme of a lynchsong

I can hear Rosalee
See the eyes of Willie McGee
My mother told me about
Lynchings
My mother told me about

The dark nights
and dirt roads
and torch lights
and lynch robes

    sorrow night
    and a
    sorrow night

The
faces of men
Laughing white
Faces of men
Dead in the night

    sorrow night
    and a
    sorrow night.[27]

NOTES

1. Billie Holiday (with William Dufty), *Lady Day Sings the Blues*, (New York: Penguin Books, 1984), p. 84.

2. William Z. Foster, *The Negro People in American History*, (New York: International Publishers, 1954), p. 480.

3. Ralph Ginzberg, *One Hundred Years of Lynching*, (New York: Lancer Books, 1969), p. 222.

4. Franz Fanon, "Racism and Culture," *Toward the African Revolution* (New York: Grove Press, 1964), p. 41.

5. Holiday, p. 84.

6. Ibid. pp. 68–69; John Chilton, *Billie's Blues*, (New York: Stein and Day, 1978), p. 75.

7. William Dufty, Liner Notes, *The Billie Holiday Story*, Decca DXB 161.

8. Holiday, p. 84.

9. Ibid., p. 83.

10. Chilton, p. 68.

11. Foster, p. 479.

12. Ibid. p. 480.

13. Ibid.

14. Phillip Bonosky, "The 'Thirties' in American Culture," *Political Affairs*, May 1959.

15. Ibid.

16. Holiday, p. 74.

17. Ibid.

18. Ibid.

19. Ibid. p. 76.

20. Chilton, p. 69.

21. Ibid., p. 104.

22. Ibid., p. 217.

23. Charles E. Smith, "Billie Holiday," in Nat Shapiro and Nat Hentoff, *The Jazz Makers* (New York: Da Capo Press, 1979), p. 288.

24. Leonard Feather, Liner Notes, "Billie Holiday: Strange Fruit," Atlantic Records SD 1614, 1972.

25. Joachim Berendt, *The Jazz Book: From New Orleans to Rock and Free Jazz* (New York: Lawrence Hill and Company, 1975), p. 310.

26. Feather, op. cit.

27. Lorraine Hansberry, "Lynchsong," *Masses and Mainstream*, Vol. 4, No. 7, July, 1951.

WHO SAYS BLACK FOLKS COULD SING AND DANCE?

"Dance Black America," at the Brooklyn
Academy of Music,
April 21–24, 1983

NTOZAKE SHANGE was born in 1948. She is a
playwright, poet, novelist, and essayist. Her most famous and
controversial work is *For Colored Girls Who Have Considered Suicide,
When the Rainbow Is Enuf: A Choreopoem* (1977). She was good friends
with the late controversial photographer Robert Mapplethorpe and each
has work featured in the other's books. "Who Says Black Folks Could
Sing and Dance?", a review of the program, was published in
Dancemagazine in August 1983. It was reprinted in Shange's collection
of essays, *See No Evil: Prefaces, Reviews, and Essays, 1974–1983* (1984).

JOURNAL ENTRY #692
what does it mean that blk folks cd sing n dance?
why do we say that so much/we dont know what we mean/
i saw what that means/good god/did i see/like i cda
walked on the water myself/i cda clothed the naked & fed
the hungry/with what dance i saw tonite/i don't mean dance
i mean a closer walk with thee/a race thru swamps that fall
off in space/i mean i saw the black people move the ground
& set stars beneath they feet/so what's this mean that
black folks cd dance/well/how abt a woman like dyane har-
vey who can make
her body the night riders & the runaways/the children han-
gin
on they mama's dress/while they father's beat to death/the
blood/from the man's wounds/his woman's tears/the night
riders

goin off in darkness/the silence of the night

how abt bernadine j. whose body waz all of that in 5 min-
utes/& whose very presence humbled all but the drum/
now that's a dance/like rael lamb careenin cross
the stage on his bare stomach/fifty feet/
sounds like possums n rattlesnakes/mississippi undercurrents
& steamin hog mawls/tossin him from decatur to south texas/
tearin him from contraction to leaps so expansive/his body
took the space allowed thirty redwood trees/& those sounds
kept pushin him/little racing motors like the cops waz
round the bend/windows opened & shut cuz there are things
others ought not hear/feet on stairways of burned out homes/
the sounds pushed him/& there was a dance that was a black
dance/that's what it means that black folks cd dance/it
dont mean we got rhythm/it dont mean the slop or the hully
gully/
or this dance in houston callt "the white boy"/it dont mean
just
what what we do all the time/it's how we remember what
cannot be said/
that's why the white folks say it aint got no form/what was
the form
of slavery/what was the form of jim crow/& how wd they
know . . .

—N. SHANGE,
Sassafrass, Cypress & Indigo, 1982

What do we mean by this racist cliché that all black folks can sing and dance? Some answers were provided by Dance Black America, April 21 through 24, 1983, at the Brooklyn Academy of Music. The festival afforded us an intellectual as well as aesthetic immersion in the realms of Afro-American movement since the Diaspora, also known as slavery. Colloquia examining regional and folk dance, the legacy and implications of Dunham, our relationships to Latin and African forms were preparations for performances and choreographic exploration by Afro-Americans from all over the country.

Many of these movers I have seen before:

In the basement of a church in Harlem, Chuck Davis teaches till sweat seeps from the floor and the spirits of the drums push ancient Africa from our modern black bodies. On East 12th Street in New York City, Rod Rodgers is free in movement and committed, through dance, to the end of racism, nuclear war, and hunger. Uptown at Sounds-in-Motion on Lenox Avenue, Dianne McIntyre utilizes what we know of Cunningham, Horton, and Graham with the force of her slight body: herself, dance. Downtown Eleo Pomare in his dances addresses muscle and the patient strength that has kept Afro-Americans in the New World from disappearing from the face of the earth. His *Las Desenamorados* is more than a realization of the pain of being "the unbeloved." It is a singular effort to find the believable in the midst of despair: the impossible.

Chuck Davis's *Lenjen-Go Mandiani*, Rod Rodger's *Box*, Dianne McIntyre's *Etude in Free*—only part of this marvelous distillation of our struggle to survive: Dance Black America.

Talley Beatty's *Rainbow* is one gift my mother gave me; his lyricism is still "una regalia," a gift. *The Road of the Phoebe Snow*, Beatty's contribution to the program, is one of the more technically difficult pieces of our time. I saw it performed admirably, courageously, by the Alvin Ailey Repertory Ensemble. Blondell Cummings performed her *Chicken Soup*, in which the kitchen is the center of our lives. Once in San Francisco, she and I planted fifty-five bulbs of flowers, to bloom as black dance in America should bloom. We are a blossoming people, "floras negras." Louis Johnson once stopped me on Grove Street to say we must dance. His *Forces of Rhythm*, performed impeccably by the Philadelphia Dance Company, fuses classical, modern, ethnic, and jazz styles, showing us how to dance, and why.

We must sing and dance or we shall die an inert, motionless, "sin ritmo" death. "Negros muertos," killed by a culture afraid of who we are and what we have to say with our bodies, our music, and our brains. Black folks do have brains. We even have ideologists, scholars, choreographers, and always the grace of the gods . . . although my teacher, Fred Benjamin, sometimes tests Christ, inviting Mary Magdalene to pick up her skirts and switch a bit to the beat of her soul: our souls—a collective whole. One people, one motion in myriad forms. Ask Vèvè Clark, the dance scholar, what she does in Haiti. I assure you, bad back or not, she's not reading books. She's dancing. Between the legendary feet of Pepsi Bethel and the jazz of us all, between Charles Moore and "el afro-latino de nosotros," there is a space open to all human beings unafraid of the ferocity of a people who take dance seriously, who seriously dance, and are generous enough to share.

Such as *Lenjen-Go Mandiani*, performed by the Chuck Davis Dance Company:

Listen to the drum from Congo Square to East 110th. Lift those feet! Swing those arms! Become a swan who sees something she can't resist up in the sky somewhere. Chuck Davis lifts us off our feet. A scenario, life uptown moving to the beat. What beat? "Say, man, where's the party at? Right there under your feet!" in the words of the rock group Time, the slick-headed boys from Minnesota. Chuck Davis demonstrates it, brightly.

Lots of critics only talk about our costumes, our colors. That's true, we are a people of color, with color. We cula ful: yellow, violet, green, orange, pink, and always black. Many rows of women, hips back and forth, east to west; young men in the throes of the drum as we all are, if we feel it. Never forgetting the flexibility of our backs—say our necks, in more unfortunate circumstances. We sing. We dance. As Vèvè Clark said at one of the festival's symposia, the question is not "What is black dance?" but what *it* is—what the spirit is. Dance on. Pat those feet through the soil. Let those toes grip the earth we worked. Take back the land, the souls of our great-grandparents in the earth. We don't need no shoes. We need to dig and jump into the land we come from; one woman after another, one dream upon the other, calling up who we are. If there are still questions about the angers of Afro-American dance, look only at the bent knees, fluid backs, vigorous arms of the Chuck Davis Dance Company. "No hay nada mas de discutar."

Such as Arthur Hall's *Marie Laveaux and Danse Congo Square*, performed by Arthur Hall's Afro-American Ensemble:

Through a remarkable golden raffia emerge dancers as slaves, looking for a moment to, as Larry Graham says, "puleese release yourself." In this piece the European influence of the New World is already apparent in the "danzon" nature of the movement and the coupling off of male and female. At that time we were merely property with rhythm. In Curaçao, Martinique, Vera Cruz, and Charleston we danced these dances—a strange syncretism for "Las Siete Potencias," the Seven Powers, and for what we had become in the New World, manifest in the walk of Arthur Hall.

The excerpt from Hall's *Fat Tuesday*, a high ceremony of candles, sequins, and drums, with a deity draped in yellow and black, undulating under marvels of feathers, takes us back once again to some form of parity. A movement not defiled— or at least not violated. Though we all know the truth of the matter. In West Africa, Elégua was a young man, virile guard of the crossroads. In the New World, Elégua is an old and crippled man. Think for a moment: Our crossroads was an ocean. Double-dutch to sand-dancing, roller-disco to Lucumbe, alive and well in Cuba. There is always a continuity to our movement. Subtle, erotic, informed by history, known and unknown.

"Hambone, Hambone, have you heard. . . . " Seven young men stomp out, letting us know that the gracious beauty of the disco dances emerges from the crudity and unselfconsciousness of our workers—our ancestors, called slaves. We make minstrelsy our own, even wearing red velvet, but no burnt cork. Our dance reflects the many ways we've avoided death, insisted on living. For the beat, for the heat, for the freedom of dance. Ain't no way to keep us down on no ground. We just jump up, again and again and again.

A brass band and saxophones leading us to someone's promised land. An old New Orleans procession, right here in Brooklyn. Like we don't have to go so far to get home. Déjan's Olympia Brass Band of New Orleans can always see me "home," by the mercy of our Lord Jesus Christ, whose cross appears in the sky as the band escorts the lost soul to the Promised Land. Very bright colors, of course, because nothing stops Carnival.

Such as Lenwood Sloan's *Darktown Strutter's Ball/Strut Miss Lizzie* , danced by Halifu Osumare and Leon Jackson, with Neal Tate on the piano and Ruth Brisbane singing:

So black et rouge. We've been everywhere; ask Josephine or Katherine. Our music and dance is our answer to our interaction with the world—all of it, from Clark Air Force Base in Manila to Guantanamo. A black somebody felt something enough to move him/her: "Let's do it, let's do it till we can't stand no mo'."

In Oakland, California, at Everybody's Creative Arts Center Halifu Osumare breathes, relaxes. Her movement reflects today and yesterday. Tonight at BAM, in "All the Dusky Gals Were There," Osumare is as enchanting as any Southern belle could be, including Scarlett O'Hara. She and her partner, Leon Jackson, exhibit the delicacy we have managed to sustain throughout the bombing of Tulsa, the riots of Liberty City, and "white only" water fountains. We have a grace about us that Dunham may have called the ability to stretch. We are all ready at the barre. The stretch is survival.

Such as the Navy Yard Boys Club Sea Cadets' *Pickin' Em Up and Puttin' Em Down*:

Military grouping. "Cultura y armas." In case we forgot there's a struggle going on here. In Nicaragua, El Salvador, St. Alban's, Angola—seems like everywhere black folks live, we gotta be ready to fight. Turn about and open ranks in your sunglasses and apple jack caps. Defend our right to make art. 1–2–3–4. Turn to the rear. Cover your back. You are too precious to lose, to abandon here in Brooklyn. Dance on, guns in hand. Who would know which was make-believe, the guns or our spirit? Who would dare take a chance on making a mistake?

Such as *Harlem Rent Party*, an assembly of dances performed by Mama Lu Parks' Jazz Dancers:

Take some tap dancing, a boa or two, and black hips: "now that gonna be a dance." Our bodies become our instruments. No trumpets, but some feet that don't miss a beat, and never missed the "A Train." Shakin', shakin' on up past 59th Street, straight to 125th, where we all know what the step is. Especially for a rent party, where we doin "Sweet Georgia Brown." Pick up them feet. Pass the hat. Oh, remember the Apollo amateur nights. Now Mama Lu Parks with a young Sammy Davis tap dancing with a younger Debbie Allen. Time step, triple that, and break it on down. Where'd you put that accent, boy? This is the real deal. Don't mess around 'less you really plannin on "messin" with it.

In Brazil, we play the dozens with "Capoeira." Here in America, English-speaking, we play the dozens with taps and our tongues. But there's always a winner—an older man, experienced warrior of rhythm like Al Perryman. For without our drums, there's only our hands and feet, the voice of a people supposedly inarticulate, assumed inaudible. But James Brown and Little Anthony never had problems being heard, nor did George Jackson. Silently, moving along like Sojourner in the night, moving on toward liberty.

But right now, we gonna Lindy Hop. Pachucos and black folks living for the moment of glory, when we move. War or no war, what has our life been: one long marathon dance. Pass that hat. The rent's due. Dance it up. Dance it away. Ballet shoes aren't enough to say alla this. Get those feet up off the ground and put them women up in the air. This here's a life dance. It's hard, and full of travail. Get them feet off of the ground. Reach for the world. Take it.

"You Could Have Been Anything You Wanted To," the BISS Harmonizers sing for us, bringing us to our childhoods and recent history of corner du-wop. "Babee, how could I let you get away?" Where did we let black dancers go? Can we find a place in our hearts for all we been missing? Can we get a hold to it now? Who is looking for Sonora Matancera or Celia Cruz? Who is looking for Pepsi

Bethel or Sounds-in-Motion? Elijah said we were the lost-found people. Let's find ourselves now. It's in the beat, the beat called destiny.

We could paint our way out like Doze, spray can in hand behind the Jazzy Double Dutch Jumpers, but foreigners to our culture call that graffiti. Fab 5 Freddy says we can rap our way out, but the foreigners call that illiterate. What is the path to freedom, and how many ways can we get there? Dance on. Rap on. "Don't Stop 'Til You Get Enough." Smurf on, brothers. Just don't hurt yourself, man. Be a little more gentle on them black bones. Listen to Master Blaster. He say, "It's called survival. Only the strong can survive." And it's true, black folks do sing, and glory hallelujah, we do dance. Dance we do.

WHAT "JAZZ"
MEANS TO ME

MAX ROACH, drummer, composer, MacArthur Fellow, is one of the most famous jazz musicians in the world. A child of the bebop era that produced the likes of Charlie Parker, Dizzy Gillespie, Thelonious Monk, Miles Davis, and others, Roach also became noted for his legendary 1960 album, *We Insist—The Freedom Now Suite*, part of an era of politicized jazz music which featured work by Oscar Brown, Jr., and Nina Simone, among others. "What 'Jazz' Means to Me," published in *The Black Scholar* in the Summer 1972 issue, is Roach's further exploration of the political significance of the music through a discussion of how and why the music got its name.

While it is apparent to many of us that a transformation in black consciousness is taking place throughout the political, social and cultural framework of the United States, it is not always clear, the relationship which black music has to that transformation. Nor is it clear, the impact which this transformation of black consciousness has had on black musicians, and on the black man's perception of his music.

What I shall do here is attempt to make those relationships more clear, drawing upon my own lifetime of experience in the black music industry. Since the essence of black consciousness is the recognition of a distinct black identity, it is essential for us to recognize the black nature of our music, and develop the appropriate terms and nomenclature for that music and the things which relate to it.

Let us first eliminate the term "jazz." It is not a term or a name that we, as black musicians, ever gave to the art which we created. It is a name which was given to the Afro-American's art form by white America, . . . which therefore inherits all the racist and prurient attitudes which have been directed to all other aspects of the black experience in this country.

If we check out the etymology of the word "jazz," we find that it has its roots in 19th-century Afro-American slang. "Jazz" was a term referring to the act of sexual intercourse and other aspects of the sexual experience. According to Webster's *New World Dictionary*, College Edition, jazz has the following origins: "Creole patois *jass*, sexual term applied to the Congo dances (New Orleans); present use from Chicago, c. 1914 but ? from earlier similar use in the vice district of New Orleans." The history of the word "jazz" tells us much about the entry of this Afro-American music into the white American experience, and the attitudes toward it.

From the etymology just outlined, we see that the term "jazz" first entered the vocabulary of white America in 1914, and it carried with it, loose, free-swinging, bawdy-house connotations. It's not surprising, therefore, that a period of permissive behavior thereafter came to be known as The Jazz Age—the 1920s. It was a period of self-avowed irresponsibility, related morality and gay behavior. Black musicians, presumably as some kind of sexual totem, were sought out, courted and listened to in the black bowels of Harlem and Chicago, New Orleans, and other cities, by the swinging white set of that era.

Furthermore, when "jazz" did become acceptable and assimilated throughout white America on a mass basis, it was taken over by white production-recording and managing industries. This became the period of the big bands in the '30s, promoting white musicians such as Bix Beiderbeck, Benny Goodman, the Dorsey brothers and others.

It is of course a crowning irony that Paul Whiteman became named as "the King of Jazz." And, during the same period, the foremost black musician was labelled, "the Duke"—Duke Ellington. It is sufficient to point out here that Duke Ellington has continued into the 1970s as a vital force in black music, and that his Twenties and Thirties compositions are still alive—"Caravan," "Black, Brown and Beige," "Mood Indigo"—and still played. Whereas there's not a single Paul Whiteman tune or arrangement still alive.

The point is not to debate the relationship of black and white musicians throughout the history of black music. But, instead, to delineate a clear line of black musical development from Duke (and before Duke) on into the present, to indicate that black music was and still is locked in the jaws of racism and exploitation.

What "jazz" means to me is the worst kind of working conditions, the worst in cultural prejudice. I could go down a list of club names throughout the country which are a disgrace to somebody who has been in the business as long as I have and who has attained "the kind of status" in the black music world that I have, who has been called "one of the giants," one of the founders of this, that and the other. Club conditions and expenses are such—especially transportation costs—that increasingly fewer musicians are making night club tours. The musician has to have at least four weeks at a club, as well as a concert or two to defray the cost of transportation—especially if he takes his whole group, four or five men, with him. Typically, the clubs are owned by persons who have no cultural or musical appreciation of black music. The prevailing attitude is, "Play 40 minutes on the bandstand, come off and take 20 minutes," then back on the set—which is impossible to do.

So jazz to me has meant small dingy places, the worst kinds of salaries and conditions that one can imagine. With the leading clubs, it takes years to develop a reputation before you can demand more than "the union scale." Take for instance in Harlem, the Village of Harlem. There, the union wages for a black musician who doesn't have the stature of a Miles Davis or Dizzy Gillespie or Duke Ellington, or a record album, the scale is so low I hesitate to mention it. It is $90 a week. A man who might have majored in music and has decided to pursue black music as his life work and to take care of his family until he achieves stature, is subject to these dismal wages and treatment. The same situation prevails the length and breadth of this country, of course.

Furthermore, clubs in the black areas of town of course pay lower than in the white sections of the city. The argument is that the poverty of black people as an audience keeps the club from making money. However, of course, people come from all over the area to these clubs when some musician of stature works there. Whereas, in the downtown area a man can have a club half the size of the club in the black area and his scale goes up to $175 to $200 a week.

The term "jazz" has come to mean the abuse and exploitation of black musicians; it has come to mean cultural prejudice and condescension. It has come to mean all of these things, and that is why I am presently writing a book, *I Hate Jazz*. It's not my name and it means my oppression as a man and musician.

Of course I do not hate black music, of which I am a part, which is a part of me, and which expresses the vision of black people here in America. My point is that we must decolonize our minds and re-name and re-define ourselves. What is "jazz?" It is the cultural expression of Africans who are dispersed on this North American continent. It derives in a continuing line from the musical and cultural traditions of Africa.

We must recognize what those traditions are, what it is we are doing musically, how we learn our music, how it pleases and has meaning, and what its significance is.

First of all, the "jazz musician" spends as much time developing his craft as any musician in the world. It is a 24-hour thing with us. We learn it mostly from mouth to mouth in rap sessions, in practice and improvisation with each other. We do not learn our craft by going to schools or academies, complete with blackboards, text books and rigid homework assignments. But there is tremendous "homework" and discipline going on.

We have to listen to records. The kid who plays like John Coltrane today can't read Coltrane in a book. He gets it from records. He has to listen, to learn by his ears, which constantly sharpens his rhythm, timing, tone and musicality.

I remember myself, one day I asked Sidney Cabot, who is a great innovator and also a great musician, "How could I develop my left hand? I've got to get a fast left hand." So he said to me, which was really a very fine technique, "The simple things you do with your right hand, do with your left hand. If you open the house door with the key in your right hand, put your key in your left-hand pocket." He did not tell me to go home and practice with my left hand for 20 hours a day. His approach gave my left hand more sense of belonging to me than going home and practicing with the drumsticks. Consequently, over a period of time, I found myself doing things I ordinarily would not have done—musically and personally, with this new dexterity.

By contrast, some years ago in the '40s, I had been playing on 52nd street and had a little loot. So I enrolled in a conservatory, with a percussion major. I went the first day to my percussion teacher and he asked me to play something for him. Well, the first thing he said to me was *that I held the sticks wrong.* Now I was on 52nd street working with Charlie Parker, Coleman Hawkins, making more money than he was making. He said, "You are holding the sticks wrong." Well, his point of reference was how to drum, in a symphony orchestra. Whereas, my thing was down close to everything, settled into the drums so that any of them could be reached instantly. So I said, "Man, if I change the way I hold the sticks and everything, I wouldn't be able to pay my tuition to this place."

Or let us take singing, for example. To develop the kind of quality Mahalia Jackson developed as a singer takes a lot of time and training. Black people come up in the church at 5, 6, 7, 8 years old. Instead of playing or singing a piece at graduation to show what you have learned the four years you have been in the conservatory, there is, instead, the way a Mahalia Jackson or an Aretha Franklin has developed and demonstrates ability. It is a much stronger form because they have to sing before a group of people and either make somebody cry or jump up and shout for joy.

Now that, to me, is what an artist is all about. No matter how much technique you have got, if you don't create some kind of emotion or some kind of electricity between yourself and somebody else, it doesn't mean a damned thing—whether you are a writer, a painter, a musician, what have you. We have come from that school as black people, that when somebody doesn't get something from you, then you don't have anything anyway.

I am often asked, "Can whites play your kind of music?" My answer is, "Yes, anybody can play something that's already been set out there. If a painter paints a certain thing, I can imitate it. But no whites have ever contributed to the creative or innovative aspects of black music." White musicians have not contributed for the same reason that no blacks have come to the stature of Debussy and Schönberg and others in Western European music. For, society has forbidden either musician to be fully engaged in the other's culture. And, all of our art forms grow out of culture. Our way of life is a culture—the way we eat, the way we look at our women, the way we swagger when we walk, the way black women have big fannies— this is all part of the culture, nor is the value of that culture sufficiently appreciated. Nobody has ever bestowed a doctorate upon musicians like Charlie Parker or Duke Ellington, yet both are past masters of creativity.

But beyond recognizing the esthetics and the learning processes involved in black music, we must cleanse our minds of false categories which are not basic to us and which divide us rather than unite us. They are misnomers: jazz music, rhythm and blues, rock and roll, gospel, spirituals, blues, folk music. Regardless of what they are called, they are various expressions of black music, black culture itself, the expression of Africans in the diaspora. Yet black musicians are placed in these categories, their works are merchandised and they face financial success or failure depending upon the popularity of their classification at a given time. Take Ray Charles, for example. He's a black musician—and he does everything. He sings everything, plays piano and alto saxophone, composes, writes, arranges in the complete range of black music. Once it's boiled down, he is a black musician playing black music. Period. Nor is he unique, unusual, or an exception. He is typical.

The categories and misnomers extend beyond music, as well. Take the term "civil rights." What do you mean, I don't have my civil rights. When I tumbled out of my mother's womb, I had my rights to everything that everybody else has. It was never a matter of my getting my civil rights; it was a matter of my regaining something wrongfully taken from me. Yet, in its context, "civil rights" was a shadow which someone else placed before me, saying, "Well, your problem is that you don't have civil rights." So, I fought for this shadow called civil rights, at that time. And there are other terms: "black power, black studies, revolutionary, ghetto, slums, avant garde, black experience, militant, integration, non-violence, etc." I often wonder when I hear black people talking and using these terms constantly, if they ever realize that this terminology did not come from black people to describe the black condition, but instead came overwhelmingly from white media, academia and politicians?

In all respects, culturally, politically, socially, we must re-define ourselves and our lives, in our own terms. As we continue this process, we will more accurately see indeed what we are, and what power we do have. The power is there. Music is a 20-billion-dollar-a-year industry, and it has been built and sustained by the talents of black people. We must see this fact as a prime example of the power and capability black people possess. And we must learn to translate this new vision into effective management and practice, to control our lives, to liberate the basic black creativity and ingenuity that have allowed us to survive, and move beyond survival to power and dominion.

THE ETHOS OF
THE BLUES

LARRY NEAL's "The Ethos of the Blues" appeared in *The Black Scholar*, Summer 1972.

It's the mood. . . . That's the carry-over from slavery—nothing but trouble in sight for everyone. There was no need to hitch your wagon to a star because there wasn't any stars. You got only what you fought for. Spirituals were the natural release—"Times gonna git better in de promised land"— but many a stevedore knew only too well that his fate was definitely tied up in his own hands. If he was clever and strong, and didn't mind dying, he came through—the weak ones always died. A blue mood—since prayers often seemed futile the words were made to fit present situations that were much more real and certainly more urgent.

—CLARENCE WILLIAMS talking to E. SIMMS CAMPBELL in *Jazzmen*

This "mood" to which Clarence Williams refers is the characteristic personality or ethos that informs the spirituals and the gospel songs. This "mood" or mode is the emotional archetype from which the blues spring. The blues, with all of their contradictions, represent, for better or for worse, the essential vector of the Afro-American sensibility and identity. Birthing themselves sometimes between the end of formal slavery and the turn of the century, the blues represent the ex-slave's confrontation with a more secular evaluation of the world. They were shaped in the context of social and political oppression, but they do *not*, as Maulana Karenga said, *collectively* "teach resignation." To hear the blues in this manner is to totally misunderstand the essential function of the blues, because the blues are basically defiant in their attitude toward life. They are about survival on the meanest, most gut level of human existence. They are, therefore, lyric responses to the facts of life. The essential motive behind the best blues song is the acquisition of insight, wisdom.

Now the spirituals and the gospels are obviously concerned with moral wisdom, but encounter here takes place against a specific symbolic text, i.e. the Bible and its attendant folklore; while, for the blues singer, the world is his text. In the social sense, therefore, we sometimes find an implicit conflict between gospel people and blues people. In some parts of the South, the known blues singer was often not even welcomed in the church. This is ironic since both forms of music spring from the same esthetic; and also, there is no disputing the number of popular blues-oriented singers who had their apprenticeship in the church.

What we have here is not merely a social dichotomy along simplistic tribal lines, but different metaphysical attitudes toward existence. The blues impulse was very early associated with the more sinister aspects of life. It was perceived as springing from a deep dark place within the black ethos. Here, Dude Botley talks about Buddy Bolden, who in the historiography of the music, is seen as the major synthesizing agent—i.e. legend has it, that he was one of the first to infuse the voice of the blues into the European horn:

> And I got to thinking about how many thousands of people Bolden had made happy and all them women who used to idolize him and them supposed to be friends. Where are they now? I say to myself. Then I hear Bolden's cornet. I look through the crack (in door) and there he is, *relaxed* back in the chair, blowing that silver cornet *softly*, just above a *whisper*, and I see he's got his hat over the bell of the horn. I put my ear close to the keyhole. I thought I had heard Bolden play the *blues* before, and play the *hymns* at *funerals*, but what he is playing now is *real strange* and I listen carefully, because he's playing something that, for a while sounds like the blues, then like a hymn. I cannot make out the tune, but after awhile I catch on. He is *mixing* up the blues with the hymns. He plays the blues *real* sad and the hymn sadder than the blues and then the blues sadder than the hymn. That is the first time that I had ever heard hymns and blues cooked up together. Strange cold feeling comes over me; *I get sort of scared because I know the Lord don't like that mixing the Devil's music with his music.* But I still listen because the music sounds so strange and I am sort of hypnotized. I close my eyes, and *when he blows the blues I picture Lincoln Park with all them sinners and whores shaking and belly rubbing. Then, as he blows the hymn, I picture my mother's church on Sunday, and everybody humming with the choir.* The picture in my mind kept changing with the music as he blew. It sounded like a *battle between the Good Lord and the Devil.* Something tells me to listen and see who wins, if he stops on the blues, the Devil wins.

Obviously, the two modes of musical expression are seen as antithetical to each other. I am sure that some of the readers remember how adamantly the late Mahalia Jackson refused to sing the blues. The blues undoubtedly owe something to that sense of body-reality depicted in Botley's description of the "sinners" in Lincoln

Park. For is not the "shaking and belly rubbing" finally the expression of the larger will to survive—to feel life in ones innermost being, even though it takes place in an oppressive political context?

Consider, for example, the manner in which Afro-Americans use the word "mean" to describe a piece of music: "Monk's solo was *mean*," or "Trane blows a *mean* horn." What about the expression "mean and evil" which we often find in the blues? And could the "Devil" in Dude Botley's description of the Bolden solo, symbolize not the Christian Satan, but a cluster of deeply felt emotional experiences that manifest themselves in the ethos and the esthetic of the blues? Therefore, Dude Botley gives us two kinds of ritual. One is Secular and African—"shaking and belly rubbing"—the other is institutionalized ritual—his mother's church where "everybody" is humming. Two forms of ritual, one associated with acceptance of the ways of the Hebrew Jesus, i.e., the Lamb of God. The other ritual, on the outside of the church, in the green park, stands in opposition to the value system of Christianity. There are obviously contending angels here. The Blues Spirit, the dark angel of the African voice is in a tug-of-war for Bolden's soul with the white voice of the Christian missionaries. To be "mean" in the lexicon of the blues is to express one's emotional experiences in the most profound, most intense manner possible. It means daring to be, to feel, to see.

The ex-slave questions the morality and religion of the over-all white society. This was a natural reaction to the world he saw around him. It was a place of torture and pain. But the world is also a place of wonder and encounter. Occasionally, one glimpsed some promise. But the immediate circumstances of one's life [were] often at odds with any of the idealistic aspirations outlined again and again in the spirituals. Therefore, although the blues are an extension of emotional and tonal qualities inherent in the spirituals, their chief emphasis is on the material world—the world as flesh, money, survival, freedom, lost love, unrequited love, and instable love. The emergence of the blues marks the important stage of the Afro-American musical identity.

In simplistic dialectical terms, the spirituals stand for one level of ritual con-sciousness—the blues for another. Both forms are primarily fundamental types of folk poetry. For example, the emphasis in blues songs is on the immediacy of life, the nature of man, and human survival in all of its physical and psychological manifestations. The blues are informed by a social history of mental and physical hardships; they lyrically address themselves to concrete life situations. And if life is perceived to be a battle of the sexes, or a quest for pleasure, that's just the way it is. The blues singer, acting as ritual poet, merely reflects the horrible and beautiful realities of life. He didn't make it that way, that is just the way things are. Hardships can conquer you, or you can conquer them. Therefore, toughness of spirit is an essential aspect of the ethos of the blues.

An ideal approach to the blues would be that of seeing them as an extensive body of folk literature, and therefore subject to all of the laws of folklore. That means where we have a variety of primary sources. The blues should be categorized according to subject matter (content), lyric and musical structure, style, region of origin and probable audience. There have been extensive field recordings of some of the earlier blues, but there does not appear to have been a conscientious attempt to systematize even these. Paul Oliver's study, *Blues Fell This Morning*, comes close, but more work is needed. The blues have their roots in the oral literature of black America; and a careful analysis of them as Oliver, Jones and Kiel have observed would reveal some very essential things about the Afro-American ethos.

No one has been able to ascertain precisely in what Southern localities the blues were born. Several writers have placed their origins in Mississippi or Alabama. Dating the origins of oral material is a difficult task. Blues songs could have had an "underground" existence anytime between 1860 and 1900. This is often the case with material which a folk population considers illicit or sinful, and as we have noted the blues were considered sinful songs by religious black folks. Therefore, it is highly possible that no white collector heard any such songs until they were popularized by W. C. Handy in 1912. It was not until about 1920 that serious study was devoted to the blues.

Handy's most famous piece of music was "Saint Louis Blues," which was originally refused by the publishers. Handy then set up his own company and published the song himself. ("Saint Louis Blues" is one of the world's best-known songs; but, strictly speaking, it is not a blues in the technical sense of the word. That is because it slightly alters the character and form of blues by the addition of a very pronounced tango rhythm. However, the song is fundamentally rooted in the blues tradition. It has a blues orientation and the general organization of its images is the same as that found in the blues.) By 1920 record companies were turning out a great deal of blues recordings directed at what the industry called the "race trade." But chances of examining the blues in their natural environment had somewhat diminished by then. The "devil songs," as religious black people called the blues, had become an integral part of the American music scene. If the early scholars of Afro-American music had been black men, and had not perhaps been so puritanical, our knowledge of the folk origins of the blues would not be so theoretical.

By the time the first blues, Hart Wand's "Dallas Blues," was published in 1912, the migratory process which had helped to disperse the blues had been well under way. The songs were popping up in minstrel and vaudeville shows throughout the South. Itinerant troubadours were singing them in dance halls, cotton fields, whore houses, torpentine camps and barrooms. The country blues singers were already stamped in the eyes of the black community as men of sin. Many Negro ministers warned their congregations against associating with blues singers. A black man traveling with a guitar ("devil box") was not allowed to pass even into the front yard of the church unless he left his guitar outside.

The social impulse in the blues, its raw quality, is almost completely at odds with the moral attitudes which the Negro ministers attempted to instill in the religious community. The music had arisen out of the same feeling which produced the spirituals, jubilees, gospel songs, and work songs. But the overt literary content of the blues was radically different from the view of the world as expressed in the spirituals.

To the blues singer the spirituals, finally, were the expression of beliefs not grounded in pressing reality. The blues are primarily the expression of a post-slavery view of the world. They are linked to a freeing of the individual spirit. Slavery leans towards obliterating the individual's sense of *himself* as a person with particular needs and a particular style or manner of doing things. Every aspect of one's life is controlled from the outside by others, and the sense of one's individual body is diminished. It follows then, that the intensely *personal* quality of the blues is a direct result of freeing of the individual personality which was often held in check by slavery. The ex-slave, therefore, accepted the Western concept of man, what other concept did he know? And furthermore, as Albert Murray observed in *The Omni-Americans*: "They were slaves who were living in the presence of more human freedom and individual opportunity than they or anybody else had ever seen before." The end of formal slavery would therefore alter the slave's horizon of experience. He would have to confront his own name. He would have to accept the fact that his life was in his own hands in a more immediately physical manner. He had seen slavery and survived it, and he wasn't going to be anybody's slave again. Herein would reside his essential strengths and contradictions for the political activists who would later try to organize him. Imamu Baraka explains this development in the following manner:

> . . . But the insistence of blues verse on the life of the individual and his individual trials and successes on the earth is a manifestation of the whole Western concept of man's life, and it is a development that could only be found in an American black man's music. From the American black leader's acceptance of Adam Smith['s] *laissez-faire* social inferences to some less fortu- nate black man's relegation to a lonely path of useless earth in South Carolina, the weight of Western tradition, or to make it more specific and local, the weight of just what social circumstances and accident came together to produce the America that the Negro was part of, had to make itself part of his life as well. . . .

What the ex-slave, in fact, did was to adopt one of the main tenets of the democratic American ideal. His adoption of the philosophy of rugged individualism was a natural out-growth of once having had his individual liberty curtailed. It was not necessarily an attempt to succeed in terms of capitalist ideals. This was to come later with the rise of the Negro bourgeoisie.

The blues are the ideology of the field slave—the ideology of a new "proletariat" searching for a means of judging the world. Therefore, even though the blues are cast in highly personal terms, they stand for the collective sensibility of a people at particular stages of cultural, social, and political development. The blues singer is not an alienated artist attempting to impose his view of the world on others. His ideas are the reflection of an unstated general point-of-view. Even though he is a part of the secular community, his message is often ritualistic and spiritual. Therefore, it is his ritual role in the community which links him to the traditional priests and poets of Africa. And ironically enough, a cursory examination of the lives of many ritual artists everywhere in the world. Let us keep in mind, therefore, that the blues are primarily folk expression. Consequently, they are subject to the processes of myth and ritual out of which all folklore is derived. Ralph Ellison makes a similar point in a review of Baraka's *Blues People*:

> . . . Classic blues were both entertainment *and* form of folklore. When they were sung professionally in theatres, they were entertainment; when danced to in the form or recordings or used as a means of transmitting the traditional verses and their wisdom, they were folklore. There are levels of time and function involved here, and the blues which might be used in one place as entertainment (as gospel music is now being used in night clubs and on theatre stages) might be put to a ritual use in another. Bessie Smith might have been a "blues queen" to the society at large, but within the tighter Negro community where the blues were part of a total way of life, and a major expression of an attitude toward life, she was a priestess, a celebrant who affirmed the values of the group and man's ability to deal with chaos.

Like any artist, the blues singer has the task of bringing order out of chaos. The songs he sings, whether his own creations or others, are reenactments of his life and the lives of his people. The immediate emotional projections of what he has seen and felt are certainly personal, but they never remain simply that. Because they are in reality only symbolic of the larger human dilemma:

> There's several types of blues—there's blues that connects you with per-sonal life—you can tell it to the public as a song. But I mean, they don't take seriously what you are tellin' the truth about. At the same time it could be you, more or less it *would* be you for you to have the feelin'. You express yourself in a song like that. *Now this particular thing reaches others because they have experienced the same condition in life so naturally they feel what you are sayin' because it happened to them* [emphasis mine]. It's a sort of thing that you kinda like to hold to yourself, yet you want somebody to know it. I don't know how you say that two ways: you like somebody to know it, yet you hold it to yourself. Now I've had the feelin' which I have disposed it in a song, but there's some things that have happened to me that I wouldn't dare tell, not to tell—but I would *sing* about them. Because people in general they takes the song as an explanation for *themselves*—they believe this song is expressing *their* feelin's instead of the one that singin' it. They feel that maybe I have just hit upon somethin' that's their lives, and yet at the same time it was some of the things that went wrong with me too.

The singer is aware that his audience has been through the same changes as he has. His task is to express through his craft their suffering and his. Everything and everyone who he encounters on his journey of the soul is mirrored in his art. He is appreciated as a meaningful member of the community to the degree to which he expresses the conscious and unconscious spirit of that community. Therefore, the blues singer should not be viewed apart from the community ethos that produced him. He is a product of a long chain of historical and social events. The blues people, as Imamu Amiri Baraka calls them, are really the true heroes and poets of the community; because they are able to reveal the essential essence of human experiences. In this sense they are spiritually dedicated to their tasks as any minister or social revolutionary. Here is John Lee Hooker, one of the best known of the country blues singers, speaking on the role of the singer. He is speaking to a concert audience at the Newport Jazz Festival:

> To you and all of my friends . . . especially my fellow mens. I'm so glad that we're here. . . . It's a big wide world. . . . We come a long ways. . . . We trying to throw a program me, Brownie [McGhee], Sonny [Terry], everybody . . . all folk singers. We are here to pay our dues to the natural facts. You know . . . we have come a long ways . . . we all . . . we entertainers trying to reach you to bring you the message of the blues . . . and folk. Sometimes we traveling late at night. We are trying to reach you . . . to pay our dues to the natural facts . . . to you, for your enjoyment. All entertainers . . . sometimes . . . you tired when you reach your destination. But you're paying your dues to the facts. But we are here to please you the best way we know. I hope you accept . . . thanks.

Hooker gives this monologue running short riffs on his guitar. Each riff is a comment on his verbal statements, and a kind of musical extension of the ideas he is trying to present to his audience. The key phrases in this monologue refer to "paying dues," bringing "the natural facts," "trying to reach you," and bringing "the messages of the blues."

"Paying dues" is an expression quite common in the black community. Roughly, it means that an individual has undergone a great many emotional and physical catastrophies, and that he has, somehow, overcome them. Paying one's dues could mean anything from losing your woman to having been in jail all of one's life. It is a highly important group value, and there is almost a religious attitude about it. The same is true for telling the "natural facts." Note that the facts are *natural*; earth-centered, rather than focused on some metaphysical realm. And there is an obvious didactic reason for conveying these "natural facts."

The didactic and moralistic impulse underlying the blues is often obscured by the fact that many blues songs seem to be inordinately concerned with the sex act; the constant allusions to "jellyroll" and "cake" for example. It also is true that the sexual content of the blues has been exploited by the record industry. The high preponderance of blues songs dealing with the sex act, apart from any reasons integral to the song itself, may stem from the tendency of some blues singers to give the record companies a great amount of marketable materials. However, any extensive survey of the blues indicates that they cover a broad range of subject matter. In the most meaningful blues, sex fits neatly into the overall meaning of the song. Even in the most salacious of blues songs, however, the import is still didactic: Here is Eugene Rhodes's version of Josh White's "Jelly, jelly."

Hello, baby, I had to call you on the phone
Hello, baby, I had to call you on the phone
Yes, I'm so sad and lonely, need the baby home
Downright rotten, lowdown dirty shame
Downright rotten, lowdown dirty shame
Way you treat me woman; know I'm not to blame.
Jelly, jelly, jelly, jelly stays on my mind,
Jelly, jelly, jelly, jelly stays on my mind,
Jellyroll killed my mother, ran my daddy stone blind

The blues are not concerned with middle-class morality, black or white. That is because the audience that they address is forced to confront the world of the flesh; the body is real, the source of much joy and pain. There is very little attempt to euphemize the realities of male-female relationship. It is the evangelical mind that often rejects these realities that are appalled by the fleshy reality of the blues. Tinpan Alley popular songs sing of "making whoopee," or "making love." The blues singer exclaims, "My man, he rocks me with one steady roll." Bessie Smith sings: "He's a deep sea diver with a stroke that can't go wrong." Certainly, these lines show more appreciation of the sex act than that of making "whoopee" or "making love." They are certainly more poetic. They celebrate the sex act in the fullest most complete manner. The blues sing the joys and the pain of the world of flesh, while the pop songs of America rehash the dullness of a dying society.

The ethos of the blues, then, is the musical manifestation of one's individual, cultural experiences in Afro-America with which members of the black community can identify. The blues performer has a talk with himself about the problem, analyzes the situation, and then takes his own advice to remedy it. He thereby opens up his soul to the world and allows it to see the sadness, the heartache and the joys he has sustained in life—the trials and tribulations that get him down, but nevertheless, his determination to "make it"—and if he can get a witness, someone who can testify to the same feelings and experiences, then he has succeeded in revealing the essential essence of human experiences.

ON AFRO-AMERICAN POPULAR MUSIC: FROM BEBOP TO RAP

CORNEL WEST is a philosopher and religious scholar. One of his most recent books, *American Evasion of Philosophy: A Genealogy of Pragmatism*, was published in 1989 by the University of Wisconsin Press. "On Afro-American Popular Music: From Bebop to Rap" is from his collection, *Prophetic Fragments* (1988), and reveals his continued involvement with the synthesis of black American popular culture (particularly black American popular music) and African-American Christianity.

The salient feature of popular music in first-world capitalist and third-world neocolonialist societies is the appropriation and imitation of Afro-American musical forms and styles. The Afro-American spiritual-blues impulse—of polyphonic, rhythmic effects and antiphonal vocal techniques, of kinetic orality and affective physicality—serve as major sources for popular music in the West. This complex phenomenon, the Afro-Americanization of popular music, prevails owing to three basic reasons. First, the rise of the U.S.A. as a world power focused international attention more pointedly to native U.S. cultural forms and styles. Second, vast technological innovations in mass media and communications facilitated immediate and massive influence of certain forms and styles upon others. Third, and most important, Afro-American music is first and foremost, though not exclusively or universally, a countercultural practice with deep roots in modes of religious transcendence and political opposition. Therefore it is seductive to rootless and alienated young people disenchanted with existential meaninglessness, disgusted with flaccid bodies, and dissatisfied with the status quo.

Afro-American popular music constitutes a crucial dimension of the background practices—the ways of life and struggle—of Afro-American culture. By taking seriously Afro-American popular music, one can dip into the multileveled life-worlds of black people. As Ralph Ellison has suggested, Afro-Americans have had rhythmic freedom in place of social freedom, linguistic wealth instead of pecuniary wealth. I make no attempt here to come to terms with the complexity of the evolving forms and content of Afro-American popular music. Rather I simply try to provide a cognitive mapping of the major breaks and ruptures in Afro-American popular music in light of their changing socioeconomic and political contexts from bebop to rap, from Charlie Parker to the Sugarhill Gang.

Our starting point is the grand break with American mainstream music, especially imitated and co-opted Afro-American popular music, by the so-called bebop jazz musicians—Charlie Parker, Theolonius Monk, Dizzy Gillespie, and others. Their particular way of Africanizing Afro-American jazz—with the accent on contrasting polyrhythms, the deemphasis of melody, and the increased vocalization of the saxophone—was not only a reaction to the white-dominated, melody-obsessed "swing jazz"; it also was a creative musical response to the major shift in sensibilities and moods in Afro-America after World War II. Through their technical facility and musical virtuosity, bebop jazz musicians expressed the heightened tensions, frustrated aspirations, and repressed emotions of an aggressive yet apprehensive Afro-America. Unlike the jazz of our day, bebop jazz was a popular music, hummed on the streets, whistled by shoeshine boys, and even danced to in the house parties in urban black communities.

Yet the bebop musicians, like Thomas Pynchon in our time, shunned publicity and eschewed visibility. Their radical nonconformist stance—often misunderstood as a repetition of the avant-garde attitude of the *fin de siècle* artists—is reflected in their famous words "We don't care if you listen to our music or not." Their implicit assumption was that, given the roots of their music, black folk could not *not* listen to it and others had to struggle to do so. Yet as the ferment of the short-lived "bebop era" subsided into the "cool" style of the early fifties, it was clear that bebop had left an indelible stamp on Afro-American popular music. Despite the brief ascendancy of black "cool" artists such as (the early) Miles Davis and John Lewis and white "cool" musicians like Chet Baker and David Brubeck, the Afro-American spiritual-blues impulse (always alive and well in Count Basie's perennial band) surfaced quickly in the sounds of Charles Mingus, Ray Charles, and Art Blakey's hard bebop Jazz Messengers who all paved the way to the era of soul and funk.

Needless to say, most black folk in the fifties listened weekly to spiritual and gospel music in black churches—sung by young choir members such as Sam Cooke, Dionne Warwicke, Aretha Franklin, Gladys Knight, and Lou Rawls. With increased strata and class differentiation in the ever-blackening urban centers throughout the U.S.A., secular attitudes proliferated and financial rewards for nonreligious and nonjazz black popular music escalated. On the one hand, jazz—under the influence of John Coltrane, Miles Davis, Ornette Coleman, and others—became more and more a kind of highbrow, "classical" avant-garde music its originators and innovators abhorred. On the other hand, black churches turned their theological guns on "the devil's music" (traditionally pointed at the blues), resulting in more and more marginality for black religious music. So the stage was set for a black popular music which was neither jazz nor gospel: soul music.

Soul music is more than either secularized gospel or funkified jazz. Rather, it is a particular Africanization of Afro-American music with intent to appeal to the black masses, especially geared to the black ritual of attending parties and dances. Soul music is the populist application of bebop's aim: racial self-conscious assertion among black people in light of their rich musical heritage. The two major artists of soul music—James Brown and Aretha Franklin—bridge the major poles in the Afro-American experience by appealing to agrarian and urban black folk, the underclass and working class, religious and secular men and women. Only the black upper middle class of long standing—and most of white U.S.A.—initially rejected them. Ironically, though unsurprisingly, none of James Brown's and few of Aretha Franklin's gold records were or are played by non-black-oriented radio stations. Yet their influence, including white appropriations and imitations, flourished.

As the black baby boom catapulted and black entrepreneurial activity in mass communications expanded, it became apparent that a youthful black market could support a black recording industry. In the South, Otis Redding, the great soul singer, had moved far along on this road, yet white power stubbornly resisted. So when in 1958 Berry Gordy, a black industrial worker in one of Detroit's Ford plants, decided to establish Motown, black popular music took a tremendous leap forward. Far ahead of black literary artists and scholars in this regard, major black popular musicians, writers, singers, and producers could now work in a production unit owned by and geared toward black people.

Motown was the center of Afro-American popular music in the sixties and early seventies—with the phenomenal success of over 75 percent of its records reaching the Top Ten rhythm and blues tune charts in the mid-sixties. The musical genius of Stevie Wonder, Michael Jackson, and Lionel Richie; the writing talents of Smokey Robinson, Nicholas Ashford, Valerie Simpson, Norman Whitfield, Barrett Strong, Eddie and Brian Holland, Lamont Dozier, and Marvin Gaye; and the captivating performances of the Temptations, the Miracles, the Supremes, the Four Tops, Gladys Knight and the Pips, the Jackson Five and the Commodores set Motown far above any other recording company producing Afro-American popular music.

Motown was the Jackie Robinson of black popular music: it crossed the color line for the first time, then proceeded to excel and thereby win the hearts and souls of vast numbers of nonblack folk. The most successful Motown figures—Diana Ross, Stevie Wonder, Michael Jackson, and Lionel Richie—now have secure status in mainstream American popular music. And outside of Motown, the only black singers or groups to achieve such transracial acceptance are Nat King Cole, Louis Armstrong, Johnny Mathis, Dionne Warwicke, Jimi Hendrix, Sly and the Family Stone, Lou Rawls, and Earth, Wind and Fire.

Like Jackie Robinson, Motown reflected the then stable, persevering, upwardly mobile working class in Afro-America. At its height, Motown produced smooth, syncopated rhythms, not funky polyrhythms (like James Brown or the Watts 103rd Street Rhythm Band); restrained call-and-response forms, not antinomian antiphonal styles (as with Aretha Franklin or the late Donny Hathaway); and love-centered romantic lyrics, not racially oriented social protest music (like Gil-Scott Heron or

Archie Shepp). Yet Motown delicately and wisely remained anchored in the Afro-American spiritual-blues impulse.

There is little doubt that Motown produced some of the great classics in Afro-American and American popular music. The Temptations' "My Girl," "Since I Lost My Baby," "You're My Everything"; the Miracles' "OOO Baby Baby," "Choosey Beggar," "Here I Go Again"; Marvin Gaye and Tammi Terrell's "Your Precious Love," "If This World Were Mine," "Ain't Nothing Like the Real Thing"; Stevie Wonder's "For Once in My Life," "My Cherie Amour," "You Are the Sunshine of My Life"; and Gladys Knight and the Pips' "Neither One of Us" will stand the test of time.

As Motown became more commercially successful with the larger white American audience, it began to lose ground in Afro-America. On two musical fronts—fast funk and mellow soul—Motown faced a serious challenge. On the first front, Motown had never surpassed James Brown. Yet Motown had produced music for Afro-America to dance—to twist, jerk, boogaloo, philly dog, and skate. With the appearance of George Clinton's innovative Funkadelic and Parliament, a new wave of funk appeared: technofunk. Never before had black folk heard such deliberately distorted voice and contrapuntal rhythmic effects filtered through electronic instrumentalities. Building principally on James Brown, the Funkadelic's "I Wanna Know If It's Good to You," "Loose Booty," and "Standing on the Verge of Getting It On" sounded musically revolutionary to the ears of the masses of black folk. Motown quickly moved into technofunk with the Temptations' successful "Cloud Nine," "I Can't Get Next to You," and "Psychedelic Shack," but it was clear that the change of image (and personnel) could not give Motown hegemonic status on fast funk.

On the second front, that of mellow soul, Motown had no peer until the rise—precipitated by the roaring success of the Delfonics—of the Philly Sound at Sigma Sound Studio in Philadelphia. The poignant music and lyrics of Kenneth Gamble and Leon Huff, Thom Bell and Linda Creed, Joseph Jefferson, Bruce Hawes and Yvette Davis, Norman Harris, and Allen Felder surfaced in the late sixties and early seventies with force and potency, as witnessed by the popular songs sung by the O'Jays, the Spinners, Harold McIvin and the Blue Notes, Blue Magic, Teddy Pendergrass, Major Harris, the Jones Girls, Lou Rawls, and even Johnny Mathis. Furthermore, the noteworthy presence of Harlem's Main Ingredient, Chicago's Chi-Lites, Detroit's (non-Motown) Dramatics, Jersey City's Manhattans, and Los Angeles's Whispers on this front yielded a more diverse situation.

The early seventies witnessed slightly more political overtones in Afro-American popular music. Surprisingly, the political ferment of the late sixties did not invoke memorable musical responses on behalf of popular Afro-American musicians, with the exception of James Brown's "Say It Loud I'm Black and I'm Proud." The youthful black market thrived on music for dance and romance; and such music was the mainstay of the late sixties. As the Vietnam War intensified (with over 22 percent of its U.S. victims being black), the drug culture spread, and black elected officials emerged, recordings such as the Temptations' "Ball of Confusion," the Chi-Lites' "Give More Power to the People," James Brown's "Funky President (People, It's Bad)," and the Isley Brothers' "Fight the Power" revealed more explicit concern with the public life and political welfare of Afro-America. Ironically, this concern was exemplified most clearly in the greatest album produced by Motown: Marvin Gaye's *What's Going On*. True to their religious roots, Afro-American popular musicians and writers couched their concerns in highly moralistic language, devoid of the concrete political realities of conflict and struggle. Marvin Gaye's classical recording openly evoked Christian apocalyptic images and the love ethic of Jesus Christ.

The watershed year in Afro-American popular music in this period was 1975. For the first time in Afro-American history, fast funk music seized center stage from mellow soul music. In the past, it was inconceivable that a black rhythm and blues group or figure—no matter how funk-oriented—not possess a serious repertoire of slow mellow, often ballad, music. It is important to remember that James Brown's early hits were mellow soul, such as "Please, Please, Please," "Bewildered," "It's a Man's World." Given the demand for nonstop dance music in discotheques in the early seventies and the concomitant decline of slow dancing and need for mellow soul, black dance music became dominant in Afro-American popular music. Barry White's sensual upbeat tunes, Brass Construction's repetitive syncopations, Kool and the Gang's distinctive Jersey funk, and Nile Rogers and Bernard Edwards's classy chic are exemplary responses to the disco scene. Yet the most important Afro-American response to this scene occurred in 1975 when George Clinton and William "Bootsy" Collins released two albums: Parliament's *Chocolate City* and *Mothership Connection*.

By building directly upon Clinton's Funkadelic, such as deploying the same musicians, Parliament ushered forth the era of black technofunk—the creative encounter of the Afro-American spiritual-blues impulse with highly sophisticated technological instruments, strategies, and effects. Parliament invited its listeners, especially the dwellers of "Chocolate cities" and to a lesser extent those in the "Vanilla suburbs," to enter the "Fourth World," the world of black funk and star wars, of black orality, bodily sensuality, technical virtuosity, and electronic adroitness. The cover of the first Parliament album, *Chocolate City*, portrayed Washington, D.C.'s, Lincoln Memorial, Washington Memorial, Capitol Building, and White House melting presumably under the heat of black technofunk and the increasing "chocolate" character of the nation's capital. The album contained only one mellow soul song ("I Misjudged You"), a mere ritualistic gesture to the mellow pole of Afro-American popular music. The second album, *Mothership Connection*—now joined with the leading saxophonists of James Brown's band, Maceo Parker and Fred Wesley—literally announced the planetary departure to the "Fourth World" on the mothership, with not one earthbound mellow love song.

The emergence of technofunk is not simply a repetition of black escapism nor an adolescent obsession with "Star Trek." In addition to being a product of the genius of George Clinton, technofunk constitutes the second grand break of Afro-American musicians from American mainstream music, especially imitated and co-opted Afro-American popular music. Like Charlie Parker's bebop, George Clinton's technofunk both Africanizes and technologizes Afro-American popular music— with polyrhythms on polyrhythms, less melody, and freaky electronically distorted vocals. Similar to bebop, technofunk unabashedly exacerbates and accentuates the "blackness" of black music, the "Afro-Americanness" of Afro-American music—its irreducibility, inimitability, and uniqueness. Funkadelic and Parliament defy nonblack emulation; they assert their distinctiveness—and the distinctiveness of "funk" in Afro-America. This funk is neither a skill nor an idea, not a worldview nor a stance. Rather, it is an existential capacity to get in touch with forms of kinetic orality and affective physicality acquired by deep entrenchment in—or achieved by pretheoretical styles owing to socialization in—the patterns of Afro-American ways of life and struggle.

Technofunk is a distinctive expression of postmodern black popular music; it constitutes a potent form of the Afro-American spiritual-blues impulse in the pervasive computer phase and hedonistic stage of late capitalist U.S. society. Ironically, the appeal of black technofunk was not a class-specific phenomenon. Technofunk invigorated the "new" politicized black middle class undergoing deep identity-crisis, the stable black working class fresh out of the blues-ridden ghettos, the poor black working class hungry for escapist modes of transcendence, and the hustling black underclass permeated by the drug culture. Black technofunk articulated black middle-class anxieties toward yet fascination with U.S. "hi-tech" capitalist society; black working-class frustration of marginal inclusion within and ineffective protest against this society, and black underclass self-destructive dispositions owing to outright exclusion from this society. For black technofunk, in a period of increasing black strata and class divisions, there are no fundamental cleavages in Afro-America, only the black nation. The cover of George Clinton's 1978 Funkadelic album, *One Nation under a Groove*, portrays black folk from all walks of life hoisting up Marcus Garvey's Afro-American liberation flag (of red, black, and green stripes) with "R & B" printed on it—the initials not for rhythm and blues but rhythm and business. In vintage black nationalist patriarchal fashion, the inside of the album contains a beautiful naked black woman lying on her back, signifying the biological source and social "backbone" of the black nation.

Again like bebop, technofunk's breakthrough was brief. Its intensely Africanizing and technologizing thrust was quickly diluted and brought more and more into contact with other nonblack musical currents, as witnessed in Prince's creative Minneapolis sound and Midnight Star's "freakazoid funk." Since 1975, four noteworthy trends have surfaced: the invasion of Afro-American popular music by ex-avant-garde jazz musicians, the meteoric rise of Michael Jackson (aided by Rod Temperton and especially Quincy Jones) as a solo performer, the refreshing return of gospel music, and the exuberant emergence of black rap music. Miles Davis's canonical album, *Bitches Brew*, in 1970 already displayed the influence of soul music on jazz; his admiration of the California funk of Sly and the Family Stone is well known. Yet by the late seventies the influx of bonafide jazz musicians—most notably George Benson, Quincy Jones, Herbie Hancock, and Donald Byrd—into Afro-American popular music (rhythm and blues) was phenomenal. The motivation was not simply financial; it also was symptomatic of perceived sources of vitality and vigor in black music in late capitalist U.S. society and culture. In avant-garde jazz, Ornette Coleman's and John Coltrane's free jazz—like Arnold

Schönberg's atonal music in the Western classical tradition—symbolized both grand achievements and dead ends. For example, Pharaoh Sanders, who briefly upheld the rich legacy of Coltrane's "new wave" jazz, was soon recording with B. B. King, the great blues singer and musician, at the Fillmore East. In short, jazz musicians were not only making a monetary bid for musical popularity; more important, they were acknowledging the legitimacy of the music of the black masses. In short, they were reaffirming the original vision of the great revolutionary figure in jazz, Louis Armstrong. White middlebrow audiences and black old-timers continued to support the great jazz singers—such as Ella Fitzgerald, Sarah Vaughan, Carmen McRae, Billy Eckstine, and Joe Williams—but jazz instrumentalists could hardly make it. In many ways, this continues to be so, though the youthful genius of Wynton Marsalis may rearrange the terrain of jazz itself. Notwithstanding the present predicament of jazz musicians, George Benson, a superb jazz guitarist, acquired immediate fame as a Motown-like smooth, mellow soul singer; Herbie Hancock, a "cool" jazz pianist with the early Miles Davis, moved into his own brand of technofunk; and the Van Gelder studio group—Bob James, Grover Washington, Eric Gale, and others—produced an ingenious "pop jazz," often based on rhythm and blues tunes. The most successful jazz musician turned rhythm and blues producer, Quincy Jones, joined his immense talent with that of the leader of the most beloved of black singing groups—Michael Jackson of the Jackson Five.

The distinctive talent of Michael Jackson is that he combines the performative showmanship of James Brown (whom he imitated in his first 1968 exhibition to gain a contract with Motown), the lyrical emotional intensity of Smokey Robinson, the transracial appeal of Dionne Warwicke, and the aggressive though attenuated technofunk of the Isley Brothers. In this regard, Michael Jackson stands shoulders above his contemporaries. He is the musical dynamo of his generation. This became quite clear with his highly acclaimed 1979 *Off the Wall* album and [was] further confirmed by his record-setting 1982 *Thriller* album. The point here is not simply that the albums sell millions of copies and stay on top of the tune charts for several months. Rather, the point is that Michael Jackson is the product of the Afro-American spiritual-blues impulse which now has tremendous international influence, thereby serving as a major model for popular music in the world, especially first-world capitalist and third-world neocolonialist countries. Like Muhammed Ali—and unlike most of his musical contemporaries—Michael Jackson is an international star of grand proportions, the most prominent world-historical emblem of the Afro-American spiritual-blues impulse.

Ironically, and unlike the only other comparable figure, Louis Armstrong, Michael Jackson is not a musical revolutionary within Afro-American history. Rather, he is a funnel through which flow many of the diverse streams and currents of the Afro-American musical tradition. It is precisely his versatility and diversity—from old funk, technofunk, and mellow soul to ballads with the ex-Beatle, Paul McCartney—which marks his protean musical identity. The only contemporary figure comparable to Michael Jackson is Stevie Wonder and though Stevie Wonder is more musically talented and daring (as well as more politically engaged), Jackson possesses a more magnetic magic on stage and in the studio. Yet neither Wonder nor Jackson explore the musical genre which exploded on the scene in the late seventies and early eighties: gospel music.

The black church, black-owned and black-run Christian congregations, is the fountainhead of the Afro-American spiritual-blues impulse. Without the black church, with its African roots and Christian context, Afro-American culture—in fact, Afro-America itself—is unimaginable. Yet, as should be apparent, the black church has suffered tremendous "artistic drainage." The giant talents of Mahalia Jackson, James Cleveland, and Clara Ward prove that the black church can keep some of its sons and daughters in the artistic fold, but for every one who stayed with the gospels, there have been four who went to rhythm and blues. In the late sixties Edwin Hawkins's "Oh Happy Day" received national visibility, but the gospel explosion—partly spawned by the Pentecostal thrust in the black religious community—did not take off until the reunion of James Cleveland and Aretha Franklin in their historic 1972 double album set *Amazing Grace*. The towering success of this live concert at the New Temple Missionary Baptist Church in Los Angeles convinced many reluctant recording companies that gospel music was marketable. And soon superb albums such as Andraé Crouch's *Take Me Back*, Walter Hawkins's (Edwin's brother) *Love Alive* and *Love Alive II* proved them correct. Although gospel music remains primarily a black affair—written and performed by and for black people—the recent Christian conversions of the popular Deneice Williams and disco queen Donna Summer may broaden the scope.

The most important development in Afro-American popular music since 1979 is black rap music. This music has been performed on ghetto streets and between stage acts during black concerts for many years. In 1979, Sylvia Robinson, the major songwriter for the mellow soul group The Moments (recently renamed Ray, Goodman and Brown), decided to record and release "Rapper's Delight" by Harlem's Sugarhill Gang. Within months, black rap records were filling record shops around the country. Most of the first black rap records were musically derived from big hits already released and lyrically related to adolescent love affairs. Yet as more sophisticated rap performers, such as Kurtis Blow and Grandmaster Flash and the Furious Five, emerged, the music became more original and the lyrics more graphic of life in the black ghetto. Kurtis Blow's "The Breaks" and "125th Street" and Grandmaster Flash and the Furious Five's "The Message" and "New York, New York" are exemplary in this regard.

Black rap music is more important than the crossover of jazz musicians to rhythm and blues, the rise of the "older" Michael Jackson, and the return of gospel music because, similar to bebop and technofunk, black rap music is emblematically symptomatic of a shift in sensibilities and moods in Afro-America. Black rap music indeed Africanizes Afro-American popular music—accenting syncopated poly-rhythms, kinetic orality, and sensual energy in a refined form of raw expressive-ness—while its virtuosity lies not in technical facility but rather street-talk quickness and linguistic versatility. In short, black rap music recuperates and revises elements of black rhetorical styles—some from our preaching—within black musical and rhythmic production. Black rap music recovers and revises elements of black rhetori-cal styles—some from black preaching—and black rhythmic drumming. In short, it combines the two major organic artistic traditions in black America—black rhetoric and black music. In this sense, like bebop and technofunk, black rap music resists nonblack reproduction, though such imitations and emulations proliferate. Yet unlike bebop and technofunk—and this is a crucial break—black rap music is primarily the musical expression of the paradoxical cry of desperation and celebration of the black underclass and poor working class, a cry which openly acknowledges and confronts the wave of personal cold-heartedness, criminal cruelty, and existential hopelessness in the black ghettos of Afro-America. In stark contrast to bebop and technofunk, black rap music is principally a class-specific form of the Afro-American spiritual-blues impulse which mutes, and often eliminates, the utopian dimension of this impulse. The major predecessor of black rap music was the political raps of Gil-Scott Heron and the powerful musical poems of the Last Poets over a decade ago; their content was angry, funky, and hopeful. Black rap music is surely grounded in the Afro-American spiritual-blues impulse, but certain versions of this music radically call into question the roots of this impulse, the roots of transcendence and opposition. Without a utopian dimension—without transcendence from or opposition to evil—there can be no struggle, no hope, no meaning. Needless to say, the celebratory form of black rap music, especially its upbeat African rhythms, contains utopian aspirations. But this form is often violently juxtaposed with lyrical hopelessness of the oppressed poor people of Afro-America. My hunch is that the form (the funky rhythms) have basically a ritualistic function: music for cathartic release at the black rituals of parties and dances. In short, even the rhythms conceal the unprecedented phenomenon in Afro-American life; the slow but seemingly sure genocidal effects upon the black underclass and poor working class in late capitalist U.S. society and the inability of poor black folk to muster spiritual, let alone political and economic, resources to survive. This is especially so for young black people. The black suicide rate among 18-to-30-year-olds has quadrupled in the past two decades; black homicide is the leading cause of death among young black men; over 50 percent of black households are headed by abandoned and abused young black women; the black prison population has doubled since the 1960s; and black churches, led by either rip-off artists like Rev. Ike, devout denominational leaders such as Rev. Jemison of the National Baptist Convention, or dedicated prophets like Rev. Daughtry of the National Black United Front, do not reach the vast majority of young black people.

Black rap music is the last form of transcendence available to young black ghetto dwellers, yet it, tellingly, is often employed to subvert, undermine, and parody transcendence itself. Such artistic strategies—such as play, silence, and performance—are typical postmodern ones in which petit bourgeois artists, philosophers, and critics wallow. Yet the indigenous proliferation of these strategies among the (once most religious) now most degraded and oppressed people in the urban centers of the richest country in the history of humankind signifies a crisis of enormous proportions for Afro-America.

It is ironic that the Afro-Americanization of popular music around the world occurs at the time that the transcendent and oppositional roots of the Afro-American spiritual-blues impulse is radically challenged from within the Afro-American musical tradition. This challenge occurs not simply because of lack of will or loss of nerve but primarily because of treacherous ruling-class policies, contemptuous black middle-class attitudes, and the loss of existential moorings due to the relative collapse of family structures and supportive networks. To put it bluntly, the roots of the Afro-American spiritual-blues impulse are based on the supposition that some-body—God, Mom, or neighbors—cares. Some expressions of black rap music challenge this supposition. The future of the Afro-American spiritual-blues impulse may well hang on the quality of the response to this challenge. In this sense, the vitality and vigor of Afro-American popular music depends not only on the talents of Afro-American musicians, but also on the moral visions, social analyses, and political strategies which highlight personal dignity, provide political promise, and give existential hope to the underclass and poor working class in Afro-America.

THE AMERICAN NEGRO'S NEW COMEDY ACT

LOUIS LOMAX (1922–1970) was one of the most famous African-American journalists of his generation. Among his books are *The Reluctant African* (1960); *When the Word Is Given* (1964), one of the better books on the Nation of Islam; *Thailand: The War That Is, The War That Will Be* (1966); and *To Kill a Black Man* (1968), an intriguing look at the deaths and careers of Malcolm X and Martin Luther King. Lomax died in an automobile accident in New Mexico, and many have come to believe that his death involved some sort of foul play. "The American Negro's New Comedy Act" appeared in the June 1961 issue of *Harper's*.

Laughter has always been his sharpest weapon.
 . . . but now its tone is more self-confident.
 . . . and a lot healthier for all of us.

High noon in New York, August: The crowded bus jogged to a stop at Fourteenth Street. All the passengers got off, except two women who had been sharing a seat—one Negro, the other white. Both were stout.
If I move to another seat, the white woman thought, *this Negro will think I don't want to sit by her.*

Two stops later the Negro looked at her seat-mate and said:

"Honey, there's plenty room on this bus; why for then are you crowding me?"

This story, now going around among Negroes and their white friends, may be apocryphal. Its meaning, however, is certain: Negroes and white people are beginning to laugh together about the most serious affliction of American society. True, we Negroes have been laughing at white people for years. I suspect—in fact I know—they have been laughing at us. But until recently the laughters have not been mutual or the same: our comic response was born of hurt; theirs, I regret to say, of malice. We were not the same order of fool: the Negro was Falstaff, acting the idiot not only to survive but to say the truth; the white man was the ancient Athenian comic staging a fertility rite during which the tribe reaffirmed its value system by pillorying a scape-goat—the outsider.

The Negro's oblique assault upon segregation has often had practical value as well as style. During the summer between my freshman and sophomore years in college, I worked as an orderly at the Little-Griffin Hospital in Valdosta, Georgia. My first duty each morning was to put chairs in the hallway leading to Dr. Griffin's office. By nine-thirty these chairs would be filled with white ladies seeking the services of the best-known gynecologist in south Georgia. For a Negro woman to be treated by Dr. Griffin, and in his office at that, was unthinkable.

I was out in the hospital yard raking leaves one morning when Sister Lucy— a woman of middle age and a stalwart member of my grandfather's church—came strolling up carrying a Jewel lard bucket filled with fresh eggs.

"Mornin', Louis."

"Howdy, Sister Lucy."

"That Dr. Griffin," she said pointing to the hospital, "he there?"

"Yes, ma'am."

"Thank you, Jesus," Sister Lucy intoned, "cause I needs treatin'."

This I had to see. I followed Sister Lucy as she made her way through the back door of the hospital and into the corridor leading to Dr. Griffin's office.

"Mornin', daughter," Sister Lucy beamed to the first white woman in line. "Why you here? You gonna have another baby?"

"Ain't three enough, Lucy?" the woman asked, beginning to laugh.

"Honey, I had two and that enough for me!" The corridor rang with laughter and Sister Lucy walked past the next eight women in line.

"How's that husband of yours?" Sister Lucy asked, leaning over a woman at the head of the line.

"He's fine, Lucy. How you?"

"Praise God. I'm fine! You know, I brought that husband of yours into this world."

"I'm gonna tell him I saw you, Lucy."

"You do that and the Lord'll bless you." With this, Sister Lucy had made her way to Dr. Griffin's secretary nurse.

"Is Dr. Griffin in there?" Lucy asked, widening her eyes with expectation.

"Yes, Lucy, he's there. How you?"

"With the help of Jesus, I'll make it."

Dr. Griffin's office door opened, a patient walked out. Sister Lucy walked in. Whatever was wrong with Sister Lucy, Dr. Griffin fixed it. He was paid with a Jewel lard bucket full of eggs. Sister Lucy made her way back down the hall laughing and joking with the waiting women. "Give the preacher my prayers when you get home," she said to me, once we were again out in the back yard. Then she added, almost in an undertone, "Lord, honey, white folks sure are foolish!"

THE WAR DID IT

But humor and sorrow are allies, opposite sides of the same coin. Three incidents of my early youth made me painfully aware of this ambivalence. There was a deacon in my grandfather's church who used to break into gales of laughter while shouting.

I would watch his face as he shouted, "Hallelujah, ha, ha, ha," and saw in its contortions the betrayal of inner stress.

And there was also the day my Uncle James (who was a Baptist minister and principal of the Negro school) lectured us about the fact that Negroes "laughed at the wrong time." Uncle was irked because we had laughed during the film *Imitation of Life*. What tickled us was Peola, the light-skinned Negro girl who passed for white and then confessed all at the funeral of her dark mother whom she had mistreated.

The third incident involved turnabout but the motivation was the same. I was delivering groceries: my bicycle turned over, threw me to the ground, and my hand was badly crushed by the loaded wooden box. The accident sent a white woman into hysterical laughter—perhaps not unlike that of the shouting Negro deacon. She called to her next door neighbor to come out and "see the bleeding nigger!"

Comedy is one way of looking at a social situation. Tragedy is another. But comedy can tell us some things about a situation that tragedy cannot. The tragedian told us that the race problem was immoral—that if we weren't careful somebody might go to Hell for it. The comic told us the race problem was absurd—that it would change as Americans became involved in bigger, even more absurd, problems. World War II proved to be that involvement.

Take the Negro sergeant who explained to his French girl friend that he wasn't *really* a Negro; that he was, rather, an intelligence officer and that the Army had painted him brown for special night fighting!

Or take this tribute to the most brilliant all-Negro infantry unit to serve in the last war. I don't know whether the story was Negro or white in origin. An all-white unit slogging up through Italy came upon the ruins of the Colosseum in Rome. "Damn," the commanding officer snapped, "those niggers from the 92nd got here ahead of us!"

These were the things we laughed about during the war. The Negro had been dumped in the most tragic absurdity of all: despite the killing and dying, there was something funny about being loyal and brave and skillful in defiance of warnings that we were unreliable and dumb. And it was the war that destroyed segregation. Colored troops didn't march straight from Berlin to Mississippi as one Negro comic suggested. Rather, they changed weapons—substituted law books for guns—and marched on the United States Supreme Court.

"Dear father," the Negro Harvard Law School freshman wrote. "I have just unearthed a law that will end segregation overnight."

The father, whose income came from prosecuting discrimination cases for the NAACP, wired back: "Keep that law buried until I get you through law school!"

And anyone who has heard the spontaneous poetic repartee between the Southern Negro preacher and his congregation will believe that this happened:

"And this is the way the new freedom came about," the preacher began, his singsong voice rattling the rafters.

"We marched on Washington . . ."

"Amen," the congregation shouted back.

"Like Moses we made our way down to the waters, singing " 'Let my folks go.' "

"Yes, praise the Lord."

"Only we didn't walk to the Red Sea, we marched down to the Potomac . . ."

"Amen, preach the word."

"But, praise God, instead of Moses and Joshua, we had Thurgood Marshall, Roy Wilkins, and A. Philip Randolph . . . ain't that right?"

"Hallelujah, amen."

"And we begin to sing and pray and clap our hands and do the holy dance."

"Yes, Lord," Sister Minnie screamed, leaping to her feet to dance for joy.

"And our voices got louder," the preacher continued, his voice now sounding like a March wind blowing through dry shingles. "We was heading toward Zion . . . just about the crack of dawn, the Lord pulled back the sky. He told the rising sun, the sinking moon, the fading stars, and the floating clouds to get out of his way so he could see. And the Lord poked his head down through the elements . . . "

"Well, do Jesus," Sister Louise intoned, leaping to her feet.

"And the Lord said, 'What you colored people doing making all that noise so early in the morning?' and we told him, 'Lord, we want to be free. No more back doors; no more back seats; no more schools we pay for and can't go to.' And the Lord smiled and said, 'Look behind you!' And we looked, like Moses searching for a rod to part the waters. But instead of a rod we saw a building. A high building with tall columns . . . and with a picture of blind justice holding a pair of unprejudiced scales. And the Lord said, 'You colored people go in that building. There's a man in there named Earl Warren, he's a servant of mine. Tell him your troubles and cut out all that noise so I can go back to sleep.' "

RACE PREJUDICE TURNED INSIDE OUT

I was in the center of "colored town," perched on the side of a mountain overlooking Clinton, Tennessee. Mob violence over school integration was into its third night. The Negro community was an arsenal; we stood in knots looking down into the center of town as John Casper ranted before a crowd in front of the courthouse. Negro citizens voluntarily stayed out of town and the sheriff advised me, the lone Negro newsman on the scene, against being on the downtown streets after dark. Had the segregationist mob decided to storm the mountain road leading to the Negro section, it would have been a massacre. Scores of Negro men, many of them war veterans, were crouched behind trees and bushes waiting for just such a move. I was waiting for the Western Union clerk to come up to "colored town" and get my overnight story and file it to Chicago. Shortly before eleven o'clock, a small Negro boy came running up to me:

"Mr. Lomax," he panted, "there's a white man down at the foot of the mountain in a car. He's a-honking his horn and a-blinking his lights and he shouted and told me to tell you he's as scared to come up here as you are to come down there where he is." I walked down the mountain road and onto a small stretch of no man's land. The Western Union man met me. He took my copy, we shook hands, laughed, and said good night.

When we Negroes think of present-day race tensions in Alabama, the serious face of Dr. Martin Luther King usually dominates our minds; but in spite of the painful events in Montgomery, we can laugh when we get a chance—even in

Alabama. One Friday the thirteenth, Dr. Ralph Bunche, Undersecretary of the United Nations, was scheduled to speak before a Negro women's group in Birmingham. Because of bad weather, his plane was forced to land in Macon, Georgia, at three in the afternoon. He called his hostess to say that he could not possibly make it in time for the eight o'clock engagement. Advised that the airline was transporting Bunche along with the other passengers to Atlanta by bus, the hostess said they would hire a limousine to bring him from Atlanta to Birmingham (a distance of some 180 miles) and that the audience would wait for him until midnight if necessary.

Bunche covered the first hundred miles without incident. Just inside the Alabama border, however, the limousine broke down. Bunche called his hostess and said things looked worse than ever. After a moment of thought she told him to hang up and sit tight. Fifteen minutes later Bunche heard the wail of police sirens. The local sheriff—white—pulled up and asked for Dr. Bunche. "I'm he," Bunche said, with justifiable trepidation.

"By God, git in the car."

Dr. Bunche got in. Despite the blinding rain, the sheriff raced across the county and at the line transferred his passenger to the waiting car of another sheriff, who opened his siren, turned on his blinking lights, and zoomed off into deep Alabama. With the sheriffs working in relays, Bunche was whisked across four counties, covering eighty miles in less than an hour, while his demon-drivers barked progress reports over the short-wave radio.

Only after he arrived at the Birmingham church where the crowd was patiently waiting did Bunche discover that the progress reports were being relayed to white policemen stationed in a car outside the church. At the end of each report the policemen raced into the church and announced Bunche's current position to the resounding shouts of "amen" and "hallelujah." The white policemen then accompanied Bunche into the church and sat in the pulpit while Dr. Bunche proceeded to give segregation hell.

Ralph Bunche is by no means the only outstanding Negro spokesman who has had humorous bouts with race prejudice in reverse. Dr. Robert Weaver, former chairman of the NAACP executive board and now Administrator of the U. S. Housing and Home Finance Agency, was a member on the UNRRA team sent to the Ukraine in 1945 to administer relief. In addition to being a bearer of gifts, Weaver, a tall handsome football hero, was the first Negro most of the Ukrainians had seen. The men were overwhelmed by his good nature and rapid jokes; the women were impressed by his agility and graciousness on the dance floor. In city after city, Weaver found himself the object of ardent and, for him, arduous admiration. Finally in Kharkov, his energy drained. The town fathers feted Weaver and his teammates in a long night of celebration. Shortly before eight the next morning, the tireless comrades banged on Weaver's door and said that he had to start immediately on an inspection tour of city housing projects. His eyes bleary, Weaver turned to his roommate and fellow UNRRA representative—a white man from Texas—and said, "I never thought I would see the day when I would long for a little racial discrimination."

This ability to laugh not only at racism but at themselves sustained Negroes through the turbulent first days of integration. And, as the excellent NBC-TV White Paper on the sit-ins showed, humor has proved to be one of the Negro's most effective weapons:

Fifty dignified Fisk University students were jailed because they participated in the Nashville sit-ins. "Hey, man," one student shouted to a cell mate, according to the TV script. "I sat down in Kress and the white waitress told me, 'We don't serve Negroes.' I told her that was good because I don't eat them."

"Dig this," another student added. "There is this cartoon of a Negro student sitting alone at a lunch counter. The caption reads: *The customer is always white!*"

Then the TV camera closed in on a Negro mother. "I got this letter from Junior," she said, alternately laughing and crying. "And he said, 'Mamma, I'm in jail, but everything is all right. Be cool, Mamma, be cool.' I can't say it like he can," she added to the camera, "but he said, 'Be cool, Mamma, be cool'."

The Supreme Court has yet to rule on the legality of the sit-ins. It may never have to for lunch-counter discrimination has been all but laughed out of existence.

And while in New Orleans segregationists were bringing public education to a lamentable halt because of the school integration issue, subdued laughter was pulsating throughout the Negro community. Fact of the matter is that New Orleans schools have been integrated since the turn of the century. The white schools are peppered with light-skinned Negroes passing for white. They pass during the school day and then go home to social life among their Negro friends and relatives. Fear of detection caused them to join the white boycott of the integrated schools and when segregationist Judge Leander Peters of nearby St. Bernard Parish threw open the door of that community's all-white schools to accommodate the boycotters, the light-skinned Negroes were among the first to go over and register.

FOR "RACE" READ "STATUS"

Negroes are now laughing at themselves as Negroes, and they are doing it without the old overtone of self-effacement. Much of Negro humor is still tribal but it is beginning to take on a tinge of interracial status-consciousness. It was a white Southerner, in fact, who told me the story of the Negro woman who decided to buy a mink with her sweepstakes winnings. Standing in front of the store mirror, the mink down to her ankles, the Negro woman looked at the white sales lady and asked:

"Do you think this coat makes me look too Jewish?"

This is social comedy that hurts; badly. Here the Negro is saying how much the noose burns by looping it around the neck of another tribe. With a single laugh, then, racism and the vulgarity of the new-rich come in for scathing criticism. This double-barreled humor began to appear shortly after the school desegregation decision. It emerged cautiously, demanding that the Negro first laugh at himself as a Negro; only then was he ready to laugh at himself as a human being.

A priest approaching a young Harlemite asked, "Are you Catholic?"

"Lord, no," the young man replied. "Ain't I got problems enough being colored?"

Two Mississippi-born Negro brothers had been living in New York for ten years. Their favorite pastime was talking about how difficult things were in the South. One night they received word of their mother's death. Early the next morning they drove southward, one brother driving, the other riding shotgun. They arrived in Mississippi without incident. After the funeral came the long drive back to New York. Taking turns, one brother drove while the other rode shotgun. Once through Central Park and onto Lenox Avenue in Harlem, the brothers began to laugh for joy. Their roars attracted the attention of a Negro policeman—who halted the car and put them both in jail for having a concealed weapon.

The focus of this humor is the emerging status-conscious Negro who seems to be more status-conscious than Negro. And he can share these raucous stories with his white friends. And they laugh together, at the same thing, because they are members of a rapidly growing tribe of new Americans who don't have to repair to their ethnic roots for a sense of identity. As with any social evolution, there are some uneasy members of this new tribe and their laughter is still troubled.

Harry Ashmore was the first to prick my skin with one of these cauterizing needles of humor. In his Southern drawl, he told me of the two small boys, one Indian, the other Negro, who got into an argument over which of their tribes had contributed the most to modern civilization.

"We got Ralph Bunche and Jackie Robinson and Joe Louis," the Negro boy said. "You Indians ain't done *nothing* to help things along. You made no contribution to our culture at all."

"Well, we had Sitting Bull and Jim Thorpe," the Indian said defensively.

"That was three days before God," the Negro snapped. "What contribution have you made to *modern* culture?"

The Indian thought a long moment and then asked: "How many children in America?"

"Oh," said the Negro imperiously, "about eleventy billion, I suppose."

"How many of them you ever seen playing cowboy and nigger?"

The same meaning gives the sting to the story of the elegant Negro, wearing a Brooks Brothers suit, a Homburg, and gray gloves, who boarded a New York bus, sat down and began to read his copy of the *Wall Street Journal*. His white seatmate leaned over and shouted, "Nigger!"

Whereupon the Negro leaped from the seat in total alarm and asked, "Where? Where? Where?"

IT HAPPENED IN HARLEM

These are jokes, stories cooked up by wags who help us laugh at ourselves. But the controversy over hiring Negro waiters at Frank's, Harlem's most elegant restaurant, a few years ago was quite real, and just as revealing.

Militant Negro groups threatened to picket Frank's because the white owners refused to hire Negro waiters. The owner stood his ground, explaining that he had two restaurants, one in Harlem, the other on the East Side, in the upper Sixties. "I have all white waiters in my Harlem restaurant," the owner explained, "and all Negro waiters in my East Side restaurant."

Then, with an eye at the men in the protest group, the owner added: "Suppose you were out for an evening with . . . shall we say someone other than your wife; would you want your next-door neighbor serving as your waiter? You can come here with your guests and nobody, at least not the waiter, knows who you are. I give the same protection to my East Side clients by having nothing but Negro waiters there."

That ended that. The protest group withdrew their demand. Frank's continued to employ only white waiters until early in 1961 when the new mood of black militancy forced integration at the restaurant.

It takes Frazier's *Black Bourgeoisie*, Galbraith's *The Affluent Society*, and Mills's *The Power Elite* combined to say in serious terms what these stories say with a guffaw: something ails American class values; the disease is catching and many Negroes have caught it. As more Negroes become integrated—that is to say, become responsible as well as complaining members of American society—the more of them are apt to come down with "middle-class sickness." And this, perhaps, is the most comic aspect of all—under segregation the American Negro was a tragic figure; now, with integration coming, he is a comic. He summons the nation's highest court, to say nothing of the nation's Army, to kick down a door and let him into a burning building.

"Lord, honey," a Negro woman remarked as a group of Negro and white teen-agers walked by arm in arm, equally disheveled, "integration is fine. But sometimes I wish they had integrated with us rather than us with them."

Dick Gregory, a rising young comic and a Negro, is perhaps the best evidence of the Negro's new comedy act. "I sat-in at a restaurant for three years," Gregory said. "Then they finally integrated the place and I found out they didn't have what I wanted!"

When David Susskind introduced Gregory on "Open End" as the "Negro Mort Sahl" Gregory quipped, "If we were in the Congo they would call *him* the white Dick Gregory!"

LO, THE AFRICANS

A truly integrated society in America is, at least, twenty-five years off. But humor, blistering prophet that it is (and with a lusty shove from the newly arrived African delegates to the United Nations), has raced on ahead.

Recently I went up the Hudson on a boat ride sponsored by the American Society for African Culture. All of the African delegates to the UN were invited as "guests" and some one hundred Negroes were invited to be "hosts." For the most part, each group thought the other rather quaint and, frankly, primitive.

The big moment came just after the boat passed under the George Washington Bridge and the Society unleashed its entertainment. To help the Africans know us better, the Society had, alas, brought on board a spiritual-singing choir. As the "Sweet Chariot" began to swing low, the American Negroes—many of whom had frequently denounced spirituals as a stigma of the past—began to squirm in their seats and eye the life jackets in the overhead racks. When the choir swung into "O Lord I want two wings to veil my face, two wings to fly away," the Americans eased up slowly and began to creep down to the first deck and into the washrooms. Then came "In that great glitin' up mawning," and long before the choir ascended to the top of "Jacob's Ladder," the Negroes were lined along the bottom rail—there wasn't a drop of Scotch on board—pondering the wisdom of swimming back to Manhattan.

I have since attended several East Side parties given by liberal white Americans who are determined to woo the Africans away from neutralism and, if necessary, Khrushchev. The principal guests are always the African diplomats, some bewildered whites, and just enough Negroes to make the function look kosher.

"Now don't you Africans cluster together," one hostess cooed to a prominent Nigerian and me. "Come mingle with the Americans." Whereupon she pulled us from our conversation and proceeded to introduce me to my wife who, I suppose, looks less African than I do. During another such Western onslaught against Communism, one young woman made her way about shaking every colored hand, saying: "I'm Mary Strickland. What delegation are you with?" As Miss Strickland (this, of course, is not her real name) neared me, my African friends began to laugh and gather for the inevitable. I acknowledged Miss Strickland's greetings and unblinkingly told her I was the delegate from Long Island. Then we really had a party.

Those of us who are laughing about racial matters are making a game of serious issues. This is the way of comedy: its essence is sacrilege. Nothing destroys racism more effectively, for laughter is a criticism, not an endorsement, of things as they are. I will never forget the night Len Gumley, one of my closest friends and a Jew, pulled the scales from my eyes. The story is part of the apocrypha, no doubt.

A chap from Tel Aviv found himself stranded in Hong Kong at the Jewish New Year. With the aid of a policeman, he located the Hong Kong Orthodox Synagogue, Rabbi Yen Su Yung presiding. After the service, the Israeli went up to shake the Rabbi's hand and say what a spiritual comfort it was to have been there. Squinting his slant eyes, his head—adorned with two pig tails—bent low, Rabbi Yen Su Yung commented:

"Oh, so, you Jewish? Velly, velly funny, you don't look Jewish to me!"

Now the Negro adds his new act to the unfolding human comedy. There is seriousness in this comedy act and we who laugh about it are neither nihilists nor clowns. We are, rather, men afflicted with the passionate faith that man can be better than he is and with the equally passionate conviction that honest laughter under-scores the need to close the gap between human aspirations and human performances. This is not to say that the Negro will save modern society, only that he is a part of it.

For we all recall that in the year two thousand and sixty-six, Zeb and Zeke, the last two segregationists on earth, were killed at a grade crossing by a supersonic train. Zeb got to Heaven first and was fully outfitted with wings, halo, and a jar of honey by the time Zeke arrived.

"How are things up here?" Zeke asked, spotting his earthly friend.

"Watch yourself," a thoroughly reformed Zeb counseled, "I just saw God and she's a Nigrah!"

II

THE BLACK WRITER

The following essays are among the most significant writings by black writers about black writing and black writers. The intention here is to give the reader a range of views of how black writers over the present century have seen the act and the art of writing.

THE NEGRO-ART HOKUM

GEORGE S. SCHUYLER. "The Negro-Art Hokum" is the most famous essay George S. Schuyler ever wrote and one of the most noted essays of the Harlem Renaissance. It appeared in *The Nation* on June 16, 1926.

Negro art "made in America" is as non-existent as the widely advertised profundity of Cal Coolidge, the "seven years of progress" of Mayor Hylan, or the reported sophistication of New Yorkers. Negro art there has been, is, and will be among the numerous black nations of Africa; but to suggest the possibility of any such development among the ten million colored people in this republic is self-evident foolishness. Eager apostles from Greenwich Village, Harlem, and environs proclaimed a great renaissance of Negro art just around the corner waiting to be ushered on the scene by those whose hobby is taking races, nations, peoples, and movements under their wing. New art forms expressing the "peculiar" psychology of the Negro were about to flood the market. In short, the art of Homo Africanus was about to electrify the waiting world. Skeptics patiently waited. They still wait.

True, from dark-skinned sources have come those slave songs based on Protestant hymns and Biblical texts known as the spirituals, work songs and secular songs of sorrow and tough luck known as the blues, that outgrowth of ragtime known as jazz (in the development of which whites have assisted), and the Charleston, an eccentric dance invented by the gamins around the public market-place in Charleston, South Carolina. No one can or does deny this. But these are contributions of a caste in a certain section of the country. They are foreign to Northern Negroes, West Indian Negroes, and African Negroes. They are no more expressive or characteristic of the Negro race than the music and dancing of the Appalachian highlanders or the Dalmatian peasantry are expressive or characteristic of the Caucasian race. If one wishes to speak of the musical contributions of the peasantry of the South, very well. Any group under similar circumstances would have produced something similar. It is merely a coincidence that this peasant class happens to be of a darker hue than the other inhabitants of the land. One recalls the remarkable likeness of the minor strains of the Russian mujiks to those of the southern Negro.

As for the literature, painting, and sculpture of Aframericans—such as there is—it is identical in kind with the literature, painting, and sculpture of white Americans: that is, it shows more or less evidence of European influence. In the field of drama little of any merit has been written by and about Negroes that could not have been written by whites. The dean of the Aframerican literati is W. E. B. Du Bois, a product of Harvard and German universities; the foremost Aframerican sculptor is Meta Warwick Fuller, a graduate of leading American art schools and former student of Rodin; while the most noted Aframerican painter, Henry Ossawa Tanner, is dean of American painters in Paris and has been decorated by the French Government. Now the work of these artists is no more "expressive of the Negro soul"—as the gushers put it—than are the scribblings of Octavus Cohen or Hugh Wiley.

This, of course, is easily understood if one stops to realize that the Aframerican is merely a lampblacked Anglo-Saxon. If the European immigrant after two or three generations of exposure to our schools, politics, advertising, moral crusades, and restaurants becomes indistinguishable from the mass of Americans of the older stock (despite the influence of the foreign-language press), how much truer must it be of the sons of Ham who have been subjected to what the uplifters call Americanism for the last three hundred years. Aside from his color, which ranges from very dark brown to pink, your American Negro is just plain American. Negroes and whites from the same localities in this country talk, think, and act about the same. Because a few writers with a paucity of themes have seized upon imbecilities of the Negro rustics and clowns and palmed them off as authentic and characteristic Aframerican behavior, the common notion that the black American is so "different" from his white neighbor has gained wide currency. The mere mention of the word "Negro" conjures up in the average white American's mind a composite stereotype of Bert Williams, Aunt Jemima, Uncle Tom, Jack Johnson, Florian Slappey, and the various monstrosities scrawled by the cartoonists. Your average Aframerican no more resembles this stereotype than the average American resembles a composite of Andy Gump, Jim Jeffries, and a cartoon by Rube Goldberg.

Again, the Aframerican is subject to the same economic and social forces that mold the actions and thoughts of the white Americans. He is not living in a different world as some whites and a few Negroes would have us believe. When the jangling of his Connecticut alarm clock gets him out of his Grand Rapids bed to a breakfast similar to that eaten by his white brother across the street; when he toils at the same or similar work in mills, mines, factories, and commerce alongside the descendants of Spartacus, Robin Hood, and Erik the Red; when he wears similar clothing and speaks the same language with the same degree of perfection; when he reads the same Bible and belongs to the Baptist, Methodist, Episcopal, or Catholic church; when his fraternal affiliations also include the Elks, Masons, and Knights of Pythias; when he gets the same or similar schooling, lives in the same kind of houses, owns the same makes of cars (or rides in them) and nightly sees the same Hollywood version of life on the screen; when he smokes the same brands of tobacco and avidly peruses the same puerile periodicals; in short, when he responds to the same political, social, moral, and economic stimuli in precisely the same manner as his white neighbor, it is sheer nonsense to talk about "racial differences" as between the American black man and the American white man. Glance over a Negro newspaper (it is printed in good Americanese) and you will find the usual quota of crime news, scandal, personals, and uplift to be found in the average white newspaper—which, by the way, is more widely read by the Negroes than is the Negro press. In order to satisfy the cravings of an inferiority complex engendered by the colorphobia of the mob, the readers of the Negro newspapers are given a slight dash of racialistic seasoning. In the homes of the black and white Americans of the same cultural and economic level one finds similar furniture, literature, and conversation. How, then, can the black American be expected to produce art and literature dissimilar to that of the white American?

Consider Coleridge-Taylor, Edward Wilmot Blyden, and Claude McKay, the Englishmen; Pushkin, the Russian; Bridgewater, the Pole; Antar, the Arabian; Latino, the Spaniard; Dumas, *père* and *fils*, the Frenchmen; and Paul Laurence Dunbar, Charles W. Chesnutt, and James Weldon Johnson, the Americans. All Negroes; yet their work shows the impress of nationality rather than race. They all reveal the psychology and culture of their environment—their color is incidental. Why should Negro artists of America vary from the national artistic norm when Negro artists in other countries have not done so? If we can foresee what kind of white citizens will inhabit this neck of the woods in the next generation by studying the sort of education and environment the children are exposed to now, it should not be difficult to reason that the adults of today are what they are because of the education and environment they were exposed to a generation ago. And that education and environment were about the same for blacks and whites. One contemplates the popularity of the Negro-art hokum and murmurs, "How come?"

This nonsense is probably the last stand of the old myth palmed off by Negrophobists for all these many years, and recently rehashed by the sainted Harding, that there are "fundamental, eternal, and inescapable differences" between white and black Americans. That there are Negroes who will lend this myth a helping hand need occasion no surprise. It has been broadcast all over the world by the vociferous scions of slaveholders, "scientists" like Madison Grant and Lothrop Stoddard, and the patriots who flood the treasury of the Ku Klux Klan; and is believed, even today, by the majority of free, white citizens. On this baseless premise, so flattering to the white mob, that the blackamoor is inferior and fundamentally different, is erected the postulate that he must needs be peculiar; and when he attempts to portray life through the medium of art, it must of necessity be a peculiar art. While such reasoning may seem conclusive to the majority of Americans, it must be rejected with a loud guffaw by intelligent people.

THE NEGRO ARTIST
AND THE RACIAL MOUNTAIN

LANGSTON HUGHES's response to Schuyler's "The Negro-Art Hokum" became even more famous than Schuyler's essay, probably because most black writers and blacks in general have found its politics more to their liking. "The Negro Artist and the Racial Mountain" appeared in *The Nation* on June 23, 1926.

One of the most promising of the young Negro poets said to me once, "I want to be a poet—not a Negro poet," meaning, I believe, "I want to write like a white poet"; meaning subconsciously, "I would like to be a white poet"; meaning behind that, "I would like to be white." And I was sorry the young man said that, for no great poet has ever been afraid of being himself. And I doubted then that, with his desire to run away spiritually from his race, this boy would ever be a great poet. But this is the mountain standing in the way of any true Negro art in America—this urge within the race toward whiteness, the desire to pour racial individuality into the mold of American standardization, and to be as little Negro and as much American as possible.

But let us look at the immediate background of this young poet. His family is of what I suppose one would call the Negro middle class: people who are by no means rich yet never uncomfortable nor hungry—smug, contented, respectable folk, members of the Baptist church. The father goes to work every morning. He is a chief steward at a large white club. The mother sometimes does fancy sewing or supervises parties for the rich families of the town. The children go to a mixed school. In the home they read white papers and magazines. And the mother often says "Don't be like niggers" when the children are bad. A frequent phrase from the father is, "Look how well a white man does things." And so the word white comes to be unconsciously a symbol of all the virtues. It holds for the children beauty, morality, and money. The whisper of "I want to be white" runs silently through their minds. This young poet's home is, I believe, a fairly typical home of the colored middle class. One sees immediately how difficult it would be for an artist born in such a home to interest himself in interpreting the beauty of his own people. He is never taught to see that beauty. He is taught rather not to see it, or if he does, to be ashamed of it when it is not according to Caucasian patterns.

For racial culture the home of a self-styled "high-class" Negro has nothing better to offer. Instead there will perhaps be more aping of things white than in a less cultured or less wealthy home. The father is perhaps a doctor, lawyer, landowner, or politician. The mother may be a social worker, or a teacher, or she may do nothing and have a maid. Father is often dark but he has usually married the lightest woman he could find. The family attend a fashionable church where few really colored faces are to be found. And they themselves draw a color line. In the North they go to white theaters and white movies. And in the South they have at least two cars and a house "like white folks." Nordic manners, Nordic faces, Nordic hair, Nordic art (if any), and an Episcopal heaven. A very high mountain indeed for the would-be racial artist to climb in order to discover himself and his people.

But then there are the low-down folks, the so-called common element, and they are the majority—may the Lord be praised! The people who have their nip of gin on Saturday nights and are not too important to themselves or the community, or too well fed, or too learned to watch the lazy world go round. They live on Seventh Street in Washington or State Street in Chicago and they do not particularly care whether they are like white folks or anybody else. Their joy runs, bang! into ecstasy. Their religion soars to a shout. Work maybe a little today, rest a little tomorrow. Play awhile. Sing awhile. O, let's dance! These common people are not afraid of spirituals, as for a long time their more intellectual brethren were, and jazz is their child. They furnish a wealth of colorful, distinctive material for any artist because they still hold their own individuality in the face of American standard-izations. And perhaps these common people will give to the world its truly great Negro artist, the one who is not afraid to be himself. Whereas the better-class Negro would tell the artist what to do, the people at least let him alone when he does appear. And they are not ashamed of him—if they know he exists at all. And they accept what beauty is their own without question.

Certainly there is, for the American Negro artist who can escape the restrictions the more advanced among his own group would put upon him, a great field of unused material ready for his art. Without going outside his race, and even among the better classes with their "white" culture and conscious American manners, but still Negro enough to be different, there is sufficient matter to furnish a black artist with a lifetime of creative work. And when he chooses to touch on the relations between Negroes and whites in this country with their innumerable overtones and undertones, surely, and especially for literature and the drama, there is an inexhaustible supply of themes at hand. To these the Negro artist can give his racial individuality, his heritage of rhythm and warmth, and his incongruous humor that so often, as in the Blues, becomes ironic laughter mixed with tears. But let us look again at the mountain.

A prominent Negro clubwoman in Philadelphia paid eleven dollars to hear Raquel

Meller sing Andalusian popular songs. But she told me a few weeks before she would not think of going to hear "that woman," Clara Smith, a great black artist, sing Negro folksongs. And many an upper-class Negro church, even now, would not dream of employing a spiritual in its services. The drab melodies in white folks' hymnbooks are much to be preferred. "We want to worship the Lord correctly and quietly. We don't believe in 'shouting.' Let's be dull like the Nordics," they say, in effect.

The road for the serious black artist, then, who would produce a racial art is most certainly rocky and the mountain is high. Until recently he received almost no encouragement for his work from either white or colored people. The fine novels of Chesnutt go out of print with neither race noticing their passing. The quaint charm and humor of Dunbar's dialect verse brought to him, in his day, largely the same kind of encouragement one would give a side-show freak (A colored man writing poetry! How odd!) or a clown (How amusing!).

The present vogue in things Negro, although it may do as much harm as good for the budding colored artist, has at least done this: it has brought him forcibly to the attention of his own people among whom for so long, unless the other race had noticed him beforehand, he was a prophet with little honor. I understand that Charles Gilpin acted for years in Negro theaters without any special acclaim from his own, but when Broadway gave him eight curtain calls, Negroes, too, began to beat a tin pan in his honor. I know a young colored writer, a manual worker by day, who had been writing well for the colored magazines for some years, but it was not until he recently broke into the white publications and his first book was accepted by a prominent New York publisher that the "best" Negroes in his city took the trouble to discover that he lived there. Then almost immediately they decided to give a grand dinner for him. But the society ladies were careful to whisper to his mother that perhaps she'd better not come. They were not sure she would have an evening gown.

The Negro artist works against an undertow of sharp criticism and misunderstanding from his own group and unintentional bribes from the whites. "O, be respectable, write about nice people, show how good we are," say the Negroes. "Be stereotyped, don't go too far, don't shatter our illusions about you, don't amuse us too seriously. We will pay you," say the whites. Both would have told Jean Toomer not to write *Cane*. The colored people did not praise it. The white people did not buy it. Most of the colored people who did read *Cane* hate it. They are afraid of it. Although the critics gave it good reviews the public remained indifferent. Yet (excepting the work of DuBois) *Cane* contains the finest prose written by a Negro in America. And like the singing of Robeson, it is truly racial.

But in spite of the Nordicized Negro intelligentsia and the desires of some white editors, we have an honest American Negro literature already with us. Now I await the rise of the Negro theater. Our folk music, having achieved world-wide fame, offers itself to the genius of the great individual American Negro composer who is to come. And within the next decade I expect to see the work of a growing school of colored artists who paint and model the beauty of dark faces and create with new technique the expressions of their own soul-world. And the Negro dancers who will dance like flame and the singers who will continue to carry our songs to all who listen—they will be with us in even greater numbers tomorrow.

Most of my own poems are racial in theme and treatment, derived from the life I know. In many of them I try to grasp and hold some of the meanings and rhythms of jazz. I am sincere as I know how to be in these poems and yet after every reading I answer questions like these from my own people: Do you think Negroes should always write about Negroes? I wish you wouldn't read some of your poems to white folks. How do you find anything interesting in a place like a cabaret? Why do you write about black people? You aren't black. What makes you do so many jazz poems?

But jazz to me is one of the inherent expressions of Negro life in America: the eternal tom-tom beating in the Negro soul—the tom-tom of revolt against weariness in a white world, a world of subway trains, and work, work, work; the tom-tom of joy and laughter, and pain swallowed in a smile. Yet the Philadelphia clubwoman is ashamed to say that her race created it and she does not like me to write about it. The old subconscious "white is best" runs through her mind. Years of study under white teachers, a lifetime of white books, pictures, and papers, and white manners, morals, and Puritan standards made her dislike the spirituals. And now she turns up her nose at jazz and all its manifestations—likewise almost everything else distinctly racial. She doesn't care for the Winold Reiss portraits of Negroes because they are "too Negro." She does not want a true picture of herself from anybody. She wants the artist to flatter her, to make the white world believe that all Negroes are as smug and as near white in soul as she wants to be. But, to my mind, it is the duty of the younger Negro artist, if he accepts any duties at all from outsiders, to change through the force of his art that old whispering "I want to be white," hidden in the aspirations of his people, to "Why should I want to be white? I am a Negro—and beautiful!"

So I am ashamed for the black poet who says, "I want to be a poet, not a Negro poet," as though his own racial world were not as interesting as any other world. I am ashamed, too, for the colored artist who runs from the painting of Negro faces to the painting of sunsets after the manner of the academicians because he fears the strange un-whiteness of his own features. An artist must be free to choose what he does, certainly, but he must also never be afraid to do what he might choose.

Let the blare of Negro jazz bands and the bellowing voice of Bessie Smith singing Blues penetrate the closed ears of the colored near-intellectuals until they listen and perhaps understand. Let Paul Robeson singing Water Boy, and Rudolph Fisher writing about the streets of Harlem, and Jean Toomer holding the heart of Georgia in his hands, and Aaron Douglas drawing strange black fantasies cause the smug Negro middle class to turn from their white, respectable, ordinary books and papers to catch a glimmer of their own beauty. We younger Negro artists who create now intend to express our individual dark-skinned selves without fear or shame. If white people are pleased we are glad. If they are not, it doesn't matter. We know we are beautiful. And ugly too. The tom-tom cries and the tom-tom laughs. If colored people are pleased we are glad. If they are not, their displeasure doesn't matter either. We build our temples for tomorrow, strong as we know how, and we stand on top of the mountain, free within ourselves.

THE DILEMMA OF
THE NEGRO AUTHOR

JAMES WELDON JOHNSON's discussion of the
problems of the black writer trying to deal with two distinct
audiences—one black, the other white—is quite perceptive and
remains timely today. The piece appeared in *The American Mercury*
in December 1928.

The Negro author—the creative author—has arrived. He is here. He
appears in the lists of the best publishers. He even breaks into the lists of
the best-sellers. To the general American public he is a novelty, a strange
phenomenon, a miracle straight out of the skies. Well he is a novelty, but he is by
no means a new thing.

The line of American Negro authors runs back for a hundred and fifty years,
back to Phillis Wheatley, the poet. Since Phillis Wheatley there have been several
hundred Negro authors who have written books of many kinds. But in all these
generations down to within the past six years only seven or eight of the hundreds
have ever been heard of by the general American public or even by the specialists
in American Literature. As many Negro writers have gained recognition by both in
the past six years as in all the generations gone before. What has happened is that
efforts which have been going on for more than a century are being noticed and
appreciated at last, and that this appreciation has served as a stimulus to greater
effort and output. America is aware today that there are such things as Negro
authors. Several converging forces have been at work to produce this state of mind.
Had these forces been at work three decades ago, it is possible that we then should
have had a condition similar to the one which now exists.

Now that the Negro author has come into the range of vision of the American
public eye, it seems to me only fair to point out some of the difficulties he finds in
his way. But I wish to state emphatically that I have no intention of making an

apology or asking any special allowances for him; such a plea would at once disqualify him and void the very recognition he has gained. But the Negro writer does face peculiar difficulties that ought to be taken into account when passing judgment upon him.

It is unnecessary to say that he faces every one of the difficulties common to all that crowd of demon-driven individuals who feel that they must write. But the Aframerican author faces a special problem which the plain American author knows nothing about—the problem of the double audience. It is more than a double audience; it is a divided audience, an audience made up of two elements with differing and often opposite and antagonistic points of view. His audience is always both white America and black America. The moment a Negro writer takes up his pen or sits down to his typewriter he is immediately called upon to solve, consciously or unconsciously, this problem of the double audience. To whom shall he address himself, to his own black group or to white America? Many a Negro writer has fallen down, as it were, between these two stools.

It may be asked why he doesn't just go ahead and write and not bother himself about audiences. That is easier said than done. It is doubtful if anything with meaning can be written unless the writer has some definite audience in mind. His audience may be as far away as the angelic host or the rulers of darkness, but an audience he must have in mind. As soon as he selects his audience he immediately falls, whether he wills it or not, under the laws which govern the influence of the audience upon the artist, laws that operate in every branch of art.

Now, it is axiomatic that the artist achieves his best when working at his best with the materials he knows best. And it goes without saying that the material which the Negro as a creative or general writer knows best comes out of the life and experience of the colored people in America. The overwhelming bulk of the best work done by Aframerican writers has some bearing on the Negro and his relations to civilization and society in the United States. Leaving authors, white or black, writing for coteries on special and technical subjects out of the discussion, it is safe to say that the white American author, when he sits down to write, has in mind a white audience—and naturally [so]. The influence of the Negro as a group on his work is infinitesimal if not zero. Even when he talks about the Negro he talks to white people. But with the Aframerican author the case is different. When he attempts to handle his best-known material he is thrown upon two, indeed, if it is permissible to say so, upon three horns of a dilemma. He must intentionally or unintentionally choose a black audience or a white audience or a combination of the two; and each of them presents peculiar difficulties.

If the Negro author selects white America as his audience he is bound to run up against many long-standing artistic conceptions about the Negro; against numerous conventions and traditions which through age have become binding; in a word, against a whole row of hard-set stereotypes which are not easily broken up. White America has some firm opinions as to what the Negro is, and consequently some pretty well-fixed ideas as to what should be written about him, and how.

What is the Negro in the artistic conception of white America? In the brighter light, he is a simple, indolent, docile improvident peasant; a singing, dancing, laughing, weeping child; picturesque beside his log cabin and in the snowy fields of cotton; naively charming with his banjo and his songs in the moonlight and along the lazy Southern rivers; a faithful ever-smiling and genuflecting old servitor to the white folks of quality; a pathetic and pitiable figure. In a darker light, he is an impulsive, irrational, passionate savage, reluctantly wearing a thin coat of culture, sullenly hating the white man, but holding an innate and unescapable belief in the white man's superiority; an everlastingly alien and irredeemable element in the nation; a menace to Southern civilization, a threat to Nordic race purity; a figure casting a sinister shadow across the future of the country.

Ninety-nine one-hundredths of all that has been written about the Negro in the United States in three centuries and read with any degree of interest or pleasure by white America has been written in conformity to one or more of these ideas. I am not saying that they do not provide good material for literature; in fact, they make material for poetry and romance and comedy and tragedy of a high order. But I do say they have become stencils inadequate for the portrayal and interpretation of Negro life today. Moreover, when [the Negro author] does attempt to make use of them he finds himself impaled upon the second horn of his dilemma.

II

It is known that art—literature in particular, unless it be sheer fantasy—must be based on more or less well established conventions, upon ideas that have some roots in the general consciousness, that are at least somewhat familiar to the public mind. It is this that gives it verisimilitude and finality. Even revolutionary literature, if it is to have any convincing power, must start from a basis of conventions, regardless of how unconventional its objective may be. These conventions are changed by slow and gradual processes—except they be changed in a flash. The conventions held by white America regarding the Negro will be changed. Actually they are being changed, but they have not yet sufficiently changed to lessen to any great extent the dilemma of the Negro author.

It would be straining the credulity of white America beyond the breaking point for a Negro writer to put out a novel dealing with the wealthy class of colored people. The idea of Negroes of wealth living in a luxurious manner is still too unfamiliar. Such a story would have to be written in a burlesque vein to make it at all plausible and acceptable. Before Florence Mills and Josephine Baker implanted a new general idea in the public mind it would have been worse than a waste of time for a Negro author to write for white America the story of a Negro girl who rose in spite of all obstacles, racial and others, to a place of world success and acclaim on the musical revue stage. It would be proof of little less than supreme genius in a Negro poet for him to take one of the tragic characters of American Negro history—say Crispus Attucks or Nat Turner or Denmark Vesey—put heroic language in his mouth and have white America accept the work as authentic. American Negroes as heroes form no part of white America's concept of the race. Indeed, I question if three out of ten of the white Americans who will read these lines know anything of either Attucks, Turner or Vesey, although each of the three played a role in the history of the nation. The Aframerican poet might take an African chief or warrior, set him forth in heroic couplets or blank verse and present him to white America with infinitely greater chance of having his work accepted.

But these limiting conventions held by white America do not constitute the whole difficulty of the Negro author in dealing with a white audience. In addition to these conventions regarding the Negro as a race, white America has certain definite opinions regarding the Negro as an artist, regarding the scope of his efforts. White America has a strong feeling that Negro artists should refrain from making use of white subject matter. I mean by that, subject matter which it feels belongs to the white world. In plain words, white America does not welcome seeing the Negro competing with the white man on what it considers the white man's own ground.

In many white people this feeling is dormant, but brought to the test it flares up, if only faintly. During his first season in this country after his European success a most common criticism of Roland Hayes was provoked by the fact that his program consisted of groups [of] English, French, German and Italian songs, closing always with a group of Negro Spirituals. A remark frequently made was, "Why doesn't he confine himself to the Spirituals?" This in face of the fact that no tenor on the American concert stage could surpass Hayes in singing French and German songs. The truth is that white America was not quite prepared to relish the sight of a black man in a dress suit singing French and German love songs, and singing them exquisitely. The first reaction was that there was something incongruous about it. It gave a jar to the old conventions and something of a shock to the Nordic superiority complex. The years have not been many since Negro players have dared to interpolate a love duet in a musical show to be witnessed by white people. The representation of romantic love-making by Negroes struck the white audience as somewhat ridiculous; Negroes were supposed to mate in a more primeval manner.

White America has for a long time been annexing and appropriating Negro territory, and is prone to think of every part of the domain it now controls as originally—and aboriginally—its own. One sometimes hears the critics in reviewing a Negro musical show lament the fact that it is so much like white musical shows. But a great deal of this similarity would be hard to avoid because of the plain fact that two of the four chief ingredients in the present day white musical show, the music and the dancing, are directly derived from the Negro. These ideas and opinions regarding the scope of artistic effort affect the Negro author, the poet in particular. So whenever an Aframerican writer addresses himself to white America and attempts to break away from or break through these conventions and limitations he makes more than an ordinary demand upon his literary skill and power.

At this point it would appear that a most natural thing for the Negro author to do would be to say, "Damn the white audience!" and devote himself to addressing his own race exclusively. But when he turns from the conventions of white America he runs afoul of the taboos of black America. He has no more absolute freedom to speak as he pleases addressing black America than he has in addressing white America. There are certain phases of life that he dare not critically discuss, certain manners of treatment that he dare not use—except at the risk of rousing bitter resentment. It is quite possible for a Negro author to do a piece of work, good from every literary point of view, and at the same time bring down on his head the wrath of the entire colored pulpit and press, and gain among the literate element of his own people the reputation of being a prostitutor of his talent and a betrayer of his race—not by any means a pleasant position to get into.

This state of mind on the part of the colored people may strike white America as stupid and intolerant, but it is not without some justification and not entirely without precedent; the white South on occasion discloses a similar sensitiveness. The colored people of the United States are anomalously situated. They are a segregated and antagonized minority in a very large nation, a minority unremittingly on the defensive. Their faults and failings are exploited to produce exaggerated effects. Consequently, they have a strong feeling against exhibiting to the world anything but their best points. They feel that other groups may afford to do otherwise but, as yet, the Negro cannot. This is not to say that they refuse to listen to criticism of themselves, for they often listen to Negro speakers excoriating the race for its faults and foibles and vices. But these criticisms are not for the printed page. They are not for the ears or eyes of White America.

A curious illustration of this defensive state of mind is found in the Negro theaters. In those wherein Negro players give Negro performances for Negro audiences all of the Negro weaknesses, real and reputed, are burlesqued and ridiculed in the most hilarious manner, and are laughed at and heartily enjoyed. But the presence of a couple of dozen white people would completely change the psychology of the audience, and the players. If some of the performances so much enjoyed by the strictly Negro audiences in Negro theaters were put on, say, in a Broadway theater, a wave of indignation would sweep Aframerica from the avenues of Harlem to the canebrakes of Louisiana. These taboos of black America are as real and binding as the conventions of white America. Conditions may excuse if not warrant them; nevertheless, it is unfortunate that they exist, for their effect is blighting. In past years they have discouraged in Negro authors the production of everything but *nice* literature; they have operated to hold their work down to literature of the defensive, exculpatory sort. They have a restraining effect at present time which Negro writers are compelled to reckon with.

This division of audience takes the solid ground from under the feet of the Negro writer and leaves him suspended. Either choice carries hampering and discouraging conditions. The Negro author may please one audience and at the same time rouse the resentment of the other; or he may please the other and totally fail to rouse the interest of the one. The situation, moreover, constantly subjects him to the temptation of posing and posturing for the one audience or the other; and the sincerity and soundness of his work are vitiated whether he poses for white or black.

The dilemma is not made less puzzling by the fact that practically it is an extremely difficult thing for the Negro author in the United States to address himself solely to either of these two audiences. If he analyzes what he writes he will find that on one page black America is his whole or main audience, and on the very next page white America. In fact, a psychoanalysis of the Negro authors of the defensive and exculpatory literature, written in strict conformity to the taboos of black America, would reveal that they were unconsciously addressing themselves mainly to white America.

III

I have sometimes thought it would be a way out, that the Negro author would be on surer ground and truer to himself, if he could disregard white America; if he could say to white America, "What I have written, I have written. I hope you'll be interested and like it. If not, I can't help it." But it is impossible for a sane American Negro to write with total disregard for nine-tenths of the people of the United States. Situated as his own race is amidst and amongst them, their influence is irresistible.

I judge there is not a single Negro writer who is not, at least secondarily, impelled by the desire to make his work have some effect on the white world for the good of his race. It may be thought that the work of the Negro writer, on account of this last named condition, gains in pointedness what it loses in breadth. Be that as it may, the situation is for the time one in which he is inextricably placed. Of course, the Negro author can try the experiment of putting black America in the orchestra chairs, so to speak, and keeping white America in the gallery, but he is likely at any moment to find his audience shifting places on him, and sometimes without notice.

And now, instead of black America and white America as separate or alternating audiences, what about the combination of the two into one? That, I believe, is the only way out. However, there needs to be more than a combination, there needs to be a fusion. In time, I cannot say how much time, there will come a gradual and natural rapprochement of these two sections of the Negro author's audiences. There will come a breaking up and remodelling of most of white America's traditional stereotypes, forced by the advancement of the Negro in the various phases of our national life. Black America will abolish many of its taboos. A sufficiently large class of colored people will progress enough and become strong enough to render a constantly sensitive and defensive attitude on the part of the race unnecessary and distasteful. In the end, the Negro author will have something close to a common audience, and will be about as free from outside limitations as other writers.

Meanwhile, the making of a common audience out of white and black America presents the Negro author with enough difficulties to constitute a third horn of his dilemma. It is a task that is a very high test for all his skill and abilities, but it can be and has been accomplished. The equipped Negro author working at his best in his best-known material can achieve this end; but, standing on his racial foundation, he must fashion something that rises above race, and reaches out to the universal in truth and beauty. And so, when a Negro author does write so as to fuse white and black America into one interested and approving audience he has performed no slight feat, and has most likely done a sound piece of literary work.

NEGRO POETS
AND THEIR POETRY

WALLACE THURMAN was another black writer very
influenced by H. L. Mencken. "Negro Poets and Their Poetry," which
appeared in *The Bookman* in July 1928, and "Negro Artists and the
Negro," which appeared in *The New Republic* on August 31, 1927,
taken together are scathing denunciations of both the philistinism of the
black writer and the black audience.

J upiter Hammon, the first Negro in this country to write and publish poetry,
was a slave owned by a Mr. Joseph Lloyd of Queens Village, Long Island.
Hammon had been converted to the religion of Jesus Christ and all of his
poems are religious exhortations, incoherent in thought and crudely executed. His
first poem was published in 1761, his second, entitled "An Address to Miss Phillis
Wheatley, Ethiopian Poetess in Boston, who came from Africa at eight years of age
and soon became acquainted with the Gospel of Jesus Christ," in 1768.

This Miss Phillis Wheatley, who had been bought from a slave-ship by a family
named Wheatley in Boston Harbor and educated by them, wrote better doggerel
than her older contemporary Hammon. She knew Alexander Pope and she knew
Ovid—Hammon only knew the Bible—and she knew Pope so well that she could
write like a third-rate imitator of him. Phillis in her day was a museum figure who
would have caused more of a sensation if some contemporary Barnum had exploited
her. As it was she attracted so much attention that many softhearted (and, in some
cases, soft-headed) whites and blacks have been led to believe that her poetry deserves
to be considered as something more than a mere historical relic. This is an excerpt
from her best poem:

Imagination! who can sing thy force?
Or who describe the swiftness of thy course?

Soaring through the air to find the bright abode,
The empyreal palace of the thundering God,
We on thy pinions can surpass the wind,
And leave the rolling universe behind,
From star to star the mental optics rove,
Measure the skies, and range the realms above,
There in one view we grasp the mighty whole,
Or with new worlds amaze the unbounded soul.

She never again equalled the above, far less surpassed it. And most of the time she wrote as in the following excerpt from "On Major General Lee." (This poem would warm the heart of "Big Bill" Thompson of Chicago; he really should know about it.) A captured colonial soldier is addressing a British general:

O Arrogance of tongue!
And wild ambition, ever prone to wrong!
Believ'st thou, chief, that armies such as thine
Can stretch in dust that heaven defended line?
In vain allies may swarm from distant lands,
And demons aid in formidable bands,
Great as thou art, thou shun'st the field of fame,
Disgrace to Britain and the British name.

She continues in this vein, damning the British and enshrining the Americans until she reaches a climax in the following priceless lines:

Find in your train of boasted heroes, one
To match the praise of Godlike Washington.
Thrice happy chief in whom the virtues join,
And heaven taught prudence speaks the man divine.

Thomas Jefferson is quoted as saying that "Religion has produced a Phillis Wheatley, but it could not produce a poet. Her poems are beneath contempt." Nevertheless, Phillis had an interesting and exciting career. The Wheatleys carried her to London, where her first volume was published in 1773. She was exhibited at the Court of George III, and in the homes of the nobility much as the Negro poets of today are exhibited in New York drawing-rooms. She wrote little about slavery, which is not surprising considering that save for her epic trip across the Atlantic in a slave-ship, she had never known slavery in any form. She often mentioned her homeland and once spoke of herself as "Afric's muse," but she was more interested in the religion of Jesus Christ and in the spreading of piety than in any more worldly items, save perhaps in her patriotic interest for the cause of the American colonists.

Heretofore every commentator, whether white or black, when speaking of Phillis Wheatley,, has sought to make excuses for her bad poetry. They have all pointed out that Phillis lived and wrote during the eighteenth century, when, to quote from the introduction to White and Jackson's *Poetry of American Negro Poets,* "the great body of contemporary poetry was turgid in the style of debased Pope." It would be too much, they continue, to expect "a poet of Phillis Wheatley's rather conventional personality to rise above this influence." In his preface to *The Book of American Negro Poetry*, James Weldon Johnson contends that "had she come under the influence of Wordsworth, Byron, Keats or Shelley, she would have done greater work." Does it smack too much of lese-majesty to suggest that perhaps Phillis wrote the best poetry she could have written under any influence, and that a mediocre imitation of Shelley would have been none the less mediocre than a mediocre imitation of Pope? Phillis was also influenced by the Bible, but her paraphrases of the scripture are just as poor as her paraphrases of "debased Pope."

Phillis died in 1784 and until Paul Lawrence Dunbar published his *Oak and Ivy*, in 1892, American Negro poetry stayed at the level at which she had left it, although there must have been over one hundred Negroes who wrote and published poetry during this period. Most of them came into prominence during and after the Civil War, and were encouraged by abolitionists to write of their race and their race's trials. Frances Ellen Harper is probably the best of this period. One volume, *On Miscellaneous Subjects*, was published with an introduction by William Lloyd Garrison. Over ten thousand copies were circulated. Mrs. Harper also wrote and published *Moses, a Story of the Nile*, in verse covering fifty-two closely printed pages. Many of her contemporaries were equally ambitious. Length was a major poetic virtue to them.

It seems highly probable that these people wrote in verse because neither their minds nor their literary tools and backgrounds were adequate for the task of writing readable and intelligent prose. They could be verbose and emotional in verse, and yet attain a degree of coherence not attainable when they wrote in prose. George M. Horton is a good illustration. He was born a slave in Chatham County, North Carolina, in 1797. It is said that he "was not a good farm worker on account of devoting too much time to fishing, hunting and attending religious meetings." He taught himself to read with the aid of a Methodist hymn-book and a red-backed speller. In 1830 he secured work as a janitor at Chapel Hill, the seat of the University of North Carolina. Here he made extra money writing love poems for amorous students. Desiring to obtain his freedom and migrate to Liberia, Horton, aided by some of his white friends, published a volume of verse entitled *The Hope of Liberty*, but the returns from the sale of this volume were not sufficient for his purpose. But he remained more or less a free agent, and was allowed to hire himself out instead of having to remain on his master's plantation. In 1865, a troop of Federal soldiers, who had been quartered in Chapel Hill, were ordered north. Horton left with them and went to Philadelphia, where he eventually died.

Here is a sample of his prose: "By close application to my book and at night my visage became considerably emaciated by extreme perspiration, having no lucu-bratory apparatus, no candle, no lamp, not even lightweed, being chiefly raised in oaky woods." And here is a sample of his verse:

> Come liberty. Thou cheerful sound
> Roll through my ravished ears;
> Come, let my griefs in joy be drowned
> And drive away my fears.

Further comment would be superfluous.

After the Civil War, the Negro found himself in a dilemma. He was supposed to be free, yet his condition was little changed. He was worse off in some respects than he had been before. It can be understood, then, that the more articulate Negroes of the day spent most of their time speculating upon this thing called freedom, both as it had been imagined and as it was in actuality.

However, none of the poetry written at this time is worthy of serious critical consideration. It was not even a poetry of protest. Although Negro poets objected to the mistreatment of their people, they did not formulate these objections in strong, biting language, but rather sought sympathy and pled for pity. They wept copiously but seldom manifested a fighting spirit. The truth is, only one American Negro poet has been a fighting poet, only one has really written revolutionary-protest poetry, and that is Claude McKay, who will be considered later.

Paul Laurence Dunbar was the first American Negro poet whose work really merited critical attention. Dunbar was the son of two ex-slaves, both supposedly full-blooded Negroes, a fact flagrantly paraded by race purists, to controvert the prevalent Nordic theory that only Negroes with Caucasian blood in their veins ever accomplish anything. He was born in Dayton, Ohio, June 27th, 1872. His father had escaped from his master and fled to Canada, but later returned to the States and enlisted for military service during the Civil War in a Massachusetts regiment. Dunbar may have inherited his love for letters and writing from his mother, whose master had often read aloud in her presence.

Dunbar attended the public schools in his home town, and was graduated from the local high-school, where he had edited the school paper. Then he found employment as an elevator operator. In 1892 he delivered an address in verse to the Western Association of Writers, and shortly afterwards he published his first volume, *Oak and Ivy*. In 1896, through the subscription method, he was able to publish another volume, entitled *Majors and Minors*. William Dean Howells wrote a most favorable review of this volume and later paved the way for Dodd, Mead and Company to publish *Lyrics of Lowly Life*, for which he wrote an introduction. Meanwhile Dunbar had visited England, and had become a great friend with Coleridge-Taylor, the Negro composer, with whom he collaborated on many songs. On his return to the United States, another friend, Robert G. Ingersoll, helped him to get a position in the Library of Congress. He was only able to keep this job two years, for meanwhile he had developed pulmonary tuberculosis, and despite pilgrimages to such lung-soothing climates as the Adirondacks, the Rockies, and Florida, he finally succumbed to the disease and died in Dayton, Ohio, on February 9, 1908.

From 1892 until the time of his death Dunbar published five volumes of verse, four volumes of collected short stories, and four novels. Not only was he the first Negro to write poetry which had real merit and could be considered as having more than merely sentimental or historical value, but he was also the first Negro poet to be emancipated from Methodism, the first American Negro poet who did not depend on a Wesleyan hymn-book for inspiration and vocabulary. Most of the poets preceding him were paragons of piety. They had all been seized upon by assiduous missionaries and put through the paces of Christianity, and their verses were full of puerile apostrophizing of the Almighty, and leaden allusions to Scriptural passages.

Yet Dunbar was far from being a great poet. First of all, he was a rank sentimentalist, and was content to let surface values hold his interest. He attempted to interpret the soul of his people, but as William Stanley Braithwaite has said, he succeeded "only in interpreting a folk temperament". And although he was, as William Dean Howells affirmed, the first "man of pure African blood of American civilization to feel Negro life aesthetically and express it lyrically," neither his aesthetic feeling nor his expression ever attained enough depth to be of permanent value.

Dunbar is famous chiefly for his dialect poetry. Yet he often regretted that the world turned to praise "a jingle in a broken tongue." He was ambitious to experiment in more classical forms, and to deal with something less concrete than the "smile through your tears" plantation-darky of reconstruction times. Here perhaps was his greatest limitation. Being anxious to explore the skies, he merely skimmed over the surface of the earth.

After Dunbar, there was a whole horde of Negro poets who, like him, wrote in dialect. The sum total of their achievement is zero, but happily, in addition to these parasitic tyros there were also two new poets who had more originality and more talent than their contemporaries. And though neither of these men produced anything out of the ordinary, they did go beyond the minstrel humor and peasant pathos of Dunbar, and beyond the religious cant and doggerel jeremiads of Dunbar's predecessors. One of these men, William Stanley Braithwaite, is best known as a student and friend of poets and poetry rather than as a poet. He has yearly, since 1913, issued an anthology of American magazine verse, and has also published some academic studies of English literature.

The second, James Weldon Johnson, achieved little as a poet until recently, when he published God's Trombones, a volume of Negro sermons done in verse. His first volume, Fifty Years and Other Poems, contains little of merit. The title poem, which recounts in verse the progress of the race from 1863 to 1913, has, because of its propagandist content, been acclaimed as a great poem. No comment or criticism is necessary of this opinion when part of the poem itself can be quoted:

Far, far, the way that we have trod
From heathen trails and jungle dens
To freedmen, freedmen, sons of God,
Americans and citizens.

Mr. Johnson, it seems, has also been fairly intimate with Methodist hymn books.

His sermon poems, while at times awkward and faulty in technique, have an ecstatic eloquence and an individual rhythm which immediately place them among the best things any Negro has ever done in poetry. Although this may not be saying much, and although, as a poet Mr. Johnson may not be adequate to the task of fully realizing the promise of these sermon poems, he has at least laid a foundation upon which a new generation of Negro poets can build. He will have to be remembered as something more than just a historical or sentimental figure. He, like Dunbar, is an important, if a minor bard; and if the Negro poet of the future is to make any individual contribution to American literature he must derive almost as much from the former's God's Trombones as from the latter's Lyrics of Lowly Life.

To consider all the Negro poets who since 1913 have lifted up their voices in song would necessitate using an entire issue of any journal. It is not only an impossible task but one not worth the time and space it would require. For our present study we will touch only the high spots, passing over such people as Fenton Johnson, whose early promise has never been fulfilled; Joseph Cotter, Jr., who, it is alleged by most critics in this field, would have been a great poet had he lived but whose extant work belies this judgment; Georgia Douglas Johnson, whose highly sentimental and feminine lyrics have found favor; Arna Bontemps, who specializes in monotonous and wordy mystic evocations which lack fire and conviction; and Helene Johnson, who alone of all the younger group seems to have the "makings" of a poet.

But taking up the contemporary triumvirate—McKay, Cullen, and Hughes—all of whom have had volumes published by reputable houses and are fairly well known to the poetry-reading public, we have poets of another type. Each one of them represents a different trend in Negro literature and life.

Claude McKay was born in Jamaica, British West Indies, where he received his elementary education, served a while in the constabulary, and wrote his first poems. A friend financed his journey to America to finish his scholastic work, but McKay found himself at odds with the second-rate schools he attended here, and finally fled to New York City, where he became a member of the old *Masses*, *Seven Arts*, *Liberator* group of radicals and artists. During this period he received a legacy which, he tells us, was spent in riotous living. Broke, he attempted to make a living by washing dishes, operating elevators, doing porter work—the usual occupations engaged in by Negro artists and intellectuals.

McKay's first volume was published while he was still in Jamaica, a compilation of folk-verse done in the native dialect. The Institute of Arts and Science of Jamaica gave him a medal in recognition of this first book. It is in many ways remarkable, and in it the poet gives us a more substantial portrait and delves far deeper into the soul of the Jamaican than Dunbar was ever able to in the soul of the southern Negro in America.

McKay's latter poetry is often marred by bombast. He is such an intense person that one can often hear the furnace-like fire within him roaring in his poems. He seems to have more emotional depth and spiritual fire than any of his forerunners or contemporaries. It might be added that he also seems to have considerably more mental depth too. His love poems are not as musical or as haunting as Mr. Cullen's, but neither are they as stereotyped. His sonnet to a Harlem dancer may not be as deft or as free from sentiment as "Midnight Nan" by Langston Hughes, but it is far more mature and moving. All of which leads us to say that a study of Claude McKay's and of the other better Negro poetry convinces us that he, more than the rest, has really had something to say. It is his tragedy that his message was too alive and too big for the form he chose. His poems are for the most part either stilted, choked, or over-zealous. He could never shape the flames from the fire that blazed within him. But he is the only Negro poet who ever wrote revolutionary or protest poetry. Hence:

If we must die, let it be not like hogs
Hunted and penned in an inglorious spot,

Oh, Kinsman! We must meet the common foe;
Though far outnumbered, let us still be brave,
And for their thousand blows, deal one death blow!
What though before us lies the open grave?
Like men we'll face the murderous pack,
Pressed to the wall, dying—but fighting back.

There is no impotent whining here, no mercy-seeking prayer to the white man's God, no mournful jeremiad, no "ain't it hard to be a nigger," no lamenting of or apologizing for the fact that he is a member of a dark-skinned minority group. Rather he boasts:

Be not deceived, for every deed you do,
I could match—out match; Am I not Africa's son,
Black of that black land where black deeds are done?

This is propaganda poetry of the highest order although it is crude and inexpert. Contrast it with these lines from Countee Cullen's sonnet "From the Dark Tower":

We shall not always plant while others reap
The golden increment of bursting fruit,
Nor always countenance abject and mute
That lesser men should hold their brothers cheap.

Countee Cullen is the symbol of a fast disappearing generation of Negro writers. In him it reaches its literary apogee. On the other hand Langston Hughes announces the entrance of a new generation, while Claude McKay, glorious revolutionary that he is, remains uncatalogued. For two generations Negro poets have been trying to do what Mr. Cullen has succeeded in doing. First, trying to translate into lyric form the highly poetic urge to escape from the blatant realities of life in America into a vivid past, and, second, fleeing from the stigma of being called a *Negro* poet, by, as Dunbar so desired to do, ignoring folk-material and writing of such abstractions as love and death.

There is hardly anyone writing poetry in America today who can make the banal sound as beautiful as does Mr. Cullen. He has an extraordinary ear for music, a most extensive and dexterous knowledge of words and their values, and an enviable understanding of conventional poetic forms. Technically, he is almost precocious, and never, it may be added, far from the academic; but he is also too steeped in tradition, too influenced mentally by certain conventions and taboos. When he does forget these things as in his greatest poem, "Heritage":

What is Africa to me:
Copper sun or scarlet sea,
Jungle star or jungle track,
Strong bronzed men, or regal black
Women from whose loins I sprang
When the birds of Eden sang?
One three centuries removed

> From the scenes his fathers loved,
> Spicy grove, cinnamon tree,
> What is Africa to me?

and the unforgettable:

> All day long and all night through,
> One thing only must I do:
> Quench my pride and cool my blood,
> Lest I perish in the flood,
> Lest a hidden ember set
> Timber that I thought was wet
> Burning like the dryest flax,
> Melting like the merest wax,
> Lest the grave restore its dead,
> Not yet has my heart and head
> In the least way realized
> They and I are civilized.

or his (to illustrate another tendency):

> I climb, but time's
> Abreast with me;
> I sing, but he climbs
> With my highest C.

And in other far too few instances he reaches heights no other Negro poet has ever reached, placing himself high among his contemporaries, both black or white. But he has not gone far enough. His second volume is not as lush with promise or as spontaneously moving as his first. There has been a marking time or side-stepping rather than a marching forward. If it seems we expect too much from this poet, we can only defend ourselves by saying that we expect no more than the poet's earlier work promises.

Mr. Cullen's love poems are too much made to order. His race poems, when he attempts to paint a moral, are inclined to be sentimental and stereotyped. It is when he gives vent to the pagan spirit and lets it inspire and dominate a poem's form and context that he does his most impressive work. His cleverly turned rebellious poems are also above the ordinary. But there are not enough of these in comparison to those poems which are banal, though beautiful.

Langston Hughes has often been compared to Dunbar. At first this comparison seems far-fetched and foolish, but on closer examination one finds that the two have much in common, only that where Dunbar failed, Langston Hughes succeeds. Both set out to interpret "the soul of his race"; one failed, the other, just at the beginning of his career, has in some measure already succeeded.

The younger man has not been content to assemble a supply of stock types who give expression to stock emotions which may be either slightly amusing or slightly tragic, but which are never either movingly tragic or convincingly comic.

When Langston Hughes writes of specific Negro types he manages to make them more than just ordinary Negro types. They are actually dark-skinned symbols of universal characters. One never feels this way about the people in Dunbar's poetry. For he never heightens them above their own particular sphere. There is never anything of the universal element in his poems that motivates Mr. Hughes's.

Moreover, Langston Hughes has gone much farther in another direction than any other Negro poet, much farther even than James Weldon Johnson went along the same road in *God's Trombones*. He has appropriated certain dialects and rhythms characteristically Negroid as his poetic properties. He has borrowed the lingo and locutions of migratory workers, chamber-maids, porters, boot-blacks, and others, and woven them into rhythmic schemes borrowed from the blues songs, spirituals and jazz and with them created a poetic diction and a poetic form all his own. There is danger in this of course, for the poet may and often does, consider these things as an end in themselves rather than as a means to an end. A blues poem such as:

> I'm a bad, bad man
> 'Cause everybody tells me so.
> I'm a bad, bad man,
> Everybody tells me so.
> I takes ma meaness and ma licker
> Everywhere I go.

or:

> Ma sweet good man has
> Packed his trunk and left.
> Ma sweet good man has
> Packed his trunk and left.
> Nobody to love me:
> I'm gonna kill ma self.

may be poignant and colorful but the form is too strait-laced to allow much variety of emotion or context. The poems produced are apt to prove modish and ephemeral. But when this blues form is expanded, as in:

> Drowning a drowsy syncopated tune,
> Racking back and forth to a mellow croon,
>   I heard a Negro play.
> Down on Lenox Avenue the other night
> By the pale dull pallor of an old gas light
>   He did a lazy sway
>   He did a lazy sway
> To the tune o' those Weary Blues.
> With his ebony hands on each ivory key
> He made that poor piano moan with melody.
> O Blues!
> Swaying to and fro on his rickety stool

He played that sad raggy tune like a musical fool.
　　Sweet Blues!
Coming from a black man's soul.

the poet justifies his experiment, and finds at the same time the most felicitous and fruitful outlet for his talent.

Mr. Hughes, where his race is concerned, is perfectly objective. He is one of them so completely that he, more than any other Negro poet, realizes that after all they are human beings; usually the articulate Negro either regards them as sociological problems or as debased monstrosities. To Mr. Hughes, certain types of Negroes and their experiences are of permanent value. He is not afraid of, nor does he ignore, them. He can calmly say:

Put on yo' red silk stockings,
Black gal.
Go an' let de white boys
Look at yo' legs.

An' tomorrow's chile'll
Be a high yaller.

or:

My old man's a white old man
And my old mother's black

My old man died in fine big house.
My ma died in a shack.
I wonder where I'm gonna die,
Being neither white nor black?

and reach the heights of his achievement in "Mulatto," one of the finest and most vivid poems written in the past few years. But Mr. Hughes has also written some of the most banal poetry of the age, which has not, as in the case of Mr. Cullen, even sounded beautiful.

The future of Negro poetry is an unknown quantity, principally because those on whom its future depends are also unknown quantities. There is nothing in the past to crow about, and we are too close to the present to judge it more than tentatively. McKay is exiled in France, an alien and a communist, barred from returning to this country. Once in a while a poem of his appears, but the period of his best work in this field seems to be at an end. Langston Hughes and Countee Cullen are both quite young, as poets and as individuals. Neither can be placed yet, nor can their contributions be any more than just intelligently commented upon. Whether they are going or will continue to go in the right direction is no more than a matter of individual opinion. All of us do know that as yet the American Negro has not produced a great poet. Whether he will or not is really not at all important. What does matter is that those who are now trying to be great should get intelligent guidance and appreciation. They seem to have everything else except perhaps the necessary genius.

NEGRO ARTISTS
AND THE NEGRO

WALLACE THURMAN

W hen the Negro art fad first came into being and Negro poets, novelists, musicians and painters became good copy, literate and semi-literate Negro America began to strut and to shout. Negro newspapers reprinted every item published anywhere concerning a Negro whose work had found favor with the critics, editors, or publishers. Negro journals conducted contests to encourage embryonic geniuses. Negro ministers preached sermons, Negro lecturers made speeches, and Negro club women read papers—all about the great new Negro art.

Everyone was having a grand time. The millennium was about to dawn. The second emancipation seemed inevitable. Then the excitement began to die down and Negroes as well as whites began to take stock of that in which they had revelled. The whites shrugged their shoulders and began seeking for some new fad. Negroes stood by, a little subdued, a little surprised, torn between being proud that certain of their group had achieved distinction, and being angry because a few of these arrived ones had ceased to be what the group considered "constructive" and had in the interim produced works that went against the grain, in that they did not wholly qualify to the adjective "respectable."

Langston Hughes was the major disturbing note in the "renaissance" chorus. His first volume of verse, *The Weary Blues*, introduced him as a poet who was interested in artistic material rather than in sociological problems. He went for inspiration and rhythms to those people who had been the least absorbed by the quagmire of American Kultur, and from them he undertook to select and preserve such autonomous racial values as were being rapidly eradicated in order to speed the Negro's assimilation.

The Weary Blues did not evoke much caustic public comment from Mr.

Hughes's people. Negroes were still too thrilled at the novelty of having a poet who could gain the attention of a white publisher to pay much attention to what he wrote. Quietly, and privately, however, certain Negroes began to deplore the author's jazz predilections, his unconventional poetic forms, and his preoccupation with the proletariat. But they were hopeful that he would reform and write in a conventional manner about the "best people."

Mr. Hughes's second volume, *Fine Clothes to the Jew*, a hard, realistic compilation, happened to be published while Negroes were still rankling from Carl Van Vechten's novel of Negro life in Harlem, *Nigger Heaven*. It seemed as if this novel served to unleash publicly a store of suppressed invective that not only lashed Mr. Van Vechten and Mr. Hughes, but also the editors and contributors to *Fire*, a new experimental quarterly devoted to and published by younger Negro artists. Under the heading "Writer Brands Fire as Effeminate Tommyrot," a reviewer in one of the leading Negro weeklies said: "I have just tossed the first issue of *Fire*—into the fire, and watched the cackling flames leap and snarl as though they were trying to swallow some repulsive dose."

Fire, like Mr. Hughes's poetry, was experimental. It was not interested in sociological problems or propaganda. It was purely artistic in intent and conception. Its contributors went to the proletariat rather than to the bourgeoisie for characters and material. They were interested in people who still retained some individual race qualities and who were not totally white American in every respect save color of skin.

There is one more young Negro who will probably be classed with Mr. Hughes when he does commence to write about the American scene. So far this writer, Eric Walrond, has confined his talents to producing realistic prose pictures of the Caribbean regions. If he ever turns on the American Negro as impersonally and as unsentimentally as he turned on West Indian folk in *Tropic Death*, he too will be blacklisted in polite colored circles.

The Negro plastic artists, especially Aaron Douglas and Richard Bruce, are also in disfavor, Douglas because of his advanced modernism and raw caricatures of Negro types, Bruce because of his interest in decadent types and the kinks he insists on putting upon the heads of his almost classical figures. Negroes, you know, don't have kinky hair; or, if they have, they use Madame Walker's straightening pomade.

Moreover, when it first became popular to sing spirituals for public delectation, the mass of Negroes objected vigorously. They did not wish to become identified again with what the spirituals connoted, and they certainly did not want to hear them sung in dialect. It was not until white music critics began pointing out the beauty of the spirituals, and identifying the genius that produced them, that Negroes joined in the hallelujah chorus.

Negroes are, of course, no different in this from any other race. The same class of Negroes who protest when Mr. Hughes says:

Put on yo' red silk stockings
Black gal.

Go out an' let the white boys
Look at yo' legs.

Put on yo' red silk stockings, gal
An' tomorrow's chile 'll
Be a high yaller

have their counterpart in those American whites who protest against the literary upheavals of a Dreiser, an Anderson, or a Sandburg. And those American Negroes who would not appreciate the spirituals until white critics sang their praises have their counterpart in the American whites who would not appreciate Poe and Whitman until European critics classed them as immortals.

The mass of American Negroes can no more be expected to emancipate themselves from petty prejudices and myopic fears than can the mass of American whites. They all revere Service, Prosperity and Progress. True, the American Negro may be the more pitiful figure, since he insists on selling every vestige of his birthright for a mess of pottage.

The American Negro feels that he has been misinterpreted and caricatured so long by insincere artists that once a Negro gains the ear of the public he should expend his spiritual energy feeding the public honeyed manna on a silver spoon. The mass of Negroes, like the mass of whites, seem unable to differentiate between sincere art and insincere art. They seem unable to fathom the innate differences between a dialect farce committed by an Octavus Roy Cohen to increase the gaiety of Babbitts, and a dialect interpretation done by a Negro writer to express some abstract something that burns within his people and scars him. They seem unable to differentiate between the Uncle Remus tales and a darky joke told by Irvin Cobb, or to distinguish the difference, in conception and execution, between a "Lulu Belle," with its cheap gaudiness and blatant ensemble, and an *All God's Chillun Got Wings* by a sympathetic, groping Eugene O'Neill. Even such fine things as a "Porgy" or a "Green Thursdays" are labeled inadequate and unfair. While *Nigger Heaven*—ask Carl Van Vechten!

Negroes in America feel certain that they must always appear in public butter side up, in order to keep from being trampled in the contemporary onward march. They feel as if they must always exhibit specimens from the college rather than from the kindergarten, specimens from the parlor rather than from the pantry. They are in the process of being assimilated, and those elements within the race which are still too potent for easy assimilation must be hidden until they no longer exist.

Thus, when the publishers of Mr. Hughes's second volume of verse say on the cover that "These poems, for the most part, interpret the most primitive types of American Negro, the bell boys, the cabaret girls, the migratory workers, the singers of blues and spirituals, and the makers of folk songs," and that they "express the joy and pathos, the beauty and ugliness of their lives," Negroes begin to howl. This is just the part of their life which experience has taught them should be kept in the background if they would exist comfortably in these United States. It makes no difference if this element of their life is of incontestable value to the sincere artist.

It is also available and of incontestable value to insincere artists and prejudiced white critics.

The Negro artist is in a no more enviable position than is the emerging, or sometimes, for that matter, even the arrived artist, of other races or countries. He will receive little aid from his own people unless he spends his time spouting sociological jeremiads or exhausts his talent in building rosy castles around Negro society. He will be exploited by white faddists, and sneered at by nonfaddists. He will be overrated on the one hand, and under-praised on the other.

Neither is the position of the bourgeois Negro an enviable one. Fearing as he does what his white compatriots think, he feels that he cannot afford to be attacked realistically by Negro artists who do not seem to have the "proper" sense of refinement or race pride. The American scene dictates that the American Negro must be what he ain't! And despite what the minority intellectual and artistic group may say, it really does seem more profitable for him to be what he ain't, than for him to be what he is.

The first literary works that came out of the so-called "Negro renaissance" were not of the riling variety. *Cane*, by Jean Toomer, was really pre-renaissance, as it was published too soon to be lifted into the best-seller class merely because its author was a Negro. And, as Waldo Frank forewarned in his introduction to *Cane*, Jean Toomer was not a *Negro* artist, but an *artist* who had lost "lesser identities in the great well of life." His book, therefore, was of little interest to sentimental whites or to Negroes with an inferiority complex to camouflage. Both the personality of the author and the style of his book were above the heads of these groups. Although *Cane* reeked with bourgeois-baiting revelations, it caused little excitement among the bourgeois sector of Negro society, save in Mr. Toomer's home town, Washington, D.C., where the main criticisms were concerning his treatment of Negro women.

Fire in the Flint by Walter White, *Flight* by the same author, and *There Is Confusion* by Jessie Fauset were just the sort of literary works both Negroes and sentimental whites desired Negroes to write. The first, a stirring romantic propaganda tale, recounted all the ills Negroes suffer in the inimical South, and made all Negroes seem magnanimous, mistreated martyrs, all southern whites evil transgressors of human rights. It followed the conventional theme in the conventional manner. It was a direct descendant of *Uncle Tom's Cabin*, and it had the same effect on the public. White latter-day abolitionists shook their heads, moaned and protested. Negroes read, boiled and bellowed.

Less sensational and more ambitious, the second novel from this author's pen sought to chronicle the emotional and physical peregrinations of a female mulatto with such a preponderance of white blood in her veins that she could be either Caucasian or Negro at will. Miss Fauset's work was an ill-starred attempt to popularize the pleasing news that there were cultured Negroes, deserving of attention from artists, and of whose existence white folk should be apprised.

All of these works of fiction, as well as the two outstanding works of nonfiction, *The Gift of Black Folk* by W. E. B. Du Bois, and *The New Negro*, edited by Alain Locke, that appeared during the heated days of the "renaissance" were considerate of the Aframerican's *amour propre*, soothing to his self-esteem and stimulating to his vanity. They all treated the Negro as a sociological problem rather than as a human being. I might add that only in "The New Negro" was there even an echo of a different tune. The rest were treatises rather than works of art.

These works were all designed to prove to the American white man that the American Negro was not inferior *per se* and, therefore, were honored and blessed by Negroes.

Color, a volume of verses by Countee Cullen, was also conventional in theme and manner. True, Mr. Cullen was possessed by a youthful exuberance that occasionally flamed with sensual passion, but for the most part he was the conventional Negro litterateur in all respects save that he had more talent than most of his predecessors. He could say:

> Yet do I marvel at this curious thing:
> To make a poet black, and bid him sing.

or wish

> To do a naked tribal dance
> Each time he hears the rain

and finally

> Once riding in old Baltimore,
> Heart-filled, head-filled with glee,
> I saw a Baltimorean
> Keep looking straight at me.

> Now I was eight and very small
> And he was no whit bigger,
> And so I smiled; but he poked out
> His tongue, and called me, "Nigger."

> I saw the whole of Baltimore
> From May until December;
> Of all the things that happened there
> That's all that I remember.

This last poem was enough to endear Mr. Cullen to every bourgeois black soul in America, as well as to cause white critics to surpass themselves in calling attention to this Negro poet's genus, a thing far more important to them than his genius. And, since Mr. Cullen, unlike his contemporary, Mr. Hughes, has not and perhaps never will seek the so-called lower elements of Negro life for his poetic rhythms and material, and since he, too, assumes the conventional race attitude toward his people rather than an artistic one, he will probably remain endeared to both bourgeois black America and sentimental white America, more because of this attitude than because of his undisputed talent or his intense spiritual sensitivity.

Fortunately, now, the Negro art "renaissance" has reached a state of near sanity. Serious and inquisitive individuals are endeavoring to evaluate the present and potential significance of this development in Negro life. They are isolating, interpreting, and utilizing those things which seem to have a true esthetic value. If but a few live coals are found in a mountain of ashes, no one should be disappointed. Genius is a rare quality in this world, and there is no reason why it should be more ubiquitous among Blacks than Whites.

OUR LITERARY AUDIENCE

STERLING A. BROWN's "Our Literary Audience"
takes up issues discussed in both Johnson's "Dilemma of the Negro
Author" and Thurman's "Negro Artists and the Negro." His criticism
of black audiences runs along the same lines. His essay appeared in
Opportunity, February 1930.

W e have heard in recent years a great deal about the Negro artist. We
have heard excoriations from the one side, and flattery from the
other. In some instances we have heard valuable honest criticism.
One vital determinant of the Negro artist's achievement or mediocrity has not been
so much discussed. I refer to the Negro artist's audience, within his own group.
About this audience a great deal might be said.

I submit for consideration this statement, probably no startling discovery:
that those who might be, who should be a fit audience for the Negro artist are,
taken by and large, fundamentally out of sympathy with his aims and his genuine
development.

I am holding no brief for any writer, or any coterie of writers, or any racial
credo. I have as yet no logs to roll, and no brickbats to heave. I have however a
deep concern with the development of a literature worthy of our past, and of our
destiny; without which literature certainly, we can never come to much. I have a
deep concern with the development of an audience worthy of such a literature.

"Without great audiences we cannot have great poets." Whitman's trenchant
commentary needs stressing today, universally. But particularly do we as a racial
group need it. There is a great harm that we can do our incipient literature. With
a few noteworthy exceptions, we are doing that harm, most effectually. It is hardly
because of malice; it has its natural causes; but it is none the less destructive.

We are not a reading folk (present company of course forever excepted). There are reasons, of course, but even with those considered, it remains true that we do not read nearly so much as we should. I imagine our magazine editors and our authors if they chose, could bear this out. A young friend, on a book-selling project, filling in questionnaires on the reason why people did not buy books, wrote down often, with a touch of malice—"Too much bridge." Her questionnaires are scientific with a vengeance.

When we do condescend to read books about Negroes, we seem to read in order to confute. These are sample ejaculations: *"But we're not all like that." "Why does he show such a level of society? We have better Negroes than that to write about." "What effect will this have on the opinions of white people."* (Alas, for the ofay, forever ensconced in the lumber yard!) . . . *"More dialect. Negroes don't use dialect anymore."* Or if that sin is too patent against the Holy Ghost of Truth— *"Negroes of my class don't use dialect anyway."* (Which *mought* be so, and then again, which *moughtn't*.)

Our criticism is vitiated therefore in many ways. Certain fallacies I have detected within at least the last six years are these:

> We look upon Negro books regardless of the author's intention, as representative of all Negroes, i.e., as sociological documents.
> We insist that Negro books must be idealistic, optimistic tracts for race advertisement.
> We are afraid of truth telling, of satire.
> We criticize from the point of view of bourgeois America, of racial apologists.

In this division there are, of course, overlappings. Moreover all of these fallacies might be attributed to a single cause, such as an apologistic chip on the shoulder attitude, imposed by circumstance; an arising snobbishness; a delayed Victorianism; or a following of the wrong lead. Whatever may be the primary impulse, the fact remains that if these standards of criticism are perpetuated, and our authors are forced to heed them, we thereby dwarf their stature as interpreters.

One of the most chronic complaints concerns this matter of Representativeness. An author, to these sufferers, never intends to show a man who happens to be a Negro, but rather to make a blanket charge against the race. The syllogism follows: Mr. A. shows a Negro who steals; he means by this that all Negroes steal; all Negroes do not steal; Q.E.D. Mr. A. is a liar, and his book is another libel on the race.

For instance, *Emperor Jones* is considered as sociology rather than drama; as a study of the superstition, and bestiality, and charlatanry of the group, rather than as a brilliant study of a hard-boiled pragmatist, far more "American" and "African," and a better man in courage and resourcefulness than those ranged in opposition to him. To the charge that I have misunderstood the symbolism of Brutus Jones's visions, let me submit that superstition is a human heritage, not peculiar to the Negro, and that the beat of the tom-tom, as heard even in a metropolitan theater, can be a terrifying experience to many regardless of race, if we are to believe testimonies. But no, O'Neill is "showing us the Negro race," not a shrewd Pullman

Porter, who had for a space, a run of luck. By the same token, is Smithers a picture of the white race? If so, O'Neill is definitely propagandizing against the Caucasian. O'Neill must be an East Indian.

All God's Chillun Got Wings is a tract, say critics of this stamp, against intermarriage; a proof of the inferiority of the Negro (why he even uses the word Nigger!!! when he could have said Nubian or Ethiopian!); a libel stating that Negro law students all wish to marry white prostitutes. (The word prostitute, by the way, is cast around rather loosely, with a careless respect for the Dictionary, as will be seen later.) This for as humane an observation of the wreck that prejudice can bring to two poor children, who whatever their frailties, certainly deserve no such disaster!

This is not intended for any defense of O'Neill, who stands in no need of any weak defense I might urge. It is to show to what absurdity we may sink in our determination to consider anything said of Negroes as a wholesale indictment or exaltation of all Negroes. We are as bad as Schuyler says many of "our white folks" are; we can't admit that there are individuals in the group, or at least we can't believe that men of genius whether white or colored can see those individuals.

Of course, one knows the reason for much of this. Books galore have been written, still are written with a definite inclusive thesis, purposing generally to discredit us. We have seen so much of the razor-toting, gin-guzzling, chicken-stealing Negro; or the pompous walking dictionary spouting malapropisms; we have heard so much of "learned" tomes, establishing our characteristics, "appropriativeness," short memory for joys and griefs, imitativeness, and general inferiority. We are certainly fed up.

This has been so much our experience that by now it seems we should be able to distinguish between individual and race portraiture, i.e., between literature on the one hand and pseudo-science and propaganda on the other. These last we have with us always. From Dixon's melodramas down to Roark Bradford's funny stories, from Thomas Nelson Page's "Ole Virginny retainers" to Bowyer Campbell's *Black Sadie* the list is long and notorious. One doesn't wish to underestimate this prejudice. It is ubiquitous and dangerous. When it raises its head it is up to us to strike, and strike hard. But when it doesn't exist, there is no need of tilting at windmills.

In some cases the author's design to deal with the entire race is explicit, as in Vachel Lindsay's *The Congo*, subtitled "A Study of the Negro Race"; in other cases, implicit. But an effort at understanding the work should enable us to detect whether his aim is to show one of ours, or all of us (in the latter case, whatever his freedom from bias, doomed to failure). We have had such practice that we should be rather able at this detection.

We have had so much practice that we are thin-skinned. Anybody would be. And it is natural that when pictures of us were almost entirely concerned with making us out to be either brutes or docile housedogs, i.e., infra-human, we should have replied by making ourselves out superhuman. It is natural that we should insist that the pendulum be swung back to its other extreme. Life and letters follow the law of the pendulum. Yet, for the lover of the truth, neither extreme is desirable. And now, if we are coming of age, the truth should be our major concern.

This is not a disagreement with the apologistic belief in propaganda. Propaganda must be counterchecked by propaganda. But let it be found where it should be found, in books explicitly propagandistic, in our newspapers, which perhaps must balance white playing up of crime with our own playing up of achievement; in the teaching of our youth that there is a great deal in our racial heritage of which we may be justly proud. Even so, it must be artistic, based on truth, not on exaggeration.

Propaganda, however legitimate, can speak no louder than the truth. Such a cause as ours needs no dressing up. The honest, unvarnished truth, presented as it is, is plea enough for us, in the unbiased courts of mankind. But such courts do not exist? Then what avails thumping the tub? Will that call them into being? Let the truth speak. There has never been a better persuader.

Since we need truthful delineation, let us not add every artist whose picture of us may not be flattering to our long list of traducers. We stand in no need today of such a defense mechanism. If a white audience today needs assurance that we are not all thievish or cowardly or vicious, it is composed of half wits, and can never be convinced anyway. Certainly we can never expect to justify ourselves by heated denials of charges which perhaps have not even been suggested in the work we are denouncing.

To take a comparison at random. Ellen Glasgow has two recent novels on the Virginia gentry. In one she shows an aging aristocrat, a self-appointed lady killer, egocentric, slightly ridiculous. In another she shows three lovely ladies who stooped to "folly." It would be a rash commentator who would say that Ellen Glasgow, unflinching observer though she is, means these pictures to be understood as ensemble pictures of all white Virginians. But the same kind of logic that some of us use on our books would go farther; it would make these books discussions of *all* white Americans.

Such reasoning would be certainly more ingenious than intelligent.

The best rejoinder to the fuming criticism "But all Negroes aren't like that" should be "Well, what of it. Who said so?" or better, "Why bring that up?" . . . But if alas we must go out of our group for authority, let this be said, "All Frenchwomen aren't like Emma Bovary but *Madame Bovary* is a great book; all Russians aren't like Vronsky, but *Anna Karenina* is a great book; all Norwegians aren't like Oswald but *Ghosts* is a great play." Books about us may not be true of all of us; but that has nothing to do with their worth.

As a corollary to the charge that certain books "aiming at representativeness" have missed their mark, comes the demand that our books must show our "best." Those who criticize thus want literature to be "idealistic"; to show them what we should be like, or more probably, what we should like to be. There's a great difference. It is sadly significant also, that by "best" Negroes, these idealists mean generally the upper reaches of society; i.e., those with money.

Porgy, because it deals with Catfish Row, is a poor book for this audience; *Green Thursday*, dealing with cornfield rustics, is a poor book; the *Walls of Jericho*, where it deals with a piano mover, is a poor book. In proportion as a book deals with our "better" class it is a better book.

According to this scale of values, a book about a Negro and a mule would be, because of the mule, a better book than one about a muleless Negro; about a Negro and a horse and buggy a better book than about the mule owner; about a Negro and a Ford, better than about the buggy rider; and a book about a Negro and a Rolls Royce better than one about a Negro and a Ford. All that it seems our writers need to do, to guarantee a perfect book and deathless reputation, is to write about a Negro and an aeroplane. Unfortunately, this economic hierarchy does not hold in literature. It would rule out most of the Nobel prize winners.

Now Porgy in his goat cart, Kildee at his ploughing, Shine in a Harlem poolroom may not be as valuable members of the body economic and politic as "more financial" brethren. (Of course, the point is debatable.) But that books about them are less interesting, less truthful, and less meritorious as works of art, is an unwarranted assumption.

Some of us look upon this prevailing treatment of the lowly Negro as a concerted attack upon us. But an even cursory examination of modern literature would reveal that the major authors everywhere have dealt and are dealing with the lowly. A random ten, coming to mind, are Masefield, Hardy, Galsworthy in England: Synge and Joyce in Ireland; Hamsun in Norway; O'Neill, Willa Cather, Sherwood Anderson, Ernest Hemingway in America. Not to go back to Burns, Crabbe, Wordsworth. The dominance of the lowly as subject matter is a natural concomitant to the progress of democracy.

This does not mean that our books must deal with the plantation or lowly Negro. Each artist to his taste. Assuredly let a writer deal with that to which he can best give convincing embodiment and significant interpretation. To insist otherwise is to hamper the artist, and to add to the stereotyping which has unfortunately been too apparent in books about us. To demand on the other hand that our books exclude treatment of any character other than the "successful Negro" is a death warrant to literature.

Linked with this is the distaste for dialect. This was manifested in our much earlier thrice told denial of the spirituals. James Weldon Johnson aptly calls this "Second Generation Respectability."

Mr. Johnson is likewise responsible for a very acute criticism of dialect, from a literary point of view, rather than from that of "respectability." Now much of what he said was deserved. From Lowell's *Bigelow Papers* through the local colorists, dialect, for all of its rather eminent practitioners, has been a bit too consciously "*quaint,*" too *condescending.* Even in Maristan Chapman's studies in Tennessee mountainers there is a hint of "outlandishness" being shown for its novelty, not for its universality.

Negro dialect, however, as recorded by the most talented of our observers today, such as Julia Peterkin, Howard Odum, and Langston Hughes, has shown itself capable of much more than the "limited two stops, pathos and humor." Of course, Akers and Octavus Roy Cohen still clown, and show us Negroes who never were, on land or sea, and unreconstructed Southrons show us the pathetic old mammy weeping over vanished antebellum glories. But when we attack these, we do not attack the medium of expression. The fault is not with the material. If Daniel

Webster Davis can see in the Negro "peasant" only a comic feeder on hog meat and greens, the fault is in Davis's vision, not in his subject.

Lines like these transcend humor and pathos:

"I told dem people if you was to come home cold an' stiff in a box, I could look at you same as a stranger an' not a water wouldn' drean out my eye."

Or this:

"Death, ain't yuh got no shame?"

Or this:

"Life for me ain't been no crystal stair."

Or:

"She walked down the track, an' she never looked back,
I'm goin' whah John Henry fell dead."

Julia Peterkin, Heyward, the many other honest artists have shown us what is to be seen, if we have eyes and can use them.

There is nothing "degraded" about dialect. Dialetical peculiarities are universal. There is something about Negro dialect, in the idiom, the turn of the phrase, the music of the vowels and consonants that is worth treasuring.

Are we to descend to the level of the lady who wanted "Swing Low, Sweet Chariot" metamorphosed into "Descend, welcome vehicle, approaching for the purpose of conveying me to my residence?"

Those who are used only to the evasions and reticences of Victorian books or of Hollywood (!) (i.e., the products of Hollywood, not the city as it actually is) are or pretend to be shocked by the frankness of modern books on the Negro. That the "low" rather than the "lowly" may often be shown, that there is pornography I do not doubt. But that every book showing frankly aspects of life is thereby salacious, I do stoutly deny. More than this, the notions that white authors show only the worst in Negro life and the best in theirs; that Negro authors show the worst to sell out to whites, are silly, and reveal woeful ignorance about modern literature.

Mamba and Hagar are libellous portraits say some; *Scarlet Sister Mary* is a showing up of a "prostitute" say others. "Our womanhood is defamed." Nay, rather, our intelligence is defamed, by urging such nonsense. For these who must have glittering falsifications of life, the movie houses exist in great plenty.

The moving picture, with its enforced happy ending, may account for our distaste for tragedy; with its idylls of the leisure class, may account for our distaste for Negro portraiture in the theatre. Maybe a shrinking optimism causes this. Whatever the reason, we do not want to see Negro plays. Our youngsters, with some Little Theatre Movements the honorable exceptions, want to be English dukes and duchesses, and wear tuxedoes and evening gowns. Our "best" society leaders want to be mannequins.

Especially taboo is tragedy. Into these tragedies, such as *In Abraham's Bosom,* we read all kinds of fantastic lessons. "Intended to show that the Negro never wins out, but always loses." "Intended to impress upon us the futility of effort on our part." Some dramatic "critics" say in substance that the only value of plays like *Porgy* and *In Abraham's Bosom* is that they give our actors parts. "Worthwhile," "elevating" shows do not get a chance. They are pleading, one has reason to suspect, for musical comedy which may have scenes in cabarets, and wouldn't be confined to Catfish Row. With beautiful girls in gorgeous "costumes;" rather than Negroes in more but tattered clothing.

"These plays are depressing," say some. Alas, the most depressing thing is such criticism. Should one insist that *In Abraham's Bosom* is invigorating, inspiring; showing a man's heroic struggle against great odds, showing the finest virtue a man can show in the face of harsh realities—enduring courage; should one insist upon that, he would belong to a very small minority, condemned as treasonous. We seem to forget that for the Negro to be conceived as a tragic figure is a great advance in American Literature. The aristocratic concept of the lowly as clowns is not so far back. That the tragedy of this "clown" meets sympathetic reception is a step forward in race relations.

I sincerely hope that I have not been crashing in open doors. I realize that there are many readers who do not fit into the audience I have attempted to depict. But these exceptions seem to me to fortify the rule. There are wise leaders who are attempting to combat supersensitive criticism. The remarks I have seen so much danger in are not generally written. But they are prevalent and powerful.

One hopes that they come more from a misunderstanding of what literature should be, than from a more harmful source. But from many indications it seems that one very dangerous state of mind produces them. It may be named—lack of mental bravery. It may be considered as a cowardly denial of our own.

It seems to acute observers that many of us, who have leisure for reading, are ashamed of being Negroes. This shame makes us harsher to the shortcomings of some perhaps not so fortunate economically. There seems to be among us a more fundamental lack of sympathy with the Negro farthest down, than there is in other groups with the same Negro.

To recapitulate. It is admitted that some books about us are definite propaganda; that in the books about us, the great diversity of our life has not been shown (which should not be surprising when we consider how recent is this movement toward realistic portraiture), that dramas about the Negro character are even yet few and far between. It *is* insisted that these books should be judged as works of literature; i.e., by their fidelity to the truth of their particular characters, not as representative pictures of all Negroes; that they should not be judged at all by the level of society shown, not at all as good or bad according to the "morality" of the characters; should not be judged as propaganda when there is no evidence, explicit or implicit, that propaganda was intended. Furthermore those who go to literature as an entertaining building up of dream worlds, purely for idle amusement, should not pass judgment at all on books which aim at fidelity to truth.

One doesn't wish to be pontifical about this matter of truth. "What is truth, asked Pontius Pilate, and would not stay for an answer." The answer would have been difficult. But it surely is not presumptuous for a Negro, in Twentieth Century America, to say that showing the world in idealistic rose colors is not fidelity to truth. We have got to look at our times and at ourselves searchingly and honestly; surely there is nothing of the far-fetched in that injunction.

But we are reluctant about heeding this injunction. We resent what doesn't flatter us. One young man, Allison Davis, who spoke courageously and capably his honest observation about our life, has been the target of second-rate attacks ever since. George Schuyler's letter bag seems to fill up whenever he states that even the slightest something may be rotten on Beale Street or Seventh Avenue. Because of their candor, Langston Hughes and Jean Toomer, humane, fine-grained artists both of them, have been received in a manner that should shame us. This is natural, perhaps, but unfortunate. Says J. S. Collis in a book about Bernard Shaw, "The Irish cannot bear criticism; for like all races who have been oppressed they are still *without mental bravery*. They are afraid to see themselves exposed to what they imagine to be adverse criticism. . . . But the future of Ireland largely depends upon *how much she is prepared to listen to criticism* and how far she is capable of preserving peace between able men." These last words are worthy of our deepest attention.

We are cowed. We have become typically bourgeois. Natural though such an evolution is, if we are *all* content with evasion of life, with personal complacency, we as a group are doomed. If we pass by on the other side, despising our brothers, we have no right to call ourselves men.

Crime, squalor, ugliness there are in abundance in our Catfish Rows, in our Memphis dives, in our Southwest Washington. But rushing away from them surely isn't the way to change them. And if we refuse to pay them any attention, through unwillingness to be depressed, we shall eventually be dragged down to their level. We, or our children. And that is true "depression."

But there is more to lowliness than "lowness." If we have eyes to see, and willingness to see, we might be able to find in Mamba an astute heroism, in Hagar a heartbreaking courage, in Porgy, a nobility, and in E. C. L. Adams's Scrip and Tad, a shrewd, philosophical irony. And all of these qualities we need, just now, to see in our group.

Because perhaps we are not so far from these characters, being identified racially with them, at least, we are revolted by Porgy's crapshooting, by Hagar's drinking, by Scarlet Sister Mary's scarletness. We want to get as far away as the end of the world. We do not see that Porgy's crapshooting is of the same fabric, fundamentally, psychologically, as a society lady's bridge playing. And upon honest investigation it conceivably might be found that it is not moral lapses that offend, so much as the showing of them, and most of all, the fact that the characters belong to a low stratum of society. Economically low, that is. No stratum has monopoly on other "lowness."

If one is concerned only with the matter of morality he could possibly remember that there is no literature which is not proud of books that treat of characters no better "morally" than Crown's Bess and Scarlet Sister Mary. But what mature audience would judge a book by the morality of its protagonist? Is *Rollo* a greater book than *Tom Jones* or even than *Tom Sawyer?*

Negro artists have enough to contend with in getting a hearing, in isolation, in the peculiar problems that beset all artists, in the mastery of form and in the understanding of life. It would be no less disastrous to demand of them that they shall evade truth, that they shall present us a Pollyanna philosophy of life, that, to suit our prejudices, they shall lie. It would mean that as self-respecting artists they could no longer exist.

The question might be asked, why should they exist? Such a question deserves no reply. It merely serves to bring us, alas, to the point at which I started.

Without great audiences we cannot have great literature.

THE NEGRO WRITER:
PITFALLS AND COMPENSATIONS

WILLIAM GARDNER SMITH's "The Negro
Writer: Pitfalls and Compensations" appeared in *Phylon*, Fourth
Quarter, 1950.

his is, as everyone recognizes by now, a world of relativity. We measure
the rights of individuals against the rights of the society; the rights of the
artist against the rights of his public; the right of free speech against the
right of the individual to protection from slander. Degrees of good and evil are
measured against other degrees of good and evil.

This apprehension of infinite relativity is, I think, instructive in considering
the position of the Negro writer—I speak particularly of the novelist—in American
society. For a moment, disregard the mechanical pros and cons, debits and credits—
whether it is easier, or more difficult, for a Negro writer to have his work published;
consider the purely esthetic question: What handicaps, and what advantages, does
the American writer possess by virtue of being a Negro?

Because the handicaps are better known, and perhaps easier to understand, I
will consider them first. The Negro writer is, first of all, invariably bitter. There
are degrees of this bitterness, ranging from the anger of Richard Wright and the
undercurrent of contempt for the white world in Chester Himes to the cruel satire
exhibited by George Schuyler in his semi-classic *Black No More*. A writer is a man
of sensitivity; otherwise, he would not be a writer. The sensitivities of the Negro
writer react, therefore, more strongly against the ignorance, prejudice and discrimi-
nation of American society than do those of the average Negro in America.

There are all forms and varieties of this inevitable strain of bitterness in the
Negro writer. Sometimes it results in militancy; sometimes in contempt for race
and self; sometimes in hatred for the whole of American society, with blindness for
the good things contained therein. It is often hard for the Negro writer to resist

polemicizing. He is driven often to write a tract, rather than a work of art. So conscious is he of the pervading evil of race prejudice that he feels duty-bound to assault it at every turn, injecting opinion into alleged narration and inserting his philosophy into the mouths of his characters.

Writing of Negroes, the novelist has difficulty with his characterizations. His people usually become walking, talking propaganda, rather than completely rounded individuals. The Negro writer hesitates, perhaps unconsciously, to temper the goodness of his Negro characters with the dialectical "evil." Fearful of re-enforcing stereotypes in the white reader's mind, he often goes to the other extreme, idealizing his characters, making them flat rather than many-sided. Or, conscious of the pitfalls listed above, and anxious to prove that he is not idealizing his Negro characters, the writer goes to the other extreme—in the name of naturalism—and paints the American Negro as an exaggerated Bigger Thomas, with all the stereo-typed characteristics emphasized three times over. To strike a compromise—and, incidentally, the truth—is possibly the most difficult feat for a Negro writer. Proof of this is the fact that I have not read one Negro novel which has truthfully represented the many-sided character of the Negro in American society today. Chester Himes, perhaps, has come closer than any other Negro author to such a representation.

It seems that it is difficult for the Negro writer to add to his weighty diatribes the leaven of humor. Writing is an art; the writer works upon the emotions of his reader. Every sentence, every cadence, every description, every scene, produces an emotional response in this reader. Consciously did Shakespeare lead his audiences through one powerful emotion after another to achieve the final, powerful effect of the death of Desdemona at the hands of Othello; consciously did Marlowe lead to the final descent into hell of Faust. In each of these journeys through dramatic experience there were rises and falls; there were moments of stern conflict and moments of relative relaxation; there were moments of tears and moments of relieving laughter.

Too often, however, in Negro novels do we witness the dull procession of crime after crime against the Negro, without relief in humor or otherwise. These monotonous repetitions of offenses against the Negro serve only to bore the reader in time; and in so doing, they defeat the very purpose of the writer, for they become ineffective. One might even say that the chronicles of offenses constitute truth; however, they do not constitute art. And art is the concern of any novelist.

Novels which last through all time are concerned with universal themes. Dostoievski's great Raskolnikov is all of us in the aftermath of great crime; Tolstoi describes the universal ruling class in time of national crisis. The Negro writer is under tremendous pressure to write about the topical and the transient—the plight of the Negro in American society today. It may be that the greatest of such novels will last because of their historical interest. It may even be that one or two will last because the writer has managed to infuse into his work some universal elements— as Dickens did, even when writing about the social conditions in the England of his day. But most Negro writers do not inject the universal element. They write only about the here and the now. Thus, their novels come and they go: in ten years, they are forgotten.

At this point, let me emphasize that the drive of the Negro writer to write about purely topical themes is of fantastic strength, and difficult for the non-Negro to appreciate. Starving and land-hungry Chinese want food and land: they are not much concerned about such abstractions as the rights of free speech, habeas corpus, the ballot, etc. When day to day problems press upon the individual, they become, in his mind, paramount. This sense of the immediate problem confronts the Negro writer. But it is significant to note that we do not today consider highly that literature which arose in protest against, say, the system of feudalism, or even, in the United States, slavery.

But there are compensations for these difficulties confronting the Negro writer. They are great compensations.

Writing is concerned with people, with society and with ethics. Great writing is concerned with the individual in the group or tribe; obedience to or deviation from the laws of that tribe, and the consequences. Usually, by the very process of selection, omission and arrangement of his material, the author implies a judgment—approval or rejection of the laws of the society, be they in legal, ethical or religious form. Basic to such writing, obviously, is some understanding of both the society and the people in it.

To grasp social and individual truth, it is my opinion that the novelist must maintain emotional contact with the basic people of his society. At first glance, this appears a simple thing; but, in reality, it is difficult. Consider the material circumstances of the "successful" writer. He becomes a celebrity. He makes money. Usually, he begins to move in the sphere of people like himself—authors, artists, critics, etc. He purchases a home on Long Island. He no longer uses the subway; for now he has an automobile. He lectures; he speaks at luncheons; he autographs books; he attends cocktail parties; he discusses style, form, and problems of psychology with friends in a rather esoteric circle; and he writes. In a word, he moves, to some degree, into an ivory tower; he becomes, in a fashion, detached from the mainstream of American life.

In times of stability this detachment is often not too harmful: for the moral code remains what it was at the moment of the writer's detachment and, despite its rarification in his new environment, still may serve as the wellspring for vital work. In moments of social crisis, however, the established moral code comes into violent conflict with the desires of the people of society. Thus, immediately prior to the French Revolution, the ethics of feudalism, though still officially recognized, actually were outdated and in conflict with the democratic tendencies of the people; and thus, today, the individualistic and basically selfish ethic of capitalism, while still officially proclaimed, is in reality contrary to the socialist tendency which has spread over the world, and even made itself felt in America through Roosevelt's New Deal and Truman's election on a Fair Deal program.

The writer who is detached from society does not perceive this contradiction; and thus is missing from his writing some element of social truth. He is behind the times; he is holding on to a shell. Part of the greatness of Tolstoi is that he perceived the ethical, i.e., social, conflict, and accurately recorded it.

The Negro writer cannot achieve—at least, not as easily as the white American writer—this social detachment, however much he might desire it. The very national prejudice he so despises compels him to remember his social roots, perceive the social reality; in a word, compels him to keep his feet on the ground. He cannot register at the Mayflower Hotel. He cannot loll on the Miami Beach. He cannot ignore disfranchisement, epithets, educational and employment discrimination, mob violence. He is bound by unbreakable cords to the Negro social group. And so his writing, however poor artistically, must almost invariably contain some elements of social truth.

The Negro writer is endowed by his environment with relative emotional depth. What does a writer write about? We have said: people, and their problems, conflicts, etc. But—what problems, what conflicts? Pick up any popular American magazine or book and you will find out—the problem of whether John D., a thoroughly empty individual, should leave his wife Mary C., a thoroughly empty individual, to marry Jane B., a thoroughly empty individual. To this problem are devoted hundreds of pages; hundreds of thousands of words. And in the end the reader of intelligence must ask the question: So what?

Emotional depth, perception of real problems and real conflicts, is extremely rare in American literature—as it is in American society generally. Instead of issues of significance, our fiction (our serious fiction) is overladen with such trite themes as that of Tennessee Williams's *The Roman Spring of Mrs. Stone*. America's is a superficial civilization: it is soda-pop land, the civilization of television sets and silk stockings and murder mysteries and contempt for art and poetry. It is difficult, out of such environment, to bring forth works with the emotional force of, say, *Crime and Punishment*.

Here again the Negro writer's social experience is, despite its bitterness, also an artistic boon. To live continually with prejudice based on the accident of skin color is no superficial experience; and neither is the reaction produced by such constant exposure superficial. There is a depth and intensity to the emotions of Negroes—as demonstrated in "Negro music"—which is largely lacking in white Americans. How often has the Negro maid or housecleaner come home to laugh at her white mistress's great concern about the color of a hat, the shape of a shoe, keeping up with the next-door Joneses? How often have Negroes, on the job, laughed in amazement at the inane trivialities which occupy the thoughts of their white fellow workers? And this laughter is logical. The Europeans would understand it. For, what man or woman who has seen a lynching, or been close to the furnaces of Dachau, or been rebuffed and rejected because of his skin color, can really seriously concern himself with the insipid and shallow love affair between Susie Bell and Jerry?

Thus, the Negro writer, if he does not make the tragic error of trying to imitate his white counterparts, has in his possession the priceless "gift" of thematic intuition. Provided he permits his writing to swell truthfully from his deepest emotional reaches, he will treat problems of real significance, which can strike a chord in the heart of basic humanity. He will be able to convey suffering without romanticizing; he will be able to describe happiness which is not merely on the surface; he will be able to search out and concretize the hopes and ambitions which are the basic stuff of human existence. And he will, in Hemingway's words, be able to do this "without cheating." For the basic fact about humanity in our age is that it suffers; and only he who suffers with it can truthfully convey its aches and pains, and thwarted desires. And now, speaking only of this period in which now we live, I should like to point out one last advantage which I feel accrues to the writer by virtue of being a Negro. It concerns the international power struggle.

We live, it appears, in an age of struggle between the American brand of Capitalism and the Russian brand of Communism. This is the obvious struggle; and most of the individuals in the world seem to feel that one must choose between one or the other. But is this, really, the root struggle? Or is mankind, the great majority of it, not actually groping for a rational social order, free from the tensions of economic and political crisis, free from war and from dictatorship, in which the individual will be permitted to live according to an ethic all sensible and truly just men can subscribe to?

For a moment, leave the last question. Consider the writer in the American scene, in this day and age. Picture him as being young and filled with ideals; consider him intelligent, sensitive and understanding. Ask the question: Can he approve of American society as it exists today?

I say, on the basis of experience and of individual reaction, no! The young writer will notice many good things, worthy of retention, in the America of today. He will approve of free speech (now being seriously curtailed); he will approve the idea of a free press (even though becoming a monopoly because of the economics involved); he will believe in free artistic expression, realizing that only through freedom can real art survive. But can he approve of the dog-eat-dog existence we glorify by the name of Free Enterprise?—an existence which distorts the personality, turns avarice into virtue and permits the strong to run roughshod over the weak, profiteering on human misery? Can he approve chronic depressions and endless wars? Can he approve racial and religious prejudice?

The young writer of ideas and ideals, I say, must instantly be repelled by the ugly aspects of American society. The history of our literature will bear this out— at a swift glance, I think of Emily Dickinson, Thoreau, Emerson, Hawthorne, Dos Passos, Faulkner, Henry James, Melville and, recently, Norman Mailer. And, being repelled, the writer seeks a substitute, something which offers hope of cure. Today, at first glance, the only alternative seems to be Russian Communism.

To list the important American writers who have turned from American Capitalism to Communism since the latter part of the nineteenth century would take up more space than this article is permitted. Suffice it to say that nearly every naturalistic writer in America has made this turn. Our young writer of intelligence and ideals, then, makes this turn. He embraces Communism of the Russian brand. And, immediately, he begins to feel uncomfortable.

For he discovers, in the folds of Russian Communism, the evils of dictatorship. He learns about purge trials; and is handed fantastic lies, which insult his intelligence, to justify them. He learns of the stifling of literature, art and music in the Soviet Union. He learns that Hitler is one day evil, the next day (following a pact with the Soviet Union) good, and the next day evil again. He discovers that Roosevelt is today a warmonger, tomorrow a true democrat and peoples' friend, whose "grand design" the Communist Party, U.S.A., seeks only to imitate. He learns that Tito, only yesterday a Communist hero only a little lower than Stalin, has in reality been a spy and a Fascist since 1936. He learns that a book which is "good" today becomes "bad," "bourgeois" and "decadent" tomorrow when the Party Line changes.

In panic does our idealistic and intelligent writer flee from alliance with the Communist Party. And at this point, the advantage of the Negro writer is discovered. For, having become disillusioned with the Soviet dictatorship, where does the white writer turn for political truth? Back to Capitalism, in ninety-nine out of a hundred cases; back to the very decaying system which lately he had left, a system he now calls "Democracy," "Freedom" and "Western Culture." He repeats the performance of John Dos Passos and, more recently and more strikingly (though in another field) Henry Wallace. The things he formerly found unbearable in Capitalism—he now ignores. Prejudice, depressions, imperialism, political chicanery, support of dictators, dog-eat-dog, strong-kill-the-weak philosophy—these things no longer exist. Black becomes white again. And the creative artist is dead! For he is blind.

The Negro writer, too, makes this retreat from Communism—for he, too, is opposed to lies, deceit, dictatorship and the other evils of the Soviet regime. But— and this is the significant point—the Negro writer does not, in most cases, come back to bow at the feet of Capitalism. He cannot, as can the white writer, close his eyes to the evils of the system under which he lives. Seeing the Negro ghetto, feeling the prejudice, his relatives and friends experiencing unemployment, injustice, police brutality, segregation in the South, white supremacy—seeing these things, the Negro writer cannot suddenly kiss the hand which slaps him. Looking at China, at Indo China and at Africa, he cannot avoid the realization that these are people of color, struggling, as he is struggling, for dignity. Again, prejudice has forced him to perceive the real, the ticking world.

Denied many freedoms, robbed of many rights, the Negro—and the Negro writer—rejects those aspects of both American Capitalism and Russian Communism which trample on freedoms and rights. Repelled now by both contending systems, the Negro writer of strength and courage stands firmly as a champion of the basic human issues—dignity, relative security, freedom and the end of savagery between one human being and another. And in this stand he is supported by the mass of human beings the world over.

So add it up. The handicaps are great. Many Negro writers—the majority, I should say, so far—have been unable to overcome them. The work of others is impaired by them. But if the handicaps can be overcome, the advantages remain. And, as I said before, they are great advantages. Because I believe that an increasing number of Negro writers will be able to overcome the disadvantages inherent in their social situation, I predict that a disproportionate percentage of the outstanding writers of the next decade will be Negroes.

THE NEGRO WRITER AND HIS ROOTS: TOWARD A NEW ROMANTICISM

LORRAINE HANSBERRY (1930–1965) grew up in Chicago. Her first play, A *Raisin in the Sun,* opened on Broadway in 1959 and won the New York Drama Critics Circle Award. "The Negro Writer and His Roots: Toward a New Romanticism," considered by many her manifesto for the black writer and perhaps her most important nondramatic piece of writing, was first delivered as a speech on March 1, 1959. It was revised and posthumously published in the March–April 1981 issue of *The Black Scholar.*

At the end of his last autobiography, *Sunset and Evening Star,* the great and beloved poet-dramatist of the Irish people, Sean O'Casey, writes:

> Even here, even now, when the sun had set and the evening star was chastely touching the bosom of the night, there were things to say, things to do. A drink first! What would he drink to—the past, the present, the future? To all of them! He would drink to the life that embraced the three of them! Here, with whitened hair, desires falling, strength ebbing out of him, with the sun gone down, and with only the serenity and the calm warming of the evening star left to him, he drank to Life, to all it had been, to what it was, to what it would be. Hurrah!

This, even in the autumn years of his life, is Sean O'Casey: warrior against despair and lover of humankind.

A few weeks ago the following appeared in the newspapers, the remarks of another poet-dramatist of stature, Tennessee Williams:

> Life is cannibalistic. Truly. Egos eat egos, personalities eat personalities. Someone is always eating at someone else for position, gain, triumph, greed, whatever. The human individual is a cannibal in the worst way.

That, in the middle years of life, at the height of all critical and monetary rewards, is the American dramatist Tennessee Williams.

Let it be said immediately and emphatically that the use of these two quotations is not intended to vilify a great creative artist. That gentleman with the painfully sympathetic eyes and the sweetest of smiles who is the gifted playwright Tennessee Williams, has presented to American culture a great body of work which significantly embodies the particular death agonies of a dying and panic-stricken social order. With horror and fear he has presented anguished indictments of that which too many others would actually celebrate. The poet Tennessee Williams is a mourner of beauty and decency, not their enemy.

It is, however, to the point of a discussion of the writer and his roots to pose the social viewpoints of two of the modern world's most important writers one against the other. They serve as poles of clarity in the great intellectual controversy now raging among thinking men and women everywhere. For at the core of these two expressions lies the essence of all arguments concerned with the destiny of the human race.

Tennessee Williams is, after all, a product of what the brilliant young Negro novelist James Baldwin has called "perhaps the loneliest country in the world." Williams himself has said, "Desire is rooted in a longing for companionship, a release from the loneliness which haunts every individual." The implications of his sense of defeat and futility transcend mere vilification or stupid, empty-headed hostility. They invite study and concern and involvement—and argument of equal stature.

TRUTH AND ART

I choose this introduction to a discussion of the Negro writer because I energetically suffer the view that, more than anything else, the compelling obligation of the Negro writer, as writer and citizen of life, is participation in the intellectual affairs of all men, everywhere. The foremost enemy of the Negro intelligentsia of the past has been and in a large sense remains—isolation. No more than can the Negro people afford to imagine themselves removed from the most pressing world issues of our time—war and peace, colonialism, capitalism vs. socialism—can I believe that the Negro writer imagines that he will be exempt from the artistic examination of questions which plague the intellect and spirit of man. If the world is engaged in a dispute between survival and destruction, involving the most fundamental questions of society and the individual—in a dispute between the champions of despair and those of hope and glorification of man—then we, as members of the human race, must address ourselves to that dispute.

I can no longer remember who it was who said, in effect, that the most gentle lie is ultimately more harmful than the most painful truth. That is a terrifying assertion, shattering in its simple assessment of at least one feature of life. It is so terrifying in fact that the immediate temptation on hearing it is to quickly assign its origin to some brutal cynic and pass on, in defense of ourselves, to all those situations in life which we *know* warrant fragile, life-giving lies: lies told with skill and confidence to the dying, to the romantically deceived—and, of course, to those stout-hearted but untalented performers we all seem to know, whose recitals we all seem obliged to attend at some point in life.

Yet, in the larger sense, in the more deeply philosophical sense, I think it remains virtually as John Keats insists: "Beauty is truth, truth beauty / That is all ye know on earth and all ye need to know." This idea, this idea of the inseparability of truth and beauty, and therefore of truth and art, will be at the heart of these remarks.

A DELUDED AMERICAN CULTURE

There is a desperate need in our time for the Negro writer to assume a partisanship in what I believe has been the traditional battleground of writers of stature for centuries, namely the war against the illusions of one's time and culture. And there are several illusions rampant in contemporary American culture, which, in my opinion, deserve the critical attention of black artists in particular.

First of all, it seems to me from my reading and from the popular cultural media, that we are beset with the most fundamental illusion of all—and one which is, in its operation, the most contradictory. This is the notion put forth that art is not, and *should* not and, when it is at its best, *cannot* possibly be "social." The most eminent scholars and critics do not hesitate to suggest that social consciousness can be the product of anything—bad manners, psychoses, infantilism, lack of sophistication, or almost anything else *other than* a reaction to the world around us. "Social statement" is excluded from the realm of true art, and true art is not social. At the same time they must insist, necessarily, that permissible content— that is, that which merely accepts or affirms things as they are—is not social statement, not a judgement, but merely entertainment (if it is popular), or "Art" (if it is not). Yet I think you will agree with me that some or all of the following topical ideas are fairly certain to pound at one in the course of a year's steady diet of television, motion pictures, the legitimate stage and the novel. These are ideas to the effect that:

- Most people who work for a living (and they are few) are executives and/or work in some kind of office.
- Women are idiots.
- People are white.
- Negroes do not exist.
- When a girl takes off her glasses and unpins her hair, she becomes a *woman.*
- Sex is the basis of all psychological, economic, political, historical, social, in fact *known*, problems of man.
- Sex is very bad.
- Sex is very good and the solution to all psychological, economic, political, historical, social, in fact *known*, problems of man.
- Sexual ideas of the past will be the sexual ideas of the future.
- Things as they are, are as they are and have been and will be that way because they got that way because things were as they were in the first place.

- The present social order is here forever and this is the best of all possible worlds.
- The present social order is here forever and this is the best of all possible worlds but there-is-nothing-we-can-do-about-it-anyway-"human-nature"-being-what-it-is.
- The present social order does not exist. It is all in the mind.
- Women long to castrate men and are doing so and taking the "man's place" in society and thereby causing a national neurosis.
- Women are also causing the increase in juvenile delinquency, divorce, hypertension, and, of course, they elected Eisenhower to office because they liked his smile.
- Businessmen are hard-headed if slightly adorable realists who are also the supreme moralists of our culture who work like fury keeping the world going in spite of people who lack drive and initiative like intellectuals and most working people.
- Intellectuals are unattractive people who wear oversize glasses and baggy clothes and are very boring and who make life dull for truly romantic people who know how to get the most out of life.
- War is inevitable.
- So are armies.
- Conservatives are the only real radicals.
- Radicals are infantile, adolescent, or senile. Any form of radicalism (except conservatism) is latent protest against Mom, toilet-training, or heterosexuality.
- Belief in God is instinctual to man.
- The Supreme Good, the ultimate achievement, is—"balls."

And of course, finally:

- European culture is the culture of the world.

It seems to me that these ideas, even presented in this topical form, offer profoundly social points of view—and deeply controversial ones insofar as I for one would beg to differ with all or most of them. I persist in the simple view that all art is ultimately social: that which agitates and that which prepares the mind for slumber. The writer is deceived who thinks that he has some other choice. The question is not whether one will make a social statement in one's work—but only *what* the statement will say, for if it says anything at all, it will be social.

The attack on this particular illusion is of vital importance for the Negro writer in particular, because those who say they do not wish to have "social" material on the stage, motion picture or TV screen are the same persons who in the past have not hesitated to relegate *all* black material, save hip-swinging musicals, to the "social" category—which, as we can see, becomes a vicious circle and demands that we be in the forefront of those who insist on a more rational discussion of the meaning of social statement in art.

A second great illusion which seems to me rampant in the cultural sphere of our lives is the assumption prevalent among so many artists that people exist independent of the world around them. This has given rise to an entire body of literature, among which are what Arthur Miller calls the "adolescent plays": plays in which the adolescent spirit endlessly beats itself against the imprisonment of its tortured soul. In and of itself, as Miller carefully notes, this a valid area for the exploration of human experience. But as the sum total of the greater weight of literary statement in our time, it is a sterile and deceiving force. The problem is that the spirit portrayed is *inexplicably* adolescent, and the nature of the torture undefined. It becomes the essence of the literature of man who simply is: unformed and uncertain, helpless in the face of a fate he cannot call by name.

Like Miller I do not believe that a proper or successful attack on this particular illusion should unleash the old horrors of so-called "problem dramas" or "agit prop" pieces. On the contrary, there is a simple and beautiful fusion of the two sides of the artistic inspection of any question when it is *genuinely* inspected. Miller says it more complicatedly, but also more handsomely, when he writes: "The shadow of a cornstalk on the ground is lovely, but it is not a *denial* of its loveliness to see as one looks at it that it is telling the time of day, the position of the earth and the sun, the size of our planet and its shape and perhaps even the length of its life and ours among the stars. . . ."

In other words, let there be no rush in the name of a "socially conscious" attack in literature to throw out the anguish of man; but let there be magnificent efforts to examine the sources of that anguish. We must have the cornstalk for itself and for what it can tell us about the world and the nature of itself in that world.

A third illusion which it seems must be dealt with is the idea that our country is made up of one huge sprawling middle class whose problems, valid though they are as subject matter, are considered to represent the problems of the entire nation and whose values are thought to be not only the values of the nation but, significantly enough, of the whole world!

The simple fact is that sections of the world's people remain unimpressed, to say the least, and even aloof from our efforts at demonstrating leadership and seem, at this point, perfectly capable of omitting from their historical destinies much of what we have thought was the very essence of the American past and the great American dream. That is to say—our particular form of organization of industrial society. It is idle to argue the patriotism of those who call this question to our attention. It is more relevant to recognize its truth and to alert the people of this nation to that truth.

Which brings me to the last great illusion that I think still clings to the cultural fabric of the country like dampness to wool on a rainy day. This is the all-important illusion in America that there exists an inexhaustible period of time during which we as a nation may leisurely resurrect the promise of our Constitution and begin to institute the equality of man within the frontiers of this land.

The truth is of course that a deluded and misguided world-wide minority is rapidly losing ground in the area of debating time alone. The unmistakable roots of the universal solidarity of the colored peoples of the world are no longer "predictable" as they were in my father's time—they are here. And I for one, as a black woman in the United States in the mid-twentieth century, feel that I am more typical of the present temperament of my people than not, when I say that I cannot allow the devious purposes of white supremacy to lead me to any conclusion other than what may be the most robust and important one of our time: that the ultimate destiny and aspirations of the African people and twenty million American Negroes are inextricably and magnificently bound up together forever.

THE BEAT

Is it really true that everything our parents longed for is now really too much *trouble?* Has aspiration really become too exhausting? Or, love too adolescent?

It is a curious thing, but I am not the first to note that when hope begins to die, reason is often swift to follow. Thus, reason is under attack in some quarters and some now turn to one form or another of medieval mysticism for escape. Having discovered that the world is incoherent, they have, some of them, come to the conclusion that it is also unreal. Having determined that life is in fact an absurdity, they have not yet decided that the task of the thoughtful is to try to help impose purposefulness on the absurdity. In these same circles display of emotion is considered the mark of the unspeakably unsophisticated, while a sense of fraternity with the human race is but of course, the accoutrement of the most outlandish, utter "square."

The current vogue for certain European dramatists favors Genet, Beckett, and Ionesco. Among the novelists and essayists, the name of Albert Camus now enjoys an almost holy stature. People seem to have become obsessed with the almost sudden universality of "guilt." We are told to stop feeling partisan about Jesus upon the cross because he bore his own guilt. Those who find issues to fight are only "sublimating" this or that sexual neurosis. I have watched these ideas take hold and become fast in the minds of certain of my generation: brilliant and thoughtful young people searching actively for a way out of what they perceive as the human condition—without commitment to anything.

In pursuit of the defeat of illusions it is important that we black writers not get lost in the various revolts of the merely revolted. I refer now to that small segment of the literati who have broken away to form their own vague, non-inspirational rebellion of rejection and nothingism: the Beat. They are a failure. They disturb no one because they attack everything and nothing. They are a source of amusement and confused misunderstanding to the very people who should feel most indicted by their emergence. They serve no significant purpose, neither to art nor society. Perhaps they are angry young men, but insofar as they do not make it clear with whom or *at what* they are angry, they can be said only to add bedlam to his already chaotic house. Beyond observing that here is the logical projection of a culture steeped in aimlessness and placing too much of a premium on sophistication for the sake of sophistication, it is idle to speak of the respective degrees of talent among them: it is talent which exhausts itself in its own negation. As unruly as the source of its birth, it feeds and distills agonies it will not by name indict.

There is a uselessness in the Beat. They are a second part of one illusion: the illusion that man possesses a choice as to whether or not he will participate in the creation of the present and the future. Like it or not, by his silence or his raised voice—his freely given commitment to what can be, or his merely passive acquiescence in what is—he participates.

THE BLACK ARTIST'S HISTORICAL RECLAMATION

The Negro writer, then, stands surrounded by these whirling elements in this world. He stands neither on the fringe nor utterly involved: the prime observer waiting posied for inclusion. For two hundred and fifty years he shouted because he found it difficult to be heard. Then, on occasion, he allowed his voice to drop to a whisper, stillness even. Now it is time to shout again.

O, the things that we have learned in this unkind house that we have to tell the world about! *Despair?* Did someone say "despair" was a question in the world? Well, then, listen to the sons of those who have known little else if you wish to know the resiliency of this thing you would so quickly resign to mythhood, this thing called the human spirit! *Life?* Ask those who have tasted of it in pieces rationed out by enemies! *Love?* Ah, ask the troubadours who come from those who have loved when all reason pointed to the uselessness and foolhardiness of love! Perhaps we shall be the teachers when it is done. Out of the depths of pain we have thought to be our sole heritage in this world—O, we know about love!

Thus comes the Negro writer. And, thus, does his mid-twentieth century task bear within it an explosive artistic potential that must not escape us for lack of awareness. We must turn our eyes outward—but, to do so, we must also turn them *inward* toward our people and their complex and still transitory culture. There is much to celebrate, there always has been. We have given the world many of its heroes and the marching feet have not stopped yet. Turn inward to where a culture has never, as Alain Locke pointed out thirty years ago, been adequately understood.

It was true thirty years ago and it is still true today that the soaring greatest of the spirituals begin and end in some minds as the product of religious childishness; they do not hear, even yet, in the "black and unknown bards" of whom James Weldon Johnson sang, the enormous soul of a great and incredibly courageous people who have known how to acknowledge pain and despair as one hope. In jazz rhythms, alien minds find only symbols for their own confused and mistaken yearnings for a return to primitive abandon: Norman Mailer writes, "For jazz is orgasm; it is the music of orgasm, good orgasm and bad. . . ." They do not hear as yet the tempo of an impatient and questioning people. Above all, in the murmur of the blues, they believe they know communion with naked sexual impulses peculiar to imperfect apes or noble savages; they miss the sweet and sad indictment of misery that forms that music. They "done taken our blues and gone."

And similarly the speech of our people has been the victim of hostile ears and commentary. That there are tones and moods of language that the African tongue prefers escapes attention, when that attention would demand admiration of beauty and color rather than mere amusement or derision. The educated are expected to apologize for slurrings that haunt our speech; the mark of ascendancy is the absence of recognizable Negro idiom or inflection. It is an attitude that suggests that we should most admire the peacock when he has lost his colors. Perhaps someday they will know it is not mere notes of music which command us—"when Malindy sings."

And make no mistake, these very cultural values have spilled in malignant portions into the life of our people. A minute and well-groomed black bourgeoisie is cautious of the implications of a true love of the folk heritage. Sophistication allows the listening to spirituals if performed by concert artists, but in church— Bach chorales and Handel, please!

There is a job to be done. White supremacy has long accustomed our enemies to assume that to the most oppressed is due the most amount of brainwashing. Thus, our children grow up believing:

1. That the African continent was merely a handy place for catching slaves for plantations and lions for circuses.

2. That we endured—and on occasion rejoiced—in bondage that was impaired unwittingly by an unfortunate and unnecessary war which had "nothing to do with slavery anyway," a war imposed on a genteel and delicate civilization by a villainous Congress and a bemused president with a beard who really hated Negroes anyway.

3. Moreover, that following that destructive war, there was apparently a lapse in American civilization when barbarians with carpet bags invaded the South and wrecked its ancient democratic culture.

4. That with the exception of George Washington Carver, Marian Anderson, Ralph Bunche, Joe Louis, and a slave girl who wrote poems back in the 17th century, we have really been a burden and a task on an otherwise smoothly functioning society.

And so on.

If this be unreasonable and unwieldy exaggeration, then more the pain for the indisputable recognition of truth in such enlargement. I shall never forget once being on a pilgrimage to the shrine which is the former home of Frederick Douglass, in the company of a group of women who had traveled many miles from many parts of the country. When I expressed my excitement at the possibility of seeing the home of this perhaps greatest of all Americans, I was asked quite sincerely by one of the group whether or not I thought, "Mr. Douglass will be home?"

Such then be the arena into which our people must thrust their destiny. The work of the Negro artist is cut out for him: the vast task of cultural and historical reclamation—to reclaim the past if we would claim the future.

But this alone is not enough. I began these remarks by saying that truth has pains that lies could only seemingly assuage. If the Negro writer would confound the hearts of his readers with unassailable dimensionality, with the complexity of man and not symbolic figures that can speak only to the already persuaded, then we, too, must discard some of the paraphernalia of our former selves. What are the sores within our people that bear exposure and examination?

I say that foremost are the villainous and often ridiculous money values that spill over from the dominant culture and often make us ludicrous in pursuit of that which has its own inherently ludicrous nature: acquisition for the sake of acquisition. The desire for the possession of "things" has rapidly replaced among too many of us the impulse for the possession of ourselves, for freedom. The exploration of babbitry would have been unwarranted twenty years ago in whatever there was of a black middle class. That is not the case today, and Dr. E. Franklin Frazier has made this clear in brutally painful clinical portraiture which would bear extension to fiction.

The war against illusions must dispel the romance of the black bourgeoisie. Nor does this imply the creation of a modern kind of buffoon dressed up in a business suit, haplessly trying to imitate the white counterpart. On the contrary. These values have their root in an *American* perversion and no place else. The man in pursuit of idle dreams is a man in pursuit of idle dreams. His color does not confound this to the point of absurdity—it merely makes it complex.

We do not laugh at Willy Loman, white or black—the impulse is more to cry. We do not reject him: we worry for him. He is the spawn of something he never really understood, its victim and its product. Sooner or later between the man and his source we must indict something if we agree that Willy Loman is a failure. But when we have seen his helplessness—the limitation of the choices his world (or his understanding of it) has offered him—it will not be Willy we indict. It is again Sean O'Casey who tells us that he does not think the world will be blown up because: "Mankind is foolish, but men are not fools." In the act of living and overcoming the destitution of much that surrounds him, man commits many an outlandish and cruel act; but we are not outlandish and cruel—or else how could we have measured our desires in such noble turns, lo these many centuries?

There are many facets of our life that cry out for attention. Let us look, for example, at color prejudice—perhaps the most hideous malignancy yet lingering from the slave history of this country. Does it persist among black men? Then let us hold it up to the light and examine it for all the ugliness that is there, and when we are done, perhaps the only thing it will be fit for is the trash can. And similarly, let the Negro writer begin to examine much that has formerly been romanticized about Negro urban life in particular. If "the numbers" are basically a prey upon our people, then it should be inconceivable that that particular aspect of gambling should emerge as a folksy and harmless pastime in our novels. The evils of the ghetto, whatever they are, must emerge as evils—not as the romantic and exotic offshoots of a hilarious people who can simply endure anything. Dope addiction, alcoholism, prostitution—all deserve this kind of treatment. In the effort to make the people beautiful we must not beautify the disease.

On the contrary, I do not believe that the deep-seated propensity for cultural apology which affects such a large section of the Negro middle class should or must affect the Negro writer: the attitude that any reminder of the slave past or the sharecropper and ghetto present is an affront to the dignity of every Negro who wears a shirt and tie. I submit that much of what is noble and most of what is distinctive in true native American culture has its origins in those very areas of the life and history of our people. In fact this spiritual self-denigration is itself deserving of literary treatment that would analyze it for its interesting indications of the confusion that can sometimes reign among oppressed peoples.

And finally there is the matter of political naivete: the isolation and insularity of our struggles. Too often has political leadership fallen to those who seem only to have the most ambitious paths on which to lead us. Obsessive over-reliance upon the courts, legalistic pursuit of the already guaranteed aspects of our Constitution (if, that is, there were but the will to enforce them) preoccupies us at the expense of more potent political concepts. I suspect, for example, in my heart of hearts, that the longings of twenty million black folk in America will lie idle until half their number still living in the Southern states of this nation enjoy complete and utter political representation in the national government. The Negro writer has a role to play in shaming, if you will, the conscience of the people and the present national government, executive and legislative, into action on behalf of the free and unharassed voting rights of all people of the South.

I suspect, again, that equality—which above all must mean equal *job* opportunity, the most basic right of all men in all societies anywhere in the world—implies vast economic transformations far greater than any our leaders have dared to envision. Until such time, on behalf of an oppressed people who yet labor daily under the rigors of second-class citizenship in these United States, the Negro artist must display wit and imagination, and energy to the depths of our beings. And until such time, the artist who participates in programs of apology, of distortion, of camouflage in the depiction of the life and trials of our people, behaves as the paid agent of the enemies of Negro freedom.

Our objective is art, not distortion, and this in itself is a reflection of the maturation of any artist. Moreover, we know that a presentation of the full-scale nature of all the complexities and confusions and backwardnesses of our people will, in the end, only heighten and make more real the inescapable image of their greatness and courage.

However, we see no reason to stop there. Let no Negro artist who thinks himself deserving of the title take pen to paper—or, for that matter, body to dance or voice to speech or song—if in doing so the content of that which he presents or performs suggests to the nations of the world that our people do not yet languish under privation and hatred and brutality and political oppression in every state of the forty-eight. The truth demands its own equals. Therefore, let an America that respects its name and aspirations in the world anticipate the novels and plays and poetry of Negro writers that must now go forth to an eager world. For we are going to tell the truth from all its sides, including what is the still bitter epic of the black man in this most hostile nation.

As it is, so shall it be recorded in fiction and essay and drama.

And, because it is as it is, when the questions are asked in Bombay and Peking and Budapest and Laos and Cairo and Jakarta—so I will tell it. And, as of today, if I am asked abroad if I am a free citizen in the United States of America, I must say only what is true: No.

If I am asked if my people enjoy equal opportunity in the most basic aspects of American life, housing, employment, franchise—I must and will say: No.

And, shame of shames, under a government that wept for Hungary and sent troops to Korea, when I am asked if that most primitive, savage and intolerable custom of all—lynching—still persists in the United States of America, I will say what every mother's child of us knows: that they are still murdering Negroes in this country, with *and without* rope and faggot, in all the old ways and many new ones. Lest We Forget, I give you the name of an American boy, Emmett Till. But more: that the social and economic havoc wreaked on the American Negro takes some ten to fifteen years off the life-expectancy of our people. There are some passionate people in this world who would not hesitate to call this last fact— murder.

I am prepared to tell all America and the world about our people. That we are yet backward and ourselves mired in many of the corruptions of our culture. I am saying that whatever the corruption within our people, tear it out and expose it and let us then take measure of what is left. I believe in the truth of art and the art of truth and the most painful exigency of cultural and social life will not be exempt from exploration by my mind or pen.

CONCLUSION

I must share with you now a part of a conversation I had with a young New York intellectual a year ago in my living room in Greenwich Village. It is to the essence of these remarks and it will bring me full circle—back to O'Casey, Williams, and what I posed as "the great intellectual controversy" now raging among thinking men and women everywhere. He was a young man I had known, not well, but for a number of years, who was, by way of description, an ex-Communist, a scholar and a serious student of philosophy and literature, and whom I consider to possess quite a fine and exceptionally alert mind. In any case, he and I had wandered conversationally into the realm of discussion which haunts the days of humankind everywhere: the destruction or survival of the human race.

"Why," he said to me, "are you so sure the human race *should* go on? You do not believe in a prior arrangement of life on this planet. You know perfectly well that the *reason* for survival does not exist in nature!"

I was somewhat taken aback by the severity that this kind of feeling has apparently reached among a generation that presumably should be lying on its back in the spring woods somewhere, contemplating lyrics of love and daring and the wonder of wild lilies.

I answered him the only way I could. I argued on his own terms, which are also mine: that man is unique in the universe, the only creature who has in fact the power to transform the universe. Therefore, it did not seem unthinkable to me that man might just do what the apes never will—*impose* the reason for life on life. That is what I said to my friend. I wish to live because life has within it that which is good, that which is beautiful, and that which is love. Therefore, since I have known all of these things, I have found them to be reason enough and—I wish to live. Moreover, because this is so, I wish others to live for generations and generations and generations and generations.

I was born on the South Side of Chicago. I was born black and a female. I was born in a depression after one world war, and came into my adolescence during another. While I was still in my teens the first atom bombs were dropped on human beings at Nagasaki and Hiroshima, and by the time I was twenty-three years old my government and that of the Soviet Union had entered actively into the worst conflict of nerves in human history—the Cold War.

I have lost friends and relatives through cancer, lynching and war. I have been personally the victim of physical attack which was the offspring of racial and political hysteria. I have worked with the handicapped and seen the ravages of congenital diseases that we have not yet conquered because we spend our time and ingenuity in far less purposeful wars. I have known persons afflicted with drug addiction and alcoholism and mental illness. I see daily on the streets of New York street gangs and prostitutes and beggars. I have, like all of you, on a thousand occasions seen indescribable displays of man's very real inhumanity to man; and I have come to maturity, as we all must, knowing that greed and malice and indifference to human misery, bigotry and corruption, brutality and, perhaps above all else, ignorance—the prime ancient and persistent enemy of man—abound in this world.

I say all of this to say that one cannot live with sighted eyes and feeling heart and not know and react to the miseries which afflict this world.

I have given you this account so that you know that what I write is not based on the assumption of idyllic possibilities or innocent assessments of the true nature of life—but, rather, my own personal view that, posing one against the other, I think the human race does command its own destiny and that that destiny can eventually embrace the stars.

If man is as small and ugly and grotesque as his most inhuman act, he is also as large as his most heroic gesture, and he is therefore a hero manyfold. Not only yesterday, as some insist, but today. Not only yesterday when Spartacus rose against the Romans; not only yesterday when the Jews of Poland rose in the ghetto—but today. Heroic still and—make no mistake—triumphant still, for the gesture of his heroism is many things. Who could watch the epic magnitude of fifty thousand Negroes in Montgomery, Alabama, walking their way to freedom, and doubt the heroism of the species? Or the nine small children who insisted on going to school in a town called Little Rock?

I think of Leonardo, contemplating man in the sky—and finding about him demons of ignorance and intolerance insisting that if man had been meant to fly, God would have given him wings. I think of Leonardo, nonetheless patiently filling his notebooks with geometric studies and algebraic equations and anatomic diagrams, and literally writing his exercises and conclusions *backwards* to escape the wrack of the inquisitor. And I think: Ah, but it is still the dark ages. And while it is true that the figurative descendants of his persecutors do not hesitate to get on an airplane to go and torment his spiritual descendants—true that the shadows have never been light enough, and that there never will be enough light in these shadows—the fact is that it is *still* the dark ages. And because now, at last, on the upward ladder toward human enlightenment, we find that man's relationship to man seems by far the most precarious, the most dangerous, and in that sense the newest of our terrors, we fear for the future itself.

Let us take courage. Once physics overwhelmed the minds of men. And it came to pass, that he who had no wings came to command the air at speeds no bird can manage. Surely then, as we turn our full attention to the hearts and minds of men, we shall see that if man can fly—he can also be free.

CULTURAL STRANGULATION: BLACK LITERATURE AND THE WHITE AESTHETIC

ADDISON GAYLE, JR., was born in 1932 and has been a professor, writer, critic, and lecturer. Among his books are *The Black Aesthetic* (editor, 1971), *Oak and Ivy: A Biography of Paul Laurence Dunbar* (1971), and *The Way of the New World: The Black Novel in America* (1975). He is also author of an autobiography, *Wayward Child: A Personal Odyssey* (1977). "Cultural Strangulation: Black Literature and the White Aesthetic" is from *The Black Aesthetic* (1971).

This assumption that of all the hues of God, whiteness is inherently and obviously better than brownness or tan leads to curious acts. . . .
—W. E. B. Du Bois

T he expected opposition to the concept of a "Black Aesthetic" was not long in coming. In separate reviews of *Black Fire*, an anthology edited by LeRoi Jones and Larry Neal, critics from the *Saturday Review* and the *New York Review of Books* presented the expected rebuttal. Agreeing with Ralph Ellison that sociology and art are incompatible mates, these critics, nevertheless, invoked the clichés of the social ideology of the "we shall overcome" years in their attempt to steer Blacks from "the path of literary fantasy and folly."

Their major thesis is simple: There is no Black Aesthetic because there is no white aesthetic. The Kerner Commission Report to the contrary, America is not two societies but one. Therefore, Americans of all races, colors and creeds share a common cultural heredity. This is to say that there is one predominant culture—the American culture—with tributary national and ethnic streams flowing into the larger river. Literature, the most important by-product of this cultural monolith, knows no parochial boundaries. To speak of a Black literature, a Black aesthetic, or a Black state, is to engage in racial chauvinism, separatist bias, and Black fantasy.

The question of a white aesthetic, however, is academic. One has neither to talk about it nor define it. Most Americans, black and white, accept the existence of a "White Aesthetic" as naturally as they accept April 15th as the deadline for paying their income tax—with far less animosity towards the former than the latter. The white aesthetic, despite the academic critics, has always been with us: for long before Diotima pointed out the way to heavenly beauty to Socrates, the poets of biblical times were discussing beauty in terms of light and dark—the essential characteristics of a white and black aesthetic—and establishing the dichotomy of superior vs. inferior which would assume body and form in the 18th century. Therefore, more serious than a definition, is the problem of tracing the white aesthetic from its early origins and afterwards, outlining the various changes in the basic formula from culture to culture and from nation to nation. Such an undertaking would be more germane to a book than an essay; nevertheless, one may take a certain starting point and, using selective nations and cultures, make the critical point, while calling attention to the necessity of a more comprehensive study encompassing all of the nations and cultures of the world.

Let us propose Greece as the logical starting point, bearing in mind Will Durant's observation that "all of Western Civilization is but a footnote to Plato," and take Plato as the first writer to attempt a systematic aesthetic. Two documents by Plato, *The Symposium* and *The Republic*, reveal the twin components of Plato's aesthetic system.

In *The Symposium*, Plato divides the universe into spheres. In one sphere, the lower, one finds the forms of beauty; in the other, the higher, beauty, as Diotima tells Socrates, is absolute and supreme. In *The Republic*, Plato defines the poet as an imitator (a third-rate imitator—a point which modern critics have long since forgotten) who reflects the heavenly beauty in the earthly mirror. In other words, the poet recreates beauty as it exists in heaven; thus the poet, as Neo-Platonists from Aquinas to Coleridge have told us, is the custodian of beauty on earth.

However, Plato defines beauty only in ambiguous, mystical terms; leaving the problem of a more circumscribed, secular definition to philosophers, poets, and critics. During most of the history of the Western world, these aestheticians have been white; therefore, it is not surprising that, symbolically and literally, they have defined beauty in terms of whiteness. (An early contradiction to this tendency is the Marquis DeSade who inverted the symbols, making black beautiful, but demonic, and white pure, but sterile—the Marquis is considered by modern criticism to have been mentally deranged.)

The distinction between whiteness as beautiful (good) and blackness as ugly (evil) appears early in the literature of the middle ages—in the Morality Plays of England. Heavily influenced by both Platonism and Christianity, these plays set forth the distinctions which exist today. To be white was to be pure, good, universal, and beautiful; to be black was to be impure, evil, parochial, and ugly.

The characters and the plots of these plays followed this basic format. The villain is always evil, in most cases the devil; the protagonist, or hero, is always good, in most cases, angels or disciples. The plot then is simple; good (light) triumphs over the forces of evil (dark). As English literature became more sophisticated, the symbols were made to cover wider areas of the human and literary experience. To love was divine; to hate, evil. The fancied mistress of Petrarch was the purest of the pure; Grendel's mother, a creature from the "lower regions and marshes," is, like her son, a monster; the "bad" characters in Chaucer's *Canterbury Tales* tell dark stories; and the Satan of *Paradise Lost* must be vanquished by Gabriel, the angel of purity.

These ancients, as Swift might have called them, established their dichotomies as a result of the influences of Neo-Platonism and Christianity. Later, the symbols became internationalized. Robert Burton, in *The Anatomy of Melancholy*, writes of "dark despair" in the seventeenth century, and James Boswell describes melancholia, that state of mind common to intellectuals of the 17th and 18th centuries, as a dark, dreaded affliction which robbed men of their creative energies. This condition—dark despair or melancholia—was later popularized in what is referred to in English literature as its "dark period"—the period of the Grave Yard School of poets and the Gothic novels.

The symbols thus far were largely applied to conditions, although characters who symbolized evil influences were also dark. In the early stages of English literature, these characters were mythological and fictitious and not representative of people of specific racial or ethnic groups. In the 18th-century English novel, however, the symbolism becomes ethnic and racial.

There were forerunners. As early as 1621, Shakespeare has Iago refer to Othello as that "old Black ewe," attaching the mystical sexual characteristic to blackness which would become the motive for centuries of oppressive acts by white Americans. In *The Tempest*, Shakespeare's last play, Caliban, though not ostensibly black, is nevertheless a distant cousin of the colonial Friday in Daniel Defoe's *Robinson Crusoe*.

Robinson Crusoe was published at a historically significant time. In the year 1719, the English had all but completed their colonization of Africa. The slave trade in America was on its way to becoming a booming industry; in Africa, Black people were enslaved mentally as well as physically by such strange bedfellows as criminals, businessmen, and Christians. In the social and political spheres, a rationale was needed, and help came from the artist—in this case, the novelist—in the form of *Robinson Crusoe*. In the novel, Defoe brings together both Christian and Platonic symbolism, sharpening the dichotomy between light and dark on the one hand, while on the other establishing a criterion for the inferiority of Black people as opposed to the superiority of white.

One need only compare Crusoe with Friday to validate both of these statements. Crusoe is majestic, wise, white and a colonialist; Friday is savage, ignorant, black and a colonial. Therefore, Crusoe, the colonialist, has a double task. On the one hand he must transform the island (Africa—unproductive, barren, dead) into a little England (prosperous, life-giving, fertile), and he must recreate Friday in his own image, thus bringing him as close to being an Englishman as possible. At the end of the novel, Crusoe has accomplished both undertakings; the island is a replica of "mother England"; and Friday has been transformed into a white man, now capable of immigrating to the land of the gods.

From such mystical artifacts has the literature and criticism of the Western world sprung; and based upon such narrow prejudices as those of Defoe, the art of Black people throughout the world has been described as parochial and inferior. Friday was parochial and inferior until, having denounced his own culture, he assimilated another. Once this was done, symbolically, Friday underwent a change. To deal with him after the conversion was to deal with him in terms of a character who had been civilized and therefore had moved beyond racial parochialism.

However, Defoe was merely a hack novelist, not a thinker. It was left to shrewder minds than his to apply the rules of the white aesthetic to the practical areas of the Black literary and social worlds, and no shrewder minds were at work on this problem than those of writers and critics in America. In America, the rationale for both slavery and the inferiority of Black art and culture was supplied boldly, without the trappings of 18th-century symbolism.

In 1867, in a book entitled *Nojoque: A Question for a Continent*, Hinton Helper provided the vehicle for the cultural and social symbols of inferiority under which Blacks have labored in this country. Helper intended, as he states frankly in his preface, "to write the negro out of America." In the headings of the two major chapters of the book, the whole symbolic apparatus of the white aesthetic handed down from Plato to America is graphically revealed: the heading of one chapter reads: "Black: A Thing of Ugliness, Disease"; another heading reads: "White: A Thing of Life, Health, and Beauty."

Under the first heading, Helper argues that the color black "has always been associated with sinister things such as mourning, the devil, the darkness of night." Under the second, "White has always been associated with the light of day, divine transfiguration, the beneficent moon and stars . . . the fair complexion of romantic ladies, the costumes of Romans and angels, and the white of the American flag so beautifully combined with blue and red without ever a touch of the black that has been for the flag of pirates."

Such is the American critical ethic based upon centuries of distortion of the Platonic ideal. By not adequately defining beauty, and implying at least that this was the job of the poet, Plato laid the foundation for the white aesthetic as defined by Daniel Defoe and Hinton Helper. However, the uses of that aesthetic to stifle and strangle the cultures of other nations is not to be attributed to Plato but, instead, to his hereditary brothers far from the Aegean. For Plato knew his poets. They were not, he surmised, a very trusting lot and, therefore, by adopting an ambiguous position on symbols, he limited their power in the realm of aesthetics. For Plato, there were two kinds of symbols: natural and proscriptive. Natural symbols corresponded to absolute beauty as created by God; proscriptive symbols, on the other hand, were symbols of beauty as proscribed by man, which is to say that certain symbols are said to mean such and such by man himself.

The irony of the trap in which the Black artist has found himself throughout history is apparent. Those symbols which govern his life and art are proscriptive ones, set down by minds as diseased as Hinton Helper's. In other words, beauty has been in the eyes of an earthly beholder who has stipulated that beauty conforms to such and such a definition. To return to Friday, Defoe stipulated that civilized man was what Friday had to become, proscribed certain characteristics to the term "civilized," and presto, Friday, in order not to be regarded as a "savage under Western eyes," was forced to conform to this ideal. How well have the same stipulative definitions worked in the artistic sphere! Masterpieces are made at will by each new critic who argues that the subject of his doctoral dissertation is immortal. At one period of history, John Donne, according to the critic Samuel Johnson, is a second-rate poet; at another period, according to the critic T. S. Eliot, he is one of the finest poets in the language. Dickens, argues Professor Ada Nisbet, is one of England's most representative novelists, while for F. R. Leavis, Dickens's work does not warrant him a place in *The Great Tradition.*

When Black literature is the subject, the verbiage reaches the height of the ridiculous. The good "Negro Novel," we are told by Robert Bone and Herbert Hill, is that novel in which the subject matter moves beyond the limitations of narrow parochialism. Form is the most important criterion of the work of art when Black literature is evaluated, whereas form, almost non-existent in Dostoyevsky's *Crime and Punishment,* and totally chaotic in Kafka's *The Trial,* must take second place to the supremacy of thought and message.

Richard Wright, says Theodore Gross, is not a major American novelist; while Ralph Ellison, on the strength of one novel, is. LeRoi Jones is not a major poet, Ed Bullins not a major playwright, Baldwin incapable of handling the novel form—all because white critics have said so.

Behind the symbol is the object or vehicle, and behind the vehicle is the definition. It is the definition with which we are concerned, for the extent of the cultural strangulation of Black literature by white critics has been the extent to which they have been allowed to define the terms in which the Black artist will deal with his own experience. The career of Paul Laurence Dunbar is the most striking example. Having internalized the definitions handed him by the American society, Dunbar would rather not have written about the Black experience at all, and three of his novels and most of his poetry support this argument. However, when forced to do so by his white liberal mentors, among [whom] was the powerful critic, William Dean Howells, Dunbar deals with Blacks in terms of buffoonery, idiocy and comedy.

Like so many Black writers, past and present, Dunbar was trapped by the definitions of other men, never capable of realizing until near the end of his life, that those definitions were not god-given, but man-given; and so circumscribed by tradition and culture that they were irrelevant to an evaluation of either his life or his art.

In a literary conflict involving Christianity, Zarathustra, Friedrich Nietzsche's iconoclast, calls for "a new table of the laws." In similar iconoclastic fashion, the proponents of a Black Aesthetic, the idol smashers of America, call for a set of rules by which Black literature and art is to be judged and evaluated. For the historic practice of bowing to other men's gods and definitions has produced a crisis of the highest magnitude, and brought us, culturally, to the limits of racial armageddon. The trend must be reversed.

The acceptance of the phrase "Black Is Beautiful" is the first step in the destruction of the old table of the laws and the construction of new ones, for the phrase flies in the face of the whole ethos of the white aesthetic. This step must be followed by serious scholarship and hard work; and Black critics must dig beneath the phrase and unearth the treasure of beauty lying deep in the untoured regions of the Black experience—regions where others, due to historical conditioning and cultural deprivation, cannot go.

NECESSARY DISTANCE: AFTERTHOUGHTS ON BECOMING A WRITER

CLARENCE MAJOR was born in 1936 in Atlanta, Georgia. He is a novelist, poet, and essayist. His works include *Emergency Exit* (1979, a novel), and "Observations of a Stranger at Zuni in the Latter Part of the Century" (1989, a book-length poem). He also compiled the *Dictionary of Afro-American Slang* (1970). "Necessary Distance: Afterthoughts on Becoming a Writer" appeared in *Black American Literature Forum*, Summer 1989.

People have a tendency to ask a writer, *Why* did you become a writer? *How* did you become a writer? Every writer hears such questions over and over. You ever hear anybody ask a butcher a question like that?

So, what's so special about being a writer? Maybe we are simply fascinated by people who are brave (or foolish) enough to go against—and lucky enough to beat—the odds.

We seem fascinated in the same way by the lives of people in show business, and probably for the same reasons the lives of writers interest us.

It is also always amazing to see someone making a living doing something he or she actually enjoys.

I never seriously tried to deal with the questions till I was asked to write my life story. If my autobiography were going to make sense, I thought I'd better try my best to answer both questions.

So, my speaking on the page to you is—in a way—an effort to answer those questions—for myself and possibly for others. I don't expect to succeed—but here goes.

It seems to me that the impulse to write, the *need* to write, is inseparable from one's educational process—which begins at the beginning and never ends.

In some sort of nonobjective way, I can remember being an infant and some of the things I thought about and touched. I had a sister, but my sister didn't have a brother. I had no self because I was *all* self. Gradually, like any developing kid, I shed my self-centered view of the world: saw myself reflected in my mother's eyes, began to perceive the idea of a self. In a way it was at this point that my *research* as a writer, and as a painter, began. (For me, the two impulses were always inseparable.) The world was a place of magic, and everything I touched was excruciatingly *new*. Without knowing it, my career had begun.

In his meditation on the art of fiction, *Being and Race*, novelist Charles Johnson says: "All art points to others with whom the writer argues about what is. . . . He must have models with which to agree . . . or outright oppose . . . for Nature seems to remain silent . . . ." Reading this passage reminded me of Sherwood Anderson's short story "Death in the Woods," in which the narrator retells the story (we are reading) because his brother, who had told it first, hadn't told it the way it was supposed to be told. In a similar way, that early self of mine, then, had already started its long battle with the history of literature and art.

In the early stages of that battle, some very primary things were going on. By this, I mean to say that a writer is usually a person who has to learn how to keep his ego—like his virginity—and lose it at the same time. In other words, he becomes a kind of twin of himself. He remains that self-centered infant while transcending him to become the observer of his own experience and, by extension, the observer of a wide range of experience within his cultural domain.

Without any rational self-consciousness at all, early on, my imagination was fed by the need to invent things. My older cousins taught me how to make my own toys—trucks, cars, houses, whole cities. We used old skate wheels for tires. Our parents couldn't afford such luxuries as toys—we were lucky if we got new clothes. Watching physical things like the toys we made take shape, I think, showed me some possibilities. (William Carlos Williams said a poem is like a machine. If I understand what he meant, I can see a connection between what I was making at age seven and poems and stories I tried to write later on.)

Plus the *newness* of everything—trees, plants, the sky—and the *need* to define everything, on my own terms, was a given. At my grandparents' farm, my cousins and I climbed trees and named the trees we climbed. Painfully, I watched my uncle slaughter hogs and learned about death. I watched my grandmother gather eggs from the chicken nests and learned about birth. I watched her make lye soap and the clothes we wore. But I didn't fully trust the world I was watching. It seemed too full of *danger*, even while I dared to explore it and attempt to imprint the evidence of my presence upon it—by making things such as toys or drawing pictures in the sand.

Daydreaming—as a necessity in the early disposition of a writer—is not a new idea. Whether or not it was necessary in my case, I was a guilty practitioner. I say this because I had an almost *mystical* attachment to nature. If looked at from my parents' point of view, it was not a good sign. I could examine a leaf for hours or spend hours on my knees watching the way ants lived. Behaving like a lazy kid, I followed the flights and landings of birds with spiritual devotion. The frame of mind that put me through those motions was, later, the same frame of mind from which

I tried to write a poem or a story: daydreaming, letting it happen, connecting two or three previously unrelated things, making them mean something—together—entirely new. I was hopeless.

And dreams—in dreams I discovered a self going about its business with a mind of its own. I began to watch and to wonder. I was amazed by some of the things I had the nerve to dream about. Sex, for example. Or some *wonderful*, delicious food! One guilty pleasure after another! This other self often invented these wonderful ways for me to actually get something—even a horse once—that I *knew* I wanted, something no one *seriously* wanted to give me.

At times, waking up was the hard part. Dream activity was all invention—maybe even the rootbeds of all the conscious, willful invention I wanted to take charge of in the hard indifference of daylight. Unlike the daydreams I spent so much time giving myself to, *these* dreams were not under my control. Later, I started trying to write them down, but I discovered that it was impossible to capture their specific texture. They had to stay where they were. But I tried to imitate them, to make up stories that *sounded* like them. The pattern of these dreams became a model for the imaginative leaps I wanted to make (and couldn't—for a long time!) in my poetry and fiction.

My first novel, written at the age of twelve, was twenty pages long. It was the story of a wild, free-spirited horse, leading a herd. Influenced by movies, I thought it would make a terrific movie, so I sent it to Hollywood. A man named William Self read it and sent it back with a letter of encouragement. I never forgot his kindness. It was the beginning of a long, long process of learning to live with rejection—not just rejection slips. And that experience too was necessary as a correlation to the writing process, necessary because one of the most *important* things I was going to have to learn was *how* to detect my own failures and be the first to reject them.

Was there, then, a particular point when I said: *Hey! I'm going to become a writer!* I think there *was*, but it now seems irrelevant because I must have been evolving toward that conscious moment long, long before I had any idea what was going on. (I was going to have to find my way—with more imperfection than not—through *many* disciplines—such as painting, music, anthropology, history, philosophy, psychology, sociology—before such a consciousness would begin to emerge.)

I think I was in the fifth grade when a girl who sat behind me snuck a copy of Raymond Radiguet's *Devil in the Flesh* to me. This was *adult fiction!* And judging from the cover, the book was going to have some good parts. But as it turned out the *single* good part was *the writing itself.* I was reading that book one day at home, and about halfway through, I stood and went crazy with an important discovery: *Writing had a life of its own!* And I soon fell in love with the *life* of writing, by way of this book—Kay Boyle's translation of Radiguet.

From that moment on, up to about the age of twenty, I set out to discover other books that might change my perception—forever. Hawthorne's *The Scarlet Letter* showed me how *gracefully* a story could be told and how *terrifying* human affairs—and self-deception within those affairs—can be. Conrad's *Heart of Darkness*

caught me in an aesthetic network of *magic* so powerful I never untangled myself.
I then went on to read other nineteenth-century—and even earlier—works by
Melville, Baudelaire, Emerson, Dostoyevsky, and the like.

But I always hung on—with more comfort—to the twentieth century. I read
J. D. Salinger's *The Catcher in the Rye* early enough for it to have spoken profoundly
and directly to me about what I was *feeling* and *thinking* about the adult world at
the time that its agony affirmed my faith in life. Richard Wright's *Native Son* was
an overwhelming experience, and so was Rimbaud's poetry. But the important thing
about these discoveries is that each of them led to Cocteau and other French writers,
going back to the nineteenth century; Salinger led me to a discovery of modern and
contemporary American fiction—Hemingway, Faulkner, Sherwood Anderson, and
on and on. Wright led to Dos Passos, to James T. Farrell, to Jean Toomer, to
Chester Himes, to William Gardner Smith, to Ann Petry, to Nella Larsen and
other Afro-American writers; and Rimbaud led to the discovery of *American po-*
etry—which was not so much of a leap as it sounds—to Williams, to Marianne
Moore, to Eliot, to cummings. This activity began roughly during the last year of
grade school and took on full, focused direction in high school. Now, none of these
writers was being taught in school. I was reading them *on my own*. In school we
had to read O. Henry and Joyce Kilmer.

But during all this time, it was hard to find books that came *alive*. I had to go
through *hundreds* before hitting on the special ones, the ones with the power to
shape or reshape perception, to deepen vision, to give *me* the means to understand
myself and other things, to drive away fears and doubts. I found the possibilities of
wedding the social and political self and the artistic self in the essays of James
Baldwin. Autobiographies such as Billie Holiday's *Lady Sings the Blues* and Mezz
Mezzrow's *Really the Blues* were *profound* reading experiences: These books, and
books like them, taught me that even life, with more pain than one individual had
any right to, was still worth spending some time trying to get *through*—and, like
Billie's and Mezz's, with dignity and inventiveness.

Although I was learning to appreciate good writing, I had no command of the
language myself. I had the *need* to write well, but that was about all. Only the most
sensitive teacher—and there were two or three along the way—was able to detect
some talent and imagination in my efforts. Every time I gathered enough courage
to dream of writing seriously, the notion ended in frustration or, sometimes, despair.
Not only did I not have command of the language, I didn't have the *necessary*
distance on experience to have anything important to say about even the things I
knew something about.

I daydreamed about a solution to these problems: I could *learn* to write and I
could go out and *live it up* in order to have experience. But this solution would
take time. I was not willing to *wait* for time. In my sense of urgency, I didn't have
that much time.

Meanwhile, there were a few adults I ventured to show my efforts to. One
teacher told me I couldn't *possibly* have written the story I showed her. It was *too*
good—which meant that it was a hell of lot better than I had thought. But rather
than gaining more self-confidence, the experience became grounds for the loss of

respect for *her* intelligence. Among the other adults who saw my early efforts were my mother—who encouraged me as much as her understanding permitted—and a young college-educated man who was a friend of the family's. He told me I was pretty good.

I was growing up in Chicago, and my life therefore had a particular social shape. The realities I was discovering in books didn't—at first—seem to correspond to the reality around me. At the time, I didn't have enough distance to see the connections.

The fact is, the writerly disposition that was then evolving was *shaped* by my life in Chicago—in the classroom and on the playground—as well as it was being shaped during the times I spent alone, with books, and anywhere else, for that matter. Which is only one way of saying that a writer doesn't make most of his or her own decisions about personal vision or outlook.

Jean Paul Sartre, in *What Is Literature?*, makes the observation that Richard Wright's destiny as a writer was chosen *for* him by the circumstances of birth and social history. One can go even further and say that it's as difficult to draw the line between *where* a sensibility is influenced by the world around it and where it is asserting its own presence in that world, as it is to say whether or not essence precedes existence.

To put it *another* way, the educational process against which my *would-be* writerly disposition was taking formation was *political*. Political because I quickly had to learn how to survive—for example, on the playground. It was not easy since I had an instinctive dislike for violence. But the playground was a place where the *dramas* of life were acted out. Radiguet's book (and Jean Paul Rossi's *Awakening*, too) had—to some extent—dealt with the same territory. As a microcosm of life, it was no doubt one of the *first* social locations in which I was forced to observe some of the ways people relate—or don't relate—to each other. Among a *number* of things, I learned how to survive the *pecking-order* rituals—with my wits rather than my fists. This was an area where books and art could not save me. But later on, I was going to see how what I *had* to learn—in self-defense—carried over to the creative effort.

The classroom, too, was *not* a place where one wanted to let one's guard down for too long. To be liked and singled out by a teacher often meant getting smashed in the mouth or kicked in the stomach on the playground. If one demonstrated intelligence in school, one could almost certainly expect to hear about it later, on the way home. It was simply not cool for *boys* to be smart in class. A smart boy was a sissy and deserved to get his butt kicked.

I had to be very quiet about my plans to become a writer. I couldn't talk with friends about what I read. I mean—why wasn't I out playing basketball?

All of this, in terms of education—or plans to become a writer—meant that, if you wanted to learn anything (or try to write something, for example), you had to do it without *flaunting* what you were doing. Naturally, some smart but less willful kids gave in, in the interest of survival; they learned how to *fail* in order to live in the safety zone of the majority. And for those of us who didn't *want* to give in, it was hard to keep how well we were doing a *secret* because the teacher would tell the class who got the best grades.

I was also facing another crisis. If, for example, I wanted to write, eventually I had to face an even larger problem—publication. I thought that, if I were ever lucky enough to get anything published (say, in a school magazine or newspaper), that would be a success I would have to keep quiet about among most of my friends and certainly around those out to put me in my place. And God forbid that my first published work should be a poem. Only sissies wrote poetry.

But I couldn't go on like that. I remember once breaking down and saying to hell with it. I walked around the school building with a notebook, writing down *everything* I saw, trying to translate the life around me, minute by minute, into words. I must have filled twenty pages with very boring descriptions. A girl I liked, but didn't have the nerve to talk to, saw me. She thought I was doing homework. When I told her what I was up to, she gave me this strange, big-eyed look, then quickly disappeared—*forever*—from my life.

I now realize that I must have been a *difficult* student for teachers to understand. At times I was sort of smart, at other times I left a *lot* to be desired. One teacher thought I might be retarded, another called me a genius. Not knowing what else to do with me, the administrators—in frustration—appointed me art director of the whole school of 8,000 students, during my last year.

Why art director? Actually, as I implied, my first passion was for painted pictures rather than the realities I discovered in books. Before my first clear memories, I was drawing and painting, while the writing started at a time within memory. So, I think it is important (in the context of "how" and "why," where the writing is concerned) to try to understand what this visual experience has meant for me.

At about the age of twelve, I started taking private art lessons from a South Side painter, Gus Nall. I even won a few prizes. So, confidence in an ability to express myself *visually* came first. But what I learned from painting, I think, carried over into the writing from the beginning.

My first articulate passion was for the works of Vincent van Gogh. This passion started with a big show of his work the Art Institute of Chicago hung in the early fifties. There were about a hundred and fifty pieces.

I pushed my way through the crowded galleries—stunned every step of the way. I kept going back. I was not sophisticated enough to know how to articulate for myself what these things were doing to me, but I knew I was *profoundly* moved. So—on some level—I no doubt did sense the *power of the painterliness* of those pictures of winding country paths, working peasants, flower gardens, rooftops, the stillness of a summer day. They really got to me.

Something in me went out to the energy of Vincent's "Sunflowers," for example. I saw him as one who broke the rules and transcended. Where I came from, no socially well-behaved person, for example, ever went out and gathered *sunflowers* for a vase in the home. No self-respecting *grown man* spent ten years painting pictures he couldn't sell. On the South Side of Chicago everything of value had a price tag.

Vincent, then, was at least one important model for my rebellion. The world I grew up in told me that the only proper goal was to make money and get an education and become a productive member of society and go to church and have a family—pretty much in that order. But I had found my alternative models, and it was too late for my world to get its hooks in me. I wasn't planning to do anything less than the greatest thing I could think of. I wanted to be like van Gogh, like Richard Wright, like Jean Toomer, like Rimbaud, like Bud Powell.

In the meantime, I went home from the van Gogh exhibition and tried to create the same effects from the life around me: I drew my stepfather soaking his feet in a pan of water, my older sister braiding my younger sister's hair, the bleak view of rooftops from my bedroom window, my mother in bed sick, anything that struck me as compositionally viable. In this rather haphazard way, I was learning to *see*. I suspect there was a certain music and innocence in Vincent's lines and colors that gave me a foundation for my own attempts at representing—first, through drawing and painting, and very soon after, in poetry I was writing. The poems I first tried to write were strongly imagistic in the Symbolist tradition.

I made thousands of sketches of this sort of everyday thing. I was responding to the things of *my* world. And I had already lived in two or three different worlds: in a Southern city, Atlanta; in a rural country setting; and now in Chicago, an urban, brutal, stark setting. We moved a lot—so much so that my sense of place was always changing. Home was where we happened to be. Given this situation, I think the fact that Vincent felt like an alien in his own land (and was actually an alien in France, and that this sense of being estranged carried over emotionally into his work) found a strong correlating response in me.

If there were disadvantages in being out of step, there were just as many advantages. I was beginning to engage myself passionately in painting and writing, and this passion would carry me through a lot of difficulties and disappointments— simply because I *had* it. I saw many people with no passionate interest in *anything*. Too many of them perished for lack of a passionate dream long before I thought possible.

At fourteen, this passionate need to create (and apparently the need to *share* it, too) caused me to try to go public—despite the fact that I knew I was doing something eccentric. One of my uncles ran a printing shop. I gathered enough confidence in my poetry to pay him ten dollars to print fifty copies of a little booklet of my own poetry. The poems reflect the influence of Rimbaud, van Gogh, and Impressionism generally—even used French words I didn't understand.

Once I had the books in hand, I realized that I didn't know more than *three* people who might be interested in seeing a copy. I gave one to one of my English teachers. I gave my mother three copies. I gave my best poet friend a copy. I may have also given my art teacher, Mr. Fouche, a copy. And the rest of the edition was stored in a closet. They stayed there till, by chance, a year or two later, I discovered how bad the poems were and destroyed the remaining copies.

Shortly after the van Gogh exhibition, the Institute sponsored a large showing of the works of Paul Cézanne, whose work I knew a bit from the few pieces in the permanent collection. I went to the exhibition not so much because I was *attracted* to Cézanne but because it was *there*—and I felt that I *should* appreciate Cézanne. At fifteen that was not easy. And the reasons I found it difficult to appreciate Cézanne as much as I thought I should had to do with (I later learned) my inability to understand, at a gut level, *what* he was about, what his *intentions* were. Cézanne's figures looked stiff and ill-proportioned. His landscapes, like his still lifes, seemed made of stone or wood or metal. Everything in Cézanne was unbending, lifeless.

I looked at the apples and the oranges on the table and understood their *weight* and how important the *sense* of that weight was in understanding Cézanne's intentions. I wanted to say, yes, it's a great accomplishment. But why couldn't I *like* it? I was not yet sophisticated enough to realize that all great art—to the unsophisticated viewer—at first, appears *ugly*—even repulsive. And I had yet to discover Gertrude Stein in any serious way, to discover her attempts to do with words what Cézanne was doing with lines and color.

It took many years to acquire an appreciation for Cézanne—but doing so, in its way, was as important to my development as a writer as was my passion for van Gogh. But the appreciation started, in its troubled way, with that big show. When I finally saw the working out of the *sculpturing* of a created reality (to paraphrase James Joyce), I experienced a breakthrough. Cézanne appealed to my *rational* side. I began going to Cézanne for a knowledge of the inner, mechanical foundation of art, and for an example of a self-conscious exploration of composition. All of this effort slowly taught me how to *see* the significant aspects of writing and how they correspond to those in painting. Discovering *how* perspective corresponded to point of view, for example, was a real high point.

These two painters, van Gogh and Cézanne, were catalysts for me, but there were other painters important for similar reasons: Toulouse-Lautrec, Degas, Bonnard, Cassatt, Munch—for intensely scrutinized private and public moments—; Edward Hopper for his ability to invest a view of a house or the interior of a room with a profound sense of mortality; Matisse—for his play, his rhythm, his design. I was attracted by the intimacy of subject matter in their work.

I also had *very* strong responses to Gauguin. He excited and worried me at the same time. At first, I was suspicious of a European seeking *purity* among dark people. (And I placed D. H. Lawrence in the same category.) Later, I realized Gauguin's story was more *complex* than that (as was Lawrence's). But more important to me was the fact of Gauguin's work: paintings with flat, blunt areas of vivid colors. Their sumptuousness drew a profoundly romantic response in me. Not only did I try to paint *that way* for a period, I also thought I saw the possibility of creating simple, flat images with simple sentences or lines.

For a while I was especially attracted to painters who used paint thickly. Turner's seascapes were incredible. Up close they looked abstract. Utrillo's scenes of Paris, Rouault's bumpy people, Albert Ryder's horrible dreams, Kokoschka's profusion of layered effects—these rekindled feelings that had started with van Gogh. (Years later, I came to appreciate Beckman and Schiele for similar reasons.) To paint that way—expressively, and apparently fast—had a certain appeal. It was just a theory but worth playing with: In correlation, it might be possible to make words move with that kind of self-apparent urgency, that kind of reflexive brilliance. The expressionistic writers—Lawrence, Mansfield, Joyce, and others—had done it.

I kept moving from one fascination to another. Later, the *opposite* approach attracted me. The lightness of Picasso's touch was as remarkable as a pelican in flight. If I could make a painting or poem *move* like that—like the naturalness of walking or sleeping—I would be lucky.

I was easily seduced. I got lost in the dreams of Chagall, in the summer laziness of Monet, in the waves of Winslow Homer, in the blood and passion of Orozco, in the bright, simple designs of Rivera, in the fury of Jackson Pollock, in the struggle of de Kooning, in the selflessness of Vermeer, in the light and shadow of Rembrandt, in the plushness of Rubens, in the fantastic mystery of Bosch, in the power of Michelangelo and Tintoretto, in the incredible sensitivity and intelligence of Leonardo da Vinci, in the earthly dramas of Daumier and Millet. (Later on, when I discovered Afro-American art, I got equally caught up in the works of Jacob Lawrence, Archibald Motley, Henry Tanner, Edward Bannister, and others. I was troubled from the beginning at the absence of Afro-American painters, novelists, poets, generally, I might turn to as models. I was seventeen before—on my own—I discovered the *reason* they were absent: The system had hidden them. It was that simple. They had existed since the beginning but were, for well-known reasons, made officially nonexistent.)

Although this learning process was a slow and very long one, and I wasn't always conscious of even the things I successfully managed to transfer into my own painting and writing, I can now look back and realize that I must always have been more fascinated by technique—in painting and in writing—than I was by subject matter. The subject of a novel or a painting seemed irrelevant: a nude, a beach scene, a stand of trees, a story of an army officer and a seventeen-year-old girl in a foreign country, a lyrical view of a horrible accident. It didn't matter! What did matter was *how* the painter or storyteller or poet had seduced me into the story, into the picture, into the poem.

I guess I also felt the need to submerge myself in the intellectual excitement of an artistic community—but I couldn't find one. Just about every writer I'd ever heard of seemed to have had such nourishment: Hemingway in Paris among the other expatriates. . . . But I was not in touch with any sort of *exciting* literary or artistic life (outside of visits to the Institute) on the South Side. True, I had met a couple of writers—Willard Motley and Frank London Brown—and a few painters—Gus Nall, Archibald Motley, and a couple of others—; but I felt pretty isolated. Plus these people were a lot older and didn't seem to have much time to spare. So, I had clumsily started my own little magazine—a thing called *Coercion Review*. It became my substitute for an artistic community and, as such, a means of connecting (across the country and even across the ocean) with a larger, cultural world—especially with other writers and poets.

I published the works of writers I corresponded with, and they published mine; and in a way this became our way of *workshopping*—as my students say—our manuscripts. When we found something acceptable, it meant—or so we thought—that the particular piece had succeeded. We were wrong more often than not. It was an expensive way to learn what *not* to publish (and how to live with what couldn't be unpublished).

Seeing my work in print increased my awareness of the many problems I still faced in my writing at, say, the age of eighteen. I wrote to William Carlos Williams for help. I wrote to Langston Hughes. They were generous. (In fact, Williams not only criticized the poetry but told me of his feelings of despair as a poet.)

Rushing into print was teaching me that I not only needed distance on approach (the selection of point of view, for example) and subject matter *before* starting a work, but I needed also to slow down, to let a manuscript wait, to see if it could stand up under my own developing ability to edit during future readings, when my head would be clear of manuscript birth fumes. As a result, my awareness of what I was doing—of its aesthetic value—increased. I became more selective about what I sent out.

During all this time, I was also listening to music. Critics of Afro-American writing often find reason to compare black writing to black music. Each of my novels, at one time or another, has been compared to either Blues songs or jazz compositions. I've never doubted that critics had a right to do this. But what was *I* to make of the fact that I had *also* grown up with Tin Pan Alley, Bluegrass, and European classical music? I loved Chopin and Beethoven.

Something was wrong. It seemed to me that Jack Kerouac, for example, had gotten as many jazz motifs into his work as had, say, James Baldwin. At a certain point, when I noticed that critics were beginning to see rhythms of music as a basis for my lines or sentences—to say nothing of content—I backed up and took a closer look. I had to argue—at least with myself—that *all* of the music I'd loved while growing up found its aesthetic way into my writing—or *none* of it did.

True, I had been overwhelmingly caught up in the Be-bop music of Bud Powell when I was a kid—I loved "Un Poco Loco," thought it was the most inventive piece of music I had ever heard, loved all of his original compositions ("Hallucinations," "I Remember Clifford," "Oblivion," "Glass Enclosure," and on and on—and as I said before, I swore by the example of his devotion to his art).

But I soon moved on out, in a natural way, from Powell into an appreciation of the progressive music of other innovators—such as Thelonius Monk, Lester Young, Sonny Stitt, John Coltrane, Clifford Brown, Miles Davis, Dizzy Gillespie, Charlie Parker, Dexter Gordon, and Ornette Coleman—and, at the same time, I was discovering Jimmy Rushing, Bessie Smith, Billie Holiday, Joe Turner, Dinah Washington—singers of my father's generation and before.

My feeling, on this score, is that Afro-American music generally (along with other types of music I grew up hearing) had a pervasive cultural importance for me. I think I need to take this assumption into consideration in trying to trace in myself the shape of what I hope has become some sort of sensitivity not only to music but also to poetry, fiction, painting, and the other arts—film, photography, dance.

I've already mentioned the importance of other disciplines—anthropology, history, philosophy, psychology, sociology—in an attempt to lay some sort of intellectual foundation from which to write. Without going through the long, hopelessly confusing tangle of my own confusion and profoundly troubled questing, I think I can sum up what I came away with (as it relates to themes I chose or the themes that *chose me*) in pretty simple terms.

I remember my excitement when I began to understand cultural patterns. Understanding the nature of kinship—family, clan, tribe—gave me insight into relationships in the context of my own family, community, country. I was also fascinated to discover, while reading about tribal people, something called a caste system. I immediately realized that I had grown up in communities, both in the South and the North, where one kind of caste system or another was practiced. For one to be *extremely* dark or *extremely* light often meant that one was penalized by the community, for example.

Totem practices also fascinated me because I was able to turn from the books and see examples in everyday life: There were people who wore good-luck charms and fetishes such as rabbits' feet on keychains. I became aware, in deeper ways, of the significance of ritual and ceremony—and how to recognize examples when I saw them. It was a breakthrough for me to begin to understand *how* cultures—my own included—rationalized their own behavior.

The formation of myths—stories designed to explain why things were as they were—was of deep interest to me. Myths, I discovered, governed the behavior and customs I saw every day—customs concerning matters of birth, death, parents, grandparents, marriage, grief, luck, dances, husband-and-wife relationships, siblings, revenge, joking, adopting, sexual relations, murder, fights, food, toilet training, game playing. You name it.

Reading Freud (and other specialists of the mind) I thought would help me understand better how to make characters more convincing. At the same time I hoped to get a better insight into myself—which in the long run would also improve my writing. I read Freud's little study of Leonardo da Vinci. I was interested also in gaining a better understanding of the nature of creativity itself.

But even more than that, I was interested in the religious experience psychologists wrote about. I consciously sought ways to understand religious frenzy and faith in rational terms. I was beginning to think how, as too much nationalism tends to lead to fascism, too much blind religion could be bad for one's mental health. To me, the human mind and the human heart began to look like very, very dangerously nebulous things. But at the same time, I kept on trying to accept the world and its institutions at face value, to understand them on their own terms. After all, who was I to come along and seriously question *everything*? The degree to which I *did* question was more from innocence than from arrogance.

I was actually optimistic because I thought *Knowledge* might lead me somewhere refreshing, might relieve the burden of ignorance. If I could only understand schizophrenia or hysteria, mass brainwashing and charisma, paganism, asceticism, brotherly love . . . ? Why did some individuals feel called to preach and others feel overwhelmed with galloping demons? What was the function of dreaming? I skimmed the Kinsey reports and considered monastic life. I read Alan Watts and was a Buddhist for exactly one week.

I liked the gentle way Reich criticized Freud and, in the process, chiseled out his own psychoanalytical principles. If I ever thought psychoanalysis could help me personally, I was not mad enough to think we could afford it. I did notice, though, how writers of fiction and poets too, from around the turn of the century on, were using the principles of psychoanalysis as a tool for exploring behavior in fiction and poetry. So I gave it a shot. But the real challenge, I soon learned, was to find a way to absorb some of this stuff and at the same time to keep the *evidence* of it out of my own writing.

Yet I kept hoping for some better—more suitable—approach to human experience. If a better one existed, I had no idea. But there wasn't much to hold on to in psychoanalysis or psychology, and even less in sociology—where I soon discovered that statistics could be made to prove anything the researcher wanted to prove. If the *very presence* of the researcher were itself a contamination, what hope was there for this thing everybody called objectivity?

While I was able to make these connections between theory and reality, I was still seeking answers to questions I had asked since the beginning—*Who and what am I?* Questions we discover later in life are not so important. Everywhere I turned—to philosophy, to psychology—I was turned back upon myself and left with *more* questions than I had had at the start.

Growing up in America when I did, while aiming to be a writer, was a disturbing experience. (Every generation is sure it is more disturbed than the previous one and less lucky than the forthcoming one.) This troublesome feeling was real, though; it wasn't just growing pains. There was something else, and I knew it. And I finally found part of the explanation. My *sense* of myself was hampered by my country's sense of *itself*. My country held an idealistic image of itself that was, in many aspects of its life, vastly different from its actual, unvarnished self. Examples: There was severe poverty, ignorance, disease, corruption, racism, sexism, and there was war—*all* too often undeclared.

But I, as a writer, could not afford the luxury of a vision of my own experience as sentimental as the one suggested by my country (of itself, of me). As I grew up, I was trying to learn *how* to *see* through the *superficial* and to touch, in my writing, the essence of experience—in all of its possible wonderment, agony, or glory.

Despite the impossibility of complete success, I continue.

I want to be as forthright as possible with these afterthoughts because I know that afterthoughts can never *truly* recapture the moments they try to touch back upon. Each moment, it seems to me, in which a thought occurs has more to do with *that moment itself* than with anything in the past. This, to my way of thinking, turns out to be more positive than negative, because it supports the *continuous* nature of life—and that of *art*, too. The creative memory, given expression, is no enemy of the past, nor does its self-focus diminish its authority.

ON BECOMING
AN AMERICAN WRITER

JAMES ALAN MCPHERSON is a professor of English at the University of Iowa. He has won the Pulitzer Prize and Guggenheim and MacArthur fellowships. His books include *Elbow Room* (1977). "On Becoming an American Writer" was published in the *Atlantic Monthly* in December 1978.

In 1974, during the last months of the Nixon Administration, I lived in San Francisco, California. My public reason for leaving the East and going there was that my wife had been admitted to the San Francisco Medical Center School of Nursing, but my private reason for going was that San Francisco would be a very good place for working and for walking. Actually, during that time San Francisco was not that pleasant a place. We lived in a section of the city called the Sunset District, but it rained almost every day. During the late spring Patricia Hearst helped to rob a bank a few blocks from our apartment, a psychopath called "the Zebra Killer" was terrorizing the city, and the mayor seemed about to declare martial law. Periodically the FBI would come to my apartment with pictures of the suspected bank robbers. Agents came several times, until it began to dawn on me that they had become slightly interested in why, of all the people in a working-class neighborhood, I alone sat at home every day. They never asked any questions on this point, and I never volunteered that I was trying to keep my sanity by working very hard on a book dealing with the relationship between folklore and technology in nineteenth-century America.

In the late fall of the same year a friend came out from the East to give a talk in Sacramento. I drove there to meet him, and then drove him back to San Francisco. This was an older black man, one whom I respect a great deal, but during our drive an argument developed between us. His major worry was the recession, but eventually his focus shifted to people in my age group and our failures. There were a great many of these, and he listed them point by point. He said, while we drove through a gloomy evening rain, "When the smoke clears and you start counting, I'll bet you won't find that many more black doctors, lawyers, accountants, engineers, dentists. . . ." The list went on. He remonstrated a bit more, and said, "White people are very generous. When they start a thing they usually finish it. But after all this chaos, imagine how mad and tired they must be. Back in the fifties, when this thing started, they must have known anything could happen. They must have said, 'Well, we'd better settle in and hold on tight. Here come the niggers.' " During the eighteen months I spent in San Francisco, this was the only personal encounter that really made me mad.

In recent years I have realized that my friend, whom I now respect even more, was speaking from the perspective of a tactician. He viewed the situation in strict bread-and-butter terms: a commitment had been made to redefine the meaning of democracy in this country, certain opportunities had been provided, and people like him were watching to see what would be made of those opportunities and the freedom they provided. From his point of view, it was simply a matter of fulfilling a contractual obligation: taking full advantage of the educational opportunities that had been offered to achieve middle-class status in one of the professions. But from my point of view, one that I never shared with him, it was not that simple. Perhaps it was because of the differences in our generations and experiences. Or perhaps it was because each new generation, of black people at least, has to redefine itself even while it attempts to grasp the new opportunities, explore the new freedom. I can speak for no one but myself, yet maybe in trying to preserve the uniqueness of my experience, as I tried to do in *Elbow Room*, I can begin to set the record straight for my friend, for myself, and for the sake of the record itself.

In 1954, when *Brown v. Board of Education* was decided, I was eleven years old. I lived in a lower-class black community in Savannah, Georgia, attended segregated public schools, and knew no white people socially. I can't remember thinking of this last fact as a disadvantage, but I do know that early on I was being conditioned to believe that I was not *supposed* to know any white people on social terms. In our town the children of the black middle class were expected to aspire to certain traditional occupations; the children of the poor were expected not to cause too much trouble.

There was in those days a very subtle, but real, social distinction based on gradations of color, and I can remember the additional strain under which darker-skinned poor people lived. But there was also a great deal of optimism, shared by all levels of the black community. Besides a certain reverence for the benign intentions of the federal government, there was a belief in the idea of progress, nourished, I think now, by the determination of older people not to pass on to the next generation too many stories about racial conflict, their own frustrations and failures. They censored a great deal. It was as if they had made basic and binding agreements with themselves, or with their ancestors, that for the consideration represented by their silence on certain points they expected to receive, from either Providence or a munificent federal government, some future service or remuneration, the form of which would be left to the beneficiaries of their silence. Lawyers would call this a contract with a condition precedent. And maybe because they did tell us less than they knew, many of us were less informed than we might have been. On the other hand, because of this same silence many of us remained free enough of the influence of negative stories to take chances, be ridiculous, perhaps even try to form our own positive stories out of whatever our own experiences provided. Though ours was a limited world, it was one rich in possibilities for the future.

If I had to account for my life from segregated Savannah to this place and point in time, I would probably have to say that the contract would be no bad metaphor. I am reminded of Sir Henry Maine's observation that the progress of society is from status to contract. Although he was writing about the development of English common law, the reverse of his generalization is most applicable to my situation: I am the beneficiary of a number of contracts, most of them between the federal government and the institutions of society intended to provide people like me with a certain status.

I recall that in 1960, for example, something called the National Defense Student Loan Program went into effect, and I found out that by my agreeing to repay a loan plus some little interest, the federal government would back my enrollment in a small Negro college in Georgia. When I was a freshman at that college, disagreement over a seniority clause between the Hotel Restaurant Employees and Bartenders Union and the Great Northern Railway Company, in St. Paul, Minnesota, caused management to begin recruiting temporary summer help. Before I was nineteen I was encouraged to move from a segregated Negro college in the South and through that very beautiful part of the country that lies between Chicago and the Pacific Northwest. That year—1962—the World's Fair was in Seattle, and it was a magnificently diverse panorama for a young man to see. Almost every nation on earth was represented in some way, and at the center of the fair was the Space Needle. The theme of the United States exhibit, as I recall, was drawn from Whitman's *Leaves of Grass*: "Conquering, holding, daring, venturing as we go the unknown ways."

When I returned to the South, in the midst of all the civil rights activity, I saw a poster advertising a creative-writing contest sponsored by *Reader's Digest* and the United Negro College Fund. To enter the contest I had to learn to write and type. The first story I wrote was lost (and very badly typed); but the second, written in 1965, although also badly typed, was awarded first prize by Edward Weeks and his staff at *The Atlantic Monthly*. That same year I was offered the opportunity to enter Harvard Law School. During my second year at law school, a third-year man named Dave Marston (who was in a contest with Attorney General Griffin Bell earlier this year) offered me, through a very conservative white fellow student from Texas, the opportunity to take over his old job as a janitor in one of the apartment buildings in Cambridge. There I had the solitude, and the encouragement, to begin writing seriously. Offering my services in that building was probably the best contract I ever made.

I have not recalled all the above to sing my own praises or to evoke the black

American version of the Horatio Alger myth. I have recited these facts as a way of indicating the haphazard nature of events during that ten-year period. I am the product of a contractual process. To put it simply, the 1960s were a crazy time. Opportunities seemed to materialize out of thin air; and if you were lucky, if you were in the right place at the right time, certain contractual benefits just naturally accrued. You were assured of a certain status; you could become a doctor, a lawyer, a dentist, an accountant, an engineer. Achieving these things was easy, if you applied yourself.

But a very hard price was extracted. It seems to me now, from the perspective provided by age and distance, that certain institutional forces, acting impersonally, threw together black peasants and white aristocrats, people who operated on the plane of the intellect and people who valued the perspective of the folk. There were people who were frightened, threatened, and felt inferior; there were light-skinned people who called themselves "black" and darker-skinned people who could remember when this term had been used negatively; there were idealists and opportunists, people who seemed to want to be exploited and people who delighted in exploiting them. Old identities were thrown off, of necessity, but there were not many new ones of a positive nature to be assumed. People from backgrounds like my own, those from the South, while content with the new opportunities, found themselves trying to make sense of the growing diversity of friendships, of their increasing familiarity with the various political areas of the country, of the obvious differences between their values and those of their parents. We *were* becoming doctors, lawyers, dentists, engineers; but at the same time our experiences forced us to begin thinking of ourselves in new and different ways. We never wanted to be "white," but we never wanted to be "black" either. And back during that period there was the feeling that we could be whatever we wanted. But, we discovered, unless we joined a group, subscribed to some ideology, accepted some provisional identity, there was no contractual process for defining and stabilizing what it was we wanted to be. We also found that this was an individual problem, and in order to confront it one had to go inside one's self.

Now I want to return to my personal experience, to one of the contracts that took me from segregated Savannah to the Seattle World's Fair. There were many things about my earliest experiences that I liked and wanted to preserve, despite the fact that these things took place in a context of segregation; and there were a great many things I liked about the vision of all those nations interacting at the World's Fair. But the two seemed to belong to separate realities, to represent two different world views. Similarly, there were some things I liked about many of the dining-car waiters with whom I worked, and some things I liked about people like Dave Marston whom I met in law school. Some of these people and their values were called "black" and some were called "white," and I learned very quickly that all of us tend to wall ourselves off from experiences different from our own by assigning to these terms greater significance than they should have. Moreover, I found that trying to maintain friendships with, say, a politically conservative white Texan, a liberal-to-radical classmate of Scottish-Italian background, my oldest black friends, and even members of my own family introduced psychological contradictions that became tense and painful as the political climate shifted. There were no contracts covering such friendships and such feelings, and in order to keep the friends and maintain the feelings I had to force myself to find a basis other than race on which such contradictory urgings could be synthesized. I discovered that I had to find, first of all, an identity as a writer, and then I had to express what I knew or felt in such a way that I could make something whole out of a necessarily fragmented experience.

While in San Francisco, I saw in the image of the nineteenth-century American locomotive a possible cultural symbol that could represent my folk origins and their values, as well as the values of all the people I had seen at the World's Fair. During that same time, unconsciously, I was also beginning to see that the American language, in its flexibility and variety of idioms, could at least approximate some of the contradictory feelings that had resulted from my experience. Once again, I could not find any contractual guarantee that this would be the most appropriate and rewarding way to hold myself, and my experience, together. I think now there are no such contracts.

I quoted earlier a generalization by Sir Henry Maine to the effect that human society is a matter of movement from status to contract. Actually, I have never read Sir Henry Maine. I lifted his statement from a book by a man named Henry Allen Moe—a great book called *The Power of Freedom*. In that book, in an essay entitled "The Future of Liberal Arts Education," Moe goes on to say that a next step, one that goes beyond contract, is now necessary, but that no one seems to know what that next step should be. Certain trends suggest that it may well be a reversion to status. But if this happens it will be a tragedy of major proportions, because most of the people in the world are waiting for some nation, some people, to provide the model for the next step. And somehow I felt, while writing the last stories in *Elbow Room*, that the condition precedent the old folks in my hometown wanted in exchange for their censoring was not just status of a conventional kind. I want to think that after having waited so long, after having seen so much, they must have at least expected some new stories that would no longer have to be censored to come out of our experience. I felt that if anything, the long experience of segregation could be looked on as a period of preparation for a next step. Those of us who are black and who have had to defend our humanity should be obliged to continue defending it, on higher and higher levels—not of power, which is a kind of tragic trap, but on higher levels of consciousness.

All of this is being said in retrospect, and I am quite aware that I am rationalizing many complex and contradictory feelings. Nevertheless, I do know that early on, during my second year of law school, I became conscious of a model of identity that might help me transcend, at least in my thinking, a provisional or racial identity. In a class in American constitutional law taught by Paul Freund, I began to play with the idea that the Fourteenth Amendment was not just a legislative instrument devised to give former slaves legal equality with other Americans. Looking at the slow but steady way in which the basic guarantees of the Bill of Rights had, through judicial interpretation, been incorporated into the clauses of that amendment, I began to see the outlines of a new identity.

You will recall that the first line of Section 1 of the Fourteenth Amendment makes an all-inclusive definition of citizenship: "All persons born or naturalized in the United States and subject to the jurisdiction thereof, are citizens of the United States. . . ." The rights guaranteed to such a citizen had themselves traveled from the provinces to the World's Fair: from the trial and error of early Anglo-Saxon folk rituals to the rights of freemen established by the Magna Carta, to their slow incorporation into early American colonial charters, and from these charters (especially George Mason's Virginia Declaration of Rights) into the U.S. Constitution as its first ten amendments. Indeed, these same rights had served as the basis for the Charter of the United Nations. I saw that through the protean uses made of the Fourteenth Amendment, in the gradual elaboration of basic rights to be protected by federal authority, an outline of something much more complex than "black" and "white" had been begun.

It was many years before I was to go to the Library of Congress and read the brief of the lawyer-novelist Albion W. Tourgée in the famous case *Plessy v. Ferguson*. Argued in 1896 before the United States Supreme Court, Tourgée's brief was the first meaningful attempt to breathe life into the amendment. I will quote here part of his brief, which is a very beautiful piece of literature:

> This provision of Section 1 of the Fourteenth Amendment *creates a new* citizenship of the United States embracing *new* rights, privileges and immunities, derivable in a *new* manner, controlled by *new* authority, having a *new* scope and extent, depending on national authority for its existence and looking to national power for its preservation.

Although Tourgée lost the argument before the Supreme Court, his model of citizenship—and it is not a racial one—is still the most radical idea to come out of American constitutional law. He provided the outline, the clothing, if you will, for a new level of status. What he was proposing in 1896, I think, was that each United States citizen would attempt to approximate the ideals of the nation, be on at least conversant terms with all its diversity, carry the mainstream of the culture inside himself. As an American, by trying to wear these clothes he would be a synthesis of high and low, black and white, city and country, provincial and universal. If he could live with these contradictions, he would be simply a representative American.

This was the model I was aiming for in my book of stories. It can be achieved with or without intermarriage, but it will cost a great many mistakes and a lot of pain. It is, finally, a product of culture and not of race. And achieving it will require that one be conscious of America's culture and the complexity of all its people. As I tried to point out, such a perspective would provide a minefield of delicious ironies. Why, for example, should black Americans raised in Southern culture *not* find that some of their responses are geared to country music? How else, except in terms of cultural diversity, am I to account for the white friend in Boston who taught me much of what I know about black American music? Or the white friend in Virginia who, besides developing a homegrown aesthetic he calls "crackertude," knows more about black American folklore than most black people? Or the possibility that many black people in Los Angeles have been just as much influenced by Hollywood's "star system" of the forties and fifties as they have been by society's response to the color of their skins? I wrote about people like these in *Elbow Room* because they interested me, and because they help support my belief that most of us are products of much more complex cultural influences than we suppose.

What I have said above will make little sense until certain contradictions in the nation's background are faced up to, until personal identities are allowed to partake of the complexity of the country's history as well as of its culture. Last year, a very imaginative black comedian named Richard Pryor appeared briefly on national television in his own show. He offended a great many people, and his show was canceled after only a few weeks. But I remember one episode that may emphasize my own group's confusion about its historical experience. This was a satiric takeoff on the popular television movie *Roots*, and Pryor played an African tribal historian who was selling trinkets and impromptu history to black American tourists. One tourist, a middle-class man, approached the tribal historian and said, "I want you to tell me who my great-great-granddaddy was." The African handed him a picture. The black American looked at it and said, "But that's a *white* man!" The tribal historian said, "That's right." Then the tourist said, "Well, I want you to tell me where I'm from." The historian looked hard at him and said, "You're from Cleveland, nigger." I think I was trying very hard in my book to say the same thing, but not just to black people.

Today I am not the lawyer my friend in San Francisco thought I should be, but this is the record I wanted to present to him that rainy evening back in 1974. It may illustrate why the terms of my acceptance of society's offer had to be modified. I am now a writer, a person who has to learn to live with contradictions, frustrations, and doubts. Still, I have another quote that sustains me, this one from a book called *The Tragic Sense of Life*, by a Spanish philosopher named Miguel de Unamuno. In a chapter called "Don Quixote Today," Unamuno asks, "How is it that among the words the English have borrowed from our language there is to be found this word *desperado*?" And he answers himself: "It is despair, and despair alone, that begets heroic hope, absurd hope, mad hope."

I believe that the United States is complex enough to induce that sort of despair that begets heroic hope. I believe that if one can experience its diversity, touch a variety of its people, laugh at its craziness, distill wisdom from its tragedies, and attempt to synthesize all this inside oneself without going crazy, one will have earned the right to call oneself "citizen of the United States," even though one is not quite a lawyer, doctor, engineer, or accountant. If nothing else, one will have learned a few new stories and, most important, one will have begun on that necessary movement from contract to the next step, from province to the World's Fair, from a hopeless person to a desperado. I wrote about my first uncertain steps in this direction in *Elbow Room* because I have benefited from all the contracts, I have exhausted all the contracts, and at present it is the only new direction I know.

PHILOSOPHY AND
BLACK FICTION

CHARLES JOHNSON was awarded the National Book
Award for fiction in 1990 for his novel *Middle Passage* and is also the
author of *Ox-Herding Tale* (1982), another well-received novel. He was a
writing student of John Gardner's, and received an M.A. in philosophy
from Southern Illinois University. Both of these connections are made
explicit in "Philosophy and Black Fiction," published in *Obsidian* in the
Spring–Summer 1980 issue, a rumination on the limitations and
potentialities of black fiction.

Concluding his 1953 study, *The Negro Novelist*, Carl Milton Hughes
complained that "the philosophical novel [depicting] some system of
thought as it affects the life of the Negro has yet to appear."[1] If ideas
alone—doctrines and theories—are the basic stuff of philosophical novels, then
recent Black fiction has clearly put Hughes's complaint to rest: James Baldwin
probed storefront Christianity in *Go Tell It on the Mountain*; in *The Outsider* and
"The Man Who Lived Underground," Richard Wright explored aspects of Euro-
pean existentialism, as did Cyrus Colter, brooding upon determinism in a distinctly
Sartrean novel called *The Hippodrome*; Ralph Ellison treated, among other things,
problems of perceptual experience and meaning in *Invisible Man*; and Ishmael
Reed, still scathing after all these years, continues to rummage through Egyptian
and vodoun [voodoo] mythology for a humanism that might speak significantly to
us in *The Last Days of Louisiana Red* and *Flight to Canada*.

But there is a deeper issue at the heart of Black philosophical fiction, a problem
that we should air frequently, because, for all our talk of "Telling it like it is," and
for all our fidelity to Black life, we often betray our experience by blinking too
quickly [at] the analytic dimension native to literary art. Especially now, during the
rather heated debate of novelist John Gardner's angry yet important essay called

"On Moral Fiction"—a manifesto that claims, and rightly so, that "fiction is a form of philosophical method, the writer's equivalent to the scientific process," but which mentions only five Black writers[2]—it is important to clarify the area where fiction and philosophy overlap, and develop a feeling for how race (better to say *raciality*, thereby clarifying race as a structure of all perception, like sexuality, spaciality, temporality) figures into how we give form, in literature and life, to our experience.

Clearly, the menagerie of Black caricatures and clichéd situations so popular today in Hollywood, so frequent in trashy fiction—the motor-mouthed dandy, two-faced preacher, hopheads, the spiritual African, ball-busting women, meek Christians, blind Caucasians, fiery Black social activists, all those frustrated, butchered lives—fail, fail utterly to express authentic ways of seeing (and let us assume that there *are*, can be, authentic Black ways of seeing). We wonder, What, Lord, are Black artists *doing*? Our *interpretation* of our experience, as Ishmael Reed has written in numerous articles, has become rigid, forced into formulae; it does not permit, as all philosophically (and aesthetically) genuine fiction must, an efflorescence of meaning or a clarification of perception. We have so stylized our sense of the Black world that gifted white writers can conjure the world and speech of Black maids, athletes, and revolutionaries with apparent fidelity: Black life, in fine, has become a frozen gesture, a one-dimensional style of being. How can we, then, salvage Black fiction from calcification? The answer is deceptively simple, yet often difficult to achieve, and serves therefore as an ideal against which we can measure ourselves. Realizing that my arguments are likely to anger and annoy, I will first proceed methodologically, at the risk of appearing obtuse, and leave my cranky opinions for last.

Philosophical Black fiction—art that interrogates experience—is, first and foremost, a mode of thought. It is the process of *interpretation*, or hermeneutics in the higher sense. One need not write *about* ideas, putting clothes on concepts as Wright did in *The Outsider*, or as Cyrus Colter did in *The Hippodrome* for a literary work to have philosophical integrity; in fact, that approach often poisons, if one is not careful, the slow process of discovery, which is the first goal of fiction. We have been at theoretical war too long over the problem of reconciling universality with the particulars of Black life (even claiming, madly, that there are no universals worth talking about) when a procedure exists for reconciling universality, or the dominant sense of experience, with Black life. I mean what the philosopher does when he applies the *epoche*, or so-called "phenomenological reduction" to experience. A full description of phenomenological techniques and strategies is not possible here, but I would like to sketch the aspects of the *epoche* that speak most significantly to the process of philosophically serious fiction.[3]

A *fresh* encounter with Black life requires: (1) All presuppositions, whatever we think we know about Black life, all our cherished beliefs in what *is* and how it appears must be suspended, shelved, "bracketed." Aspects of the Black world become, after the *epoche*, only the occasion for universal reflection. (2) With this "bracketing" accomplished, Black experience becomes a pure field of appearances with but two important poles: consciousness and the objects, others, to which it is related intentionally. We describe *how* these appear, and note that Black subjectivity (memory, desire, anticipation, will) stain them with a particular sense. (Here, the poetic act, perhaps even neologism—bending language like soft plastic—is necessary for describing without prejudice what has not been seen, or seen so deeply, before.) (3) Finally, we ask if this look at Black life—stripped in the first stage of all Black particulars, purified or irrealized such that it now stands before us as an instance of *all* experience (storefront Christianity, say, as the occasion for reflection on the universal theme of religion) of its type—exhibits traits that illuminate our theme. Surely, it must. Buried in the particulars of storefront Christianity—the *way* we approach the supernatural—the theme of religion shows a new face. How, then, does its specific occurrence in Black life *vary* our conception of religion?

Because all conception—philosophy—is grounded in perception, there is no reason, in principle, that we cannot work through the particulars of Black life from *within* and discover there not only phenomena worthy of philosophical treatment in fiction, but also—and here I'll make my wildest claim today—significant new perceptions. Universals are not static (as Robert Bone believes in *The Negro Novel in America*, nor empty as Stephen Henderson argues) but changing, historical, *evolving* and enriched by particularization; the lived Black world has always promised a fresh slant on structures and themes centuries old.

"The world in which we live," writes Ellison of B. P. Rinehart in *Invisible Man*, "was without boundaries. A fast seething, hot world of fluidity . . . ."[4] From the fibrous particulars of Black life a perception anchored *in* racial experience is bodied forth, and we come to understand somewhat how new seeing—revitalized vision—occurs in Black fiction. First, Ellison, through a *saying* that is *showing* (a new disclosure of the Real that brings it from concealedness, which phenomenologist Max Scheler has called *alethia*; a revealing based upon the writer's Black situation in the world) is "in-formed" by Black life and simultaneously *gives form* to it. Furthermore, his perception is *a* truth. This is so because art expressed the meaning of the Real *through* a (Black) subjectivity rooted in the specifics of race and class. These contingencies, these very particulars of Black life which seemed so at odds with universality make the universal utterance possible. But, as Blyden Jackson argues in "The Negro's Image of the Universe as Reflected in His Fiction," many Black fictional worlds are dominated by stasis, not fluidity. These expressions are also a truth, but not *the* truth, and at any given time, by a slight modulation of your perception (the subject-pole of our previous discussion), you can see Black life as *either* fluid *or* static (but not both at the same time because the world outruns our perceptual grasp). There is no single true image of the Black world; but neither is each image merely subjective. We can liken the Black world to a tree branching forth innumerable appendages in an endless explosion of meaning. The Black world *appears* in countless guises. For Richard Wright in *Lawd Today* and *American Hunger* South Side Chicago in the 1930s is a cesspool, but for Ronald Fair in "We Who Came After," his prologue to *We Can't Breathe*, Chicago is an almost pastoral setting for Black childhood. The point, which has been made elsewhere and more eloquently, is that our experience as Black men and women completely outstrips our perception—Black life is ambiguous, and a kaleidoscope of meanings rich, multi-sided, and what the authentic Black writer does is despoil meanings to pin down the freshest interpretation given to him. This is genuine fiction. It is also hermeneutic philosophy, in the sense that the writer is an archaeologist probing the

Real for veiled sense. Surely a man should cease writing and shut up when he can no longer peer into Black life and give birth to a new universal. But you are still thinking of universality as a static mold that violates Black life; this is a very dull notion.

What is dangerous, maybe even disastrous, for Black fiction as we approach the 1980s is a self-satisfied acceptance of what we've already seen, codified and institutionalized in the 1960s and 1970s. Fresh perception easily sours into formulae, into typicality, which is the end of thought. We've reached a point where to *be* Black (and, yes, we are talking about Black literature and Being here) is to exist within the easy categories of racial existence outlined by Stephen Henderson's *Understanding the New Black Poetry*, Eugene Redmond's *Drumvoices*, or the visceral but truncated vision of *Roots*; the sum and substance of our lives, to hear our writers tell it, is Black music, Creole dishes, dancing, sass, and certain African survivalisms. Accepting this interpretation (which, like all true perceptions, is partial, one-sided, and badly in need of completion) kills as surely as a knife thrust the evolution—expansion and efflorescence—of Black life.

In their probings, our younger Black novelists have turned in strangely similar Black worlds: cloned worlds. These writers differ in certain respects that are doubtlessly important to them, as they explain in their interviews, but seen from a philosophical distance they show a marked similarity in their ways of seeing. In *Corregidora* and *Eva's Man*, Gayl Jones finds, like Cyrus Colter in "Mary's Covert," Richard Wright, and Ernest Gaines in "Three Men," a Black world without freedom, grimy with sexual humiliation, shame, where human contact is a variation on Hegelian master-slave bondage, and escape is possible only through death and deeper levels of self-betrayal. Hal Bennett's books like *Lord of Dark Places*, as well as John A. Williams's *Mothersill and the Foxes*, offer us a sideshow of Black sexual gymnastics, as if Black being was predominantly venereal. Vern E. Smith's highly commercial *The Jones Men* gives us Lennie Jack, who sums up the sense of the contemporary Black world with the observation, "It's cold out there, brother." Perhaps only Ishmael Reed, Al Young in such gentle fictions as *Sitting Pretty*, and Toni Morrison in *Song of Solomon* are exceptions today. Reacting against the Black world-qua-sewer, they unearth worlds with a preestablished harmony, a range of humor, the fantastic, everyday experience, and grace. If there are dominant philosophical traits in Black fiction, however, they are the particular pain of the Black self in search of an *amonea deverticula*, its agonizings over the paradox of change in the Black world: stasis and flux. Like the Milesians, we seem baffled by motion and identity, and end, curiously like Parmenides, denying changes of state or knowledge for our characters. The sense of *Weltanschauung* in these Black worlds, as Washington poet Colleen McElroy once remarked, "is that everything fails."

Despite modulations in the lived worlds of these writers, and more I haven't mentioned, there is dangerously little variety of vision, interpretation, or thought. Neither is there completeness, or a full exhibition of multiple interpretations. Intellectual life, for example, is seldom portrayed, and Hughes's conclusion still seems sadly correct (our only exceptions to this unhappy judgment are Toomer, Wright, and Ellison, whose fictions are the fruit of a process where feeling and thought co-mingle to *change*, deepen our perception of the Lifeworld in general, and the Black world in particular).

To a degree, I get panicky, peer round, and wait for a kick in the pants when speaking of Black fiction and philosophy in the same breath. As a down-to-earth people, we are, like most Americans, suspicious of philosophy. We value, or so we say, feelings, emotions, actions. You know. Concrete things. Axe-handles. Tea cups. Objects. But even this flimsy dodge does not excuse us from developing serious philosophical fictions—interpretive art that deepens perceptual experience. Feelings are, after all, shamelessly analytic. We aim perceptually at something and, through the emotions of anger or love, cause it to *appear* before us as it could not otherwise. The emotions (and all subjective operations) doorway onto the world, end in knowledge, and therefore are instrumental as a mode for analyzing the appearance (being) of phenomena in Black life. Secondly, a fictional world is a coherent deformation of Black life (in itself silent as to its meaning) so it makes sense. The writer's shaping process—plotting, characterization, description, dialogue, what he includes *and* excludes—illuminates the Black world. "It seems to me," wrote Blyden, "that few if any literary universes are as impoverished as the universe of Black fiction. [Of greatest interest] . . . are the things that cannot be found there."[5] Isn't the Black world *also* a field where men interrogate morality? Don't we wonder about religion, political philosophy, the existence of others, the Good, meaning, duty, or thought itself? (Samuel R. Delany, it must be said, struggles with thought and language in such sci-fi fabulations as *Babel-17* and, although his ambition is delightful, it is the world of *Star Wars* aliens, not Black people, where the probing occurs.) No one much cares these days about the particulars of Black life only (this always borders on the exotic, voyeuristic, the sociological). We read the fictions of the racial Other because they disclose the world—a common world, finally—as it might appear if we could be over there in that body, behind those eyes that see a slant on things denied us by the accidents of birth.

I have argued that philosophical hermeneutics and the exploration of meaning are native to all literary production; that universality is embodied in the particulars of the Black world; and that the final concern of serious fiction is the liberation of perception. And I have also argued—without malice, for all our writers are dear to me and struggle against stupendous odds in a white-dominated marketplace—that we abdicate our responsibility as Black creators by embracing all too easy interpretations of our being-in-the-world. We "control" our images too rigidly and, consequently, stifle our fictions with worlds so ossified, so stamped with *sameness* they seem to be the product of a committee, not an individual consciousness grappling with meaning. Personally, I have nothing against *The Jeffersons*, Papa LaBas, Richard Pryor records, or Kunte Kinte; but the cold facts are that we have frozen our vision in figures that caricature, at best, the complexity of our lives and leave the real artistic chore of interpretation unfinished.

NOTES

1. Carl Milton Hughes, *The Negro Novelist* (New York: The Citadel Press, 1953), p. 251.

2. John Gardner, *On Moral Fiction* (New York: Basic Books, 1978). The writers mentioned, very briefly,

are Ralph Ellison, Amiri Baraka, Ed Bullins, Toni Morrison, and I, which indicates that the community of black literary artists should add its voice to this theoretical debate, if only for the sake of completeness.

3. Phenomenology is, or so its founder Edmund Husserl claimed, more than a "philosophy"—it is a method for examining experience without presuppositions. Important works for a complete discussion of this method are Husserl's *Cartesian Meditations* (Paris: Martinus Nijhoff, 1973); Ronald Bruzina's *Logo and Eidos* (Paris: Mouton, 1970); and Mikel Dufrenne's monumental work, *The Phenomenology of Aesthetic Experience*, trans. Edward S. Casey (Evanston: Northwestern University Press, 1973).

4. Ralph Ellison, *Invisible Man* (New York: Random House, Vintage Books, 1972), p. 487.

5. Blyden Jackson, "The Negro's Image of the Universe as Reflected in His Fiction," *Black Voices*, ed. Abraham Chapman (New York: New American Library, 1968), p. 631.

BLACK CRITIC

HAKI R. MADHUBUTI was known in the 1960s as the exciting and popular poet Don L. Lee. Madhubuti has in the last dozen years or so concentrated on prose works and on his publishing house, Third World Press, which is also the home of the Institute of Positive Education, an Afrocentric organization dedicated to the reorientation of the black educational experience. Madhubuti's essay "Black Critic" appeared in the anthology *Jump Bad: A New Chicago Anthology*, edited by Gwendolyn Brooks, which was published by Third World Press in 1971.

The best critics are creative writers, especially published writers who are confident of their worth—which as critics puts them above the common *hatchet men*; Gore Vidal calls them *literary gangsters*. The "frustrated writer" out to build a literary reputation at the expense of others. The competent critic is not a "frustrated writer," he is a writer who chooses criticism as an extension of his craft. He is also one who goes into criticism with the same honesty and fairness that should be a part of his other creative works.

The black critic is first a black man, who happens to write; just [like] the poet, he has the same, if not more, responsibility to his community to perform his function to the best of his ability. He understands the main dilemma of the black writer; "Is he a *writer* who happens to be *black* or is he a *black* man who happens to *write?*" The argument is not a new one. Arna Bontemps speaks of it in connection with some of the post–Harlem Renaissance poets: "But in those days a good many of the group went to the Dark Tower to weep because they felt an injustice in the critics' insistence upon calling them Negro poets instead of just poets. That attitude was particularly displeasing to Countee Cullen." This was the type of illusion that not only would plague the poets but was definitely felt in the other art forms that black people ventured into. As with Countee Cullen, another well-known poet of the post–Harlem Renaissance period, Robert Hayden, refused to acknowledge that he was a "Negro" or black poet. Bontemps relates it this way: "One gets the impression that Hayden is bothered by this Negro thing. He would like to be considered simply as a poet." Which is almost like *any* black man in the world saying to the worldrunners that he would like to be considered a man, not a black man. Nonsense! The mere fact that a request of that type is put forth denies the chance of one's being considered anything else. So the point is to stop asking those who can't grant the wish in the first place, and to deal positively with the situation (Addison Gayle calls it the *Black Situation*).

Claude McKay, whom Wallace Thurman has referred to as "the only Negro poet who ever wrote revolutionary or protest poetry," was able, like Gwendolyn Brooks, Frank Marshall Davis, Margaret Walker, Melvin B. Tolson, Langston Hughes and Sterling Brown, to deal with the dilemma so that it did not affect his work to the point of *color distortion*, i.e., being one thing and trying to write as another, what Fanon calls black skins, white masks.

We must understand that this will be the decade of the black critic. It will be his responsibility not only to define and clarify, but also to give meaningful direction and guidance to the young, oncoming writers. To perform that function the critic must, if possible, remain detached from his material so that he can fairly filter the music from the noise. So we reiterate that good criticism calls for detachment and fairness, not pseudo-objectivity.

Objectivity at its best is a myth and a very subtle game played on black people. We are a very *subjective* people. All people are. In the final analysis, all one can really try to be is *fair*. One immediately obliterates the whole concept of objectivity when he takes into account the different variables that helped shape our lives. How can one be "objective" about, say, good housing if he has never lived in such; or about hunger if one has been *truly* hungry. How can you be objective about black music if it has played an important part in *your* general survival; or about Christianity even though it was forced on you; or about the war if you don't have any power over foreign affairs; or about anything, for that matter, if it involves the human predicament. Objectivity, in matters of importance, such as in the arts, cannot truly exist; true art is as much a part of the culture as is the critic who judges it. So from the get-go the critic is at a disadvantage because he can't dissociate himself fully from that which he is to "objectively" criticize. Some black critics, however, having been schooled in academia, tried to criticize black literature from a different, conventional perspective—and failed. James T. Stewart relates the reason for such failure in this way: "His assumptions were based on white models and on a self-conscious 'objectivity.' This is the plight of the 'negro' man of letters, the intellectual who needs to demonstrate a so-called academic impartiality to the white establishment."

We must understand that white critics write for white people; they are *supposed* to; they owe their allegiance and livelihood to white people. The black critic is in a very precarious position at this time in history; we agree with Albert Murray (and that's unusual) when he said that "being black is not enough to make anybody an authority on U.S. negroes." Being black *is not enough*, but is, at this time, a necessary prerequisite.

It has become increasingly clear that one starts with the roots and then defines the type of tree. That is to say, *any* writer was first black, white, yellow or red before he became a writer. Like the tree, the *to-be-writer* acquired certain characteristics notable in his particular lineage, such as language, religion, diet, education, daily life-style. So up to a certain point the *to-be-writer* was just another black, white, yellow, or red manchild, right? This is universal: naturally development into manhood is partially predetermined—which is to say that because of the different cultural patterns of black, white, yellow, and red men, there exist normal differences and variety in each of the four mentioned; and each type will look at the world the way he/she has been taught to view it. The core of my argument is that I, as a black man/critic, cannot possibly accurately judge or assess, let's say, Chinese literature. And, if we look at the reasons why unemotionally, I'm sure you would agree:

> First I can't speak the Chinese language (which means I can't read the literature in the original); second, I never lived among the Chinese people—so I know very little about their daily life style; third, my only knowledge of Chinese religion comes from what I read—which puts me at the disadvantage of accepting someone else's interpretation, which is always dangerous; fourth, my knowledge of Chinese music is terribly limited; fifth, my knowledge of Chinese folklore and dance is negligible; and finally, I've never been to China, so would be unfamiliar with many of the references used in the literature.

Have I made myself clear? The critic is first and foremost a black man, red man, yellow man, or white man who writes. And as a critic, he must stem from the same roots that produced him. How else can his style and content presently be understood? Which brings us to whites who study from the outside looking in, maintaining that they can learn as much about the tree from distant observation as from intimacy, or that they can interpret by anatomically dissecting the organism (keep in mind that even in dissection one has to touch that which one dissects).

With a tree, they may be successful in some of their findings. But in dealing with humans, one has to almost become a part of the humans he wishes to understand. When looking from the outside, one almost has to use the tools of the anthropologist—has to live, sleep, eat, suffer, and laugh among the people about whom one is trying to gain some insight. No white critic has done this. Sure, Robert Bone may have had some in-depth conversations with Sterling Brown, but that doesn't give him the tools that are necessary to pass judgment on the entirety of black literature. William Styron may have let James Baldwin spend some time on his farm, but obviously knowing and listening to Baldwin, as perceptive as Baldwin is, doesn't give Styron the sensitivity necessary for recording the adventures of one of our greatest black heroes, Nat Turner. David Littlejohn may have taken a few courses in black literature and sat in on some of the black writers' conferences, but obviously for him all of that was a prerequisite for a bad, pretentious book that Hoyt Fuller rightly maintains should be avoided "like the plague." Edward Margolies lives in the heart of the literary capital; that's where he should stay, and leave the native sons alone. Irving Howe and Richard Gilman had best stay with Jewish and WASP literature respectively, and leave their natural opposites alone; their ignorance is showing in whiteface.

The argument intensifies as the "negro" apologists say the reason Bone, Styron, Littlejohn, Margolies and others tried to write about the black writer is that there were no *black critics* willing to do it. Well, we can look at that statement from two points of view. There have always been black critics, e.g., James Weldon Johnson, William Stanley Braithwaite, Benjamin Griffith Brawley, Sterling A. Brown, Alain Locke, and Nick Aaron Ford, just to mention a few of the earliest. The problem, however, was not that there weren't any competent black critics; the problem was getting into print. Some of our contemporary "black" critics found it not beneficial to make a life out of the study of black literature—still leaving out Africa, the West Indies, and many of the Asian countries. World literature to them meant, naturally, that which was white and western. But there's still time for them to come back; James A. Emanuel pulls their coats when he says that "the pages of *CLA Journal*, to select but one representative, Negro-managed scholarly publication, are regularly filled with excellent Negro commentary on the works of white authors. If more of such professionally trained Negro critics were to turn their energies to the explication of literature by authors of their race, the enrichment in the feeling and knowledge of both black and white readers would be imponderable."

The black critic—as a black man first and writer second—illustrates a profound understanding of his responsibility to himself and to his community. He is what he reflects or projects. If he moves throughout the world quoting the qualities of John Donne and F. Scott Fitzgerald, that's where he's at; if he marvels at the achievements of William Dean Howells and Francois Rabelais, that's probably where he wants to be, and to try to move him from that point may be an exercise in futility. The black critic like the black creative writer is a part of a people and should not isolate himself into some pseudo-literary wishing land. The black critic/writer must understand that writing is, after all is said and done, a *vocation* like that of a teacher, doctor, historian etc., and becomes a way of life only when established within a concept and identity compatible with the inner workings of the self. That is to say, some of us blacks may *think* we are white, but that concept comes under daily question and contradiction, and is forever inflicting pain on the inner self. We are black men who happen to write, not *writers* who happen to be black. If the latter were true, Richard Wright, Ted Joans, William Gardner Smith and Chester Himes would not have left this country; Ralph Ellison would have published another novel by now; Sam Greenlee wouldn't have had to go to England to get his book published; John A. Williams would be as secure and rich as Norman Mailer; *Black World* wouldn't exist; and Frank Yerby, after a long record of denials of his "negroness," wouldn't have published *Speak Now*.

What the black critic must bring to us is an extensive knowledge of world literature, along with a specialized awareness of his own literature. He must understand that a "mature literature has a history behind it," and that that which is being written today is largely indebted to the mature black literature that came before. Thus, if looked at from the proper perspective, the whole of black literature can provide reliable criteria for the new critic to use. The competent black critic will have a love for and an intimate experience with the literature on which he is passing judgment. This will give him a basic philosophy for such judgment. As Stephen Coburn Pepper puts it, "It follows that good criticism is criticism based on a good philosophy. For a good philosophy is simply the best disposition of all evidence available."

We agree with T. S. Eliot in "The Frontiers of Criticism" when he states that "Every generation must provide its own literary criticism, each generation brings to the contemplation of art its own categories of appreciation, makes its own demand upon art, and has its own uses for art." The poet/writer will take the language of others and of his own generation and extend and revitalize it. The poet/writer as critic is at his best when he uses his own poetic talents—for as a poet/writer he is uniquely capable of knowing and understanding the potential of other poet/writers. What the critic does in many cases is make people more aware of what they already feel but can't articulate. The black critic understands that today's poets have revitalized and enriched the language, and in doing so have opened up new avenues of communication among the world's people.

The black critic, like the black poet, must start giving some leadership, some direction. We agree with Darwin T. Turner when he states that "despite fifty years of criticism of Afro-American literature, criteria for the criticism have not been established. Consequently, some readers judge literature by Afro-Americans according to its moral value, a few for its aesthetic value, most by its social value, and too many according to their response to the personalities of the Black authors." This narrow-mindedness must end and substantial criteria must come into existence. We can see innovative movement by looking at the statement of purpose of *The Writers' Workshop* of the *Organization of Black American Culture* (OBAC) under the direction of Hoyt Fuller.

That purpose includes the following:

1. The encouragement of the highest quality of literary expression reflecting the black experience.
2. The establishment and definition of the standards by which that creative writing which reflects the black experience is to be judged and evaluated.
3. The encouragement of the growth and development of black critics who are fully qualified to judge and evaluate black literature on its own terms while at the same time cognizant of the traditional values and standards of western literature and fully able to articulate the essential differences between the two literatures.

We're sure that other writers in different parts of the states have traveled or are beginning to travel in similar directions.

We must pull in the brothers and sisters [who] are academically involved, people like Darwin T. Turner, James A. Emanuel, Addison Gayle, Jr., Richard Long, Catherine Hurst, Stephen Henderson, George Kent, Helen Johnson, Sarah Webster Fabio, W. Edward Farrison, Richard Barksdaie, and Dudley Randall. We must optimistically encourage the young to continue to see innovative change and standards; let them know that we hear them and are listening to them, because without Carolyn Rodgers, Mary Helen Washington, Johari Amini, David Llorens, Carolyn Gerald, Larry Neal, Toni Cade, Clayton Riley, and others, the controversy over criteria and a black aesthetic might not ever have existed.

Lastly, a word of caution to our new and established critics. You cannot be concerned continuously with the intellectual diplomacy such as that of the white critic who before placing his stamp of approval on some studies must first check indexes to see if his name is listed as a reference, thereby perpetuating a closed literary system dangerous for the benefit of black people. For rhetoric can be a dangerous communicative device if it is not correctly used, especially in the world of letters. Black critics who do not have a tradition of social rhetoric must now become masters of an alien language, that is, if black people are to survive. And survival is what we are about. Not individually, but as a people. To quote Addison Gayle, Jr., "The dedication must be to race"; you see, the wolves, ours and theirs, are waiting for us to fail. We have a surprise for them.

III

CULTURAL AND
POLITICAL ESSAYS

Probably the most diverse of any group of works in this book, these essays cover a multitude of views, from James Weldon Johnson on Haiti to Gordon Parks on the Nation of Islam (or, as they were called in the press, the Black Muslims), from the literary and cultural gossip columns of Gwendolyn Bennett and Countee Cullen in *Opportunity* magazine in the 1920s to A. Philip Randolph's theories of mass civil disobedience in the 1940s. Here is the richness of black intellectuality and literary style that defines what the possibility of the essay as a literary genre in the hands of blacks is really about.

THE DARK RACES
OF THE TWENTIETH CENTURY

PAULINE E. HOPKINS (1859–1930) was a novelist, playwright, short-story writer, editor, actress, and singer. Her most widely known work is *Contending Forces: A Romance Illustrative of Negro Life North and South* (1900). "The Dark Races of the Twentieth Century" is a series of four articles that appeared in *The Voice of the Negro* from February to June 1905. It is a panoramic look at the dark-skinned races of the world at a time when the imperialist aggressions of the white western world were particularly intense.

> Mislike me not for my complexion
> The shadowed livery of the burnished sun.
>
> —SHAKESPEARE, *Othello*

I. Oceanica: The dark-hued inhabitants of New Guinea, the Bismarck Archipelago, New Hebrides, Solomon Islands, Fiji Islands, Polynesia, Samoa, and Hawaii

The earnest plea of Portia's somber-hued lover for fair play at her hands despite his "shadowed livery," is but an apt illustration of the firmness with which color-prejudice had fixed itself upon the social life of those distant centuries. It had become in Shakespeare's time an important factor in social science, and has been steadily growing in its proportions to the present date. So important was the quality of color that we find the greatest of all English poets making place for this question in the greatest work of his hands. He had already written *Hamlet* and *Macbeth* and *Lear* was about to follow. There is no such group in the literature of any country or any age as the "four great tragedies"—*Hamlet*, *Macbeth*, *Othello* and *Lear*. And of the four great tragedies, many critics assign the foremost place to *Othello*. Wordsworth says: "The tragedy of *Othello*, Plato's records of the last scenes in the career of Socrates, and Izaak Walton's *Life of George Herbert*, are the most pathetic of human compositions." Born with a vision so keen as to pierce the veil swinging between the Present and the Future, Shakespeare left, in perhaps his greatest work, a silent protest against the unjustness of man to man.

So strong is the question of color that all information possible is sought for in reply, and every theory imaginable is advanced by men who should know better. What causes the color of the dark races of the globe? What is it and of what does it consist? Dr. Delaney in his eminent work on the Origin of Races answers the question explicitly and clearly. He says:

> All coloring matter which enters into the human system is pigment—*pigmentum*—that in the fair race is *red*, that in the tawney being *yellow*, the red being modified by elaboration according to the economy of the system of each particular race. In the Caucasian, it is in its most simple elementary constituent; in the Mongolian, in a more compound form. But that which gives complexion to the blackest African, is the *same red matter; concentrated rouge*, in its most intensified state.

The word of God as given to Paul should settle the question of color origin of the human species beyond a peradventure: "God hath made of one blood all the nations of men for to dwell on all the face of the earth." But the sons of Japheth are a stiff-necked people, prone to improve upon God's work, if possible, and so we have [at the] opening of the twentieth century "perils" yellow and black [borne] alone on an unreasoning insanity on the question of color.

Many causes have lately arisen to augment the desire of thinkers to know all possible of the origin and relationship of the dark-hued races, and the time is ripe for a popular study of the science of ethnology. The rise of new powers and the decline of old powers, the great expansion in the business world or the growth of commercialism, the remarkable development of the imperialistic fever among governments, has caused a searching of the obscure corners of the globe even among untutored savages for world markets and for world conquests. Nor is this new knowledge and insatiable curiosity of little value. It is all in accord with the plan of salvation from the beginning. At the dispersion of the Tower Builders of Babylon the confusion of tongues caused a separation; and so another change is already inaugurated which is compelling a reunion of the scattered members of the great human family. We may always be sure of one fact, "creation had a method." For the benefit of scientific opinion we again quote Dr. Delaney:

> The first son of Noah, Shem, was born with a high degree of complexion or color; the second son, Ham, with a higher degree or intensity of the same color, making a different complexion; and the third son, Japheth, with the least of the same color, which gives an entirely different complexion. The three brothers were all of the *same colour—rouge*—which being possessed in a different degree gave them different complexions.

> Ham was positive, Shem medium, and Japheth negative. And here it may be remarked as a curious fact, that in the order of these degrees of complexion

which indicated the ardor and temperament of the races they represented, so was the progress of civilization propagated and carried forward by them.

Physiology classifies the admixture of the races by a cross between the White and Black, as a Mulatto; between the Mulatto and White, a Quadroon; between a Quadroon and White, a Quintroon; between a Quintroon and White, a Sextaroon; between the Sextaroon and White, a Septaroon; between the Septaroon and White, an Octoroon. The same numerical classifications are given a like number of crosses between the offsprings of the Black and Mulatto, with a prefix of the adjective black; as a Black Quadroon, and so on to Octoroon. A cross between an American Indian and a White, is called a Mustee or Mestizo; and a cross between the Indian and Black, is called a Sambo or Zambo.

Now, what is here to be observed as an exact and with little variation, almost never-failing result, in this law of pro-creation between the African and Caucasian, or White and Black races is, that these crosses go on with a nicety of reducing and blending the complexion, till it attains its original standard to either pure white or pure black, on the side by which the cross is continued from the first. By this it is seen that each race is equally reproducing, absorbing and enduring, neither of which can be extinguished or destroyed, all admixtures running out into either of the original races, upon the side which preponderates. This is an important truth, worth the attention and serious consideration of the social scientist, philosopher, and statesman.

"And the Lord said, Behold the people is one, and they have all one language. So the Lord scattered them abroad from thence upon the face of all the earth." And this separation of the three brothers was the origin of races. Each brother headed and led his people with a language, and in all reasonable probability, a complexion similar to his own, each settling the then known three parts of the earth—Asia, Africa and Europe.

The inhabitants of Oceanica form a large proportion of the living dark races, and a curious fact becomes apparent in studying their characteristics: Miscegenation is supposed to destroy a sterling race but this is an *impossible theory*. As stated above, the sterling races when crossed, reproduce themselves in their original purity. The offspring of two sterling races becomes an abnormal or mixed race, and to this abnormal race the Malays and Papuans of Oceanica belong. They are, no doubt, composed of the three original races formed by an intermingling of Egypto-Ethiopian, Persian, Assyrian, Greco-Macedonian and Tartar conquerors who conquered the original natives. They will, no doubt, become extinct by the resolvent European and Mongolian races settling among them.

The region of Melanesia includes all the islands from New Guinea in the west to Fiji in the east, a region inhabited by the black Papuan race—hence the word *black* describes the people of New Guinea, the Bismarck Archipelago, the Solomon Islands, the New Hebrides and New Caledonia. These people all have frizzly hair. It is a race characteristic, and the whole head of hair has much the appearance of a mop.

The people of New Guinea have been known as Papuans for more than three hundred years. The race is mixed but is very different from its neighbors, the Malays. The average height of a New Guinea native is five feet eight inches. He is strongly built. The skull long, lower jaw prominent, nose large with broad nostrils, lips full, face oval. The dress of a native man is a breech-cloth of bark, while the women wear a fringed girdle of woven grass. Manners and customs vary in the island. Hereditary chiefs are unknown, and there is no recognized form of government, the people having unwritten rules of conduct.

Bismarck Archipelago lies to the east of New Guinea, and belongs to Germany. The inhabitants live in huts similar in shape to bee-hives, small and surrounded by palisades of bamboo. Unmarried men live in a community. Cannibalism is more or less general and polygamy is common. They have the remarkable custom of putting young girls of six or eight years in cages made of palm leaves, which they can never leave until their wedding day. Old women guard them.

The Solomon group comprises seven large islands which belong to Great Britain. Formerly the natives were so treacherous that Europeans had but little intercourse with them, but now traders come frequently and mission work is spreading rapidly.

The New Hebrides are a group of volcanic islands named by Captain Cook in 1774. They have an area of 5,000 square miles with a population of 70,000, governed by a commission of officers of the British and French warships in the Pacific. In the five Southern islands there are more than forty schools under the patronage of the Presbyterian Church.

South of this group lies the New Caledonia. The people are called Canakas by the French. They wear very little clothing and were cannibals when the French first colonized the island.

FIJI ISLANDS, POLYNESIANS, SAMOA, AND SANDWICH ISLANDS

The inhabitants of Fiji—a group of more than two hundred islands—are Papuans, properly speaking. They have greatly declined in numbers since white men brought them the vices of civilization. They are a fine race, some standing six feet in height. They were cannibals and still practice this horror at intervals. Like most primitive people, they have no fear of death. A missionary was once invited to attend the funeral of the mother of a young Fijian, and great was his surprise upon joining the funeral procession to see the old lady cheerfully walking to her grave. Favorite wives of chiefs cheerfully submit to be strangled at the death of the husband, they believing that in this way they secure happiness and honor after death.

Eastward from Fiji lies Polynesia. Polynesians are supposed to be one of the finest races in the world. One of their games resembles draughts, the same played ages ago by Egyptian Pharaohs and their wives. "Animism," universal animation, or the endowing of all things with a soul is their religion.

The Samoans are a handsome, well-built people, hospitable, courteous, honest and affectionate—a nation of gentlemen. Nominally, they are Christians, the London Missionary Society having over 200 native missionaries in these islands.

The annexation of the Sandwich Islands to the United States is a matter of history and brought the inhabitants prominently before the civilized world. The population is now about 40,000, although at the time of discovery by Captain Cook there were 300,000 inhabitants. The capital is Honolulu. The people have adopted the Christian religion and civilized customs. A melancholy interest is felt in these people because of their misfortunes and the prevalence of that dread disease leprosy among them.

From 1820 to 1860 the Congregationalists held this mission field in Hawaii, and now the Anglican Church has begun work there.

II. THE MALAY PENINSULA
BORNEO, JAVA, SUMATRA, AND THE PHILIPPINES

The Eastern Archipelago which extends westward and northwest from New Guinea, contains among its important islands the Timor group: the Moluccas, Celebes, Flores, the Sunda Islands, and Sumatra, Borneo and the Philippines. The Negritos are found in the Philippines; but the chief race of this vast archipelago is the Malay.

Most of the islands are mountainous, and many of them contain active volcanoes. The climate is very hot, but at an elevation of a few hundred feet, becomes healthful; and, by ascending still higher, we reach a delightful region of perpetual spring. No part of the world is richer in its vegetable productions than these islands. The minerals are also very valuable. All of our spices—cinnamon, cloves, nutmegs and pepper—are raised on these islands. Here also grow the bread-fruit tree, sago, the cocoa-nut palm, bananas and yams. Guttapercha grows in the forests of Borneo and of other islands in the archipelago. Rice is cultivated in most of the islands. Java exports great quantities of coffee and sugar. Borneo furnishes gold, diamonds and tin. From the Philippines we receive sugar, hemp and tobacco. Many of the animals are among the fiercest and largest upon the earth.

The Malays who inhabit this region are a branch of the great Mongolian or Yellow species of the divisions of mankind. They are described as of medium stature, three or four inches below the European height. Complexion light brown, square face with high cheek bones, black eyes and a short nose quite unlike that of the white man or Negro.

Socially they are divided into three distinct groups: the "Men of the Soil" or the aborigines, who inhabit Molucca and Sumatra in the accessible wooded highlands, and belong to the Negritos; the "Men of the Sea" or Sea Gypsies, who live by fishing and robbing; and the civilized class, known as "Malay Men," who possess a certain culture and religion. They constitute a section of the race which under the Hindus settled in Sumatra about the fourth century, after which came the Arabs, developing national life and culture and political states.

The chief characteristic of the Malay is his easy-going nature. Generally they are gentle and extremely civil in speech and courteous in manner, and very particular in all matters of etiquette; the upper classes behave with all the dignity of European gentlemen. However, they lack the frankness of Englishmen, being by nature suspicious. The dark side of the Malay character as given by many travelers is not reassuring. Gambling and cock fighting are the greatest amusements.

In the domestic circle we find that the position of woman is not very low, the

Moslem Malays treating their womankind much better than the heathen Malays do. One writer says: "The husbands never beat the wives; it is quite the other way." In truth, the woman is highly valued, and a man must pay a heavy price for a wife. These are interesting facts to the student of ethnology, for a hopeful future for a people can generally be determined by the development of its women along the lines of virtue and intelligence.

BORNEO

The island of Borneo is not thickly inhabited and is divided into four territories: North British Borneo and the Rajah of Sarawak in the northwest; between these lies the small State of the Sultan of Brunei; the remainder of the island belongs to the Dutch. The entire population may be roughly estimated at 2,000,000.

Numerous ruins of Hindu temples are scattered over the island, reminding one forcibly of the first immigrants to this country. But always predominating, we find the incisive Anglo-Saxon marching along triumphantly toward the sovereignty of the world. An account of the work of Rajah Brooke in Sarawak is interesting and instructive. Mr. Brooke went to Borneo in 1839, and found the country in a chronic state of insurrection. Two years afterward he was made rajah, or king. The personal courage exhibited by Mr. Brooke, and the firmness with which he put down the earlier conspiracies against his rule, won the better class of chiefs to his side. He administered the law with strict justice. A writer says: "The success of this policy was never better shown than during the Chinese insurrection, when having narrowly escaped with his life, his friends killed or wounded, his house burned and much of the town destroyed, the whole population rallied around the English rajah, driving out and almost exterminating the invaders, and triumphantly brought him back to rule over them. In what country shall we find rulers, alien in race, language and religion, yet so endeared to their subjects? It requires no peculiar legal or diplomatic or legislative doctrine, but chiefly patience and good feeling, and the absence of prejudice. The great thing is not to be in a hurry; to avoid over-legislation, law forms and legal subtleties; to aim first to make the people contented and happy in every way, even if that way should be quite opposite to European theories of how they ought to be happy. On such principles Sir James Brooke's success was founded. True, he spent a fortune instead of making one, but he left behind him a reputation for goodness, wisdom and honor which dignifies the name of Englishmen for generations to come." If our powerful American leaders might be brought to emulate the example of Sir James Brooke in dealing with the race question in the United States, how matters would be simplified, and peace take the place of suspicion and hatred. But greed and the desire for high place will eventually override all humane suggestions for the upbuilding of humanity, and we may expect to see the present state of things continue to the end.

SUMATRA

The population of Sumatra is about 3,500,000. These people are fairly civilized and cultivate the land. Many of the inhabitants have intermarried with the Arabs, consequently they are mostly Mohammedans and their language is written in Arabic. They are clever craftsmen and build good ships; every man is a soldier.

PHILIPPINE ISLANDS

This beautiful group of islands has been destined to bring America, or more properly speaking the United States, prominently before the civilized world in the character of the promoter of human progress. The population of these islands is about 10,000,000, divided among the following tribes: Tagalo, Ilocano, Visayan, Igorrote and Negrito. The Spaniards divided the inhabitants of the Philippines into three classes: Indus or Christians, Infeles or Pagans of the interior, and the Moros or Sulus. They are divided into many tribes speaking different dialects, so that on the island of Luzon we find as many as twenty dialects.

The Tagalo is the leading race and has had the advantages of education and culture. The Ilocano is, however, the hope of the "New Philippines" under the rule of the American Republic, and he will prove a blessing to his countrymen. The Visayan tribe inhabits the Visayas. The Mestizo and Macabebe are interesting. The latter, like the Negrito, is becoming extinct. One is struck with the strong resemblance to the Chinese in all the photographs of the natives. This is accounted for by the fact that the islands have been overrun with Chinese for centuries and they have taken native women as wives. The confusion of types continues and one may trace the Mexican, Peruvian, Japanese and Spaniard. No part of Australasia presents so great a confusion of races.

At the time of Magellan's discovery of these islands lying washed by the Pacific Ocean and the China Sea, the country was peopled by the tribes of Negritos, or descendants of African tribes. Wars and intermarriage have very nearly obliterated the traces of the original stock, and the remaining numbers live in the mountains and cultivate the land. Many interesting theories are offered as to the origin of Negroes in this archipelago. Some scientists say that he was driven from Africa, and others that he came from New Guinea. All we know is that he is there safely housed in the mountains. The Negritos are a most interesting people. Mr. Abraham Hale spent some time among the primitive race and has given much valuable information to the Anthropological Institute of Great Britain. He says that in those districts where the Negritos live to themselves, untouched by the Malays, they are simple-hearted, kind, always anxious to please and are very hospitable.

Professor Keene says of the Sakai, a tribe of Negritos: "Surrounded from time out of mind by Malay peoples, some semi-civilized, some nearly as wild as themselves, but all alike taking from them their land, these aborigines have developed defensive qualities unneeded by the more favored insular Negritos and are doomed to extinction before their time. They have never had a chance in the race of life."

We suffer yet a little space
   Until we pass away,
The relics of an ancient race
   That ne'er has had its day.

The cities of the archipelago are beautiful and picturesque; they all have their plazas and churches generally the centers of the respective cities.

Manila, the capital, is the metropolis and the principal port. It is situated on the east of Manila bay, twenty-nine miles from the China Sea, whose breezes make it very pleasant in the afternoon.

New Manila is the home of all commercial enterprise and holds the hotels and places of amusement. The streets are clean and the houses are surrounded by the most beautiful palms, thus presenting a most imposing spectacle to the visitor's eye. The city has improved greatly since its occupation by the Americans. Streets have been widened, driveways repaired and sanitary and water systems perfected.

In this study of the dark races actually living today upon the globe, the reader or student is deeply impressed with the infinite variety of mixture in these races. This very mingling of races proves the theory of "one blood." Indeed, the principle that the human species is *one* cannot be disputed, and all men that inhabit the earth are but varieties of this one species. Next to the curiosity aroused by these so-called "human leopards" comes wonder at the persistent efforts of scientists to separate the dark races endowed with European characteristics, from any possible connection with the Negro, or more properly speaking, African race.

The question is: Was man created in one center or in several centers of the earth? The consensus of opinion is with those scientists who claim one center of creation and a triple complexion in the family of Noah.

The presence of man in all sections is easily explained by migration, and there is nothing to show several distinct nuclei. Man started from one point alone, and by the power of adaptation he has finally covered the entire face of the habitable globe. Therefore we must conclude that the Negritos of the Philippines and the other dark races of Australasia are of the family of Ham.

Buffon supports the theory of three fundamental types of man—white, black and yellow. We believe this theory to be true.

All men, we then conclude, were once upon one plane; hunting and fishing, then herdsmen, and lastly husbandmen. Through these three stages in all countries mankind has passed of necessity before becoming civilized, and why not the Negro or Black?

Says Figuier, "Nations whom we find at the present day but little advanced in civilization, were once superior to other nations" we may point out. The Chinese were civilized long before the inhabitants of Europe, at the very time when the Celts and Aryans, clothed in the skins of wild beasts and tattooed, were living in the woods in the condition of hunters. The Babylonians were occupied with the study of astronomy, and were calculating the orbits of the stars two thousand years before Christ, for the astronomical registers brought by Alexander the Great from Babylon refer back to celestial observations extending over more than ten centuries. Egyptian civilization dates back to at least four thousand years before Christ, as is proved by the magnificent statue of Gheffrel, which belongs to that period, and which, as it is composed of granite, can only have been cut by the aid of iron and steel tools, in themselves indications of an advanced form of industry.

"This last consideration should make us feel modest. It shows that nations whom we now crush by our intellectual superiority were once far before us in the path of civilization."

Then why not allow that the theory of Ethiopia as the mother of science, art and literature is true? Surely we the descendants of Ham cannot be condemned and ridiculed for claiming that the ancient glory of Ethiopia was the beacon light of all intellectual advancement now enjoyed by mankind. History and the fragments found in buried cities, though meager, give us a strong claim upon the attention of the world.

III. THE YELLOW RACE
SIAM, CHINA, JAPAN, KOREA, THIBET

The Yellow race is also known as the Mongol race because of the family characteristics common to both. These characteristics are, high cheek-bones, a lozenge-shaped head, flat nose, flat face, narrow obliquely-set eyes, coarse, black hair, scanty beard and a greenish yellow complexion.

In many of the features which distinguish this race we notice the very objectionable ones supposed to distinguish the black race alone. We find the same flat nose that marks the Guinea Negro and the same peculiar shape of the head—dolichocephalous, elongated cranium from front to rear—which is supposed to be a characteristic also of the same Negro race. But this resemblance to the Negro does not end with the Yellow race, for North Germans of the Caucasian race have the same head development, and we are surprised to note that among the lower classes of the Irish peasantry the flat feet, bent, shapeless body, etc., are seen. Mr. Fred Douglass spoke of this striking likeness among Irishmen to the Negro upon his return from a visit to Ireland. We contend that the characteristics supposed to be peculiar to the Negro are common to all members of the human species under conditions which tend to leave undeveloped the faculties of the mind. From this state of degradation all classes of men may be raised by the cultivation of the intellectual or spiritual part of this body. There alone is the difference; it is the portion of the spirit in every being which raises up to the heights of civilization and eliminates the purely animal, for man is a spirit shining within the body of an animal.

SIAM

The kingdom of Siam embraces part of the Indo-Chinese and part of the Malay peninsular. The delta of the Me Nam river is the natural and economic centre of Siam which is flooded every year between June and November. The population of Siam has never been known, but nine millions is a probable fair estimate. France has taken about 80,000 square miles of her territory.

Within the dominion of Siam we find three representatives of the world's races: the Caucasian, Mongolian and the Negro. Ethnologists are puzzled by the mixture of these races. But the most recent investigation seems to show that the modern

Indo-Chinese are Malay races sprung from an original tattooing race that occupied the hills of Thibet and drifted down into the plain.

The Siamese are well-formed, of olive complexion, darker than the Chinese but fairer and handsomer than the Malays. Their eyes are well-shaped, lips prominent, noses slightly flattened, a wide face across the cheek-bones, top of the forehead pointed and the chin short. They are very fond of the bath. The men shave the head leaving only a tuft of hair on the top. The preservation of this tuft is a matter of considerable social importance. On a child's head it is knotted and held together by a gold or silver pin. The shaping of the hair tuft of the children is an important event, being made a family festival to which friends and relatives are invited. Long nails are considered aristocratic. Opium smoking is indulged but is not on the increase. Marriage takes place at an early age. Marriage for love is rare, and a man may have as many wives as he likes. Education of the females is much neglected, although many girls are taught accomplishments for the amusement of the future husband and his guests. The Siamese are a musical people and possess many wind and string instruments, although they play entirely by ear.

Siam is an absolute monarchy without any limit to right and legislation. There is no army, but in time of war everybody is conscripted. Schools are few and poor but she is sending her boys to Europe and America to be educated. They have telegraph connections established and have begun to build up a good national trade. Siam promises to follow in the wake of Japan in adopting modern civilization, and for this reason, as well as for racial considerations, should be interesting to us.

Socially the government of Siam is a serfdom, and every subject is a slave to the king. The abolishment of slavery did away with caste, but under the corvee system which operates in this government, a free man is a slave still because he has no one to succor him, and finds himself better off under a master. Such conditions may prevail in the United States in a few years under the slavery of caste to which we now seem doomed unless the spirit of humanity is aroused in the nation in behalf of the blacks.

CHINA

The Chinese Empire includes China, Thibet, Korea, Mongolia, Manchuria Soongaria and Little Bokhara. The last four named divisions are called Chinese Tartary. Thibet and Chinese Tartary are thinly-settled regions.

Lassa, the capital of Thibet, is the residence of the Grand Lama, who is worshipped as the Supreme Being. His followers believe that he never dies, and that his soul passes into another body—that of some child selected by the priests. This country is of extraordinary interest to all civilized races. No white man living has ever seen Lassa and returned to tell the tale. Thibet is the last land of mystery remaining in the world and is guarded by the highest mountains in the center of which lies the valley which contains Lassa.

In Thibet a woman may have many husbands, but a man may have only one wife.

The general description given of the Mongolian race applies to the Chinese, amongst whom of all the yellow race, civilization was the first to develop itself in former centuries, but in recent years they have remained stationary, and their culture is now second rate compared with the advanced state of civilization reached by Europe and America. The government is a despotic monarchy, the emperor possessing unlimited power over all beneath him. The officers of the government are styled mandarins. Laws are severe, and for trifling offences the bamboo punishment is inflicted, while serious crimes meet with death.

The position of woman in China is a very humble one. Her birth is often regarded as unfortunate. The young girl lives shut up in her father's house. Her place is that of a servant. She is given in marriage without being consulted, and often in ignorance of her future husband's name.

Ancient writers speak of China as the people of the land of Seres. The present area of China is about 4,500,000 square miles, only Great Britain and Russia exceeding it in extent. The early history is obscure; their "Book of History" records events said to have occurred as far back as 2350 B.C., but gives no account of the origin of the race. A few learned Chinese say that the race now dominating China was not the original race which possessed the land.

The Chinaman is not endowed with much imagination, or it may be that centuries of rigorous training along material lines have practically so clogged his mental faculties that it is impossible for it now to act under normal conditions.

Education is widely spread in China. The education of the wealthy child commences from the hour of its birth. At six years of age he learns the elementary principles of arithmetic and geography; at seven he is separated from his mother and sisters and takes his meals alone; at eight he is taught the usages of politeness; at nine he is taught the astrological calendar; at ten he is sent to a public school; between thirteen and fifteen he is taught music; at fifteen come gymnastics, the use of arms and riding, at twenty he is often married.

The Chinese have practiced the typographical art from time immemorial; but as their alphabet is composed of more than forty thousand letters, they could not use movable type. There are in Pekin several daily papers. There is no country in the world where the walls are so thickly covered with bills and advertisements.

The great movement of the twentieth century is seen in the banding together of all white races as against the darker races, and in the Geary law which excludes Chinese from the United States. It excludes them all and provides a police at an expense of more than $200,000 a year to prevent their coming; yet a considerable number find an entrance each year.

JAPAN

The Empire of Japan embraces the islands of Nippon, Shikoke, Kiusiu and Yezo besides some of smaller size. The country is aptly described as an empire of islands.

Several different races are blended in the Japanese type of today and this is explained by the geographical situation of the country: it is connected with the Malay group by a chain of islands and by a narrow strait with the Peninsula of Korea and the mainland of Asia. It is also connected with Kamchatka. The Japanese may be considered skilful and daring navigators, and in this way have blended their race with other races.

Political power is divided between an hereditary and despotic governor, the Taicoon, and a spiritual chief, the Mikado. The creed of Buddhism, that of the Kamis, and the doctrines of Confucius equally divide the religious tendencies of the Japanese.

The worship of Buddha and Confucius is carried on in the same manner in China and Japan. The pagodas are similar, the ministers are the same bonzes with shaven heads and long gray robes. The buildings and junks of both nations are identical. Their food is the same—a diet of vegetables, principally rice and fish, washed down by plenty of tea and spirits. Coolies carry their loads in the same way in each country. Japanese women wear their hair in the same style as the Chinese women do, but the resemblance stops there. The Japanese are a warlike, and feudal nation as they have proved in their present war with Russia, surprising the entire world by their endurance and prowess, and they would be indignant at being confounded with the servile and crafty inhabitants of the Celestial Empire, who despise war, and whose sole aim is commerce.

Japanese have but one wife; polygamy is sometimes practiced in China.

Since the war between Russia and Japan began, there has been great talk of the "yellow" peril. As against this gossip, Prime-Minister, Count Katsura, has made a remarkable statement of Japan's motives: "The struggle is in the interest of justice and humanity, and of the commerce and civilization of the world. Should Japan ever become the leader of the Orient, her influence will be exercised to turn her neighbors' feet into the path she has herself irrevocably chosen—the path of close community with the Occident.

"In this struggle, standing as we do for principles, which we believe, are identical with those cherished by all enlightened nations, we look to the United States for that sympathy which we think our cause deserves; and especially do we turn to the people of the universities of America, which have given to so many of us a cordial welcome, and to whose teachers, alumni and students many of us are bound by ties of gratitude and friendship."

Although the Geary law bears on its face an injustice, yet to the student it but marks another mile-stone in the march of human progress.

Japanese prowess has astonished the world. A strike among Russian laborers is no less remarkable.

Cui bono? we ask.

Time will solve the riddle.

Says an eminent writer: "We wage a two-fold struggle: the struggle for bread and the struggle for freedom. We wrestle on the one hand with nature, seemingly niggard; and on the other, with principalities and powers, with laws and systems.

"At times the odds appear too great; those who are against us seem stronger than those who are for us. We think to surrender. We are tempted to accept the idler's philosophy and turn over to 'Evolution' the task to which we believed God had called us."

Cui bono? Centuries ago the most civilized nations fell a prey to barbarians who overturned dynasty after dynasty and completely changed the character of races and governments, thus placing scientists at fault in the twentieth century in their attempt to classify the living races of their time. Those barbarians were known to the dark races who ruled the world then, as the "white" peril. To those white barbarians the civilized world of today owes the supremacy of the white races.

Silently God demonstrates His power and the truth of His words: "Of one blood have I made all races of men to dwell upon the whole face of the earth."

No amount of scientific reasoning, no strenuous attempts of puerile rulers or leaders can hope to prevail against Omnipotence.

IV—AFRICA: ABYSSINIANS, EGYPTIANS, NILOTIC CLASS, BERBERS, KAFFIRS, HOTTENTOTS, AFRICANS OF NORTHERN TROPICS (INCLUDING NEGROES OF CENTRAL, EASTERN AND WESTERN AFRICA), NEGROES OF THE UNITED STATES

When we consider the fact that there are 1,300,000,000 people in the world and that only about 375,000,000 are white (or one-quarter of the globe's population), we are not surprised that the dominant race dreads a "dark peril," and sees in every movement made by the leading representatives of dark peoples, a menace to his future prosperous existence.

Most of the 1,000,000,000 of dark-skinned brethren are found in Africa, the vast southwestern peninsula of the Old World: No other division of land on the globe has such a compact and rounded outline. Access to the interior is rendered difficult because of the general absence of gulfs and large inlets. With the rapid advance which exploration has made in Africa in recent years, there has followed a great rivalry among European nations for colonies and protectorates; but while great wealth and boundless avenues for commerce have been opened up, civilization has been a mixed blessing to the natives, and today the eyes of Christendom are fastened upon the Congo Free State and its attendant acts of atrocity in the enforcement of slavery within its borders. The regeneration of Africa is upon us, but blood and tears flow in its train.

The characteristics of the people comprising African stock may be described as having heads rather long than broad, hair black and rarely straight, and the skin almost invariably black or very dark.

ABYSSINIANS

The Abyssinians, or Ethopians, comprise the people of the elevated plateau of Abyssinia. Under this general designation are comprehended many tribes—speaking different languages, but whose origin has long been a puzzle to historians. In stature they are rather below than above six feet, and are fairer than Negroes, with an oval face, a thin, finely-cut nose, good mouth, regular teeth, and frizzled hair. Abyssinia is interesting both in geographical and ethnological features. So striking is the resemblance between the modern Abyssinian and the Hebrews of old that we are compelled to look upon them as branches of one nation in spite of strong evidence to the contrary. As this theory is forbidden us, how are historians to account for the existence of this almost Israelitish people, and the preservation of a people so nearly approaching to the Hebrew in intertropical Africa? Very recently Abyssinia has become a place of great interest to Americans. A treaty has just been signed between the United States government and "Menelik II, by the Grace of God King of Kings of Ethiopia." It is a curious fact that the United States authorities maintain friendly relations with all independent black governments, although dealing severely with its own Negro population. To what end is this?

The United States Consul-General gives an interesting description of the military manœuvres of Menelik's troops. He says in an extended article: "The escorting troops then wheeled, and moved on in advance. Their numbers increased so rapidly as we approached the city that we were finally preceded by 3,000 men.

"Surrounding their chief, the warriors marched in most extraordinary confusion, sometimes performing evolutions, sometimes walking their horses, and sometimes galloping. It was a beautiful spectacle. No two costumes were alike. Saddles and bridles were decorated with gold and silver fringe. Bucklers of burnished gold were carried by soldiers, and from their shoulders flew mantles of leopard and lion skins, of silk, satin and velvet. Only the bright rifle-barrels marked the difference between these Ethiopians and the army of their forbears who followed the Queen of Sheba when she went down into Judea. We were spellbound by the moving mass of color, across which floated the weird music of a band of shawm players—playing as they had played when Jericho fell.

"At the farther end of the audience-hall sat the Emperor upon his divan or throne. On each side of the throne stood two young princes holding guns, and back of it and extending on both sides until they merged into the crowds waiting in the aisles, stood the ministers, judges, and officers of the Court. A subdued light softened the colors and blended them harmoniously."

THE EGYPTIANS, BERBERS, AND NILOTIC PEOPLE

Egypt, as we all know, was once the scene of a noble civilization. Egypt was in close proximity to Arabia, but the two people have met very different destinies. The Arabian worshipped one god; the Egyptians paid homage to foul deities. Their physical characteristics were also different; the Arabian had a restless visage, lean and active figure. The Egyptians had voluptuous forms, long, almond-shaped eyes, thick lips, large , smiling mouths; complexions dark and coppery—the whole aspect that of the genuine African character, of which the Negro is called an exaggerated type.

The Berbers comprise the native population of the Sahara desert [and] of the country north of it, and the original population of the Canary Islands. This section of African stock is near the Egyptian frontier in Fezzan Tunis, Algeria, and Morocco. Their language is allied to the Hebrew and Arabic, and hence is called sub-Semitic. The tribes bearing this name are very numerous. One very interesting fact in reference to the Berbers is that the extinct aboriginal inhabitants of the Canary Islands owed to them their origin. These were the "fortunate isles" of the early Roman poets, the "Hesperides," or "isles of the blest," of many a song-writer.

The Gallas are spread over eastern intertropical Africa and are a formidable and warlike people. In complexion they are brown, their hair worn in tresses over the shoulders. They are of the type which fill up the transition from the Armenian type and the Western and Central African Negro. The Gallas come under the Nilotic class who inhabit the Valley of the Nile.

The Nubians are a most interesting class also. They are of reddish-brown complexion, but of a shade not as deep as the East African Negro. The hair is frizzled and thick. Under the name "Nubian" are comprehended two sections of people alike in physical character, but speaking distinct languages. These are the Eastern Nubians and the Nubians of the Nile. The Eastern Nubians are a handsome people living near the Red Sea. The Nubians of the Nile extend from Egypt to the borders of Sennaar.

KAFFIRS

Under this name are comprehended all the South African races. Many tribes and even nationalities, all allied, however, by common customs and similar dialects, come under their name. The word "Kaffir" is considered by them a term of contempt; but as each division of the nation to which it applies has a separate name, their language supplies no substitute, unless the general terms Sechuano, Bantu or Zingian—all of which terms have been applied to the Kaffir race by different ethnologists—be received in its place. The Kaffirs are one of the widest spread of the African families. The Kaffirs are blackish-red in complexion and the hair crisp. The men are a handsome set, very tall with an intellectual cast of countenance. They show much aptitude for civilization, but their origin is a mystery to scientists. The Kaffirs are great warriors.

Hottentots are supposed to be the original inhabitants of South Africa, and were conquered by the Kaffirs. Between the two tribes there exists undying hatred. Bushmen and other allied tribes are found in South Africa. A number of African kingdoms have become famous among civilized peoples: The Kingdoms of Dahomey, Ashanti, etc.

Everyone is familiar with the story of the conquest of Dahomey by General Dodds. The Amazon warriors of this kingdom are women of prowess who have astounded and amazed the world. General Dodds was himself of Negro descent; he was accorded high honors for his victory upon his return to France.

The Ashantis have been the Spaniards of Southwest Africa, and they have persecuted other tribes assiduously. They are a famous tribe and of a warlike disposition.

Africa is such a wide ethnological region that were we to attempt to describe it even in the most abstract manner, we would need as many volumes at our command as we have had pages in this short sketch. When Africa is mentioned, people instantly associate the tribes as one vast mass of hideous ignorance. Such is far from the case. Some of the tribes are as fine specimens of manhood as one could wish to meet. In proof of the versatility of its people we have but to refer to the great advance of the Negroes of the United States—a heterogeneous mass composed of contributions from nearly all the tribes of the fatherland. In America a great problem has been worked out—the problem of the brotherhood of man, represented by the highest intellectual culture among Negroes, that can be shown by any other race in our cosmopolitan population. "God's image he, too, although made out of ebony." Says Blumenback: "I am acquainted with no single bodily characteristic which is at once peculiar to the Negro, and cannot be found to exist in many other and distant nations."

Le Maire says in his travels through Senegal and Gambia, that there are Negresses as beautiful as European ladies.

The Negro Freidig was well-known in Vienna as a masterly concertist on viol and violin. The Russian colonel of artillery, Hannibal, and the Negro Lislet of France, who on account of his superior meteorological observations and trigonometrical measurements was appointed correspondent for the *Paris Academy of Sciences*.

In an able article of the *Southern Quarterly Review*, 1855, we note these facts:

"In the whole range of the African continent we discover the same endless variations and gradational blending between the widest extremes, exhibited by all the other people of the earth. In color they vary through every shade from the European that sometimes appear in Egypt, and still exists in the neighborhood of Mount Atlas, to the polished ebony of the thoroughly dyed Negro. In physiognomy, they range between the elegant Grecian outline, and the exaggerated monstrosity of prognathous development. In texture of hair they exhibit every grade from the soft Asiatic and even auburn locks of some Egyptians, to the Auranian Berbers, through the long, plaited ringlets of the Morooran Kaffirs, and short, crisp curls of the Nubian, the thick and frizzled, wolf-like covering of the diffused Gallas and the still more woolly-headed growth of the Fellahs, and the thoroughly developed Negro tufts of the Guinea tribes. In every important part that marks varieties in man, the inhabitants of Africa vary with such indefinite blendings of one grade into another, between the Caucasian standard and the lowest Negro specimen, that it is impossible to draw a line of division at any point of the skull, and affirm that here one type ends and another begins."

SELF-DETERMINING HAITI

JAMES WELDON JOHNSON'S famous four-part essay, "Self-Determining Haiti," was published in *The Nation* in August and September 1920, some five years after the United States invasion of Haiti. Johnson's pieces were the most comprehensive and informative examination of U.S. occupation of the island.

I. THE AMERICAN OCCUPATION

To know the reasons for the present political situation in Haiti, to understand why the United States landed and has for five years maintained military forces in that country, why some three thousand Haitian men, women, and children have been shot down by American rifles and machine guns, it is necessary, among other things, to know that the National City Bank of New York is very much interested in Haiti. It is necessary to know that the National City Bank controls the National Bank of Haiti and is the depository for all of the Haitian national funds that are being collected by American officials, and that Mr. R. L. Farnham, vice-president of the National City Bank, is virtually the representative of the State Department in matters relating to the island republic. Most Americans have the opinion—if they have any opinion at all on the subject—that the United States was forced, on purely humane grounds, to intervene in the black republic because of the tragic coup d'etat which resulted in the overthrow and death of President Vilbrun Guillaume Sam and the execution of the political prisoners confined at Port-au-Prince, July 27–28, 1915; and that this government has been compelled to keep a military force in Haiti since that time to pacify the country and maintain order.

The fact is that for nearly a year before forcible intervention on the part of the United States this government was seeking to compel Haiti to submit to "peaceable" intervention. Toward the close of 1914 the United States notified the government of Haiti that it was disposed to recognize the newly elected president, Theodore Davilmar, as soon as a Haitian commission would sign at Washington "satisfactory protocols" relative to a convention with the United States on the model of the Dominican-American Convention. On December 15, 1914, the Haitian government, through its Secretary of Foreign Affairs, replied: "The Government of the Republic of Haiti would consider itself lax in its duty to the United States and to itself if it allowed the least doubt to exist of its irrevocable intention not to accept any control of the administration of Haitian affairs by a foreign Power." On December 19, the United States, through its legation at Port-au-Prince, replied, that in expressing its willingness to do in Haiti what had been done in Santo Domingo it "was actuated entirely by a disinterested desire to give assistance."

Two months later, the Theodore government was overthrown by a revolution and Vilbrun Guillaume was elected president. Immediately afterwards there arrived at Port-au-Prince an American commission from Washington—the Ford mission. The commissioners were received at the National Palace and attempted to take up the discussion of the convention that had been broken off in December, 1914. However, they lacked full powers and no negotiations were entered into. After several days, the Ford mission sailed for the United States. But soon after, in May, the United States sent to Haiti Mr. Paul Fuller, Jr., with the title Envoy Extraordinary, on a special mission to apprise the Haitian government that the Guillaume administration would not be recognized by the American government unless Haiti accepted and signed the project of a convention which he was authorized to present. After examining the project the Haitian government submitted to the American commission a counter-project, formulating the conditions under which it would be possible to accept the assistance of the United States. To this counter-project Mr. Fuller proposed certain modifications, some of which were accepted by the Haitian government. On June 5, 1915, Mr. Fuller acknowledged the receipt of the Haitian communication regarding these modifications, and sailed from Port-au-Prince.

Before any further discussion of the Fuller project between the two governments, political incidents in Haiti led rapidly to the events of July 27 and 28. On July 27 President Guillaume fled to the French Legation, and on the same day took place a massacre of the political prisoners in the prison at Port-au-Prince. On the morning of July 28 President Guillaume was forcibly taken from [the] French Legation and killed. On the afternoon of July 28 an American man-of-war dropped anchor in the harbor of Port-au-Prince and landed American forces. It should be borne in mind that through all of this the life of not a single American citizen had been taken or jeopardized.

The overthrow of Guillaume and its attending consequences did not constitute the cause of American intervention in Haiti, but merely furnished the awaited opportunity. Since July 28, 1915, American military forces have been in control of Haiti. These forces have been increased until there are now somewhere near three thousand Americans under arms in the republic. From the very first, the attitude of the Occupation has been that it was dealing with a conquered territory. Haitian forces were disarmed, military posts and barracks were occupied, and the National Palace was taken as headquarters for the Occupation. After selecting a new and acceptable president for the country, steps were at once taken to compel the Haitian government to sign a convention in which it virtually foreswore its independence. This was accomplished by September 16, 1915; and although the terms of this convention provided for the administration of the Haitian customs by American civilian officials, all the principal custom houses of the country had been seized by military force and placed in charge of American Marine officers before the end of August. The disposition of the funds collected in duties from the time of the military seizure of the custom houses to the time of their administration by civilian officials is still a question concerning which the established censorship in Haiti allows no discussion.

It is interesting to note the wide difference between the convention which Haiti was forced to sign and the convention which was in course of diplomatic negotiation at the moment of intervention. The Fuller convention asked little of Haiti and gave something, the Occupation convention demands everything of Haiti and gives nothing. The Occupation convention is really the same convention which the Haitian government peremptorily refused to discuss in December, 1914, except that in addition to American control of Haitian finances it also provides for American control of the Haitian military forces. The Fuller convention contained neither of these provisions. When the United States found itself in a position to take what it had not even dared to ask, it used brute force and took it. But even a convention which practically deprived Haiti of its independence was found not wholly adequate for the accomplishment of all that was contemplated. The Haitian constitution still offered some embarrassments, so it was decided that Haiti must have a new constitution. It was drafted and presented to the Haitian assembly for adoption. The assembly balked—chiefly at the article in the proposed document removing the constitutional disability which prevented aliens from owning land in Haiti. Haiti had long considered the denial of this right to aliens as her main bulwark against overwhelming economic exploitation; and it must be admitted that she had better reasons than the several states of the United States that have similar provisions.

The balking of the assembly resulted in its being dissolved by actual military force and the locking of doors of the Chamber. There has been no Haitian legislative body since. The desired constitution was submitted to a plebiscite by a decree of the President, although such a method of constitutional revision was clearly unconstitutional. Under the circumstances of the Occupation the plebiscite was, of course, almost unanimous for the desired change, and the new constitution was promulgated on June 18, 1918. Thus Haiti was given a new constitution by a flagrantly unconstitutional method. The new document contains several fundamental changes and includes a "Special Article" which declares:

All the acts of the Government of the United States during its military Occupation in Haiti are ratified and confirmed.

No Haitian shall be liable to civil or criminal prosecution for any act done by order of the Occupation or under its authority.

The acts of the courts martial of the Occupation, without, however, infringing on the right to pardon, shall not be subject to revision.

The acts of the Executive Power (the President) up to the promulgation of the present constitution are likewise ratified and confirmed.

The above is the chronological order of the principal steps by which the independence of a neighboring republic has been taken away, the people placed under foreign military domination from which they have no appeal, and exposed to foreign economic exploitation against which they are defenseless. All of this has been done in the name of the Government of the United States; however, without any act by Congress and without any knowledge of the American people.

The law by which Haiti is ruled today is martial law dispensed by Americans. There is a form of Haitian civil government, but it is entirely dominated by the military Occupation. President Dartiguenave, bitterly rebellious at heart as is every good Haitian, confessed to me the powerlessness of himself and his cabinet. He told me that the American authorities give no heed to recommendations made by him or his officers; that they would not even discuss matters about which the Haitian officials have superior knowledge. The provisions of both the old and the new constitutions are ignored in that there is no Haitian legislative body, and there has been none since the dissolution of the assembly in April, 1916. In its stead there is a Council of State composed of twenty-one members appointed by the president, which functions effectively only when carrying out the will of the Occupation. Indeed the Occupation often overrides the civil courts. A prisoner brought before the proper court, exonerated, and discharged, is, nevertheless, frequently held by the military. All government funds are collected by the Occupation and are dispensed at its will and pleasure. The greater part of these funds is expended for the maintenance of the military forces. There is the strictest censorship of the press. No Haitian newspaper is allowed to publish anything in criticism of the Occupation or the Haitian government. Each newspaper in Haiti received an order to that effect from the Occupation, *and the same order carried the injunction not to print the order.* Nothing that might reflect upon the Occupation administration in Haiti is allowed to reach the newspapers of the United States.

The Haitian people justly complain that not only is the convention inimical to the best interests of their country, but that the convention, such as it is, is not being carried out in accordance with the letter, nor in accordance with the spirit in which they were led to believe it would be carried out. Except one, all of the obligations in the convention which the United States undertakes in favor of Haiti are contained in the first article of that document, the other fourteen articles being made up substantially of obligations to the United States assumed by Haiti. But nowhere in those fourteen articles is there anything to indicate that Haiti would be subjected to military domination. In Article I the United States promises to "aid the Haitian government in the proper and efficient development of its agricultural, mineral, and commercial resources and in the establishment of the finances of Haiti on a firm and solid basis." And the whole convention and, especially, the protestations of the United States before the signing of the instrument can be construed only to mean that that aid would be extended through the supervision of civilian officials.

The one promise of the United States to Haiti not contained in the first article of the convention is that clause of Article XIV which says, "and, should the necessity occur, the United States will lend an efficient aid for the preservation of Haitian independence and the maintenance of a government adequate for the protection of life, property, and individual liberty." It is the extreme of irony that this clause which the Haitians had a right to interpret as a guarantee to them against foreign invasion should first of all be invoked against the Haitian people themselves, and offers the only peg on which any pretense to a right of military domination can be hung.

There are several distinct forces—financial, military, bureaucratic—at work in Haiti which, tending to aggravate the conditions they themselves have created, are largely self-perpetuating. The most sinister of these, the financial engulfment of Haiti by the National City Bank of New York, already alluded to, will be discussed in detail in a subsequent article. The military Occupation has made and continues to make military Occupation necessary. The justification given is that it is necessary for the pacification of the country. Pacification would never have been necessary had not American policies been filled with so many stupid and brutal blunders; and it will never be effective so long as "pacification" means merely the hunting of ragged Haitians in the hills with machine guns.

Then there is the force which the several hundred American civilian place-holders constitute. They have found in Haiti the veritable promised land of "jobs for deserving democrats" and naturally do not wish to see the present status discontinued. Most of these deserving democrats are Southerners. The head of the customs service of Haiti was a clerk of one of the parishes of Louisiana. Second in charge of the customs service of Haiti is a man who was Deputy Collector of Customs at Pascagoula, Mississippi (population, 3,379, 1910 Census). The Superintendent of Public Instruction was a school teacher in Louisiana—a State which has not good schools even for white children; the financial advisor, Mr. McIlhenny, is also from Louisiana.

Many of the Occupation officers are in the same category with the civilian place-holders. These men have taken their wives and families to Haiti. Those at Port-au-Prince live in beautiful villas. Families that could not keep a hired girl in the United States have a half-dozen servants. They ride in automobiles—not their own. Every American head of a department in Haiti has an automobile furnished at the expense of the Haitian Government, whereas members of the Haitian cabinet, who are theoretically above them, have no such convenience or luxury. While I was there, the President himself was obliged to borrow an automobile from the Occupation for a trip through the interior. The Louisiana school-teacher Superintendent of Instruction has an automobile furnished at government expense, whereas the Haitian Minister of Public Instruction, his supposed superior officer, has none. These automobiles seem to be chiefly employed in giving the women and children an airing each afternoon. It must be amusing, when it is not maddening to the Haitians, to see with what disdainful air these people look upon them as they ride by.

The platform adopted by the Democratic party at San Francisco said of the Wilson policy in Mexico:

> The Administration, remembering always that Mexico is an independent nation and that permanent stability in her government and her institutions could come only from the consent of her own people to a government of her own making, has been unwilling either to profit by the misfortunes of the people of Mexico or to enfeeble their future by imposing from the outside a rule upon their temporarily distracted councils.

Haiti has never been so distracted in its councils as Mexico. And even in its moments of greatest distraction it never slaughtered an American citizen, it never molested an American woman, it never injured a dollar's worth of American property. And yet, the Administration whose lofty purpose was proclaimed as above—with less justification than Austria's invasion of Serbia, or Germany's rape of Belgium, without warrant other than the doctrine that "might makes right," has conquered Haiti. It has done this through the very period when, in the words of its chief spokesman, our sons were laying down their lives overseas "for democracy, for the rights of those who submit to authority to have a voice in their own government, for the rights and liberties of small nations." By command of the author of "pitiless publicity" and originator of "open covenants openly arrived at," it has enforced by the bayonet a covenant whose secret has been well guarded by a rigid censorship from the American nation, and kept a people enslaved by the military tyranny which it was his avowed purpose to destroy throughout the world.

II. WHAT THE UNITED STATES HAS ACCOMPLISHED

When the truth about the conquest of Haiti—the slaughter of three thousand and practically unarmed Haitians, with the incidentally needless death of a score of American boys—begins to filter through the rigid Administration censorship to the American people, the apologists will become active. Their justification of what has been done will be grouped under two heads: one, the necessity, and two, the results. Under the first, much stress will be laid upon the "anarchy" which existed in Haiti, upon the backwardness of the Haitians and their absolute unfitness to govern themselves. The pretext which caused the intervention was taken up in the first article of this series. The characteristics, alleged and real, of the Haitian people will be taken up in a subsequent article. Now as to results: The apologists will attempt to show that material improvements in Haiti justify American intervention. Let us see what they are.

Diligent inquiry reveals just three: The building of the road from Port-au-Prince to Cape Haitien; the enforcement of certain sanitary regulations in the larger cities; and the improvement of the public hospital at Port-au-Prince. The enforcement of certain sanitary regulations is not so important as it may sound, for even under exclusive native rule, Haiti has been a remarkably healthy country and had never suffered from such epidemics as used to sweep Cuba and the Panama Canal region. The regulations, moreover, were of a purely minor character—the sort that might be issued by a board of health in any American city or town—and were in no wise fundamental, because there was no need. The same applies to the improvement of the hospital, long before the American Occupation, an effectively conducted institution but which, it is only fair to say, benefited considerably by the regulations and more up-to-date methods of American army surgeons—the best in the world. Neither of these accomplishments, however, creditable as they are, can well be put forward as a justification for military domination. The building of the great highway from Port-au-Prince to Cape Haitien is a monumental piece of work, but it is doubtful whether the object in building it was to supply the Haitians with a great highway or to construct a military road which would facilitate the transportation of troops and supplies from one end of the island to the other. And this represents the sum total of the constructive accomplishment after five years of American Occupation.

Now, the highway, while doubtless the most important achievement of the three, involved the most brutal of all the blunders of the Occupation. The work was in charge of an officer of Marines, who stands out even in that organization for his "treat 'em rough" methods. He discovered the obsolete Haitian *corvée* and decided to enforce it with the most modern Marine efficiency. The *corvée*, or road law, in Haiti provided that each citizen should work a certain number of days on the public roads to keep them in condition, or pay a certain sum of money. In the days when this law was in force the Haitian government never required the men to work the roads except in their respective communities, and the number of days was usually limited to three a year. But the Occupation seized men wherever it could find them, and no able-bodied Haitian was safe from such raids, which most closely resembled the African slave raids of past centuries. And slavery it was—though temporary. By day or by night, from the bosom of their families, from their little farms or while trudging peacefully on the country roads, Haitians were seized and forcibly taken to toil for months in far sections of the country. Those who protested or resisted were beaten into submission. At night, after long hours of unremitting labor under armed taskmasters, who swiftly discouraged any slackening of effort with boot or rifle butt, the victims were herded in compounds. Those attempting to escape were shot. Their terror-stricken families meanwhile were often in total ignorance of the fate of their husbands, fathers, brothers.

It is chiefly out of these methods that arose the need for "pacification." Many men of the rural districts became panic-stricken and fled to the hills and mountains. Others rebelled and did likewise, preferring death to slavery. These refugees largely make up the "caco" forces, to hunt down which has become the duty and the sport of American Marines, who were privileged to shoot a "caco" on sight. If anyone doubts that "caco" hunting is the sport of American Marines in Haiti, let him learn the facts about the death of Charlemagne. Charlemagne Peralte was a Haitian of education and culture and of great influence in his district. He was tried by an American court martial on the charge of aiding "cacos." He was sentenced, not to prison, however, but to five years of hard labor on the roads, and was forced to work in convict garb on the streets of Cape Haitien. He made his escape and put himself at the head of several hundred followers in a valiant though hopeless attempt to free

Haiti. The America of the Revolution, indeed the America of the Civil War, would have regarded Charlemagne not as a criminal but a patriot. He met his death not in open fight, not in an attempt at his capture, but through a dastard deed. While standing over his camp fire, he was shot in cold blood by an American Marine officer who stood concealed by the darkness, and who had reached the camp through bribery and trickery. This deed, which was nothing short of assassination, has been heralded as an example of American heroism. Of this deed, Harry Franck, writing in the June *Century* of "The Death of Charlemagne," says: "Indeed it is fit to rank with any of the stirring warrior tales with which history is seasoned from the days of the Greeks down to the recent world war." America should read "The Death of Charlemagne" which attempts to glorify a black smirch on American arms and tradition.

There is a reason why the methods employed in road building affected the Haitian country folk in a way in which it might not have affected the people of any other Latin-American country. Not since the independence of the country has there been any such thing as a peon in Haiti. The revolution by which Haiti gained her independence was not merely a political revolution, it was also a social revolution. Among the many radical changes wrought was that of cutting up the large slave estates into small parcels and allotting them among former slaves. And so it was that every Haitian in the rural districts lived on his own plot of land, a plot on which his family has lived for perhaps more than a hundred years. No matter how small or how large that plot is, and whether he raises much or little on it, it is his and he is an independent farmer.

The completed highway, moreover, continued to be a barb in the Haitian wound. Automobiles on this road, running without any speed limit, are a constant inconvenience or danger to the natives carrying their market produce to town on their heads or loaded on the backs of animals. I have seen these people scramble in terror often up the side or down the declivity of the mountain for places of safety for themselves and their animals as the machines snorted by. I have seen a market woman's horse take flight and scatter the produce loaded on his back all over the road for several hundred yards. I have heard an American commercial traveler laughingly tell how on the trip from Cape Haitien to Port-au-Prince the automobile he was in killed a donkey and two pigs. It had not occurred to him that the donkey might be the chief capital of the small Haitian farmer and that the loss of it might entirely bankrupt him. It is all very humorous, of course, unless you happen to be the Haitian pedestrian.

The majority of visitors on arriving at Port-au-Prince and noticing the well-paved, well-kept streets, will at once jump to the conclusion that this work was done by the American Occupation. The Occupation goes to no trouble to refute this conclusion, and in fact it will by implication corroborate it. If one should exclaim, "Why, I am surprised to see what a well-paved city Port-au-Prince is!" he would be almost certain to receive the answer, "Yes, but you should have seen it before the Occupation." The implication here is that Port-au-Prince was a mudhole and that the Occupation is responsible for its clean and well-paved streets. It is true that at the time of the intervention, five years ago, there were only one or two paved streets in the Haitian capital, but the contracts for paving the entire city had been let by the Haitian Government, and the work had already been begun. This work was completed during the Occupation, *but the Occupation did not pave, and had nothing to do with the paving of a single street in Port-au-Prince.*

One accomplishment I did expect to find—that the American Occupation, in its five years of absolute rule, had developed and improved the Haitian system of public education. The United States has made some efforts in this direction in other countries where it has taken control. In Porto Rico, Cuba, and the Philippines, the attempt, at least, was made to establish modern school systems. Selected youths from these countries were taken and sent to the United States for training in order that they might return and be better teachers, and American teachers were sent to those islands in exchange. The American Occupation in Haiti has not advanced public education a single step. No new buildings have been erected. Not a single Haitian youth has been sent to the United States for training as a teacher, nor has a single American teacher, white or colored, been sent to Haiti. According to the general budget of Haiti, 1919–1920, there are teachers in the rural schools receiving as little as six dollars a month. Some of these teachers may not be worth more than six dollars a month. But after five years of American rule, there ought not to be a single teacher in the country who is not worth more than that paltry sum.

Another source of discontent is the Gendarmerie. When the Occupation took possession of the island, it disarmed all Haitians, including the various local police forces. To remedy this situation the Convention (Article X), provided that there should be created—

> without delay, an efficient constabulary, urban and rural, composed of native Haitians. This constabulary shall be organized and officered by Americans, appointed by the President of Haiti upon nomination by the President of the United States. . . . These officers shall be replaced by Haitians as they, by examination conducted under direction of a board to be selected by the Senior American Officer of this constabulary in the presence of a representative of the Haitian Government, are found to be qualified to assume such duties.

During the first months of the Occupation officers of the Haitian Gendarmerie were commissioned officers of the marines, but the war took all these officers to Europe. Five years have passed and the constabulary is still officered entirely by Marines, but almost without exception they are ex-privates or non-commissioned officers of the United States Marine Corps commissioned in the gendarmerie. Many of these men are rough, uncouth, and uneducated, and a great number from the South, are violently steeped in color prejudice. They direct all policing of city and town. It falls to them, ignorant of Haitian ways and language, to enforce every minor police regulation. Needless to say, this is a grave source of continued irritation. Where the genial American "cop" could, with a wave of his hand or club, convey the full majesty of the law to the small boy transgressor or to some equally innocuous offender, the strong-arm tactics for which the Marines are famous, are apt to be promptly evoked. The pledge in the Convention that "these officers be replaced by Haitians" who could qualify, has, like other pledges, become a mere scrap of paper. Graduates of the famous French military academy of St. Cyr, men who have actually qualified for commissions in the French army, are denied the opportunity to fill even a lesser commission in the Haitian Gendarmerie, although such men, in addition to their pre-eminent qualifications of training, would, because of their understanding of local conditions and their complete familiarity with the ways of their own country, make ideal guardians of the peace.

The American Occupation of Haiti is not only guilty of sins of omission, it is guilty of sins of commission in addition to those committed in the building of the great road across the island. Brutalities and atrocities on the part of American Marines have occurred with sufficient frequency to be the cause of deep resentment and terror. Marines talk freely of what they "did" to some Haitians in the outlying districts. Familiar methods of torture to make captives reveal what they often do not know are nonchalantly discussed. Just before I left Port-au-Prince an American Marine had caught a Haitian boy stealing sugar off the wharf and instead of arresting him he battered his brains out with the butt of his rifle. I learned from the lips of American Marines themselves of a number of cases of rape of Haitian women by Marines. I often sat at tables in the hotels and cafes in company with Marine officers and they talked before me without restraint. I remember the description of a "caco" hunt by one of them; he told how they finally came upon a crowd of natives engaged in the popular pastime of cock-fighting and how they "let them have it" with machine guns and rifle fire. I heard another, a captain of Marines, relate how he at a fire in Port-au-Prince ordered a "rather dressed up Haitian," standing on the sidewalk, to "get in there" and take a hand at the pumps. It appeared that the Haitian merely shrugged his shoulders. The captain of Marines then laughingly said: "I had on a pretty heavy pair of boots and I let him have a kick that landed him in the middle of the street. Someone ran up and told me that the man was an ex-member of the Haitian Assembly." The fact that the man had been a member of the Haitian Assembly made the whole incident more laughable to the captain of Marines.

Perhaps the most serious aspect of American brutality in Haiti is not to be found in individual cases of cruelty, numerous and inexcusable though they are, but rather in the American attitude, well illustrated by the diagnosis of an American officer discussing the situation and its difficulty: "The trouble with this whole business is that some of these people with a little money and education think they are as good as we are," and this is the keynote of the attitude of every American to every Haitian. Americans have carried American hatred to Haiti. They have planted the feeling of caste and color prejudice where it never before existed.

And such are the "accomplishments" of the United States in Haiti. The Occupation has not only failed to achieve anything worthwhile, but has made it impossible to do so because of the distrust and bitterness that it has engendered in the Haitian people. Through the present instrumentalities no matter how earnestly the United States may desire to be fair to Haiti and make intervention a success, it will not succeed. An entirely new deal is necessary. This Government forced the Haitian leaders to accept the promise of American aid and American supervision. With that American aid the Haitian Government defaulted its external and internal debt, an obligation, which under self-government the Haitians had scrupulously observed. And American supervision turned out to be a military tyranny supporting a program of economic exploitation. The United States had an opportunity to gain the confidence of the Haitian people. That opportunity has been destroyed. When American troops first landed, although the Haitian people were outraged, there was a feeling nevertheless which might well have developed into cooperation. There were those who had hopes that the United States, guided by its traditional policy of nearly a century and a half, pursuing its fine stand in Cuba, under McKinley, Roosevelt, and Taft, would extend aid that would be mutually beneficial to both countries. Those Haitians who indulged this hope are disappointed and bitter. Those members of the Haitian Assembly who, while acting under coercion were nevertheless hopeful of American promises, incurred unpopularity by voting for the Convention, are today bitterly disappointed and utterly disillusioned.

If the United States should leave Haiti today, it would leave more than a thousand widows and orphans of its own making, more banditry than has existed for a century, resentment, hatred and despair in the heart of a whole people, to say nothing of the irreparable injury to its own tradition as the defender of the rights of man.

III. GOVERNMENT OF, BY, AND FOR THE NATIONAL CITY BANK

Former articles of this series described the Military Occupation of Haiti and the crowd of civilian place-holders as among the forces at work in Haiti to maintain the present status in that country. But more powerful though less obvious, and more sinister, because of its deep and varied radications, is the force exercised by the National City Bank of New York. It seeks more than the mere maintenance of the present status in Haiti; it is constantly working to bring about a condition more suitable and profitable to itself. Behind the Occupation, working conjointly with the Department of State, stands this great banking institution of New York and elsewhere. The financial potentates allied with it are the ones who will profit by the control of Haiti. The United States Marine Corps and the various office-holding "deserving Democrats," who help maintain the status quo there, are in reality working for great financial interests in this country, although Uncle Sam and Haiti pay their salaries.

Mr. Roger L. Farnham, vice-president of the National City Bank, was effectively instrumental in bringing about American intervention in Haiti. With the administration at Washington, the word of Mr. Farnham supersedes that of anybody else on the island. While Mr. Bailly-Blanchard, with the title of minister, is its representative in name, Mr. Farnham is its representative in fact. His goings and comings are aboard vessels of the United States Navy. His bank, the National City, has been in charge of the Banque Nationale d'Haiti throughout the Occupation.[1] Only a few weeks ago he was appointed receiver of the National Railroad of Haiti, controlling practically the entire railway system in the island with valuable territorial concessions in all parts.[2] The $5,000,000 sugar plant at Port-au-Prince, it is commonly reported, is about to fall into his hands.

Now, of all the various responsibilities, expressed, implied, or assumed by the United States in Haiti, it would naturally be supposed that the financial obligation would be foremost. Indeed, the sister republic of Santo Domingo was taken over by the United States Navy for no other reason than failure to pay its internal debt. But Haiti for over one hundred years scrupulously paid its external and internal debt—a fact worth remembering when one hears of "anarchy and disorder" in that land—until five years ago when under the financial guardianship of the United States interest on both the internal and, with one exception, external debt was defaulted; and this in spite of the fact that specified revenues were pledged for the payment of this interest. Apart from the distinct injury to the honor and reputation of the country, the hardship on individuals has been great. For while the foreign debt is held particularly in France which, being under great financial obligations to the United States since the beginning of the war, has not been able to protest effectively, the interior debt is held almost entirely by Haitian citizens. Haitian Government bonds have long been the recognized substantial investment for the well-to-do and middle class people, considered as are in this country, United States, state, and municipal bonds. Non-payment on these securities has placed many families in absolute want.

What has happened to these bonds? They are being sold for a song, for the little cash they will bring. Individuals closely connected with the National Bank of Haiti are ready purchasers. When the new Haitian loan is floated it will, of course, contain ample provisions for redeeming these old bonds at par. The profits will be more than handsome. Not that the National Bank has not already made hay in the sunshine of American Occupation. From the beginning it has been sole depositary of all revenues collected in the name of the Haitian Government by the American Occupation, receiving in addition to the interest rate a commission on all funds deposited. The bank is the sole agent in the transmission of these funds. It has also the exclusive note-issuing privilege in the republic. At the same time complaint is widespread among the Haitian businessmen that the Bank no longer as of old accommodates them with credit and that its interests are now entirely in developments of its own.

Now, one of the promises that was made to the Haitian Government, partly to allay its doubts and fears as to the purpose and character of the American intervention, was that the United States would put the country's finances on a solid and substantial basis. A loan for $30,000,000 or more was one of the features of this promised assistance. Pursuant, supposedly, to this plan, a Financial Adviser for Haiti was appointed in the person of Mr. John Avery McIlhenny. Who is Mr. McIlhenny? That he has the cordial backing and direction of so able a financier as Mr. Farnham is comforting when one reviews the past record and experience in finance of Haiti's Financial Adviser as given by him in Who's Who in America, for 1918–1919. He was born in Avery Island, Iberia Parish, La.; went to Tulane University for one year; was a private in the Louisiana State militia for five years; trooper in the U.S. Cavalry in 1898; promoted to second lieutenancy for gallantry in action at San Juan; has been member of the Louisiana House of Representatives and Senate; was a member of the U.S. Civil Service Commission in 1906 and president of the same in 1913; Democrat. It is under his Financial Advisership that the Haitian interest has been continued in default with the one exception above noted, when several months ago $3,000,000 was converted into francs to meet the accumulated interest payments on the foreign debt. Dissatisfaction on the part of the Haitians developed over the lack of financial perspicacity in this transaction of Mr. McIlhenny because the sum was converted into francs at the rate of nine to a dollar while shortly after the rate of exchange on French francs dropped to fourteen to a dollar. Indeed, Mr. McIlhenny's unfitness by training and experience for the delicate and important position which he is filling was one of the most generally admitted facts which I gathered in Haiti.

At the present writing, however, Mr. McIlhenny has become a conspicuous figure in the history of the Occupation of Haiti as the instrument by which the National City Bank is striving to complete the riveting, double-locking and bolting of its financial control of the island. For although it would appear that the absolute military domination under which Haiti is held would enable the financial powers to accomplish almost anything they desire, they are wise enough to realize that a day of reckoning, such as, for instance, a change in the Administration in the United States, may be coming. So they are eager and anxious to have everything they want signed, sealed, and delivered. Anything, of course, that the Haitians have fully "consented to" no one else can reasonably object to.

A little recent history: In February of the present year, the ministers of the different departments, in order to conform to the letter of the law (Article 116 of the Constitution of Haiti, which was saddled upon her in 1918 by the Occupation[3] and Article 2 of the Haitian-American Convention[4]) began work on the preparation of the accounts for 1918–1919 and the budget for 1920–1921. On March 22 a draft of the budget was sent to Mr. A. J. Maumus, Acting Financial Adviser, in the absence of Mr. McIlhenny, who had at that time been in the United States for seven months. Mr. Maumus replied on March 29, suggesting postponement of all discussion of the budget until Mr. McIlhenny's return. Nevertheless, the Legislative body, in pursuance of the law, opened on its constitutional date, Monday, April 5. Despite the great urgency of the matter in hand, the Haitian administration was obliged to mark time until June 1, when Mr. McIlhenny returned to Haiti. Several conferences with the various ministers were then undertaken. On June 12, at one of these conferences, there arrived in the place of the Financial Adviser a note stating that he would be obliged to stop all study of the budget "until the time when certain affairs of considerable importance to the well-being of the country shall be finally settled according to recommendations made by me to the Haitian Government." As he did not give in his note the slightest idea what these important affairs were, the Haitian Secretary wrote asking for information, at the same time calling attention to the already great and embarrassing delay, and reminding Mr. McIlhenny that the preparation of the accounts and budget was one of his legal duties as an official attached to the Haitian Government, of which he could not divest himself.

On July 19 Mr. McIlhenny supplied his previous omission in a memorandum which he transmitted to the Haitian Department of Finance, in which he said: "I had instructions from the Department of State of the United States just before my departure for Haiti, in a part of a letter of May 20, to declare to the Haitian Government that it was necessary to give its immediate and formal approval to:

1. A modification of the Bank Contract agreed upon by the Department of State and the National City Bank of New York.
2. Transfer of the National Bank of the Republic of Haiti to a new bank registered under the laws of Haiti, to be known as the National Bank of the Republic of Haiti.
3. The execution of Article 15 of the Contract of Withdrawal prohibiting the importation and exportation of non-Haitian money except that which might be necessary for the needs of commerce in the opinion of the Financial Adviser.

Now, what is the meaning and significance of these proposals? The full details have not been given out, but it is known that they are part of a new monetary law for Haiti involving the complete transfer of the Banque Nationale d'Haiti to the National City Bank of New York. The document embodying the agreements, with the exception of the clause prohibiting the importation of foreign money, was signed at Washington, February 6, 1920, by Mr. McIlhenny, the Haitian Minister at Washington and the Haitian Secretary of Finance. *The Haitian Government has officially declared that the clause prohibiting the importation and exportation of foreign money, except as it may be deemed necessary in the opinion of the Financial Adviser, was added to the original agreement by some unknown party.* It is for the purpose of compelling the Haitian Government to approve the agreements, including the "prohibition clause," that pressure is now being applied. Efforts on the part of business interests in Haiti to learn the character and scope of what was done at Washington have been thwarted by close secrecy. However, sufficient of its import has become known to understand the reasons for the unqualified and definite refusal of President Dartiguenave and the Government to give their approval. Those reasons are that the agreements would give to the National Bank of Haiti, and thereby to the National City Bank of New York, exclusive monopoly upon the right of importing and exporting American and other foreign money to and from Haiti, a monopoly which would carry unprecedented and extraordinarily lucrative privileges.

The proposal involved in this agreement has called forth a vigorous protest on the part of every important banking and business concern in Haiti with the exception, of course, of the National Bank of Haiti. This protest was transmitted to the Haitian Minister of Finance on July 30 past. The protest is signed not only by Haitians and Europeans doing business in that country but also by the leading American business concerns, among which are the American Foreign Banking Corporation, the Haitian-American Sugar Company, the Panama Railroad Steamship Line, the Clyde Steamship Line, and the West Indies Trading Company. Among the foreign signers are the Royal Bank of Canada, Le Comptoir Français, Le Comptoir Commercial, and besides a number of business firms.

We have now in Haiti a triangular situation with the National City Bank and our Department of State in two corners and the Haitian government in the third.

Pressure is being brought on the Haitian government to compel it to grant a monopoly which on its face appears designed to give the National City Bank a stranglehold on the financial life of that country. With the Haitian government refusing to yield, we have the Financial Adviser who is, according to the Haitian-American Convention, a Haitian official charged with certain duties (in this case the approval of the budget and accounts), refusing to carry out those duties until the government yields to the pressure which is being brought.

Haiti is now experiencing the "third degree." Ever since the Bank Contract was drawn and signed at Washington, increasing pressure has been applied to make the Haitian government accept the clause prohibiting the importation of foreign money. Mr. McIlhenny is now holding up the salaries of the President, ministers of departments, members of the Council of State, and the official interpreter. (These salaries have not been paid since July 1.) And there the matter now stands.

Several things may happen. The Administration, finding present methods insufficient, may decide to act as in Santo Domingo, to abolish the President, cabinet, and all civil government—as they have already abolished the Haitian Assembly—and put into effect, by purely military force, what, in the face of the unflinching Haitian refusal to sign away their birthright, the combined military, civil, and financial pressure has been unable to accomplish. Or, with an election and a probable change of Administration in this country pending, with a Congressional investigation foreshadowed, it may be decided that matters are "too difficult" and the National City Bank may find that it can be more profitably engaged elsewhere. Indications of such a course are not lacking. From the point of view of the National City Bank, of course, the institution has not only done nothing which is not wholly legitimate, proper, and according to the canons of big business throughout the world, but has actually performed constructive and generous service to a backward and uncivilized people in attempting to promote their railways, to develop their country, and to shape soundly their finance. That Mr. Farnham and those associated with him hold these views sincerely, there is no doubt. But that the Haitians, after over one hundred years of self-government and liberty, contemplating the slaughter of three thousand of their sons, the loss of their political and economic freedom, without compensating advantages which they can appreciate, feel very differently, is equally true.

IV. THE HAITIAN PEOPLE

The first sight of Port-au-Prince is perhaps most startling to the experienced Latin American traveler. Caribbean cities are of the Spanish-American type—buildings square and squat, built generally around a court, with residences and business houses scarcely interdistinguishable. Port-au-Prince is rather a city of the French or Italian Riviera. Across the bay of deepest blue the purple mountains of Gonave loom against the Western sky, rivaling the bay's azure depths. Back of the business section, spreading around the bay's great sweep and well into the plain beyond, rise the green hills with their white residences. The residential section spreads over the slopes and into the mountain tiers. High up are the homes of the well-to-do, beautiful villas set in green gardens relieved by the flaming crimson of the poinsettia. Despite the imposing mountains a man-made edifice dominates the scene. From the center of the city the great Gothic cathedral lifts its spires above the tranquil city. Well-paved and clean, the city prolongs the thrill of its first unfolding. Cosmopolitan yet quaint, with an old-world atmosphere yet a charm of its own, one gets throughout the feeling of continental European life. In the hotels and cafes the affairs of the world are heard discussed in several languages. The cuisine and service are not only excellent but inexpensive. At the Café Dereix, cool and scrupulously clean, dinner from *hors d'œuvres* to *glaces*, with wine, of course, recalling the famous ante-bellum hostelries of New York and Paris, may be had for six gourdes ($1.25).

A drive of two hours around Port-au-Prince, through the newer section of brick and concrete buildings, past the cathedral erected from 1903 to 1912, along the Champ de Mars where the new presidential palace stands, up into the Peu de Choses section where the hundreds of beautiful villas and grounds of the well-to-do are situated, permanently dispels any lingering question that the Haitians have been retrograding during the 116 years of their independence.

In the lower city, along the water's edge, around the market and in the Rue Républicaine, is the "local color." The long rows of wooden shanties, the curious little booths around the market, filled with jabbering venders and with scantily clad children, magnificent in body, running in and out, are no less picturesque and no more primitive, no humbler, yet cleaner, than similar quarters in Naples, in Lisbon, in Marseilles, and more justifiable than the great slums of civilization's centers— London and New York, which are totally without aesthetic redemption. But it is only the modernists in history who are willing to look at the masses as factors in the life and development of the country, and in its history. For Haitian history, like history the world over, has for the last century been that of cultured and educated groups. To know Haitian life one must have the privilege of being received as a guest in the houses of these latter, and they live in the beautiful houses. The majority have been educated in France; they are cultured, brilliant conversationally, and thoroughly enjoy their social life. The women dress well. Many are beautiful and all vivacious and chic. Cultivated people from any part of the world would feel at home in the best Haitian society. If our guest were to enter to the Cercle Bellevue, the leading club of Port-au-Prince, he would find the courteous, friendly atmosphere of a men's club; he would hear varying shades of opinion on public questions, and could scarcely fail to be impressed by the thorough knowledge of world affairs possessed by the intelligent Haitian. Nor would his encounters be only with people who have culture and savoir vivre; he would meet the Haitian intellectuals—poets, essayists, novelists, historians, critics. Take for example such a writer a Fernand Hibbert. An English authority says of him, "His essays are worthy of the pen of Anatole France or Pierre Loti." And there is Georges Sylvaine, poet and essayist, *conférencier* at the Sorbonne, where his address was received with acclaim, author of books crowned by the French Academy, and an Officer of the Légion d'Honneur. Hibbert and Sylvaine are only two among a dozen or more contemporary Haitian men of letters whose work may be measured by world standards. Two names that stand out preeminently in Haitian literature are Oswald Durand, the national poet, who died a few years ago, and Damocles Vieux. These people, educated, cultured, and intellectual, are not accidental and sporadic offshoots of the Haitian people; they *are* the Haitian people and they are a demonstration of its inherent potentialities.

However, Port-au-Prince is not all of Haiti. Other cities are smaller replicas, and fully as interesting are the people of the country districts. Perhaps the deepest impression on the observant visitor is made by the country women. Magnificent as they file along the country roads by scores and by hundreds on their way to the town markets, with white or colored turbaned heads, gold-looped-ringed ears, they stride along straight and lithe, almost haughtily, carrying themselves like so many Queens of Sheba. The Haitian country people are kind-hearted, hospitable, and polite, seldom stupid but rather, quick-witted and imaginative. Fond of music, with a profound sense of beauty and harmony, they live simply but wholesomely. Their cabins rarely consist of only one room, the humblest having two or three, with a little shed front and back, a front and rear entrance, and plenty of windows. An aesthetic touch is never lacking—a flowering hedge or an arbor with trained vines bearing gorgeous colored blossoms. There is no comparison between the neat plastered-wall, thatched-roof cabin of the Haitian peasant and the traditional log hut of the South or the shanty of the more wretched American suburbs. The most notable feature about the Haitian cabin is its invariable cleanliness. At daylight the country people are up and about, the women begin their sweeping till the earthen or pebble-paved floor of the cabin is clean as can be. Then the yards around the cabin are vigorously attacked. In fact, nowhere in the country districts of Haiti does one find the filth and squalor which may be seen in any backwoods town in our own South. Cleanliness is a habit and a dirty Haitian is a rare exception. The garments even of the men who work on the wharves, mended and patched until little of the original cloth is visible, give evidence of periodical washing. The writer recalls a remark made by Mr. E. P. Pawley, an American, who conducts one of the largest business enterprises in Haiti. He said that the Haitians were an exceptionally clean people, that statistics showed that Haiti imported more soap per capita than any country in the world, and added, "They use it, too." Three of the largest soap manufactories in the United States maintain headquarters at Port-au-Prince.

The masses of the Haitian people are splendid material for the building of a nation. They are not lazy; on the contrary, they are industrious and thrifty. Some observers mistakenly confound primitive methods with indolence. Anyone who travels Haitian roads is struck by the hundreds and even thousands of women, boys, and girls filing along mile after mile with their farm and garden produce on their heads or loaded on the backs of animals. With modern facilities, they could market their produce much more efficiently and with far less effort. But lacking them they are willing to walk and carry. For a woman to walk five to ten miles with a great load of produce on her head which may barely realize her a dollar is doubtless primitive, and a wasteful expenditure of energy, but it is not a sign of laziness. Haiti's great handicap has been not that her masses are degraded or lazy or immoral. It is that they are ignorant, due not so much to mental limitations as to enforced illiteracy. There is a specific reason for this. Somehow the French language, in the

French-American colonial settlements containing a Negro population, divided itself into two branches, French and Creole. This is true of Louisiana, Martinique, Guadeloupe, and also of Haiti. Creole is an Africanized French and must not be thought of as a mere dialect. The French-speaking person cannot understand Creole, excepting a few words, unless he learns it. Creole is a distinct tongue, a graphic and very expressive language. Many of its constructions follow closely the African idioms. For example, in forming the superlative of greatness, one says in Creole, "He is great among great men," and a merchant woman, following the native idiom, will say, "You do not wish anything beautiful if you do not buy this." The upper Haitian class, approximately 500,000, speak and know French, while the masses, probably more than 2,000,000, speak only Creole. Haitian Creole is grammatically constructed, but has not to any general extent been reduced to writing. Therefore, these masses have no means of receiving or communicating thoughts through the written word. They have no books to read. They cannot read the newspapers. The children of the masses study French for a few years in school, but it never becomes their everyday language. In order to abolish Haitian illiteracy, Creole must be made a printed as well as a spoken language. The failure to undertake this problem is the worst indictment against the Haitian Government.

This matter of language proves a handicap to Haiti in another manner. It isolates her from her sister republics. All of the Latin American republics except Brazil speak Spanish and enjoy an intercourse with the outside world denied Haiti. Dramatic and musical companies from Spain, from Mexico and from the Argentine annually tour all of the Spanish-speaking republics. Haiti is deprived of all such instruction and entertainment from the outside world because it is not profitable for French companies to visit the three or four French-speaking islands in the Western Hemisphere.

Much stress has been laid on the bloody history of Haiti and its numerous revolutions. Haitian history has been all too bloody, but so has that of every other country, and the bloodiness of the Haitian revolutions has of late been unduly magnified. A writer might visit our own country and clip from our daily press accounts of murders, robberies on the principal streets of our larger cities, strike violence, race riots, lynchings, and burnings at the stake of human beings, and write a book to prove that life is absolutely unsafe in the United States. The seriousness of the frequent Latin American revolutions has been greatly overemphasized. The writer has been in the midst of three of these revolutions and must confess that the treatment given them on our comic opera stage is very little farther removed from the truth than the treatment which is given in the daily newspapers. Not nearly so bloody as reported, their interference with people not in politics is almost negligible. Nor should it be forgotten that in almost every instance the revolution is due to the plotting of foreigners backed up by their Governments. No less an authority than Mr. John H. Allen, vice-president of the National City Bank of New York, writing on Haiti in the May number of *The Americas*, the National City Bank organ, says, "It is no secret that the revolutions were financed by foreigners and were profitable speculations."

In this matter of change of government by revolution, Haiti must not be compared with the United States or with England; it must be compared with other Latin American republics. When it is compared with our next door neighbor, Mexico, it will be found that the Government of Haiti has been more stable and that the country has experienced less bloodshed and anarchy. And it must never be forgotten that throughout not an American or other foreigner has been killed, injured or, as far as can be ascertained, even molested. In Haiti's 116 years of independence, there have been twenty-five presidents and twenty-five different administrations. In Mexico, during its 99 years of independence, there have been forty-seven rulers and eighty-seven administrations. "Graft" has been plentiful, shocking at times, but who in America, where the Tammany machines and the municipal rings are notorious, will dare to point the finger of scorn at Haiti in this connection.

And this is the people whose "inferiority," whose "retrogression," whose "savagery," is advanced as a justification for intervention—for the ruthless slaughter of three thousand of its practically defenseless sons, with the death of a score of our own boys, for the utterly selfish exploitation of the country by American big finance, for the destruction of America's most precious heritage—her traditional fair play, her sense of justice, her aid to the oppressed. "Inferiority" always was the excuse of ruthless imperialism until the Germans invaded Belgium, when it became "military necessity." In the case of Haiti there is not the slightest vestige of any of the traditional justifications, unwarranted as these generally are, and no amount of misrepresentation in an era when propaganda and censorship have had their heyday, no amount of slander, even in a country deeply prejudiced where color is involved, will longer serve to obscure to the conscience of America the eternal shame of its last five years in Haiti. *Fiat justitia, ruat coelum!*

NOTES

1. The National City Bank originally (about 1911) purchased 2,000 shares of the stock of the Banque Nationale d'Haiti. After the Occupation it purchased 6,000 additional shares in the hands of three New York banking firms. Since then it has been negotiating for the complete control of the stock, the balance of which is held in France. The contract for this transfer of the Bank and the granting of a new charter under the laws of Haiti were agreed upon and signed at Washington last February. But the delay in completing these arrangements is caused by the impasse between the State Department and the National City Bank, on the one hand, and the Haitian Government on the other, due to the fact that the State Department and the National City Bank insisted upon including in the contract a clause prohibiting the importation and exportation of foreign money into Haiti subject only to the control of the financial adviser. To this new power the Haitian Government refuses to consent.

2. Originally, Mr. James P. McDonald secured from the Haitian Government the concession to build the railroads under the charter of the National Railways of Haiti. He arranged with W. R. Grace & Company to finance the concession. Grace and Company formed a syndicate under the aegis of the National City Bank which issued $2,500,000 bonds, sold in France. These bonds were guaranteed by the Haitian Government at an interest of 6 per cent on $32,500 for each mile. A short while after the floating of these bonds, Mr. Farnham became President of the company. The syndicate advanced another $2,000,000 for the completion of the railroad in accordance with the concession granted by the Haitian Government. This money was used, but the work was not completed in accordance with the contract made by the Haitian Government in the concession. The Haitian Government then refused any longer to pay the interest on the mileage. These happenings were prior to 1915.

3. "The general accounts and the budgets prescribed by the preceding article must be submitted to the

Legislative Body by the Secretary of Finance not later than eight days after the opening of the Legislative Session."

4. "The President of Haiti shall appoint, on the nomination of the President of the United States, a Financial Adviser who shall be attached to the Ministry of Finance, to whom the Secretary (of Finance) shall lend effective aid in the prosecution of his work. The Financial Adviser shall work out a system of public accounting, shall aid in increasing the revenues and in their adjustment to expenditures."

THE VIRGIN ISLANDS

CASPER HOLSTEIN's series of three articles on the
Virgin Islands, which appeared in *Opportunity* in June, July, and
November of 1926, are concerned, as were Johnson's pieces, with
United States imperialism and the relationship of the dark-skinned and
white peoples internationally. *Opportunity*, like *The Crisis* (the official
publication of the NAACP), ran several articles about what we would
now call third world countries, particularly articles denouncing U.S.
occupation of Haiti.

The tourist in search of romance can find its footprints in the Virgin Islands
of the United States. The grim walls of Bluebeard's Castle on the heights
overlooking the town of Charlotte Amalia, in St. Thomas, recall the days
when the black flag with its skull and crossbones threw terror into the hearts of
peaceful merchants and other travellers. The Salt River plantation still stands at the
mouth of a lagoon, up which tradition says that Columbus sailed on St. Ursula's
Day, when he named the group of islands in honor of St. Ursula and her eleven
thousand virgins.

It was in the little town of Bassin, or Christiansted, in St. Croix, that the boy
Alexander Hamilton grew up and labored as clerk, under Nicholas Kruger, and first
exhibited those remarkable powers that took him through what is now Columbia
University in New York at the age of sixteen and made him the active genius and
"father of the American Constitution." It should be said here that the natives of the
Island of St. Croix raised the funds to send the young Hamilton to New York by
popular subscription. The tomb of his mother, Rachall Fawcett Levine, may still
be seen by the inquiring tourist at the Grange Estate in St. Croix.

On the same island slavery was abolished by the slaves themselves after a bloody
uprising in 1848. But long before this, the fierce love of freedom characteristic of

the Danish Negroes had blown a spark over the mainland, where, in 1822, one of them, by the name of Denmark Vesey, organized a slave-revolt in Charleston, South Carolina, which all but succeeded. And since that time the Virgin Islands have sent many famous sons to mingle their blood, brains and initiative with those of their brethren under the Stars and Stripes on the mainland. It is an interesting list which includes such names as Hamilton, Blyden, Roberts, Harrison, Benjamin Banaeker, Jackson and many others. It is an outstanding fact, testified to by the American rulers of the Islands, that illiteracy in the Danish West Indies when they were taken over was less that 5 per cent, and as the editor of *The New York World* put it: "That is more than we on the mainland can boast of."

Under Danish rule the islanders were more or less happy and contented. It is true that the decline of the sugar industry in the West Indies brought the pressure of poverty into the scheme of things in every West Indian Island, including those of Denmark. But the source of this pressure was economic rather than bureaucratic. Today, after eight years of American rule, the population is discontented, clamoring for changes in the fundamental law under which they are governed, and in the personnel of the governing body. What is the cause of this disastrous change? The answer will be found in the following brief narration of the events which have transpired since 1917. In that year the American Government bought the islands for twenty-five million dollars as the first point in the strategic defense of the Panama Canal. Soon after the islands were taken over we entered the war against Germany. At that time it was necessary to establish what Mr. Lloyd George described as a "practical dictatorship." During our dictatorship most of the functions of Congress were taken over by the Executive. It was perfectly natural, therefore, that the Government then set up in the Virgin Islands should have followed the fashion of autocracy. And it did. The government has been administered by the Navy Department—which is the first instance in our History, or that of any other Colonial power, of putting the government of a tropical dependency (not acquired through conquest) under a war-making branch of the government. Against this brutal anomaly the common-sense of the Virgin Islanders cries out.

In the beginning the government in the islands quite frankly described itself on its seal and official letterhead, "The Naval Government of the Virgin Islands." When the democratic agitation of the Virgin Islands Congressional Council began to make headway on the mainland, the Navy's officials quickly changed the legend on the seal and letter-heads and have been declaring ever since that there is no naval government in the Virgin Islands. In the eight years since the transfer there have been six naval governors, each one taken from active duty in the Navy Department. But, as it was recently and wittily put by *The Nation*, "It is not a change of governors, but a change of government that the Virgin Islands need." Their objection to the rule of the Navy Department is based not only on the fact that it is anomalous and undemocratic, but also on the policies which the Navy's personnel have promulgated. American race-prejudice, from which the islands had been free, has been officially introduced by the Department's officials. While Mr. Woodrow Wilson's government, backed by some weak-kneed "liberals," was dealing out ferocious hanging sentences to the Negro soldiers who shot in defense of their lives at Houston, Texas, white marines were rampaging in the islands and shooting up the inoffensive black citizens in their peaceful homes. For these light diversions hardly any official punishment has been meted out. On the higher levels, Naval judges have used their power to pay off personal scores and the Navy officials in the islands have deported and imprisoned editors and other critics of their misconduct.

In the meantime the islands have suffered both from official neglect and official unconcern. As is well known, the bay-rum industry has been the main-stay of the island of St. Thomas, together with the coaling and provisioning of the numerous ships that entered the harbor in the days before the Volstead disaster. But the application of the 18th Amendment and a new Port Law have almost wiped out the bay-rum industry and the income from the ships which now go elsewhere for coal and provisions. That this is either ill-will or deliberate indifference appears from the fact that the rest of the United States Constitution—and especially those parts which guarantee the right of full manhood and womanhood suffrage—are kept in abeyance by the Naval officials in the islands, who declare that the United States Constitution does not apply to the Virgin Islands. And, in many instances there has been glaring disregard of that great document. As Mr. George Washington Williams, District Judge of the Virgin Islands, in conversation with a high government official of Porto Rico, said: "What is the Constitution among friends?"

The Islanders may very well ask why apply the recent 18th Amendment to their detriment while withholding the application of the 14th and 15th, which, with some others, would be to their benefit?

To this simple reasoning Naval officials, like Judge George Washington Williams (of Baltimore), who is the chief exponent of Naval rule in the islands, reply that they are enforcing a *Danish law*. This law deprives nineteen-twentieths of the population from exercising the franchise. But when this law is examined, it is found that it went into effect in 1906 and that it provides explicitly that the restrictions on the franchise were to be revised ten years later. *But in 1917 the American Navy took over the administration of the islands!* So it is evident that this continued limitation of the franchise is the product of an American policy rather than a Danish intent—as Lieut. Commander Wm. S. Zane, of the Navy, Executive Secretary, while representing the Governor at a recent meeting of the Colonial Council in St. Croix, said: "We have broken the laws so long we may as well break them a little longer." But it is quite in keeping with the purpose of the Navy Department to keep these darker nephews and nieces of Uncle Sam forever on the outside of Democracy's backyard.

For the removal of this and other disabilities the Virgin Islanders are looking forward confidently to the next session of Congress and are putting forward their claims for consideration on grounds of patriotism, justice and democracy. They want a decided change in their present status, which is neither that of citizens nor aliens. They want to be happy and contented citizens of the United States, and since the present Naval regime stands as an absolute bar to that, they are seeking the *abolition* of Naval Rule and the *establishment* of civil government.

SENATOR WILLIS (OHIO) AND THE VIRGIN ISLANDS

CASPER HOLSTEIN

I t is a rather common thing for a white politician to be the friend of the Negroes in words, especially when those Negroes are in his own constituency. But Senator Frank B. Willis of Ohio has had his friendship put to a severe test of sincerity and has come out true blue. During the present session of Congress Senator Willis as Chairman of the Senate Committee on Territories and Insular Possessions has taken up the cudgels for a people of whom the greater majority are Negroes more than fifteen hundred miles away from his home state. On the pure ground of justice, the people of the Virgin Islands have had their cause championed by the senior Senator from Ohio all through the present session of Congress. He has shown himself unmistakably their friend in urging his fellow senators to grant to those islands the blessings of civil liberty and to bring them from under the heavy hand of the Navy, whose officers have been running things there on the basis of their racial superiority dogmas. The representatives of the Virgin Islanders receive the most courteous and cordial cooperation from Senator Willis in making clear the unfortunate pass to which their people have been reduced by nine years of Naval rule. It has been a great fight for justice to the weak and oppressed and in this fight the senior Senator from Ohio has shone in the forefront of the battle.

Like another Theodore Roosevelt, he has dared to champion the cause of a downtrodden people and has stuck manfully by his guns all the way through. His generous heart and chivalrous bearing in this conflict has won to him not only Virgin Islanders but thousands of American Negroes. And if it were in our power to make him some suitable acknowledgement in return we should gladly do so. But we trust that the Negro people in his own constituency will bear in mind his service to their fellow Negroes under the same flag in the islands of the Caribbean when he comes before them for reelection this Fall. By so doing they can make clear to the rest of the American nation that we are not unmindful of good will and friendly favors when they have been lavished on members of our race. The bonds of national citizenship still bind the black people and the white under the one common title of American. The history of this land with its ideal of liberty under the law is the equal heritage of both sides of the family tree. In the cause of justice and freedom from oppression the black man needs the white man's helping hand, the white man needs black men's good will and cooperation. It is such men as Senator Willis who help to keep alive the great American tradition of inter-racial good will and reciprocal kindliness. And so long as the Negro American values his friendships so long will the good work done by this Ohio Senator follow him with [its] fruitage of good works.

CONGRESS AND
THE VIRGIN ISLANDS

CASPER HOLSTEIN

The present problem of the Virgin Islands is a legitimate though neglected offspring of the United States Congress. For it was by congressional action that Uncle Sam's new acquisition was robed in the rags of a demonstrative foundling and committed to the rough hands of the Navy Department until such time as Congress might be able to resume its rightful prerogative of legislating them back into the family mansion where a republican form of government is assured to the humblest member. In the hands of the dry nurse the fate of the infant has been a far from happy one. Sounds expressive of pain, anguish and discontent have been rife and the rightful parent is preparing to re-assert his authority. In brief, Congress is about to do something definite for the legislative relief of the harassed islands.

Some time in July a commission made up of senators and representatives will leave these shores with a mandate from Congress to inquire into the facts of the present unsatisfactory situation in the Virgin Islands. And with authority to subpoena witnesses and records the commission is a result of the hearings recently held before the Insular Affairs Committee in Washington, out of which emerged two bills designed to put an end to the present haphazard idea of administrative responsibility and to set up a form of civil government in the Islands. These bills were presented in the Senate and in the House of Representatives. The bills were put on the calendar and had been advanced for favorable consideration when the passage of the motion creating the Congressional Commission of Investigation caused them to be temporarily withheld. This will work well in the end because the report of the Commission upon its return will serve as the basis of immediate and conclusive action.

On this Commission there will be men who have already demonstrated their friendship for the Virgin Islands and their sympathy with their efforts to secure an unequivocal status of American citizenship. Their ears will be open to the cry for justice and the Islanders will be free to present before them the full facts of the case. Virgin Islanders in Continental America have full faith in the personnel of the Commission and have no fear that the hearings before them will be hocussed by back-stairs influence or monopolized by those whose policy has been responsible for the present plight of the Islanders and the rapid and unfortunate depopulation of their island homes. The impressions which will be made on the minds of the members of the Commission will depend entirely upon the resident Islanders' handling of their case and presentation of the facts. But we may rest assured Naval rule in the Virgin Islands is doomed. The discussions in Congress and the hearings before the Insular Affairs Committee clearly indicated as much. When to the surprise of outsiders the Southern members of the Committee assumed the offensive on behalf of the Virgin Islands it was obvious that that phase of Prussianism in Uncle Sam's Caribbean possessions against which they were contending was on its last legs, [and] members of Congress were surprised to learn that the Islanders have been going to pot under the irresponsible rule of the Navy camouflaged as non-Naval and were not at all backward in expressing their dissatisfaction with the facts which they found. And oddly enough the representatives of the Navy who testified at the hearings expressed themselves as willing and even eager to rid the Navy of the continued responsibility of administering the Islands. The Navy seemed resigned and inclined to self-effacement. The persistent exposure of the maladministration of the Islands during the past four years is thus seen to have yielded good fruit. The public opinion of the United States was slow in swinging into action, but when it did it exerted a pressure which was irresistible and out of which was heard the insistent voice of justice and fair play. Newspapers and magazines from New York to California rose in a swelling chorus of criticism and a cry for reform. And now that Congress is on the very verge of the required reforms the thanks of the people of the Virgin Islands are due to all those who thus demonstrated that the heart of this great nation is still sound and dependable and that even for a handful of people recently acquired by it, justice and democracy are available; if they are willing to work hard without ceasing in order to secure these modern safeguards of existence.

WOMAN'S MOST SERIOUS PROBLEM

ALICE DUNBAR-NELSON (1875–1935) was a
regular contributor to *The Messenger* in the 1920s. A noted journalist,
educator, and fiction writer, she was married to Paul Laurence Dunbar
from 1898 to Dunbar's death in 1906, although the couple had separated
in 1902. "Woman's Most Serious Problem," a discussion of the
sociological significance of working black women which sounds strangely
contemporary, was published in *The Messenger* in March 1927. "The
Negro Woman and the Ballot" was published in April 1927.

E   B. Reuter in his latest book, *The American Race Problem*, makes this
      comment: "During the past decade there has been a somewhat marked
❖   improvement in the economic conditions of the Negroes. This reflected
in the decline of the number of women employed, and in the shift in the numbers
in different occupations." This statement is followed by a table showing shift in
occupational employment.

From one elevator operator in 1910, the number jumped to 3,073 in 1920.
Those engaged in lumber and furniture industries in 1910 were 1,456. In 1920,
4,066. Textile industries jumped from 2,234 to 7,257. On the other hand, chamber-
maids in 1910 were numbered 14,071, but in 1920 they had declined to 10,443.
Untrained nurses from 17,874 to 13,888; cooks from 205,584 to 168,710; laun-
dresses, not in public laundries, from 361,551 to 283,557. On the other hand, cigar
and tobacco workers jumped from 10,746 to 21,829, and the teaching profession
showed a normal increase from 22,528 to 29,244.

Just what do these figures indicate? That the Negro woman is leaving the
industries of home life, cooking, domestic service generally, child nursing, laundry
work and going into mills, factories, operation of elevators, clerking, stenography
(for in these latter occupations there is an almost 400 per cent increase). She is

doing a higher grade of work, getting better money, commanding better respect from the community because of her higher economic value, and less menial occupation. Domestic service claims her race no longer as its inalienable right. She is earning a salary not wages.

This sounds fine. For sixty-three years the Negro woman has been a co-worker with the Negro man. Now that she is more than ever working by his side, she feels a thrill of pride in her new economic status.

But—"the ratio of children to women has declined from census to census for both races. The decline has in general been more rapid for the Negro than for the white elements in the population." In 1850 the number of children under five years of age per 1,000 women from 15 to 44 years of age for Negro women was 741, for white women, 659. In 1920 the Negro birth rate had decreased to 439, the white to 471, while the percentage of children under five years of age had decreased in the case of Negro women from 13.8 in Negro families to 10.9, and in white families from 11.9 to 10.9.

"In spite of the considerable increase in the Negro population, and in the increase of the marriage rate, the actual number of Negro children under five years of age was less in 1920 than at any of the previous enumerations. In 1900 the number of Negro children under five years of age was 1,215,655; in 1910 the number was 1,263,288; in 1920 it was 1,143,699.

And this sharp decline in the face of increased knowledge of the care and feeding of infants, the work of insurance companies in health, Negro Health Week, public health nurses, clinic dispensaries, and all the active agencies for the conservation and preservation of health.

One startling fact is apparent. Negro women are exercising birth control in order to preserve their new economic independence. Or, because of poverty of the family, they are compelled to limit their offspring.

The same author, Dr. Reuter, tells us that a recent study showed that fifty-five Negro professors at Howard University had come from families averaging 6.5 children, while the professors themselves had an average of 0.7 children. Some were unmarried, but for each family formed, the average number of children was 1.6. "The birth rate of the cultured classes is apparently only one-third of the masses."

The race is here faced with a startling fact. Our birth rate is declining; our infant mortality is increasing; our normal rate of increase must necessarily be slowing up; our educated and intelligent classes are refusing to have children; our women are going into the kind of work that taxes both physical and mental capacities, which of itself, limits fecundity. While white women are beginning to work more away from home, at present, even with the rush of all women into the wage earners class, in New York City alone, seven times as many colored as white women work away from home.

The inevitable disruption of family life necessitated by the woman being a co-wage earner with the man has discouraged the Negro woman from child-bearing. Juvenile delinquents are recruited largely from the motherless home. That is the home that is without the constant care of the mother or head of the house. For a child to arise in the morning after both parents are gone, get itself an indifferent breakfast, go to school uncared for, lunch on a penny's worth of sweets, and return to a cold and cheerless house or apartment to await the return of a jaded and fatigued mother to get supper, is not conducive to sweetness and light in its behavior. Truancy, street walking, petty thievery and gang rowdyism are the natural results of this lack of family life. The Negro woman is awakening to the fact that the contribution she makes to the economic life of the race is too often made at the expense of the lives of the boys and girls of the race—so she is refusing to bring into the world any more potential delinquents.

This is the bald and ungarnished statement of a startling series of facts. The decline in the birth rate of the Negro. The rise in the economic life of the Negro woman. The sharpest peak of the decline—if a decline can be said to have a peak—is in the birth rate of the more cultured and more nearly leisure classes. The slow increase in the national family life, caused by the women workers not having time to make homes in the strictest sense of home-making. The sharp rise in juvenile delinquency—in the cities, of course, and among the children of women workers. And worst of all because more subtle and insinuating in its flattering connotation of economic freedom, handsome salaries and social prestige—the growing use of married women of the child-bearing age as public school teachers, with the consequent temptation to refrain from child-bearing in order not to interfere with the independent life in the school room.

This is the situation. I would not suggest any remedy, make any criticism, raise any question, nor berate the men and women who are responsible for this crisis. For it is a serious crisis. I would only ask the young and intelligent women to give pause.

The new Negro is the topic most dwelt upon these days by the young folks, whom some call, frequently in derisive envy, the "Intelligentsia." In every race, in every nation and in every clime in every period of history there is always an eager-eyed group of youthful patriots who seriously set themselves to right the wrongs done to their race, or nation or sect or sometimes to art or self-expression. No race or nation can advance without them. Thomas Jefferson was an ardent leader of youthful patriots of his day, and Alexander Hamilton would have been dubbed a leader of the intelligentsia were he living now. They do big things, these young people.

Perhaps they may turn their attention, these race-loving slips of girls and slim ardent youths who make hot-eyed speeches about the freedom of the individual and the rights of the Negro, to the fact that at the rate we are going the Negro will become more and more negligible in the life of the nation. For we must remember that while the Negro constituted 19.3 per cent of the population in 1790, and 18.9 in 1800, he constitutes only 9.9 per cent today, and his percentage of increase has steadily dropped from 37.5 in 1810 to 6.3 in 1920.

No race can rise higher than its women is an aphorism that is so trite that it has ceased to be tiresome from its very monotony. If it might be phrased otherwise to catch the attention of the Negro woman, it would be worthwhile making the effort. No race can be said to be a growing race whose birth rate is declining, and whose natural rate of increase is dropping sharply. No race will amount to anything economically, no matter how high the wages it collects or how many commercial enterprises it supports, whose ownership of homes has not kept proportionate pace with its business holdings. Churches, social agencies, schools and Sunday schools cannot do the work of mothers and heads of families. Their best efforts are as cheering and comforting to the soul of a child in comparison with the welcoming smile of the mother when it comes from school as the machine-like warmth of an incubator is to a chick after the downy comfort of a clucking hen. Incubators are an essential for the mass production of chickens, but the training of human souls needs to begin at home in the old-fashioned family life, augmented later, if necessary, in the expensive schools and settlements of the great cities.

THE NEGRO WOMAN
AND THE BALLOT

ALICE DUNBAR-NELSON

I
t has been six years since the franchise as a national measure has been granted
women. The Negro woman has had the ballot in conjunction with her white
sister, and friend and foe alike are asking the question, What has she done
with it?

Six years is a very short time in which to ask for results from any measure or
condition, no matter how simple. In six years a human being is barely able to make
itself intelligible to listeners; is a feeble, puny thing at best, with undeveloped
understanding, no power of reasoning, with a slight contributory value to the human
race, except in a sentimental fashion. Nations in six years are but the beginnings
of an idea. It is barely possible to erect a structure of any permanent value in six
years, and only the most ephemeral trees have reached any size in six years.

So perhaps it is hardly fair to ask with a cynic's sneer, What has the Negro
woman done with the ballot since she has had it? But, since the question continues
to be hurled at the woman, she must needs be nettled into reply.

To those colored women who worked, fought, spoke, sacrificed, traveled,
pleaded, wept, cajoled, all but died for the right of suffrage for themselves and their
peers, it seemed as if the ballot would be the great objective of life. That with its
granting, all the economic, political and social problems to which the race had
been subject would be solved. They did not hesitate to say—those militantly gentle
workers for the vote—that with the granting of the ballot the women would step
into the dominant place politically, of the race. That all the mistakes which the
men had made would be rectified. The men have sold their birth-right for a mess
of pottage, said the women. Cheap political office and little political preferment
had dazzled their eyes so that they could not see the greater issues affecting the
race. They had been fooled by specious lies, fair promises and large-sounding words.

Pre-election promises had inflated their chests, so that they could not see the post-election failures at their feet.

And thus on and on during all the bitter campaign of votes for women.

One of the strange phases of the situation was the rather violent objection of the Negro man to the Negro woman's having the vote. Just what his objection racially was, he did not say, preferring to hide behind the grandiloquent platitude of his white political boss. He had probably not thought the matter through; if he had, remembering how precious the ballot was to the race, he would have hesitated at withholding its privilege from another one of his own people.

But all that is neither here nor there. The Negro woman got the vote along with some tens of millions of other women in the country. And has it made any appreciable difference in the status of the race?

Unfortunately, statistics are not available to determine just how the additional vote has affected communities for the better. The Negro woman was going to be independent, she had averred. She came into the political game with a clean slate. No Civil War memories for her, and no deadening sense of gratitude to influence her vote. She would vote men and measures, not parties. She would scan each candidate's record and give him her support according to how he had stood in the past on the question of the race. She owed no party allegiance. The name of Abraham Lincoln was not synonymous with her for blind G.O.P. allegiance. She would show the Negro man how to make his vote a power, and not a joke. She would break up the tradition that one could tell a black man's politics by the color of his skin.

And when she got the ballot she slipped quietly, safely, easily and conservatively into the political party of her male relatives.

Which is to say, that with the exception of New York City, and a sporadic break here and there, she became a Republican. Not a conservative one, however. She was virulent and zealous. Prone to stop speaking to her friends who might disagree with her findings on the political issue, and vituperative in campaigns.

In other words, the Negro woman has by and large been a disappointment in her handling of the ballot. She has added to the overhead charges of the political machinery, without solving racial problems.

One or two bright lights in the story hearten the reader. In the congressional campaign of 1922 the Negro woman cut adrift from party allegiance and took up the cudgel (if one may mix metaphors) for the cause of the Dyer Bill. The Anti-Lynching Crusaders, led by Mrs. Mary B. Talbot, found in several states—New Jersey, Delaware, and Michigan particularly—that its cause was involved in the congressional election. Sundry gentlemen had voted against the Dyer Bill in the House and had come up for re-election. They were properly castigated by being kept at home. The women's votes unquestionably had the deciding influence in the three states mentioned, and the campaign as conducted by them was of a most commendable kind.

School bond issues here and there have been decided by the colored woman's votes—but so slight is the ripple on the smooth surface of conservatism that it has attracted no attention from the deadly monotony of the blind faith in the "Party of Massa Linkum."

As the younger generation becomes of age it is apt to be independent in thought and in act. But it is soon whipped into line by the elders, and by the promise of plums of preferment or of an amicable position in the community or of easy social relations—for we still persecute socially those who disagree with us politically. What is true of the men is true of the women. The very young are apt to let father, sweetheart, brother or uncle decide her vote. The next in years prefer not to take the thorny path of independence because it involves too many strained relations in the church or social club. Being human and gregarious, she follows along the line of least resistance, and rightly dubs politics a bore.

Whether women have been influenced and corrupted by their male relatives and friends is a moot question. Were I to judge by my personal experience I would say unquestionably so. I mean a personal experience with some hundreds of women in the North Atlantic, Middle Atlantic and Middle Western States. High ideals are laughed at, and women confess with drooping wings how they have been scoffed at for working for nothing, for voting for nothing, for supporting a candidate before having first been "seen." In the face of this sinister influence it is difficult to see how the Negro woman could have been anything else but "just another vote."

All this is rather a gloomy presentment of a well-known situation. But it is not altogether hopeless. The fact that the Negro woman can be roused when something near and dear to her is touched and threatened is cheering. Then she throws off the influence of her male companion and strikes out for herself. Whatever the Negro may hope to gain for himself must be won at the ballot box, and quiet "going along" will never gain his end. When the Negro woman finds that the future of her children lies in her own hands—if she can be made to see this—she will strike off the political shackles she has allowed to be hung upon her, and win the economic freedom of her race.

Perhaps some Joan of Arc will lead the way.

NORDIC EDUCATION FOR THE NEGRO: A CURSE OR A BOON?

(A Personal Reflection)

E. FREDERICK MORROW, born in 1909, is most
famous for having been the first black to become a presidential adviser.
He served in this capacity under President Eisenhower, and related these
experiences in his 1963 book, *Black Man in the White House.* "Nordic
Education for the Negro: A Curse or a Boon? (A Personal Reflection),"
published in *Opportunity* in January 1931, is a provocative complement
to William Melvin Kelley's "The Ivy League Negro," which appears in
Part VI of this volume.

M y education started fifteen years ago at the age of six. One year from
now I shall be at the end of the long tether. An A.B. shall be conferred
upon me, and thus equipped I shall be ushered out into the world to
make my way.

So far that is the same process undergone by myriads of other men for many
decades. They have come and gone, either to achieve or fail. If they come to the
end of their course with any regrets or haunting questions as to the value of having
spent four formative years in college, they probably were questions or regrets viewed
from a financial or economic standpoint. They were seldom of a racial nature. That
then is where many men have differed from me.

I am a Negro. That fact explains everything pertinent to my being. Raised in
a Northern community where the pressure of making a living prevents many Negro
children from enjoying to the full the advantage of secondary schools, I fortunately
was one of the few able to carry on through high school. My companions and
playmates were mostly white. My activities and courses were different from those
taken by the other members of my race. Hence, after four years together, Nordic
girls and boys began to look upon me as some glorified black of white culture,
different from what that color was supposed to indicate.

Surrounded on all sides by this condition, it was only natural that traits and idiosyncrasies peculiarly Nordic should be incorporated into my personal culture pattern. My whole destiny was being shaped by this metamorphosis. But fond parents sensed the change coming over me. They were sickened by the unfortunate condition. I was becoming a snob, a "hi-hatter." Dad spared the rod, but not his two-edged tongue!

When it came time to choose a college, they sought to quell my conceit by sending me to a Negro college, where an appreciation could be acquired for all that which is really Negro. I had picked Harvard. We compromised, however, upon my agreeing to stay at the college they had chosen for a year, and then transfer to one of my choice. They hoped that a year would be sufficient to remake me. They overlooked one fact—my age. I was only 17.

In February I withdrew from the college they had chosen. That unfortunate difference (acquired) between other men and myself, made my life miserable. They could not stand my self-assuredness and superiority complex while I could not understand their disdainful attitude. Yet this contact had done one thing for me, although it did not come to light until a year or two later. The glimpse into their beautiful society, the sight of their loyalty to the race, devotion to the right, and desire to achieve, thrilled me, and turned my mind toward one end—the desire to share their ideals and to be of their brotherhood.

It was easy, therefore, to persuade my father to send me to Bowdoin College. That little aristocratic college appealed, because there would be there the opportunity to *belong*, and to test my power among men typical of those found out in the trying world. I wanted to see if it were possible for men of different races to dwell side by side in brotherhood and unity, each bending its labors and efforts towards the uplifting and betterment of the other.

So, for about four years at Bowdoin I have dwelt intimately among the Nordics. Played, dined, slept, talked, laughed, cried, fought with them. There is one other Negro lad here—brilliant beyond description. So together we have lived within these walls. We have known what it means to be white. That is, how easy life seems, what benefits are derived, and what opportunities are open if one is not cursed by a color. The doors that will be closed to us later on have been opened for four years. Those trivial comforts of life—good hotels, luxurious Pullmans, fast motors, interesting people, brilliant society, superb golf courses, palatial homes, have all been ours. To what end has all this been? Are we farther away now or closer to our race than before? I fear the truth.

Thus, as the first chapter of my life is about to close, I timidly reflect, and fearfully wonder what tomorrow will bring.

Up to now what is to be said in favor of a Negro seeking education in white institutions? No matter where it may be, it is inevitable that some men should question his being there. They cannot be blamed. Many of his associates have never before come in contact with Negroes, and if so, only those in menial occupations. It is only natural, therefore, that their reaction should be based upon information disseminated by their parents, acquaintances, books, press articles, especially those relating to crimes. Some of those whose opinions are unfavorable assume that birds of a feather flock together and relegate every Negro to the unfavorable class. This condition, then, offers a splendid opportunity to the able, intelligent and cultured Negro lad to expunge such bigoted judgment. Since these conditions exist, a loyal Jeremiah is needed to preach the doctrine of good will toward all men. At first he, too, may be stoned and mocked—but final opinion will always be that of respect.

Secondly, there is a chance to compete with men who have always looked upon the Negro as inferior to them, in intellect and capacity. Of course, that is an asinine idea conclusively proved false by eminent scholars—yet white men are [loath] to believe, and very often even after seeing are not convinced. But the opportunity is there.

What about social opportunities? Here is a situation that varies with individuals. How far it goes depends upon the compatibility of the different persons. There are always some men who accept other people for what they are (as regards character and culture) and not what they may be (as regards race, creed or color). There are a courageous few who see in the Negro all the human qualities of a really fine person. These men form his friendships and each search[es] out the things in the character of the other that will be serviceable, and the things that will constitute an essential and harmonious counterpart to their own existences. This is one of the great joys of living—the ability to attract other men by one's personality. It is one of the finest assets a Negro can have. At times it is the only thing that will gain him admittance to circles outside of the one into which he is born, or thrust by reason of color.

Certainly something should be said upon the educational side of this discussion. In one phase particularly do white colleges overshadow Negro colleges, and that is in endowment. Yet this fund in Negro institutions is increasing every year. It is no fault of theirs that the endowment is not larger. It is interesting to note, moreover, that this fact has not prevented many of them from becoming first-rate institutions.

One has to admit, however, that the size of the endowment does make a difference. It means acquiring the best of professors, providing the finest of equipment, affording infinite opportunities for research. Likewise can larger scholarships and prizes be granted. A greater variety of courses are available. In short, every phase of education is adequately provided for—the convenience as well as training and learning of the student. This factor lures quite a few young Negroes away from their own colleges to others. The burning desire that they have to equip themselves for a useful life, causes them to seek those places where the opportunities are the greatest.

There may be other things on this score that are significant—but they are perhaps personal things (like one's taste for caviar—or clothes) that are not talked about. The things that really matter have been named. So much then for the boon of this type of education.

What is to be said against a Negro seeking education in a white college? First and foremost is the fact that he unavoidably acquires a white perspective—a white sense of values as it were. The next step is that of seeing very little if anything in all things Negro—that is, always finding fault, always unpleased, always peeved or ungrateful for any enterprise undertaken by this race. This condition is fatal. The man rapidly deteriorates into a snob, and all race pride goes up in smoke. To what end then has all his education been? To no end! Dissatisfied with everything, he spends all his life criticising and opposing, and such a miserable being benefits neither race nor self. If he had not had that prolonged glimpse into that imagined paradise, his attention would never have been centered in that direction. But having glimpsed, he cannot forget, and he cruelly snubs his people for things they cannot help—lack of money—lack of pomp and ceremony—lack of worldly things. The superficial has overcome him, and he has mistaken it for the all and end all of everything. Do not misunderstand me. This is not true of every Negro who has been educated in a white college. Many have not entered into college life or activities sufficiently to have felt this blight. But there are some.

Another difficulty comes to the fore when one is in the society of one's own racial group. One has lost one's sense of ease and the habit of feeling entirely at home. Personally, I never know when to laugh or cry, speak or keep silent. A sorry state!

In Negro colleges there is the opportunity to meet the chosen of the race—the intelligent, the clean, the splendid, the loyal type of youth. There is the finest opportunity to become race conscious and build up race pride. There are beautiful and noble women that some day will become the wives of those men who deserted and went elsewhere. There the hope of the entire race is focused—and the fire of achievement and industry is kindled and kept alive.

The Negro who has chosen the white university misses all this—and yet he is preparing himself to go out among these same people to make his way. The valuable knowledge that makes for harmony and understanding he does not acquire. Do you wonder I ask, is Nordic education for the Negro a curse or a boon?

All those vital things which the Negro college has to offer, I have in part missed—and may later lament. But in the last analysis, there seems to me to be one defense at least for these four experimental years spent among the Nordics. "As citizens we are to live many years in this world along side of each other, united in all mutual enterprises; loyal to a common government; sharing the same uplifting hopes and desires—and feeling the same oppressions and social wounds. We need therefore to understand each other." That being so, perhaps these four years have not been without their value after all.

THE MIND OF
THE AMERICAN
NEGRO

E. FRANKLIN FRAZIER (1894–1962) was a
noted sociologist, anthropologist, historian, and educator. He received his
Ph.D. from the University of Chicago. His books include *The Negro in
the United States* (1949), *The Negro Church in America* (1962), and his
most famous and controversial work, *Black Bourgeoisie* (1957). "The
Mind of the American Negro" was published in *Opportunity* in
September 1928 and argued against then current scientific methods
designed to prove the Negro's mental inferiority.

I

Henri Grégoire, at one time Bishop of Blois, wrote in France at the
beginning of the nineteenth century that Dr. Gall, the formulator of
phrenology, had assured him that the organs of music were lacking in
the Negro. When the Bishop subjected this generalization to objective verification
and "on the first head . . . observed that one of the most distinguishing characters
of the Negroes is their invincible taste for music," Dr. Gall acknowledged the fact,
"but denied that they have capacity for improving this fine art." Thus speculation
concerning the intellectual capacity and mental traits of the Negro has appeared
under different garbs according to the current philosophic and scientific concepts.
At one time the Bible was invoked to prove the inferior position of the Negro among
the human races. When this type of authority declined, the evolutionary hypothesis
was brought to the support of prevailing sentiments and beliefs. Even the masses who
unconsciously assimilated a naive and crude interpretation of evolution believed that
a Negro could only "ape" the thoughts and ways of the whites. At the present time
the mental tests are affording a basis for the rationalization of beliefs concerning
the Negro's mental capacity.

The most important sources of beliefs concerning the Negro's mind are the theories about the mental traits of primitive peoples. Therefore, since the Negro constitutes the most important primitive group in the world today it will not be out of place to review briefly those theories and their present status among authorities. When the ideas of organic evolution became a philosophic principle, it was applied by the classical anthropologists to social development. According to these thinkers contemporary peoples with simpler cultures represented an arrested stage in the development through which modern man had passed. In order to make primitive man fit into their generalizations concerning mental and social evolution, data were selected from the observations of anyone who had been among primitive peoples in order to endow them with those mental characteristics which were indicative of low mental development. It was held that primitive man possessed a keenness of sensory powers unknown in civilized man. Moreover primitive peoples were supposed to lack emotional control and the capacity for intellectual concentration and abstract thought.

These assumptions have been disproved by the field studies of modern ethnologists. The so-called primitive races do not show superior sensory faculties: and in emotional control they are undoubtedly the equals of civilized man in the realm of their own interests. They will starve in the presence of food rather than break taboos or obligations which they recognize towards their fellowmen. Concerning their intellectual traits, Rivers, one of the world's greatest ethnologists, wrote: "Summing up my own experience—and I believe this will be confirmed by anyone who has used the methods of modern ethnology—I may say that in intellectual concentration, as well as in many other psychological processes, I have been able to detect no essential difference between Melanesian or Toda and those with whom I have been accustomed to mix in the life of our own society." Likewise, Paul Radin attempts to show in his richly documented book just published, *Primitive Man as Philosopher*, that primitive peoples give evidence of the same range of intellectual capacity and temperamental endowment as modern man. Levy-Bruhl's recent theory—based mainly upon the observations of missionaries and travellers—that primitive man was incapable of logical thought and possessed a mentality that does not differentiate between subject and object has been disproved by critical field studies. In the secular sphere of life, according to these studies, primitive peoples are as logical in their use of data as civilized man. In fact, because of the connotations of the term "primitive," and more especially because the essential difference between so-called primitive peoples and civilized man seems to be the lack of a written tradition among the former, the term "preliterate" is coming into use among ethnologists.

Numerous attempts have been made to assess the mentality of the Negro in America. On the anatomical side, we have the claim of Dr. Bean that the Negro's brain showed certain characteristic traits, which we disproved by the subsequent investigations of Dr. Mall at Johns Hopkins University. As to the specific anatomical traits which would show affinity with the anthropoid apes, it should be mentioned in passing that they are about evenly divided between the whites and the Negroes. The most recent attempts to determine the mental status of the Negro have been through the use of mental tests. These newly devised tests are supposed to give quantitative expression to a fixed and unalterable capacity in the individual known as intelligence. These tests have been applied to Negroes all over the country and on a large scale in the draft. The results of these tests generally have been to show the Negro inferior to the whites. Although many anthropologists, psychologists, and sociologists have refused not only to accept these findings as conclusive, but have refused to accept even the assumption that intelligence as a hereditary trait can be isolated, we cannot enter into a criticism of the tests here. We shall note, however, that northern Negroes were shown in the army tests to be superior to southern Negroes . . . while in the Alpha tests for literates New York Negroes made scores equal to Alabama whites. Even those authorities like Professor Hankins, who hold that whites are superior intellectually to Negroes, do not predicate this of all whites. They hold that the range of intellectual traits is the same, but that the relative frequency of those individuals of exceptional intellectual endowment is not as great among the Negroes as among the whites. As a corollary to this assumption, it is held that while all races may show the same capacity for assimilating modern culture, they show unequal capacity for continuing it through progressive inventions and discoveries.

Two other hypotheses have also been utilized to fix the mental traits of the Negro. During the vogue of the instinct psychology, one of its foremost adherents sponsored the opinion that the sex instinct and the instinct of submission were stronger in the Negro than in the whites. The potency of the first was supposed to prevent the development of great mentality; while the prominence of the latter fitted the Negro by nature for an inferior social status. Likewise a theory of psychological types has differentiated the Negro from the whites. According to this theory the Negro's mind is orientated towards the objective world and tends to be free from a subjective evaluation of things. This involves the question of racial temperament which we shall consider later.

II

Most if not all of the attempts to determine the mental traits of the Negro have been barren in so far as they have given any indication of his psychological adjustment to the American cultural environment. The contradictory results which we have noted in the results of the mental tests are due undoubtedly to the failure to take the environment into account. A more promising approach to the determination of the mental characteristics of the Negro is found in the analysis of those collective phenomena which represent his responses to the social milieu in which he has been placed. Therefore in analyzing the mind of the American Negro from our point of view we must first of all consider the social matrix in which it has been formed.

It is necessary at the beginning of our analysis to rid ourselves of a very widespread misconception which vitiates most attempts to arrive at an understanding of the psychology of the Negro; namely, the attribution of every characteristic divergence from American cultural forms to African survivals. We must recognize the fact that the introduction of the Negro into America meant stripping him of his entire cultural heritage. The break with the African tradition was rendered complete by the destruction of the tribal organization. In Plateau, near Mobile, Alabama, a ninety-year-old Negro, the last survivor of a slaver that smuggled in a cargo of slaves in 1858, preserves only dim memories of his African past and is in good standing in the Baptist Church. In America the Negro has had no neighboring African culture in which he could live his life and thereby resist assimilation of western culture as he has done in South Africa. Nevertheless, the Negro has lived in some degree of isolation and has taken over the culture about him in proportion to the extent he has participated in the common social heritage. Where he has lived under a system of domestic slavery, assimilation has progressed more rapidly than where he worked on the plantation. A differentiation in social classes among Negroes has been influenced to a large extent by the cleavage between types which developed under these two systems of slavery.

Because of the importance of literacy in taking over the social heritage, the extent to which the Negro has become literate gives some indication of his assimilation of western civilization. However, the fact that he has reduced his illiteracy seventy per cent since 1860 should not be taken literally as a measure of his progress in this direction. A more significant indication of the importance of the written tradition is to be found in the growth of Negro newspapers, magazines and books with chiefly a Negro public, during the past decade. The urbanization of the Negro has not only contributed to the decrease in his illiteracy but has increased the necessity for a written form of communication.

The social configuration in which the Negro's mind has assumed its characteristic forms has embraced chiefly those economic, religious, educational and political influences to which he has been subjected in the past. Economically the Negro has adjusted himself to American civilization in the role of a personal servant and a plantation farmer. While in the first role he has enjoyed an intimacy with the whites which has facilitated his taking over the social forms of American culture, it has caused him to make many false valuations of life and to fail to develop the self-sufficiency and initiative which are required in a competitive individualistic civilization. On the other hand, the sloth and improvidence of the plantation Negro have become the symbols of the traits which many regard as the racial inheritance of the Negro. Although Mr. Mencken in commenting on the influence of the Negro on American culture is of the opinion that the religion of the United States is African Methodist, the presence of three million Baptists and over a million Methodists among Negroes can be accounted for by the activities of these evangelizing churches among the slaves and freedmen. We can find the pattern for the religious emotionality of the American Negro in the early revivals in America without going to Africa. The half remembered fetishistic practices of Africa were soon degraded to the level of superstitions. When we consider the educational background of Negroes we find that until recent years the intellectual classes among them came almost entirely from the missionary schools of the South. Nearly all of these schools were founded in order to develop an educated ministry for the masses. Later when they were developed to give general intellectual culture, these schools took over the classical tradition. The whole atmosphere of these schools was such as to inculcate in the Negro a sentimental evaluation of life and to continue magical attitudes which are latent in the purely literary aspect of culture. Although obscured by controversial issues the rationalistic evaluation of life potential in industrial education was of primary importance in the mental development of the Negro. While the role which the Republican party played in the emancipation of the Negro offers an adequate explanation for his loyalty to the party, for the fundamental influences in shaping his political conceptions and attitudes, one must go to the arbitrary government of slavery to which he was subjected.

III

If the mind of the Negro is the result of the social configurations briefly indicated above, what are its characteristic forms? In answering this question we are brought face to face with the question of racial temperament. Many authorities who find no adequate ground for essential intellectual differences between races still feel that differences in temperamental endowment are responsible for the characteristic collective responses of the races. According to this theory different races tend to select different aspects of the same culture when brought into contact with it. In considering what appears to be characteristic in the Negro's responses to western civilization, we shall endeavor to assess the probable influence of this factor. The temperamental factor has often been invoked to explain the ease with which the Negro was fitted into the plantation system and personal service. But the diversity of racial groups represented in the slave population will suggest at once the inadequacy of this simple explanation. An adequate explanation is found in the fact that the subordination of the Negro was achieved by a people possessing a superior technology and that he was thoroughly disorganized and conquered by his own people before he was finally stripped of his culture, including language.

But a more fundamental characteristic which has been charged to the Negro's temperamental endowment is his seeming lack of appreciation of economic value. In this respect he has often been contrasted to his disadvantage with the Jew. He has apparently been interested in consumption rather than production. Illustrative of this often repeated charge is Dean Kelly Miller's recent observation, which can easily be corroborated, that it was possible to indicate those cars in front of Freedman's Hospital in Washington belonging to Negro doctors simply by placing a chalk mark on the most expensive ones. Similarly someone else has observed that in the Pullman porter's present struggle for the right of collective bargaining, the economic values have often been obscured by the opportunities which association has offered for the enjoyment of the amenities of social life. In defense of this supposedly temperamental trait of the Negro a white friend stated at a conference on Negro labor in reply to a white employer who had experienced difficulties in employing Negroes, that the artistic nature of the Negro resisted the mechanization of American life. Do we need to resort to an unknown quantity such as racial temperament to explain these deviations from the social forms of American culture, or are there adequate explanations in the social milieu in which the Negro's mental life has been shaped?

Those who regard racial temperament as an explanation for the Negro's attitude towards economic values should not go to Africa. If in America the Negro would seemingly prefer being a chauffeur to hazarding a living as a small merchant, his brother in Africa is a "born" trader and has made his markets a conspicuous part of his culture. It is in the plantation system and the fact that the Negro has served in the capacity of a personal servant that we find adequate explanation for the Negro's attitude towards industrial life and economic enterprises. The studies which have been made by the National Urban League indicate that the Negro is overcoming the habits acquired under the plantation system and is becoming a well disciplined industrial worker. In fact the tendency towards personal loyalty which he acquired under the agricultural system is regarded by some as an asset in his adjustment to the industrial system. In regard to business enterprise, the numerous failures, especially of banks, have become the source of amusing anecdotes and cited as evidence of economic inefficiency more or less attributable to racial inheritance. But a business tradition has never been built up among Negroes and there has never been an opportunity for acquiring it through apprenticeship in white enterprises. The insurance companies which are enjoying the greatest well founded success among Negroes have been made possible through men who have acquired the knowledge in schools of a business technique that can be formulated. Out of the business world which the Negro is slowly building up, we see emerging black Babbitts who do not differ in their mental attitudes from the same white social type.

But how do we account for the Negro's seeming interest in production rather than consumption values? Any adequate analysis of the mental reactions of the Negro involving his attitudes towards certain values must take into consideration the central fact in his life, namely, his struggle for status. In this respect he shows many of the characteristic reactions of other oppressed groups, the variations being due to his peculiar economic and social situation. With the Negro the consumption values have chiefly given status. We see the same role of consumption in the life of the leisure class. The struggle for status is equally apparent when a Negro doctor acquires an expensive car, or the Pullman porters give a ball or a Negro laborer bedecks himself in a silk shirt. In fact social differentiation corresponding to the social valuation of economic classes, has not reached the point which it has attained among the whites, and many Pullman porters feel a spiritual affinity with the leisure class in the Negro group. A study of Negro newspapers affords a fine insight into the social differentiation which is occurring among Negroes. We see emerging from the mass the same social types with the same attitudes which we find among the whites. To say that this is mere imitation of modes of behavior and thought which are out of harmony with the racial temperament of the Negro, is to overlook the civilizational processes which are taking place. Since a relatively significant group of successful men has emerged, the status which economic success brings is a sufficient motive to make a large number of Negroes subject themselves to long hours of dull business routine to the exclusion of the enjoyment of life which, it was believed, was in harmony with his temperament. Probably the Negro's marked inclination towards social life was due to his struggle for status rather than to temperamental qualities. Certainly social differentiation has progressed far enough to create valuations of life among the educated Negroes that were scarcely heard of among Negroes twenty years ago.

The religious life of the Negro which has so often been regarded as characteristic of his temperament, exhibits all the traits of an adaptation to his environment. It was easy for an organized religion like Christianity to displace the remnants of fetichism among the enslaved Negroes whose social life was atomized. Not only did the Christian religion give organization to the universe of the Negroes, but it afforded a compensation for the hardships of his earthly lot in another world. Nevertheless, it cannot be said that the Negro became a mystic. There was no denial of life, but a healthy acceptance of reality. The ecstatic element in his religion has always predominated over the ritualistic and ceremonial aspects. The ritualistic practices have developed on the basis of the practices of the evangelical churches. The lodges, which have been second only to the churches in social significance among Negroes, have offered a larger opportunity for ritualistic practices. The religious imagery has been taken over from biblical lore and combined with the experiences of his daily life. Its simplicity is well known in the spirituals. While the absence of genuine mysticism may lead us at first to find an explanation in an extroverted temperament, the fact that tendencies towards genuine mysticism can be found among certain isolated Negroes who have acquired a literary tradition makes even this assumption questionable. A somewhat similar tendency can be seen among educated religious leaders who are winning a reputation for deep spirituality that tends to ignore and deny social realities. In this tendency the same old compensatory mechanism is apparent. On the other hand there is a drift of the educated Negroes from the Methodist and Baptist denominations to the Congregational and Episcopal churches and Christian Science.

The political consciousness of the masses of Negroes has developed chiefly in response to the social configuration of the plantation and the personal relations which he has sustained to the whites. His political activities have never been directed towards changing his subordinate economic position into one of power. Though largely agricultural, the Negro has supported the party of industrial exploitation because he has regarded himself as the ward of that party. When in recent years a small group of young radicals attempted to persuade him that his advancement because of his economic position should be sought in allying himself with radical groups, their language was entirely unintelligible to the average Negro. Even when the Negro possessed political power, the early political leaders never urged a program that was out of harmony with the existing agricultural system. Besides regarding political activities as an occupation, they were in favor of such measures as popular education and civil rights which would give the Negro the external signs, at least, of equal status. It has only been since large numbers of Negroes have come to northern cities that the idea of self determination in politics has appeared and expressed itself in the Negro's refusal to give his traditional support to the Republican party, especially in local elections.

We shall consider finally the Negro's mind as it is reflected by the intellectual classes. At the present time the artistic productions of the Negro are attracting attention. In fact, the Negro has been popularly regarded as especially endowed with musical ability. This belief has not been the result of the creations of his conscious artists but because of his folk music. There is a rather general belief that the Negro's signal contribution to the world's spiritual goods will be in the form of art. But the assumption of a specially inherited capacity for music will have to reckon with the quantitative tests which Guy Johnson has been carrying on among Negroes. In a preliminary statement of his results which he sets forth in the *Southern Workman*, he states that these tests do not show any "significant differences in the musical capacities between the whites and the Negroes." Mr. Johnson shows appreciation of the fact that psycho-physical measurements of sensory faculties give no indication of the extent of potential achievement which depends upon motivation. In fact, the studies of Adler tend to show that imperfections in sensory apparatus may become the basis of motivation for compensations which result in high achievement. Likewise in assessing the intellectual potentialities of the Negro, the results of tests of sensory faculties or acquired abilities cannot be an infallible index of capacity. The question of intellectual capacity of the Negro has been the chief issue in the matter of his psychological characteristics. The lack of opportunity has often been urged as an explanation of the meager intellectual attainments of the Negro, only to be countered by numerous examples of whites with limited opportunities who rose to the highest realms of intellectual achievements. Even in music it is generally asserted that the Negro has not shown the creative genius which might have been expected. But in assessing the opportunities of the Negro for achievement the cultural influences have been considered in their subtler forms. Opinions concerning the nature of genius and the originality of intellectual creations are being revised today. In our brief analysis of the Negro's mind we can only touch on one or two influences which are stimulating the Negro to greater intellectual achievement.

It cannot be gainsaid that Negro schools, even those of higher learning, have been sterile in the production of men of high intellectual calibre. The products of the classical tradition of these schools have enjoyed prestige among their own people. But even here the influence of the struggle for status is apparent; for as Professor Robert Park has observed, when the white man made the measure of the Negro's intellect his capacity to master Greek and Latin, he studied the classics. In this connection one is reminded of the gibe of Will Rogers that the teachers in a Negro school in the South spoke English with such grammatical correctness that he could not understand them. The most important influence in the quickening of the Negro's intellectual powers has been the urbanization of the race, which has destroyed the isolation in which it has lived. The urbanization of the Negro was stimulated by the World War which uprooted the whole mass. Among the masses this movement has destroyed the magical mental attitudes and among the intellectuals it has created the present so-called renaissance. Heretofore, the Negro who showed promise of brilliant attainments measured by universal standards has found himself isolated without status in either the white or colored group. Without the stimulus or motivation for intellectual achievements he has fallen back upon his own where he has played a different role. As a scientific and scholarly tradition is being built up chiefly at Howard University and Fisk University, and the Negro scholar is achieving a place in the scientific world just as the Negro artist is winning his way, the intellectuals of the race are finding a congenial atmosphere in which the Negro's mind is flowering. While on the one hand, the intellectual development of Negro leaders because of the status of the race in America has been dependent to some extent upon the general culture of the race, on the other hand the Negro's mind has been quickened chiefly by the breaking down of the isolation in which the race has lived.

THE EBONY FLUTE

GWENDOLYN BENNETT (1902–1981) began to
write "The Ebony Flute" column for *Opportunity* in August 1926. As
the editorial in *Opportunity* that announced the start of the column put
it: "The growth of Negro literary groups throughout the country and their
manifest concern about the activities of other writers prompts the
introduction of a column carrying informal literary intelligence. It begins
under the hand of Gwendolyn Bennett, one of the most versatile and
accomplished of our younger group of writers." Countee Cullen began
"The Dark Tower" column later that same year, announced in the
November 1926 number of *Opportunity*: "His opinion on books and
events of literary significance will appear regularly as a special new
department, and there will be occasional articles and poetry from his
pen." Together, "The Ebony Flute" and "The Dark Tower," the first
columns of their sort by blacks, have become the most important
historical artifacts that provide a picture of black literary and artistic
activity in the 1920s. Included here are the first two columns by
Bennett—August and September 1926—and the first by Cullen, which
appeared in *Opportunity* in December 1926.

I

With timely alacrity Langston Hughes has thrown his hat into the
intellectual ring with the pretty compliment of one poet to an-
other. . . .["] I think Countee's lines,

The dead are wisest for they know
How deep the roots of roses grow.

is very beautiful." . . . There has been a goodly response to the question as to what is the greatest or most beautiful line of poetry written by a Negro. . . . It is of incident interest that Robert Frost says the finest lines submitted to the 1926 *Opportunity* contest are from Helene Johnson's "The Road," namely:

Ah, little road, brown as my race is brown,
Your trodden beauty like our trodden pride,
Dust of the dust, they must not bruise you down.

Kinckle Jones suggests that his favorite is:

Yet would we die as some have done:
Beating a way for the rising sun.

from Arna Bontemps' "The Daybreakers" . . .
And Aaron Douglas chooses from Jean Toomer's "Georgia Dusk" these lines:

A feast of moon and men and barking hounds,
An orgy for some genius of the South
With blood-hot eyes and cane-lipped scented mouth,
Surprised in making folk-songs from soul sounds.

. . . speaking of poetry calls to mind the announcement of William Stanley Braithwaite's *Anthology* for 1926. It is to have a larger scope this year. It is to be divided into four parts, i.e., The Poetry of the United States, Anthology of Poems 1926, Yearbook of American Poetry, and A Biographical Dictionary of Poets in the United States. The first section includes articles by Jessie B. Rittenhouse, Glenn Hughes, James Southall Wilson, Dawson Powell, Willard Johnson, George Sterling, Thomas Walsh, Henry Harrison, Alain Locke, Josel Washington Hall, Marianne Moore, Joseph Auslander, and E. Merrill Root . . . . There will be many of the younger Negro writers represented in his coming volume. *Golgotha is a Mountain* by Arna Bontemps; *No Images,* by Waring Cuney; *Northboun',* by Lucy Ariel Williams; *Tragedy of Pete,* by Joseph Cotter; *Lines to Elders, Scornful Lady* and *Confession,* by Countee Cullen; *Magula, Fulfillment* and *Calla Bella,* by Helene Johnson . . . these are to be among those printed this year . . . they are either prize or mention winners in the 1926 *Opportunity* Contest . . . the book will be ready October twenty-first and its price is to be four dollars. . . . William Rose Benet writes me ever so pleasant a letter in which he says: "I am flattered that you like 'Harlem,' and glad that you should use the term 'The Ebony Flute' for a heading to your column, which column seems to me an excellent idea." . . .

Bruce Nugent, whose *Sahdji* appeared in the *New Negro,* has finished his first novel. As yet he has not named it . . . by the way, *Nigger Heaven,* by Carl Van Vechten, is to be on the stands the twentieth of August. However, the review copies are out and I was fortunate enough to see and read one of them. For me it is a splendid book. Mr. Van Vechten has done what I choose to call a perfect piece of research work . . . of it Isabel M. Paterson says in "Turns With a Bookworm": "It is going to occupy much the same position this coming autumn as *The Green Hat* did last year." . . . We also had the rare privilege of glancing hurriedly over the proof for *Tropic Death*, Eric Walrond's book . . . it certainly has "flights of bright delight." He weaves the warm magic of the tropics with simple words and bright colors. *Drought*, which appeared in the London *New Age*, is heavy with its weight of heat and aridity. The author's careful description leaves the reader's lips parched and dry. This excerpt fairly bakes with white heat:

> The sun had milked the land of its moisture—pressed it dry. Star apples, sugar apples, husks, transparent on the dry sleepy trees. Savagely prowling through the orchards blackbirds stopped at nothing . . . turtle doves rifled the pods of green peas and purple beans and even the indigestible Brazilian bonavis. Potato vines yellow as the leaves of autumn severed from their roots by the pressure of the sun, stood on the ground, the winds eager prey. Undug, stemless—peanuts, carrot—seeking balm, relief, the caress of a passing wind, shot dead unlustered eyes up through sun etched cracks in the withering earth. The sugar corn went to the birds. Ripening prematurely breadfruits fell swiftly on the hard naked soil, half ripe, good only for fritters . . . fell in spatters . . . and the hungry dogs, anticipating the children, lapped up the mellow fruit.

And we have much cause for being glad that Langston Hughes has won the 1926 Witter Bynner Contest. The prize was awarded for a group of five poems called *A House in Taos*. The prize is $150 . . . the judges were Rose O'Neill, Vachel Lindsay and Witter Bynner. There were six hundred entries from forty-nine colleges in twenty-six states . . . the contest is for undergraduates in American colleges . . . Tenth honorable mention was awarded to Waring Cuney, who won a half of the first prize of the *Opportunity* poetry contest for his poem "No Images." Both Mr. Hughes and Mr. Cuney are students at Lincoln University. This year the prize winner was to have received a year's tuition to a Mexican University, with carfare from the United States border into Mexico . . . Mr. Hughes is rejecting this part of the winnings and allowing it to pass on to the first honorable mention which goes to Josephine Jackson of Mt. Holyoke College. He puts it very nicely— "You see this way it makes it possible for two people to win prizes."

Contests grow thickly about us as the summer wears on . . . The Survey Associates Incorporated offers a prize of $250 for the best account of the "most interesting thing you know about plays for grown-ups." . . . The manuscripts must not be less than 1,000 nor more than 2,500 words in length, typewritten, double spaced, and on one side of the paper . . . the last date is September thirteenth and the address is—Jury, Harmon-Survey Award 3, care of *The Survey*, 112 East 19th Street, New York City. . . . *College Humor* offers $10,000 in prizes for the best novel or story adaptable to magazine and motion picture production. . . . Midnight, February first, 1927, is the last date and the address is: Contest Editor, *College Humor*, 1050 La Salle Street, Chicago, Illinois.

Which reminds me that Donald J. Hayes is said to be at work on a new literary monthly of the Negro race, called *Vision* . . . to be published from Atlantic City . . . the editors characterize their hopes for the magazine in these words: "In contrast to other Negro magazines, it will have no chip on its shoulder, but will attempt to win friends by giving the Negro writer opportunity for development and by presenting work of distinction. The magazine will be published with white cooperation." . . . It pleases me to see that *American Life*, which had its *premiere* in June, is still in the running.

John Matheus' *Fog* is being translated into German by Dr. Herman Muller for a syndicate which supplies matter for literary publications in Germany. . . . O'Brien has written asking Arthur Huff Fauset for a hundred and fifty word biography of himself for this year's *Best Short Stories* . . . that means that "Symphonesque" goes in this year's honor roll . . . . Countee Cullen writes from Paris that it is the "only city" and that he'd like to stay ever so much. . . .

The Krigwa Little Theater has decided upon the plays that it will produce in the fall. . . . *Blue Blood*, by Georgia Douglas Johnson, which was awarded honorable mention in the play section of the *Opportunity* Contest: *Her*, by Eulalia Spence; *No Count Boy*, by Paul Green, which was produced in New York by the Dallas Little Theater in 1925 and was awarded the Belasco Cup in the National Little Theater Tournament . . . this movement plans working up a repertoire of both Negro and general plays which will be given alternately during the season. Aaron Douglas is decorating the walls of the Krigwa Little Theater which holds its meetings in the basement of the 135th Street Public Library.

Rudolph Fisher has had two stories accepted by the *Cosmopolitan Magazine* . . . . "Fire By Night" and "The Back-slider" are their names. Edwin Morgan's "Prayer" is to appear in *The Bookman* . . . he is spending his summer in Europe. Frank Horne, winner of the second prize of the *Crisis* Literary Contest for 1925, is assistant director of the Boys' Camp Welcome Hall which is situated at Saltaire, Fire Island . . . his "To Chick" from *Letters Found by a Suicide* is to appear in Braithwaite's *Anthology*.

I am particularly interested in reading *Beyond the Rockies*, by William Augusta Banks, published by Dorrance and Company in Philadelphia . . . it is a book of poetry written by a young man who has had an unbelievably hard time of it . . . in fact his struggle for a livelihood has been almost of a storytale quality . . . the verse is carefully done and I find much of it worthy of special note . . . this particular verse has a wistful quality that pleases me: . . .

When January locks me in
Cool mists come dimming down.
The winter is suggesting then
The cool of Twilight Town.

. . . two other books of poetry have come to no notice recently: . . . *Gems of Inspiration*, by A. R. Schooler; *Poems* by Sarah C. Fernandis.

Richard Reid is doing a portrait of Reverend John Haynes Holmes, pastor of the Community Church. . . . Mr. Reid is the artist whose work was in last year's Exhibit of Independent Artists. . . .

Yone Noguchi is criticizing the Japanese themes as presented by Lewis Alexander . . . he lives in Japan and had a book of *Hokku* published in 1920 by the

Four Seas Company. . . . This poem, "To Countee Cullen," appeared in the
Chicago Tribune in the column entitled "Line o'Type or Two by the Faun":

It matters not if your skin is dark
    As the midnight jungle track
I thrill to the beat of the song you sing
    Feeling the torture and rack
That sundered the souls of your broken slaves
    For hundreds of dead years back.

Under the march of your musical lines,
Under the tread of their feet,
I hear the wind in the jungle pines
And the drone of the tom-tom's beat,
With ebon savage under the sun
    In the shimmering tropic heat

Chance gave you the soul of a minstrel fair
    Housed in a blackamoor's frame,
With your heart tuned high to the upper air
    Though a scion of scorn and shame,
Refusing a outcast's usual lot
    And turning it into fame!

. . . So the talk of this and that comes to a close. . . . I wonder how the manuscripts
for the *Boni Contest* are coming along . . . and hope that there will be a novel
come out of it worthy of the name of *the* Negro novel. . . .

II

In searching about for a heading that would make a fit label for literary chit-chat
and artistic what-not I stumbled upon "The Ebony Flute." So lovely a name it is
that I should like to have made it myself, but I didn't. I say "stumbled" advisedly.
Reading again William Rose Benet's poem, "Harlem," in the *October Theatre Arts
Magazine* I was struck by the exceeding great beauty of his use of the "ebony flute"
as an instrument upon which one could "sing Harlem." An ebony flute ought to
be very effective for most any sort of singing for that matter. Ebony, black and of
exquisite smoothness. . . . And a flute has that double quality of tone, low and
sweet or high and shrill, that would make of Harlem or any other place a very
human song. No better instrument then for the slim melody of what book one has
read or who is writing what new play than an ebony flute . . . speaking of Benet's
"Harlem," what a lovely thing it is! It opens with:

I want to sing Harlem on an ebony flute
While trap-drums ruffle to a crash and blare,
With a clear note
From a sylvan throat

Of a clarinet—of a clarinet!
God and brute, black god and brute
Grinning, brooding in the murk air,
Moons of flame and suns of jet,
Hurricane joy and dumb despair.

Vermillion, black and peacock blue,
Pink, plum-purple, zig-zag green—
I want to sing Harlem with a paint-box too,
Shaking out color like a tambourine,
Want a red
Like a furious fire;:
Want a black
Like a midnight mire;
Want a gold
Like golden wire;
Want a silver
Like Heaven entire
And God a-playing at his own front door
On a slide trombone with a conical bore!

And on through line on line of beauty that coins a Harlem as a poet would see it, lush and colorful . . . fertile like rich earth. On and on to its close which ends with the crooning of his "Mammy Earth. . . ."

O child of the wild, of the womb of the night,
Rest, and dream, my dark delight!

Tropic Death, a book of short stories by Eric Walrond, will come out in October. Boni and Liveright are the publishers. I can scarcely wait for this book to be on the market. . . . Few of the Negro writers that are being heralded on all sides today can begin to create the color that fairly rolls itself from Mr. Walrond's facile pen. *Tropic Death* ought to have that ripe color that is usually the essence of Mr. Walrond's writing . . . and also a simple forcefulness that the author often achieves. . . . A new magazine is added to the Chicago list of Negro publications: *American Life Magazine*, Moses Jordan editing . . . the same Mr. Jordan whose book, *The Meat Man*, was published a few years back. The June issue, Volume One—Number One, carried "From Venice to Vienna" by Jessie Redmon Fauset and "Pale Lady" by Langston Hughes. I have not seen the July issue of this magazine but look forward to seeing the future copies that will come out. . . . Maude Cuney Hare has an article on "Creole Folksongs" in the July number of the *Musical Observer*. Needless to say, Mrs. Hare's article is adequate . . . certainly there are few people more authoritative in their speaking of Creole folksongs than she.

Aaron Douglas is doing the illustrations for Carl Van Vechten's *Nigger Heaven* which will appear August the twentieth. *The Publisher's Weekly* says that Mr. Douglas' advertisement for this book in the current magazines is the best for the month of June . . . but by far the most important thing about Mr. Douglas these days is his new wife. He married Miss Alta Sawyer of Kansas City, Missouri, on Friday June eighteenth. . . . The English edition of Langston Hughes' *Weary Blues* came out on July ninth . . . the second edition of *The New Negro* will be out in the fall. . . . The Negro writers must not let the first of September slip up on them without having their manuscripts ready for the Albert and Charles Boni contest. The address for sending the novels to the judges is 66 Fifth Avenue. . . . Thinking of novels makes me recall what Simeon Strunsky of the *New York Times Book Review* said not so long ago about beautifully written books. . . . "The Beautifully written book as a rule is the over-written book. One sinks into beauty ankle-deep." He goes to quite some trouble to poke fun at the elegant conservatism of what is called beautiful prose today. But even in the face of Mr. Strunsky's caustic remarks on the question of beautiful writing, properly so-called, I should be ever so happy to find some of that ankle-deep beauty in the things that come out of the Boni contest . . . what of it, if some Negro should write a *Marie Chapdelaine* with its wistful but perfect simplicity or perhaps an *Ethan Frome*. . . . Mr. Strunsky rambles on to the amazing consolation that "We still have our newspapers. In them are the reservoirs of simple health upon which we can draw when the English language threatens to cave in under heavy doses of beauty between bound covers" . . . and we can do little else but wonder how any one can live in New York and see the rife yellow journalism of the daily news sheets and speak of them as the salvation of the English language . . . nor even the aridity of the *New York Times* could be set on the pinnacle that had been built for "beautiful writing."

"George Sand Reigns Again for a Day" in the *Times* for June twenty-seventh made me think of a young newspaper writer I knew in Paris who was always breaking into any conversation that chanced to be going on at the time with the information that he lived in the back part of a house the front part of which had belonged to George Sand . . . and I always think within myself that I could see in that about as much claim to fame as any. . . . F. Fraser Bond in reviewing *The Best Love Stories of 1925*: "Something has come over the American love story. . . . It seems to have grown up. No longer does it find its chief concern in the billings and cooings of tepid adolescents" . . . he goes on further to observe that "Peter Pan has put on long trousers." Can't you see some E. E. Cumings-John V. Weaver person coming forward with a "Come out of it Lovers" to scare away that something that has "come over" the love story of today. . . .

Hall Johnson's Negro operetta, *Goophered*; with the libretto by Garret is to have in it three lyrics by Langston Hughes: "Mother to Son"; "The Midnight Blues"; and "Song for a Banjo." This operetta is for early fall or late summer production. Mr. Johnson is the winner of the third prize of the music section of the *Opportunity* Contest . . . and by the way, Zora Neale Hurston and Langston Hughes are collaborating on an operetta the libretto of which is to be by Miss Hurston and the lyrics by Mr. Hughes . . . they are also writing a musical comedy together. . . . Mentioning musical comedies of a dusky character reminds me of the ill-fated *My Magnolia* which ran for a single week at the Mansfield Theater.

Jean Toomer, author of *Cane*, is spending the summer at the Gurdjieff Institute in Fountainbleau, France. . . . Countee Cullen and his father, Reverend Cullen, are travelling through Europe for the summer months . . . they will make many interesting stops chief among them a pilgrimage to the Holy Land. . . . Arthur Huff Fauset whose "Symphonesque" won first prize in the short story section of the *Opportunity* contest is to be a member of their party. . . . Dr. Rudolph Fisher has very endearingly nick-named his new baby "the new Negro."

Friday, July sixteenth, the annual reception for summer school students was given at the 135th Street Library. Mr. Johnson of *Opportunity* spoke on the *Opportunity* contests and what they had meant to the younger school of writers. When Mr. Johnson had finished his speech he called on several of the prize winners of the first and second *Opportunity* contests who chanced to be in the audience and asked them to read. . . . "Golgatha [sic] Is a Mountain" was never so lovely for me until I heard Mr. Arna Bontemp read it himself. He reads with a voice as rich in its resonance as his prize-winning poem is in its imagery and beauty. It was good to see so many of the people who are writing and doing things together . . . Zora Neale Hurston, Bruce Nugent, John Davis . . . Langston Hughes who talked a bit about blues and spirituals and then read some of the new ones he had been doing . . . and just before he sat down he read a poem called "Brass Spittoons" . . . as lovely as are many things with much more delectable names.

Horace Liveright is busy casting his play *Black Boy* for its fall production. Paul Robeson is to play the lead which I understand is to be a prize-fighter. I heard Mr. Liveright say the other night that he was having difficulty in finding an actress for the role of Irene who plays in the lead opposite Mr. Robeson. This part is difficult to fill since the heroine is supposed all during the play to be white and is discovered at the end to be a colored girl who "passes." Remembering the harmful publicity that attended the opening of *All God's Chillun* because of a white woman's playing opposite a Negro, Mr. Liveright has been leaving no stone unturned to find a Negro girl who can take the part. There are hundreds who are fitted for the physical requirements of the piece but few whose histrionic powers would measure up to the standard of Broadway production.

Clarissa Scott of Washington dropped into the office the other day on her first trip in the interest of the new social investigation work she is to be doing in New York this summer . . . the same Clarissa Scott whose "Solace" won a prize in the *Opportunity* contest for last year . . . and it was good to see her again and to know that she would be in New York all the summer . . . sandwiched between talk of what was happening in Washington and at Howard the question arose as to what was the most beautiful line of poetry written by a Negro . . . her first thought was:

> Dark Madonna of the grave she rests
> Lord Death has found her sweet.

from Countes Cullen's *A Brown Girl Dead* . . . strange how discussions of this sort get started, isn't it? I had never thought in terms of the best or most beautiful or the greatest line of Negro poetry before . . . there are several that come in line for the distinction now that I come to think of it . . . without thinking too long my first choice is from Langston Hughes' new blues poem called "The Railroad Blues." . . .

A railroad bridge is a sad song in de air

or

Where twilight is a soft bandanna handkerchief

. . . or perhaps Lewis Alexander's

A *body smiling with black beauty* . . .

or Jean Toomer's

Above the sacred whisper of the pines,
Give virgin lips to cornfield concubines,
Bring dreams of Christ to dusky, cane-lipped throngs.

We wonder what William Stanley Braithwaite would say . . . or Claude McKay . . . or Jessie Fauset. . . . But all that resolves itself into the hopelessness of deciding what the greatest of anything is . . . nothing is really greatest but greatness itself. . . .

THE DARK TOWER

COUNTEE CULLEN

"The last week of 'White Wings'! Step up, boys and girls, and see how a gay and gallant gentleman may die.'" Thus Miss Edna Ferber, in an open letter to Mr. Alexander Woollcott of the *New York World*, baited the younger generation to a last minute attendance at a play that after an all too brief run was closing because it was too beautiful and rare and gay to be a financial success. Those of us whose nostrils can still quiver in the sulphurous atmosphere of a challenge, went and laughed and applauded, to come away indignant but helpless in a world that, for the most part, lets the fine decline and the stupid flourish like the green bay. To be sure, most of us didn't understand it all right down to the last elusive symbol, but we knew that it was a riotously jubilant and a pitifully whimsical drama of the thing we are in arms against: the attempt of old uncompromising patterns to rule in a world needing the robust and the new, not because they are novel, but because they fit into the shifting grooves of our times. The younger generation went, Miss Ferber, and they laughed at and pitied the stiff-backed Inches; they fought along with Mary Todd; and best of all they appreciated to the fullest Joseph, that marvelous horse of totally unequine parts who could enjoy a joke and tell one, and die that the things which were beating in the womb of time might have a birth. It *was* a gay and gallant death!

On the whole it was a month of catastrophes for performances in which we were more than passingly interested, for both *Deep River* and *Black Boy*, which we had expected to hold the boards for a large part of the season, the one because of its inveigling music topped with a most adequate cast that included Julius Bledsoe, Lottice Howell, Frank Harrison and Rose McClendon; the other because we felt that any play could stand for a while that gave Paul Robeson a chance to exercise his vibrant personality, and to sing a stave or two. Paul Robeson can act as well as he can sing; it is even probable that the thespian heritage in him outvalues the melodic, and one would like to see him in another play worthy of his powers. That calls for stalwart writing when you remember *The Emperor Jones*. It is a far cry from Eugene O'Neill to William Shakespeare, but after *The Emperor Jones*, to bill Robeson in anything except *Othello* seems retrogressive to us on more points than that of time.

At last we have had explained to our satisfaction the identity of that gay ebony Harlemite whom, at odd moments of the day and night, we have met, with his limping gait and his feet encased in the queerly-patterned shoes, which we now suspect were expressly made to conceal the cloven hooves within them. Witter Bynner in the *New Yorker* has tracked the Prince of Darkness to his lair—Harlem. "Black Lucifer" is the poem.

> He was always as blithe, always as black
>   As any boy in Harlem:
> Light used to glitter on his back
>   In heaven as it does in Harlem.
> He sang hosannas to the Lord
> And watched what he was bowing toward,
> Till Lucifer at last was bored
>   And came away to Harlem.
>
> And now you can find him any night,
>   Glittering in Harlem,
> Thanking God that he isn't white
>   Like visitors in Harlem.
> With a paler skin he might have stayed
> And tinkled a harp and sung and prayed.
> And where would you rather be on parade—
>   In heaven, or in Harlem?

What seems to us the high water mark in race consciousness was exhibited by the gentleman who recently inquired at the new circulating library in Harlem for a copy of *Negro Heaven*. Happily the young lady who served him was not meticulous as far as titles go.

Courage is costly, and in this world a departure from precedent costlier, as Julian S. Starr and R. K. Fowler, erstwhile editor and assistant editor respectively of the *Carolina Magazine*, literary mouthpiece of the University of North Carolina, have undoubtedly learned by now. For they have both been deposed because, in the last edition of the magazine they published a story in which the principal characters were a white girl and a mulatto. And this just after we had been turning double somersaults and triple handsprings because that same issue carried a sketch by Eric Walrond, along with a pronunciamento asking for contributions from people of all races, colors, creeds, and political leanings!

Apparently we belong to a race that with charming inappreciation of the rights due the planter insists upon reaping where it has not sown. And once in a while the rightful heir, apparent to all except ourselves, is moved to feeble protest. Some of us fail to see that the various excitements of Negro living can appeal to writers who share no blood relationship with us at all, whose interest in us does not go beyond the perfectly legitimate and dispassionate concern of the artist for his plastic materials. Because Miss Lenore Ulric plays Lulu Belle with an uncanny certainty, and because Miss Lottice Howell in *Deep River* was an entrancing quadroon both visibly and vocally is no reason why the geneses of these actresses should be amiably reconstructed to make them, as it were, to the manner born, as an explanation of their felicitous portrayals of their roles. Nor should the fact that *Porgy*, in our opinion, is to date the best novel woven around Negro characters, subject its author, Du Bose Heyward, to gratuitous and unwilling adoption into the Negro race. A recent note in the *Saturday Review of Literature* informs us that Mr. Heyward is "more moved than delighted at the question which is being asked about his degree of pigmentation." His friend Hervey Allen is even preparing a brief critical biography of Mr. Heyward which Doran will publish as a booklet, and which "ought to stop any question as to Heyward's color and quality." Long ago Carl Van Vechten was taken into the fold, but we fancy more to his amusement than to his alarm, if any word of his initiation has come to him.

We believe that what is being read at the Harlem library is a fair index of what books are most in demand by Negroes, and in a measure indicative of the Negro's literary mind. The list for November is distinguished, almost highbrow. The books, listed according to the number of reservations on them, are: fiction: Dreiser's *American Tragedy*, Erskine's *Private Life of Helen of Troy*, Ferber's *Show Boat*, Fauset's *There is Confusion*, Van Vechten's *Nigger Heaven*, White's *Flight*, and Wren's *Beau Geste* and *Beau Sabreur*; nonfiction: De Kruif's *Microbe Hunters*, Dell's *Intellectual Vagabondage*, Dorsey's *Why We Behave Like Human Beings*, Durant's *Story of Philosophy*, Locke's *The New Negro*, and Niles' *Black Haiti*.

Our mind refuses to carry us back to a book by a new writer that has so completely ingratiated itself into our esteem, as has *The Time of Man* by Elizabeth Madox Roberts. (The Viking Press, $2.50), with such a lack of insinuating effort on the part of its author. This first novel by a woman whose fame heretofore was secured only to a discriminating few by her delightful book of children's verses, shows how incontestable is the affiliation between fine prose and fine poetry. The reader cannot turn the most casual page of this book without finding himself confronted by something unalterably and irrevocably said. The author's style is a heaven-made marriage of words, with no incompatibility of phrase or sentence; divorce would be disastrous to this perfect mating. There has always been room to question the flat assertion frequently encountered that poets never write distinguished prose; now there is more room than ever, with the publication of *The Time of Man*. Read the following representative passage describing the marriage of Ellen Chesser, and see if its aloof dignity does not both hurt and heal you, silence you and cause you to sing:

"Then they went, all, into the outer room and stood about the walls. Ellen's eyes followed the child as she slipped in unpremeditated motions from place to place or stood in unfixed quiet. The room became very still as Ellen and Jasper stood beside the man, the brother who had been brought; or the man faced them, and joining their hands, said ceremonial words. His face was thin and set with ceremony, his hands moving rigidly over the words or settling down in hard, firm finality over the said word, fixed and done. Fixed forever, pronounced, finished, said and unrevoked, his words flowed down through the great hardness of his voice, a groundwork on which to lean, a foundation beneath a foundation, the framework of the house set and fixed in timbers and pinned together with fine strong wedges of trimmed hard wood. His voice trembled a little with its own fixity and hardness, but it erected a strong tower. In the end he made a prayer for herself and Jasper, and gave her a paper on which their names were written. The women shook her hand, and then the men came, their handshakes reserved and ceremonious. The child stood beside the wall, her gaze light and aloof, or she tapped her shoulder softly against the door or touched the latch, her look free and her way unhampered, and the beauty of her look came about Ellen as she gave her hand to the men."

This is a book to bow before in humble, breathless acknowledgment. Like the manner in which it is written, the story is simple and close to the earth, concerning one Ellen Chesser whose life seems a series of moving from place to place from the time we first encounter her as a backwoods girl to the time we leave her, a matron with many children, setting out with calm acceptance to accompany her husband in his search for a new home. Of great struggle there is none in the book, but whosoever starts it will end it, and relinquish it feeling that perfect performances are not solely of the past. Do you remember Maria Chapdelaine? You will remember Ellen Chesser also.

For your Christmas book list we recommend William Stanley Braithwaite's *Anthology of Magazine Verse for 1926*, and Elizabeth Madox Robert's *The Time of Man*. We assume that *Tropic Death* is already on your list.

William Stanley Braithwaite's anthologies of magazine verse are a yearly confirmation of what a greater poet than any therein assembled realized when he said "The poetry of earth is never dead." This year's edition (*Anthology of Magazine Verse for 1926*, B. J. Brimmer Co., Boston, $4.00), the Sesqui-Centennial number and the fourteenth annual issue, is, aside from being an anthology of the best magazine verse of 1926, a survey of American poetry from 1912 to 1926. No serious student of our verse can afford to neglect this volume. If American verse is going the way of all flesh with alarming alacrity, these poems collected by Mr. Braithwaite cannot be arraigned as evidence.

Besides the list of poems honored by inclusion in the anthology, a heady and stimulating symposium is offered in the section "Poetry of the United States," where some of the most distinguished poets and critics of today discuss American verse somewhat geographically. Of special interest to us were the articles by Jessie B. Rittenhouse on the poetry of New England, that by Marianne Moore on the "New" Poetry since 1912, the caustic essay "On Poetry" in which E. Merrill Root takes up the cudgels for the poets against H. L. Mencken, and the article on the Negro Poets of the United States, by our fervent arch-stimulator of the younger generation, Alain Locke.

Some—but these will not be the younger Negro poets—may take exception to Alain Locke's appraisal of the work of Negro poets in this statement: "Therefore I maintain that the work of Negro poets in the past has its chief significance in what it has led up to; through work of admittedly minor and secondary significance and power a folk consciousness has slowly come into being and a folk tradition has been started on the way to independent expression and development." Truths the most self-evident are rarely accepted with corresponding immediacy.

There can be no question of the growth of expression in Negro poets in the past year or two when we consider that Mr. Braithwaite's anthology, in which poems are reprinted solely on their merits as poetry, contains this year works by no less than twelve Negro poets: Gwendolyn Bennett, Arna Bontemps, Joseph Cotter, Waring Cuney, Frank Horne, Langston Hughes, Helene Johnson, Georgia Douglas Johnson, Chaliss Silvay, Wallace Thurman, and Lucy Ariel Williams. And with all the respect due our racial magazines from which most of these poets' work is reprinted, it is good to see the horizon widening in that Langston Hughes is reprinted from *The New Republic* and *The New York Herald-Tribune*, and Chaliss Silvay, a newcomer, from *The Will o' the Wisp*.

Braithwaite's anthology has always been, to quote an appreciative reviewer, "a national institution," but we may for all that be pardoned a bit of selfish pride in this nationally recognized work of one of ours.

ONCE MORE THE GERMANS FACE BLACK TROOPS

CLAUDE MCKAY (1889–1948) was born in Jamaica and came to the United States in 1912. Although associated with the Harlem Renaissance, McKay spent virtually no time at all in the United States during the 1920s, traveling to the Soviet Union, other parts of Europe, and northern Africa. A poet, novelist, essayist, and nonfiction writer, McKay wrote the best-selling book by a black author of the 1920s, the novel *Home to Harlem* (1928). McKay gained a considerable reputation as a poet with *Spring in New Hampshire* (1920) and *Harlem Shadows* (1922) many years before he established himself as a novelist. He also wrote an autobiography and a study of Harlem. McKay was very sympathetic to communism in the 1920s but he was to change and become virulently anticommunist by the late 1930s. His essay "Once More the Germans Face Black Troops" is a startling interpretation of the meaning of the presence of black colonial and African-American troops in Europe during World War I and the interwar years. It was published in *Opportunity*.

Again African soldiers bivouac on the Rhine. And Aframerican newspapers dramatize the news in deep black headlines, with striking photographs of stalwart native warriors led by French officers against a silhouette of palm trees, as if by a geographical miracle an oasis of the Sahara had been transplanted to the Franco-German frontier. This second extensive marshalling of an African army in Europe may evoke conflicting thoughts in many who think back to the hectic vacillating era of the Allied Occupation of the Rhineland. To perform that onerous duty France called upon her dependable African soldiers. And that action started a bitter, vicious propaganda which poisoned the minds of thousands of Germans and ultimately culminated in Hitler's mad onslaught against the Jews.

In the name of the German people, the German Kaiser had angrily protested against the Africans fighting in Europe during the first World War. The German propagandists maintained that the superior German race should not be subjected to fighting against inferior Africans. Curiously interesting is the fact that the most eloquent exponent of the Nordic theory of German racial superiority was a German-ized Englishman, Housten Chamberlain, who had chosen to reside in Germany. Another ironical item in the development of the propaganda is that it originated in the ideas of the French diplomat, Count Gobineau. In his book, *The Inequality of Races*, Gobineau exalted the Nordic above all other types of humanity. He died in 1882, the same year in which Darwin died.

There was no compunction among the Germans regarding the arming of their natives to fight the British in Africa, during the Great War. And if Britain had not swept the seas clear of them, they also might have transported African soldiers to fight in Europe. Commanding the sea routes, Britain and France availed themselves of colored man power from Africa, Asia, and America; and later the United States sent over her Negro soldiers.

The colored soldiers on the Allied side were eager fighters. White men had trained them for many decades in the tactics of modern warfare. White officers had led them in battle, to subdue independent and revolting native tribes and bring wild virgin regions of the globe into the orbit of the expanding domain of Civilization. But it was their first experience of girding to fight an army of white men in a great war.

The Africans lent a certain exotic flavor to the long, grim fighting in Europe. There were touching stories of their hard disciplined conduct and primitive simplic-ity, accompanied by striking photographs in newspapers and magazines. Some particularly painful items, such as the gruesome trophy of a German head trium-phantly carried by a Senegalese in his knapsack, were delicately and humorously handled to appease the public taste.

In the famous World War novel, *Le Feu* [The Fire], Henri Barbusse gives an unforgettable glimpse of the African soldiers marching to the front lines:

> Africans! They march past with faces red-brown, yellow or chestnut. . . . Their eyes are like balls of ivory or onyx, angular. Now and again comes swaying along above the line the coal-black mask of a Senegalese sharp-shooter. . . . We watch them in silence. They command respect and even a little fear. These Africans seem jolly and in high spirits. They are going, of course, in the front line. That is their place, and in their passing is the sign of an imminent attack. They are made for the offensive. Those and the 75 gun we can take our hats off to. They're everywhere sent ahead at big moments, the Moroccan Division.
>
> We talk over the characteristics of these Africans; their ferocity in attack, their devouring passion to be in with the bayonet. . . . We recall those tales that they tell. They raise their arms above their heads. . . . "Comrade, Com-rade!" "No, not Comrade." And in pantomime they drive a bayonet forward at belly-height. . . .

One of the sharp-shooters overhears our talk as he passes. He laughs abundantly in his helmeted turban and repeats our words with significant shakes of his head: "Not Comrade, not Comrade, never! Cut head off!"

"They're a different race from us," said Barque. . . "they only live for the minute. . . In fact, they're real soldiers."

"*We* are not soldiers," said Big Lamuse, "we're men."

Perhaps the arrival of the Aframericans to join their African brothers on the battle-fields of France perceptibly diminished the exotic status of the Colonials. In custom and outlook the Aframericans were closer to the Europeans than the Africans. Their thought processes, being American, were a part of the European stream. They spoke the same vernacular as their white American comrades, while the *petit-negre* jargon of the majority of Senegalese was barely intelligible to the *poilu* [First World War French soldier—Ed.]. The Germans may have expected a warm American response to their gospel of racial superiority, being quite aware of the extent of racial bigotry in America. They must have been confounded to confront Aframericans in Europe, valiantly fighting for the Allied cause.

Then came Armistice and Peace. And amidst the debris of German Empire, misery, hunger, internal strife and social revolutionary movements, the racial theory of German superiority apparently seemed lost, forgotten. But the ink was scarcely dry on the Treaty of Versailles before it was discovered, revived, and served as Germany's first effective appeal to the sentiment of the outside world.

The Great War had shot Europe to pieces, increasing and nourishing all the petty national and racial hatreds. And the black man who had fought for something that was quite incomprehensible to him was one of the first victims of the reaction. Before the war, old and ripely cultured Europe had tolerated him as a rarity. He was accommodated as a student, or a musician, actor or occasional tourist.

But the war had compelled colored men to Europe by hundreds of thousands: Africans, Aframericans and West Indians. Besides fighting in Flanders and Champagne, thousands were concentrated in French and English ports to work as stevedores. West Indian regiments saw service in Egypt and Arabia. The war's end found thousands of colored men congregated in the Allied capitals and the great French and English ports. Their unusual presence in such huge numbers stirred trouble between them and the common people, especially in England. Rioting broke out between blacks and whites for the first time in Britain. Particularly savage incidents occurred in London, Cardiff and Liverpool, where the homes of colored men were burned. Even in Marseille and Bordeaux there were dangerous flare-ups. The root of the disorders was social: economic and sexual maladjustment.

Of piquant interest is the story of the West Indian regiments. Those black regiments were formed soon after the emancipation of the slaves. They were the military pride of the West Indies. Their picturesque zouave uniform was adapted from the Moroccan native costume. It was either especially chosen or approved by Queen Victoria. The black regiments actively served in the conquest and pacification of Britain's West African colonies. Their regimental bands were famous at home and in England, where they had been sent [for] coronation ceremonies and other official celebrations.

The regiments were largely expanded during the World War. Abroad there developed friction between the colored and the white soldiers, especially the South Africans. The South Africans were ardent partisans of Nordic ideas of racial superiority, such as were propagated by the Germans. But, although they are a colonial and subject people, the West Indians were not accustomed to the special form of discrimination which was practiced against South African natives and which obtusely white South Africans desired to impose upon black soldiers abroad. As a consequence South Africans and West Indians became involved in grave conflicts. In that period of utmost peril the British command had to deal with the perplexing problem of keeping apart white soldiers of their great Dominion and colored soldiers from the colonies. The West Indians returned home with dangerous feelings of injustice and resentment. Serious disorders accompanied their return. They broke barracks and participated in civil strife to the point of mutiny. Finally the British Government abolished the black regiments. . . It is of interest to note that the Government of South Africa in its recent declaration of war upon Germany decided against sending troops to fight in Europe.

There were also serious differences between white and colored American soldiers in France. But there was no racial trouble between French *poilus* and French colonials. Senegalese, Moroccans, Annamites and French West Indians—France saw no reason why she should not employ her colored soldiers to do duty in the occupied zones, exactly as she had in actual warfare. But grunting and squirming under the heavy pressure of the Treaty of Versailles, the Germans accused the French of special vengeance. They said the French desired to humiliate them to the utmost by dominating them with savages. The French ridiculed the charges in their inimitable witty spirit.

In the Chamber of Deputies the black deputy from Martinique interrogated Premier Poincaré on the subject. Why did the Germans single out the colored troops for attack? Was their behavior less circumspect than the white troops? Had the German Government cited any specific act of the brutality or savagery of colored soldiers against German citizens? Poincaré replied that there were no specific charges. He charged the Germans with objecting to the African troops because of their race and color. And he declared that France would not tolerate an appeal to race prejudice. If Africans were brave enough to fight the foe in war, they were good enough to guard France in time of peace. Poincaré added in his dry humorless tone that the Germans hated the Africans because they, the Germans, were still uncivilized; they were the real savages. The Chamber of Deputies was convulsed with hilarity.

Excepting for such rare intervention as that of the black deputy, the poor and unorganized Africans could not defend themselves. So the insidious propaganda against them went merrily along. The French, however, considered the German appeal to world opinion against the African troops in the Rhineland just a stratagem to circumvent the Treaty of Versailles. The French position on the issue of the colonial troops was patently honest. Any one with observant eyes who has lived in France can attest that. African and other colonial conscripts are called to service in the same manner as Frenchmen. Many Colonials prefer to do their military service in France, while many Frenchmen choose the colonies. Senegalese soldiers may be seen all over France, in small towns like Langedoc, Gascogne, Burgundy, Brittany and Normandie as if, designedly, the French Government desires the inhabitants to become familiar with their presence.

The Chief of the French General Staff declared some years ago that France possessed an unlimited reserve of men in her African Empire. Because of this dependence upon their African man power, Germans and other foreigners have made doleful and silly predictions about the hybridization of the French and its danger to European civilization. But the calamity mongers must be either ignorant or wilfully blind to the close pattern of French social life. For in spite of all the naughty French letters and novels and revues and pictures and peep shows and what not, the French are really the most moral people in Europe. Family life is precious and bourgeois family life is sacred. Strangers are not permitted to break in easily as they may in some European countries. Excepting in unusual cases, the French do not generally mate with strangers and a foreign wife or husband in France is not an exotic social asset as it may be in Britain or America. If the hybridization of the French cannot be effected by other white people, there is little likelihood of native Africans becoming the instruments of hydridization. But the French are self-contained and so can permit many things that other people don't. Shut out from the sanctuary of their family life there are varied amusement features. And they grant strangers who can pay for it a license to play and some may imagine that that is looseness. These strangers may conjure up a lot of things when they happen to see Africans also having a good time like themselves. Perhaps because they lack the balance, self-assurance, and cultural unity which distinguish the French people.

The German agitation against the African troops in the Army of Occupation did not move the French. But it reached and stirred the English and Americans. In fact, some of the leading agitators were Germans who had lived in America. Eloquently they dwelt upon the status of Negroes in America, especially the South, and demanded whether the German people would stand for "*Neger-regierung*" (Negro-rule). By insistently harping upon this aspect of the Occupation of the Rhineland, the Germans created the first rift between the English and the French as early as 1920.

First receptive to the subtle propaganda in Britain were the Laborites and Leftists. Their sympathy naturally went to the newly-established Social-Democratic republic in Germany. The new regime was struggling against internal enemies, militarists and Junkers on the right and Communists on the left, while victorious France threatened with its black guard on the Rhine. The French were moving deeper and deeper into the Rhineland. In 1920 they entered the cities of Darmstadt, Dusseldorf and Frankfurt.

The British Leftists were convinced that the French were not giving the German republic a fair chance. But how could public opinion be aroused in the interest of a Germany that so recently had been a ruthless enemy? Employing the methods of all unscrupulous agitators, who sway the people with slogans little related to the real issues involved, the British Leftists took up the German cry of, "Black Troops on the Rhine!" The Germans had emphasized the humiliation of a Nordic people policed by African savages. But Britons preferred to dwell upon the erotic implications of the occupation. The labor paper, *The Daily Herald*, devoted liberal space to curious details of African *eroticism*. And its sales jumped sensationally, it was rumored, during the period of the agitation. More dignified was the *New Statesman*, but equally eminently disapproving. Marshalled by E. D. Morel, M.P., who was famous for exposing the Belgian atrocities in the Congo, leading liberals such as George Lansbury, M.P. and H. G. Wells joined the crusade.

The British people were profoundly moved. Protest meetings were organized throughout Britain. The African occupation of the Rhineland was not the only issue, but also the spectre of France massing African troops to dominate Europe by force. It had been rumored that African soldiers had acted to dislodge German workers from an industrial plant, which had been seized in the occupied territory. This was a serious incident to the labor leaders, who thought ahead to the future when African troops might possibly be hurled against the advance of Labor.

It was an era of violent social upheaval. Extreme Leftists cherished hopes of winning the armed forces to their side as had the Bolsheviks in Russia. But they felt less hopeful of influencing African troops. Among the British upper classes the reaction was different, of course. They disapproved of African troops in the Army of Occupation, but because of its effect upon European prestige in Africa. However, the Conservative press did not join in the protest.

The French were only irritated. The people as a whole, even organized labor, were not perturbed. Instinctively committed to the highly civilized custom of the small family, they had accepted with fatality the fact that as long as the maintenance of an immense army was necessary to the preservation of their national life, they must needs depend upon the African reservoir for an adequate supply of man power.

But the Germans had won with flying colors their appeal to world opinion and succeeded in ideologically dividing the allies. The political repercussions were stupendous. The Black-Troops-on-the-Rhine campaign was the entering wedge of the split between French and British policy, which carried Europe drifting and floundering down the years into another war.

The British and French viewpoints were irreconcilable, perhaps because the French are obstinately hard about practical facts and, unlike the British, little swayed by puritan sensibility. At the time of the Washington Conference, four years after the Armistice, relations between France and Britain had become so strained that the British, conjuring up a sudden French attack, were demanding the limitation of their submarine and air fleet building. The tension was eased by the advent to power of the Labor Government in 1924. The French also got rid of Poincaré le Ruhr (as the Premier was nicknamed) to put in a radical government. Meeting at Geneva, Prime Minister Ramsay MacDonald and Premier Hernot staged a dramatic demonstration of friendship by publicly embracing each other.

Yet it is of interest to remember that the presence of the Africans in the Rhineland and in Europe had been protested primarily by members of the Labor Government and its prominent supporters. The Laborites were opposed to further occupation of the Rhineland by any troops, black or white, and were demanding the withdrawal of the Army of Occupation. But the Labor Government survived a few months only and the French Radical Socialist government only a little longer. When the Labor Government returned to power in 1929 it withdrew the British troops of the occupation, leaving the French alone to continue the policing of the Rhineland for another year.

The agitation against the African troops had caught the attention of the world. Emerging triumphant from the Russian Civil War, the Bolshevik masters of the Kremlin were also interested. With fresh eager minds and a radically new outlook on international affairs, they were not, like the British, concerned about the moral implications of the African troops on the continent of Europe. The Bolsheviks saw in the Africans vigorous virgin human material which could be moulded to the interest of the proletariat in the world struggle between labor power and capitalist power.

Chinese peasants and primitive Mongolian nomads fighting on their side during the Civil War had proved themselves dependable and indomitable. The Bolsheviks believed that Africans also could be trained in the service of the Social Revolution. Their policy of special sympathy and encouragement to Africans and other colored peoples was based upon this premise. Africans, Aframericans, Indians, Chinese—all colored delegates and students in Moscow were always accorded preferential treatment.

The policing of the Rhineland with African troops was one of the issues discussed at the Fourth Congress of the Communist International, which was held in Moscow in 1922–23. The writer was in Moscow then. The leader of the German delegation from the Ruhr declared that the agitation against the African troops was purely political propaganda. The population, he said, was friendly towards the Africans and even treated them with more consideration than the European troops. A similar point of view was expressed by Clara Zetkin, the first woman member of the Reichstag.

I was invited to visit the Rhineland to make my own observations. I did later, when I returned to Germany. Personally, I was treated with perfect courtesy everywhere. And the cordial relationship which existed between the African troops and the common people was quite amazing. It appeared even more natural and intimate than what I have observed in France. And also it set me thinking as to what might have been the original germ of the propaganda. For though the issues may be distorted and deliberately confused to deceive the people, propaganda does not come out of the air, but has its roots in something real.

It seemed evident that it was the over friendliness of the population to the Africans, rather than their presence as French soldiers, which aggravated the propagandists. When excited by agitation and led as soldiers the Germans may be savage and ruthless, but the common folk seemed to be the kindliest and most considerate in Europe. I was often asked almost childishly: "Do you like us Germans?" "Do they like us in America?" As if I could answer for American majority opinion! People in France don't ask such questions. They consider it natural that France should be admired by any visitor as the most civilized country in the world.

The propagandists might have started with the idea that the friendliness and familiarity of the German folk with the Africans may be demoralizing for a conquered people. The motives of Hitler and his henchmen were almost identical when they made a bonfire of books and works of art and science, which they considered un-German and defeatist, and proscribed international culture.

Hitler himself must have been quite receptive to the propaganda against the Africans. Although it started when he was unknown, three years before the Munich putsch, his *Mein Kampf* reveals that his extraordinarily alert mind was attuned to every echo of the grievances of the defeated German nation. Probably as he brooded over the idea of *Mein Kampf*, the issue of Nordic superiority and African inferiority might have appeared as live as any.

But he was no Frobenius, scientifically interested in Africans, no Gobineau dealing in abstract ideas. A realist, he may have reflected that Germany was stripped of her African colonies and that the Africans were merely the pliant instruments of a victorious power, that would undoubtedly be dealt with some day. Also although Africa was vastly rich, native Africans possessed no great individual wealth or political power.

So Hitler may have pondered, why continue the empty issue of Nordic superiority and African inferiority, when the Army of Occupation was entirely withdrawn? But the dogma of the superiority of the German race was still a wonderful whip to excite the pride of a humiliated nation. And instead of the poor transient African there was the eternal Jew, comfortably ensconced in Germany, possessing enormous wealth and political power, and stirring Hitler's imagination with the attractive possibility of LOOT! So in the place of the African scapegoat, Hitler put the Jew.

But now the African troops have returned to the Rhineland again, fighting Fascism, fighting for Democracy and the liberation of Christian and Jew. Will Hitler like the Kaiser bellow against Africans fighting in Europe? Will he try to revive the old prejudice about Black Troops on the Rhine? British Labor cannot heed, for it is the spearhead of British antagonism to Hitler. And Britons—British workers—are fighting side by side with those Africans, who are fighting for the freedom of Labor against Dictatorship, fighting for the triumph of Democracy.

A REPLY TO MY CRITICS

Randolph Blasts
Courier a "Bitter Voice
of Defeatism"

A. PHILIP RANDOLPH (1889–1979) was one of the
greatest labor leaders and civil disobedience strategists in American social
history. He was the editor of *The Messenger,* and organizer of The
Brotherhood of Sleeping Car Porters, whose key victories in the 1930s in
negotiating with the Pullman Company opened the door for the gains of
the Civil Rights movement 25 to 30 years later. Randolph was also the
organizer of the March on Washington Movement which was
instrumental in the integration of defense plants during World War II
and eventually led to the integration of the armed services in 1948.
These three articles, from the six that Randolph wrote in the June and
July 1943 issues of the *Chicago Defender,* largely in response to his
critics, particularly the *Pittsburgh Courier,* one of the leading black
newspapers of the day, virtually lays out the format, strategy, philosophy,
and tactics of the civil rights movement; taken together, these pieces rank
as one of the most important pieces of political writing by a black
American.

T he noble editorial pose of the *Pittsburgh Courier* as the High Command
and Infallible Arbiter on the grand strategy of organization for the solution
of the Negro problem during these times of storm and stress, would be
humorous were it not so tragically disastrous.

With a mere flourish of flippancy the strident voice of the petty black bourgeoisie
buries the March on Washington under a mountain of words and bids it ever to be
silent. Yes, strange as it may seem the *Pittsburgh Courier* disposes of a movement as
simple as that, as it innocently thinks, which has staged the greatest anti-discrimination
and anti-segregation demonstrations in the history of the Negro people, and won the

biggest economic victory for the masses in securing Executive Order No. 8802, which has been the means of securing thousands of jobs for Negroes.

Says the *Courier* in the issue of May 8: "The March on Washington leadership is completely visionary and has succeeded merely in staging a few giant mass meetings and stirring indignation and unrest which it lacks the administrative genius to constructively canalize. The measure of this leadership is evidenced by irresponsible talk about suicidal civil disobedience and mass marches which never materialize."

VALUE OF MEETINGS

And so giant mass meetings against jim-crow don't count, although the government of the United States uses them to whip up patriotism to increase war bond sales. Labor stages them to safeguard its rights and to win new ones; the Jews and other minority groups spend thousands of dollars and give months in sweat and toil to build them. From the very foundation of our republic and among all of the free and oppressed peoples of the world, the public meeting has been the chief agency for creating cause consciousness for freedom and peace. But to the *Courier* great public meeting demonstrations mean nothing.

Thus, despite these solid and constructive achievements, the *Courier* which would claim credit for every step of progress the Negro people make, elects hysterically and frantically to deride, berate and decry the March on Washington Movement, its leadership, and all its works. If something isn't done to cause M.O.W.M. to do a disappearing act, this self-proclaimed incomparable paragon of journalistic wisdom will simply go beserk and possibly pass out.

The *Courier* is hell-bent upon selling the people a bill of goods to the effect that the March on Washington is going to cause our white folks to get so crazy, dizzy-mad that they will swing a shillelah on our dolicho-meso-brachycephalic skulls and knock our Hottentot brains out.

COURIER'S LACKS

But happily, the inexorable law of diminishing returns will take care of the editorial struggles of the *Courier* to tear the March on Washington Movement limb from limb and give it the old run-out powders—even were we to refrain from saying "It ain't so." From M.O.W.M.'s diagnosis of the condition of the *Courier*, the conclusion is unavoidable that it is suffering from an acute masochistic complex. It feels sorry for itself despite its material affluence. And why? It lacks something.

We can understand why it cannot comprehend the deeper spiritual implications of the March Movement and the inescapable challenge of moving masses for a free world.

It lacks a cause.

It lacks a mission.

It lacks dedication to an ideal or principle bigger than itself.

It has no faith in the masses, black or white.

Its editorials breathe the lifeless air of defeatism, cynicism, supersophistica-
tionism and futilitarianism.

It sneers and snubs the people's struggles for economic, political and social
   righteousness.
With all of its ink and paper, it is the victim of editorial frustration.

GESTAPO JOURNALISM

Obsessed with its editorial personality inadequacy, it manifests homicidal tendencies
toward the March on Washington Movement and militant struggles for social
justice, believing with a sort of cruel religious faith that it is ordained to serve as the
propaganda Gestapo of the M.O.W.M. But the March on Washington Movement
is certain to survive the ravings of this commercial champion of comfort and
conservatism.

Listen to the Jesuitical casuistry of the editorial Solon of the *Courier* and one
would think that the March on Washington Movement is a throw-back to Neander-
thal Man, and, withal, even without benefit of his primitive tools of fire and
stone.

We hasten to assure our friends and foes that we only claim to be the "little
men" of the specie[s]. Homo Sapiens, who humbly seek to play our part without
hope of pomp or glory or thirty pieces of silver in making America a free land for
black men.

AIMS OF MARCH

Now why does this journalistic colussus thunder his wrath against M.O.W.M.?
Only because the March on Washington Movement proposes to march on Washing-
ton against Jim Crow.

Only because it proposes to hold a great "We Are Americans, Too" conference
in Chicago June 30 to July 4, to proclaim that jim-crow must go and march to help
make it go.

Only because M.O.W.M. proposes to ponder and to discuss as a form of
strategy, to fight jim-crow, nonviolent, good-will direct action, which is a modified
expression of the principle of non-violent civil disobedience and non-cooperation
set forth by Gandhi in India.

Only because M.O.W.M. proposes that the Negro people no longer rely solely
upon the Republican, Democratic, Socialist or Communist parties but that they
should build a powerful non-partisan political block without the benefit of the flesh-
pots of either of the parties, but that they depend upon their own right financial
arm.

Only because the March on Washington Movement is an expression of mass
pressure as a technique of action and socio-racial instrumentation for the achieve-
ment of Negro rights.

Only because the M.O.W.M. is an all-Negro movement, though not anti-
white or anti-semitic or anti-American or anti-labor or anti-democratic.

Only because the M.O.W.M. preaches the doctrine of self-reliance to the
Negro people, but with collaboration with other groups, white or otherwise, that
seek to wipe out jim-crow.

HOW IT STARTED

But a word now about how the March on Washington came into being and how it functions.

The present crisis gave birth to the March on Washington Movement. It was formed in protest against a wild and reckless exhibition of racial discrimination and segregation in [the] defense industry and the government. Although the United States was working feverishly to become the arsenal of democracy, and hence needed skilled and unskilled manpower, Negroes were shunted from pillar to post, given the run-around and oft-times insulted when they applied for war jobs to help make our country an arsenal of democracy.

Young Negro men and women who had passed civil service examinations with unusually creditable ratings, found a cold, if not hostile reception when applying for jobs even in government departments.

Negroes were turned down by defense personnel managers for many and sundry reasons such as, they simply had not worked Negroes before, or that they were lazy or incompetent or were too slow, or wouldn't make time or that the white employees would strike if Negroes were taken on. It did not matter that Negro workers had a record for high productive ability in the First World War. It did not matter that Negroes had given and were giving satisfactory performance of skilled tasks in private peacetime industry. Discrimination was riding the high winds of race hate.

Meanwhile, billions of dollars of the taxpayers, of whom Negroes represent no inconsiderable section, were being appropriated by the Congress for war contracts. Powerful captains of industry, waving the flag and proclaiming their patriotism the while, set up exacting profit-making demands as the only condition under which they would agree to transform and gear their plants for war production to defeat the Axis powers. Albeit, they got what they wanted. Moreover, they put dollar-a-year men on OPM and WPB and other agencies to see to it that their contractual rights are protected.

Organized labor through the A. F. of L. and C.I.O. denounced no-strike legislation for the duration but agreed to waive the right to strike if the government set up the War Labor Board with labor possessing equal representation with capital and the public to settle disputes over wages, working conditions and union recognition that arose in defense plants. Labor also demanded equal participation in all government defense agencies to help run the war. It has not won all of its demands but it has not surrendered. It is still fighting and it is winning step by step.

But what about the Negro? Negroes never got and do not now have any real representation in anything. They were thrown the sop of "advisers" and "aides" although nobody accepted their advice or aid either in or out of the government. Negroes were and still are segregated in the Army, Navy, Marine Service Air Corps, WAACS, and rejected by the WAVES and SPARS.

PARLEYS FAIL

Efforts to correct this outrageous, unjust and undemocratic condition through the ordinary conference technique with President Roosevelt and government department heads failed and failed miserably. Top government spokesmen gave generously of their charm and courtesy in receiving Negro leaders but no jobs. They went to great pains not to offend Negro leaders in these conferences. In fact, their impeccable politeness without action was definitely boring, especially when everybody knew that Negro workers were being kicked around and Negro soldiers called "nigger" by bumptious, Negro-hating southern white officers.

Yes, the conference method of handling Negro problems collapsed. The truth is, it never had worked. Negroes simply thought it worked. Negroes had never realized that a conference does not amount to a picayune unless there is power behind the representatives in the conference. The so-called good-will, interracial conferences don't mean a thing. They are chloroform for the masses. When the chloroform wears off, the passions of the beast of race prejudice flare up again.

Organized labor has long since learned the lesson of the value of organized power behind its leaders in conference. If the words of leaders cannot be backed by the deeds of the people, they are empty and futile and the leaders are useless and helpless.

DESPERATION APPARENT

A sense of utter helplessness came over the Negro leaders when nothing but glowing unfulfilled promises came out of conference after conference with government heads. Negroes became disillusioned and desperate.

While Negroes wanted to join the armed forces and produce ships and planes, guns and ammunition to help defeat the Axis nations, opinions were expressed from jitterbugs to Ph.D.'s alike, to the effect that there was no difference between Hitler of Germany and Talmadge of Georgia or Tojo of Japan and Bilbo of Mississippi so far as Negroes were concerned. This was the outcry of bitterness and resentment. Negroes were wounded.

In the midst of these conditions the March on Washington Movement was born.

In the March on Washington Movement, the voiceless and helpless "little men" became articulate. Though jobless, for the first time they experienced a thrill from a sense of their importance and worthwhileness. In meeting after meeting, the "forgotten black man" could rise and tell an eager and earnest crowd about jobs he sought but never got, about the business agent of the union giving him the brush-off, how he had gone to the gates of defense plants only to be kept out while white workers walked in, how he cooled his heels in an office and finally was told with a cold stare, "no more workers wanted" or how the government employment services would not permit him to enroll as a skilled worker but only as a porter or janitor or how he was denied entrance into certain government training courses for skilled defense jobs.

In very truth, in the March on Washington, little men can tell their story their own way.

Randolph Tells Philosophy Behind "March" Movement

Negroes are at the crossroads. They face new problems. These problems are made bigger, more complex and baffling by this global war.

The solution of these problems requires a re-orientation in program, strategy, method and technique. What is true of the Negro is also true of labor, all minorities, all oppressed groups, and the champions of the liberal democratic tradition.

But before we settle upon the pattern of this re-orientation, it is well to explore the nature of the times through which we are passing. This is no longer a period of capitalist democratic, social, economic and political equilibrium. Times have changed. We are living in a period of social acceleration. The tempo of our social metamorphosis has been stepped up. It continues to step up.

What has happened?

What is happening?

What may happen?

CLASH OF COLOR

World War II has brought into focus a sharp and threatening clash of color. It has deepened the conflict between monopoly, capitalistic democracy and totalitarian fascist autocracy.

The foundations of the century of financial imperialism and colonialism are cracking. The progress of science and industrialism, the deepening revolt against the master race ideology and the decisive challenge for ethnic democracy by the darker races, are bringing this about.

But what of the future?

Gandhi and Nehru and the All-India Congress leaders uncompromisingly defy the rule of Britain and demand independence and freedom for India.

China, not long from under the yoke of the white power European nations, Great Britain only yesterday having been expelled from Hongkong by Japan, wars against imperialist Nippon for peace and freedom.

AFRICA RESTIVE

While little or nothing is said in the news about Africa, except as the battle ground of the tanks and airplanes of the Allied and Axis powers, and as providing strategic military and naval bases for the United Nations, it is a matter of common knowledge that the natives in North Africa and in Africa south of the Sahara Desert, are restive and stirring under the imperialist rule of the old mandate system of the League of Nations and the colonial policies of Great Britain, France, Italy, Spain, Portugal, Holland and Belgium.

And what of the natives? Is this war being fought to restore the rule of these imperialist powers? Will Singapore be handed back to Britain?

In the West Indies, there are riots and rebellion of the natives for work and wages and against British colonialism. Black militant leaders of the natives are thrown into concentration camps. They are hounded and harassed but not silenced.

Negroes in the United States of America smart under a socio-economic, political racial chauvinism. They are awakening. They are questioning the domination of the so-called master white race. And they are re-examining their own moral, spiritual and intellectual armament.

THESIS OF MARCH

In the midst of this economic chaos, political disorder, social confusion, conflict of world ideologies, intellectual uncertainty and international unpredictability, the March on Washington Movement was born. Immediately it struck its roots deep in the soil of the Negro masses.

Its program and strategy, technique and methodology are set forth in the following thesis of the March on Washington Movement:

1. That this is a period of revolutionary ferment in which the patch-work, compromise and appeasement policy type of action is futile, useless and unnecessary in seeking a solution to the problems of race, labor or society.

2. That the Negro is passing through his darkest hour in the United States of America and throughout the world, and that his lot as a citizen has grown worse since Pearl Harbor, and will continue to grow worse unless some basic change is made in the policy of the Federal Government toward the citizenship status of the Negro.

SUPREME STRUGGLE

3. That the Negro must make his supreme struggle for his democratic rights and the status of first-class citizenship, now while conditions are fluid and unsettled for after the war is over it will be too late, since the social, economic, political, and racial relations will tend to become crystallized with encrusted dogmas that will resist change.

4. That the government is an accommodative and repressive organism which is constantly balancing pressures from conflicting social forces in the local and national communities, and without regard to the question of right or wrong, it inevitably moves in the direction of the pressure of the greatest challenge.

5. That the methodology and technique in an epoch of revolutionary ferment must be revolutionary, unusual, extraordinary, dramatic and drastic in order to be effective in placing the cause of a minority into the mainstream of national and international public opinion.

SELF-RELIANCE

6. That Negroes must develop the spirit of self-reliance, and take the initiative and assume the responsibility for the solution of their problem, but collaborate with their natural allies such as the trade union movement, and other oppressed minorities including the Jews and Catholics and those liberal forces that seek to extend the frontiers of a true democracy.

7. That the goal of the Negro is complete equality, economic, political, social and racial, with the immediate objectives of abolishing discrimination and segregation in the defense and peacetime industries, the Government and the Army,

Navy, U.S. Marines, Air Corps, WAACS, WAVES, and SPARS, in housing, education, transportation, places of service accommodation, such as hotels, restaurants and places of amusement, including theaters, dance halls, etc.

9. That the law of the achievements of freedom, justice and equality is the law of the Seed and the Cross. This is the law of struggle, sacrifice, suffering. It is the law of death. Death precedes life. The seed must decay and die before the tree can live. Jesus Christ had to bear the cross and die in order to give life everlasting. Verily, there is no royal road to freedom.

10. That the power resides in the masses and they must be organized and mobilized and disciplined to struggle for equality.

This is the philosophy of the March on Washington Movement. Without some such chart and compass, Negro movements and leadership will ever be hopelessly and distressingly unwitting of their way.

Their efforts and struggles will be purposeless and planless. And such is the case with a large section of Negro leadership today. It has no system of thinking by which to interpret events and issues and problems as they arise from day to day that affect the Negro and the workers. There is no well-developed philosophy of thought and struggle by which the Negro leaders evaluate the importance and significance of political movements, economic policies and social systems, to the Negro.

In fact, our leadership is dangerously divided. There is no agreement on segregation, whether it is a menace or promise. Note the fact that the *Pittsburgh Courier* has gone on record as suggesting and advocating a jim-crow army. It is not alone. Dr. DuBois [sic] quit the National Association for the Advancement of Colored People on the theory of utilizing segregated opportunity. In the First World War, Negro leadership accepted Jim Crow in the armed forces uncomplainingly.

But the March on Washington Movement rejects segregation as the main pillar of racial chauvinism, oppression and exploitation. And segregation is the one pillar of the temple of racial fascism and oppression, which southern race bigotry will guard zealously and not surrender without a struggle.

In the "We Are Americans, Too" Conference which will be held in Chicago June 30 to July 4, segregation in labor, industry, government, education, housing, entertainment and transportation will be described and plans mapped to attack it as the major problem which confronts the Negro today.

Randolph Tells Technique of Civil Disobedience

A major strategy which will be thoroughly explored at the "We Are Americans, Too" conference in Chicago will be what is generally known as non-violent civil disobedience and non-cooperation.

According to the program of the March on Washington Movement this same principle will be expressed through what we elect to designate as constitutional obedience or non-violent good will direct action.

But this strategy has been condemned and denounced by critics on the grounds that we are attempt to introduce as a method for solution of the Negro problem, a strategy which was born in a foreign and oriental situation.

NOT VALID

However, this criticism is not valid. By the same token of reasoning one could condemn Christianity and reject it as a product of an oriental clime. Jesus Christ, like Gandhi, was born in the eastern world.

But there are certain basic principles of human behavior that are well-nigh universal, one, is some form of religious worship, Christianity, Confucius, Buddhist, or pagan. It is practically a universal trait also for people everywhere constantly to seek to achieve freedom and relief from pain, physical and social, and the securing of pleasure and happiness, individual and collective.

The difference between non-violent civil disobedience and non-cooperation as advocated by Gandhi in India and non-violent good-will direct action is set forth by the March on Washington Movement is that in India the objective is to effect a transition of governmental power from the hands of the British imperialists into the hands of the Indian people as represented by the all-India Congress. It practically amounts to the breaking down of British Civil government and the establishment of an Indian Civil government. Were this not so, the fight for Indian independence would have no point or meaning.

PURPOSE IN AMERICA

But in America the March on Washington Movement does not seek to bring about any transition of governmental power from the hands of the white people to the Negro people. There is no desire to see the collapse of American civil government. Negroes are not seeking independence as a racial unit. On the contrary we want to maintain American civil government because wherever it ceases to function, mob law reigns and Negroes are the victims.

But it is contended that the program of the March on Washington in advocating constitutional obedience will be provocative of violence, bloodshed and trouble. This allegation is doubtless based upon the theory that the March on Washington Movement will call upon Negroes in the armed forces, and in the defense industries to refuse to obey orders and commands and stop work at a given time, because this method of action is comparable to that which is practiced in India during the non-violent civil disobedience campaign.

This construction of non-violent goodwill action as espoused by the March on Washington Movement is wholly erroneous and misrepresents it. The March on Washington will not call on the Negroes of the armed forces or defense industries to disobey commands or stop work at any time. These groups will not come within the category of Negroes who will be expected to comply with the program of non-violent goodwill direct action nor will the procedure and technique of behavior be of a piece with the Indian Nationalist pattern.

BASED ON COMMON UNITY

Non-violent goodwill direct action in the first place is based upon the theory of the common unity of all peoples and the possible modification of behavior patterns by a process of reconditioning through the word and the deed, but fundamentally through the deed. While language plays an important role in the transformation of human action and human institutions, action, the deed is far more potent and in fact it is perhaps the human crucible through which the language forms are developed.

Now for a long time the Negro has relied rather completely on the processes of persuasion through the written word such as, petitions and statements and eloquent orations of condemnation to and of the white ruling class. But the Negro people as such have never been thrown into actual physical motion against jim-crow, discrimination and segregation in America. Because of this fact the word or statement and oratorical method of dealing with the question of Negroes has been quite ineffective because they could not be descriptive of any basic actual human struggle Negroes were waging to achieve the objectives, namely, freedom, justice and equality.

While the use of the word will still be of paramount importance, the word will play an entirely different role according to the program of the March on Washington Movement in as much as it will reflect and portray human effort that the social and physical movements of Negroes are carrying on to bring about the abolition of jim-crow in America today.

OUTLINES PROCEDURE

For instance, when the March on Washington Movement projects constitutional obedience as an instrument to change the racial exclusion policy of a given restaurant, hotel or place of entertainment with respect to the Negro, it will proceed through the action technique, namely by having a group of Negroes visit the restaurant, hotel, or said place of entertainment preceded by a group of whites.

If the Negroes are refused, the whites who have been trained with the Negroes as to the procedure, will join with the Negroes and call upon the management for a reason for the racial exclusion policy. If it is not possible to change the policy through negotiation then a civil action suit will be planned with the white persons cooperating as witnesses.

When the negotiation period has ended and it is recognized as being impossible to change the position and policy of the enterprise, non-violent goodwill action calls for the next step which is possibly the staging of a sitdown strike of white and colored citizens who have been well trained with respect to technique of action and procedure.

The picketline may also be employed. When this is done and the law is invoked by the proprietor, the March on Washington's policy will be for the Negroes and whites to stand their ground in the said restaurant even to the point of being thrown out physically, in which event, action will not be taken for damages for physical injury but only for civil rights on the grounds that physical injury is an incident of the struggle and that some suffering and sacrifice must be made by Negroes if they expect to win their freedom.

Should Negroes March On Washington— If So, When?

Is Jim Crow in Washington? What a question! Is water wet? Is fire hot? Is Mississippi's Senator Bilbo anti-Negro? Is Texas's Congressman Dies against racial equality?

Yes "Mr. James H. Crow" has his habitat in Washington. In the capital of our republic, Negro citizens are segregated in life and segregated in death. In the capital of the arsenal of democracy Negro citizens cannot buy a sandwich beyond the Black-Belt except at the railroad station.

Verily, Washington is not only the capital of the nation. It is the capital of Dixie, of 20th Century Copperheaded Confederacy. There, crackerocracy is in the saddle. Ku Klux Klanism runs riot. Here, the alleged headquarters of the democracy of the world, an anti–poll tax bill is filibustered to death by a tiny fraction of "little wilful men"—southern senators, and an anti-lynching bill cannot survive.

Not only is Jim Crow in Washington. Jim Crow is running Washington. Negroes cannot eat in the restaurant of the Congress. They cannot even sit in the peanut gallery of any cheap theater in downtown Washington.

This is an affront. It is an insult. Here is the Negro's dilemma. They are not first-class citizens because they are jim-crowed and they are jim-crowed because they are not first-class citizens. Thus, to win first-class citizenship is to abolish jim-crow and to abolish jim-crow is to win first-class citizenship.

JIM CROW RUNNING D.C.

But, the tragedy is not only that Jim Crow is in the District of Columbia, but that the pattern of Washington's Jim Crow is being spread by "official" Washington into areas of our country—North, East and West, where it was hitherto unknown. Our federal government in Washington has become an official carrier of the germ of Jim-Crow throughout the length and breadth of our land, and is infecting the body politic everywhere and poisoning the blood stream of national public opinion. Official Washington is freezing Jim Crow. It is perpetuating the pattern of segregation. It is crystallizing second-class citizenship.

What can be done about it? This question is naturally posed.

Why is Washington such an important center for the Negro to direct his forces upon? In short, why march on Washington? The answer is, Washington is the head and front and nerve center of the world. Washington is the political symbol of the greatest power on earth today. Prime ministers and kings of all of the nations of the earth look to Washington, not so much for ideas as for lend-lease, and they accept America's ideas on race and color. Because of the billions now being appropriated by the Congress in Washington to help the United Nations win the war and for the promotion of plans for the post-war rehabilitation of both the Allies and enemy powers, Washington is the financial and economic powerhouse of the entire world. Upon the well-known theory that politics is a reflex of economics, the political influence of Washington is destined to grow into towering proportions.

Thus, if the Negro people permit Washington to continue and develop as a symbol of color and racial Jim-Crow-ism, the colored and subject peoples everywhere will look with contempt upon the Negro as the classic second-class citizens of all times.

ECONOMIC AND POLITICAL CENTRALISM

Under our monopoly capitalistic economy, economic power and control are being steadily concentrated into the hands of the few. There has been no appreciable modification of the fact that two percent or less of the population own ninety percent of the wealth in the last decade. Pari-passu with this amazing economic concentration has gone the centralization of political power in our federal system. The existing gross inequalities in wealth and natural resources in our geographical regions, makes federal control and determination of broad economic and legislative policies well nigh inevitable. Then, Washington is required not only to provide lend-lease for Russia but also lend-lease or WPA for Georgia, one of the southern states, distinguished for its backwardness in racial relations, [and] social and labor legislation.

But political centralism is condemned and rejected by the Southern bourbon politicians and branded as "bureaucracy" and the antithesis of the American democratic system whose roots are deep in the soil of the village and town meeting where all policies affecting the local communities are aired and made. This theory, if followed, will safeguard the poll tax, white primaries and other discriminatory registration devices and the right of the South to handle and settle the race problem in its own sweet way.

Hence, the doctrine of States' rights is being revived with all of its old-time virulence and vitality by the Southern political theoreticians. A break with the New Deal Democratic party and an alliance with the Middle Western Republicans that also views this trend of political centralism with alarm, is threatened. These two political doctrines are now coming to grips. Which will survive?

FOR POWERFUL FEDERAL SYSTEM

Where should the Negro stand? It is almost axiomatic that the hope of the Negro in the South lies in the decreasing influence of states' rights and the increasing power of the federal government. If Negroes are ever to get an equal break in educational, farming and labor opportunities in the South, they will get it through enlightened and liberal federal government policies and financial subsidy, with some voice in the application of the basic principles of democracy.

But Negroes must be realistic. Dangers lurk in increasing federal power. It's the danger of a Jim-Crowized and segregationized federal system. If this obtains, the South won't need states' rights anymore. They will have control over federal rights. In which event, it is possible that the Negroes in America, like the Jews in the Third Reich of Hitler, may be sentenced by federal state decree to official Jim-Crowism.

Whether this happens or not, will depend largely upon the Negro himself and the extent and effectiveness he is able to convince labor and liberal America that the spread of Jim-Crowism or anti-Negroism is a pre-condition to the rise and progress of Fascist forces and the Nazi theories of racialism that may destroy our democratic system, such as it is.

If the South succeeds in selling the federal government and America as a whole its doctrine of racism, it is conceivable that the time may come when Jim-Crow may become constitutional fiat. Note the laws against the Jews in Germany and France.

A CENTRAL POINT OF STRATEGY

But with all of the real and imaginary dangers involved in the possible control of our federal system by the apostles of Southernism, since the Negroes' legal and constitutional status as citizens in our Republic has its origin and source in federalism through the specific adoption of the Fourteenth Amendment following the Civil War, and since under the shibboleth of states' rights, Negroes have been shorn of the rights they theoretically possess, we have no choice save to stand for the strengthening of our federal political organism.

However, this does not mean that Negroes in the hinterlands of Mississippi and Alabama and in the big metropolitan centers should sit down, fold their arms and wait on Uncle Sam to make all things wrong right. No, not at all. Because even if the federal state apparatus had not fallen under the dominion of Southernocracy, it would not voluntarily take up the cause of the Negro or any other group in the national community and fight for it. Governments don't act that way. Whatever concession any group secures from the American state is either the result of control or pressure.

Because the head of every organism is its most sensitive part, the head of every state usually registers the slightest adumbration of the social forces, Negroes, like the South, labor, business and farmers, must carry their problems to Washington with increasing force, intelligence and drama. And the extent to which either one of the aforementioned social forces get[s] a favorable hearing at the capital is in virtually direct ratio to the amount of pressure-power it can mobilize and exercise upon the machinery of the federal state. Risking a possible over-simplification in the statement of the situation, it practically amounts to this: No pressure, no concession. Even the justice of a group's cause is not sufficient. A group must not only be right, it must have might. Even the decisions of the Supreme court of the United States as Mr. Dooley says, oftentimes follow public sentiment.

PRESSURE ON GOVERNMENT

The question of whether the Negroes shall put pressure upon the local, state and federal governments to achieve their rights, is tantamount to asking shall the Negroes seek to survive. But Negroes want more than survival. They want to survive as equals, as first-class citizens, possessing and enjoying all of the rights, privileges and immunities of any other citizen.

However, Negroes will not survive as equals unless they are fit to survive as equals. And they are not fit to survive as equals unless they have the power to survive as equals. They will not possess the power to survive as equals unless they are organized upon a mass basis from the so-called bottom to the top, including the so-called uneducated and the educated, the poor and the well-to-do, the jitterbug and Ph.D.s, the sharecroppers and city workers.

Not only must the chasm between the uneducated and educated Negro be abolished and all brought into a common mass struggle to develop the maximum striking and pressure power of the Negro in the liberation movement to attack jim-crow but the "little Negro" must be drawn into the fight by actual participation and given a sense of his importance, responsibility, obligation and ability to share in the performance of vital tasks that are nominally thought to be the exclusive function of the educated and professional Negro.

CANNOT WIN WITHOUT THE MASSES

The fact is the Negroes' cause cannot win without the masses. Negroes of talent, genius and ability are about at the end of their ropes. The demonstration of the Negroes' capacity for cultural advancement has been a necessary stage in the evolution of Negro life. And it must continue to go forward. But the Negroes' primary problem now is to survive as an economic, political, social and racial equal.

This involves power, economic, social and political power. The masses alone can supply that power. The masses have numbers. Effective public demonstrations need numbers. The public is always affected by numbers. It is also affected by the purpose for which great masses demonstrate. The public, Negro and white, is affected by large number of people in physical motion. Great mass formations affect all of the physical senses. They stir the feelings of the people. They provoke thought. They cause officials of state to pause and wonder.

Demonstrations of great masses of workers in strikes, on the picket line, is the chief strategy of the trade union movement. It has gotten results and will continue to get results. But the demonstration must be non-violent. The demonstrators must not possess offensive deadly weapons such as knives, razors or guns of any kind. The Negro's most effective weapon is his purpose, cause, moral courage and non-violent mass demonstration.

Thus, it appears that an important part of the future strategy and technique of the Negro must be in the field of demonstration, both non-violent mass activity and disciplined non-violent demonstration of small Negro and white groups for civil and economic justice.

And it does not appear that anything is calculated to awaken both white and black America to the justice and necessity of the Negroes being recognized and accepted as a full-fledged American citizen except some demonstration with the drama of a March on Washington. But when? The answer is: when the people are ready and the times and conditions give such a program strategic power. Even the much talked about Second Front is considered from the point of view of time strategy or its whole point may be lost.

Moreover, the people must not only be ready but they must be prepared and disciplined to march on Washington. And this may have to be done. Such a comprehensive maneuver will require the support and cooperation of Negro leadership from church, labor, business and the people.

But a March on Washington must be the Negroes' last resort.

Randolph Tells Program To Win Full Race Equality

Before a program for any oppressed minority or majority can be formulated, it ought to be determined what the group needs and wants. A discussion of needs and wants is timely because a group may need what it does not want and it may want what it does not need.

Since Negroes in the United States of America live under a democracy—though limited—especially in terms of race, where public opinion—the most powerful single force in modern society—is created, or rather ought to be created by the free interplay and free competition of ideas in the arena of public discussion, they, the Negroes, need the status of free and equal citizens. They must be free and equal in order to participate in and help shape and determine constructive and creative human action and human institutions.

Negroes must be free in order to be equal, and they must be equal in order to be free. These are complementary and supplementary rights and conditions. The existence of one is a condition to the existence of the other. Under the terms of our liberal democratic traditions, the absence of freedom or equality means the absence of democracy. Men cannot win freedom unless they win equality. They cannot win equality unless they win freedom. Men cannot remain free unless they remain equal. They cannot remain equal unless they remain free. These are axioms of a democratic, progressive society. Their validity and verity are as unquestionable as the mathematical statement two plus two equals four.

NEGRO NOT FREE

But the Negro is not free. He never has been free. He is not free because he is not equal to other citizens within the framework of the laws, institutions, customs and practices of our so-called democratic government.

Why?

The answer is: the Civil War, the American liberal bourgeois, democratic, socio-economic, political revolution failed to complete its basic historical mission.

Unlike the European liberal, bourgeois, socio-political revolutions of the 18th and 19th centuries in France, England, Italy and Germany, the Civil War or the American Revolution, was aborted. It did not run its course. It was of the pattern of the Russian Revolution under the Czar of 1905.

What is the path of history of the liberal bourgeois democratic socio-political revolution?

What are its objectives?

They are as follows:

1. The overthrow of the old slave or feudal governmental regime and the establishment of a democratic republic.

2. The breakup of the slave or feudal economy and the creation in its stead [of] a free, competitive capitalist order.
3. The transition of the power to rule from the agrarian slave or feudal class to the industrial and financial bourgeoisie.
4. The transformation of the slaves or serfs into free workers and independent peasant proprietors.
5. The creation of an economic stake for the former slaves or serfs in the new social order.
6. The adoption of a universal free suffrage.
7. The establishment of a free public school system.
8. The recognition not only of the right of the former slaves or serfs to vote but to be voted for and to share in the operation and direction of the governmental apparatus and to rule.
9. The economic unification of the national community.
10. The centralization of political power in a strong, federal, or national system.

TASK OF NEGRO

Only a casual examination of the historical, political and social economy of the United States of America will reveal that the American Revolution was arrested and only those aims were realized that contributed to the consolidation of the power of the new ruling class, namely, the capitalists.

What then is the immediate task of the Negro?

It is to complete an uncompleted liberal bourgeois democratic socio-political revolution—commonly known as the Civil War.

What does this involve?

It involves giving life, reality and force to those basic, substantive, organic, social and political principles of freedom, equality and justice, set forth in the Declaration of Independence, the Federal Constitution, and, especially, the 13th, 14th and 15th Amendments, the Proclamation of Emancipation and the recent Rooseveltian Four Freedoms, in relation to the Negro.

While the slave power was broken, the slave masters were not eliminated. They rose and seized the reins of state rule and served as industrial and plantation padrones or an absentee owning capitalist class of the North. Soon the newly emancipated slaves found themselves hedged in, limited and handicapped by the old remnants, hangovers and vestiges of a pre-capitalist era.

HANGOVER OF SLAVE ERA

For a free suffrage, the freedmen were given Grandfather clauses, Poll-Taxes, White Primaries and other restrictive registration devices.

For a free public school system, they received a segregated pattern, in which the strongest lesson Negro students are taught is that they are inferior to white boys and girls.

For the status of free workers and independent peasant proprietors, Negroes, by peonage, vagrancy laws, sharecrop and the company store system, were reduced to the lot of serfs bound to the land, turpentine stills and lumber mills, in a semicapitalist plantation economy, and whipped and frightened into submission and docility by a lynch-rope, Ku Klux terrorism.

How can this problem be met?

This question suggests method.

Around method invariably revolve multiple opinions.

Now the most basic phase of the Negro problem is economic.

Why?

The origin of the Negro problem was economic—namely; the slave trade.

The reason for putting Negroes in slavery was economic—cheap labor.

The reason for the abolition of slavery was economic—the rise of capitalism and the uneconomic character of the slave-labor production of cotton, rice, sugar and tobacco.

And the biggest problem confronting Negroes today is economic, that is, getting work and wages to buy food, clothing and shelter.

Thus, the M.O.W.M. sets as the cardinal and primary cornerstone of its program, economic action.

LABOR UNIONS

And the major and paramount form of economic action is the building of trade and industrial unions and the employment of the technique of collective bargaining.

Why?

Because well-nigh 99%⁄10 percent of the Negro people are workers—who sell their labor power in the market for wages. Hence, the biggest business of the Negro is to sell at the highest price that which he has the most of—namely, his ability to work.

But labor, through trade unions, may win decent wages at the point of production and lose them at the point of consumption, when, as a consumer, they go back in to the market to buy back, with their wages, the goods they have produced with their labor. Consumers' co-ops provide an agency through which the workers, of hand and brain, can conserve and increase their purchasing power by buying from themselves on the Rochedale principle. This form of economic action may include retail, wholesale, trade, manufacturing, giant agriculture and dairy farming and every form of modern enterprise. It is an important key to economic security and economic democracy for the little man.

NEGROES IN BUSINESS

Now, much controversy has ranged around the so-called Negro business. But there should be no such thing as a Negro business. There should be such a thing as a Negro in business and he should do business as a business man and not as a Negro business man. When a Negro who is in business does business as a business man and employs sound purchasing and selling principles and managerial and accounting standards, he will succeed.

But when a Negroes goes into business as a Negro business and expects to trade upon race loyalty, without competing in the market in terms of price, quality and service, he is attempting to perform an uneconomic task and is quite certain to fall, and, of course, he should fail. Negroes should be encouraged to go into all kinds of businesses and to cater to the wide public without regard to race or color. And as business men they should employ workers upon a basis of need and efficiency, without regard to race, color, religion or national origin.

Negroes should also go into business with white, as well as Negro partners, and co-ops may have Negro and white members. This is just as practical and proper as are mixed trade unions. And, of course, Negroes, like white men in business, have a right to choose whomever they wish as partners.

EMPLOYMENT FOR NEGROES

Concerning the employment of Negroes:

The March on Washington Movement takes the position that Negroes should fight for integration on a basis of equality in all American businesses and into all categories of work, skilled, unskilled, technical and professional. This may be effected through various forms of pressures, such as: mass marches, picketing and the boycott, following systematic efforts at negotiations.

Of course, the M.O.W.M. maintains and fights for Negroes to be employed in every department of the government, municipal, state and federal; from a porter or janitor to the highest form of technical, skilled and professional order, upon a basis, naturally, of merit and ability.

Since Negroes as workers and consumers are tax-makers and tax payers, they should fight for placement in all types of employment in public utilities. Public utilities in every city should have their Negro motormen, conductors, bus drivers, ticket agents, telephone girls, gas meter readers, bookkeepers, stenographers and foremen and places in the supervisory departments.

How to get them?

Answer:

1. Negotiation
2. Mass marches
3. Picketing
4. Boycott
5. Inter-racial, inter-faith pressures
6. Seek trade union cooperation
7. Inform and propagandize consumer-public on right of Negroes to jobs
8. Membership in trade union

ROLE OF F.E.P.C.

Because the March on Washington has a policy of putting first things first, it launched its first campaign to win jobs and justice in national defense plans and the government. Executive Order 8802 and the President's Committee on Fair Employment Practice were its first fruit. While war manpower shortage had a great influence in opening up new employment opportunities for Negroes, no one can gainsay the fact that Executive Order 8802 and F.E.P.C. has opened many doors of opportunity for jobs hitherto closed to Negroes.

While most people, including Negroes, have jobs, the problem of upgrading Negroes upon a basis of skill is still far from being solved. Twenty thousand white workers in the Pickard automobile plant struck because three or more Negro workers were placed in skilled jobs and a race riot broke out in the Mobile shipyards because three or more Negroes were made welders.

Unfortunately Monsignor Francis J. Haas, newly appointed chairman of F.E.P.C., accepted the dangerous and unjustifiable compromise of segregation to effect a settlement. It goes without saying that this is no solution of the problem but complicates the matter and creates a new problem.

The M.O.W.M. will continue to press for the immediate rescheduling of the railroad hearings, an adequate budget and office and field personnel, rescheduling of the Capitol Transit hearings, the hearings in Detroit, St. Louis, El Paso, Baltimore, Buffalo and Cleveland. The March on Washington Movement will also project a fight to secure federal legislative sanction and permanence for F.E.P.C.

Need For Race Political Bloc Seen By Randolph

As a major strategy for the effective employment of Negro political power, the March on Washington advocates . . . building in every local community and also on a national scale a powerful non-partisan political bloc.

This does not require that Negroes come out of either the Republican, Democratic, Socialist or Communist parties. But it does require that when a crucial question of universal concern and importance to the Negroes arise, that Negroes will express their united political strength regardless of party politics on the issue.

When this is done, it will strengthen the position of the Negro leaders in the Republican and Democratic parties and make the white boss politicians more disposed to give serious consideration to all questions affecting the interests of the Negro. Negroes as Democrats are not so strong. Negroes as Republicans are not very strong. Negroes as Socialists or Communists are helpless.

But when Negro Republicans and Democrats step forward face to face with a powerful political boss or mayor, governor, President, Senate or House committee and demand consideration for the Negro or ELSE, they will get consideration. For politicians and office holders respect nothing but VOTES.

They are seldom moved by questions of principles, ideals, human justice or injustice. Politicians are hungry for power and jobs. They fear votes and the righteous wrath of the people. They will only do the right thing for the people when they are made to do so by pressure-power, public opinion and votes.

Therefore, upwards of 15 million Negroes don't need to beg anybody for anything. They have power if they will mobilize it by registering and organizing it into one powerful non-partisan political bloc which can be thrown against or for a public official or measure.

FINANCED BY NEGROES

Such a political bloc should be financed by Negroes entirely, for he who pays "the fiddler" calls the tune. Such a bloc should not accept any money from Republican, Democratic, Socialist or the Communist parties.

This political bloc should send speakers into districts to oppose the enemies of the Negro and support their friends on a basis of their record in office. This piece of political machinery could have experts draft campaign literature on the issues and the candidates and distribute it widely throughout the country, expressing the position of the Negro on vital questions and men seeking office. It could take whole page advertisements in strategic papers, white and colored, at the strategic time during a campaign to let the world know that the Negroes are not asleep or dumb.

If such a powerful non-partisan political bloc was honestly, courageously and intelligently directed, it could transform the political status of the Negro people; put a Negro on the U.S. Supreme Court, on federal courts, in the Cabinet, on policy-making commissions, get Negroes their rightful share of jobs in government agencies, abolish anti-Negro legislation, reverse anti-Negro court decisions, eliminate discriminations in administrative agencies and secure for Negroes the respect enjoyed by other citizens.

How can this bloc be built?

It could be set up by a federated body of religious, fraternal, civic, labor, educational, woman, business, and political groups that would agree upon a minimum program.

Labor is now in the process of building such a bloc through the federation of the A.F. of L. [and] C.I.O., the Big Four Railroad Brotherhoods and the National Farmers Union.

The farmers already possess a powerful non-partisan political bloc. So has big business.

And it works.

Meanwhile, Negro political leaders could continue to carry on their activities in the respective parties and in a more effective way.

SOCIAL ACTION

M.O.W.M. advocates and practices the following forms of social action procedures and techniques:

1. Social pressure through mass action: mass marches, mass picketing, mass boycott, mass letter writing, mass telephoning, mass telegraphing to public officials concerning vital social issues affecting the Negro.
2. Pressure through organized, disciplined, non-violent, good-will direct action.
3. Social pressure through giant public mass meetings.

The immediate positive and direct value of mass action pressure consists in two things: one, it places human beings into physical motion which can be felt, seen and heard. Nothing stirs and shapes public sentiment like physical action. Organized labor and organized capital have long since recognized this. This is why the major weapon of labor is the STRIKE. It is why the major weapon of business is the lock-out—the shut-down.

All people feel, think and talk about a physical formation of people whoever they may be. This is why wars grip the imagination of man. Mass demonstrations against jim-crow is worth a million editorials and orations in anybody's paper and on any platform. Editorials and orations are only worthwhile when they are around and on actual human struggles for specific social and racial rights and against definite wrongs.

AWAKEN AMERICA

Mass social pressure in the form of marches and picketing will not only touch and arrest the attention of the powerful public official but also the little man in the street. And, before this problem of jim-crow can be successfully attacked, all of America must be shocked and awakened. This has never been done, except by race riots that are dangerous social-racial explosions. Mass efforts are a form of struggle for Negro rights in which all Negroes can participate, including the educated and uneducated, the rich and poor. It is a technique and strategy which the little Negro in the tavern, pool-room, on the streets, jitterbug, store-front preacher and share-cropper, can use to help free the race.

While constitutional obedience or non-violent Good-Will Direct Action cannot be executed through the mass action technique, it tends to arouse and educate mass interest and thinking.

Now, the March on Washington Movement is an all-Negro movement, but it is not anti-white, anti-American, anti-labor, anti-Catholic or anti-Semitic. It's simply pro-Negro.

Why?

Because Jim Crow is primarily anti-Negro.

Since no other group in the country is jim-crowed but the Negro, it seems to be as simple as water tends to run down hill that the Negro must take the initiative and assume the responsibility to abolish Jim Crow. This does not mean that Negroes should not invite Catholic, Jewish, labor and business groups of white people to help them win this fight. While labor unions are only composed of workers, they seek the help of clergymen, housewives and liberals who may be non-workers. During strikes, unions form citizens committees to help the workers but they do not take the citizens into the unions.

It is well-nigh axiomatic that white citizens may sympathize with the cause of striking miners or autoworkers or lumberjacks, but the fact remains that the miners, autoworkers and lumberjacks must take the initiative and assume the responsibility themselves to win higher wages and shorter hours.

By the same token, white liberals and labor may sympathize with the Negro's fight against Jim Crow, but they are not going to lead the fight. They never have and they never will. The fight to annihilate Jim Crow in America must be led by Negroes with the cooperation and collaboration of white liberals and labor.

BLACK BOURGEOISIE SCARED

But the black petit bourgeoisie and intelligentsia are scared. They write about a struggle in which they have never participated. Columns of words are written about the Negro problem and the writer assumes that a great and satisfactory job has been done. Newspaper labor experts who have never organized the first couple of workers into anything, talk omnisciently about labor strategy and presume to tell the workers what to do. But fortunately, the workers follow their own mind.

They, the intellectual with white-collaritis, magnify the dangers of any proposal for action against jim-crow. They want to abolish it with words, that is, some of them do and some of them want to keep jim-crow to continue to shoot at. They advise the use of the type of technique which involves no personal risks and requires nothing more than ink and paper. They always seek an escape mechanism in ponderous, wordy and clever defeatist dissertations. And they always attempt to get solace for the avoidance of action techniques by viewing with alarm any forward, aggressive program which may be branded as out of the framework of the so-called American way of life, whatever that is.

The petit black bourgeoisie whose proud vocal representative is the *Pittsburgh Courier* which is likely to be on anybody's side at any time, regardless of the principles involved, are like one of two mules of an old farmer. One mule was willing to pull the load and the other old mule was willing to let him pull it. The petit black bourgeoisie are always hunting for some white angel at whose feet they may place the Negroes' problems. At one time they unloaded on the G.O.P. on the grounds that it was the party of "Father" Abraham Lincoln. Then when the political pickings got kind of slight they fled to the Democratic Jackass. Ere long they will learn that there is no fundamental difference between Democrats and Republicans either with regards to Negroes or labor, that they are like two peas in a pod, two souls with a single thought—tweedledee and tweedledum.

The *Courier's* reaction to suggested new ethnic techniques is like that of the old ape preceding the age of the Piltdown Skull Man, who in a convention of anthropods, woke up in time to hear one young radical ape proposing that all apes henceforth stop hanging by their tails and walking on all fours like they didn't have any sense but that they stand up erect on their hind legs and walk. He let out a squawk that no good would come of this new-fangled notion because any ape with two grains of brains could see that it was easier to walk on four legs than on two. But the anthropods that became man and built a civilization, as bad as it is, stood on their hind legs and walked forward. That is the admonition of the March on Washington Movement to the Negro: STAND UPON THY FEET AND THE GOD OF JUSTICE, FREEDOM AND PROGRESS WILL SPEAK UNTO THEE.

RACE RIOTS

The March on Washington Movement urges Negroes to hold public meetings and discuss the epidemic of race riots now sweeping the country to bring the issue intelligently into the open.

People's committees should be picked in the meetings from the floor by the people and given a mandate to go to see the mayor of the city—and to join with other committees of similar cities to see the governor to urge and demand that commissions on race relations be appointed to study the labor, economic, housing, recreational, educational and law enforcement policies and forces with a view to making recommendations to the mayor and governor to take measures to prevent riots and to stop them promptly and effectively when they start.

These public meetings should also call upon President Roosevelt to appoint a National Commission on Race to perform the aforementioned task on a national scale. They should also call upon Congressman Sam Rayburn, Democratic Speaker of the House of Representatives, and Congressman Martin, Republican Minority Leader, to set up machinery for a Congressional investigation of the Detroit race riot and the riots in Beaumont, Texas; Mobile, Alabama; Los Angeles, California; and other places.

The public meetings should also plan the formation of city-wide interracial-interfaith committees, composed of trade unionists, business, educational and political representatives to serve as a public group of citizens to cooperate in the study and maintenance of law and order and to cooperate with all public officials.

Such meetings should also call upon the President to send Negro and white troops into riot areas and to keep them there to insure the right and opportunity of the Negro workers to continue with the white workers in the production of war materials, ships and planes to enable the United Nations to win the war and destroy Axis tyranny.

Negroes must not be deceived into thinking that Hitler caused the Detroit race riot or any other riot. These riots are the result of our government's policy of segregating and discriminating against Negroes for decades, long before Hitler was ever heard of, and riots will continue long after Hitler is dead and forgotten if our government does not stop practicing the segregation of Negro citizens and integrate the Negro into the government and war and peace time industry on a basis of equality with their white brothers and sisters. Of course, these riots help the cause of Hitler and fascism.

Let the Negro masses speak. Demand that organized labor join the fight to abolish the cause of race riots and fascism.

OUR WHITE FOLKS

GEORGE S. SCHUYLER's satirical attack against
racism in "Our White Folks," an essay that H. L. Mencken liked very
much, was printed in the *American Mercury* in December 1927.

Numerous and ponderous tomes have been written about Negroes by
white folks. With a pontifical air they rush into print on the slightest
provocation to tell the world all about the blackamoor. These writings
range all the way from alarmist gabble about the Black Menace or the tragedy of
the dark brethren suffocating in the midst of white civilization to sloppy sentimentali-
ties by the lunatic fringe of Liberals and the mooney scions of Southern slaveholders
who deplore the passing of Uncle Tom and Aunt Beckie, who knew how to "act
properly" and did not offend them by being self-respecting or intelligent. This
fervent scribbling has been going on for a dozen decades or more, until today the
libraries and attics of the country are crammed with more books and papers on the
Negro than on any other American group. With so much evidence of what the
Nordic thinks of his black brother, no one need remain ignorant on the subject.
And if one doesn't read one may learn his attitude and opinion by observing the
various Jim Crow laws and other such exhibits throughout this glorious land.

We Ethiops, one gathers from this mass of evidence, are a childish, shiftless,
immoral, primitive, incurably religious, genially incompetent, incredibly odorifer-
ous, inherently musical, chronically excitable, mentally inferior people with pro-
nounced homicidal tendencies. We are incapable of self-government or self-
restraint, and irresponsible except when led by white folks. We possess a penchant
for assaulting white females and an inordinate appetite for chicken, gin and water-
melon. While it is finally and reluctantly admitted that we belong to the human
race, we are accorded only the lowest position in the species, a notch or two above
the great apes. We make good domestics but hopeless executives. Even at this late

date, all coons look alike to the great majority of Nordic Americans, and even the highest type of Negro is under no consideration to be accorded a higher position than the lowest type of white. In short, from examining the bulk of the evidence, the impartial investigator must conclude that the Negro has almost a monopoly of all the more discreditable characteristics of mankind. But at the same time one is effusively informed that he is deeply loved and thoroughly understood, especially by his pork-skinned friends of southern derivation.

As a result of this attitude of his pale neighbors, the lowly moke has about ten times as many obstacles to hurdle in the race of life as the average peckerwood. It is difficult enough to survive and prosper in this world under the best of conditions, but when one must face such an attitude on the part of those who largely control the means of existence, the struggle is great indeed. Naturally there is deep resentment and bitterness among the more intelligent Negroes, and there always has been. Nothing else could be expected from a people who confront a continuous barrage of insult and calumny and discrimination from the cradle to the grave. There are Negroes, of course, who publicly claim to love the white folks, but privately the great majority of them sing another tune. Even the most liberal blacks are always suspicious, and have to be on the alert not to do or say anything that will offend the superior race. Such an atmosphere is not conducive to great affection, except perhaps on the part of halfwits.

Is it generally known that large numbers of Negroes, though they openly whooped it up for Uncle Sam, would have shed no tears in 1917–18 if the armies of the Kaiser had by some miracle suddenly swooped down upon such fair cities as Memphis, Tennessee, Waycross, Georgia, or Meridian, Mississippi? The Negro upper class, in press and pulpit, roared and sweated to keep the dinges in line by telling them how much the white folks would do to improve their status after the war if they would only be loyal, but the more enlightened Ethiops were frankly skeptical, a skepticism justified later on. On several occasions during that struggle for democracy I sounded out individual Sambos here and there, and was somewhat surprised to find many of them holding the view that it made no difference to them who won the war, since the Germans could hardly treat them any worse than the Nordics of the U.S.A., and might treat them a lot better. Any number of intelligent Negroes expressed the opinion under the breath that a good beating would be an excellent thing for the soul of America. Even some of the actual black soldiers were observed on occasion to indulge in cynical smirks and sarcastic exclamations during the reading of tracts from Mr. Creel's propaganda mill.

II

Of course the attitude of the Negro toward the Nordics varies with the locality he lives in, the conditions under which he lives, and the class to which he belongs. Traveling in the south, it is difficult to get the truth about race relations in a given community unless one is very painstaking. This is due to the fact that among both whites and blacks down there, there is a great deal of local patriotism, no matter how bad conditions may actually be. The whites will claim that their niggers are the best in the world and that those in all of the surrounding towns are gorillas, while the Ethiops will speak highly of their own white folks, but heap maledictions upon the heads of the crackers further down the line. It is always wise to let them talk themselves out of breath in praise of their particular community, and then inquire discreetly about the schools, the courts, the franchise, economic opportunities, civic improvements, health conditions, and so forth. As the Negroes discuss such things one begins to get an indication of their real feelings, which are seldom flattering to their townsfolk of paler hue.

Curiously enough, the majority of Nordics seem to believe that all Negroes look upon them as some sort of demigods—as paragons of intelligence, efficiency, refinement and morality. No doubt they have arrived at this curious conclusion by observing how the blackamoors ape their appearance with skin whiteners and hair straighteners, and how they are given to disparaging the efforts and attainments of other Negroes. They have probably heard such Negroisms as "A nigger ain't nuthin," "What more can you expect from a nigger?" and "Why don't you be like white folks?"

The Negro, it is true, is cynical and skeptical about his own, and often his castigations of his brethren are more devastating than any administered by the white folks. In this respect, he resembles his Jewish brother. But the crow is equally critical of his red-necked comrades. Only infrequently do the white folks perceive that this indirect flattery is a sort of combination of protective coloration, group discipline, and feeling of annoyance and futility. It does not in the majority of cases mean that the individual Negro they see in front of them thinks that they are his superiors—except in power.

If the Southern white, as is his wont, can with any justification trumpet to the world that he knows the Negro, the Aframerican can with equal or greater truth claim to have the inside information on the cracker. Knowing him so intimately, the black brother has no illusions about either his intelligence, his industry, his efficiency, his honor, or his morals. The blacks haven't been working with and for the white folks all these decades and centuries for nothing. While the average Nordic knows nothing of how Negroes actually live and what they actually think, the Negroes know the Nordics intimately. Practically every member of the Negro aristocracy of physicians, dentists, lawyers, undertakers and insurance men has worked at one time or another for white folks as a domestic, and observed with cynical detachment their orgies, obsessions and imbecilities, while contact with the white proletariat has acquainted him thoroughly with their gross stupidity and often very evident inferiority.

Toward the white working classes, indeed, there is a great suspicion and ill-feeling among the Negroes of the United States, much to the discomfiture of labor organizers and radicals. The superior posture of the poor whites is based on nothing but the fortuitous circumstance that created them lighter in color. The Negro puts this down to mere ignorance and a fear of competition for jobs. He believes that the white workers would have nothing to lose by ditching their color prejudice and aligning themselves with him. Ever since the so-called Civil War, he has been attempting to make the white proletariat see the light, but the mudsill Caucasians are obdurate. They think far more of an empty color superiority than they do of labor solidarity. Even the Jewish working-people, of whom solidarity might be expected, are far from being free of color prejudice.

Quite naturally, the Negroes feel far more kindly toward the whites of wealth and influence. From them they have obtained quite a few favors and largesses, but they do not lose sight of the fact that in the face of a group crisis, such as a lynching or a race riot, they cannot depend upon these upper class Nordics, who invariably desert when the mob heaves into sight, if indeed they do not join it. Directing and controlling the social and economic life of the country, they have allowed to go almost unquestioned all sorts of legislation inimical to the Negro's advancement. Toward individual Negroes they may be kindly and helpful, but except in the case of those who support Negro colleges and schools, they do not seem to care a rap about how the mass of blacks gets along. They allow gross inequalities in the appropriation of school funds; they allow Negro residential sections to go without adequate health inspection; they allow the compulsory school laws to remain unenforced in so far as the blacks are concerned; they make little or no protest against peonage and the horrors of Southern prisons and chain-gangs; they allow petty officials to make a mockery of the judicial system where Negroes are involved; and they refuse to see to it that the Negro is given the means to protect himself, if possible, through the franchise.

These upper class white folks contend that the workings of democracy prevent them from forcing the poor whites to toe the mark, but the Negroes observe that when it is desired to put over anything else that is deemed important, some way is always found. It seems to the thinking black man that, even granting that the white ruling class is incapable of assisting the masses of his people, they could at least openly enlist themselves on the side of honesty, fairness and square dealing, and thereby set an example to the others. But in the main they prefer to remain silent, and so leave the Negro to the mercies of the white rabble. Is it any wonder that he views them with distrust?

The attitude of the Northern white folks, in particular, puzzles and incenses him. Very often he feels that they are more dangerous to him than the Southerners. Here are folks who yawp continuously about liberty, justice, equality and democracy, and whoop with indignation every time a Senegambian is incinerated below the Potomac or the Belgians burn another village in the Congo, but toward the Negro in their midst they are quite as cruel as the Southern crackers. They are wont to shout, in their liberal moments, that the Negro is as good as they are—as if that were a compliment!—and to swear by all the gods that they want to give him a square deal and a chance in the world, but when he approaches them for a job they offer him a mop and pail or a bellhop's uniform, no matter what his education and training may be. And except in isolated instances they see that he remains permanently in the lowly position they have given him.

The majority of them are almost as prejudiced as their Southern brethren, as any Negro knows who has ever attempted to enter a public place or to attend their social gatherings. Unlike the crackers, they only grudgingly give him a chance to earn a living, even as a menial. The restriction of European immigration has helped the Negro in the North considerably in the field of industry, but in the marts of commerce there seems to be an impression that he is incapable of functioning in the field of general business. At present, in the city of New York, which is considered a heaven for Negroes, and the tolerance and liberality of which are widely advertised throughout the nation, it is harder for a capable young Negro to get a decent job in a business house than it is for a comely Negro girl to escape being approached by white men in a Southern town.

To the intelligent Aframerican, an individual who has color prejudice seems manifestly to belong in the same intellectual class as the Holy Rollers and the Ku Kluxers. To judge an individual solely on the basis of his skin color and hair texture is so obviously nonsensical that he cannot help classing the bulk of Nordics with the inmates of an insane asylum. He views with mingled amusement and resentment the stupid reactions of white folks to a black skin. It excites his bitter mirth to observe how his entrance into almost any public place is sufficient to spoil the evening of the majority of the proud Caucasians present, no matter how intelligent they may claim to be. Nor is this insanity restricted alone to Anglo-Saxons, for Jews, Irish, Greeks, Poles, Russians, Italians, and Germans, even those who know little of the American language and less of the national customs, grow quite as apoplectic at the sight of a sable countenance.

III

Because the whites bellow so much about their efficiency and thrift, the Negro marvels that they go to the expense of a dual school system, Jim-crow railroad coaches and waiting-rooms, separate cemeteries, and segregated parks, libraries and street cars, with the obvious economic waste entailed, when the two peoples are so intimately associated all day, not to mention at night. Indeed, an examination of family trees will reveal that a large number of the whites and blacks are really related, especially in the land of cotton, where most of the hue and cry is raised about Anglo-Saxon purity. The South, the Negro does not fail to note, has actually retarded its own progress by maintaining this hypocritical double standard. And now it is threatening the standards of living in the New England mill towns and Northern coal fields by offering cheaper labor and lower taxes—an offer that it can make only because of the ready acceptance of low living standards by the Southern white mob out of fear that Negroes will take its poorly paid jobs. Thus the results of the stupid system are felt in sections where hardly any Negroes live at all.

Almost every thoughtful Negro believes that the scrapping of the color caste system would not hinder but rather help the country. In their zeal to keep the black brother away from the pie counter, the whites are depriving the nation of thousands of individuals of extraordinary ability. The rigid training and discipline that the Negro has received since his arrival on these sacred shores has left him with a lower percentage of weaklings and incompetents than is shown by any other group. He has always had to be on the alert, ever the diplomat and skillful tactician, facing more trying situations in a week than the average white citizen faces in a year. This experience has certainly fitted him for a more important position than he now holds in the Republic. He is still imbued with the pioneering spirit that the bulk of the whites have had ironed out of them. He has energy and originality, the very qualities being sought today in business and government. Yet narrow bigotry and prejudice bar his way.

When the Southern white man asks the liberal Caucasian, "Do you want your daughter to marry a nigger?" he is probably hitting the nail on the head, for that is the crux of the entire color problem. Fear of economic and political competition is a factor, but above it is the bogey of sex competition. Equality in one field will unquestionably lead to equality in the other. And yet there is no law compelling blacks and whites to intermarry, and if the natural aversion that the scientists shout of really exists there need be no fears on that score. The Anglo-Saxons will retain their polyglot purity if they wish to do so—and if they actually find the Ethiops as repellant as the authorities on the subject allege.

But there is considerable doubt in the mind of the Negro as to whether this aversion actually exists, and whether the Anglo-Saxons actually *think* it exists. He tries to reconcile the theory that it does with the fact that nearly thirty States have laws prohibiting intermarriage between the so-called races, and with the additional fact that half of the Negroes in America obviously possess more or less Caucasian blood, thus being neither black nor white. The dark brother is convulsed with mirth over the famous one-drop theory, that distinctive American contribution to the science of anthropology which lists as Negroes all people having the remotest Negro ancestry, despite the fact that they may be, and often are, indistinguishable from the purest Nordic. He whoops with glee over the recent incident in Virginia, where the workings of the new Racial Integrity Law caused fifty white children to be barred from the white schools and ordered to attend Negro schools on the ground that they were Negroes, although no one knew it except the official genealogists, whereas all the while, in the States of Texas and Oklahoma, dark brown Mexicans and Indians were listed as white, and their children attended white schools. Knowing how much racial intermixture has been going on in this country since the Seventeenth Century, he is eager to see racial integrity laws passed in all of the States, as has been done in Georgia and Virginia, so that the genealogists may get busy on a national scale and thus increase the "Negro" population to at least four times its present number.

The Negro listens with a patient tolerance born of much knowledge and observation to the gabble of white gentlemen concerning the inferior morality of black women. These chivalrous folk, in some sections, do not hesitate to discuss these illicit amours within hearing of their Negro servitors, who boil within as they listen to the racy conversation of the advocates of racial separatism. The whites, of course, never hear the Negro's side of the story. Indeed, it is doubtful whether they realize that he *has* a side. For many and obvious reasons, he keeps his very interesting information to himself and grins along his way. He knows that no one group in this country monopolizes sex morality. Some day a black American Balzac is going to gather material for another volume of Droll Stories that will be quite as interesting and entertaining as the original.

The attitude of the whites toward the Negro's participation in politics seems very absurd to the contemplative dinge. He is a part of American life and he knows very well what is going on in politics. If his sooty brethren are not yet ready to be trusted with the ballot, neither for that matter are the ruck of peckerwoods. He has heard the yells and moans of the ex-Confederates about the alleged horrors of the Reconstruction period, when Negro legislators (who never controlled a single Southern state) are said to have indulged in graft on a great scale and squandered the public funds, but after careful investigation he has failed to learn of a single state or community in the whole country in which precisely the same thing is not true of white politicians. If Negroes sell their votes for a quart of corn liquor and two dollars, they are, he observes, by no means alone. Surely, he concludes, no legislature composed of Negroes could pass more imbecile legislation than is the annual product of every legislative body in the land, not by any means excluding Congress. He concludes that he is barred from the ballot in the South only in order to keep capable Negroes from competing with broken-down Nordic lawyers for political sinecures. The excuse that his inability to use the ballot intelligently is the cause of his disfranchisement is highly amusing to him after a glance at the national scene.

The amazing ignorance of whites—even Southern whites—about Negroes is a constant source of amusement to all Aframericans. White men who claim to be intelligent and reasonable beings persist in registering surprise whenever they hear of or meet a Negro who has written a novel, a history, or a poem, or who can work a problem in calculus. Because of this naïveté, many mediocre Negroes are praised to the high heavens as geniuses of the first flight, and grow sleek and fat. Such fellows are frequently seized upon by gullible whites and labeled as leaders of the Negro race, without the Negroes being consulted on the matter. It seems incredible to most white folks that within the Negro group are social circles quite as cultured and refined as those existing among whites. I recall with amusement the story circulating the rounds of Aframerica concerning a wealthy white woman in a Southern city who asked her Negro maid if it was true that there were Negro homes in New York City such as those described by Carl Van Vechten in *Nigger Heaven*, and who was quite astonished and incredulous when the girl informed her that not only were there such homes in New York but also in that town as well.

IV

Those Negroes who have entrée to white intellectual circles do not return to their own society with regret, but rather with relief, for they rightly observe that the bulk of the white intellectuals have more form than content; that they have a great deal of information but are not so long on common sense; and that they lack that sense of humor and gentle cynicism which one expects to find in the really civilized person, and which are the chief characteristics of even the most lowly and miserable Aframerican.

These so-called sophisticated whites leap from one fad to another, from mah jong to "Ask Me Another," with great facility, and are usually ready to embrace any cause that comes along thirsting for supporters. They are obsessed by sex and discuss it interminably, with long dissertations on their moods and reactions, complexes and sublimations. Life to them seems to be one perpetual psychoanalytical clinic. This appears to the Negro observer as a sure sign of sexual debility. The lusty, virile fellow, such as is the average shine, is too busy really living to moon overly much about the processes of life. It is difficult to imagine a group of intelligent Negroes sprawling around a drawing-room, consuming cigarettes and synthetic gin while discussing their complexes and inhibitions.

The Negroes have observed, too, that they know how to have a good time, despite all their troubles and difficulties, while the majority of white people certainly do not. Indeed, the frantic efforts of the crackers to amuse themselves is a never-ending source of amusement to the blacks. The Nordics take all amusements so seriously! They cannot swim without attempting to cross the English Channel or the Gulf of Mexico; they cannot dance without organizing a marathon to see which couple can dance the longest. They must have their Charleston contests, golf contests, coffee-drinking contests, frankfurter-eating contests. In short, they always go to extremes. The Negroes, on the other hand, have learned how to enjoy themselves without too much self-consciousness and exhibitionism.

The efforts of the Nordics to be carefree are grotesque; the so-called emancipated whites being the worst of the lot. No group of Negroes anywhere could be louder or rowdier than they are in their efforts to impress the neighborhood with the fact that they are having a good time. Look, for example, at their antics in Greenwich Village. It is not without reason that those white folks who want to enjoy themselves while in New York hustle for Harlem. The less emancipated ones go to the cabarets, where they can sit and watch Negroes dance and caper; the more sensible go to a Negro dance-hall, where they can participate in the fun. It is not uncommon to hear them say that the only time they thoroughly enjoy themselves is when they journey to the so-called Black Belt, where joy is not shackled or saddled.

This is probably the reason why, to the white brethren, the blacks are supposed to be happy-go-lucky children, with never a serious thought in their polls. But the Negro, recalling how the white folks swarm to hear such mountebanks as Billy Sunday, Krishnamurti, Conan Doyle, Imperial Wizard Evans and William Hale Thompson, and eagerly swallow all of the hokum flowing through the Republic, concludes that the Sambos have no monopoly on intellectual infantilism.

The Negro is a sort of black Gulliver chained by white Lilliputians, a prisoner in a jail of color prejudice, a babe in a forest of bigotry, but withal a fellow philosophical and cynical enough to laugh at himself and his predicament. He has developed more than any other group, even more than the Jews, the capacity to see things as they are rather than as he would have them. He is a close student of the contradictory pretensions and practices of the ofay gentry, and it is this that makes him really intelligent in a republic of morons. It is only during the last few years that the cracker *intelligentsia* have begun to sniff suspiciously at the old Anglo-Saxon slogans and concepts of justice, democracy, chivalry, honor, fair play, and so forth. The Negro has always been skeptical about them, knowing that they were conditioned by skin color, social position and economic wealth.

He is sick and tired of the holier-than-thou attitude of the white folks. On what, he inquires, do they base the contention that they are superior? He puts the history of the blacks down through the ages alongside that of the whites and is not ashamed of the comparison. He knows that there is as much evidence that black men founded human civilization as there is that white men did, and he doubts whether the occidental society of today is superior to the monarcho-communist society developed in Africa. He knows that neither intellectually nor physically is he inferior to the Caucasians. The fact is that in America conditions have made the average Negro more alert, more resourceful, more intelligent, and hence more interesting than the average Nordic. Certainly if the best measure of intelligence is ability to survive in a changing or hostile environment, and if one considers that the Negro is not only surviving but improving all the time in health, wealth, and culture, one must agree that he possesses a high degree of intelligence. In their efforts to fight off the ravages of color prejudice, the blacks have welded themselves into a homogeneity and developed a morale whose potentialities are not yet fully appreciated.

V

They laugh to themselves when they hear white folks refer to them as ugly and black. Thanks to the whites who are always talking about racial purity, the Negroes possess within their group the most handsome people in the United States, with the greatest variety of color, hair and features. Here is the real melting-pot, and a glorious sight it is to see. Ugly people there are, certainly, but the percentage of beautiful folk is unquestionably larger than among the ofay brethren. One has but to venture abroad in a crowd of whites and then go immediately to a fashionable Negro thoroughfare to be impressed with this fact. Black? Well, yes, but how beautiful! How well it blends with almost every color! How smooth the skin; how soft and rounded the features! But there are browns, chocolates, yellows and pinks as well. Here in Aframerica one finds such an array of beauty that it even attracts Anglo-Saxons, despite their alleged color aversion.

The dark brother looks upon himself as an American, an integral part of this civilization. To him it is not a white civilization, but a white and black civilization. He rightly feels that it is partially his, because for three hundred years he toiled to make it possible. He wants no more than an equal break with everybody else, but he feels that he has much greater contributions to make to our national life than he has so far been allowed to make. There is hope among the more enlightened Negroes that the similar group among the Nordics can be educated to see the social value and necessity of removing the barriers that now hamper the black citizen. The country can lose nothing and may gain much by a step. Strange as it may seem, many Negroes look to the enlightened Southern whites as the force that will help bring about the change. While these ofays do not understand the blacks as well as they think, they do at least know them fairly well, and there is, propaganda to the contrary, some good feeling between the two groups. This emerging group of Southern whites is gradually becoming strong enough to make its voice heard and respected, and in the years to come it will have more and more influence.

The Aframerican, being more tolerant than the Caucasian, is ready to admit that all white people are not the same, and it is not unusual to read or hear a warning from a Negro orator or editor against condemning all crackers as prejudiced asses, although agreeing that such a description fits the majority of them. The Ethiop is given to pointing out individual pinks who are exceptionally honorable, tolerant and unprejudiced. In this respect, I venture to say, he rises several notches higher than the generality of ofays, to whom, even in this day and time, all coons look alike.

NEGROES WITHOUT SELF-PITY

ZORA NEALE HURSTON's "Negroes Without Self-Pity" and "The Rise of the Begging Joints," both of which espouse the conservative view of self-reliance and work, were published in the *American Mercury* in November 1943 and March 1945, respectively. Hurston (1891–1960), a Floridian, is perhaps the most renowned and critically examined of all black women writers. Although she died in virtual obscurity, her work (novels, short stories, anthropological studies) has acquired the status of classic or seminal among both feminist and black scholars.

I may be wrong, but it seems to me that what happened at a Negro meeting in Florida the other day is important—important not only for Negroes and not only for Florida. I think that it strikes a new, wholesome note in the black man's relation to his native America.

It was a meeting of the Statewide Negro Defense Committee. C. D. Rogers, President of the Central Life Insurance Company of Tampa, got up and said: "I will answer that question of whether we will be allowed to take part in civic, state and national affairs. The answer is—yes!" Then he explained why and how he had come to take part in the affairs of his city.

"The truth is," he said, "that I am not always asked. Certainly in the beginning I was not. As a citizen, I saw no reason why I should wait for an invitation to interest myself in things that concerned me just as much as they did other residents of Tampa. I went and I asked what I could do. Knowing that I was interested and willing to do my part, the authorities began to notify me ahead of proposed meetings, and invited me to participate. I see no point in hanging back, and then complaining that I have been excluded from civic affairs.

"I know that citizenship implies duties as well as privileges. It is time that we

Negroes learn that you can't get something for nothing. Negroes, merely by being Negroes, are not exempted from the natural laws of existence. If we expect to be treated as citizens, and considered in community affairs, we must come forward as citizens and shoulder our part of the load. The only citizens who count are those who give time, effort and money to the support and growth of the community. *Share the burden where you live!"*

And then J. Leonard Lewis, attorney for the Afro-American Life Insurance, had something to say. First he pointed to the growing tension between the races throughout the country. Then he, too, broke tradition. The upper-class Negro, he said, must take the responsibility for the Negro part in these disturbances.

"It is not enough," he said, "for us to sit by and say 'We didn't do it. Those irresponsible, uneducated Negroes bring on all this trouble.' We must not only do nothing to whip up the passions among them, we must go much further. We must abandon our attitude of aloofness to the less educated. We must get in touch with them *and head off these incidents before they happen.*

"How can we do that? There is always some man among them who has great prestige with them. He can do what we cannot do, because he is of them and understands them. If he says fight, they fight. If he says, 'Now put away that gun and be quiet,' they are quiet. We must confer with these people, and cooperate with them to prevent these awful outbreaks that can do no one any good and everybody some harm. Let us give up our attitude of isolation from the less fortunate among us, and do what we can for peace and good-will between the races."

Not anything world-shaking in such speeches, you will say. Yet something profound has happened, of which these speeches are symptoms and proofs. Look back over your shoulder for a minute. Count the years. If you take in the twenty-odd years of intense Abolitionist speaking and writing that preceded the Civil War, the four war years, the Reconstruction period and recent Negro rights agitations, you have at least a hundred years of indoctrination of the Negro that he is an object of pity. Becoming articulate, this was in him and he said it. "We were brought here against our will. We were held as slaves for two hundred and forty-six years. We are in no way responsible for anything. We are dependents. We are due something from the labor of our ancestors. Look upon us with pity and give!" The whole expression was one of self-pity without a sense of belonging to America and what went on here.

Put that against the statements of Rogers and Lewis, and you get the drama of the meeting. The audience agreed and applauded. Tradition was tossed overboard without a sigh. Dr. J. R. E. Lee, president of Florida A and M College for Negroes, got up and elaborated upon the statements: *"Go forward with the nation. We are citizens and have our duties as such."* Nobody mentioned slavery, Reconstruction, nor any such matter. It was a new and strange kind of Negro meeting—without tears of self-pity. It was a sign and symbol of something in the offing.

THE RISE OF THE BEGGING JOINTS

ZORA NEALE HURSTON

People have been telling me to clap hands, crack jokes, and generally cut Big Jim by the acre. I ought to look and see. Great joy was around me.

When I turned around and asked why I should jump Juba and burn red fire without ceasing, they told me, "Look! No more slavery days, and even the Reconstruction is past and gone. Aunt Hagar's chillun are eating high on the hog."

Now, there is nothing I favor more than clapping hands in drumtime, like dancing all night long, unless it is having something to clap hands and dance over. But I didn't see too clear; so I said, "Pick up your points. Tell me, and then make see, so I can dance it off."

So they told me again and often. Sometimes they said it with arm-gestures. Same thing all over again: the Reconstruction is over. Everything is fresh and new.

But I am not cutting my capers yet awhile, because I don't know for certain.

I do see a great many Negroes with college degrees, fur coats, big houses, and long cars. That is just fine, and I like it. That looks really up-to-time. On the other hand, I see some things that look too much like 1875 in the lap of 1944, and they worry me.

Those Begging Joints, for instance. That is not the name they go by, of course. Some folks with their mouths full of flattery call them normal schools, colleges, and even universities. I'm sort of tie-tongued and short-patienced, so I call them a functional name and let it go at that.

The "puhfessahs," principals, presidents, and potentates who run these institutions seem to like them mighty fine. They will tell you without your even asking that these are "great works." Further, that they themselves are latter-day martyrs, electing to "carry on this great work for our people, so that our girls and boys may get some sort of an education." They tootch out the mouth to say this so that it oozes out in an unctuous tone of voice. There is also a ceremonial face-making, with eye-gleams, to go along with the sound. If you don't make some fast time away from there, you are going to hear all about how they were born in a log cabin. Think of that! And now, look! They have builded this g-r-e-a-t institution! The mouth-spread would take in the mighty expanse of Columbia University, but you look around and see something that would have been a miracle in 1875, but nothing to speak of in this day and year of our Lord.

The next thing you know, the talk has gotten around to funds. It always gets around to funds. Money is needed to carry on the g-r-e-a-t work. If you don't know any better, you will soon be shaking with apprehension at the prospect of this institution's closing its doors, and never another Negro girl or boy learning her or his ABCs. If you know anything about Negro education, you come out of your spasm quickly when you remember that there are such Class A seats of learning as Howard University, Fisk University, Morgan State College, Atlanta University and affiliates, Tuskegee, Morehouse, Talladega, Hampton, Florida A and M, Southern, Bennett, Virginia State and Lincoln U. In addition, there are most all the Northern white colleges except Princeton with Negro graduates and students. For those with ambition but less funds, there are the state-supported colleges for Negroes in every Southern state. Quite a number of colored folk have even earned degrees at the leading universities of Europe, from Scandinavia to Spain.

But in spite of this, you are asked to shake and shiver over the prospective fate of some puny place without a single gifted person in its meager faculty, with only token laboratories or none, and very little else besides its FOUNDER. The Founder is the thing! And the Founder exists to raise funds.

II

Where can one of these Begging Joints be found? There are two or more left in every state in the South.

With so many good colleges available to Negroes, why do these Begging Joints keep on existing? Because there are so many poor Negroes, and so many rich white people, who don't know very much. They not only do not know, but they are very incurious.

The colored families from which the Begging Joints draw their students know nothing about the importance of curricula for accrediting. They think that just finishing, "schooling out," is all that is necessary. Just so it is a school. Forty years ago, that would have been all right.

But, not only has the responsibility of the Negro population shifted, the concept of education has changed. Competition is keen, and every chick and child has to pull his weight in efficiency or get trampled in the rush. And that is the tragedy of promoting 1880 on 1944.

These institutions have two things to sell to the folks who are still living in the just-after-slavery aura. One of these is "Off" and the other is the equivalent of the medieval virtue belt. And both of these things take us back to the nineteenth century.

In those days, any kind of school education was something for a Negro to have and threw glitter all around the owner, even to distant cousins. To send your son or daughter *Off* to school marked you as a Big Negro, getting more like the white folks every day. So *Off* became the thing to strive for. It then brought the exalted job of teaching school, plus social preference in everything, including marriage.

Off has lost its glamor for the upper-class Negroes, but it still has some attraction for the lower class. Almost never will an upper-class Negro send his children away until after high school, if a fairly good school is at hand. When he does so, it is either because the local secondary school is not accredited, and will hamper the entrance to some good college, or because of some family reason. It is not because of any prestige of *Off*. But there are still those to whom *Off* is a putting-of-the-family-foot on the ladder, an offsetting of the necessity of labor over the washtub and the cookstove.

The virtue belt factor comes in like this. During slavery, there was no encouragement to continence on the plantations. Quite the contrary. So when freedom came, it is too much to expect that it would have been acquired immediately. There was little immorality really, just a lack of concept about the thing. So in the first generation or so after Emancipation, a mighty lot of girls got "ruint." Hence the first boarding schools that got started were more like reformatories with instruction on the side. You sent your daughter *Off*, if you could afford it, more to keep her from getting "ruint" than to get her educated. Naturally, even those ugly-faced, chilly, warden-like matrons were no more capable of thwarting a boy-crazy girl than her parents were. Daughter often brought her "diploma" home in her arms. Love will find a way.

The instances of this are fewer these days, but the idea is still being sold to parents—"We are not like that Howard University and Fisk. We don't allow our girls to go walking across the campus with boys. And no dancing together. No, indeed! Of course we are not so big as those places. But the students at those schools don't learn a thing! All they do is socialize."

It is true that schools like Howard and Fisk place no ban on ordinary social contacts. It is true that there is some dancing. But what the Begging Joint Puhfessahs neglect to mention is that such colleges as Fisk and Howard run small chance of getting any under-privileged, unrestrained girls among the students. They have the pick of the nation. The instances in them of the kinds of troubles the Puhfessahs suggest fearsomely are negligible.

But the simple woman toiling over a washtub or cookstove does not understand that. So she sends her daughter *Off* to get her virtue guarded, at the instigation of the Puhfessah. It may be a locking of the stable after the horse is stolen, but that is not important to the Puhfessah. If daughter is an indifferent student, that is not important either. The "Great Work" needs students.

No students, no schools. No school, no excuse to seek funds. No funds, the principal is faced with a major change in his or her way of living. A terrible loss of prestige, plus going to work with the hands. No more of giving his life and life's blood to the "doing of something for my people." The Puhfessah is in no position to pick and choose among prospective students. He must take [what] he can get or fold. And God forbid the folding!

So the doer of good works begs a good living for himself in the name of his people. And that is all right for him. But what about the poor black men and women bowed down over mops or standing over the white folks' cookstoves to send daughter or son to the Begging Joint to dress the stage for the educational Fagin? And what of the students?

After two to four years, the janitor's or cook's son or daughter has a piece of paper tied up with a snatch of ribbon. He has had several years of considering himself above the commonality of Negro existence. He thinks sweat and overalls are not for him. But after many trials he finds that he can get no better employment than the boy he used to know next door. He is Jim Jones again, instead of Mr. James Jones, prospective principal of a school. He cannot meet the requirements of the state board of education. He may have learned a smattering of some trade at his school, but not enough to help him much when skilled labor is demanded. Time and money have been wasted, and in addition, he feels a bitter loss of face.

Some, pressed by necessity, adjust themselves and do what must be done. Others, just as pressed, never do. They cannot fit in where they think they belong, but will not adjust themselves to the level of their fitness. They go through life scornful of those who work with their hands, and resentful of the better-prepared Negroes. I know one man of this type who will not wear overalls, no matter how dirty the job that he has to do, because to him overalls are the symbol of the common Negro, and he fears to be so classified. The highest "position" that he has ever held since he left college more than twenty years ago has been a minor one in a 5- and 10-cent store, but he clings to the delusion of grandeur still.

But the Begging Joint does a greater disservice still to the individual, the race and the nation. That is its perpetuation of the double standard in education. Even Southern legislators have come to realize that there must be only one, and the requirements of the Negro state and county schools are being sharply raised year by year. Beginning about 1930, the State of Florida began displacing its old-fashioned Negro teachers with more highly trained ones, preferably from the big Northern colleges. Other states have similar policies. But the little private schools are out of the jurisdiction of the state boards of education. All the state boards can do is to refuse to accredit the backward institution.

The raising of the Negro educational standard is an obvious necessity, since the inefficient are a drag on all. The city, the state and the nation need all their useful people, regardless of race and kind. There is no longer any place for the black man who "does very well for a Negro." He has got to be good these days, and I said *good*. But the Begging Joints are still doing nothing but trying to put exclamation points behind what was considered good away back in 1880 when the majority of white people thought that all Negroes were something less than human.

III

As for the white donors to these Begging Joints, they need their heads examined. I am going to give them full credit for being friends of the Negro. But even so, why can't they be intelligent about it? If they want to do something for Negro education, why not look into things and give where it will do some good?

Mind you, I am not seeking funds. I am not a Founder—and not consequently, a member of the Order of Higher Mendicants, as George Schuyler so aptly puts it. You were the one who said that you wanted to do something for Negro education. All I say is, if you really mean what you say, come out of the backwoods of your mind and do some figuring up. You must know that this is the greatest industrial nation on earth, and that during the last two generations the colleges have followed the trend of the nation's needs. Industry calls for scientists. They must be trained in laboratories, so colleges of any account must have these. Not only must they have them, but they must be able to make the constant replacements necessary to keep up with the latest developments. What would have equipped a whole college fifty years ago is required now for a comprehensive laboratory in chemistry, physics or biology.

Now, why give five thousand dollars a year to Chitterling Switch "college" in the backwoods of Mississippi, let us say, when it is some one-cylinder outfit with perhaps two hundred students? Five thousand is not going to be any help, not in the fix it is in. Five million is more like what it would take to bring it up to our time. Five thousand will just about pay for prexy's new Cadillac, with possibly enough over to put some chairs in a classroom.

Since you really want to do something for Negro education, give to one of the colleges which already has something to build on. You might, for instance, give to Howard University's great medical school. It is turning out doctors and dentists who compare favorably with the best in the nation. The money could be used for laboratory replacements, or to sponsor some serious young medico who yearns to make further research.

Or if you are inclined toward literature, give to the library fund of Morgan State College, at Baltimore. It has a fine library, and aims to make it the finest possible. Or give to the school of Social Sciences at Fisk, which, under Dr. Charles S. Johnson, has increased the sum total of knowledge in that field considerably in the last decade. Or send the check to Atlanta University. Its department of sociology is getting grand results.

I wouldn't put it past some of you to tell me that it is your own money, and you can do with it as you please. You are free, white and twenty-one. But you see, I'm free, black and twenty-one; and if you tell me that, I will know and understand that you have no genuine interest in Negro education. Or if you think you have, you haven't taken a sounding in the last forty years. You are way behind the times.

I have made it my business to talk with patrons of the Chitterling Switch kind of a school in the last three years, and I have been astonished at the number of persons giving money to a school without even inquiring into the curriculum or looking into the training of the faculty. They were under the delusion that the school to which they gave was at the top of Negro education. Indeed, the majority had the idea that there was no other kind for Negroes to go to. Some did not even know that there were colleges provided by the state. They fluttered about raising little sums impelled by the fear that if the little place were not kept in condition to keep on crippling young black folks, there would be no other chance for Negroes to get hamstrung for life.

Instead of being a help, many donors have been giving aid and assistance to the defeat of those who need a chance more than anyone else in America.

What is the general history behind these little knowledge-traps? First, there were those little piney-woods schools opened by the Abolitionist church groups immediately after the Civil War. Fired by the Cause, hundreds, perhaps thousands, of pious Northerners came South and gave themselves to teach the freemen how to read and write. But the greatest emphasis was on the Bible. Those who were first taught, were urged to go forth and spread what they had learned to others.

Then the "do something for my people" era came in on the trailing clouds of Booker T. Washington. He was responsible, but he didn't mean any harm. Tuskegee was a success, with tycoons of industry and finance rolling down in their private cars to see and be awed. They saw Booker T. Washington as the Moses of his race. They donated millions to give body to the idea of Booker T. So in the black world, the man was magical. He sat with Presidents. He went abroad and stood with kings. This school-founding thing was something!

Without the genius of his idea and the surprise of its newness, hundreds of other Negroes deserted pulpits, plows, washtubs and cookpots and went out founding schools. The outer offices of financiers began to be haunted by people "doing something for my people." There remained only one Tuskegee. But then, there was only one Booker T. Washington.

These Begging Joints were a natural part of the times when they were started and in a way they were all right for then. But they are unburied corpses in 1944. We can bury the carcasses any time we will or may. All it takes is a made-up mind.

NEGRO MARTYRS
ARE NEEDED

CHESTER B. HIMES's "Negro Martyrs Are Needed,"
which calls for blacks to take militant and aggressive political action,
was published in *The Crisis* in 1943. Himes (1909–1984), a noted
black expatriate, is most famous for his fiction, particularly his
detective novels that featured Gravedigger Jones and Coffin Ed
Johnson.

M

artyrs are needed to create incidents. Incidents are needed to create
revolutions. Revolutions are needed to create progress.
These are the tactics devised by the peoples of the world who
wanted freedom. No one has ever proved or denied that these are the best tactics
to employ for the attainment of this end; it has been proved that these are the *only*
tactics to bring about such attainment.

The American colonials were not the first to recognize the singularity of these
tactics, but they were the first to use them effectively for the benefit of a large
number of people. Since the American Revolution they have become the ABCs of
political advancement throughout the world. The first and fundamental convictions
of the political tactician fighting for the human rights of the people are: (1) Progress
can be brought about only by revolution; (2) Revolutions can only be started by
incidents; (3) Incidents can be created only by martyrs.

Of all the oppressed groups of people in the world today, racial, religious, and
political, the thirteen million Negro Americans are the only group who have not
yet employed these tactics in some manner or other in their quest for democratic
equality. This is one of the strangest conditions of history. No serious unbiased
scholar will deny that the Negro Americans have been the most oppressed minority
group in the world for the past three hundred and twenty-three years. But yet no
intelligent politician will deny that there is *no other manner* in which Negro Ameri-
cans can release themselves from this oppression.

Let us consider then what a Negro American revolution will be and what it will do.

First I must point out the possible ways of existence for all people. There are only three:

(1) *Wherein everyone is free.* As of today, citizens of the communist-dominated socialist state of the U.S.S.R. have come closest to this goal. However, it does not matter whether the structure of the government is communistic, socialistic, or democratic; this is the most preferable way of existence for the majority of the people of the world.

(2) *Wherein a ruling class or race is free.* This is the point to which citizens of the United States of America and of the British Empire have advanced. Outwardly, this would seem preferable to the ruling class or race. But the fallacy of that is that this is not a fixed stage of existence; *it is a pivot of change.* The ruling class or race must share their freedom with everyone in order to preserve it; or they must give it up.

(3) *Wherein no one is free.* Loosely we may say that this comprises dictatorships and imperialistic nations, especially if they are at this time our enemies. It is generally agreed that less than one-tenth of one per cent of the people of the world prefer this way of existence; so we may state for point of argument that no one prefers it.

AIM OF REVOLUTION

There can be only one (I repeat: *Only one*) aim of a revolution by Negro Americans: That is *the enforcement of the Constitution of the United States.* At this writing no one has yet devised a better way of existence than contained in the Constitution. *Therefore Negro Americans could not revolt for any other reason.* This is what a Negro American revolution will be: A revolution by a racial minority for the enforcement of the democratic laws already in existence.

What will a revolution by Negro Americans do:

(1) Bring about the overthrow of our present form of government and the creation of a communistic state. A communist organization of immense proportions already exists in this nation.

"I therefore defined," Engels wrote, "the objects of communists in this way: (1) To achieve the interests of the proletariat in opposition to those of the bourgeoisie; (2) To do this through the abolition of private property and its replacement by community of goods; (3) To recognize no means of carrying out these objects other than a democratic revolution by force."[1]

It is obvious that the Communist party of America will attempt to direct any revolution, whether by Negro Americans or any other group, to the accomplishment of these aims. It is equally obvious that in any nation where great numbers of people are oppressed the Communists have fair chances of success.

(2) Bring about the overthrow of our present form of government and the creation of a dictatorship.

The first reaction of the people who are endeavoring to continue the existence of white supremacy in all its vicious destructiveness will be to stamp out this revolution with a maximum of violence and a minimum of mercy. Many Negroes will be shot. Many will be imprisoned. The remainder will be literally enslaved. *If these people are successful.*

But what is more to be feared in the historic progress of the human race: *At this pivot of change where we now exist we will cease to go forward and go back.* Law, order, decency, all the democratic principles which we have so far developed in this nation will be destroyed. The white race will become barbarians. The darker races slaves.

When people become barbarians they can no longer govern themselves. They respect only might. The strongest, the most deadly, most vicious, most cunning, most murderous, will become the ruler. He will rule as long as he is feared.

(3) It may be successful and bring about the enforcement of the Constitution, democratic equality, and the acceptance of the democratic way of existence by all of the citizens of our nation.

For this to happen it will be necessary that the majority of the people of the United States believe in democracy and will join with us in bringing about its establishment. In this event a Negro American revolution will cease to be a revolution and become a movement of the people to stamp out injustices, inequalities, and violations of our laws. The people who would try to prohibit the people from so doing would become rebels, traitors, secessionists, and would be dealt with accordingly.

If the majority of the people of the United States do not believe in democracy as the best way of existence, we will not achieve democratic equality in any event. So we are forced to begin our thinking here; we have no other point from which to begin.

MARTYRS NEEDED

At this point Negro martyrs are needed. The martyr to create the incident which will mobilize the forces of justice and carry us forward from the pivot of change to a way of existence wherein everyone is free.

It is obvious that we can not stay here; we've got to go somewhere. If we can not of our own accord go forward, we will against our will be pushed backward.

The first step backward is riots. Riots are not revolutions. In the best sense revolutions are the renunciation of the existing evils of government by the governed. Revolutions are not necessarily brought about by force of arms. *They may be successfully accomplished by the manifest will of the people.* In the event of a Negro American revolution it is to be hoped there will be no shooting.

Riots are tumultuous disturbances of the public peace by unlawful assemblies of three or more persons in the execution of private objects—such as race hatreds. No matter who passes the first blow or fires the first shot, riots between white and black occur for only one reason: *Negro Americans are firmly convinced that they have no access to any physical protection which they do not provide for themselves.* It is a well-known and established fact that this conviction is rooted in history:

Negroes in fact do not have any protection from physical injury inflicted by whites other than that which they provide themselves.

It is a rather deadly joke among Negroes (especially since the Detroit riots) that the first thing to do in case of a race riot is not to call the police but to shoot them. . . . "Man, what you mean call the police; them the people gonna kill you. . . ."

White citizens who believe in democracy (and white citizens who do not believe in democracy but do not want to have race riots) can stop race riots whenever and wherever they occur by simply appearing on the scene and making it apparent to the white persons thus engaged that they do not approve. The reason for this is obvious: White persons who incite and engage in race riots are in a minority, but *they are firmly convinced that the majority of white people morally support their actions.* As a consequence most Negro Americans clearly realize that the white citizens who stay at home and remain quiet during riots are morally as guilty as those who wield the clubs and fire the guns.

Negro martyrs are needed to assemble these white citizens who believe in democracy and stay at home; and to inspire them to fight for their beliefs.

MARTYRS RARE

It is necessary that such a Negro martyr be a person of integrity who loves freedom enough to make any sacrifice to attain it. Preferably, he should be a Negro leader, a person reasonably intelligent by the accepted standards, one who is well-known to Negro and white Americans alike and who can not be ignored by either white or Negro media of news distribution. He must be a Negro who will not compromise, and who does not mind embarrassing his white liberal friends who believe sincerely that "adaptation" or "evolution" is the best policy for Negroes to follow. And, of course, he must be a Negro who will not sell out. Therefore we must get our lanterns.

He must be solidly supported by the Negro middle class for there is no Negro leader solidly supported by the Negro lower class. Not only should he be solidly supported by this group, but so identified with them as to make it impossible for them to abandon him.

It is apparent that the Negro middle class must be out in front in any Negro American revolution, so this must be fixed in mind, and further reasoning must go forward from it. *The Negro middle class must accept the responsibility for the successful culmination of any Negro attempt for democratic equality.*

Therefore it is of singular importance that members of this group be able to recognize democratic equality when it comes, and not confuse it with social acceptance by members of other groups or races. We have not achieved equality by weekending with our white friends and drinking their liquor or flirting with their wives. In fact, many of us who are Negro Americans wish to retain the right to choose our house guests and paramours as much as any white American.

The incident, of course, must be a denial of some rights guaranteed to every citizen of the United States by the Constitution, such as the right of any decent, honest person to live wherever he chooses, or the right of a citizen to vote or serve on juries. Incidents such as an unjust accusation of rape serve no primary purpose other than to agitate or inflame and fix no constructive precedent for progress.

The martyr must make the stand and refuse to yield. The Negro middle class must come to his assistance, also refusing to yield, and must influence the Negro lower classes to follow.

What is of utmost importance is the stand. All of us Negro Americans must make the stand. And after we have made it, we must not give on any point. We must not compromise a breath. *After all, we have nothing to lose, except our lives, and one preferable change to win: Democratic equality.*

NOTE

1. *Marx-Engels Selected Correspondence*, pp. 1–2.

THE BLACK YOUTH MOVEMENT

J. SAUNDERS REDDING's "The Black Youth Movement," a conservative response to the rise of militancy among black college students, was published in *The American Scholar* in 1969. Redding (1906–1988) was an old-guard black academic and critic and a writer of merit. His works include the critical classic, *To Make a Poet Black* (1939), the novel *Stranger and Alone* (1950), and *An American in India* (1954).

From its beginning in 1960 until well past the middle years of the decade, the black youth movement did not have much to do with what is commonly thought of as education. Although it began among students in exclusively black institutions, where the competence of the instructors and the quality of instruction generally left something to be desired, the average of the students had no quarrel with the learning they were getting. They lacked the sophistication to question it. After all, they understood it to be—as in fact it was—the same learning that their contemporaries in white colleges and universities were getting. And what was good enough for white folks was good enough for them. Besides, the average of black students professed to believe that Southern University, a black institution, was as good as Louisiana State, Morehouse College as good as Sewanee, Bennett College as good as Agnes Scott, and Howard University quite the equal of Harvard.

What black students of the year 1960 wanted was simply an end to segregation and discrimination. Although integration was undoubtedly their ultimate goal, they did not say so. All their talk was of "desegregation," and all they asked was that the process begin on a basic level that everyone could understand and all ordinary folk could relate to. As if to emphasize this, the students began their campaign at a lunch counter in a five and ten cent store in Greensboro, North Carolina. Inspired by the example and persuaded by the precepts of Martin Luther King, Jr. (who was soon working directly with them), students in all-black institutions organized the Student Non-Violent Coordinating Committee (S.N.C.C. or SNICK) in 1961, and the next year broadened their campaign to include, chiefly, the elimination of discrimination in voting. They were surprised when liberal and concerned white students rushed to associate with S.N.C.C., and they were pleased and proud to admit them.

Now all that is changed. It is possible to fix the date when change began, but why it began is another matter. In 1965, James Forman was ousted as head of S.N.C.C. Almost the first public announcement of his successor, Stokely Carmichael, was a declaration to the effect that henceforth S.N.C.C. would be all black. While whites would be welcome to make financial contributions, they would not be permitted to join the organization or to work in its programs.

This keep-it-black reaction gradually spread from S.N.C.C. to CORE to local branches of the Black Students Union, and now is an overriding influence on the whole black youth movement. It leaves no tenable ground between integration and alienation, and it threatens the aspirations of those who advocate it. A kind of self-defeating extremism, it is rooted in a simple assumption that whites and blacks have held for years—an assumption that is itself "the cause of all our woes": the white man is superior to the black.

The truth or falsity of this is beside the point. What is to the point is that, with all the weight of psychic and symptomatic support behind it, the assumption has operated to produce a body of alleged knowledge that, exalting the western, Anglo-Saxon tradition, is Rah! Rah! White Folks! generally, and in regard to American history, literature and culture is antiblack racist specifically. This is the knowledge, compacted of distorted fact and myth, that is taught on all levels in American schools. Once absorbed, it becomes extremely difficult for the average white to believe in equality, freedom and human dignity for the black, and equally difficult for the average black to believe himself worthy of them.

The spokesmen-leaders of black youth act upon this assumption even while the internal logic of their movement demands that they reject it. But here the rhetoric of the revolution should be mentioned as a factor. The cognitive meaning of such phrases as "cultural identity," "cultural nationalism," "ethnic monism," and "black power" has been lost. The phrases have become clichés, and you cannot fashion an ideology from clichés. So the spokesmen-leaders talk about doing their own "black thing." They inveigh against western tradition as racist, corrupt, irrelevant, and against the white man as ignorant and brutal. They pretend to draw upon the intellectual and professional resources, the existential knowledge, and the cultural inheritance of the black ghetto. But when it comes down to cases, practice subverts principle.

Take Rap Brown. Although an impassioned spouter of "black power" and an ardent advocate of "ethnic integrity," when he is indicted for a criminal offense, he retains the services of not one, but two white lawyers. Or the instance of LeRoi Jones. If he has said it once, he has said it publicly a half-dozen times over the past three years: I write for a black audience. But his works are published by white publishers for a white market and, excepting the short-lived, federally-supported experimental Black Arts theater productions, his plays have been produced and directed by whites in theaters owned and controlled by whites in off-Broadway neighborhoods where blacks seldom go—even to see LeRoi Jones's plays. And anyway, how high is the common denominator of the audience of black people he says he writes for? How many of his soul brothers would understand the symbolic and metaphorical *A System of Dante's Hell* (a novel) and *The Dutchman* (a play), both of which owe considerably to the despised western, Anglo-Saxon tradition?

To charge the spokesmen-leaders with simple mendacity is to ignore the error of understanding into which they have led the students to whom they make the strongest appeal. Neither they nor the most vocal black students seem to understand that their felt need for a change in the materials and methods of education is as yet uninformed by rational thought. Indeed, given the conditions as they themselves have stated them—white racist learning, social irrelevance, the cultural alienation of black people—given these conditions, which, they also claim, generated the keep-it-black phase of the black youth movement, the demand for a "black studies" program to which only blacks would be admitted is naïve and silly. To meet the demand would be to perpetuate the very conditions to which black students say they are opposed, and which, presumably, dictated their choice of white institutions in the first place.

It is impossible to believe that the black students who were listened to at Cornell, Northwestern and San Francisco State spoke for all, or even for a majority, of the black students enrolled in white colleges and universities. One is encouraged in this doubt by a recent letter from a black student at Yale.

> We do not [he wrote] talk of black studies here. We do speak of an Afro-American program, which we define as an American studies curriculum which structures into the corpus of historical and literary material the substantive facts about black Americans. . . . Our argument is that the course in American history that ignores or slights the black man's role is a bad course. We believe that writing by black Americans is *American* writing, and that to segregate it from the body of American expression is a ridiculous exercise of ignorance, and that it does great harm to American literature as an instrument of cultural and aesthetic diagnosis. . . .

These arguments are not easily refuted. The exploration of the black American reality within the context of the American experience is a proper scholarly activity, and courses in sociology, history, literature, political science, linguistics, and the like afford inviting opportunities to pursue it. If taught by competent instructors, the intellectual demands of such courses would be rigorous enough to satisfy the highest academic standards. The courses would be open to all who cared to take them.

For the final test of Afro-American studies will be the extent to which they rid the minds of whites and blacks alike of false learning, and the extent to which they promote for blacks and whites alike a completely rewarding participation in American life.

CHALLENGE TO NEGRO LEADERSHIP

The Case of Robert Williams

JULIAN MAYFIELD's "Challenge to Negro Leadership: The Case of Robert Williams," a sympathetic look at the challenge to the establishment civil rights movement from more radical blacks, was published in *Commentary* in April 1961.

There is one, and only one, issue in the Robert Williams case. That single issue is: Shall the National Association for the Advancement of Colored People endorse the advocacy by a local NAACP officer of stopping "lynching with lynching" or "meeting violence with violence"?

—FROM *The Single Issue*, A PAMPHLET DISTRIBUTED AT THE NAACP NATIONAL CONVENTION IN NEW YORK, JULY 1959

For some time now it has been apparent that the traditional leadership of the American Negro community—a leadership which has been largely middle class in origin and orientation—is in danger of losing its claim to speak for the masses of Negroes. This group is being challenged by the pressure of events to produce more substantial and immediate results in the field of civil rights or renounce the position it has long held. The dramatic Tuskegee and Montgomery boycotts, the rash of student sit-ins—none was inspired by the National Association for the Advancement of Colored People, the Urban League, or the established Negro church denominations, but it is to their credit that they hurriedly gave the boycotts and sit-ins their blessing and, as with the NAACP, much needed financial help. They were thereby able to present a united front to their common enemy, the system of white supremacy.

But the challenge to middle-class Negro leaders—including the newer type like Martin Luther King—remains. It is inherent in the rapid growth of the militant, white-hating Muslim movement among working-class Negroes. It can be heard in the conversations of black intellectuals and students from the South who regard the efforts of the NAACP, the Urban League, and most religious and civic leaders with either disdain or despair, in the belief that they are doing too little, too timidly and too late.

Probably nothing more clearly illustrates this challenge, however, than the case of *Wilkins vs. Williams*. Robert F. Williams is the president of the Union County, North Carolina, branch of the NAACP. *Wilkins vs. Williams* was a hearing before the board of directors of the NAACP in New York City, which grew out of three criminal cases that were disposed of in one day by the Superior Court in Monroe, the seat of Union County.

Before this court on May 5, 1959, stood James Mobley, B. F. Shaw, and Louis Medlin. Mobley, a mentally retarded colored man, was charged with assault with intent to commit rape on a white woman. (He admitted he had caught her wrist during an argument.) Shaw, a white man, was charged with assault on a Negro chambermaid who claimed he had kicked her down a flight of stairs in the hotel where she worked. The case of the other white defendant, Medlin, was the most inflammatory. He was accused of having entered the home of a Negro woman, eight months pregnant, of attempting to rape her, and, when she resisted and tried to flee across a field, of brutally assaulting her and her six-year-old son. A white woman neighbor had witnessed the assault and summoned the police.

The Union County branch of the NAACP is the only one of its kind now in existence. Its members and supporters, who are mostly workers and displaced farmers, constitute a well-armed and disciplined fighting unit. Union County Negroes have had more than their share of ugly race relations, and by 1959, their experience—which we shall examine in detail later— taught them to rely on their own resources in their dealings with the white community. After Medlin was arrested, their first impulse was to mount an assault against the Monroe jail, seize the prisoner, and kill him. It was Robert Williams who restrained them. He pointed out that murdering Medlin would place them in the position of the white men who, shortly before, had dragged Mack Charles Parker from a jail in Poplarville, Mississippi, and lynched him. Besides, Williams argued, so much national and international attention was focused on Monroe that the judge and juries would be forced to punish the white men.

But Williams was wrong. Impervious to world opinion, the court freed both Shaw and Medlin, and committed the mentally retarded Negro to prison for two years. (Only the last-minute discovery by his attorney of a technicality, which reduced the charge from rape to assault, prevented the judge from handing down a thirty-year sentence.) On the steps of the courthouse, Williams issued an angry statement to a UPI reporter:

> We cannot take these people who do us injustice to the court and it becomes necessary to punish them ourselves. In the future we are going to have to try and convict them on the spot. We cannot rely on the law. We can get no justice under the present system. If we feel that injustice is done, we must right then and there, on the spot, be prepared to inflict punishment on the people.

Since the federal government will not bring a halt to lynching in the South, and since the so-called courts lynch our people legally, if it's necessary to stop lynching with lynching, then we must be willing to resort to that method.

Roy Wilkins, executive secretary of the NAACP, called Williams from New York to ask about the statement. Williams confirmed it as his and said he intended to repeat it that afternoon for several radio and television stations eager to interview him. He would make it clear, he assured Wilkins, that he was not speaking for the NAACP but for himself, though he would stress that his views represented the prevailing feeling of the colored people in Union County. Wilkins replied that it would be virtually impossible for the general public to separate Williams's statement from the policies of the NAACP since he would be identified as an officer of the organization. Williams then made his scheduled appearances, and the next day, May 7, Wilkins sent a telegram directing him to suspend his activities as a local officer pending consideration of his status at a meeting of the Association's board of directors. Williams answered that he would attend the meeting with counsel.

Thus the stage was set for a contest between a highly respected leader of a distinguished national organization and a relatively unknown young Southerner capable of issuing rash statements on the steps of a courthouse. *Wilkins vs. Williams* aroused heated discussions in nearly every Negro community in the country, but it was obvious from the beginning that Williams was bound to lose. At a closed hearing in June, before the Committee on Branches, Williams, represented by Conrad Lynn, a veteran civil-rights attorney, asserted that his statement had been made under emotional duress, and that he had not meant to imply that Negroes should exercise anything more than their legal right to self-defense and the right to come to the defense of another party against criminal attack. The committee upheld the action of its executive secretary and suspended Williams for six months. A few weeks later, the delegates to the Association's fiftieth annual convention voted 764 to 14 against Williams and in favor of suspension.

The one-sided vote should have settled the matter, with Williams returning to obscurity. But the questions raised by *Wilkins vs. Williams* are profound, and still far from settled. A close examination of relevant documents and newspaper files, and interviews with some of the principals involved, leads one to conclude that the real issue was never raised, and that Williams was slapped on the wrist for having stated publicly what many of his fellow Negroes, even those on the board of directors of the NAACP, felt but did not think it politic to express. Indeed, a statement issued by Roy Wilkins on May 6, 1959, deploring Williams's statement might well have been written by Williams himself.

At the same time it must be recognized that the mood of Negro citizens from one end of the nation to the other is one of bitterness and anger over the lynching [of Mack Parker] in Poplarville, Mississippi, April 25, and over numerous instances of injustice meted out to Negroes by the courts in certain sections of the South. They see Negroes lynched or sentenced to death for the same crimes for which white defendants are given suspended sentences or set free. They are no longer willing to accept this double standard of justice.

If Negroes were no longer willing to accept the double standard of justice, *what were they to do about it?* Wilkins did not say, but one paragraph in the brief Williams submitted to the Committee on Branches provides the answer which he has been expounding ever since and which daily finds wider and wider acceptance:

> He [Williams] believes the message of armed self-reliance should be spread among Negroes of the South. He is convinced that a somnolent national government will only take action when it is made aware that individual Negroes are no longer facing the mobs in isolation but are acquiring the habit of coming to the aid of their menaced brothers.

But this was precisely the position which the NAACP could not publicly support. The organization was already being subjected to constant harassment by the Southern states. And to have advocated Williams's position would have exposed the NAACP to widespread criticism from many of the people who now warmly support it, those who, for the most part, prefer the legalistic or pacifist approach to American race relations. Moreover, the possible resulting violence could have shaken the nation to its very foundation, and caused it intense embarrassment in the conduct of its diplomacy with a largely non-white world. But the situation in the South that provoked Williams's statement and the ensuing controversy remains unchanged. The NAACP's rejection of Williams's position only postponed the crisis facing Negro leadership; it did not eliminate it. Because it seems probable that Williams—and other young men and women like him—will play an increasingly vocal role in the social maelstrom that is the American Southland, a closer look at him, his views, and the environment that produced him, may be revealing.

I first met Robert Williams at the center of a revolution, and I am certain that this has colored my attitude toward him. It was in Havana in the summer of 1960. Relations between the Eisenhower administration and the Castro government had deteriorated almost to the breaking point. White and black leaders in the United States had already denounced Fidel Castro's efforts to win friends and sympathy among American Negroes. Adam Clayton Powell, once a warm supporter, had disavowed the Cuban leader. Joe Louis's public relations firm, under strong public pressure, had been forced to drop its Cuban account, and Jackie Robinson had taken Castro to task in his New York *Post* column. The prominent Negroes who had flocked to Havana soon after the revolution succeeded had gone home and not returned.

Yet there at the Hotel Presidente, a guest of the Casa de las Americas, a Cuban cultural agency, was Robert Williams, a tall man in his middle thirties, of massive shoulders and thick girth. In Havana he wore the wide-brimmed hat of the *guajiro* (peasant) and a beard that would have been impressive anywhere else but in the land of Fidel Castro and his comrades. This was Williams's second visit to the island since the revolution, and he was a celebrity, applauded wherever he went. In personal appearances, and in magazine and newspaper articles, Williams had been excoriating the United States, his main charge being that America talks freedom abroad while denying it to its black citizens at home. Williams and Castro had frequently appeared together on television and a warm friendship had developed between them. The relationship had mutual advantages: the Cuban leader was furnished with a gold mine of propaganda material to use in his clash with the Eisenhower administration, and Williams had a platform from which he could speak and be heard around the world. His attacks on the United States nearly involved him in a fist fight with an American newspaperman who angrily accused him of unpatriotic behavior in airing an embarrassing domestic problem in a country that was hostile to the United States. Unwittingly the reporter had touched on one of the keystones of Williams's strategy.

"What some people don't understand," he told me one evening, "is that in the South we're fighting for our lives." He was referring to the broad economic offensive white officials and businessmen have mounted against militant Negroes throughout the South. "I'm in this struggle to win, and I'll win it any way I can. If somebody gets embarrassed, that's too bad."

An opportunity to test the effectiveness of his approach had arisen on his first trip to Cuba. A telephone call from Monroe informed him that his wife and children were receiving threats from the Ku Klux Klan. Furious, he stormed down to the United States embassy, stopping only to pick up a correspondent friend from *Prensa Latina*, the Cuban News Service. He demanded and received an audience with Ambassador Philip Bonsal with whom he lodged a vigorous protest. The harassed diplomat no doubt realized the potentially explosive propaganda material that could fall into Castro's hands. He agreed to submit Williams's written protest to Washington, and within a few hours Mrs. Williams and her children had a guard of several police cars.

Williams believes that the white supremacist system of the South could not survive very long without the support, or the tacit consent, of various agencies of the federal government. At the same time, he is convinced that the federal government offers the only real hope the Negro has of winning any large measure of his civil rights. But Washington will act only under strong pressure, and this the Negro people must create by a more militant assertion of their rights—including "meeting violence with violence." The white South, through its traditional alliance with conservative Republicans, subjects the federal government to an enormous amount of pressure and wins appreciable results. Consequently, it has been able to defy the Supreme Court's school desegregation order for seven years with little federal intervention. Williams concedes that the Negro cannot match the South's great resources in either money or Congressional influence, despite the best intentions of Northern liberals and even a liberal president. But the Negro does have a formidable weapon in his sensitive position in international affairs. Without the cold war and the competition between the colossi of West and East, it seems doubtful that the many African nations could have gained independence so rapidly. Certainly the history of U.S. intervention in Latin America indicates that the Cuban revolution would not have been permitted to swing so far to the left if not for the extreme degree of United States sensitivity to world opinion today. For the same reason (though he knows it is possible to exaggerate the similarities), Williams believes the American

Negro has been presented with the finest opportunity history is likely to offer him to obtain full participation in our national life.

Thus, when President Eisenhower was in India championing the rights of Asians to better housing, Williams wired him in care of Prime Minister Nehru (also an NAACP member) to protest a housing redevelopment scheme, largely financed by federal funds, that Union County officials had designed to destroy the best Negro neighborhood in Monroe. Eisenhower acted with unusual haste, and the project has been stalled ever since.

Nowhere was Williams's method of subjecting every racial incident to world exposure more effectively demonstrated than in the "Kissing Case." On October 28, 1958, two Monroe colored boys, James Hanover Thompson and David "Fuzzy" Sampson, eight and nine years old, were arrested and charged with assault on a white female. Earlier that afternoon, in a game with some white children, James had either kissed or been kissed by a seven-year-old white girl. The boys were held incommunicado three days before Williams knew they were under arrest. Ironically, according to Williams, his first intelligence came from the mayor of Monroe who telephoned because he said he knew Williams was a "troublemaker" and he wanted to know if Williams had any ideas about how to handle the case. (The mayor denies he made the call.) It seemed to Williams that the boys required immediate legal aid which was not available in Union County. He submitted a request to the national office of the NAACP; but meanwhile, on the sixth day after their arrest, in a closed hearing, without defense counsel, Judge J. Hamilton Price heard the case and committed the boys to indeterminate terms in reform school.

Williams, through an intermediary, was responsible for Ted Poston's breaking the story in the New York *Post*, and from there, it spread around the world with lightning-like rapidity. Demonstrations were staged against American embassies in Europe, outstanding intellectuals protested to the State Department, and Canon L. John Collins of London's St. Paul's Cathedral became involved in a lively transatlantic feud with Luther H. Hodges, then governor of North Carolina. (The governor, to his embarrassment, was first informed of the "Kissing Case" by a reporter while in the middle of a television interview in Philadelphia.) Eventually the boys were released from the reform school and allowed to go back to live with their mothers who had been forced to move out of Union County. "Without the pressure of world opinion," Williams insists, "those boys would still be in custody."

These stories, which I later verified, were related to me during long nightly conversations in Havana. One evening I asked Williams a question I thought he might not answer. What truth was there in the rumor that had been circulated during the NAACP convention that his men were not only armed (in the South, after all, a surprisingly large number of people keep guns) but that they were in fact a small army, drilled and disciplined, with access to an arsenal?

He laughed. "Hell, man, that's no secret, and I don't know why it should frighten the board of directors of the NAACP. Everybody in Monroe knows what we have, that we know how to use it, and that we are willing to use it. The mayor and the chief of police know, and so does the Klan. Come to Monroe when you get back to the States and see for yourself." This was the same kind of invitation that had taken me to Cuba and two months later I was in Monroe, North Carolina.

Some Southern towns are lovely, with great old houses that slumber on broad streets beneath spreading, ancient trees. In such towns even a Negro writer on a hurried visit can perceive that, although *his* ancestors only supplied the labor under the ante-bellum system of caste and privilege, at least there was a comprehensive society in which everyone had a place; and, dimly, he can understand why the Southern aristocracy fought so desperately to retain the cruel and dehumanizing system that was slavery. Here, at least, social relations had a symmetry wherein the dark, ugly things were hidden away, in the slave quarter or on the backstairs of the big house.

But Monroe is not such a town. It is ugly. There is little distinction in the architecture of its finest houses; and although it is built on hills, there is a dreary flatness about it. Worse, it is a composite town. Unpainted one-room Negro shacks, which rent for an inflated ten dollars a month, sit within a stone's throw of the tiny, neat, unimaginative bungalows of the white middle class. One can drive three blocks in any direction and see the graphic reality of race relations in Union County. The Northern visitor, keenly aware that violence always simmers beneath the seeming tranquility, wonders that anybody, black or white, would want to fight over this place.

In the days of the steam engine Monroe was a prosperous railroad maintenance town. A generation ago Robert Williams's father, along with a significant number of Monroe's colored men, serviced the trains and earned a steady living at it. They bought their own homes in the colored section called Newtown, sent their children to the colored school most of the year, and saw in their youngsters the hope of a better future. If they were not a genuine middle class, they were better off than the tenant farmers and sharecroppers in the county's rural population. But the diesel engine supplanted steam, and the depression and mechanization displaced most of the tenant farmers and sharecroppers; and, though Monroe did not die, it was left severely crippled.

By the time Williams had grown to adolescence, unemployment was a chronic problem in Newtown. He served a hitch in the army, somehow squeezed in three years of college at West Virginia State and Johnson C. Smith College in nearby Charlotte, and then enlisted in the Marine Corps for a tour of duty. On returning to Monroe, he entered the lists of the letters-to-the-editor columns of the Charlotte newspapers and seems to have spent most of his time incensing the local whites by debunking their notions of white supremacy. During this period he married Miss Mable Robinson, a sturdy, tall, attractive woman with whom he has had two children. He worked at his trade of machinist while he wrote his provocative letters to the newspapers. It is possible that no one outside of North Carolina would ever have heard of Williams if the Supreme Court had not ordered school desegregation in 1954.

It is still difficult to imagine the impact of the Court's decision on small Southern towns. Intercourse between the races—that is, social intercourse during the Southern day, which, as James Baldwin has pointed out, is quite different from the guilt-ridden, integrated Southern night—was the function of the local white officials and businessmen, and colored ministers and other self-appointed spokesmen who purported to represent the views of their fellow Negroes. White lawyers in Monroe often defended Negroes who were in trouble (not too vigorously, to be sure) and were paid by the NAACP chapter. There was an understanding, a working relationship, between the whites who ran the town and the colored ministers. The whites would try to control their extremists, and in return, the black men of God helped to keep the black population in its place.

But suddenly, one Monday in 1954, a long-held tradition was struck a death-blow. The NAACP, which had never claimed to be anything but a moderate organization, became the ogre of the Southland. Acknowledged membership in it could mean the loss of job, credit, and physical security. Negro doctors, lawyers, undertakers—whoever had to be licensed by the state—promptly withdrew from membership. When the Union County chapter was apparently in its last throes (with only six members), Robert Williams was drafted for the presidency. ("You're the only fool left," said one of those who urged him to accept the position.) Somewhat innocently, Williams set about trying to recruit members among the respectable middle class, and, needless to say, he failed absolutely. In desperation he turned to the lower class of the Negro community. He likes to tell of the day he walked into a pool parlor and asked if anyone there wanted to join the NAACP. The players looked at him in astonishment: "Man, do you mean *we* can belong to that organization?" From that time on, Williams has had as many members as he could manage, sometimes more. He says of that period, "I made an important discovery. The woman earning ten, fifteen dollars a week as a domestic, the share-cropper, the ditch-digger—they were more loyal to the NAACP than the Negroes who were much better off. They would stick under pressure, probably because they had less to lose and we were the only fighting organization they had."

As the Union County branch of the NAACP grew, so did the Ku Klux Klan, which had renewed its activity soon after the Supreme Court decision. Most of the Klan's wrath was directed against Dr. A. E. Perry, one of the six who had remained in the chapter when Williams assumed leadership. The popular young physician, who was fairly prosperous, had built an attractive, ranch-style home overlooking a new highway. The Klan considered the house an affront, and it believed that Perry contributed large sums of money to the NAACP chapter. It publicly announced its intention of running him out of the county.

"When we heard over the radio," Williams says, "that a Klan meeting had drawn 8,000 people, we figured it was time to take a stand. You see, there are only 13,000 people in the county." (Klansmen from surrounding counties were swelling the attendance.) The colored men of Monroe armed themselves with the heaviest weapons available, and set up an alarm system that would summon them instantly to the scene of any trouble. A regular night guard was established around Dr. Perry's home. Trenches were dug, Molotov cocktails prepared, and gas masks and helmets were distributed. At one point during this troubled period the police attempted to seize the weapons, but desisted when Williams and Perry threatened a lawsuit.

(Nothing in the laws of North Carolina and of most Southern states restricts or contravenes the constitutional right "to keep and bear arms, and be secure in one's person.")

A Klan motorcade, sixty cars strong, invaded Newtown on the evening of October 5, 1957. As was their custom, the robed Klansmen fired at the homes of the Negroes as they drove past. Near Dr. Perry's home they were confronted with the sustained fire of several scores of men who had been instructed by Williams not to injure anyone if it could be helped. At the first sign of resistance the Klan motorcade dissolved into chaos. Panicky Klansmen fled in every direction, some of them wrecking their automobiles. There have been no Klan motorcades in Monroe since.[1]

It is interesting to speculate on why this significant event received so little publicity. Monroe Chief of Police Mauney admitted to the Associated Press the next day that there had been a motorcade—he knew because it had included several police cars—but he denied that there had been an exchange of gunfire. Williams invited the press to Newtown to view the bullet-scarred houses and the wrecked automobiles whose owners did not care to come to claim them. Nevertheless, few people outside the state knew that the clash had taken place, and that the Klan had sustained a decisive defeat. Compare this with the nationwide news coverage and wide applause given the Indians in nearby Lumberton County, when they routed a Klan meeting with gunfire a few weeks later. About this Williams says, "It's as if they were afraid to let other Negroes know what we have done here. We have proved that a hooded man who thinks a white life is superior to a black life is not so ready to risk his white life when a black man stands up to him." He recalls proudly that in Monroe they have had their sit-ins and wade-ins, but none of their boys and girls has been the victim of violence from racist hoodlums. "They know, don't you see, that we are not passive resisters."

The morale of the Negroes in Union County is high. They carry themselves with a dignity I have seen in no other Southern community. Largely vanished are the slouching posture, the scratching of head, and the indirect, mumbled speech that used to characterize the Negro male in the presence of whites. It is as if, in facing up to their enemies, they have finally confronted a terrible reality and found it not so terrible after all.

But they have had to pay a price for their new self-respect. Paternalism has been destroyed in Union County. The left-over food that the colored maid could once carry home is now consigned instead to the garbage pail, and the old clothes that found their way to the colored section are now either sold or burned. The intimate communication that used to pass from mistress to maid, master to workman (seldom in the reverse direction) has largely disappeared. Negroes suspected of belonging to the NAACP are told "Let Williams feed you!" and "Let Williams find you a place to live!" as they are fired from their jobs and evicted from their homes. Northern owners of the new factories, by agreement with the city fathers, hire no Negroes but import white workers from Charlotte, twenty-five miles away. It would almost appear that the rulers of Monroe society had determined to strengthen the

Union County NAACP and Williams's influence on the colored community; and, in fact, that is what they have done.

But what role is Williams likely to play in the future? Although he has shown great personal courage and demonstrated effective leadership ability in Monroe, he can claim no large following outside his own county. True, he has a scattering of fervent supporters in the United States, Europe, and Latin America, who subscribe to *The Crusader*, the weekly newsletter in which he flays not only white supremacists but Negro moderates who accommodate themselves to the system. But he is in danger of being driven out of Monroe where his standard of living is close to penury. (No one will employ him in any capacity in Union or nearby counties.) Certainly the present national leadership of the NAACP does not fear that Williams will undermine their position in the near future. The organization is still the most effective civil rights force in the country, and few of its members have shown any inclination to abandon it.

But sooner than anyone now supposes, three factors may create a social climate in the South in which a Robert Williams will play a leading role. They are the growing militancy of Negro students; the intransigence of the Southern white oligarchy; and the depressed Negro working class and peasantry. The students and the white ruling groups of the South are locked in a struggle that has greater ramifications than perhaps even they realize. At stake is not whether a black child shall sit beside a white child in a schoolroom or at a lunch counter; it is not even whether a black *boy* sits beside a white *girl* and one day marries her. At stake is the very existence of the Southern oligarchy, its entrenched power and traditional privileges which rest on a nondemocratic political system and an economy based on a plentiful supply of cheap, unorganized labor. Ultimately the struggle in the South will determine who will represent the states and the Congressional districts in Washington, who will sit in the legislatures, the city halls, and the courts, who will operate the industries and the arable land. As the real issue becomes more apparent, two developments seem certain. First, those who now wield power will refuse to yield beyond a minimum of token desegregation and will retaliate, often violently and in defiance of federal law; and second, the students will abandon the technique of passive resistance as it proves ineffectual in seriously disturbing the power structure of Southern society.

The most decisive factor in the conflict will probably be the Negro laboring class, heretofore unheard from. These are the great masses of the unskilled, who belong to no labor unions or civic organizations, whose churches are more concerned with leading their flocks to heaven than to a fuller share of democracy on earth, whose only fraternity is that of the millions of neglected and untrained who have nothing to barter in the labor market but their willingness to work. Only yesterday the man of this class could pick the cotton, run the elevator, pack the crate, but now the machine can do it better and displaces him. Government statistics hardly suggest how great his number is, much less what he is feeling and thinking, but we know he is everywhere. (The industrialization programs of the South almost always exclude him. Fourteen percent of the black labor force is now unemployed as opposed to 7 percent for the nation as a whole.) A casual walk through any colored section of a Southern town or city will reveal him, standing on the corner, lounging near the bar, slouched on the doorstep, staring into the uncertainty that is his future. The "they" in his life, those who make decisions that vitally affect him, are not only the governments, federal, state, and local, the captains of industry and finance, but even the Negro middle class and the striking students, all of whom seem to be going someplace without him. It is not *his* children that all of the school desegregation furor is about; he is lucky if he can keep them in the colored school. No one can presently claim to speak for this man, not church, union, nor NAACP; and just as he does not yet clearly understand the social forces arrayed against him, neither do *they* understand *him* or the various stimuli to which he is likely to respond.

Predictions are risky at best, but it seems safe to say that as these forces come into sharper conflict in what is essentially an attempt to overthrow an entrenched political and economic power, the Negro leadership class will be faced with a crisis, for its purely legalistic (or passive resistance) approach will clearly not be able to control the dynamics of the Negro struggle. Then to the fore may come Robert Williams, and other young men and women like him, who have concluded that the only way to win a revolution is to be a revolutionary.

NOTE

[1] Dr. Perry has been driven out of Union County. The county's leading Catholic layman, he was arrested in 1958 and indicted on charges of performing an abortion on a white woman. Sole evidence submitted against him was her uncorroborated statement. He was convicted, sent to prison, and barred from Union County. Denied the right to practice medicine, he now works as an assistant to an undertaker in Durham.

THE AUGUST 28TH MARCH ON WASHINGTON

The Castrated Giant

MICHAEL THELWELL, born in Jamaica, is a
novelist and essayist. "The August 28th March on Washington: The
Castrated Giant" was written in 1964 and published in *Duties,
Pleasures, and Conflicts: Essays in Struggle* (1987).

The now historical March [1963] on Washington for Jobs and Freedom
was in many ways a social phenomenon that could have taken place, as
the *Readers' Digest* is fond of saying, "only in the United States." The
true significance of what happened in Washington on that day defies any simple
definition. What *really* happened on the tortuous road that the March took to
Washington will probably never be made public. This is unfortunate because
somewhere along the twisting road that stretched between the first ideas for the
March, and the abortion of those ideas that was finally delivered in Washington on
August 28, lies the corpse of what could have been a real step forward in the struggle
for Negro rights in this country.

It would be useful, especially to Negroes involved in this struggle, to know just
who was responsible for what happened to the March, and to know what forces
were at work, what kinds of pressures and bribes were tried and by whom. It would
be important to know what deals were made, and who made them. Which of the
many compromises were the results of inevitable social pressures, and which were
forced by the power machinations of the Kennedy administration? Which decisions
were sincere mistakes of timidity and of judgment, and which were deliberate
attempts to reduce the whole operation to impotence? It would be useful to know,
for example, what the real role of the middle-class Negro organizations was in this
event, and whose interests they imagined themselves to be representing, and whose
interests they did, in fact, end up representing. It would help to know these things,
but for understandable reasons, the people who have the information that would

indicate these things are silent. But there were some things that are public, like what happened—this the whole world saw, and some of these leaders *did* make public statements that said more than the words spoken.

On the day itself, as the far-flung tentacles of the sprawling organization that had materialized around the idea for the March came together, it was clear to observers that something significant was happening before their eyes. The nature of what was happening was not then, and is still not, clear. On the one hand, there was an undeniable grandeur and awesomeness about the mighty river of humanity, more people than most of us will ever see again in one place, affirming in concert their faith in an idea, and in a hope that is just. And on the other, there was an air of grotesquery as in some kind of carnival where illusion is the stock-in-trade, an impression given sustenance by the huge green and white striped carnival tent and the hordes of hucksters peddling gaudy March pins, pennants, tassels, and similar items more readily associated with sporting events than with serious social protest. It was a day of contrasts, a day of platitude and rhetoric juxtaposed with genuine passion and real anguish, a day of bitterness and disappointment for some, and of hope and inspiration for others.

One looked into the black face of a southern sharecropper, weathered and marked by privation, yet on this day filled with hope and pride, and the belief that a new day was indeed coming. Then one looked at his son, sixteen years old, fresh from the brutality of a southern jail, who did not need the abstractions about oppression and intimidation because his own body bore their marks, and one could not but share in the bitterness in his eyes. And if one looked from these two, to the small army of propagandists, wheeling cameras and masses of equipment around, intent on recording this day as some kind of triumph for the system that has oppressed these people, one could not escape the feeling that somewhere there had occurred a subtle and terrible betrayal. Because, this day that had promised so much was too sweet, too contrived, and its spirit too amiable to represent anything of the bitterness that had brought the people there. And, while the goodwill and amiability of the marchers surmounted race and class and was a heartening thing, there was an overhanging atmosphere of complete political irrelevance.

As originally conceived, the March was to come as the climax of the most tumultuous summer of Negro militance in the history of the country, and was to have been the largest single demonstration of social discontent that this government had known.

When I heard the plan articulated for the first time, and it was still embryonic then, I was told that waves of nonviolent demonstrations of civil disobedience were planned to completely immobilize the Congress. The militant student group—the Student Nonviolent Coordinating Committee (SNCC)—was already thinking out stratagems to get huge numbers of demonstrators into the halls of Congress. This is forbidden by law, and the plan was to replace the demonstrators with another wave as soon as the first was removed, and to keep this up until the jails of Washington were filled. Simultaneous with this action there were to be sit-ins in the offices of the Justice Department protesting that agency's failure to protect the constitutional rights of Negroes in the south. Similar sit-ins were planned for the offices of certain politicians from southern states where the constitutional and legal rights of Negroes were being, and are now being, violated each day by local authorities as a matter of official policy. All these activities, which were to be done by the same people who were then manning the lines in demonstrations all over the country, were to be auxiliary to the huge body of the March which would break no laws, but would come to Congress and present to it a petition for the redress of three hundred years of wrongs. The civil disobedience aspect of the demonstrations were intended to dramatize the situation of the Negro: Negroes were there offering their bodies to the jails because in this country they *are* in a jail, because they are not citizens and are not really represented by Congress, because they have no voice in the decisions that govern their living and their dying, and because they have been traditionally and deliberately excluded from full participation in the social processes of the country in which they were born.

Civil disobedience was central. Laws are for those who make them, and who give their consent to them and are protected by them. On this basis, Americans, white and black, fought one revolution, and the Negroes, by symbolically defying the laws, as they have been doing in small communities throughout the south, were again affirming that "government without representation is tyranny." And the attack was to be directed to the seat of government as that is the symbol and residence of power and represents the entire system that persecutes us.

The goal was social dislocation without violence. This is the underlying technique that informs all direct action projects in the movement toward justice for America's disinherited blacks: it is one of rendering the institution under pressure inoperable by the presence of determined black bodies. When demonstrators descend on any establishment, the purpose is to so disrupt its functioning as a segregated institution that it will become non-functional and be forced to close and reopen on an integrated basis. So in one sense the demonstrations are aimed at destroying institutions that function unjustly, and replacing them by a different institution, in the sense that the same restaurant once integrated has become a new entity in terms of its function. This was not the idea for the March, since the goal was not to attempt a permanent dislocation of the Congress, but merely to use this kind of pressure for one day. This was in May, and planning was geared toward having this action during the congressional debate on the civil rights legislation that President Kennedy had decided to introduce, largely because of "Ole Miss" and Birmingham.

Certain questions were still to be resolved at this time. The penalty for disrupting the function of the Congress is a sentence of up to five years in jail. Could, from among the thousands of Negroes who were at that time involved in demonstrations all over the country, a sufficiently large number be found who were willing to risk this long sentence? Was it justifiable to ask them to do this? Where would the money come from to stage the kind of complicated and expensive legal battle that would be required to free these demonstrators afterwards? Would the authorities use force to break the demonstrations up? This is the pattern in the south, but not in Washington. But neither is it the pattern to allow demonstrations aimed at Congress. In 1961, when 120 students from Howard University attempted to picket on the steps of the Capitol, the police broke the demonstration up with the threat of the five-year sentence. On the other hand, there was a question of whether Kennedy would risk the kind of adverse publicity that would result if the demonstrators were forcibly removed from the halls of Congress. It has been this administration's posture abroad that it is committed to equality for all Americans. The reality is that it is committed to political expediency and to containing the Negro militance by conciliation. Would it have risked giving the lie to its official image by a picture on the front pages in Africa and Asia, showing ten resisting Negroes being dragged from the steps of the Capitol—the American symbol to the world of democracy and justice? The other alternative would be either to head off the March by making real concessions to Negro demands, or else to allow civil disobedience without any police action that might have triggered off violence. The demands of the March were to be:

- "Full employment for all Americans of both races, and an appeal for a massive federal program to train all unemployed . . . in meaningful and dignified jobs at decent wages.
- "Integration of all public schools by the end of this year.
- "A federal fair employment practices law, outlawing all job discrimination.
- "Passage of the Kennedy administration's legislative package . . . without compromise or filibuster."[1]

As it turns out, the administration was spared having to make this decision. I remember leaving the conversation where the original plan for the March was told to me. I said to my friend who was to play a central role in organizing the March, "I've told you that when the 'revolution' comes it will be the Negroes who begin it." This was a joke between us, but only partially so, because we were agreed that at the time when the Negro succeeded in forcing the power structure of this country into revising its practices and this society into amending its traditional attitude of exclusion and exploitation toward him, its effects would be so far-reaching and profound as to completely remake society. It is still my conviction that this is so, because no one can look at the deeply entrenched tradition of racial injustice in America and imagine that any gradual evolution of justice is possible. It will take traumatic action of various kinds to wrench society out of the deep channels of segregation in which it moves, and which causes this evil to re-create itself. Early this year, a group of Negro students was told by a Negro official of the federal government that the latter could do nothing to enforce fair employment on one of its contracts, because the kind of extreme action that this would require in the face of the long history of exclusion would disrupt too many of the established socioeconomic patterns and affront too many powerful groups within the society. That bureaucrat really meant that the federal government *could* take this action, but that it *would* not. But this illustrates why any meaningful integration of the Negro will be accompanied by social tension, chaos, and will result in the restructuring of the extant social patterns. In this sense it will be "revolutionary" in the deepest sense of that term.

Every Negro leader, except Roy Wilkins and Whitney Young, who has felt the burden of this systematic cultural policy of exclusion, knows that he cannot integrate into this society but into a new and decent one that will have to be created from energy that must be initiated by the Negro people. For this reason, the language of every Negro leader, even those that are incredibly conservative on all other political issues, is couched in the idiom of revolution whenever he talks about integration.

Minister Malcolm X, the fiery and witty leader of the Black Muslim movement, which bases much of its social ideology on the impossibility and undesirability of integration and appeals for complete separation, sums up the totality of the Negro's exclusion in these terms: "Martin Luther King says that we are second-class citizens. That is not true, we are not citizens at all. The fact that we were here before 1776, and that we are born here does not make us citizens. A cat can have kittens in an oven, but does that mean that they are biscuits?"

It was this entrenchment of discrimination that led me to speak in terms of the "revolution." And this is why I favored, and still do favor, the tactic of disobedience to the civil law on the March, and the use of aggressive nonviolence. If these original plans had not been abandoned, a crisis might have been forced. The mere threat of using five thousand veteran demonstrators who had known jails and police brutality from demonstrations in cities like New York, Birmingham (Alabama), Cambridge (Maryland), and Danville (Virginia), and Negroes from the Deep South where the state quite literally represents a monopoly of violence against the Negro, may well have been enough to pry some action from a reluctant Congress. The history of the United States Congress over the last one hundred years is a history of racism. It has never acted in the interests of the Negro unless it was forced into doing so by political pressure. Like any other institution, its reactions are geared to practical considerations and self-interest and not moral imperatives; therefore, its actions tend to ride on the coattails of public opinion, which means in this country, white opinion and national prejudice. As a body, it will do nothing for the Negro that is likely to move against the mainstream of social momentum. This unwillingness to act for integration is compounded by the structuring of that body, which places southern politicians, who represent areas in which Negroes are effectively disenfranchised, at the head of influential parliamentary committees. Thus Congress is in great measure controlled by men who derive their power from segregation and to whom integration on a political level means the end of the system that brought them to power. The presence of these "Dixiecrats" in the Democratic party, and the essentially schizophrenic and bastard nature of that party within which an allegedly liberal president must live with the most reactionary forces in this country, is one more indication why the Negroes' posture toward the political establishment must be one of attack. It also indicates why no meaningful legislation can be induced out of a Congress with its present political composition, and why the March was originally conceived not as an appeal to conscience, but as an expression of strength.

Such a demonstration as was outlined would not have attracted anything like the 250,000 people who attended on August 28, but there can be no doubt that it would have received widespread support. This was the Negro mood at that time.

Newspapers and TV news programs were filled with the story of the "Negro upris-
ing." Demonstrations were erupting in the streets of cities across the nation, north
and south. Within a period of two weeks after the March was first mentioned to
me, upheavals were recorded in cities as far apart as Albany and Americus in
Georgia, Greenwood, Goldsboro, Jackson, and Oxford in Mississippi, and in cities
in Florida, Alabama, Louisiana, the Carolinas, California, and the "border" states
of Virginia and Maryland. Before the summer was over, outbreaks of varying
degrees of violence were to shatter the northern complacency of cities like Chicago,
Philadelphia, New York, and Boston.

In Cambridge, Maryland, some of the most critical confrontations took place,
and the possibility of a racial war was sufficiently present to warrant the imposition of
martial law. In Danville, Virginia, the tactics used by police to break up nonviolent
demonstrations were more savage than in Birmingham. On the 10th of June, of
sixty-four demonstrators, forty required medical attention after club-wielding police
and deputized garbage collectors followed blasts of water poured from fire hoses into
the group, clubbing women and children indiscriminately and strewing the street
with bloody, soaked bodies. One result of this was that three days later, the demon-
strations included 250 Negroes. These two instances illustrate the all-pervading
nature of the oppression of Negroes here. I chose them because they are both located
within a few hours drive of Washington, D.C., but similar instances of this nature
can be found all over the land.

After the much-publicized Birmingham demonstrations, the Negro mood
hardened perceptively and became more abrasive and determined. There was more
bitterness and less patience; there were also more demonstrations. On these morn-
ings, a glance through the newspapers, which generally subdue their reports of
racial unrest, revealed that Negroes, like the spring, "were breaking out all over."
Even from the relatively neutral reports, it was evident that the mood of these
demonstrations was changing. Incidents of Negroes facing up to the police and to
white mobs were more frequent. In the streets, the bars, the homes, the churches,
the mood ebony was clearly one of indignation and open anger. The landlady of a
friend of mine, a lady of some sixty-five years, and up until then, a veritable
stereotype of the respectable, religious, and passive older generation of lower-middle-
class Negro, began to seriously investigate the possibilities of purchasing a revolver.

This new mood did not escape the white press, nor did the politicians miss it
either. Great concern was expressed about the possibility of a major race riot, or a
series of race riots sweeping the country.

President Kennedy had publicly affirmed the right of peaceful demonstrations
earlier in the spring. Now, moved as much by the southern and conservative charges
that he was encouraging anarchy, as by the possibility that the Negro people would
retaliate in kind to their attackers, he took the position that, although legal, demon-
strations were irresponsible and that Negroes should return their battle to the arena
of the courts, which was, among other things, less visible. The position of the
student demonstrators was that there was nothing to be gained by keeping the
illusion of "peace." There is no real peace where there is no justice, and the white
man's peace is for us a slave's peace. The demonstrations did not stop.

In this position Kennedy was supported by the National Association for the Advancement of Colored People (NAACP), whose national secretary, Roy Wilkins, publicly questioned the effectiveness of street demonstrations. There are two important considerations which militate against this position. One, the simple fact [of] the white establishment's wish to stop demonstrations is the best possible brief for their continuance; if it becomes sufficiently threatened, it will remove the causes of the demonstrations. The other factor is that discrimination does not exist because of any absence of law affirming Negro rights. It exists, in spite of such laws and the Constitution, because the federal administration *has never acted to enforce these laws* which are blatantly broken and ignored, unless some kind of crisis seems imminent. Therefore, it is not more laws that are needed, but more pressure.

The 1954 Supreme Court decision on segregated schools directed the integration of the entire school system "with all deliberate speed." Nearly ten years later, there has been little more than token observance of this ruling in the south. One answer is direct action, and even with the schools this is possible. In Englewood, New Jersey, Negro parents took their children out of the Negro kindergarten and into the white school where the children had not been permitted to enroll. The teachers attempted to ignore these illegal infiltrators, but the white infants did not, and after three days the teachers found it simpler to include the "demonstrators" in the class activities. In Boston, Negro citizens set up "freedom schools," and withdrew thousands of Negro children from the official high schools in protest of the inferior facilities given to Negroes. The "freedom schools" included in their curriculum classes in the theory of civil disobedience, social responsibility, and Negro history. The Boston school system hastily came to terms with the Negro community.

The plans for this March were evolved by Bayard Rustin, a Negro militant and pacifist; Tom Kahn, a white student in a Negro university who was a young man with a long history of civil rights activities; and Norman Hill, an executive of the Congress on Racial Equality (CORE), a militant direct action group.

Rustin is one of the most colorful characters in the civil rights movement. In addition to being an astute tactician, and extremely politically sophisticated, he is one of the few real intellectuals that is active. He is essentially not a "leader" figure, but there is no one person who has had more direct effect in defining the direction that the struggle has taken in recent years. He was executive assistant to A. Philip Randolph in planning the March on Washington for the integration of war industries during World War II. He was Martin Luther King's adviser during the Montgomery bus boycott, the director of the Youth March on Washington for integrated schools in 1954, and has organized nonviolent demonstrations in Tanganyika and in England, and, three years ago, led a party of Africans into the Sahara in protest against French nuclear bomb tests. One of the reasons that he is not a publicly acknowledged leader in this struggle—and this does not speak too well of the courage of existing groups—is his association with the American Communist party during the depression, but he is certainly the person with the most realistically radical approach to the struggle, and one of the few adult voices that the students in the struggle respect and will listen to. Another such person is the novelist James Baldwin.

Main opposition to Rustin as organizer of the March came from Roy Wilkins of the NAACP, that huge, middle-class based and essentially conservative Negro organization. Wilkins is the "Negro leader" most appreciated by the middle-class Negro and white liberal community as being "responsible." He is roundly rejected by the students as a tool of the white power structure. It is difficult to understand how anyone can be naïve or nearsighted enough to demand sweeping changes in the area of Negro rights, in a country where any meaningful demand on behalf of the Negro is radical and yet hold conservative attitudes toward all other areas of society.

When I left Washington in June, the plans for the March were not yet made public, and it was my understanding that the first steps were already under way. A. Philip Randolph was approached, and was willing to call on the other five civil rights groups to participate. Since the appeal was for jobs and freedom, it was felt that organized labor should be involved.

Martin Luther King's Southern Christian Leadership Conference (SCLC), which had spearheaded the Birmingham demonstrations, committed itself to the idea eagerly. CORE, another militant organization, and the one responsible for the 1961 Freedom Rides, and the Student Nonviolent Coordinating Committee, which is a student organization which specializes in working only in the deepest south, were also eager to support the March in its unadulterated form. However, the heads of the NAACP and the Urban League, the two most affluent of the civil rights organizations, withheld their support on the basis that it did not appear to be worth the effort or the money. It should be pointed out that the support of these two organizations was considered essential for reasons of politics and finance.

From this point on, the March plans were subjected to the bewildering succession of changes, disputes, and distortions that resulted in the final fiasco that took place on August 28. One meeting of these leaders was described to me in these terms: "Well, we finally pinned Wilkins [of the NAACP] down and finally wrung a commitment from him." By this time he had held up the campaign for several weeks, but the support of the NAACP and the Urban League was on the condition that civil disobedience be abandoned. The first compromise was made: there were to be no sit-ins, pickets, or aggressive activity of any kind. The next issue was a strong objection to Rustin as the deputy organizer. Randolph and King were adamant on this point, and Rustin's services were retained.

My next information was to the effect that although the March was not officially announced, the Kennedys knew about it, and it was in the wind that the administration was against it. The committee was having difficulty getting support or money. "You would be surprised," my informant concluded, "how liberal doors close in your face when Kennedy is opposed to a project." Shortly thereafter, there was a public announcement, and Kennedy publicly disapproved of the idea. A Negro clergyman in New York declared that there were going to be "massive acts of civil disobedience, prostrate bodies on streets and airport runways and railroad tracks, massive and monumental sit-ins at the Congress." The white community was unanimously horrified. It then became a matter of public discussion that SNCC and CORE were preparing for "nonviolent civil disobedience, all day sit-ins at the Justice

Department, in Senator Eastland's [of Mississippi] office and in the Congress." The country's reaction was, as nearly as I could observe, one of apprehension, if not open fear. The events of the spring and early summer, especially those in Birmingham, had convinced them that the Negro community was about ready to retaliate in kind. Bloodbaths were predicted, should the March take place.

The Committee for the March, and the leaders of the Urban League and NAACP singly denied any plans for direct action, and CORE and SNCC were chastised for "irresponsibility." I was told that "the Kennedy administration was putting up unbelievable opposition," and that administration maneuvering was "fantastic." I was not told, nor did I ask, the nature of this opposition. However, after the official rejection of any kind of civil disobedience, public opinion began to veer. The entire idea of the March was no longer condemned as un-American, and groups not normally active in the Negro cause began to hint at support. Liberal columnists began to remember that the Negro had the force of morality and a history of persecution behind him. But the powerful labor federation, the AFL-CIO, still refused, and never came out in support.

Shortly thereafter, the announcement came of the rerouting of the March. Instead of going to the Capitol legally and petitioning Congress, the March would now proceed from the Washington Monument to the Lincoln Memorial and listen to the speeches of the leaders. The leaders alone would *visit* the politicians. Plans to include two unemployed Negroes in the meeting with the president were quietly forgotten. I do not know that they were ever officially changed, but I do know that no unemployed persons made that visit.

With this new announcement, President Kennedy underwent a sudden and dramatic change of heart, and publicly welcomed the March as an expression of support for the legislation that the events of the summer had convinced him to introduce. From this point on, the March became more of an expression of faith in the Kennedy administration. The changing of the route had guaranteed that the whole proceedings would be as unobtrusive as possible and that it could be isolated to one small and relatively unimportant section of Washington.

It was the second week of August before I was able to get to New York. Despite severe doubts about having anything to do with this March, I found myself being pulled, possibly by curiosity, to its headquarters. There the truth of the assertion that "Americans Love a Parade" was made evident. There was great willingness to support the project. The phones buzzed with supporters of this "social revolution" to complain "that the bus that my bridge club has chartered has no air conditioning" or that "our buses have no reclining seats." One group wanted to know if they could carry signs bearing talmudic inscriptions and whether their leader could make a speech or see the president. Others wanted to know if they would lose a day's pay by attending. . . .

In the New York headquarters, I found many students whom I knew. Their attitude was one of expectant excitement. They were all veterans of the struggle; most had prison records as a result, and were sufficiently aware as to have few illusions about what their relationship as young Negroes was to their environment. Knowing this, I had difficulty determining how they could lend their support to what the project had become. That question is still largely unanswered, but I suspect that the answer has much to do with a personal loyalty to Rustin, and the manner in which any activity can generate around itself a force and an energy that completely immerses anyone who is in too close proximity to it. For those students, the problem became one of obtaining six more buses, trying to get a train, or getting letters out, and in the solution of these individual problems, the validity of their total meaning passed unnoticed.

The scene at Washington's March headquarters ranged between irony and absurdity. The entire town buzzed with activity and speculation; the newspapers were filled with little else. In the office, the volunteers of both races, by some queer coincidence, became divided into what appeared to be racial groupings, whites to the north, Negroes to the south. This proved to be the result of coincidence and a personality conflict between two organizers, rather than any racial tension.

Quite obviously, the March was the best thing that had happened to private enterprise and small business in Washington. Three days before the event, private entrepreneurs started selling the March pins, pennants, and other assorted souvenirs that they had had the foresight to have made. It was a triumph of American ingenuity, and I calculate that the March committee lost many thousands of dollars to these opportunists who undersold the official March prices for these items.

Very clearly, the agents of the government were under orders to cooperate with the workers. One student volunteer—Stokely Carmichael—received a traffic ticket while driving a "March" car; the police captain promptly tore the ticket up. This apparently insignificant incident represents a fraudulent inversion of normalcy which can be understood if you know that the student had seen a companion assaulted two months before by a Washington policeman when they protested against brutality in the arrest of a Negro. He was arrested off a picket line a week before in Washington because of the "intimidating" nature of the sign he carried.

The cooperation of various groups was, to say the least, surprising. Huge, luxurious, and air-conditioned cars were loaned to the committee. Two of these came from a firm that had been picketed by CORE that summer because of alleged discrimination in their hiring policy. So much sweetness was generated, in fact, that one woman's conscience was moved. She wanted to help, although her attitudes toward Negroes had not been of the best in the past. She had this huge house so she decided that she'd take in marchers. She phoned the housing committee: "Yes, that's right. I can give housing to twenty marchers. Yes, that's right, twenty. Anything to help a good cause. But, one thing . . . would you please see that you only send me white marchers please?"

But it was most nauseating at the headquarters tent that was pitched by the Washington Monument. White tourists forsook the tour of the monument to photograph and gape at the volunteers at work making signs. The government photographers shot miles of film; they often interrupted the work to pose the volunteers, so as to "integrate" the work teams. "Now smile," they said, "this is going to Africa." So it happened that Negro students from the south, some of whom had still unhealed bruises from the electric cattle prods which southern police use to break up demonstrations, were recorded for the screens of the world portraying "American Democracy at Work."

The sweetness and light was so all-pervading, and the smiling official faces so numerous, that one student volunteer remarked to me: "It's incredible! Look how cooperative they are. When the 'revolution' comes, the government will be cooperating with the revolutionaries."

He was wrong. Whenever it appears that Negroes are about to change the shape of things, and to effect a more equitable distribution of power and privilege—and this is what any kind of Negro freedom in America will require—the real racism will emerge in the form of guns, clubs, police dogs, and the violent suppression that happened in Danville and Birmingham. The March no longer had pretentions of doing that. However, amid this ocean of goodwill, one or two local whites maintained their perspectives. On the night of the 26th, the telephone cables into the headquarters tent were cut. On the morning of the 28th, some of the buses en route to the demonstration were stoned. The American Nazi party contributed their usual racial abuse until one of their number was arrested. On that morning, a young Virginian was arrested while driving toward the crowd, carrying a sawed-off shotgun. One was almost grateful to these people for reaffirming reality.

Little needs to be said of the events of the day itself. One white marcher gave this account:

"From the headquarters tent they began passing out the placards. They must have had ten thousand of them all neatly lithographed, each bearing one of five officially approved slogans such as 'We March for Jobs for All.' 'If you want a sign please step up,' said a young woman, and the people who had come so far stepped up and were given their officially approved signs.

" 'Do you want a program?' asked a busy lady in white, and she made sure that the people who had come so far each had a mimeographed program, showing them which way to march, and telling them how to behave properly.

"And afterwards, through the long hot afternoon, we stood in front of the stolid Memorial while they sang at us and spoke to us of equality and justice; all, it seemed, in officially approved words. And through diligent organization and scrupulous planning, they managed to stage a mass protest against injustice *without offending anyone.*

"I suppose that this is necessary, but I am sad. I had high hopes and I came away sad. I find it sad to live in a society where a man demanding individual freedom must march into battle carrying a mimeographed map, and under a lithographed banner showing an officially approved slogan. And, I feel deeply, that in some way I don't fully understand, the people who had come so far had been betrayed."

These are sentiments that are quite understandable, but suppose the writer instead of being a white Californian, had been a Negro student out of a Mississippi jail? There are two events from the day that are illustrative. James Lee Pruitt is an eighteen-year-old Mississippi Negro. He worked on voter registration for SNCC; his job was to organize Negroes to make the attempt to register. It is dangerous and frustrating work. One student, Jimmy Lee, was shot in Mississippi for doing this two years ago. At the March, Pruitt was stopped by one of the marshals whom the committee had provided to keep the peace.

"Has that sign been approved?" asked the marshal.

"It's my sign," Pruitt said.

He was led silently to the chief marshal for judgment to be passed on his sign which simply said "STOP CRIMINAL PROSECUTIONS OF VOTER REGISTRATION WORKERS IN MISSISSIPPI." This was something that young Pruitt understood since he had recently spent four months in a five-by-eight-foot cell along with fourteen other SNCC workers. In jail they had been kept without any clothes for forty-seven days, and had the fans trained on their small cell. Pruitt had been placed into a tiny zinc cubicle set in the Mississippi sun until he passed out after twelve hours, with a reported temperature of 104 degrees. When one of the group fell ill and the services of a doctor were requested, the guard said only, "Sure, Nigger, after you are dead."

During his trip to Washington to carry that sign, the car that he was traveling in developed mechanical trouble. No garage in the town would touch the car and it had to be abandoned. Pruitt was one of those who "had come so far" and at great price. It could not have been much consolation to him that the chief marshal, after hearing his story, decided that he had a right to carry the unofficial sign. And this story, while extreme, is symbolic of a great many who had come a long way and at great sacrifice, whose stories were not told and whose anguish was not expressed on that day. There is a small footnote to the Pruitt story. Yesterday, November 15, I heard from a SNCC field secretary that Pruitt was again in Parchman Farm, the Mississippi penal farm of folk song and legend.

The other story concerns another young Negro whose name is John Henry Lewis. He is the twenty-five-year-old national chairman of SNCC, the outfit to which Pruitt belongs. He has been arrested in the south more than twenty-five times and the day of the March was one of the few times that I have seen him without some kind of bandage on his head. He was listed on the "mimeographed program" as a speaker, and, when he spoke, he would tell some of the truth, and at least the stories of the Pruitts would be heard. Of this we were sure.

However, a copy of his speech was seen by the Catholic archbishop of Washington, Patrick O'Boyle, who decided that the speech was "inflammatory" and refused to give the invocation unless it was revised. Over the strong objections of Lewis, supported by Rustin, pressure of the other leaders carried the day and the speech was changed. The final chapter in irrelevance was written. The people who had come so far were to get dreams and visions and rhetoric. Here is some of what Lewis was to have said:

> Listen, Mr. Kennedy! Listen, Mr. Congressman! Listen Fellow Citizens! The black masses are on the march for freedom and for jobs. We will march through the south, through the heart of Dixie, the way Sherman did . . . we shall pursue our own scorched earth policy.
>
> We shall take matters into our own hands to create a new source of power outside of any national structure, to splinter the segregated south into thousands of pieces and put the pieces back in the image of democracy.

So there is much to be sad about as regards the magnificent abortion of August 28. It is sad that at the end of so much activity, the best and worst that could be said is that "it was orderly and no one was offended." It is much sadder and a little obscene that if anyone gained from the day's activity it was the U.S. Department of State which converted the proceedings into a great propaganda victory. When the Telestar broadcast of the March was suddenly and inexplicably canceled by Russian TV, this was hailed by the American press and by the State Department as evidence that the "Russians were afraid to show their people this example of democracy in action." But even if this is true, who does this help? Could they not afford to allow their people to see this mammoth crowd of "free" people in a "free society" petitioning their government for the redress of wrongs? No explanation has been offered as to why a free people should need to march for freedom, or why, if the government is really theirs—i.e., really represents them—it has made no move to redress these wrongs. This exploitation of so many angry and sincere people, whose indignation was misrepresented as some kind of testimonial for the system that had oppressed them, and against which they were protesting, must qualify as one of the greatest and most shameless manipulations of recent years.

But the real political waste was that the March became a symbol and a focal point in the minds of Negroes during this explosive summer of our discontent, and in many communities where the Negro temper was right, and where there had begun meaningful protest activity, the militants were diverted into mobilization for the March. In one community the local student group was told in June that the most important activity they could undertake was to make the March preparations their summer project. This was before the emasculation process had begun, and these students decided to set aside their local program and to work toward this end. This happened in too many areas; local action slowed down, and we all looked to Washington for the climax that never came. In this way, much energy and much anger were wasted on the spectacular. Ironically, what was to have been our day of protest served a similar function to the "bread and circuses" of the Roman emperors—it drained the anger of our people into irrelevant channels.

POSTSCRIPT

Like most Americans, I watched the event on television. A group of activist students—SNCC folk mostly—had been, by default and accident, left in possession of the headquarters tent when the March began spontaneously without the leadership. There being no possible way to stop that sea of humanity, the assembled dignitaries had to scramble rather unceremoniously to overtake the masses they perceived themselves to be leading. A spectacle we found symbolically appropriate and funny.

Because we had just learned of the sanitizing of John's speech, as it turns out, for remarks critical of the Kennedy administration's civil rights agenda, our mood was not celebratory. Which is why we were quite ungracious when a messenger appeared with several large boxes of leis sent by sympathizers in Hawaii. The refrigerated garlands were accompanied by a message of heartfelt support and the hope that the leaders on the platform would wear them.

It was a touching gesture of solidarity, but in that moment it seemed entirely too festive. Besides which none of us, even were it possible, was in the mood to chase after those leaders to festoon them with the petals of orchids. So far as I know, the present was never acknowledged and the donors, watching from Hawaii, never saw their gifts on TV, nor learned what happened to them. (If they looked closely when the camera panned the crowd, they *may* have noticed that a number of attractive young women and some small children were indeed bedecked with bands of orchids.)

When the telecast began, the mood in the tent was mixed. We were respectful when the venerable A. Philip Randolph opened the program. "We are gathered here in the largest popular demonstration in the history of this nation . . . we are not an organization . . . not a pressure group . . . we are not a mob. We are the advance guard of a moral revolution. . . ."

But with each succeeding speaker, the mood in the headquarters tent grew grimmer and more sullen, all the more so because of the inescapable and confusing ambivalence we all felt—our deep-seated sense of co-optation and irrelevance in conflict with the sheer numbers and unprecedented size of the operation. So we hid our confused anger behind a screen of sarcasm. We mocked and jeered the "bullshit and rhetoric" so roundly that the few journalists who wandered in in search of "background" seemed visibly surprised and left hurriedly. Clearly they had expected jubilation.

Then something unforgettable happened. Martin Luther King, Jr., began to talk. We greeted him with crude witticisms about "De Lawd." Then that rich, resonant voice asserted itself and despite ourselves we became quiet. About half-way through as image built on stirring image, the voice took on a ringing authority and established its lyrical and rhythmic cadence that was strangely compelling and hypnotic. Somewhere in the artful repetitions of the "Let Freedom Ring" series, we began—despite our stubborn, intemperate hearts—to grunt punctuations to each pause. "Ahmen, Waal, Ahhuh."

By the time the oration triumphantly swept into its closing movement—an expression of faith and moral and political possibility, delivered in the exquisite phrasing and timing of the black preacher's art—we were transformed. We were on our feet, laughing, shouting, slapping palms, hugging, and not an eye was dry. What happened that afternoon in that tent was the most extraordinary, sudden, and total transformation of mood I have ever witnessed.

Then drowning the electronic sound from the set, like an eerie counterpoint, came the booming, indescribably deep and visceral roar of the real crowd—some 250,000 souls—half a mile away.

Seventeen days later, after I had mailed off the above, four young girls in Sunday school were murdered when their church was bombed. Two months later, in Dallas, Texas, John F. Kennedy was gunned down.—M. T. (1986)

NOTE

1. The latter is particularly interesting, since this legislation has had an unusual history. Kennedy called it the "most pressing business" of the Congress during the summer's racial turmoil. He recently made the statement that his tax cut is the most necessary, and now that the demonstrations have slowed down, and the polls say that white opinion is that the Negro "is pushing too fast," he and his brother Bobby have indicated that the civil rights legislation needs to be "watered down" to ensure that it is

passed. A strong bill at this point would not pass they say; what is already an inadequate bill must be further diluted. It is not difficult to see where the two Kennedys are looking—at the presidential elections of '64.

Yet despite this clear betrayal, Kennedy is still supported by his favorite "responsible" Negro leaders. Roy Wilkins and Whitney Young came out this week with statements that sounded alarmingly like Kennedy's, and as though they were saying that the Negro was pushing too hard. It is not difficult to understand why Malcolm X calls Wilkins "Kennedy's Nigger."

IDENTITY, DIVERSITY, AND THE MAINSTREAM

ALBERT MURRAY's "Identity, Diversity and the
Mainstream" is from *The Omni-Americans: New Perspectives on Black
Experience and American Culture* (1970). Murray, born in 1916, is a
fiction writer (*Train Whistle Guitar*, 1974; *The Spyglass Tree*, 1990)
and cultural critic (*The Hero and the Blues*, 1973; *Stomping the Blues*,
1976). He co-authored the acclaimed *Good Morning Blues: The
Autobiography of Count Basie*, published in 1985.

A SHORT HISTORY OF
BLACK SELF-CONSCIOUSNESS

The preoccupation with symbols and rituals of black consciousness currently so
noticeable among so many civil rights activists and passivists alike is frequently
misrepresented as an entirely new development. Some of the slogans and gestures
may be new; and it well may be that never before have any Americans insisted in
giving such revolutionary significance to a new fashion in *hair texture*. (Once and
for all, how much culture and identity can you get from hair texture?) But in most
other respects, the present wave of interest in self-definition and self-determination
is not an innovation but a resurgence of the exuberant self-delight that characterized
the so-called Harlem renaissance or New Negro movement no longer ago than the
nineteen-twenties.

The New Negro movement was very specifically concerned with black identity
and black heritage. Nor was it unresponsive to social and political matters. But its
most significant achievements were in literature and the arts rather than in the area
of social revolution. Its outstanding writers included James Weldon Johnson, Alain
Locke, Walter White, Claude McKay, Countee Cullen, Rudolph Fisher, Langston
Hughes, Jean Toomer, and Arna Bontemps. The artists included Aaron Douglas,

Palmer Hayden, Richmond Barthé, and Augusta Savage, and there were "black conscious" performers and entertainers beyond number.

And how can even the most casual student of black culture in the United States not take note of the fact that the decade of the nineteen-twenties is still known as the Jazz Age? It was from the Negro musician, not from a white writer named F. Scott Fitzgerald, that this title was derived. The nineteen-twenties was the first great hey-day of the jazz- or blues-idiom musician. The music of King Oliver, Bessie Smith, W. C. Handy, Louis Armstrong, Jelly Roll Morton, James P. Johnson, and hundreds of others was impressing an affirmative consciousness of blackness not only upon other Negroes and upon white Americans, but upon the world at large as never before.

Perhaps the most magnificent synthesis, historical continuity and esthetic extension of all of the best elements of the New Negro period are to be found in the music of the Duke Ellington orchestra. No other institution in the United States represents a more deliberate and more persistent effort to come to terms with black heritage as it relates to the ever shifting complexities of contemporary life. Nor has Ellington simply clung to traditional folk forms. Culture hero that he is, he has not only confronted every esthetic challenge of his times, but has grown ever greater in the process. (Someday, Ellington may well come to be regarded as the Frederick Douglass of most black artists. He is already regarded as such by most musicians.)

During the depression of the nineteen-thirties, the cultural emphasis generated by the New Negro movement gave way to a direct and very urgent concern with abstract economic theory and a general politicalization of all issues. In consequence (in part at least) black consciousness as such seems to have been de-emphasized in the interests of the polemics of class struggle dialectics, and black culture was redefined in accordance with the integration-oriented policies of friendly but paternalistic white liberals, left wing intellectuals, Communist party organizers, and other do-gooders and supporters of black causes of that period. Blackness as a cultural identity was all but replaced by blackness as an economic and political identity—or condition, plight, and blight. U.S. Negroes, that is to say, were in effect, no longer regarded as black people. They were now the black proletariat, the poor, the oppressed, the downtrodden minority. Sometimes, as a matter of fact, it was as if white left-wing intellectuals had deliberately confused cultural issues with questions of race. In any case, there came a time (which is not yet passed) when it was not at all unusual for paternalistic white friends of black sufferers to condemn any manifestations of interest in black culture as a medium for identity as racism and separatism. By this time, many white friends even refused to concede that the blues was unique to U.S. Negro lifestyle. Suddenly, music was just music and just as suddenly, non-Negro Benny Goodman, not Louis Armstrong, Fletcher Henderson, Count Basie, or Duke Ellington, was King of Swing, and Gene Krupa, not Chick Webb or Jo Jones, was their dyed-in-the-blue rhythm man. Moreover, they knighted Benny Goodman himself as a big fat liberal because he was nice enough to permit Negroes like Teddy Wilson, Lionel Hampton, and Charlie Christian to perform on the same stage with white "jazz musicians."

Perhaps the most comprehensive example of the post–New Negro attitude toward black experience is found—some current ideologists of blackness will be surprised to learn—in the fiction of Richard Wright, precisely because of its deficiencies. At times, as has been seen, it was as if Wright, who had every reason to know better, regarded Negroes not as acquaintances and relatives to be identified against a very complex cultural background, but rather as human problems struggling to become people. Sometimes Wright also gave the impression that he felt that the writer's basic function was to politicalize everything. Time and again he depersonalized the personalities as well as the motives and even the environment of his characters—in the interest (so far as one can tell) of revolutionary political theory. Few will deny that the social objectives behind Wright's theories were of the very highest order. But neither can it be denied that such theories contributed very little to the promotion of black identity in the sense in which it is being approached by the young people of today. Such theories, in fact, are most likely to lead to an oversimplification of the whole question of identity by their overemphasis on class as if it were the main clue to motives and manners. This, in any case, is where the theories led Wright. In *Black Power*, he seems to have found it easier to identify with Africa as a land of class brothers than as the homeland of some of his most important cultural antecedents.

In the fiction of Richard Wright, many of the same elements of black experience that were so fascinating to Negro writers of the renaissance period, and which the great Negro musicians have never ceased to celebrate (or to be inspired by), are subordinated to political conjecture. Some evidence of Wright's negative regard for the "black consciousness" of the nineteen-twenties may be found in his essay "Blue Print for Negro Writing." He wrote there: "Today the question is: Shall Negro writing be for the masses, moulding the lives and consciousness of those masses toward new goals, or *shall it continue begging the question of the Negro's humanity*." (Italics added.) Then several paragraphs later: "There is a Negro church, a Negro press, a Negro social world, a Negro sporting world, a Negro business world, a Negro school system, Negro professions; in short, a Negro way of life in America. The Negro people did not ask for this, and deep down, though they express themselves through their institutions and adhere to this special way of life, *they do not want it now. This special existence was forced upon them from without by lynch ropes, bayonet and mob rule.* They accepted these negative conditions with the inevitability of a tree which must live or perish in whatever soil it finds itself." (Italics added.)

Perhaps this attitude, which is very much the same as that of self-inflated white welfare workers, accounts at least in part for the fact that the identity of Bigger Thomas, the protagonist of *Native Son*, is more political than black. In any case, as Wright depicts him, such soul brother characteristics as Bigger possesses have much less to do with a total complex lifestyle than with Wright's rather academic conception of the similarity of black violence to the behavior of rats in a maze. Bigger, as Wright makes clear enough in "How Bigger Was Born," an article published in *The Saturday Review of Literature*, is a political symbol, really a parable figure in a political sermon about the revolutionary implications of the oppression of black Americans.

Thus, those who are seriously interested in the actual texture of life in the Chicago of Bigger Thomas (how it felt to be among Negroes, to walk along a South Side street, to sit in a bar, to be in love, etc.) would do well to supplement reading *Native Son* with a dozen or so recordings of Earl Hines's great Grand Terrace orchestra. Indeed, students of black heritage will find it highly rewarding to compare the images that Richard Wright felt were representative of black experience in the nineteen-thirties and -forties with the music to which black style was literally geared. Despite the fact that the musician has long occupied the position of supreme artist for U.S. Negroes, Wright almost always wrote as if he were totally unrelated to what Count Basie, Jimmie Lunceford, Fats Waller, Lionel Hampton, Louis Jordan, and others were saying about black experience during his day. At a time when Wright was making such statements as, "I thought of the essential bleakness of black life in America . . ." and ". . . I brooded on the cultural barrenness of black life . . ." Duke Ellington, whose audiences were larger than ever and whose orchestra had greater range than ever, was creating "Concerto for Cootie," "Cottontail," "Jack the Bear," "Portrait of the Lion," "Bojangles," "Jump for Joy," "In a Mellow Tone," "Sepia Panorama," "Harlem Airshaft," "Koko"; and for his first concert at Carnegie Hall, that citadel of white European identity, was attempting to make a comprehensive, affirmative statement about black heritage and identity in "Black, Brown, and Beige."

What with all the high pressure propaganda about the brotherhood of man and all the promises of one world (as opposed to the traditional self-aggrandizing nationalistic, or tribalistic, states), the trend away from any special positive emphasis on black consciousness per se continued during World War II and the first years of the United Nations.

Negroes were no less concerned about their rights as American citizens during all this time, to be sure. They made the double "V" sign and worked for victory over fascism abroad and victory over segregation and second class citizenship at home. In point of historical fact, it is the wartime generation that is most responsible for the accelerated activism that has come to be known as the Civil Rights Movement or the Negro Revolution. Nevertheless, that generation whose leaders by and large were derived directly from the same intellectual environment that had produced Richard Wright placed little emphasis on black consciousness and black culture. Perhaps the universal prominence of Ellington, Basie, Dizzy Gillespie, and Charlie Parker meant that the crucial role of black consciousness was simply being taken for granted. But the point is that spokesmen did not articulate issues in terms of it.

Given the differences between Ralph Ellison and Richard Wright on the blues idiom, it is not surprising that Ellison's novel, *Invisible Man*, published in 1952, addressed itself in an entirely different manner to the problem of black identity, black heritage, and black consciousness. The protagonist of *Invisible Man*, who becomes politically involved (much the same as Richard Wright or Angelo Herndon did) is a metaphorical ghost in spite of the fact that he has the most obvious physical features. White people see him not as an individual person, but as a problem. In a sense, he is even more invisible to himself. As Ellison once said, "The major flaw in the hero's character is his unquestioning willingness to do what is required of him by others as a way to success, and this was the specific form of his 'innocence.' He goes where he is told to go; he does what he is told to do; he does not even choose his Brotherhood name. It is chosen for him and he accepts it."

The climax of *Invisible Man* is, in itself, a highly significant statement about self-definition. The hero, as if to foreshadow the somewhat more flamboyant gestures of some of the young activists of the nineteen-sixties, disengages himself from the ever so integrated but never quite desegregated Brotherhood and goes underground to hibernate and meditate on the relationship of identity to reality.

In view of the troubles of the invisible man, there is no wonder that some older students of black identity have a number of misgivings about Eldridge Cleaver. At first they thought (or hoped) that he was the Invisible Kid coming back up out of his hole and making the scene as a cool stalking Black Panther, using the Constitution like a Mississippi gambler with a deck of cards. So they edged forward waiting for him to start riffing on all the stuff he had learned from Rinehart and Ras the Exhorter, and had been down there getting "together." And then they discovered that not only was he a member of the *Ramparts* magazine brotherhood, but had chosen to define himself largely in terms of the pseudo-existential esthetique du nastiness of Norman Mailer, who confuses militant characteristics with bad niggeristics precisely because he wouldn't know a real bad Negro until one happened to him. That such a promising young intellectual as Eldridge Cleaver would allow himself to be faked out one inch by the essentially frivolous notions of a jive-time fayboy playboy—to whom the essence of black experience seems to be the Saturday night spree, and to whom jazz is the music of orgasm—instead of utilizing the immensely superior insightfulness of the blues, is enough to scandalize any chicken-shack piano player who ever read a book by Mickey Spillane.

The point of course is not that there is anything inherently wrong about being influenced by white writers. What black writer isn't? The point is that bad taste in white intellectuals is something that black leaders and spokesmen can least afford. Whether white people, including the philanthropic foundations, can afford their customary taste for black hype artists remains to be seen. The fact that Cleaver rejects counter-racism is commendable. But who the hell needs a brown-skinned Norman Mailer?

The current campaign to stimulate greater academic interest in black studies represents a resurgence of appreciation for the black components of American culture. Such campaigns have been a long time coming. Some completely sincere but misinformed campaigners, however, are not nearly as constructive as they so obviously intend to be. They wish to establish a historical context of black achievement. But they often proceed as if respectable traditions of black heroism exist only outside the United States. Yet few glories that they may find to identify with in ancestral Africa are likely to be more directly significant or more immediately applicable than the legacy of courage and devotion to human dignity and freedom that they leave so largely unclaimed at home.

Not that the African past is unimportant. On the contrary, it represents a heritage that merits the most careful and enthusiastic study. But certainly not primarily in the interest of *race* pride, as those who have been overconditioned by the psycho-political folklore of white supremacy insist. And the danger exists that even the slightest emphasis on race pride leads all too easily to what Arthur Schomburg quite accurately labeled "puerile controversy and petty braggadocio."

Schomburg, for whom the famous Schomburg Collection of Negro Literature and History in Harlem is named, placed the fundamental relevance of African culture in clear perspective back in 1925. The following statement from "The Negro Digs Up His Past," which Schomburg contributed to Alain Locke's *The New Negro*, is as applicable to the black studies programs of today as to the Negro renaissance of the nineteen twenties. "Of course," he goes on to say, after having rejected the excesses of black counter-racism, "the racial motive remains legitimately compatible with scientific method and aim. The work our race students now regard as important, they undertake very naturally to overcome, in part, certain handicaps of disparagement and omission too well known to particularize. But they do so *not merely that we may not wrongfully be deprived of the spiritual nourishment of our cultural past, but also that the full story of human collaboration and interdependence may be told and realized.*" (Italics added.) Nor was Schomburg alone in this view. Such major U.S. Negro historians and scholars as Carter G. Woodson, Benjamin Brawley, Charles Wesley, W.E.B. Du Bois, James Weldon Johnson, Benjamin Quarles, and John Hope Franklin, have always regarded a knowledge of Africa as being basic to an adequate understanding of America—so that "the full story of human collaboration and interdependence may be told and realized."

THE ROLE OF THE PRE-AMERICAN PAST

Many Americans of African (and part-African) ancestry who are forever complaining, mostly in the vaguest of generalities, and almost always with more emotion than intellectual conviction, that their black captive forefathers were stripped of their native culture by white Americans often seem to have a conception of culture that is more abstract, romantic, and in truth, pretentious than functional. Neither African nor American culture seems ever to have been, as most polemicists perhaps unwittingly assume, a static system of racial conventions and ornaments. Culture of its very essence is a dynamic, ever accommodating, ever accumulating, ever assimilating environmental phenomenon, whose components (technologies, rituals, and artifacts) are emphasized, de-emphasized, or discarded primarily in accordance with pragmatic environmental requirements, which of course are both physical and intellectual or spiritual.

There is, to be sure, such a thing as the destruction of specific cultural configurations by barbarians and vandals. But even so, time and again history reveals examples of barbarian conquerors becoming modified and sometimes even dominated by key elements of the culture of the very same people they have suppressed politically and economically. In other words, cultural continuity seems to be a matter of competition and endurance in which the fittest elements survive regardless of the social status of those who evolved them. Those rituals and technologies that tend to survive population transplantation seem to do so because they are essentially compatible to and fundamentally useful in changed circumstances. So, for example, the traditional African disposition to refine all movement into dance-like elegance survived in the United States as work rhythms (and playful syncopation) in spite of the fact that African rituals were prohibited and the ceremonial drums were taken away. On the other hand, the medicine man was forceably replaced by the minister and the doctor—and he has met or is meeting the same fate in Africa!

As for those white American immigrants who faced no slave system and so presumably were not stripped of their "culture," in point of fact they were still stripped by the necessities of pioneer readjustment. Needless to say, they were not stripped altogether—but neither were the black chattel bondsmen. If the African in America was unable to remain an African to the extent that he may have chosen to do so, neither were very many Europeans able to remain Europeans even though they were able to construct exact duplicates of European architecture in Virginia and Maryland—and to the extent that they did remain Europeans, they often were out of practical touch with life around them. Nothing can be more obvious than the fact that for most practical everyday intents and purposes almost all non-English-speaking immigrants were stripped of their native tongue. Nor are French, German, Spanish, and Italian taught in American schools in interest of ethnic identity and pride. They are taught primarily as tools for research. In any case, that the black man was the victim of brutal treatment goes without saying, but how much of his African culture he would have or could have kept intact had he come over as a free settler is a question that should be discussed against the fact that the pressure on "free white Americans" to conform is (as non-Protestants, for example, know very well) greater than is generally admitted. The question of African survival should also be discussed in full awareness of the fact that the dynamics of American culture are such that the average American citizen is a cultural pluralist.

Many black New Yorkers seem to be insisting on their loss of African culture not so much because they actually feel deprived of it but because they have somehow allowed themselves to be theorized into imitating and competing with white and somewhat white immigrants whose circumstances are not really analogous. There is, for instance, much theorizing by the Jewish friends, sweethearts, spouses, and colleagues of black New Yorkers about the importance of a Jewish ancestral home-land—but no one has as yet demonstrated that U.S. Jews are in any practical sense better off since the establishment of the vest pocket state of Israel, as marvelous as that little nation has turned out to be—nor has it been shown that the fall of Lumumba, Tschombe, or Nkrumah added to the problems of black Americans.

It is not Jewish culture as such that accounts for the noteworthy academic performance of Jewish pupils—which performance seems to impress black New Yorkers no end. Rather it is much more likely to be the traditional Jewish cultural *orientation* to the written word as the basis of formalized and routinized education. Indeed, so far as specific cultural details are concerned, a significant number of outstanding American Jewish intellectuals appear to represent Germany to a far greater extent than they represent the Middle East.

The definitive academic conditioning or intellectual "occupational psychosis" or mental orientation of the American Jewish intellectual, scientist, technician, and even journalist seems to have been derived largely from the tradition of the Talmudic scholar, that inimitable master of research and midrash. In any case, it is the Talmudic scholar's traditional orientation to painstaking documentation which appears to be most functional. What sustains the fine Jewish student, that is to say, is neither Hebrew nor Yiddish, nor specific precepts from the synagogue, but rather his overall conditioning to (or attitude toward) written communication and linguistic discipline, plus a respect for prescribed procedures.

The Afro-American tradition, on the other hand, is largely oral rather than written. Even its music is likely to be transmitted largely through auditory means rather than by notation even when both pupil and teacher are musically literate. The great Jewish conductors, concert-masters, and virtuosi, by contrast, proceed very much as if they were Talmudic scholars with scores and instruments. Indeed, Euro-Americans in general are Talmudic scholars in the sense that they tend to read and talk about such musical qualities as, say, dissonance, cacophony, atonality, and so on perhaps nearly as much as they listen to or perform music that contains these characteristics. Afro-American performers and listeners alike tend to proceed directly in terms of onomatopoeia.

In his very perceptive books, *Made in America* and *A Beer Can by the Highway*, John A. Kouwenhoven, whose observations on the nature of America belong beside those of Constance Rourke, states that contemporary American culture is the result of the conflict or interaction of two traditions in the United States over the years. He called one the learned or academic and the other the vernacular, or folk or native. This distinction is a particularly useful one in the present context. The learned or documentary orientation to experience is of its very nature essentially conservative and even antiquarian. In traditions that are essentially learned, even revolutionary action is likely to be based almost as much on the documentation and analysis of past revolutions as upon the urgencies of a current predicament. Literacy, that is to say, is always indispensable to such a cultural orientation or lifestyle.

Americans from Africa, however, are not derived from a lifestyle that has been, or indeed has even needed to be, as concerned with preserving and transmitting the past per se as Europeans have been. Not that the past was considered entirely forgettable. Far from it. But the African concept of time and continuity (or of permanence and change) seems to have been different, and certainly the concept of history, heritage, and documentation was different. (Afro-Americans, of course, came neither from Egypt nor from the famous Lost Cities.) It is hardly surprising if African conceptions of education were also different.

In all events, it is not only possible but highly probable that the "cultural dislocation trauma" suffered by Africans transported to frontier America were considerably less than European-oriented polemicists imagine, precisely because the African's native orientation to culture was less static or structured than they assume, precisely, that is to say, because the African may have been geared to improvisation rather than piety, for all the taboos he had lived in terms of. The fact that these taboos were not codified in writing may have contributed to a sense of freedom, once he was beyond the "pale."

But perhaps most important of all, it should never be forgotten that nothing is more important to man's survival as a human being than is his flexibility, his adaptability, his talent for accommodating himself to adverse circumstances. Perhaps it is a one-dimensional and essentially snobbish conception of culture which prevents some black- and white-oriented polemicists from realizing that there is probably more to be said for the riff-style lifestyle that Negroes have developed in response to the adverse circumstances of their lives in the United States, than can be said for the culture they were so brutally stripped of. And, besides, look at what actually happened to the Africans who remained at home with their culture intact. Some "African bag" polemicists cop out at this point. But contemporary African leaders, spokesmen, and intellectuals do not. They are the first to explain that they were invaded and colonized by *Europeans*—and by European technology, upon which they are now more dependent than they ever were before. Nor do African officials hesitate to send as many students as possible to Europe and to segregationist America. Not to become white, but to enable the students to extend themselves in terms of the culture of the world at large.

Perhaps it is also pretentiousness that prevents some psychopolitical theorists from realizing that just as "Talmudic scholarship" applied to technology may account for the ability of Jewish and other literate peoples to survive and thrive in alien cultures all over the world, including South Africa, so may riff-style flexibility and an open disposition towards the vernacular underlie the incomparable endurance of black soulfullness or humanity.

There is, nevertheless, as much to be said for the vernacular tradition as for the learned tradition—and as Kouwenhoven's investigations suggest, even more to be said for the interaction of the two. At the advent of the phonograph, to take an example from recent cultural history, the typical U.S. Negro musician, not unlike his African ancestors, was clearly more interested in playing and enjoying music than in *recording* it for posterity. As a matter of fact, many Afro-Americans in general still tend to regard phonograph recordings more as current duplications (soon to be discarded as out of date) which enable them to reach more people simultaneously than as permanent documents. Euro-Americans, on the other hand, started record collections and archives, which eventually came to include the music of black Americans. Thus, it is the Euro-American whose tradition of scholarship and research has provided at least the rudiments of a source of musicological data that black historians and students in quest of musical heritage may someday make the most of.

Similarly, it is African creativity that has produced in African art one of the most marvelous achievements of the human imagination. But, as every art dealer knows, it is the Europeans who have been most interested in preserving it, and its fantastic value on the world art market is geared not to the valuation made by Africans but to the valuation of galleries and museums in Europe and America. Further, such are the practical realities that African scholars, artists, and art dealers seem far more interested in what white European and American art dealers and museum directors think about African culture than what Harlem polemicists think.

When outraged Afro-Americans indict those whose bigotry is the cause of the omissions, distortions, the wholesale falsification and outright suppression of information about black people of the United States, the merits of their case are beyond question. Indeed, the deliberate debasement of the black image has been so viciously systematic and often times so exasperatingly casual that the scope of white malevolence is hard to exaggerate.

The absence of readily available documentary materials in Africa on the history and culture of the peoples of that continent, however, can hardly be blamed on the vandalism of slave traders and certainly not entirely upon the ruthless disregard by European colonials for African culture. Though some missionaries were Huns of a sort, the British Museum, the Musée de l'Homme, and the American Museum of Natural History contain impressive evidence that not all Europeans were set on obliterating African history or denying the significance of its culture. The fact of the matter is that white archaeologists and anthropologists have been instrumental in stimulating contemporary Africans to develop a European-type concern with the documentation and glorification of the past—and glorification of the present for posterity.

It is quite true that conventional European histories of the world have largely ignored African achievements. But what of histories of the world written by Africans down through the years? Were all of these destroyed by European barbarians, or did they never exist? The chances are that those African peoples for whom there is little or no "autobiographical" record conceived of time, reckoned time, and dealt with the passage of time in ways that, as suggested earlier, belonged to an orientation that was essentially different from that of most of the peoples of Europe. It is not impossible that some African cultures were as profoundly conditioned by the vanity of vanities as was the preacher in *Ecclesiastes*—or as the traveler in Shelley's "Ozymandias."

That U.S. Negroes should enjoy the privilege of introducing additional African elements, including new fashion accents, ornaments, and trinkets, into the pluralistic culture of the United States not only goes without saying but, as the ads in *Ebony*, *Jet*, and the black weeklies suggest, give as big a boost to black business as to black vanity. Nevertheless, those who are so deeply and fervently concerned about the status of black culture and the prestige of black studies are likely to be motivated by forces and precedents that are not nearly so African as European or Euro-Talmudic, as it were. Thus, it is all too true that the "Americanization" process that captive Africans were forced to undergo stripped them of many of the native accoutrements that they held most dear and wished to retain. But it was also a process of Americanization that has now equipped and *disposed* them not only to reclaim and update the heritage of black Africa but also to utilize the multicolored heritage of all mankind of all the ages.

INSIDE THESE WALLS

ETHERIDGE KNIGHT gives a compelling view of life inside prison in the essay "Inside These Walls," which was published in his anthology, *Black Voices From Prison* (1970).

Prison legend has it that D. C. Stephenson, during the time that he was Grand Dragon of the Indiana Ku Klux Klan and a high-up in the state's politics, made a tour of the prison here and, finding the height of the walls not to his satisfaction, demanded that they be built higher "for the protection of society." Ironically, D. C. Stephenson, a few years later, found himself behind those newly heightened walls. He had been convicted of murder.

Today the walls of the Indiana State Prison are forty-three feet high; they are gray stone and concrete, surrounding twenty-three acres of land.

Inside these walls are 2,000 men, black, white, and brown, ranging in age from sixteen to eighty-three. The average age is thirty-six. The prison boasts one ex-policeman, one ex-Justice of the Peace, a bank embezzler, and four college graduates. The vast majority, however, come from the lower economic level and are small-time burglars, stickup artists, and forgers. Lifers make up the largest group; there are 450.

And what do these men do inside these walls? It's simple, maddeningly simple: At six o'clock in the morning a whistle blows. They get up and wash their faces. At six-fifteen, a bell rings, and they march off to the prison mess hall and eat a breakfast of, say, oatmeal, prunes, bread and coffee. They leave the mess hall in a line and drop their spoons in a bucket by the door, watched over by a "screw." They march to their shops—say the Tag Shop, climb upon a stool and dip license plates into a tank of paint until nine-thirty. A bell rings; they smoke. A bell rings; they go back to work.

At eleven-thirty, a bell rings again. They stop work, wash up, march back to their shelters. At twelve o'clock, a bell rings in the cellhouse; they walk to the mess hall where they eat, say, a meal of white beans, frankfurters, and cornbread. They leave the mess hall, drop their spoons into the bucket and, in line, go back to work. The morning performance is repeated. At four-thirty a whistle blows; they march to supper and then into their cellhouse for the night. Maddeningly simple.

Most of the ancient buildings in which the men work and live are made of red bricks, with green tile roofs. They rise stark and bare, ornamented only with steel-barred windows, deep-set and elongated windows that make the sides of the building look like sad-faced clowns. There are four cellhouses: A, B, C, and D; and the two dormitories: I and G. Each cellhouse shelters approximately 400 men, and the two dormitories about 400.

One of the oldest and most famous cellhouses is "B" (BCH). It was built in 1907 and was once the home of John Dillinger. The first thing that strikes you about the cellhouse is its immensity. An oblong, barnlike building, it stretches more than two-thirds of a city block, and the glaring light bulbs strung along the walkways in front of the cells give the illusion of even greater distance. The cells are stacked five tiers high, ranging back to back down the center of the cellhouse with their fronts gaping at the outer walls.

Coming in from work, the men file up the iron stairs like long lines of worker ants, their heavy steps unlike the sounds made by any other group of moving men. As they reach their respective tiers, they break off, and each man goes to his cell. A bell rings twice, and at the front end of each gallery a guard begins to lock the cells and count the men. Then it is quiet time, nervous time, until after mail call, which will occur in about thirty minutes.

The cells are ten feet long and six feet wide. (Although the practice has been discontinued, two men were once assigned to some of these cells.) On the door of each cell is a card, bearing the inmate's name, number, and job assignment. Each cell contains a toilet bowl, a wash basin, a cot, a set of earphones, and whatever small furniture the inmates can either make or scrounge. For the past few years the men have been permitted to paint their own cells, choosing their own colors. Some men keep their cells extraordinarily neat. Precise. Others barely manage to pass the occasional inspection by the cellhouse officer. By and large a man is allowed to arrange his cell as he sees fit.

And what do the men do in their cells? One young man, a muscle boy, is doing push-ups. Two hundred a night. Another man is answering a letter that he has just received. One man is pacing his cell, stopping every now and then to crack his knuckles. Another is lying on his bunk listening to his earphones. Another is standing, gripping the bars and calling down the gallery to his buddy. Another is already in bed, his knees drawn up toward his chest, his blanket pulled over his head. Most of the men read books: Westerns, blood and sex detective mysteries, Gothic romances, and current book-list novels, in that order.

Some men have lived in the same cells for eight, ten, twelve years. The pressures are heavy, and the sounds made at night by 400 caged men are lonely and empty. A clacking typewriter, a flushing toilet, a futile curse, and drifting, distorted music from a radio. An inmate spends from fourteen to sixteen hours a day in his cell. Soon it becomes, in truth, his home.

PRISON GUARDS

The primary function of prison, some say, is to isolate and punish the criminal, and to that end we have the typical prison guard.

The pay for being a prison guard is about the same as that earned by a dishwasher in a large hotel. Why then do men become prison guards? Some, the majority, simply drift into the job. They are for the most part unskilled and semiliterate; ex-farmers, factory workers, common laborers, and the like. Others, a very small minority, are sexually perverted and would take any kind of job, just so long as it is around a large number of men over whom they have near total power. (It is these men and their inmate counterparts—and sometimes lovers—who are the causes of almost all cases of brutality in prison.) There is still another microscopic group who become keepers of men. They are the do-gooders, the humanitarians. They do not last long; or if they do last and gain positions of power, their efforts are nullified by politics, public apathy, and subversion by the men with whom they have to work.

Generally, prison guards are just plain, poor men. It is the nature of the work that brings out the worst in the best of them. Most of them are not equipped mentally, spiritually, or morally to work in the swamp of brutality, loneliness, sexual depravity, and scheming without themselves being covered with the same muck. A prison guard does time and, as with the inmate, it weighs heavily on his shoulders. Two years ago, a guard, on night duty in a gun tower on the wall, phoned Center Control and said, "I quit." Then he simply walked out of the gun tower, across to the parking lot, and drove away.

Because of the low pay some guards are easily bribed to smuggle contraband inside the prison. And because of their own positions in the world, or a nagging wife, or approaching sexual impotence, some guards succumb to the insidious bootlicking and "brown-nosing" of favor-currying inmates and become petty tyrants who are manipulated by these inmates for their, the inmates', own purposes. Indeed, the competence of prison guards can be measured in direct proportion to the number of "rats" and bootlickers within a prison. Men have lost their "clear time"—their chance to go home—on the uncorroborated word of another inmate.

It is not uncommon to hear two old-timers, one of them a guard, talking longingly about the good old days when the "joint was a joint." The guard, after long years, is perhaps by now a lieutenant or a captain; and he is not about to relinquish an iota of prerogative or power to those "mother-coddling treatment guys." Such guards have been known to enlist the aid of their old buddy convicts in their fight.

There is still talk of the beatings and killings that once occurred here: of the "water cure," of the soap-filled cane, and of the "wrecking crew." Only a few years ago skeletons were unearthed where the infamous "Blue Wall" once stood. (The Blue Wall was the inmates' name for the Hospital for the Criminal Insane that was once inside the prison here.)

Physical brutality in prison, however, has, except for a few isolated cases, gone by the board. Nowadays a prison guard can be suspended or fired for striking an inmate—unless, of course, it is in self-defense or in the defense of another guard or an inmate.

Force has never proved to be an effective method for controlling men, and prison officials have come to realize this. For some reason, brutality and loose discipline in prison seem bound together; and too, there seems to be a relationship between brutality and the quality of the prison guards. Recently a new policy relating to discipline was instituted here. The Hole and other extreme forms of punishment were abolished—and there has been no breakdown in normal order. The fact is that physical brutality is as nothing compared to the brutality of the soul incurred by years and years of cancerous prison life.

Below is a copy, in the exact wording and punctuation, of a recently issued bulletin, setting forth the new policy:

OFFICE OF THE DEPUTY WARDEN
October 12, 1967

TO: Whom it may concern

CONCERNING: Conduct Adjustment Committee Policies [called the Kangaroo Court by the cons—E.K.]

Effective this date a copy of the Conduct Adjustment Committee results will be forwarded to all shelters. This procedure will insure that all supervisory officers, as well as shelter officers, are fully acquainted with the Committee's actions, and therefore able to comply with the wishes of the Committee. It will be the responsibility of the shelter officers to keep these reports in a secure place at all times. Captains and Lieutenants will check the files periodically for compliance.

For the information of everyone (Officers and Inmates), the following policies and/or procedures are hereby announced, and are effective as of this date.

MAJOR OFFENSES: Some examples of offenses included in this category are:

1. Escape or attempted escape.
2. Fighting.
3. Contraband (possession of weapon, knife, etc.)
4. Drunk.
5. Assaulting or threatening an officer.
6. Assaulting or threatening an inmate.
7. Sex offenses, also obscene literature and pictures in the nude.
8. Unauthorized medication.
9. Insolence (some instances).
10. Inciting a riot.
11. Gambling.
12. Unauthorized alteration of clothing (some instances).
13. Destroying state property (some instances).

MINOR OFFENSES: Some offenses included in this category are:

1. Out of place. [Being caught someplace without proper authorization—E.K.]
2. Contraband (food, etc.)
3. Bucking chow lines.
4. Refusing to obey orders.

5. Refusing job assignment.
6. Failure to comply with shelter rules.
7. Insolence (some instances).
8. Smoking in line.
9. Destroying state property (some instances).
10. Loud or boisterous talk.
11. Refusing to work.
12. Unauthorized alteration of clothing (some instances).

Please be advised that the above listing of offenses for which an inmate may be brought before the Conduct Committee is not intended to be all inclusive, but rather as an example. In all cases the final decision as to whether an offense is considered minor or major, rests with the Committee.

DISCIPLINARY ACTIONS OF THE CONDUCT ADJUSTMENT COMMITTEE: Cases will normally be disposed of by utilizing one or more of the following procedures. Again this is only intended to serve as a guide for all concerned and final decision rests with the committee in all cases.

a. REPRIMAND: Verbal correction or reproof.

b. LOSS OF RECREATION: Locked in personal cell at all times except for hours spent on the job. Inmate may also leave his cell for purpose of going to and from work, the dining room, church, and visits. No other exceptions will be made.

c. COMPLETE LOSS OF PRIVILEGES: Locked in personal cell at all times except for movement to and from dining room, hospital, and visits. No further exceptions will be made. When moving to and from the hospital or visits, inmate must be escorted by an officer. Commissary is restricted to 2nd Grade [See Commissary List—E.K.] ONLY for the duration of this disciplinary action. Men sheltered in dormitory or I-Cellhouse will be moved to the Idle Shelter upon receiving disciplinary action of this nature. Upon completion of the penalty assessed by the Committee, a return transfer to the dormitory or I-Cellhouse, if appropriate, will be effected. Repeated offenses may result in permanent loss of opportunity to shelter in either the dormitory or I-Cellhouse. Men who have been assessed Complete Loss of Privileges will not be allowed a change in job or shelter, other than to the Seclusion Unit [called the "Rock"—E.K.], during the period of time involved in the disciplinary action.

d. PLACEMENT IN 2ND GRADE: Men placed in 2nd Grade will lose the privileges of recreation, movies, club functions, and all related activities for a period of ninety (90) days. Commissary is restricted to 2nd Grade Items ONLY for the entire period. Loss of clear time.

e. WEEK END LOCK UP: Inmates receiving this disciplinary action will report to the Deputy's Office immediately after work on Friday for confinement in the Seclusion Unit. Release from Confinement will be effected in time to report to work on the following Monday morning.

f. BULL PEN TIME: For certain minor offenses reported on either Incident or Conduct reports, bull pen time, not to exceed two hours without a break, may be designated.

g. MAJOR OFFENSES: Offenses in this category may result in indefinite periods of confinement in the Seclusion Unit plus loss of good time and/or clear time, where the welfare of the individual or the population in general is concerned.

h. I-CELLHOUSE AND DORMITORY PRIVILEGES: A major offense will automatically cause the inmate to be removed from either of these shelters for a period of one year from the date of the offense. Two minor reports in a twelve month period will also constitute cause for removal from these shelters for one year. In this instance, eligibility date for return to one of the shelters will be one year from date of the last offense.

For your information it will be the Committee's prerogative to suspend all or any portion of any disciplinary action assessed by the committee. In cases where violation of the above policies occur, extensions of assessments in effect or new assessments will be imposed by the Committee. In all cases except the 2nd Grade ninety day period described above, duration of time involved in disciplinary actions will vary and will be determined on the merits of the individual case. Shelter Officers are charged with the responsibility of ascertaining if new men assigned to their respective shelters are currently being disciplined by action of the Conduct Adjustment Committee.

(signed)
R. Gohn
Deputy Warden

✳   ✳   ✳

We turn now to the "Treatment" department. At the head of this department is a deputy warden, who is directly responsible to the warden for all prescribed policies and procedures relative to the individualized treatment of inmates: resocialization and rehabilitation. He also directs the supervisory heads of the following departments: Classification, Education, Vocational Training, Chaplains, Recreation, Music, Psychology, and Occupational Therapy.

THE CLASSIFICATION DEPARTMENT

This department consists of a director, six full-time caseload counselors, and three part-time group counselors. The classification director functions as the supervisor of the counselors and as the coordinator of the Classification Committee which is responsible for all inmate work and shelter assignments. The Class Comm is made up of the directors of Education and Industry, along with the deputy wardens of Treatment and Custody; the committee meets twice weekly. Work and medical reports are obtained on all cases appearing before the committee; these, along with the remarks of supervisors releasing or requesting inmates, aid the committee to arrive at "objective" judgments. In the case of men appearing for Minimum Custody (trusty) consideration, the warden also interviews them.

In theory the classification program works well; in practice, however, it is a failure. Homosexuals, epileptics, the feebleminded, and the psychopaths are all lumped in with the general population. The young and the weak are mixed indiscriminately with the strong and case-hardened. Such muddling, though, cannot be avoided. The prison is overcrowded.

Men are different; and one of the aims of the Class Comm is to assign jobs and cells according to individual needs. Yet the smooth operation of the prison takes precedence over the needs of the individual. If a man is a butcher, and the Tag Shop needs more men, then the man goes there. It is hard to persuade a man who has been, say, a carpenter most of his life, and who is serving a 2–21-year sentence for killing a man in a fit of rage, that he is being "rehabilitated" when he is assigned to the mess hall to mop floors. By no stretch of the imagination can an assignment to the Tag Shop be considered rehabilitative; it is a job for which there is no demand whatsoever on the outside because all license plates throughout the country are made in the various state prisons. And, in the assigning of quarters, men are quartered in the "honor" dormitories not because of their individual needs, as such, but because of their good conduct—as a reward. Furthermore, men with long sentences are given priorities in jobs and cells simply because they have long sentences.

At present there are six counselors serving the entire prison population. Each counselor handles a caseload of approximately 350 men. He handles the mailing requests of those assigned to his caseload. He spends time at the information desk, assisting visiting friends and relatives of inmates. In case of domestic trouble, he tries to manage a workable relationship between the inmate and his family. He collects data on all new arrivals at the prison; he prepares "progress" reports for inmates appearing before the Parole Board. The counselor is in general a bridge between the inmate and the institution and the inmate and his family. Now, obviously, this large amount of work places definite limitations upon the quality of work done.

There are clearly not enough counselors; nor do those hired remain at the prison long. The work is too hard. The pay is too low. In his annual report to the warden, the present director of classification said: "The salary adjustments for counselors approved last year were expected to lower their turnover. And in spite of our continued personnel changes, there would undoubtedly have been more had it not been for these salary increases. Nonetheless, the starting rate of $450 per month for college graduates is ridiculously low. And this, coupled with annual increases of less than six dollars per week (when allowed!) makes retention of the *best* men impossible. Such a policy of salary administration guarantees retention of the *least* qualified personnel." [Emphasis and parenthetical remark in the original—E.K.]

PSYCHOLOGY DEPARTMENT

The prison maintains one full-time psychologist and one part-time psychiatrist. (Because of the pay rate and the overwork, the turnover in psychologists is almost as rapid as with the counselors.) The work of the single psychologist is reduced to administering tests to new inmates and conducting psychiatric examinations, along with the psychiatrist, of those inmates whose behavior denotes mental illness. The chances are that an inmate with a mental illness will not be noticed as long as his actions do not upset the prison routine.

EDUCATION DEPARTMENT

The aim of the Education Department is to provide academic training to those inmates who are interested. The professional staff consists of six full-time teachers who are employed the year round and three part-time teachers who are employed during the summer months. Nine inmates serve as instructors in the elementary school and four as instructors in the high school. Both schools are fully accredited by the Indiana Board of Education, and the diplomas certifying completing of required courses are issued to graduates. College and trade school courses are also available to the inmates from the Indiana University Extension Correspondence and the International Correspondence. About 200 men attend school; the majority of them are in the elementary grades.

RECREATION DEPARTMENT

Not ten years ago, in a prison in New Jersey, inmates had to pay their guards' salaries during evening yard time. Today, at the prison here some of the recreation equipment is paid for from the Inmate Recreation Fund, which consists of the profits from the prison commissary. That is to say, inmates are paying a higher price for commissary items in order to buy their own basketballs.

The recreation yard is approximately three football fields long and two football fields wide. In one corner of the yard is the gym, with a full-sized basketball floor and television sets ranged along one wall. Recreation periods are one night a week for each cellhouse and all day on weekends for all cellhouses. Inmates with spare time or off-duty are permitted on the yard during weekday mornings and afternoons. Recreation offers a variety of activities: baseball, basketball, boxing, football, tennis, weightlifting, wrestling, checkers, chess, and, along with many others, that favorite of all sports: TV watching.

In prison, recreation provides a very necessary outlet for pent-up emotions, and a majority of the men take advantage of the facilities.

VOCATIONAL TRAINING

The various courses in vocational training are taught by twenty inmates and three civilians. Courses are offered in typewriter repair, refrigeration and air conditioning, carpentry, masonry, radio and television, auto mechanics, upholstering, and photo-lithography. In 1964–65, sixty-two men graduated from the classes; in 1965–66, forty-eight graduated. The curricula for the classes have been developed and approved by the Trade and Industrial Education Department of the State of Indiana. The institution itself provides a never ending source for project work and experience in typewriter repairing, radio and television, masonry and carpentry. The furniture used by the upholstering class comes from the state hospitals; materials and wrecked autos are donated to the mechanics class by auto dealers.

All the courses in vocational training operate with little or no expenditures of state funds; most of the financial support is donated by various companies and organizations. Although the courses are devised and approved by the state, a man does not receive training from them comparable to vocational courses in the free world. There is no modern equipment; most of the televisions, radios, typewriters, autos, etc., are outdated. An effort is being made, however, to persuade large companies here in the state to send qualified instructors to the prison to train the men for possible jobs in the respective companies.

RELIGIOUS ACTIVITIES

Religious services for the men are provided by a Protestant chaplain, a Catholic chaplain and his assistant, and a Christian Science fieldworker. Jewish services are also held the first Saturday of each month by a rabbi from Michigan City. The chaplains also hold personal interviews, make hospital visits, and distribute religious literature. In his annual report to the warden, the deputy warden of treatment made the following recommendation for "the construction of a completely new physical Chapel facility. The new facility should be a centrally located building of sufficient size as to be able to house all types of religious activities, regardless of denomination. Within this building would be separate offices of the Catholic and Protestant chaplains, a common sanctuary for worship services of all denominations, classrooms for Bible study and meditation. The use of this building would be restricted to religious activities and not serve as a multipurpose building as the present Chapel does for worship, movies, concerts, meetings, etc."

PAROLE BOARD

Ninety-five percent of the sentences meted out by Indiana courts are indeterminate. Thus parole is the one thing uppermost in the minds of inmates.

Until 1967, the Indiana Parole Board was made up of three men, who held parole hearings once a month at the prison, the reformatory, the women's prison, the state penal farm, and at the institutions for boys and girls. This year there is a five-man parole board, the two men being added to it "in order to devote more time to each individual case." Over seven years ago, the *Chicago Tribune*, in an editorial, dated June 12, 1960, noted:

"At a recent one-day meeting at the Indiana State prison at Michigan City, the Indiana Parole Board interviewed 119 men. The board freed 29 on parole and recommended 20 for discharge from parole. Parole was denied to 18 applicants. Other decisions ranged from 'no change' to both parole and discharge. This volume of work no doubt involved extensive preparation by subordinates of the board. Even so, one would think the parole board members must have felt uncomfortably hurried. Some of the applicants, certainly, must have felt that in so crowded a day their interviews were disappointingly perfunctory. Unless the gentlemen on the board are supermen, or unless it is all right for interviews with parole applicants to be so brief as to be routine, the board settled entirely too much business for one day's work. The public has a stake too, in the parole process. Undue or misplaced severity adds to the state's expense and makes it responsible for waste of human life; undue or misplaced lenience denies society protection to which it is entitled. Illinois, like Indiana, has a part-time parole board. The citizens in each state share both the cost of and the responsibility for any mistakes arising from ill-considered parole board decisions."

A parole, logically, is the end, the icing for the rehabilitative cake. But is the parole system working? From 1960 to 1965, 2,652 men were paroled; of that number, 1,140 were returned as parole violators.

Parole boards are notoriously capricious. One man, after being told by the board that he was being denied a parole because of his past record, reasoned, "If they set me for that this time, then they'll have to set me for that from now on—cause my record will be the same ten years from now." Another man, a Negro, as he was being denied a parole, was asked accusingly by a member of the board, "Why do you colored guys wear those mustaches?" From then on, very few Negroes appeared before the board with mustaches! A is told that he is being denied because he has not taken advantage of the rehabilitation programs offered; B, who also did not participate in any programs, is granted a parole. These seemingly whimsical actions create a tremendous pressure on the inmates, causing some to abandon any attempts at self-improvement, causing others to become paranoid.

The unpredictability of the board, on the one hand, also creates trouble for a prison warden. Very seldom are his advice and recommendations heeded. And how does a warden explain the actions of a board to a man whose accomplice in crime, his "rap buddy," has been granted a parole when all available data on both men are the same. On the other hand, the parole board is a tremendous asset to the warden as a means of maintaining order in prison. Every inmate knows that in order to make a parole he must keep his "time clear." The queer reasoning seems to be that if a man can conform to the authoritarian routine of prison life, he will then be able to function positively in a free, competitive life on the outside.

Finally, when a man *is* paroled, he is given $15 in cash and a new suit of clothes (out of style) by the state. And most men leaving prison have nothing on which to rely until they can draw a paycheck. (During the years in prison he has earned an average of ten cents a day. A bar of soap costs twenty cents, in prison.)

Ninety-nine times out of a hundred, a man leaving prison is going to work on a blue-collar job, so the new suit of clothes is without utility. The fifteen dollars will hardly provide him with a place to stay—to say nothing of the personal necessities: work clothes, razor and toothbrush, etc. Because of all this, a man who has a wife or relatives on whom he must rely is from the outset put into an embarrassing, self-demeaning position. A man who has no wife or close relatives is forced to seek out old friends, usually those in an environment which quickly shoves him back into criminal activities.

Small wonder then that 75 percent of all ex-convicts return to crime. Men are put into prison for the protection of society, it is said, but is it being protected when 90 percent of all the men in prison will at one time or another be released and when 75 percent of them return to crime?

INSIDE THE SIT-INS AND FREEDOM RIDES: TESTIMONY OF A SOUTHERN STUDENT

DIANE NASH, a Northern black who went to Fisk in 1959 and became a Freedom Rider in 1961, tells the story of her involvement in the sit-in movement and also provides insight into the theological and tactical basis of the entire civil rights movement in her essay "Inside the Sit-ins and Freedom Rides: Testimony of a Southern Student," published in *The New Negro*, edited by Matthew H. Ahmann (1969).

I see no alternative but that this text must be a personal interpretation of my own experience within the region known as "Dixie."

My participation in the movement began in February, 1960, with the lunch counter "sit-ins." I was then a student at Fisk University, but several months ago I interrupted my schoolwork for a year in order to work full time with the movement. My occupation at present is coordinating secretary for the Nashville Nonviolent Movement.

I should not wish to infer that I speak for the southern movement, for I think that there is no single person who can do that. Although many of the following statements can be generalized for the entire movement in the south, I shall refer largely to Nashville, Tennessee, for that is where I have worked.

I submit, then, that the nonviolent movement in that city:

1. is based upon and motivated by love;
2. attempts to serve God and mankind;
3. strives toward what we call the beloved community.

This is religion. This is applied religion. I think it has worked for me and I think it has worked for you and I think it is the work of our church.

One fact occurs to me. This is that the problems of the world lie within men and women; yes, within you, me, and the people with whom we come in contact daily. Further, the problems lie not so much in our action as in our inaction. We have upon ourselves as individuals in a democracy the political, economic, sociological, and spiritual responsibilities of our country. I'm wondering now if we in the United States are really remembering that this must be a government "of the people" and "by the people" as well as "for the people." Are we really appreciating the fact that if you and I do not meet these responsibilities then our government *cannot* survive as a democracy?

The problems in Berlin, Cuba, or South Africa are, I think, identical with the problem in Jackson, Mississippi, or Nashville, Tennessee. I believe that when men come to believe in their own dignity and in the worth of their own freedom, and when they can acknowledge the God and the dignity that is within every man, then Berlin and Jackson will not be problems. After I had been arrested from a picket line about three weeks ago, I jotted down the following note, with this meeting in mind:

> If the policeman had acknowledged the God within each of the students with whom I was arrested last night, would he have put us in jail? Or would he have gone into the store we were picketing and tried to persuade the manager to hire Negroes and to treat all people fairly? If one acknowledges the God within men, would anyone ask for a "cooling off period," or plead for gradualism, or would they realize that white and Negro Americans are committing sin every day that they hate each other and every day that they allow an evil system to exist without doing all they can to rectify it as soon as they can?

Segregation reaches into every aspect of life to oppress the Negro and to rob him of his dignity in the south. The very fact that he is forced to be separated obviously implies his inferiority. Therefore the phrase "separate but equal" denies itself. The things nonblack Americans take for granted, such as a movie and dinner date for college students, or a coffee-break downtown, are usually denied the black American in the south. Sometimes he may obtain these services if he wishes to compromise his dignity. He might, for example, attend a downtown movie if he would enter through the alley entrance and climb to the balcony to be seated.

But these are not the most important things. The purpose of the movement and of the sit-ins and the Freedom Rides and any other such actions, as I see it, is to bring about a climate in which all men are respected as men, in which there is appreciation of the dignity of man and in which each individual is free to grow and produce to his fullest capacity. We of the movement often refer to this goal as the concept of the redeemed or the "beloved" community.

In September, 1959, I came to Nashville as a student at Fisk University. This was the first time that I had been as far south as Tennessee; therefore, it was the first time that I had encountered the blatant segregation that exists in the south. I came then to see the community in sin. Seeing signs designating WHITE or COLORED, being told, "We don't serve Niggers in here," and, as happened in one restaurant, being looked in the eye and told, "Go around to the back door where you belong," had a tremendous psychological impact on me. To begin with, I didn't agree with the premise that I was inferior, and I had a difficult time complying with it. Also, I felt stifled and boxed in since so many areas of living were restricted. The Negro in the south is told constantly, "You can't sit here." "You can't work there." "You can't live here, or send your children to school there." "You can't use this park, or that swimming pool," and on and on and on. Restrictions extend into housing, schools, jobs (Negroes, who provide a built-in lower economic class, are employed in the most menial capacities and are paid the lowest wages). Segregation encompasses city parks, swimming pools and recreational facilities, lunch counters, restaurants, movies, drive-in movies, drive-in restaurants, restrooms, water fountains, bus terminals, train stations, hotels, motels, auditoriums (Negro college students usually attend the most important formal dances of the year in the school gymnasium), amusement parks, legitimate theaters, bowling alleys, skating rinks—all of these areas are segregated. Oppression extends to every area of life.

In the deeper south, Negroes are denied use of public libraries, they are denied entrance even to certain department stores, are discriminated against on city buses, in taxicabs, and in voting. Failure to comply with these oppressions results in beatings, in house-burnings and bombings, and economic reprisals, as we saw in Fayette County, Tennessee, and in Montgomery in the case of the Freedom Riders. Significant, however, are the many countless incidents that the public never·even hears about.

As can easily be imagined, all this has a real effect upon the Negro. I won't attempt to analyze here the effect of the system upon the Negro, but I should like to make a few observations. An organism must make some type of adjustment to its environment. The Negro, however, continues to deny consciously to himself, and to his children, that he is inferior. Yet each time he uses a "colored" facility, he testifies to his own inferiority. Many of the values that result from this dual self-concept are amazing to note. Let me relate to you one very interesting incident.

I spent thirty days in the jail in Rock Hill, South Carolina. For the first few days the heat was intense in the cell. Breathing was difficult. Everyone was perspiring profusely. We couldn't understand why the women in the cell hesitated to ask that a window be opened or the heat be turned down. It turned out that it was because they were so often cold in their homes, and had come to value heat so highly, that they were willing to suffer from it if they could just have it.

A further example of these curious values is given by the Negro who has received several college degrees or who has a profession and who can consider himself a successful and important man, but who, at the same time, will still attest to his own inferiority by cooperating with segregation. What value, or lack of it, accounts for the fact that so many faculty members at Negro colleges have not disassociated themselves from universities which have expelled student demonstrators? Why are the faculty members and administrators of southern Negro colleges not on the picket lines and sitting at the lunch counters? I think the answer lies within the answer of what Jim Crow does to the Negro. For one thing, it stymies his ability to be free by placing emphasis on the less important things, but on things, nevertheless, which Negroes have been denied.

Segregation has its destructive effect upon the segregator also. The most outstanding of these effects perhaps is fear. I can't forget how openly this fear was displayed in Nashville on the very first day that students there sat-in. Here were Negro students, quiet, in good discipline, who were consciously attempting to show no ill will, even to the point of making sure that they had pleasant and calm facial expressions. The demonstrators did nothing more than sit on the stools at the lunch counter. Yet, from the reaction of the white employees of the variety stores and from the onlookers, some dreadful monster might just as well have been about to devour them all. Waitresses dropped things. Store managers and personnel perspired. Several cashiers were led off in tears. One of the best-remembered incidents of that day took place in a ladies restroom of a department store. Two Negro students, who had sat-in at the lunch counter, went into the ladies restroom which was marked WHITE and were there as a heavy-set, older white lady, who might have been seeking refuge from the scene taking place at the lunch counter, entered. Upon opening the door and finding the two Negro girls inside, the woman threw up her hands and, nearly in tears, exclaimed, "Oh! Nigras everywhere!"

So segregation engenders fear in the segregator, especially needless fear of what will happen if integration comes; in short, fear of the unknown. Then Jim Crow fosters ignorance. The white person is denied the educational opportunities of exchange with people of a race other than his own. Bias makes for the hatred which we've all seen stamped upon the faces of whites in newspaper pictures of the mob. The white hoodlum element is often provoked and egged on by the management or by onlookers; this is a type of degradation into which the segregator unfortunately slips.

Police departments can also sink to a sorry state. Bias lets the police turn their heads and not see the attacks made against demonstrators. In Nashville, police permissiveness has served to make the hoodlum element more and more bold, with incidents of real seriousness resulting, even a real tragedy, as was the case in the bombing of a Negro attorney's home last year during the sit-ins.

An unhappy result of segregation is that communications between the races become so limited as to be virtually nonexistent. The "good race relations" to which segregators in the south often refer, is nothing more than a complete breakdown in communication so that one race is not aware of any of the other race's objections or of interracial problems. This has been clearly exemplified in cities where race relations have been called "good" and where the masses of Negroes have rallied behind students in boycotts of downtown areas that have been, reportedly, up to 98 percent effective among the Negro population.

By not allowing all its citizens to produce and contribute to the limit of their capacities, the entire city, or region, or country, will suffer, as can be seen in the south's slow progress in industrial, political, and other areas today and in the weakening of American influence abroad as a result of race hatred.

Segregation, moreover, fosters dishonesty between the races. It makes people lie to each other. It allows white merchants to accept the customers' money, but to give them unequal service, as at the Greyhound and Trailway Bus Lines, where all customers pay the same fares but some are not free to use all the facilities in the terminals and at restaurants where rest stops are made. Fares are equal, but service is not. The system forces the Negro maid to tell her employer that everything is all right and that she's satisfied, but when she is among her friends she talks about the injustice of the system.

Worst of all, however, is the stagnancy of thought and character—of both whites and Negroes—which is the result of the rationalization that is necessary in order that the oppressed and oppressor may live with a system of slavery and human abasement.

I can remember Nashville in this stage of sin when I first came there in September, 1959, a few months before the sit-in movement was to begin. As a new student at Fisk University that September, I was completely unaware that over the next few months I would really experience segregation; that I would see raw hatred; that I would see my friends beaten; that I would be a convict several times and, as is the case at the moment, that there would be a warrant out for my arrest in Jackson, Mississippi. Expecting my life to pursue a rather quiet course, I was also unaware that I would begin to feel part of a group of people suddenly proud to be called "black." To be called "Negro" had once been thought of as derogatory and had been softened by polite company to "colored person." At one time, to have been called "Nigger" was a gross insult and hurt keenly. Within the movement, however, we came to a realization of our own worth. We began to see our role and our responsibility to our country and to our fellow men, so that to be called "Nigger" on the picket line, or anywhere, was now an unimportant thing that no longer produced in us that flinch. As to the typical white southerner who compromises with "Nigra" we only secretly wish for a moment when we could gracefully help him with his phonetics, explaining that it's "knee—grow."

The revolution in the Negro student's concept of the name of his own race is really important only as it is indicative of change in the Negro's concept of himself and of his race.

Through the unity and purposefulness of the experience of the Nashville Negro, there was born a new awareness of himself as an individual.

There was also born, on the part of whites, a new understanding and awareness of the Negro as a person to be considered and respected.

I think an outstanding example of this latter change was revealed by the negotiations which took place between Negro students and leaders and the white merchants who were the managers of downtown lunch counters. It became apparent to me during the negotiations that the white southerner was not in the habit of taking the Negro seriously. During the initial stages, the attitude of the merchants was one of sort of patting us on the head and saying, "Yes, we've listened to your story and maybe segregation is bad, but you can't have integration now, because it'll ruin our business." And they closed the matter there. However, after the sit-ins continued and after the moral weight of the community was felt, through our 98 percent effective boycott; after a number of talks in which the merchants got to know us as people and saw our problem (and we saw theirs), there was indeed a beautiful type of awareness born, to the extent that one of the merchants, who incidentally was a white southerner, made what I think was a real concession: "Well, it was simply that we didn't see they were right and we were wrong."

I think we can also see this awareness of Negro and white for each other as individuals, in the attitudes of the crowds who watched the demonstrations. In the beginning, as I mentioned, there was mostly fear. However, after the violence was allowed to go on and after the police protection broke down and officers insisted on looking the other way while people were beaten, not infrequently there was a white person in the crowd who would see someone about to tear up one of the picket signs or about to hit someone, and would go up and stop this person and say, "No, no! You can't do that." And often they would get into a discussion which sometimes looked constructive. I hope it was.

There also has been a real change in the temper of the crowd, a change from fear to, I think, just curiosity and watching because something is going on. There is not the hatred and the serious fear and emotional tension that there once was. In Nashville, since the integration of the lunch counters and dining rooms and department stores, we've been fortunate enough to have movies also integrated. As I mentioned earlier, in the downtown area Negroes could not attend movies unless they entered through an alley entrance and sat in the balcony. However, after several weeks of standing-in, they are now allowed to use the theatres' facilities on a fully integrated basis.

Swimming pools in Nashville have been closed this summer under very strange circumstances. It seems that on one particular day a group of Negroes attempted to integrate the city's swimming pools, which incidentally, of course, are tax-supported. On the next day, the park commissioners closed all the swimming pools in the city, for financial reasons. Now it seems that the mayor did not know anything about the park commission being in serious financial difficulty, nor did any of the other city officials, and strangely enough the park commissioners could not be reached for comment. But I'm afraid our swimming pools are closed for financial reasons.

The H. G. Hill food stores are currently being picketed. This is our local project for the moment. This company hires Negroes only for warehouse work and as truck drivers and, of course, pays them below union standards. Many stores are in completely Negro neighborhoods and even in these stores we cannot have Negro cashiers or personnel.

I am eager to talk with you about the Freedom Rides because I think that they denote a new and important level of effort. And I feel that more such projects will be necessary for the ultimate success of the southern movement, especially in states of the deep south, such as Alabama and Mississippi. As you know, the idea of a Freedom Ride was conceived and the project was begun by the Congress of Racial Equality. The first trip originated in Washington, D.C., in May of this year (1961). From Washington, the group traveled through most of the southern states and was repeatedly beaten and jailed as the bus made its way across Dixie. As you remember, at Anniston and Birmingham, Alabama, the bus met with mob violence; the CORE members were beaten and the bus was burned. Most of the riders were hospitalized for a short time. Mr. James Peck, who was one of the whites along with the group, had fifty stitches taken in his head as a result of the repeated beatings that he had to take. Attempting to get a bus to their destination, which was Montgomery, the riders were told that no driver would take them further. In a state of exhaustion then, after traveling hundreds of miles under tremendous tension, repeated jailings and beatings, they took a plane to New Orleans, which was the last stop of the planned itinerary.

In Nashville, the students had been closely following the Freedom Bus as it moved from town to town, for the people on the bus somehow were ourselves. Their dream of freedom in travel was our dream also. Their aspirations were our own aspirations. There is a tremendous bond between people who really stand up or ride for what they feel is just and right. You see, the CORE members were riding and being beaten for our freedom, too. Therefore, it was quite simple. Mob violence must not stop men's striving toward right. Freedom Rides and other such actions must not be stopped until our nation is really free.

In Nashville then, we were faced with a grave situation. We called a meeting of the students and adults within the movement. Talking by phone with persons who had been at the scene of the tragedies in Birmingham and Anniston, we were told, "Don't come. It's a bloodbath. Be assured, someone will be killed if you do come." Upon hearing this, the Nashville group set about preparing themselves for the fact that someone of them would be killed when they took the trip.

You see, these people faced the probability of their own deaths before they ever left Nashville. Several made out wills. A few more gave me sealed letters to be mailed if they were killed. Some told me frankly that they were afraid, but they knew that this was something that they must do because freedom was worth it. I, incidentally, feel very blessed and very grateful for knowing such people and for being able to call most of them my friends.

The purpose of any nonviolent demonstration is to focus the attention of people on how evil segregation really is and then to change their hearts. Some people have been confused about the objectives of the Freedom Rides, and I've heard it said that "the point has been made," so there is no use in going on. The objective of the Freedom Ride from Birmingham was not just to point out that people cannot ride freely but to make it possible for all persons to ride and use terminal facilities without being discriminated against. Until that objective has been attained there *is* reason for going on.

So the drama continued. The bus left Nashville about 6:00 A.M. en route to Birmingham, Alabama. My own role was to stay at the telephone, to keep contact with Birmingham, to hear from the riders as often as they could call, to make arrangements ahead in Montgomery, to keep the Justice Department advised—in short, to coordinate.

The students were held on the bus for some time when they reached Birmingham, and subsequently were taken into "protective custody." The next morning at 4:25, I received a call from them. They said that they'd been driven by the police to the Alabama-Tennessee border and had been put out of the car there on the highway and told to cross the border. At the moment they were on the open highway and felt unsafe. They did not know where shelter was, but would call again as soon as possible. They had been fasting since they had been in jail the day before.

We immediately sent an automobile to get them, and the next time we heard from them, they advised us that they were returning to Birmingham and were determined to board a bus for Montgomery. The police chief wasn't going to get off that easily.

The next night was an all-night vigil for them at the bus station. They were told, again, that no driver would drive the bus. Finally, next morning they were able to get a driver and the bus moved on to Montgomery, Alabama. We all read about that morning, I think, in Montgomery, Alabama. I wish I could have shared with you the moments in our office when that violence was taking place. It seemed that when the bus arrived and the mob attacked the students, they were immediately dispersed. People put a few of them in their cars and took them home. Within a very short time the group was scattered throughout the city.

We listed all the names of the persons who had left Nashville and began trying to account for them. We would ask the students as they called in, "When did you last see . . . ?" The reports we got that morning were: John Lewis was bleeding profusely from the head; another student seemed unconscious; Jim Swirg had been cornered by about sixteen or seventeen men and was being beaten. They had lead pipes, knives, and guns. In a relatively short time, however, we were able to account for all of the students. Miraculously, no one was dead.

Shortly afterwards, in the job of coordinator, I went down to Montgomery to help with the work there. I think you probably read about the meeting which took place in the church in Montgomery that night, at which Martin Luther King, the Freedom Riders, and a number of other people were present. When the police would not afford the church protection, a car was burned. There were incidents of violence and a mob of thousands, I understand, gathered outside. People in the church that night didn't know how close they were to real tragedy. This was the night martial law was declared in Montgomery. That night everyone remained in the church throughout the night.

Now something very interesting took place in the church that night. I think it can almost be a generalization that the Negroes in Alabama and Mississippi and elsewhere in the deep south are terribly afraid until they get into the movement. In the dire danger in which we were that night, no one expressed anything except concern for freedom and the thought that someday we'll be free. We stayed there until dawn and everyone was naturally tired, but no one said so. There were about three thousand people there that night, representing all walks of life, from young children to the elder people in the community. I don't think I've ever seen a group of people band together as the crowd in the church did that night.

Finally at dawn, we were escorted home by the troops. The students boarded the bus for Jackson, along with a second bus that had come from Nashville carrying five ministers. The buses left for Jackson, Mississippi, and I think we pretty well know the story from there on. Immediately upon arrival, the people were jailed. Since then there have been roughly three hundred people jailed for doing nothing more than riding a bus.

It interests me that the Freedom Riders have been called "trouble makers," "seekers of violence," and "seekers of publicity." Few people have seen the point: here are people acting within their constitutional and moral rights; they have done nothing more than ride a bus or use a facility that anyone else would normally expect to use any day of the year, but they have been confined and imprisoned for it. And somehow the Attorney General and the President of the United States and the Justice Department of the United States can do nothing about such a gross injustice. As far as being seekers of violence and publicity, the students have, at all times, remained non-violent. Are not the committers of violence responsible for their own actions? To date, as I've said, there have been approximately three hundred people jailed as Freedom Riders. All were returned within the last two weeks for arraignment. There stood to be lost five hundred dollars for each person who did not return to Jackson. And out of 189 who were on bond, all except nine were returned. The riders had been convicted in the city court and are currently appealing on the county court level. Their appeal trials have been set at the rate of two per day between now and January. The first trial took place yesterday. The result of that trial is that Mr. Henry Thomas was convicted of breach of peace, sentenced to four months imprisonment, and his bond was set at two thousand dollars.

Now I think that this is a serious question for the American public to consider. Is this really the country in which we live? This is a serious moment, I think, for those who take democracy and freedom seriously. Remember now that these Freedom Riders are citizens of the United States who can be called on to go to war and who are receiving treatment of this type.

If so harsh a treatment is involved for an action as right as riding a bus, perhaps one as unimportant as riding a bus, can we not draw from that an inference of what life in the south for the Negro must really be like?

I think that it is most essential that the government move at a rate of progress adequate to meet the needs of the governed. Not being able to do so has resulted in the tragedies of Little Rock, New Orleans, and Montgomery. It might be interesting to note that we have not had incidents such as New Orleans and Montgomery where there has been adequate government. There always needs to be a Faubus or a Patterson.

The Negro must be represented by those who govern. Without this representation, there is moral slavery, if not physical. No person or country can have a clear conscience and a noble mien with such a sin on its conscience. I'm interested now in the people who call for gradualism. The answer, it seems to me, is to stop sinning and stop now! How long must we wait? It's been a century. How gradual can you get? Montgomery has shown how far it has advanced on its own; we've seen this from the mob to the governor. As for the legal position about the right to serve whom one pleases, I would say that this position does not alter the fact that segregation is wrong. Segregation on the bus lines, trains, and planes is wrong *intra*state as well as *inter*state. The press has made much of the interstate passage. However, the Freedom Riders are just as concerned with intrastate travel, because we're concerned with the injustice of segregation.

The Negro is seeking to take advantage of the opportunities that society offers; the same opportunities that others take for granted, such as a cup of coffee at Woolworth's, a good job, an evening at the movies, and dignity. Persons favoring segregation often refer to the rights of man, but they never mention the rights of Negro men.

I would like to say also that the students and the adults who have taken part in this movement and who are doing so now are dead serious. We're ready to give our lives. It is a slight miracle, I think, that in the almost two years since February of 1960 there has not been a fatality. But we have come amazingly close to it several times. Let me mention the case of William Barbee who was on the Freedom Ride when it arrived at Montgomery and met with mob violence. Barbee had gone on a few hours ahead to arrange for cars and other necessities before the riders arrived. When they did get there and were attacked, he was busy trying to get them into taxi cabs or ambulances and take them where they could receive medical attention. Just as about all of them had gotten into cabs, the mob attacked him.

At that moment a Negro man was passing by. He was on his way to pay a bill. It was just a regular day in his life until he saw one of the mobsters with his foot upon William Barbee's neck. Mr. Nichols, who had lived in the south all his life, said that he started to go ahead about his business. But, he said, he knew that he would never be able to live with his conscience again if that man killed Barbee. So he turned around and pulled the man off. Well, Mr. Nichols landed in the hospital next to Barbee. But even after he had pulled the man off, the crowd went back to William Barbee, and he was again in danger of death when the head of the highway patrol came along and was able to get the mob off with a gun. This student, William Barbee, is back in the movement, has been beaten up on a picket line and jailed again. I think that this is indicative of some of the determination and the seriousness with which we take the cause.

I think that quite often today you can hear the strains of a very old spiritual that's sung quite seriously. Some of the words are: "Before I be a slave I would be buried in my grave and go home to My Lord and be free."

From those who say they approve the ends, not the means, I would be interested in suggestions for a means which would yield freedom without delay. Let us look at the means. The students have chosen nonviolence as a technique; there is no reason why they couldn't have taken up guns. It was a responsible choice, I think. We have decided that if there is to be suffering in this revolution (which is really what the movement is—a revolution), we will take the suffering upon ourselves and never inflict it upon our fellow man, because we respect him and recognize the God within him.

Let us see now what the movement needs. The movement is very much in need of a major federal decision that will result in enforcement of the Constitution and federal law. (You might be interested to know that during the Freedom Rides Governor Ross Barnett of Mississippi informed me of two very interesting things by telephone: He said (1) that he did not feel that Supreme Court decisions applied to his state, and (2) that he intended to enforce Mississippi law over and above any federal law that conflicted with it.) Along with a major federal decision to follow through on civil rights, there is needed a major decision on the part of the people. There is needed a realization that the problem lies as much in Jackson or Nashville as it does in Berlin or anywhere in the world. The problem, I think, centers around the questions of truth, honesty, justice, and democracy. What is needed is concern for human rights—not just white human rights. Until such time as this realization comes, Freedom Rides and similar such southwide projects are necessary. Count on more of them.

As far as the Catholic student and the Catholic church are concerned, from our pulpits we need directness and we need emphasis. If this is not an area in which the Church must work, what is? It seems that our role must necessarily be leadership. And anything but outspoken and direct leadership in this movement is immoral. Newman Clubs and campus organizations in the south can certainly revitalize themselves by contacting local movements or starting one, pledging their support and participation. And the same is true for the problems which exist in the north.

There are roles for all of us to play. First, of course, is the role of the participant, who really pickets or sits in. Then there is the role of the observer. I don't know if you have heard, but a number of whites are being utilized effectively as observers. In the integration of lunch counters and movie theaters, many of the older church women who have been sympathetic with the cause for a long time, but who haven't had an opportunity to speak out, have helped by doing such things as sitting next to Negroes at the lunch counters or at movies and thus creating an appearance of normalcy. These people have become quite enthusiastic about their new role. There have been several cases of—well, real "bigness." One lady is known to have drunk countless cups of coffee and gained ten pounds in sitting at lunch counters all day for several days in a row and looking normal. Several have been known to see the same picture over and over again. Also looking normal. For those in the North, as I mentioned, there are local problems, and we also need groups that we can call upon to support the southern movement.

Finally, this movement has been called one of passive resistance. But it is not that at all. Rather it might be called one of active insistence. In regard to our own roles and the role of our church, I think we need to understand that this is a question of *real* love of man and love of God. Is there such a thing as moderate love of God or moderate disdain for sin? I think we need radical good to combat radical evil. Consider the south. It can be the answer for the free world; it can be the pivot. The problem there is a vital challenge for truth; for respect for man. In a word, it is a question of dignity.

"WHAT THEIR CRY MEANS TO ME"—A NEGRO'S OWN EVALUATION

GORDON PARKS, born in 1912 in Fort Scott, Kansas, is one of the true Renaissance men of American culture: photographer, poet, autobiographer, novelist, film director, composer. There is almost nothing that Parks cannot do in the arts. " 'What Their Cry Means to Me'—A Negro's Own Evaluation," Parks's first essay on the Black Muslims, was published in *Life* magazine, May 31, 1963, and remains, alongside Baldwin's *The Fire Next Time*, one of the best impressionistic pieces on the Muslims.

A s I flew back from Phoenix, across this white Christian nation, I tried to summarize my impressions of Elijah Muhammad, whom I had just met for the first time—and to guess what he thought of me. He had made his mission and prophecy clear: as "spiritual head of the Muslims in the Western world," he would lead the black man out of his hell on earth. Both his manner and speech were subdued but his condemnation of the "enemy" was ardent and incessant.

"The white devil's day is over," he said. "There is none a black man can trust. He was given 6,000 years to rule. His time was up in 1914. These are his years of grace—70 of them. He's already used up most of those years trapping and murdering the black nations by the hundreds of thousands. Now he's worried, worried about the black man getting his revenge."

Although I was a black man in white man's clothing, sent by the very "devils" he criticized so much, he made no attempts to convert me. Once he warned, "Don't forget, young man. You've been living in the white Christians' world for a long time. Don't let them blind you. You don't need them."

But he seemed to regard me with neither favor nor scorn. He said neither yes nor no to my request for permission to do a report on the internal workings of the

Movement. (In New York, Malcolm X had told me that only Elijah Muhammad could give me the necessary clearance—and that he sternly shunned publicity.) Muhammad had consented to see me and expose me to his doctrine; then, in a matter-of-fact way, he had let me know exactly where he stood. Now, as I flew back to New York to await his decision, somehow I felt scorched from the heat of his inner burning.

The pilot announced our position over Chicago and I looked down, thinking of the three years I had lived in the infamous Black Belt of that city. I remembered the filth, fear, poverty, evictions and bloodshed; the rackets, police brutality, store-front churches—voices within praying, singing, shouting for mercy. I remembered the rat-infested tenements, the cold nights of winter when the hawk of misery spread his wings over the shivering black ghetto—and then the robberies and murders that followed, sometimes for food alone. Mostly I remembered the hopelessness that seeped into the black souls of that jungle. Now, from this height, Chicago shone clean in the afternoon sunlight. But I knew that, within the brightness below, torment and suffering filled the lives of thousands.

With my emotions oddly mixed of tenderness, pain and resentment, I wondered what Elijah Muhammad's words meant to those who had great reason to suffer. The soft-spoken, angry words kept coming back again and again. I wondered whether or not my achievements in the white world had cost me a certain objectivity. I could not deny that I had stepped a great distance from the mainstream of Negro life, not by intention but by circumstance. In fulfilling my artistic and professional ambitions in the white man's world, I had had to become completely involved in it.

At the beginning of my career I missed the soft, easy laughter of Harlem and the security of black friends about me. Although en route to my home in Westchester I occasionally drove through Harlem in those days, there was hardly ever enough time to become a physical part of it again. Eventually I found myself on a plateau of loneliness, not knowing really where I belonged. In one world I was a social oddity. In the other I was almost a stranger.

Many times I wondered whether my achievement was worth the loneliness I experienced, but now I realize the price was small. This same experience has taught me that there is nothing ignoble about a black man climbing from the troubled darkness on a white man's ladder, providing he doesn't forsake the others who, subsequently, must escape that same darkness.

In time the word came from Phoenix: Elijah Muhammad had found me worthy of his confidence. I could start my report. For the next few months I was to melt into the Muslim organization and examine its aims, its laws and the legends surrounding it. I was to eat in its restaurants, attend its rallies and most secret ceremonies. I came to know entire families who were devout members. And all the while I attempted to assess its meaning to America and to the American Negro— and to myself.

What was Elijah Muhammad's real purpose? Was his movement indeed gaining countless unshakeable adherents? And why was his voice, barely audible in person, screaming loudest in the wilderness, often drowning out the more conservative voices of the NAACP, the Urban League and other highly respected Negro organizations?

I asked Malcolm X, who served as my guide through the intricacies of Islam, some of these same questions late one night as we drove along the noisy streets of Harlem. He replied, "The thinking American Negro realizes that only Elijah Muhammad offers him a solid, united front. He is tired of the unfulfilled promises of the lethargic, so-called Negro leaders who have been so thoroughly brainwashed by the American whites. 'Have patience,' they say, 'everything is going to be all right.'

"The black man in this country has been sitting on the hot stove for nearly 400 years. And no matter how fast the brainwashers and the brainwashed think they are helping him advance, it's still too slow for the man whose behind is burning on that hot stove!"

Malcolm's caustic reply was to take on more meaning, more truth, as I read the daily newspaper accounts of the black man's interminable suffering in the South. The "white devil" seemed determined to live up to Malcolm's predictions. I thought of my youngest son, who had just received a notice from the draft board, and I thought of the words of Malcolm X:

"The black man has died under the flag. His women have been raped under it. He has been oppressed, starved and beaten under it—and still after what happened in Mississippi they'll ask him to fight their enemies under it. I'll do my fighting right here at home, where the enemy looks me in the eye every day of my life. I'm not talking against the flag. I'm talking *about* it!"

Abruptly I checked the flow of corrosive thoughts. Was I becoming too receptive to the Muslim doctrine? I began prodding myself into a more argumentative mood, re-examining my feelings so that I might honestly assess the moral convictions I had developed so painfully through the years. When I was young—penniless and obsessed with the ambition to become a photographer—Harvey Goldstein, a white man, gave me my first decent camera, along with invaluable guidance in using it. Later, William G. Haygood, a white Southerner, encouraged me and helped me win the first Julius Rosenwald Fellowship in photography. Julio de Diego, the Spanish painter, offered inspiration and advice. Jack Delano, a Jew, guided me toward the Farm Security Administration, where I fell under the influence of Roy Stryker, a Dutchman from Colorado, who taught me more about democracy and its almost infinite potential than any person I've met since.

In the course of a career that has thrust me into contact with virtually every kind of person and has taken me several times around the world, I have come to realize the universality of man.

No, I could no more dismiss the events that molded me than I could cast off the cloak of my skin—no matter how appealing Malcolm X was as an individual or as a minister of Muhammad.

Yet there must be, I concluded, some reason why the Muslims struck a responsive chord, not only in me but in so many Negroes moving in sophisticated circles who previously had held themselves aloof from the day-to-day aspects of "the problem." It came as a shock, one afternoon at a chic outdoor party, to hear well-to-do Negro women extolling black nationalism. One matron threatened to join the New York mosque of the Muslims. I heard another berate a blond woman for the Caucasians' treatment of "her people." "You mean, *our* people," retorted the fair-skinned lady. "I happen to be Negro too."

The hostess laughed and nudged me. "Neither she nor anyone in her family would have admitted that 10 years ago!"

The Muslims, with their sharp and unrelenting attack, their aggressive racial pride, have awakened Negroes long insulated by their middle-class possessions and aspirations. Behind the Islamic chanting and the semimilitary ritual there lies a cause— one which calls to Negro slum dwellers and suburbanites alike.

Particularly strong is the attraction for the Negro "lowest down on the totem pole," as labor leader A. Philip Randolph has described them. By their very nature the NAACP and the Urban League cannot match the impact of the Black Muslims. Their leaders do not have the hour-by-hour contact with people who, like the Muslims, suffer the problems each and every day of their lives. While Roy Wilkins of the NAACP is attending an integrated social gathering, or is conferring with constitutional lawyers on vital civil rights issues, Malcolm X of the Muslims is visiting prisoners in jail or a destitute family or addressing a crowd of Negroes on a street corner:

"Justice now! Freedom now! Not when the white man feels he is finally ready to give it to us!"

Although Malcolm X is the most articulate spokesman in the movement, there are some areas of Muslim philosophy into which he does not venture. One day en route to the Temple No. 7 Restaurant in Harlem I asked him, "Exactly what are Mr. Muhammad's ultimate aims?"

He paused for a moment. "It's best that you ask him on your next visit," he replied. "He loves to explain this himself. But I will tell you that he intends to unite every American black man, whether he be a Muslim, a Methodist or a Catholic. Mr. Muhammad teaches that we cannot afford the luxury of economic, religious or political difference. We must sit in counsel if we are to attain our freedom.

"Remember," Malcolm X cautioned as I left the restaurant. "To try to go it alone is to doom yourself to failure. The black attorneys, students, writers, clergy, teachers and all the rest must unite as one and take the Muslim leadership for their own salvation. If I have a bowl of soup, then you have a bowl of soup. If you die fighting for what is right, then I must die beside you—for I am your brother. You are a black man. The white man won't let you forget it. So know yourself and be yourself. We are of the black nation and we must recapture our rightful heritage and culture and live accordingly."

I started to hail a cab but Gladstone X, a Muslim who is close to Malcolm X, was already in the street, his arm raised and signaling. A taxi screeched to a stop and Gladstone opened the door for me. "Good night, brother," he called as the car pulled off.

I had just settled back when the driver, a big, broad-shouldered Negro, turned and spoke. "That was Malcolm X, wasn't it?"

"Yes, it was," I said. "Do you know him?"

"Oh, not personal like, but I hear him speakin' sometimes on the corner with the rest of those nationalist people."

"What do you think of him?"

"Me? Oh, I dig him the most. He's got somethin' goin' for you and me. He's the only one that makes any sense for my money."

"Are you a Muslim?"

"Who, me? Naw. I'm too busy makin' a buck to join anything. But those Muslims or Moslems, 'ever what you call 'em, make more sense to me than the NAACP and Urban League and all the rest of 'em put together. They're down on the good earth with the brother. They're for their own people and that Malcolm ain't afraid to tell Mr. Charlie, the FBI or the cops or nobody where to get off. You don't see him pussyfootin' round the whites like he's scared of 'em."

"Have they got many followers here in Harlem?"

"I don't know how many followers he's got, but he's sure got a hell of a lot of well-wishers."

"Do you go for all their teachings—like not smoking or drinking or eating pork or fornicating?"

"Well, I don't smoke or drink much, but I like my barbecue and I do like my women. That's about the only place the Muslims and I part company. As far as the white man is concerned, if I could get along without his dollar, I could get along without him."

"Some people say the Muslims hate all white people."

"Well, I don't know about that. But if they don't, they should, 'cause they sure don't waste no love on us. That's for sure!"

"But the Negro is making progress in this country," I reminded him. "And there are some good whites."

"Aw, yeah. And there's some good dogs, too, but all of 'em'll bite you if you don't watch 'em."

"What about that new Negro Astronaut they have just selected for training?"

"Well, that's good . . . very good. But I wouldn't be surprised if they didn't put him and a Jew in one of those capsules together and blow it to hell and gone up to the moon—just to prove a white man's the only one can really make it!"

We were at my hotel now. I paid my fare and said, "How do you think we can solve the racial question?"

"Well, I'll tell you," the cabbie replied. "I used to live in Mobile and I lived in Memphis and I've lived in New York for 15 years. I've come to one conclusion. No matter where the white man is, he's the same—the only thing he respects is force. And the only thing's gonna change him is some lead in his belly."

He lifted a cigar box from the seat beside him and opened it. "I don't like to come downtown," he said. "See this? [A black revolver glistened in the street light]. I'm always afraid I'll use it. That's why I'm headin' back uptown 'fore I get in trouble."

As I left, two white men hailed the cab. The driver slammed the door, locked it and gunned the motor. "Goin' home!" he shouted back at them.

"The dirty black bastard!" one of the men mumbled as the cab roared off toward Central Park.

* * *

Recently I sat in a Los Angeles courtroom at the trial of 14 Muslims charged with assault and interfering with an officer. They had been involved in an altercation with the police, during which one young Muslim, Ronald Stokes, was shot to death. (I had read the detailed account of the tragedy in the Muslims' newspaper, *Muhammad Speaks*. SEVEN UNARMED NEGROES SHOT IN COLD BLOOD BY LOS ANGELES POLICE! the red headline blared. The story charged that the police had entered the Muslims' temple during the fighting.) The courtroom was crowded to capacity with Negroes, not all of them Muslims.

I watched Malcolm X seated in the front row, directly across from the all-white jury. His face was sphinxlike and his eyes never left Officer Donald Weese, the killer of Stokes, from the moment the policeman took the stand until he got off. During the preliminary hearings it had been established that Weese, though he knew the Muslims were unarmed, shot at least four other men besides Stokes and beat another one down with the butt of his gun. The following questions by Attorney Earl Broady and answers from Officer Weese are from the court records of the trial:
Question—Mr. Weese, when you fired at Stokes, did you intend to hit him?
Answer—Yes, I did.
Q—Did you intend to hit him and kill him?
A—Yes. The fact that I shot to stop and the fact that I shot to kill is one and the same, sir. I am not Hopalong Cassidy. I cannot distinguish between hitting an arm and so forth, sir. I aimed dead center and I hoped I hit.
Q—You are saying, sir, to shoot to stop and to shoot to kill is one and the same thing in your mind?
A—That is correct.
Q—Did you feel to protect yourself and your partner it was necessary to kill these men?
A—That is correct, sir.

Leaving the courthouse that evening, I recognized a white reporter who was covering the trial for one of the Los Angeles dailies.

"The Muslims are going to be convicted," he said. I asked him if he thought they were guilty as charged.

"The State has no case, none whatsoever, but they can't afford to lose this one. They've got to get those cops off or the Muslims can sue them for millions," he replied.

That evening I relayed the reporter's beliefs to Malcolm X, who said, "Oh, he told you the truth, brother. He was an honest devil, because that's what will happen—but things won't end there. Believe me."

A few days later I accompanied Malcolm X to Phoenix where Elijah Muhammad discussed the trial with more emotional intensity than I had seen him show before. "Every one of the Muslims," he said, "should have died before they allowed an aggressor to come into their mosque. That's the last retreat they have. They were fearless, but they didn't trust Allah completely. If they had, it would have been a different story. A true Muslim must trust completely in Allah."

Mr. Muhammad was weak from one of his periodic fasts, which had gone on for three days, and every so often spasmodic coughing forced him to leave the room.

After each attack he returned to deride the "white devil." Although fatigue slowed his voice, he talked on, about the turmoil in Birmingham and the other parts of the South. "There is one thing good about what is happening down there," he said. "The black man at last can see what the white man is really like, what he really feels about him. Birmingham bears witness to the fact that a white man is a devil and can't do right, what with water hoses stripping dresses from our women and our youth being chased and bitten by vicious dogs. At last the black man realizes he must fight for his rights if he is to attain them. The white man is more vicious than the dogs he sets upon us. He is never satisfied with a black man no matter what his position. You can lie down and let your back be his doormat, but soon he'll get tired of that and start kicking you. 'Turn over, nigger! You're layin' on the same side too long,' he'll say."

Before leaving Mr. Muhammad, I asked two questions I had been saving: First, what is salvation for the black man?

"We must accept Islam," he said crisply. "We are the initial people."

"Why?" I asked.

"Because it is something universal, wherein man submits himself completely to God—a black God."

What is your over-all purpose—your goal?

"Universal peace and brotherly love—two things the white man will never be able to accept."

It was nearing plane time. A white-suited chauffeur ushered us out toward Muhammad's limousine. I got in, and through the rear window I could see him and Malcolm X warmly embracing, their cheeks touching as they bade farewell.

Not all of Elijah Muhammad's aims and motives are clear to me. Much of his religious philosophy appears naive and thoroughly confusing. It is obvious from which stratum of Negro society he hopes to draw support for his program: the indigent, unprivileged blacks, those still seeking a messiah to lead them into a promised land of "freedom, justice and equality."

The Muslims insist that only within a separate state can their ultimate goal be achieved. They deride the "passive resistance" preached by Martin Luther King. Malcolm X once said of King's attitude, "There is no philosophy more befitting the white man's tactics for keeping his foot on the black man's neck. If you tell someone he resembles Hannibal or Gandhi long enough, he starts believing it—even begins to act like it. But there is a big difference in the passiveness of King and the passiveness of Gandhi. Gandhi was a big dark elephant sitting on a little white mouse. King is a little black mouse sitting on top of a big white elephant."

But with the passiveness of King and the extremism of Muhammad, the Negro rebellion has come alive. Fire hoses, police dogs, mobs or guns can't put it down. The Muslims, the NAACP, the Urban League, Black Nationalist groups, the sit-inners, sit-downers, Freedom Riders and what-have-you are all compelled into a vortex of common protest. Black people who only a few months ago spoke with polite moderation are suddenly clamoring for freedom.

The leaders have lost control; instead of leading the black people they are being pulled along after them, like leaves caught up in the wake of a speeding car. Even Martin Luther King is seeing his nonviolence movement hopelessly swept into a long-fomenting universal revolt. As the Negro pushes on, the resistance of the Deep South will surely stiffen. Violence and chaos are inevitable. Anyone who can't sense it is either naive or afraid to face the uncomfortable fact. Racial strife is possible all over this land. Have we so very quickly forgotten the Harlem, Chicago, Tulsa and Detroit riots in the earlier days of our troubled generation?

"Even here in the North the 'enemy' is plentiful!" screams Malcolm X.

He is right. Because for all the civil rights laws and the absence of Jim Crow signs in the North, the black man is still living the last-hired, first-fired, ghetto existence of a second-class citizen. His children are idling into delinquency and crime; in too many places they attend schools as inferior and as neatly segregated as any in the deepest South. The revolt in Englewood, New Jersey, against segregated schools there is just as important to the cause as the revolt in Birmingham or Nashville. Truly, there has been no time like this in the U.S. since the Civil War.

Most of us are wondering about the "new" Negro—and how he got this way. But he isn't new, and he didn't get this way overnight. He has been stirring for a long time, while his country tucked the Emancipation Proclamation under her head for a pillow and went to sleep. The historic Supreme Court decision of 1954 disturbed her repose, but that was all. Now she has been jolted awake by a black militancy that will surely test her democratic conscience.

I remember once standing in a Paris bar with Todd Webb, a white man, trying to convince a Russian student that Todd and I were truly friends, that we had been so even in America. The Russian only laughed at both of us. "Ha! I read about America, you know. You are together here, but in America you stand far apart. Don't think you fool me."

And how pathetically torn I was trying to defend America against the criticisms of Europeans when papers all over the world carried the story of the lynching of the Negro boy, Emmett Till!

I also recall the time in Washington, D.C., when John Vachon, another white friend, and I walked into a Negro restaurant late one cold night. We were famished, but the owner became abusive and ordered us both out. I tried to get him to sell my friend some ribs. "Not even to take out," he said bitterly. "I'll go *his* people one better."

The times cry out for bold, principled leadership of a kind that has never really been attempted in this country before. After Attorney General Robert Kennedy ran head-on into the fanatical opposition of Alabama's Governor George Wallace on the desegregation issue, the President's brother was quoted as saying, "It's like a foreign country. There's no communication. What do you do?"

You keep trying, Mr. Kennedy. You keep going back for more, again and again, until you begin to realize what it is like for a black man to "go slow," to "take it easy" while under the bootheel of a racist like "Bull" Connor. Go down there sometime when the fire hoses are on full blast, when the dogs are snarling and tearing black flesh, when women, men and children are on their knees singing, crying and praying for deliverance from the agony of this brutal land. Then go back and tell the President that if it is greatness he seeks, this indeed is his chance for it.

I have had faith in America for as long as I can remember. But I have also been angry—even bitter. It is now time for America to justify this belief I have in her, to show me I have not believed in vain. I want my children and their children to keep this faith flowing through their veins. But in all honesty I cannot ask of them love for a country incapable of returning their love.

As for the Muslims, I dislike the fact that they exist, but I also feel this way about the NAACP, CORE, the Urban League, B'nai B'rith, the Sons and Daughters of Erin or any such group. I deplore the conditions that necessitate their existence. If and when all such organizations feel they can safely fold their tents, I believe the Muslims will begin folding theirs.

Nobody can speed this day any quicker than the White American. He should remember that the main reason for the racial strife throughout the South and parts of the North is the Negro's black skin. The Negro can't change his color; the white man must change his attitude toward that black skin. And the Negro can't go around believing that every white man who does not invite him home to dinner is his enemy.

And I, for one, don't intend to join the Muslims. I sympathize with much of what they say, but I also disagree with much of what they say.

I wouldn't follow Elijah Muhammad or Malcolm X into a Black State—even if they achieve such a complete separation. I've worked too hard for a place in this present society. Furthermore, such a hostile frontier would only bristle even more with hatred and potential violence. Nor will I condemn all whites for the violent acts of their brothers against the Negro people. Not just yet, anyway.

Nevertheless, to the Muslims I acknowledge that the circumstance of common struggle has willed us brothers. I know that if unholy violence should erupt—and I pray it won't—this same circumstance will place me, reluctantly, beside them. Although I won't allow them to be my keeper, I am, inherently, their brother.

Late one evening not long ago Malcolm X and I were driving into New York City from Brooklyn. We were talked out, and I drowsed as he fought the headlight glare of oncoming traffic. Unexpectedly he said, "We sent a little white college girl out of the restaurant in tears today." I listened uneasily, bracing myself for another diatribe against a presumptuous, if well-meaning, "devil."

But Malcolm, speaking with a gentleness he rarely exhibits when discussing whites, hastened to assure me that it was nothing any Muslim had said against her. "She had come in to see if there wasn't something she and her college friends could do to help Muslims and the whites get together," he explained.

"That's nice," I said, pushing up in my seat. "What did you say?"

I am positive he was unaware of the trace of melancholy in his voice as he answered, "I told her that there was no chance—not the ghost of a chance. She started crying, then she turned and went out."

BEAUTY IS JUST CARE . . . LIKE UGLY IS CARELESSNESS

TONI CADE BAMBARA, born in New York in 1939, is among the most significant black short fiction writers in America. Her works include "Gorilla, My Love" (1972), "The Sea Birds Are Still Alive" (1977), and the novel, *The Salt Eaters* (1980). "Beauty Is Just Care . . . Like Ugly Is Carelessness," a critique of white popular culture and the distorting and damaging images it promotes among blacks, appeared in *Essence* in January 1978.

When pressed about her beauty secrets M'Dear would shruggingly list: herbal head rinses, soda mouth baths, white-clay foot packs, sea-salt soaks in an oaken tub, visits to informed and good-humored friends, the reading of responsible newspapers, listening to joyous music, lending an ear to chatty children, engaging in meaningful work.

She frequently talked back to the radio, and when it insisted itself on her attention with commentary unbecoming to her person, she'd cut it off. When hearing news of a neighbor's misfortune, she lit the wick and prayed till the candle dwindled. News of good fortune was considered a general tonic, so she'd spread the news extravagantly. M'Dear's beauty regime was an around-the-clock attentiveness to mental, physical and spiritual hygiene.

Clothes were important and she selected them with care. Not because of her weight, as some folks hinted, or her complexion, as others came right out and said, or her standing in the community as a respectable widow woman. She favored blousey blues if her errands for the day called for ventilation and subdued discussion. Or muted flower prints 'cause she didn't want her spirit crowded or her disposition misread. She liked greens and golds, for they were in sympathy with her goals in gardening. Purple and white, she felt, strengthened her affinity with young students. Her coats and capes were dressed up with outrageous collars of coquille feathers and eye-stinging maribou because, she said, it reminded people they could soar. On the insides of her elbows she doused vanilla extract or rubbed in a dash of nutmeg, 'cause perfume interfered with luncheon aromas.

"That's it," she'd shrug. But folks would press for more, sure that some dazzling secret for gorgeous longevity would break from cover and fly out, if only they could keep the old gal talking. "Beauty is care," she'd conclude. "Just as ugly is carelessness."

M'Dear took as serious a position on the food question as she did on the race question, the woman question and the class question. She walked a lot, laughed a lot, took hospitality, birthdays, new ideas and children to heart.

At school when kids got ugly, teachers pounced with the cake of soap. M'Dear argued that this roughly administered remedy to carelessness did not promote lovelier language but simply neutralized the sewer wastes that drained from brain to tongue. The root of the nasty-mouth-kid problem, she said, was ignorance—the dread ugly of all uglies. She prescribed more direct and radical measures. A dose of the dictionary followed by a trip to the library was her recommendation. There she hovered close and monitored our selections with care. M'Dear was very careful about the mental hygiene of children.

She questioned kids about movies, comic books. She asked us then, as Aretha was to ask us later, to think about what we danced to. (And here we are now doing the hustle to "She's a brick [blankety blank] house.") Brainwashing was what M'Dear called her attempts to develop in the children around her a critical habit, an analytic habit, a 24-hour, red-alert , combat-duty guardedness. "There's a war on," M'Dear would remind us.

Odd that "brainwashing" should have such a bad reputation today. Odd that it provokes long-winded tirades on totalitarianism and torture, conjures up images of sci-fi body-snatching terrors. Considering how much filth corporate and societal institutions inflict every day on consumers of entertainment, information, education, health care and legal relief services—brain cleansing should be a welcome detoxification. Brain scrubbing, in fact, should be a routine beauty rite. More to the point we need to re-embrace the critical habit promoted in the sixties. For to be as credulous at 30 as we were at three—as though the environment holds no potential dangers and media seduction is not to be resisted—is unattractive and dangerous.

At three, when we were offered that arrogant little burglar/vandal/liar as a heroine, as a model, we'd not yet been encouraged and equipped to raise some critical questions about what constitutes a human value system. So we persisted in calling the story of that unrepentant criminal "Goldilocks and the Three Bears—A Fairytale" instead of "The Golden Bandit—A Paradigm."

We needed responsible adults to pause in the reading so we could ask that child, her parents and the PR agency hawking her, just what the hell did she call herself doing, acting so mean, low-down and disrespectful? Breaking into folks' home, smashing up their furniture, messing with their groceries, sleeping in their bed—and with her shoes on—the nasty heifer. And when the folks come home, does she beg their pardon for such gross misbehavior? Does she offer to call her dad to fix the door? Does she offer to cook dinner and launder the sheets and repair the chair? Does she at least say "Good evening"? She does not. She runs away and tells her parents some lie about bears terrorizing her. And they go for it with their bigoted, hot-headed selves. And the story ends. And aint nobody gonna tell that brat about herself or take some responsibility for civilizing her parents and their community, which obviously sanctions such anti-social behavior? Aint nobody gonna intervene before the parents pick up the shotgun or lynch rope and go after the maligned victims the bandit kid is calling out of their names? Uhh-ugh-lee.

Burn books? Close down the libraries? Board up the movie houses? The trouble is the Golden Bandit is in the air, the food, the bloodstream even.

That we have slipped and are dangerously uncritical is demonstrated by the community-wide embrace of *Star Wars*, which offers the most blatant and brazen message of white supremacy in years. White folks, a mere 20 percent of the world's population, will rule the galaxy. The film has seduced us, intoxicated us. We surely need to fashion some techniques of hygiene. Best we develop some standards, some critical criteria for the selection of books, films, music, et cetera, some habit of checking out what's being sold before buying it internally.

For the Golden Bandit idea of hero rides again and again in contemporary myth and lesson. The hero of the commercials—the mindless consumer. An addict. The western, war movie, cops and robbers—the mindless killer. An addict. The hero of the futuristic tales, the supposed figure of advanced humankind—Six Million Dollar Man, Bionic Woman, clones, DNA creatures being bred in desert labs on government grants—are menacing freaks.

Considering how relentlessly corporate and societal institutions pollute and poison the brain under the guise of entertainment, information, education, and social services—brainwashing ought to be a routine beauty rite, assuming, as M'Dear surely did, that a healthy state of mind, body, spirit and affairs is our birthright.

Perhaps we need to develop the habit of a sweet-oil bathing of the inner ear to restore one's balance after tuning into some late night show and hearing Dr. Thus-and-such discoursing on how botulism can be suspended in an aerosol spray or General Dofunny expounding on the merits of the neutron bomb. And maybe we need to resort to boric acid irrigation to clarify vision after watching the TV script-writers turn guerrilla warfare on the continent into monkey shines in the bush. And perhaps a lubricant should be taken while watching *Taxi Driver, Rocky* and a host of other movies whose battered Black-body messages stick in the mind as well as the throat. And a wake-up shampoo administered by some strong-fingered attendant when we experience our first inkling that the Western aesthetic is anesthetic.

The perception of advanced humankind in this part of the world is locked at the level of horror show. Dr. Frankenstein's answer, you recall, to the miseries and limits of civilized kind was the Monster. It was to be a superman, this patchwork creation manufactured from society's victims. But what got up from the operating table was a menace—a freak, a mutation rather than a transformed being. As it was with the good doctor, so it is with the urban designers, economic planners, social engineers and popular mythmakers—mutation not transformation.

For models of transformation, change, struggle, development, M'Dear steered us first to the biography stalls in the library and then to the church basement where the elders hung out. She steered us through Harriet Tubman, Douglass, Vesey, Toussaint and other members of our championship tradition. She also exposed us to the lessons of oral history transmitted by folks right from the block. M'Dear sought to develop in the children an immunity to debilitating lies.

To guard against those who would sell us Frankenstein, we still need only look to our own figures of change. Malcolm for example. We need to look to our own collective behavior over generations—our cultural products. The slick, well-budgeted *Star Wars, Clockwork Orange, Fahrenheit 451, Tommy, Rollerball* and the rest of the future-shock, past-tremble, anti-human-capacity nightmares that instruct us that we have no future, no past, no present, fall apart when pushed up against a film like *Willie Dynamite*—which for all its technical ineptness makes an irresistible call to develop the belief in our capacity to transform self and reconstruct society. The same goes for the infrequently shown films of Haile Gerima—*Child of Resistance, Harvest Three Thousand* and *Bush Mama*. All are powerful antidotes to other Hollywood intoxicants.

The really hurting thing about the complex of -isms that characterize America, its satellites and captive territories—racism, narcissism, opportunism, specie-ism, materialism, sexism—is that they disfigure spirit and cripple the capacity to grow, to imagine, to act. This daily dosage of poisons consumed uncritically under the guise of literature, the arts, higher education and news does not help to build an immunity to disease but rather coaxes an addiction to unhealth, unwholeness. After awhile it seems perfectly "natural" to go to the doctor, the disco, the restaurant, the university, the theater and submit to the pumping in of inert substances, dead stuff, so we can feel more akin with dead stuff. After awhile it seems perfectly "natural" to live fragmented—the mind up here, the body down there, emotions safely tucked under the soul out there, somewhere, somehow. After awhile it seems perfectly "natural" to equate kin, mate, children, friends and nature with disposable diapers and no-return bottles. Natural to be ugly.

M'Dear maintained that there are only a few truly ugly people. Most of the time it's just a case of folks being careless about their birthrights—like the right to develop, the right to a beautiful state of mind, the right to integrity, wholeness, the right to resist assaults on the nervous system. We all know people who have grown beautiful—willed it so—to recognize that resistance to madness and the embrace of good sense improves general appearance. Just as accommodation and collaboration disorient and deteriorate.

Folks who've incorporated the pathology of the system into their own system usually look the part. Drooped eyelids, slack jaw, caved-in chest, slumped-over torso. It's hard to tell whether they're standing up or falling down. They've taken on everybody and anybody's weight just for the sensation of being needed. *You need me therefore I love you / You need me therefore you oughta love me* . . . Or into your life races the hot-eyed go-getter under the spell of big business. Demands all, accepts nothing, issues ultimatums and conditions, is addicted to everything and complains loudly that he/she has never experienced enoughness, and somebody's going to pay for that. All the time running to and fleeing from, eyes and clothes askew, flight/ fight jungle mechanism the only thing well oiled and working, off balance and upset by want and need, talking 'bout *I need you, therefore I love you/I need you therefore you better love me.* What from a distance looked like a glow of health close up and all in your face proves to be an unhealthy flush from all that constriction of blood vessels and clenching of muscles.

Then there's the radar swiveling, predatory grin headhunter, scanning the terrain, stalking the community, his/her appetite making no distinction between a potato and a baby, the enemy and the kin. He/she practices the gangster lean while walking, driving, eating, sleeping lest some force or other slip round the blind side and put the heart under arrest. *I don't need no damn body so love me.*

Then there are the other folks. Folks who have taken their care about the business of being human and alive and on the earth at this particular time in history. Folks who are balanced, centered in a frame of reference that enables them to distinguish between the myths and the truths, between that which retards the self and communal agenda and that which promotes development. Folks who are alert and aglow, creating an illumined space around them to be comfortable in. Folks who have resisted the lie that alienation is the human condition. Folks who have a careful faculty operating in building relationships, spending money, using time, eating, screening films, learning skills, listening to music, dancing. Folks who view the establishing of relations, the rearing of children, the self as development questions rather than management problems. *I want a sane, full life for me and I want no less for you. I love you.*

"It has to do with foundations," M'Dear used to say. Definitely not meaning girdles or makeup. Nor the hot breakfast the school nurse insisted was the foundation for everything. For there are foods that can warm the stomach but manage to embalm tissue while they're at it. And M'Dear surely did not mean the purity and refinement that the third-grade teacher maintained was the basis of the good life, cramming as much Beethoven, Rembrandt and dreams of sailing to Europe into us as the school bell would allow.

"Stuff," M'Dear would say to me, arranging flowers in her hair. "You need a good foundation for life." And as we sat on her pillows to watch her light the candles M'Dear would finally surrender up her beauty secret—"Take care. Choose life."

THE REDEVELOPMENT OF THE DEAD BLACK MIND:

The Building of Black Extended Family Institutions

HAKI R. MADHUBUTI. Afrocentricity has become a topic of much discussion in the early nineties as educational programs in black schools, both private and public, have shown the influence of those who advocate the necessity of a nationalistic, Pan Africa–focused set of values to teach black children. Haki R. Madhubuti, born in Little Rock, Arkansas, in 1942, has been one of the leading national figures in this movement. His essay "The Redevelopment of the Dead Black Mind: The Building of Black Extended Family Institutions," from his book, *Enemies: The Clash of Races* (Third World Press, 1978), is as straightforward and compelling an account of this position as any written.

Very few people with a progressive frame of reference at this day and time in our struggle would question the reality in the United States and in much of the world [of] the existence of the concept that anything white is designated "normal" and anything black or non-white is projected as "abnormal." The mass media's effectiveness in using politics, sex, education, religion, sports, culture, entertainment, law and economics to impress upon every man, woman and child in the country that the *American Way* (the white way) is the *Right Way* is nothing less than phenomenal. For example, as painful as it is, proportionally, there are more black people wearing wigs today, men and women, than there existed in 1965; there are more beauty shops in today's black community than educational, cultural, economic or political institutions. Mass media has made it explicitly clear that the ideal is the "European natural" and that the Germanic blond is the essence of "correctness." And we in our search for meaning generally go the way of European-American "correctness," not realizing that what is "normal" for others may be deadly for us.

As soon as black babies struggle from their mothers' wombs, they are designated by this society as being "abnormal," first by color. Later incompetence will be added as a "scientific rationale" for their oppression. From birth, every minute of their lives will be a struggle to be recognized and respected as black people. This struggle will intensify to the point where it will either *make them* or *destroy them* as black men or women. The training (passed off as education) black people receive from birth through high school (and for some, college) is grounded in white nationalist history, tradition, values and culture and has worked beautifully for Aryan (white) nationalists.

Black parents and friends associated with the affirmative black independent school movement often ask, *what guarantee do we have that our children will not betray black people if black people provided their total educational experiences and needs from birth to adulthood?* Our answer to this very important question is that *the great majority of black people have not betrayed white people and the fact is a direct result of white education, socialization, and enslavement from birth.* This must be understood if we are to effectively plan for tomorrow.

As black people living in the United States, the color of our skins takes on added significance, especially since our people did not freely choose to come to this part of the world. We were raped from Africa, transported here under the most horrible of conditions, sold like pigs and turned out into the fields to be trained and broken like horses. We were *denatured*: forced to do things that were unnatural and against our very being and culture. It was like taking an elephant out of Africa and putting the elephant in a circus in the United States and making the elephant do circus tricks such as jumping through hoops. In the elephant's natural habitat he doesn't jump through hoops. In order to make him do circus tricks he must first be *denatured*. As far as black people are concerned we've been enslaved, retrained and thus transformed into imitation white people—*denatured*.

We were separated from our families (those who were not killed during the actual voyage), robbed of our spirits, redefined into slave and/or negro status and systematically beaten into a world where slave and black were to become synonymous. Black became a brand, like that given to cattle—except we were naturally born with ours in a foreign land surrounded everywhere by the most skilled outlaws ever to hit the face of the earth.

Today the major substantive change that has come about is a negative one. That is to say that the great majority of black people do not realize that we are still enslaved. The twentieth century was able to bring into being the new technology and within it a new *scientific slavery*. Slavery of today and the future concentrates on the control of the mind and thereby controls the body. Therefore, a fact that should be carefully considered is that *nothing in this world* (history, science, technology, sex, education, sports, entertainment, etc.) is value-free or valueless. Every action that transpires between peoples and cultures carries with it its own values. And if black people do not *have* and *practice* their own values, customs and traditions, other people out of their own survival-necessity will impose their values on us, i.e., that's why we speak, dress, think and act like Euro-Americans (white people) rather than like Africans (black people). Therefore, we believe that our collective movement must address itself to *life-giving* and *life-saving* values, actions and institutions that stimulate and motivate black people toward the liberation and re-development of black people.

Black re-education and re-development are dependent upon new thoughts, values and actions. In order to assure that these new thoughts, values and actions are introduced into the black communities at a meaningful level, we need *affirmative independent black institutions*. These institutions are needed at a world level if we are to seriously attack and defeat white world supremacy. As we survey the world today all too often what we pass off as black progressive values are just *white values painted black*. Therefore, we must start our re-education at the local levels first. Affirmative independent black institutions means just that: we say *affirmative* as opposed to *alternative* because when one speaks of alternative, the first question is alternative to what? Generally we are talking about alternatives to white supremacist institutions. However we maintain that to be an alternative to white supremacist institutions *is not the answer to our problems because by definition we will be defined from outside. The world, and especially the Black world, is much larger and complex than just the opposite of white.* Affirmative means to *affirm and confirm first and foremost your own beauty, values, knowledge, and worth and to move on from there using and adapting to your needs the positive elements from other parts of the world if necessary.*

The *family* as the first-line institution is the foundation upon which the new black consciousness and community can be built and sustained. However, we must understand that black consciousness is forever in a process of growth and is not an *absolute*. That is to say that the black struggle of the sixties was different from the black struggle of the seventies and that the eighties will bring with it new unknowns to adjust to and conquer. That which is "correct" today is not an absolute, the absolute is to always maintain the ability to move toward "correctness." *To maintain the ability to admit and grow from our mistakes rather than let them defeat us represents best the inner strength of a people.*

To measure a people's accomplishments you look at them and their institutions. What major institutions have we created by ourselves other than an abundance of churches that don't reflect the total journey, hurt, blood, past, present and future of the race? We frequent and support white people's museums, theaters, schools, hospitals, parks, libraries, farms, commercial outlets, etc. The institution is the reinforcer and initial direction-giver to the families. That is to say, that the working and functioning families within the institutions are at all times leaders as well as doers. Therefore *a commitment to a lifestyle that is compatible with struggle is absolutely necessary if the institution is to function within the spheres of black harmony and development.* What we mean is that all the functioning families must work, study, create and build. These are not families that do all of the work alone while other families just study or vice-versa. The extended family values are based on the African communalistic concepts of collective work, growth internally, externally and institutionally.

The people-to-people relationship within the family-institution must be of the highest level. We believe in the concepts of *work* every day for our people; *study* every day for the development of our people; *creativity* for the beauty of our people; and *building* for the future of our people. Nothing less than total respect between each other is accepted in the working institution. This respect is displayed not only among the adults but with our children (our life-line) remembering that we are the *mamas* and *babas*[1] of *all* of the institution's or community's children and not just of those we biologically bring into the world. This is important because the children see—we must *act* and *be*.

Institutions are actually *unified people* who have initiated work around agreed-upon guidelines and objectives. The strength of the institution is derived from its people-base and its value-base. The values must be livable, and workable, and above all make sense while addressing themselves to the *real world*, thus bringing meaning and purpose to the lives of those who practice them. The value system practiced at the Institute of Positive Education in Chicago is the Nguzo Saba,[2] a black value system. This value system is based upon African tradition and reason, yet speaks to our everyday associations here in the 20th century. These values briefly are Umoja (unity), Kujichagulia (Self-Determination), Ujima (Collective Work and Responsibility), Ujamaa (Cooperative Economics and Extend Family), Nia (purpose), Kuumba (Creativity) and Imani (Faith). The people must be *aware* of, *accept* and *practice* the agreed-upon values, if the institution is to develop. Hopefully, if these values and the culture from which they emanate are correct, they will enable us not only to survive but to develop and advance. If they are incorrect, they will be changed in the process of struggle and work.

The people/families who are considering the move toward the development of institutions must come together and define the type of institution they wish to give their "lives" to. At that time they would survey the basic needs they wish to commit themselves to solving; education, health, housing, food, clothing, drugs, youth development, spiritual enlightenment, day care, social and culture awareness, political development, economics, community defense, communication, community organization, aid to senior citizens, etc.

It is important that you develop around your capabilities in terms of what you can actually accomplish and not only around wishes, dreams or rhetoric which is generally exaggerated. For example, if we talk about education, a good question to ask ourselves as a group first is *can we educate our own children?* It is a contradiction to talk about re-educating the community when we can't even deal with our own sons and daughters. We are serious about this. Start with what you can do; start with your own families before you try to educate Chicago, New York, Atlanta or the world. Our experience has been that the children of some of the "blackest," most "nationalist/Pan-Africanist" parents are sometimes more undisciplined and politically backward children than some of the "Negroe" children we say we are trying to reach. The seriousness and effectiveness of any program should be actualized first and foremost in the lives of the teachers or instructors.

It is almost useless to talk about building institutional structures that will grow and endure without the involvement of the total families. We see the brothers, but not the sisters or the children. Why are the wives and the children not at the black nationalist functions? If the functions are correct they should act as part of the political and socialization process and are necessary for the total family and not just the *brothers*. Why do the brothers leave the wives and children at home? Maybe, because they may get embarrassed. You can't have the brothers saving the race, the sisters integrating the white house and the children getting high off false words and nationalist neglect. The worst type of hypocrisy which has programmed us for failure has been the internal separation of the family.

Of course, the major problem is that we are not yet *really black* because the de-slaving process has not been locally or nationally perfected so as to teach us the fundamentals of national black unity. *We have never been taught from birth to work for our own people.* That act alone is the basis for movement. It is paramount that each child knows that working for his/her people is not only a duty and a privilege, but is absolutely necessary if we are to survive, develop and remain a people. It must be understood that *nowhere in today's United States are there black men or women in positions of real power or influence who have not been trained or "educated" by white people.* If you have problems dealing with that let me put it another way, in today's United States there exist *no black men or women* in positions of real power or influence who have not been trained or "educated" by black people who have been trained or "educated" by white people. Does one need to go any further to discover the root of much of our confusion?

That's a terrible indictment of a people who talk about liberation but continue to send their children to the enemy to be liberated. The Mormons of Salt Lake City, Utah, teach their own; the Amish of Pennsylvania teach their own; the Irish of Chicago teach their own, the Italians of New Jersey teach their own; the Anglo-Saxons of Boston teach their own; the Jews of the world teach their own; and the Negroes are taught by everybody else but ourselves so we are taught to work hard for everybody else's liberation rather than that of black people. *White people are not going to teach black people to work for black people. Also, black people who've been taught by white people all their lives will have difficulty relating to and teaching black children.* We see this in the public school system every day and our experience with some black teachers with advanced degrees who join black independent school movements is that most of them are unable to put into practice much of the *theory* of education that they have learned at their colleges or universities without a total black reorientation. This is not to suggest that we do not need people who have advanced degrees. What we need are people with *advanced knowledge*, but only after the negative elements of that knowledge have been filtered out so that we do not pass it on to our children.

Revolutionary theory comes from revolutionary practice and not the other way around. The theory comes out of the day-to-day doing. Yes, we must learn from those who preceded us regardless of who they were, but all knowledge must be placed into the context of the current struggle. As much as I respect the People's Republic of China, it would be a grave error for me to adopt verbatim the tactics and strategy of their struggle for a number of reasons:

1) I am not Chinese and thus culturally would interpret and look at the world through different eyes. 2) We are currently struggling in the nerve center of the most scientifically and technologically advanced nation in the world and to pattern our struggle "totally" after the Chinese, Cubans, Angolans, or Russians or anyone

else would not only be shortsighted, but the height of naiveté. 3) Blacks in America are a minority struggling against a white majority. This fact alone requires new thought and vision. In essence, we have to stop relying on others to supply us with the revolutionary theory of struggle, because struggle in the United States has its own elements of *life* and *death* that are unlike life and death anywhere else in the world. If we do not understand this we are doomed to failure.

Therefore, blackness as we understand it is not only speaking about our *color* in all its various shades, but also defines our *culture* which must be rooted in our black past and present while at the same time negotiating and adjusting itself to any future that confronts us. Blackness also deals with our *consciousness*, which should direct us toward working and acting in the best interest of black people as well as the world's people. As far as theory is concerned, white people talk and push the theory of individualism, but act collectively, especially in dealing with us, and if you look at the strong Euro-American or Asian nations, you will see strong families because the nation is families united.

The black family must be the basis for the new institution. The mother, father and children or the core/nuclear family are first and foremost the first line politicizers and socializers of the race. The black family-institution must believe in the importance and creativity of the individual man, woman and child.

The brain of every black person should be developed to its highest, and the institution, if it is functioning at an effective level, plays a vital role in that development. The institution must allow for the greatest expression of individual creativity and expression. Yet, there must be noted a distinction between *individuality* and *individualism*. Individuality is the expression of the self in concert with the collective selves; whereas individualism is the expression of the self at the expense of and in contradiction to the collective selves. Therefore, a person working individually and at odds with the collective frame of reference of the majority is an example of individualism that can greatly and generally does immobilize the institution. There are exceptions, but the institution's strength comes from the people who have created, upheld, protected, practiced and disseminated the values and programs deemed important by that community. If the institutions are not careful, individual *disruption* can become a *tactic* and a *program* for those who wish to see them fail. However, we must not confuse new and untried ideas with individualism; it is always good and stimulative to have people in your institution that continually subject the body to innovative thoughts. If the individual, potentially, is the *single best source of creativity*, the family, potentially, is the *collective best source of creativity*. The nuclear family working within the institutional structure becomes the *extended family*. The extension of the nuclear family into the extended family now practiced through the institution is one of the most productive means in which to provide our people with much needed goods and services, such as food, housing, clothing, security, love, education and protection. Therefore, it is important that we talk about institutional structure and components:

> *People*: The lifestyle is the workstyle. There must be a serious commitment to the building of the institution and in order to have this we need serious, committed and competent men, women, and children. The actual day-to-day

work will have much to do with defining the type of people that will give their lives to such an endeavor. The majority of the people that we will be working with are inadequately educated, and unskilled. Therefore, all adult educational programs must take this into account. However, we must remember that the education of adult black men and women is a delicate undertaking and must be done with care and love.

Family: The immediate families of the people must be involved, must form the basis for the extended family which eventually will form the basis for the institution. The family is important because it is more stable and secure than the floating individual. There are exceptions, but our experiences have shown that the families who commit themselves to the institution generally are more reliable because a collective decision to work and struggle has been made by the members of the family, and a collective unit does not generally commit itself without much discussion and examination.

Work: In the beginning there are no eight-hour work days. A twelve-to sixteen-hour work day is the rule rather than the exception. If one is truly serious about building affirmative black institutions, one's total personal resources must be at the command and use of the institution. *Work for the people* should be distinguished from a *job* such as working for General Motors, etc. You go to get a job to labor for somebody else and they pay you for your labor. You work for yourself and your people and there is very little monetary pay, if any. And if you have the correct frame of reference, you must always put more into the building in order to see a meaningful return. You work to build your own institutions and your reward will aid in the liberation of our people. *In Africa, work is not only honorable but it is fruitful exercise for the mind and body.*

Finances: If you are to remain independent, you must have an independent financial base. The black church has its congregation, the N.A.A.C.P. has its membership and private and governmental grants. The first source of money should start with the institutional members who should contribute a minimum of 10 percent of their weekly salaries to the institution. We believe that all individual and family debts should be cut to the minimum. If this is done, much of the outside pressures of living which prevent financial movement will be solved. Therefore we should be able to funnel our monies into institutions that will benefit us rather than into those institutions that will benefit our enemies. There should be a standing committee working daily on raising funds for the institution. Remember, those who feed your stomach will control your diet.

Structure: Elected council of elders (elders are not necessarily defined by age— the real decision-makers should be those who do the work) to include men and women who over a given period of time have displayed a high level of work, study, creation and building. For further understanding of this concept see Chancellor Williams's *The Destruction of Black Civilization*.

Politics: Black Nationalism, Pan-Africanism and African Communalism? However, if the institution is reaching a broad base of people it should be willing to work with Black Christian, Black Muslim, Black Israelites, Black Marxists and any other black people who are genuinely working for the race. Be careful of closing oneself off from the actual black community. The study of the politics of the local areas as well as that of the national and international fronts should be an on-going program. There are few things in a capitalist society that are not racial, political or economical.

Social: It is important that the moral and morale factors remain high. The institution should adopt a value system that is compatible for growth and development. We suggest the Nguzo Saba. Brothers should not be allowed to misuse sisters and vice-versa. Relationships between men and women in the institution should be open, honest and at all times above board. That's why we believe in the family orientation. If the institution is to grow and develop and to attract the old and the young, the atmosphere that it creates must be conducive to growth and development. We believe in the concept of *marriage and of the equal work and decision-making responsibilities of both men and women at all levels of the institution.* This is to say, men and women must have an equal voice in the day-to-day operation and the work distributed in accordance with *ability* and *competence. You will not attract intelligent women unless the women are treated intelligently and given responsible work in keeping with their talents and the needs of the institution.*

Love: The love of a people is often confused with the simplified and romanti-cized reflection of daytime soap operas which is at best an insult to intelligent men, women and children. Therefore according to the western concept of life, if I don't say I love you daily or continuously smile and talk nice things to you every time I see you, I don't love you. If I don't run through the grass holding your hand, or if I am not off somewhere forever buying you gifts, I don't love you. This is nonsense. The collective and individual love of a people must be redefined out of our struggle and our traditions. So often we find that the first persons to back up when the work gets hard are the persons who are always smiling, hugging and loving everybody to death. Black love first and foremost is a display of high respect, genuine care and family cohesiveness, based on values and concepts that the people practice among themselves and others. For example, one marries a person because of respect of that person's knowledge, workstyle and lifestyle. One marries a person because over a period of their working together they grow emotionally and physically attached to each other based around the commonality of work and life practices. One marries another because after a given time the needs of the two as defined by their people's struggle become more and more the same needs. Perhaps they both are studying the same material and are both trying to create institutions for themselves and their people's tomorrow. Therefore a marriage is not only an emotional and physical choice, but also, and above all, a rational and logical choice.

Institutional image: Your institution should at all times be clean, well lighted and radiate a sense of warmth and seriousness. This cannot be stressed too much because the immediate image of your work area reflects you. If your work areas are raggedy, possibly your programs are raggedy? This is important because our people are still Cadillac-buyers and expect the best in anything that they invest their time and money in. Just think how the image changes if the institution's pictures and posters are framed rather than just tacked on the wall any old way. Remember, neatness and orderly work areas also reflect and encourage efficiency. Also, the most effective act that helps keep the family as well as new people coming in at *ease* is the ability of all those who participate to SMILE. A big sincere smile upon greeting everyone is essential for creating a warm atmosphere.

Goods and services: The institution is working at its highest when internally and externally it is able to provide itself with many of the basic goods and services needed for development. For example, a good start would be food co-ops and then, possibly, a move into day care centers and elementary schools. The major concept is to begin to cut all levels of dependency on other people for the goods and services that are life-giving and life-saving. This takes much work, but is the substance of the institution is such programs can be actualized. If we are not providing our people with life-giving and life-saving goods and services, they must be getting them from someone else and their allegiance and support may go to others first rather than to the Nationalist/Pan Africanist Institutions.

Legal and professional services: Your first move in this nation is to put yourself on a "legal" footing. It is important, if you are planning to be a "service" institution, to acquire nonprofit and tax-exempt status (two different concepts.) Try to locate a committed lawyer to aid you in this—don't beg or bargain for this type of service, *pay the going rate, because it needs to be done correctly* and as soon as possible. If you are to handle money you will need someone [who] is competent in the area of accounting. Your books must be in order for tax purposes—even if you are tax-exempt you will still have to file. There have been many individuals, institutions and businesses destroyed because of delinquent taxes. Try to get as many "professional" people involved as possible, especially in the areas of law, medicine, accounting, housing, employment, etc.

Coalitions and alliances: It is important to realize that other groups, institutions, or communities may be doing work that is also significant to the black struggle. Be willing to share your ideas as well as resources and people. Always look at the larger picture even though you may be involved with people in a twenty-block radius or less. The ultimate power of affirmative black independent institutions lies not only in their ability to organize and be productive themselves but also in their ability to form coalitions and alliances with other like and "unlike" groups. Remembering too that the struggle is not only for the space that you actually occupy but for the *planet*, and our WORLDVIEW must be one that understands and at the same time functions at many levels.

The creation of black institutions is a simple and important step in the development of a black consciousness, which is paramount and of immediate need if black people are to move forward worldwide. Therefore our concerns must be in the area of reeducation within a cultural base that is progressive as well as moral; an educational base that respects and develops the individual while at the same time fostering collective values in all life-giving areas. We need institutions that can prepare us for the 21st Century; that can turn the tide of defeatism and negativeness so pervasive among our young. Most importantly we need institutions that project a positive world future for black people and the sons and daughters of black people.

The sixties taught us that in order to gain the total and lasting support of our people one must begin to institutionalize programs that are deemed necessary by the black community. In order for this to be effective the institution by definition will bring structure and "permanency." What has happened to SNCC, CORE, SCLC, RAM and the Black Panther Party? Nationally as well as locally most of them are not with us anymore. They were valuable, needed and did much of their work as they defined it, but they were first and foremost *transient organizations*, and their long-range goals and objectives have not been met. When one talks about struggle in the proper context, one talks about *decades* of hard work and serious study. Therefore you have to talk about a sense of permanency *which means that you are not going to leave the battle-front when the fighting starts.* When we talk about permanent institutions in the black community, we immediately think about the black church, N.A.A.C.P., the Urban League and the Nation of Islam. Where are our fifty-year plans for the race? The affirmative independent Black institutions must be involved with the long-range as well as the short-range goals of a people. This above all requires definite and absolute action with the utmost sophistication. But we must not move too fast beyond the practical or the believable. We must be production-oriented. Words have always been cheap and with today's inflation our people are *not* buying programs that are merely well-written.

What I am truly interested in is moving beyond easy slogans and confused non-action. What we have proposed here is not *the* answer for everyone, but may be an answer for a few. And really at this point in our development this is about as much as we can . . . expect of each other. Define the problem and organize to solve it as best and as logically as possible. Can you organize your mother, your father or your neighbors on the block? The Black Nationalists–Pan Africanist institutions must be the focal point for the redevelopment and liberation of black people. Affirmative independent black institutions may not immediately change the world-wide image of black people but they can be a beautiful start.

The *struggle* is not for ideology, Congressional seats or state control of production, the *struggle* after all the verbiage and self-aggrandizment, after the articulate word games (mini or macro economics) and anti-this and anti-that, the *struggle* at its very foundation is for *civilization*. The *struggle* is for *results* in the *good*, is for a *harmony of people and land*, is for a *meeting* of the *minds* beyond the narrow confines of current popular thought.

Touch the mind and you touch the situation; put something on the mind of the receiver and you force him or her to confront the condition. At that point one has a choice, to work for continued enslavement or to work for liberation. We have work to do and the building of the black extended family institution is a necessary step and it will be done if we are to survive and grow. For as long as there is air to breathe, water to drink—as long as the good earth provides us with food, clothing and shelter there is nothing that black people cannot do and the first step in doing anything is also the first step toward getting it done. Look at your children and you see yourself. Our children above anything else are our impetus and *we black men and women are the change if change is to come.*

NOTES

1. Mothers and Fathers.
2. Recreated for black people in the west by Maulana Ron Karenga.

WILLIE HORTON
AND ME

ANTHONY WALTON is among the new young
nonfiction prose writers on the scene. His work has appeared in the *New
York Times* and *Callaloo*, among other places. He is currently finishing a
memoir entitled *Mississippi* for Farrar Straus & Giroux. Willie Horton,
the black Massachusetts convict who, when given a work-release during
Michael Dukakis's tenure as governor, raped and beat a white woman,
became during the 1988 presidential campaign of George Bush a symbol
of the excesses of liberal social policy. Walton's insightful and intelligent
response to the meaning of Willie Horton in the black mind first
appeared in August 20, 1989, issue of the *New York Times Magazine*.

I am a black man. I am a young black man, born, let's say, between *Brown v.
Board of Education* and the murders of Schwerner, Chaney and Goodman.
Or, in the years that followed the murder of Emmett Till, but before the
murder of Dr. Martin Luther King, Jr.

I am one of the young black Americans Dr. King sang of in his "I Have a
Dream" speech: "I have a dream that . . . the sons of former slaves and the sons of
former slave owners will be able to sit down together at the table of brotherhood . . .
that my four little children will one day live in a nation where they will not be
judged by the color of their skin, but by the content of their character. . . . I have
a dream today!"

Though I have a living memory of Dr. King, I don't remember that speech. I
do remember my parents, relatives, teachers and professors endlessly recounting it,
exhorting me to live up to the dream, to pick up the ball of freedom, as it were,
and run with it, because one day, I was assured, we would look up and the dream
would be reality.

I like to think I lived up to my part of the bargain. I stayed in school and remained home many nights when I didn't have to in the interest of "staying out of trouble." I endured a lonely Catholic school education because public school wasn't good enough. At Notre Dame and Brown, I endured further isolation, and burned the midnight oil, as Dr. King had urged.

I am sure that I represent one of the best efforts that Americans, black Americans particularly, have made to live up to Dr. King's dream. I have a white education, a white accent, I conform to white middle-class standards in virtually every choice, from preferring Brooks Brothers oxford cloth to religiously clutching my gold cards as the tickets to the good life. I'm not really complaining about any of that. The world, even the white world, has been, if not good, then acceptable to me. But as I get older, I feel the world closing in. I feel that I failed to notice something, or that I've been deceived. I couldn't put my finger on it until I met Willie Horton.

George Bush and his henchmen could not have invented Willie Horton. Horton, with his coal-black skin; huge, unkempt Afro, and a glare that would have given Bull Connor or Lester Maddox serious pause, had committed a brutal murder in 1974 and been sentenced to life in prison. Then, granted a weekend furlough from prison, had viciously raped a white woman in front of her fiancé, who was also attacked.

Willie Horton was the perfect symbol of what happened to innocent whites when liberals (read Democrats) were on the watch, at least in the gospel according to post-Goldwater Republicans. Horton himself, in just a fuzzy mug shot, gave even the stoutest, most open, liberal heart a shiver. Even me. I thought of all the late nights I had ridden in terror on the F and A trains, while living in New York City. I thought Willie Horton must be what the wolf packs I had often heard about, but never seen, must look like. I said to myself, "Something has got to be done about these niggers."

Then, one night, a temporary doorman at my Greenwich Village high-rise refused to let me pass. And it occured to me that it had taken the regular doormen, black, white and Hispanic, months to adjust to my coming and going. Then a friend's landlord in Brooklyn asked if I was living in his apartment. We had been working on a screenplay under deadline and I was there several days in a row. The landlord said she didn't mind, but the neighbors. . . . Then one day, I was late for the Metroliner, heading for Harvard and a weekend with several yuppie, buppie and guppie friends. I stood, in blazer and khakis, in front of the New York University Law School for 30 minutes, unable to get a cab. As it started to rain, I realized I was not going to get a cab.

Soaking wet, I gave up on the Metroliner and trudged home. As I cleaned up, I looked in the mirror. Wet, my military haircut looked slightly unkempt. My eyes were red from the water and stress. I couldn't help thinking, "If Willie Horton got a haircut and cooled out. . . ." If Willie Horton would become just a little middle-class, he would look like me.

For young blacks of my sociological cohort, racism was often an abstract thing, ancient history, at worst a stone against which to whet our combat skills as we went winging through the world proving our superiority. We were the children of the dream. Incidents in my childhood and adolescence were steadfastly, often laughingly, overcome by a combination of the fresh euphoria of the civil rights movement and the exhortations and Christian piety of my mother. Now, in retrospect, I can see that racism has always been with me, even when I was shielded by love or money, or when I chose not to see it. But I saw it in the face of Willie Horton, and I can't ignore it, because it is my face.

Willie Horton has taught me the continuing need for a skill W. E. B. Du Bois outlined and perfected 100 years ago: living with the veil. I am recognizing my veil of double consciousness, my American self and my black self. I must battle, like all humans, to see myself. I must also battle, because I am black, to see myself as others see me; increasingly my life, literally, depends upon it. I might meet Bernhard Goetz on the subway; my car might break down in Howard Beach; the armed security guard might mistake me for a burglar in the lobby of my building. And they won't see a mild-mannered English major trying to get home. They will see Willie Horton.

My father was born in a tar-paper, tin-roof shack on a cotton plantation near Holly Springs, Mississippi. His father was a sharecropper. *His* father had been a slave. My father came north, and by dint of a ferocity I still find frightening, carved an economic space for himself that became a launch pad to the Ivy League, to art school, to professional school, for his children.

As the song by John Cougar Mellencamp says it, "Ain't that America. . . ." But a closer look reveals that each of my father's children is in some way dangerously disgruntled, perhaps irrevocably alienated from the country, *their* country, that 25 years ago held so much promise. And the friends of my father's children, the children of the dream Dr. King died to preserve, a collection of young people ranging from investment bankers to sidemen for Miles Davis, are, to a man and woman, actively unsatisfied.

Du Bois, in "The Souls of Black Folks," posed a question perhaps more painful today than in 1903: "Training for life teaches living; but what training for the profitable living together of black men and white?"

I think we, the children of the dream, often feel as if we are holding 30-year bonds that have matured and are suddenly worthless. There is a feeling, spoken and unspoken, of having been suckered. This distaste is festering into bitterness. I know that I disregarded jeering and opposition from young *blacks* in adolescence as I led a "square," even dreary life predicated on a coming harvest of keeping-one's-nose-clean. And now I see that I am often treated the same as a thug, that no amount of conformity, willing or unwilling, will make me the fabled American individual. I think it has something to do with Willie Horton.

Black youth culture is increasingly an expression of alienation and disgust with any mainstream (or so-called white) values. Or notions. Cameo haircuts, rap music, outsize jewelry are merely symptoms of attitudes that are probably beyond changing. My black Ivy League friends and [I] are manifesting attitudes infinitely more contemptuous and insidious; I don't know of one who is doing much more on the subject of Dr. King's dream than cynically biding his or her time, waiting for some as-yet-unidentified apocalypse that will enable us to slay the white dragon, even as we work for it, live next to it and sleep with it.

Our dissatisfaction is leading us to despise the white dragon instead of the dragon of racism, but how can we do otherwise when everywhere we look, we see Willie Horton?

And we must acknowledge progress. Even in our darkest, most paranoid moments we can acknowledge white friends and lovers. I wouldn't have survived the series of white institutions that has been my conscious life without them. But it is hard to acknowledge *any* progress, because whites like to use the smallest increment of change to deny what we see as the totality. And, even in the most perfect and loving interracial relationships, racism waits like a cancer, ready to wake and consume the relationship at any, even the most innocuous, time. My best friend, white and Jewish, will never understand why I was ready to start World War III over perceived slights at an American Express office. In my darker moments, I suspect he is a bit afraid of me now. In my darkest moments, I wonder if even he sees Willie Horton.

Some of you are by now, sincerely or cynically, asking yourselves, "But what does he want?" A friend of mine says that the complaints of today's young blacks are indeed different from those of generations ago because it is very difficult to determine whether this alienation is a clarion call for the next phase of the civil rights movement or merely the whining of spoiled and corrupted minority elites who could be placated by a larger share in the fruits of a corrupt and exploitative system that would continue to enslave the majority of their brothers and sisters.

I don't think there is any answer to that question. I also think that the very fact it can be asked points to the unique character of the American race question, and the unhealable breach that manifests itself as a result in our culture and society. I don't think, for good or bad, that in any other ethnic group the fate of an individual is so inextricably bound to that of the group, and vice-versa. To use the symbol and metaphor of Willie Horton in another way, I do not think that the lives and choices of young white males are impacted by the existence of neo-Nazi skinheads, murdering Klansmen or the ordinary thugs of Howard Beach. I also, to put it plainly, do not recall any young black man, even those who deal drugs in such places, entering a playground and spraying bullets at innocent schoolchildren as happened in Stockton, California. It is not my intention to place value considerations on *any* of these events; I want to point out that in this society it seems legitimate, from the loftiest corridors of power to the streets of New York, to imply that one black man is them all.

And I want to be extraordinarily careful not to demonize Willie Horton. He should not be a symbol or scapegoat for our sins; he is a tragically troubled man— troubled like thousands of others, black and white—who was unwittingly used by a President to further division and misunderstanding. If anything, Horton is a particularly precise example of the willingness of those in power to pit us against one another. One lately fashionable statement, about to slide from truth to truism, is that blacks have the most to fear from lawless blacks. Any clear-eyed perusal of crime statistics will prove this. But what does it avail if the media, if the *President*, use this ongoing tragedy merely to antagonize and further separate Americans?

I think that what I am finally angry about is my realization of a certain hollowness at the center of American life. Earlier, I mentioned the sense of having undergone a hoax. That hoax, as I now see it, is that the American community is putatively built upon the fundamentals of liberty and justice for all, that it is to be expected that the freedom to compete will result in winners and losers, and that the goal of society is to insure fairness of opportunity. In light of the events of recent years, I begin to see that we are, competing or not, winners or not, irrevocably chained together, black and white, rich and poor. New York City is a glaring microcosm of this interrelatedness, which can be thought of as either a web of fear ensnaring and enslaving us, or as a net of mutuality that strengthens us all.

As events like the Central Park rape illustrate, the world is becoming ever smaller, and it is increasingly difficult to consign social problems to realms outside our personal arenas of concern. I see the connection between Willie Horton and me, because it affects my own liberty. It was not always an obvious connection.

Another quote from Dr. King brings the issue into focus: "Most of the gains . . . were obtained at bargain rates. The desegregation of public facilities cost nothing; neither did the election and appointment of a few black public officials. . . ." To move to the next level of progress, we must face the fact that there are going to be costs, especially economic costs. To hire two black firefighters means two white firefighters won't be hired, and this is no easy reality. Racism is ultimately based on power and greed, the twin demons of most human frailties. These demons cannot be scapegoated, as the saga of Willie Horton proves. They are more like the Hydra, and will haunt our dreams, waking and other, regardless.

IV

AFRICA AND THE
AMERICAN BLACK

Africa has been on the mind of the black American since he first arrived in bondage on the shores of the New World. As the African became more estranged and more distant from Africa and began to see himself or herself as an American, Africa became a contradiction in the black American's mind, a source of unease and irreconcilability. On the other hand, Africa (no longer understood as landscape of distinct and quite separate countries and peoples but as an entire continent of collective indistinction and blurred realities) was a sentimental home-land, a place of romantic ancestry or pioneering dreams of settlements, as in the various schemes that blacks have had since the days of slavery to modern times to return there in body or in spirit (e.g., Paul Cuffe in the 1810s and 1820s; Martin R. Delany in the 1850s; Henry McNeal Turner and Edward Wilmot Blyden in the 1890s; Marcus Garvey in the 1920s; W. E. B. Du Bois in both the 1920s and the 1950s; Malcolm X in the 1960s; the black cultural nationalism movement of the late 1960s that resulted, in part, in dashikis and Afros and the black holiday, Kwanzaa; the scholarship of Ivan Van Sertima, Chancellor Williams, and Josef Ben-Yochanan and the entire Afrocentricity movement). In addition, the black American came to believe, as the white American taught him, and as he or she perceived himself or herself when confronted by the African, that Africa was a backward land of backward unwashed people, of jungle and noncivilization, that Africa was, in short, not only incapable of containing history but it could never cease being simply uncharted territory.

And of course for so very long, for most of the memory of black people in

America, [Africa] has been a place controlled by whites. (This last point is probably why South Africa has become such a particularly meaningful location for both black and white Americans.) The black American can never understand the black African fully and think that this is what he or she [the American] is. He or she can only think that this is what he or she was. It is an antiquity that, no matter how the black American may wish to use it to illuminate his pride in his past, simply dims and stains the possibility of his future. These few essays that deal with the black American and his spiritual homeland reflect the very contradictory qualities of which I speak.

IMPRESSIONS OF THE SECOND PAN-AFRICAN CONGRESS

JESSIE REDMON FAUSET, a great admirer of
W. E. B. Du Bois, was an observer at the second Pan-African
Congress, organized by Du Bois and held in London in 1921. The
first had been held in 1919. There were to be a series of these
conferences, under Du Bois's leadership, for the rest of the decade.
Fauset's accounts of the 1921 conference appeared in the November
1921 ("Impressions of the Second Pan-African Congress") and the
December 1921 issues of *The Crisis*.

I

The dream of a Pan-African Congress had already come true in 1919. Yet
it was with hearts half wondering, half fearful that we ventured to realize
it afresh in 1921. So tenuous, so delicate had been its beginnings. Had
the black world, although once stirred by the terrific rumblings of the Great War,
relapsed into its lethargy? Then out of Africa just before it was time to cross the
Atlantic came a letter, one of many, but this the most appealing word from the
Egyptian Sudan: "Sir: We cannot come, but we are sending you this small sum
[$17.32], to help toward the expenses of the Pan-African Congress. Oh Sir, we are
looking to you for we need help sorely!"

So with this in mind we crossed the seas not knowing just what would be the
plan of action for the Congress, for would not its members come from the four
corners of the earth and must there not of necessity be a diversity of opinion, of
thought, of project? But the main thing, the great thing, was that Ethiopia's sons
through delegates were stretching out their hands from all over the black and
yearning world.

II

Then one day, the 27th of August, we met in London in Central Hall, under the shadow of Westminster Abbey. Many significant happenings had those cloisters looked down on, but surely on none more significant than on this group of men and women of African descent, so different in rearing and tradition and yet so similar in purpose. The rod of the common oppressor had made them feel their own community of blood, of necessity, of problem.

Men from strange and diverse lands came together. We were all of us foreigners. South Africa was represented, the Gold Coast, Sierra Leone and Lagos, Grenada, the United States of America, Martinique, Liberia. No natives of Morocco or of East Africa came, yet men who had lived there presented and discussed their problems. British Guiana and Jamaica were there and the men and women of African blood who were at that time resident in London.

That was a wonderful meeting. I think that at first we did not realize how wonderful. The first day Dr. Alcindor of London and Rev. Jernagin of Washington presided; the second day Dr. Du Bois and Mr. Archer, ex-Mayor of Battersea, London. Of necessity those first meetings had to be occasions for getting acquainted, for bestowing confidences, for opening up our hearts. Native African and native American stood side by side and said, "Brother, this is my lot; tell me what is yours!"

Mr. H. A. Hunt of Fort Valley, Georgia, Mr. R. P. Sims of Bluefield, West Virginia, Dr. Wilberforce Williams of Chicago, Mrs. Hart Felton of Americus, Georgia, Professor Hutto of Bainbridge, Georgia, Rev. W. H. Jernagin of Washington, D.C., Dr. H. R. Butler of Atlanta, Mr. Nelson of Kentucky, Dr. Du Bois, Mr. White, Mrs. Kelley, and Miss Fauset—all these told of America. And in return Dr. Olaribigbee and Mr. Thomas of West Africa, Mr. Augusto of Lagos, Mrs. Davis of South Africa, Mr. Marryshow of Grenada, Mr. Norman Leys, a white Englishman who knew East Africa well, Mr. Arnold, also white, who knew Morocco, Mr. Varma, and Mr. Satkalavara of India told the tale of Africa and of other countries of which the Americans knew little or nothing.

We listened well. What can be more fascinating than learning at first hand that the stranger across the seas, however different in phrase or expression, yet knows no difference of heart? We were all one family in London. What small divergences of opinion, slight suspicions, doubtful glances there may have been at first were all quickly dissipated. We felt our common blood with almost unbelievable unanimity.

Out of the flood of talk emerged real fact and purpose for the American delegate. First, that West Africa had practically no problems concerning the expropriation of land but had imminent something else, the problem of political power and the heavy and insulting problem of segregation. The East African, on the other hand, and also the South African had no vestige of a vote (save in Natal), had been utterly despoiled of the best portions of his land, nor could he buy it back. In addition to this the East African had to consider the influx of the East Indian who might prove a friend, or might prove as harsh a taskmaster as the European despoiler.

Through the interplay of speech and description and idea, two propositions flashed out—one, the proposition of Mr. Augusto, a splendid, fearless speaker from Lagos, that the Pan-African Congress should accomplish something very concrete.

He urged that we start with the material in hand and advance to better things. First of all let us begin by financing the Liberian loan. Liberia is a Negro Independency already founded. "Let us," pleaded Mr. Augusto, "lend the solid weight of the newly-conscious black world toward its development."

The other proposition was that of Mr. Marryshow, of Grenada, and of Professor Hutto of Georgia. "We must remember," both of them pointed out, "that not words but actions are needed. We must be prepared to put our hands in our pockets; we must make sacrifices to help each other." "Tell us what to do," said Mr. Hutto, "and the Knights of Pythias of Georgia stand ready, 80,000 strong, to do their part."

Those were fine, constructive words. Then at the last meeting we listened to the resolutions which Dr. Du Bois had drawn up. Bold and glorious resolutions they were, couched in winged, unambiguous words. Without a single dissenting vote the members of the Congress accepted them. We clasped hands with our newly found brethren and departed, feeling that it was good to be alive and most wonderful to be colored. Not one of us but envisaged in his heart the dawn of a day of new and perfect African brotherhood.

III

Down to Dover we flew, up the English Channel to Ostend, and thence to Brussels.

Brussels was different. How shall I explain it? The city was like most other large cities, alive and bustling, with its share of noise. All about us were beautiful, large buildings and commodious stores, except in the public squares where the ancient structures, the town hall and the like, centuries old, recalled the splendor and dignity of other days. But over Brussels hung the shadow of monarchical government. True London is the heart of a monarchy, too, but the stranger does not feel it unless he is passing Buckingham Palace or watching the London Horse Guards change.

At first it was not so noticeable.

We had been invited by Paul Otlet and Senator LaFontaine and had been helped greatly by M. Paul Panda, a native of the Belgian Congo who had been educated in Belgium. The Congress itself was held in the marvellous *Palais Mondial*, the World Palace situated in the Cinquantenaire Park. We could not have asked for a better setting. But there *was* a difference. In the first place, there were many more white than colored people—there are not many of us in Brussels—and it was not long before we realized that their interest was deeper, more immediately significant than that of the white people we had found elsewhere. Many of Belgium's economic and material interests centre in Africa in the Belgian Congo. Any interference with the natives might result in an interference with the sources from which so many Belgian capitalists drew their prosperity.

After all, who were these dark strangers speaking another tongue and introducing heaven only knew what ideas to be carried into the Congo? Once when speaking of the strides which colored America had made in education I suggested to M. Panda that perhaps some American colored teachers might be induced to visit the Congo and help with the instruction of the natives.

"Oh, no, no, no!" he exclaimed, and added the naive explanation, "Belgium would never permit that, the colored Americans are too *malins* [clever]."

After we had visited the Congo Museum we were better able to understand the unspoken determination of the Belgians to let nothing interfere with their dominion in the Congo. Such treasures! Such illimitable riches! What a storehouse it must plainly be for them. For the first time in my life I was able to envisage what Africa means to Europe, depleted as she has become through the ages by war and famine and plague. In the museum were the seeds of hundreds of edible plants; there was wood—great trunks of dense, fine-grained mahogany as thick as a man's body is wide and as long as half a New York block. Elephants' tusks gleamed, white and shapely, seven feet long from tip to base without allowing for the curve, and as broad through as a man's arm. All the wealth of the world—skins and furs, gold and copper—would seem to center in the Congo.

Nor was this all. Around us in the spacious rooms were the expression of an earlier but well developed art, wood carvings showing beyond the shadow of a doubt the inherent artistry of the African. Dearest of all, yet somehow least surprising to us, was the number of musical instruments. There is not a single musical instrument in the world, I would venture to say, of which the Congo cannot furnish a prototype.

Native wealth, native art lay about us in profusion even in the museum. Small wonder that the Belgian men and women watched us with careful eyes.

The program in Brussels was naturally different from that in London. We undertook to learn something of the culture which colored people had achieved in the different parts of the world, but we hoped also to hear of actual native conditions as we had heard of them in the first conference. M. Panda spoke of the general development of the Congo. Madame Saroléa of the Congolese woman. Miss Fauset told of the colored graduates in the United States and showed the pictures of the first women who had obtained the degree of Doctor of Philosophy. Bishop Phillips of Nashville and Bishop Hurst of Baltimore greeted the assembly. Mrs. Curtis told of Liberia, the presiding officer of the Conference, M. Diagne, and his white colleague M. Barthélemy from the Pas de Calais, in the French Chamber of Deputies, ably assisted.

Belgian officialdom was well represented. General Sorelas of Spain spoke of the problem of the mixed race. Another General, a Belgian, splendid in ribbons and orders, was on the platform, and two members of the Belgian Colonial Office were present, "unofficially."

There was no doubt but that our assembly was noted. A fine, fresh-faced youth from the International University gave us a welcome from students of all nations; we were invited to a reception at the Hotel de Ville (City Hall) in the ancient public square, and on the last day General Sorelas and his beautiful wife and daughters received us all in their home.

And yet the shadow of colonial dominion governed. Always the careful Belgian eye watched and peered, the Belgian ear listened. For three days we listened to pleasant generalities without a word of criticism of colonial governments, without a murmur of complaint of Black Africa, without a suggestion that this was an international Congress called to define and make intelligible the greatest set of wrongs against human beings that the modern world has known. We realized of course how delicate the Belgian situation was and how sensitive a conscience the nation had because of the atrocities of the Leopold regime. We knew the tremendous power of capital organized to exploit the Congo: but despite this we proposed before the Congress was over to voice the wrongs of Negroes temperately but clearly. We assumed of course that this was what Belgium expected, but we reckoned without our hosts in a very literal sense. Indeed as we afterward found, we were reckoning without our own presiding officer, for without doubt M. Diagne on account of his high position in the French Government had undoubtedly felt called on to assure the Belgian Government that no "radical" step would be taken by the Congress. He sponsored therefore a mild resolution suggested by the secretaries of the Palais Mondial stating that Negroes were "susceptible" of education and pledging cooperation of the Pan-African Congress with the international movement in Belgium. When the London resolutions (which are published this month as our leading editorial), were read, M. Diagne was greatly alarmed, and our Belgian visitors were excited. The American delegates were firm and for a while it looked as though the main session of the Pan-African Congress was destined to end in a rather disgraceful row. It was here, however, that the American delegates under the leadership of Dr. Du Bois, showed themselves the real masters of the situation. With only formal and dignified protest, they allowed M. Diagne to "jam through" his resolutions and adjourn the session; but they kept their own resolutions in place before the Congress to come up for final consideration in Paris, and they maintained the closing of the session in Brussels in order and unity. I suppose the white world of Europe has never seen a finer example of unity and trust on the part of Negroes toward a Negro leader.

But we left Belgium in thoughtful and puzzled mood. How great was this smothering power which made it impossible for men even in a scientific Congress to be frank and to express their inmost desires? Not one word, for instance, had been said during the whole Congress by Belgian white or black, or French presiding officer which would lead one to suspect that Leopold and his tribe had ever been other than the Congo's tutelary angels. Apparently not even an improvement could be hinted at. And the few Africans who were present said nothing. But at that last meeting just before we left, a Congolese came forward and fastened the button of the Congo Union in Dr. Du Bois's coat.

What lay behind that impassive face?

IV

At last Paris!

Between Brussels and the queen city of the world we saw blasted town, ravaged village and plain, ruined in a war whose basic motif had been the rape of Africa. What should we learn of the black man in France?

Already we had realized that the black colonial's problem while the same intrinsically, wore on the face of it a different aspect from that of the black Americans. Or was it that we had learned more quickly and better than they the value of organization, of frankness, of freedom of speech? We wondered then and we wonder still though heaven knows in all humility.

But Paris at last, with its glow and its lights and its indefinable attraction!

We met in the Salle des Ingénieurs (Engineers' Hall) in little rue Blanche back of the Opera. Logan was there, Béton and Dr. Jackson, men who had worked faithfully and well for us even before we had come to Paris. And around us were more strange faces—new types to us—from Senegal, from the French Congo, from Madagascar, from Annam. I looked at that sea of dark faces and my heart was moved within me. However their white overlords or *their* minions might plot and plan and thwart, nothing could dislodge from the minds of all of them the knowledge that black was at last stretching out to black, hands of hope and the promise of unity though seas and armies divided.

On the platform was, I suppose, the intellectual efflorescence of the Negro race. To American eyes and, according to the papers, to many others, Dr. Du Bois loomed first, for he had first envisaged this movement and many of us knew how gigantically he had toiled. Then there was M. Bellegarde, the Haitian minister to France and Haitian delegate to the assembly of the League of Nations. Beside him sat the grave and dignified delegate from the Liga Africana of Lisbon, Portugal, and on the other side the presiding officer, M. Diagne and his colleague, M. Candace, French deputy from Guadeloupe. A little to one side sat the American Rayford Logan, assistant secretary of the Pan-African Congress at Paris and our interpreter. His translations, made off-hand without a moment's preparation, were a remarkable exhibition.

In the audience besides those faithful American delegates who had followed us from London on, were other friends, Henry O. Tanner, Captain and Mrs. Napoleon Marshall, who had joined us in Paris, Bishop and Mrs. Hurst, who had come back from Brussels to Paris with us, Captain and Mrs. Arthur Spingarn, white delegates from America, who had attended the conferences regularly and had laughed and worked with us in between whiles.

The situation in Paris was less tense, one felt the difference between monarchy and republic. But again the American was temporarily puzzled. Even allowing for natural differences of training and tradition, it seemed absurd to have the floor given repeatedly to speakers who dwelt on the glories of France and the honor of being a black Frenchman, when what we and most of those humble delegates wanted to learn was about *us*.

The contrast between the speakers of the Eastern and Western hemispheres with but two exceptions was most striking. Messieurs Diagne and Candace gave us fine oratory, magnificent gestures—but platitudes. But the speeches of Dr. Du Bois, of Edward Frazier, of Walter White, of Dr. Jackson, of a young and fiery Jamaican and of M. Bellegarde, gave facts and food for thought. The exceptions were the speeches of M. Challaye, a white member of the Society for the Defense of African Natives, and those of the grave and courtly Portuguese, Messieurs Magalhaens and Santos-Pinto.

But this audience was different from that in Brussels. To begin with, its members were mainly black and being black, had suffered. More than one man to whom the unusually autocratic presiding officer had not given the right to speak said to me after hearing Dr. Du Bois's exposition of the meaning and purpose of the Pan-African Congress, "Do you think I could get a chance to speak to Dr. Du Bois? There is much I would tell him."

France is a colonial power but France is a republic. And so when our resolutions were presented once more to this the final session of the Pan-African Congress, that audience felt that here at last was the fearless voicing of the long stifled desires of their hearts, here was comprehension, here was the translation of hitherto unsyllabled, unuttered prayers. The few paragraphs about capitalism M. Diagne postponed "for the consideration of the next Pan-African Congress." But the rest that yearning, groping audience accepted with their souls.

The last session of the last day was over. It was midnight and spent and happy we found our way home through the streets of Paris which never sleeps.

V

Yet after all the real task was at Geneva. The city struck us dumb at first with its beauty of sky and water—the blue and white of the September heavens above, Lake Geneva and the Rhone River gliding green and transparent under stone bridges, black and white swans, red-beaked, floating lazily about green baby islands, and above and beyond all in the far distance Mont Blanc rising hoary, serene and majestic. In the sunset it looked like burnished silver.

But scant time we had for looking at that! The Assembly of the League of Nations was on. A thousand petitions and resolutions were in process of being presented. Delegates from many nations were here and men of international name and fame were presiding. How were we to gain audience?

Fortunately for us Dr. Du Bois's name and reputation proved the open sesame. He had not been in the city two hours before invitations and requests for interviews poured in. One of our staunchest helpers was an English woman, Lady Cecelia, wife of that Mr. Roberts who had worked with Montague in India. She presided at meals at a long table in the dining room of the *Hotel des Familles* and here Dr. Du Bois was made a welcome guest throughout his whole stay. Here came to meet and confer with him on our cause Mr. Roberts himself, Mr. Lief-Jones, M.P., Professor Gilbert Murray (representing South Africa at the Assembly of the League of Nations), and John H. Harris of the Anti-Slavery and Aborigines' Protection Society. M. Bellegarde, Haitian Minister to France and delegate to the Assembly, was also at that hotel and gave us generously of his aid and assistance.

On Monday night, September 13, Dr. Du Bois addressed the English Club of Geneva and conveyed to them some idea of what the black world was thinking, feeling and doing with regard to the Negro problem. I am sure that many of that group of people, thinkers and students though they were, had never dreamed before that there might even be a black point of view. But they took their instruction bravely and afterwards thanked Dr. Du Bois with shining eyes and warm hand clasps.

Besides meeting and conferring with these distinguished personages, Dr. Du Bois had luncheon conferences with Réné Claparède of the executive committee of the Société Internationale pour la Protection des Indigènes and with William Rappard, head of the Mandates Commission of the League of Nations, a dinner conference with G. Spiller, former secretary of the Races Congress, and an interview with Albert Thomas, head of the International Bureau of Labor.

At the end of a week of steady driving, by dint of interviewing, of copying, of translating, of recopying, we were ready to present and did present to Sir Eric Drummond, secretary of the League of Nations, a copy in French and English of the resolutions entitled "To the World" and of the manifesto. Mr. Thomas and M. Rappard, who both heartily endorsed the appointment of a "man of Negro descent" to the Mandates Commission, Professor Gilbert Murray, and M. Bellegarde also received copies.

And between whiles we listened to the world striving to right its wrongs at the Assembly of the League of Nations.

Of course, we were at a disadvantage because America, not being in the League of Nations, had no delegate. But Professor Murray suggested to M. Bellegarde, the Haitian delegate, that he state the second resolution (see manifesto) during the debate on Mandates. This he did, as Professor Murray writes us, with "quite remarkable success" and "I think that next year it may be quite suitable to put it down as a resolution."

VI

Results are hard to define. But I must strive to point out a few. First, then, out of these two preliminary conferences of 1919 and 1921, a definite organization has been evolved, to be known as the Pan-African Congress. There will be more of this in these pages. Naturally working with people from all over the world, with the necessity for using at least two languages, with the limited detailed knowledge which the black foreigner is permitted to get of Africa and with the pressure brought to bear on many Africans to prevent them from frank speech—action must be slow and very careful. It will take years for an institution of this sort to function. But it is on its own feet now and the burden no longer is on black America. It must stand or fall by its own merits.

We have gained proof that organization on our part arrests the attention of the world. We had no need to seek publicity. If we had wanted to we could not have escaped it. The press was with us always. The white world is feverishly anxious to know of our thoughts, our hopes, our dreams. Organization is our strongest weapon.

It was especially arresting to notice that the Pan-African Congress and the Assembly of the League of Nations differed not a whit in essential methods. Neither attempted a hard and fast program. Lumbering and slow were the wheels of both activities. There had to be much talk, many explanations, an infinity of time and patience and then talk again. Neither the wrongs of Africa nor of the world, can be righted in a day nor in a decade. We can only make beginnings.

The most important result was our realization that there is an immensity of work ahead of all of us. We have got to learn everything—facts about Africa, the difference between her colonial governments, one foreign language at least (French or Spanish), new points of view, generosity of ideal and of act. All the possibilities of all black men are needed to weld together the black men of the world against the day when black and white meet to do battle.

God grant that when that day comes we shall be so powerful that the enemy will say, "But behold! these men are our brothers."

AFRICA AND THE
AMERICAN NEGRO
INTELLIGENTSIA

W. E. B. DU BOIS's interest in Africa was abiding
and intense. He helped to organize a series of Pan-African conferences
during the 1920s. He was eventually to become a citizen of Ghana
and to die there. He wrote numerous works on Africa, African
culture, and imperialism. "Africa and the American Negro
Intelligentsia" was originally published in *Présence Africaine*,
December 1954–January 1955.

L eading American Negroes are today widely ignorant of the history and
present situation in Africa and indifferent to the fate of African Negroes.
This represents a great change from the past. In the seventeenth century
the Negroes of the Americas regarded Africa as their Fatherland and looked forward
to eventual repatriation for themselves or their posterity. They preserved African
words, phrases and customs. I have written elsewhere of the African song which
was handed down for four or five generations in my own family. My grandfather's
grandmother was seized by an evil Dutch trader two centuries ago; and coming to
the valleys of the Hudson and Housatonic, black, little and lithe, she shivered and
shrank in the harsh north winds, looked longingly at the hills, and often crooned a
heathen melody to the child between her knees, thus:

> Do ba-no co-ba, ge-ne me, ge-ne me!
> Do ba-na co ba, ge-ne me, ge-ne me!
> Ben d' nu-li, nu-li, ben d' le!

The child sang it to his children and they to their children's children, and so
200 years it has traveled down to us and we sing it to our children, knowing as little
as our fathers what its words may mean, but knowing well the meaning of its music.
Most American Negroes were landed directly in the West Indies after their

voyage from Africa, or were later transported from the West Indies to America after a period of "seasoning"; or were descended from West Indian Negroes brought from Africa. Such Negroes during the years 1619 to 1700 naturally regarded Africa as the home for which they longed and sang.

The attitude of American Negroes in the eighteenth century can be seen in the history of Philadelphia. Between 1790 and 1800, the Negroes here increased 176 percent to nearly 7,000 persons. There was much poverty and crime among these folk, who were either runaway slaves from the South or emancipated serfs from the rural districts round about. But there was also much industry and ambition. Some cases of ability occurred, like the black physician, [James] Derham; and two real social leaders in the preachers Absalom Jones and Richard Allen.

Negroes at the time were attending the white Methodist Church. As their numbers increased, an attempt was made to segregate them in the balcony. Jones and Allen refused to submit and in 1787 led out a group of blacks, who started an organization which they called significantly the Free African Society, formed without regard to religious tenets, provided the persons lived an orderly and sober life in order to support each other in sickness and for the benefit of their widows and fatherless children. Jones and Allen helped rescue the sick in the great epidemic of 1792, using their own funds in part. They were publicly commended by the mayor.

Free African societies and Negro unions were formed in other cities. They corresponded on matters of mutual interest, among others the question of migration to Africa. Eventually, the Philadelphia society divided; one became the African Methodist Church, still one of the most powerful American Negro organizations with 1,250,000 members, and property worth $35,000,000. The other section became a black church in the white Episcopalian sect, thus beginning the long trek toward integration.

The decade 1830 to 1840 was one of the severest seasons of trial through which the black American ever passed. The great economic change which made slavery the cornerstone of the cotton kingdom was definitely finished and all the subtle moral adjustments which followed were in full action. New immigrants took advantage of the growing prejudice which found a profitable place for the Negro in slavery, and was determined to keep him in it. Immigrants began to crowd the free Northern Negro in a fierce economic battle. With a precarious social foothold, little economic organization, and no support in public opinion, the Northern free Negro was forced to yield. In Philadelphia from 1829 to 1849, six mobs of hoodlums and foreigners cowed and murdered the Negroes. In the Middle West and, especially in Ohio, severe Black Laws had been enacted in 1804 to 1807.

These laws, however, were dead letters until 1829, when increased Negro migration induced the Cincinnati authorities to enforce them. The Negroes obtained a respite of thirty days and sent a deputation to Canada. They were absent for sixty days, and when the whites saw no effort to enforce the law further, they organized a riot. For three days Negroes were killed in the streets until they barricaded their homes and shot back. Meantime, the governor of upper Canada sent word that he "would extend to them a cordial welcome." He said: "Tell the republicans on your side of the line that we royalists do not know men by their color.

Should you come to us you will be entitled to all the privileges of the rest of His Majesty's subjects."

On receipt of this, fully 2,000 Negroes went to Canada and founded Wilberforce; while a national convention of Negroes was called in Philadelphia in 1830—the first of its kind.

Proposals by whites to send Negroes back to Africa were made as early as 1714. They were repeated by Samuel Hopkins and Ezra Styles after the Revolutionary War. Jefferson and a Virginia legislative committee proposed a plan for gradual emancipation and deportation in 1777. Other proposals by emancipation societies were made, and then in 1815, a Negro, Paul Cuffee, started the actual migration in 1815, carrying nine colored families, thirty-eight persons in all, to Sierra Leone, at an expense of $4,000 which he paid himself.

Two years after Paul Cuffee, the American Colonization Society was formed, with distinguished Americans like Bushrod Washington [the late President's nephew], Henry Clay, and John Randolph on the roster of members. By 1832, more than a dozen states approved. By 1830, the Abolitionists turned down the scheme. Local organizations seceded and the parent body became insolvent in 1834, and inactive about 1854. The total exportation by the society was 12,000.

The first American Negro to graduate from an American college was John Brown Russwurm, who received his bachelor's degree at Bowdoin College, Maine, in 1826. He went to New York, where he edited an Abolition paper [*Freedom's Journal*]. In 1829, he went to Liberia, Africa, as superintendent of public schools, and also carried on business activities in Monrovia. He was colonial secretary and editor from 1830 to 1834, and from 1836 to his death in 1851, was governor of Maryland Colony at Cape Palmas. "A man of strict integrity; a good husband, father, and friend."

Alexander Crummell, a leading Negro Episcopalian priest, went to Africa, and Daniel Payne was favorable. Lott Cary went in 1821 under a Negro organization, and died there in 1828.

The American Colonization Society came to have two antagonistic objects. The first was the philanthropic object of removing the Negro to Africa and starting him on the road to an independent culture in his own fatherland. The second and more influential object was to get rid of the free Negro in the United States so as to make color caste the permanent foundation of American Negro slavery. The contradiction of these two objects was the real cause of the failure of colonization, since it early incurred the bitter opposition of both Abolitionists and Negro leaders. The result of the movement was the establishment of Liberia in an inhospitable land and without adequate capital and leadership. The survival of that little country to our day is one of the miracles of Negro effort, despite all of the propaganda of criticism that has been leveled against that country.

From 1830 on the leaders of Negroes opposed migration. Then, too, the idea of migration received a setback from the Liberian experiment. American Negroes found that on arriving in Africa they were regarded as strangers by the natives. They were alien in tribal and clan relationships; they did not know the native languages or native culture patterns; as a result the open war between the emigrants to Liberia and the native tribes took up much of Liberian history, and alienated other American Negroes.

From 1830 to the Civil War, American Negroes fought for emancipation. State conventions were called, in many instances, and the most representative and intelligent national convention held up to that time met in Rochester, New York, Douglass's home, in 1853. This convention developed definite opposition to any hope of permanent relief for the colored freedman through schemes of emigration.

However, the radical stand of this assembly against emigration caused a call for a distinct emigration Negro convention in 1854. This convention was held under the presidency of the same man who afterward presided at the Chatham convention of John Brown, and with some of the same Negroes present.

There were three parties in the convention, ranged according to the foreign fields to which they preferred to emigrate. Martin R. Delaney, a major in the Civil War, headed the party which desired to go to the Niger Valley in Africa. James Whitfield led the party which preferred to go to Central America, and Bishop Holly the party which preferred to go to Haiti.

All these parties were recognized by the convention. Delaney was given a commission to go to the Niger Valley in Africa; Whitfield to go to Central America; and Holly to Haiti, all to enter into negotiations with the authorities of these various countries for Negro emigrants and to report to future conventions. Holly was the first to execute his mission, going down to Haiti in 1855, when he entered into relations with the officials, and as a result some 2,000 Negroes migrated. Dr. Delaney went on his mission to the Niger Valley, Africa, via England, in 1858. There he concluded a treaty signed by himself and eight kings, offering inducements to Negro emigrants to their territories. Whitfield reached California on his way to Central America, but died in San Francisco.

Meantime, in the South and especially in the West Indies, another variant of thinking among the Negro intelligentsia had come about because of the rise of a large mulatto element. At first the mixed bloods demanded freedom as a right because of their white fathers; in most cases they received education, usually in France or England, and on returning to the colonies often became men of property and influence. By tradition and education they refused to be considered Africans or Negroes. They supported black slavery and demanded for mulattoes treatment as whites. There arose, therefore, a fierce feud between mulattoes and blacks, until common interest united these groups in defense against the whites. In the case of Haiti, the revolt of the mulattoes against the whites was being repulsed in bloody reprisal, when the mass of 500,000 blacks arose under Toussaint and wrested the island from France, Spain, and Britain.

In the United States, a similar situation arose from the appearance of mulatto children of whites and blacks, and the migration of West Indian mulattoes to this country. Thus, a class of free colored people arose in the South and in Louisiana, and in cities like Mobile, Savannah, and Charleston, they formed a group, sometimes owning land and even black slaves. Each group started schools and social organizations. In some states they had for a time the right to vote. They were the object of increasing oppression after 1820, and numbers of them went North, where they joined leaders of the black and mulatto groups already there. Naturally, in this intelligentsia, there was no thought of Africa as Fatherland or refuge. They wanted to be Americans.

As the Negro question became prominent before the war, the project of colonization was revived by the whites, and Abraham Lincoln believed in it "as one means of solving the great race problem involved in the existence of slavery in the United States."

By an act of April 16, 1862, which abolished slavery in the District of Columbia, Congress made an appropriation of $100,000 for voluntary Negro emigrants at an expense of $100 each; and later, July 16, an additional appropriation of $500,000 was made at Lincoln's request. The President was authorized "to make provision for transportation, colonization and settlement, in some tropical country beyond the limits of the United States, of such persons of the African race, made free by the provisions of this act, as may be willing to emigrate, having first obtained the consent of the government of said country to their protection and settlement within the same, with all the rights and privileges of freemen."

In several cases, President Lincoln interviewed delegations on the subject of colonization. He believed that a good colonization scheme would greatly encourage voluntary emancipation in the border states. He received in August, 1862, a committee of colored men, and urged colonization on account of the difference of race. "You and we are different races. We have between us a broader difference than exists between almost any other two races. . . . Your race suffers very greatly, many of them, by living among us, while ours suffers from your presence. In a word, we suffer on each side. If this is admitted, it affords a reason why we should be separated. . . . If intelligent colored men, such as are before me, would move in this matter, much might be accomplished."

A bill was introduced into the House in 1862 appropriating $200,000,000— $20,000,000 to colonize and the rest to purchase 600,000 slaves of Unionist owners in border states. The bill was not passed, but the committee made an elaborate report on colonization July 16, 1862, declaring:

"The most formidable difficulty which lies in the way of emancipation in most if not in all the slave states is the belief which obtains especially among those who own no slaves that if the Negroes shall become free they must still continue in our midst, and . . . in some measure be made equal to the Anglo-Saxon race. . . . The belief [in the inferiority of the Negro race] . . . is indelibly fixed upon the public mind. The differences of the races separate them as with a wall of fire; there is no instance in history where liberated slaves have lived in harmony with their former masters when denied equal rights—but the Anglo-Saxon will never give his consent to Negro equality, and the recollections of the former relation of master and slave will be perpetuated by the changeless color of the Ethiop's skin. Emancipation, therefore, without colonization could offer little to the Negro race."

After emancipation negotiations were begun with several foreign countries that owned colonies in the West Indies, and with South American countries. The cabinet discussed the matter. Some wanted compulsory deportation, but the president objected to this. Finally, he settled on two projects: one in Panama, and the other in the West Indies, where an island was ceded by Haiti. An adventurer, named Kock, undertook to carry 5,000 colored emigrants to the land, but the result was a fiasco, and a large number of the 400 actually sent, died of disease and neglect, and were finally brought back to the United States on a war vessel.

After enfranchisement, the thought of the African Negro intelligentsia was turned entirely toward achieving citizenship and equality in the United States. Moreover, then and later, as Negroes entered public schools and colleges, their teaching belittled and sneered at Africa. They were taught that Africa had no history and no culture and they became ashamed of any connection with it. Bitter controversy arose over the name which should designate them: they resented the word "African" and later the word "Negro." Effort was made to adopt "colored" or "Afro-American" as more suitable. A distinct color line within the dark group was drawn. In the early twentieth century the attitude of the Negro intelligentsia began to change. Increasing color caste, with disfranchisement, segregation, lynching, and mob violence, began to drive all persons of Negro descent together for self-defense against law, science, and religion. The missionary efforts of the American Negro churches reached Africa and brought new knowledge of the Dark Continent. Bishop [Henry M.] Turner of the African Methodist Church strongly advocated a "Back to Africa" movement in the nineties and a few Negroes migrated to Africa.[1]

The attempt of Booker T. Washington to integrate Negro labor into white industry actually encouraged the rise of legal "color caste," and a note of resistance crept into Negro literature. My own books—*The Souls of Black Folk* (1903) and *The Negro* (1915)—led to a reassessment of the meaning and history of Africa. *The Crisis*, established in 1910, carried articles on Africa.

In *United Asia*, Vol. VII, No. 2, pp. 23–28, I have written: "At the time of the first world war there came suggestions that American participation in this war should lead to a recognition of the rights of African people as against the imperial powers."

President Wilson was approached on the subject and a memorandum was directed to the Peace Congress of Versailles. To implement this the NAACP, in sending me to Paris after the Armistice to inquire into the treatment of Negro troops, also permitted me to attempt to call a Pan-African Congress. This was an effort to bring together leaders of the various groups of Negroes in Africa and in America for consolidation and planning for the future.

I had difficulty in calling such a congress because martial law was still in force in France and the white Americans representing the United States there had little sympathy with my ideas. I was in consultation with Colonel House, who was President Wilson's spokesman, and with others, but could accomplish nothing. Finally, however, I secured the sympathy and cooperation of Blaise Diagne, who was Colonial Under-Secretary in the Cabinet of Clemenceau, and who had been instrumental in bringing to France the 700,000[2] Africans, who as shock troops saved the nation.

Diagne secured the consent of Clemenceau to our holding a Pan-African Congress, but we then encountered the opposition of most countries in the world to allowing delegates to attend. Few could come from Africa, passports were refused to American Negroes and English whites. The Congress therefore, which met in 1919, was confined to those representatives of African groups who happened to be stationed in Paris for various reasons. This Congress represented Africa partially. Of the fifty-seven delegates from fifteen countries, nine were African countries with twelve delegates. Of the remaining delegates, sixteen were from the United States and twenty-one from the West Indies.

The Congress specifically asked that the German colonies be turned over to an international organization instead of being handled by the various colonial powers. Out of this idea came the Mandates Commission. The *New York Herald* of 24 February, 1919: "There is nothing unreasonable in the program drafted at the Pan-African Congress which was held in Paris last week. It calls upon the Allied and Associated Powers to draw up an international code of law for the protection of the nations of Africa and to create as a section of the League of Nations, a permanent bureau to insure observance of such laws and thus further the racial, political and economic interests of the natives."

The National Association for the Advancement of Colored People did not adopt the "Pan-African" movement on its official program, but it allowed me on my own initiative to promote the effort. With a number of colleagues we went to work in 1921 to assemble a more authentic Pan-African Congress and movement. We corresponded with Negroes in all parts of Africa and in other parts of the world and finally arranged for a congress to meet in London, Brussels, and Paris in August and September. Of the 113 delegates to this Congress, forty-one were from Africa, thirty-five from the United States, twenty-four represented Negroes living in Europe, and seven were from the West Indies.

The London meetings of the Congress of 1921 were preceded by a conference with the international department of the English Labour Party, where the question of the relation of white and colored labor was discussed. Beatrice Webb, Leonard Woolf, M. Gillies, Norman Leyes, and others were present. Otlet and La Fontaine, the Belgian leaders of internationalism, welcomed the Congress warmly to Belgium.

Resolutions passed without dissent at the meeting in London contained a statement concerning Belgium, criticizing her colonial regime, although giving her credit for plans of reform for the future. This aroused bitter opposition in Brussels, and an attempt was made to substitute an innocuous statement concerning good will and investigation, which Diagne of France, as the presiding officer, supported. At the Paris meeting, the original London resolutions, with some minor corrections, were adopted. They said in part:

> To the World: The absolute equality of races, physical, political and social, is the founding stone of world and human advancement. No one denies great differences of gift, capacity and attainment among individuals of all races, but the voice of Science, Religion and practical Politics is one in denying the God-appointed existence of super races or of races naturally and inevitably and eternally inferior.

The Second Pan-African Congress sent me with a committee to interview the officials of the League of Nations in Geneva. I talked with Rappard, who headed the Mandates Commission; I saw the first meeting of the Assembly, and I had an interesting interview with Albert Thomas, head of the International Labor Office. Working with Bellegarde of Haiti, a member of the Assembly, we brought the status of Africa to the attention of the League. The League published our petition as an official document, saying in part:

> The Second Pan-African Congress wishes to suggest that the spirit of the world moves toward self-government as the ultimate aim of all men and nations and that consequently the mandated areas, being peopled as they are so largely by black folk, have a right to ask that a man of Negro descent, properly fitted in character and training, be appointed a member of the Mandates Commission so soon as a vacancy occurs.

We sought to have these meetings result in a permanent organization. A secretariat was set up in Paris and functioned for a couple of years, but was not successful. The Third Pan-African Congress was called for 1923, but postponed. We persevered and finally, without proper preparation, met in London and Lisbon late in the year. The London session was small. It was addressed by Harold Laski and Lord Oliver and attended by H. G. Wells. Ramsay MacDonald was kept from attending only by the pending election, but wrote: "Anything I can do to advance the cause of your people on your recommendation, I shall always do gladly."

The meeting of an adjourned session of this Congress in Lisbon the same year was more successful. Eleven countries were represented there, including Portuguese Africa. The resolutions declared:

> The great association of Portuguese Negroes with headquarters at Lisbon, which is called the Liga Africana, is an actual federation of all the indigenous associations scattered throughout the five provinces of Portuguese Africa and represents several million individuals. . . . This Liga Africana which functions at Lisbon, in the very heart of Portugal so to speak, has a commission from all the other native organizations and knows how to express to the government in no ambiguous terms but in dignified manner all that should be said to avoid injustice or to bring about the repeal of harsh laws. That is why the Liga Africana of Lisbon is the director of the Portuguese African movement; but only in the good sense of the word, without making any appeal to violence and without leaving constitutional limits.

I planned a Fourth Pan-African Congress in the West Indies in 1925. My idea was to charter a ship and sail down the Caribbean, stopping for meetings in Jamaica, Haiti, Cuba, and the French islands. But here I reckoned without my steamship lines. At first the French Line replied that they could "easily manage the trip"; but eventually no accommodations could be found on any line except at the prohibitive price of $50,000. I suspect that colonial powers spiked this plan.

Two years later, in 1927, American Negro women revived the congress idea, and a Fourth Pan-African Congress was held in New York. Thirteen countries were represented, but direct African participation lagged. There were 208 delegates from twenty-two American states and ten foreign countries. Africa was sparsely represented by representatives from the Gold Coast, Sierra Leone, Liberia, and Nigeria. Chief Amoah III of the Gold Coast, and anthropologists like [Melville] Herskovits, then of Columbia, Mensching of Germany, and John Vandercook were on the program.

In 1929 we made a desperate effort to hold a Fifth Pan-African Congress on the continent of Africa itself; we selected Tunis because of its accessibility. Elaborate preparations were begun. It looked as though at last the movement was going to be geographically African. But two insuperable difficulties intervened: first, the French government very politely but firmly informed us that the Congress could take place in any French city, but not in French Africa; and second, there came the Great Depression.

The Pan-African idea died, apparently, until twenty years afterward, in the midst of World War II, when it leapt to life again in an unexpected manner. At the Trades Union Conference in London in 1944 to plan for world organization of labor, representatives from black labor appeared from the Gold Coast, Libya, British Guiana, Ethiopia, and Sierra Leone. Among these, aided by colored persons resident in London, Lancashire, Liverpool, and Manchester, there came a spontaneous call for the assembling of another Pan-African Congress in 1945, when the World Federation of Trade Unions would hold their meeting in Paris. This proved not feasible, and the meeting place was changed to London. Here again we met difficulty in securing meeting places and hotel accommodation. However, a group of Negroes in Manchester invited us and made all accommodations.

The Fifth Pan-African Congress, therefore, met from 15 to 21 October, 1945, in Manchester, England, with some 200 delegates representing East and South Africa and the West Indies. Its significance lay in the fact that it took a step toward a broader movement and a real effort of the peoples of Africa and the descendants of Africa the world over to start a great march toward democracy for black folk.

At this meeting Africa was for the first time adequately represented. From the Gold Coast came Nkrumah, now Prime Minister of the first African British Dominion. With him was Ashie-Nikoi of the cocoa farmers' cooperative. From Kenya, Jomo Kenyatta; from Sierra Leone the trade union leader, Wallace Johnson; from Nigeria, Chief Coker; from the West Indies came a number of trade union leaders; from South Africa the writer, Peter Abrahams, acted as publicity director, while George Padmore was general director.

It was interesting to learn that from the original Pan-African Congress the idea had spread so that nearly every African province now had its national congress, beginning historically with the great Congress of West Africa held in 1920 just after the First Pan-African Congress in Paris. There are now national congresses in South Africa, Rhodesia, Nyasaland, Tanganyika, and Angola.

The following reports from the Fifth Pan-African Congress are of interest. I thus painted the general scene:

> In a great square Hall in Manchester in the midst of that England of the Economic Revolution where the slave trade first brought capitalism to Europe there met yesterday and today the Fifth Pan-African Congress.

As I entered the Hall there were about 100 black men present. They represented many parts of Africa: the Gambia, that oldest and smallest of English West African colonies that numbers 200,000 Negroes; Sierra Leone with 2,000,000, the Gold Coast with 500,000 and so to Nigeria with more than 20,000,000. They were mostly young men and full of enthusiasm and a certain exuberant determination. Around the walls were slogans—"Africa Arise, the long, long night is Over"; "Africa for the Africans"; "Down with the Color Bar." And then the slogans reached out—"Freedom for all Subject People"; "Oppressed Peoples of the Earth Unite"; "Down with Anti-Semitism"; and some specific demands like "Ethiopia wants outlet to the Sea"; "Arabs and Jews United against British Imperialism."

There were at the morning session, Tuesday, seven speakers. One from the Gold Coast, educated in America, Nkrumah. He demanded absolute independence and a Federation of West African Republics. Nikoi followed, chairman of the West African Delegation to the Colonial Office. He spoke with force and rhythmic eloquence, charging Great Britain with the beginnings of slavery and speaking as a representative of that Aborigines Protection Society, which obtained from Queen Victoria the dictum, "I had rather have your loyalty than your land." He was fierce in his demand: "Down with Imperialism! No Dominion Status—I want to be Free." He represents 300,000 farmers of the Gold Coast, the upper-class farmers who raise the greatest crop of cocoa in the world. He complained of the new Colonial Secretary of the Labour government, who refused to remove economic controls. He said that the West African Produce Control monopolizes the natural products and fixes prices for a mass of people whose average income is $20 a year.

Then came Annan, a worker delegate from the Gold Coast Railway Employees Union. He told how, in 1944, they had celebrated on the Gold Coast the Centenary of the Bond; that original effort at Black Democracy in West Africa, and a century after that Bond the issue on the Gold Coast is poverty—grinding poverty. He reminded his hearers that the workers must be able to live in order to vote, that the Gold Coast needed industrial development and that sacrifices were necessary if their demands were to be granted. They must be willing to live with the dockers and miners. "There is Imperialism among us Negroes, ourselves, and we must remember that we can expect no more from a British Labour Government than from a Tory Government."

Coker, Delegate of the Nigeria Trade Union Congress, was more measured in his demands. He, too, represents the cocoa farmers, but he stressed certain remedies like cooperation and planning, and believed that India's Gandhi had the remedy in nonviolence.

Then came perhaps the best-known man in West Africa, Wallace Johnson, Delegate of the Sierra Leone Trade Union Congress and of the Moslem League. He represents 10,000 organized workers and 25,000 unorganized workers, and in order to establish these unions he has spent five years in British West African prisons. Trade unionism in Africa, he said, was developed against and in spite of the Law, and they had a much harder time than unionism in Britain. He drew violent applause from the audience. "I have brought," he said, "a monster document to the Labour government. In 150 years Britain, in my country, has made but five percent of the population literate and today, instead of sending prepared students to England, they cater to reaction and complacency." He instanced the fact that in Sierra Leone, ginger, bringing 25 a ton in the open market before the War, had to be sold to the merchants for 11 a ton and after the fall of Singapore when the price rose to t 144 a ton, the black merchants got only t 30.

Downs-Thomas of Gambia spoke for the oldest West African colony and demanded the abolition of Crown Colony Government. "How," he said, "can forty different colonies in all stages of development be ruled by the Colonial Office?"

Perhaps the best and most philosophical speech was made by H. O. Davis, of the Nigerian Youth Movement. He said that the long-range program was Independence for Nigeria, but the short-range program had to meet internal hindrances like poverty, ignorance, and disease and the fact that the Negroes were unarmed; that the external hindrance was the British government itself, which would never willingly give up the colonies. The leaders must go down to the masses, and he agreed with the West African States Union that it is idiotic to think of the colonies as liabilities. If they were they never would be kept by the imperial government. Atrocities are not confined to German and Japanese prisons. They were all too common in the English prisons before the War and British democracy apparently was not for export.

Later speakers were:

Mr. Kenyatta, who covered the six territories: Somaliland, Kenya, Uganda, Tanganyika, Nyasaland and the Rhodesias. He gave an outline of the conditions under which the native peoples lived before the advent of Europeans. A picture of happy and contented peoples enjoying the common use of the land with an agricultural, pastoral, and hunting economy. He contrasted that picture with present-day conditions with a landless native people of 14,000,000, and a small minority of white Europeans forcing the natives to work at slave rates under appalling conditions. Mr. Kenyatta detailed the conditions obtaining in the territories upon which he was reporting, varying only in detail, and all displaying the characteristic pattern of imperialistic capitalism that Mr. Kenyatta condemned. He called for political independence for East Africa, and an end to racial discrimination.

Mr. George Padmore spoke on Southern Rhodesia, where there was a population of 50,000 Europeans and 2,000,000 Africans; before Bills concerning the black people could be made law, they must have the sanction of the Colonial Office. The land had been taken from the Africans and given to Europeans; the natives were then forced to work upon the farms and tobacco plantations at low wages. The Europeans wanted the three states to come together so that the laws now prevailing in Southern Rhodesia would be extended. Of Northern Rhodesia Mr. Padmore told of London and American controlled copper mines where the wages paid to colored workers amounted to 1s. 6d a day. White miners got £1 per day. Profits of the mining companies over the last sixty years averaged £10,000,000, and out of this there had been paid only about £1,500,000 in wages. Profits and income tax are paid to the Exchequer in London, the mining companies being registered in London, and taxes are paid to the country in which they are registered. Mr. Padmore spoke of the increasingly progressive element among the young colored people and called on the Congress to give all support for the aspirations and demands of the peoples of East African territories.

A final report of the Congress said:

The Fifth Pan-African Congress meeting in Manchester with 200 delegates representing sixty nations and groups of African descent finished their work today and will adjourn with a mass meeting tomorrow at Chorlton Town Hall. On Thursday and Friday complaints and appeals were heard from Ethiopia and the West Indies. Ethiopia demands the return of Eritrea and Somaliland and parts of the sea. She charges that England is occupying and proposing to keep some of the best grain lands of Ethiopia. The delegates from the West Indies, that former Empire of sugar by sugar for sugar, complained of poverty and neglect with land monopoly and low wages in the face of 100 percent increase in the cost of living. The situation brought revolutionary strikes and riots in 1937, led by Butler, Bustamente and Payne, who were promptly thrown in jail. Reforms followed. Something approaching Home Rule has been granted in Jamaica and other places, but insufficient reforms in various islands. Later, a black professor from Londonderry reported on French Africa and its rising nationalism.

This was the final resolution:

The 200 Delegates of the Fifth Pan-African Congress believe in peace. How could they do otherwise when for centuries they have been victims of violence and slavery? Yet if the world is still determined to rule mankind by force, then Africans as a last resort may have to appeal to force, in order to achieve freedom, even if force destroys them and the world.

We are determined to be free; we want education, the right to earn a decent living; the right to express our thoughts and emotions and to adopt and create forms of beauty. Without all this, we die even if we live.

We demand for black African autonomy and independence so far and no further than it is possible in this "One World" for groups and peoples to rule themselves subject to inevitable World Unity and Federation.

We are not ashamed to have been an age-long patient people; we are willing even now, to sacrifice and strive to correct our all too human faults; but we are unwilling to longer starve while doing the world's drudgery, in order to support by our poverty and ignorance a false aristocracy and a discredited imperialism. We condemn monopoly of capital and rule of private wealth and industry for private profit alone. We welcome economic democracy as the only real democracy; wherefore, we are going to complain, appeal and arraign; we are going to make the world listen to the facts of our conditions. For their betterment we are going to fight in any and every way we can.

Meantime, a greater change was taking place among American Negroes. Up until the close of the First World War, the "talented tenth" among Negroes had recognized leadership and the growing respect of the whites. But with the Depression and the New Deal, the American Negro intelligentsia began to lose ground. An economic and class differentiation took place and the race leadership began to shift to a new Negro *bourgeoisie*. Garvey,[3] the sincere but uneducated and demagogic West Indian leader, had helped this change during his career in America. He promoted an African movement, but it was purely commercial and based on no conception of African history or needs. It was American and not African, and it failed. But American Negro business expanded. Negroes began to enter white industry. Curiously enough, the propaganda of Booker T. Washington began with 1900 to change from efforts to interest Negroes in "working with the hands"; inducing him to invest in business and profit by exploitation of labor. The insurance companies, retail businesses, distribution of goods, and white-collar work of all kinds increased among Negroes. By the time the Second World War opened American Negro leadership was in the hands of a new Negro *bourgeoisie* and had left the hands of teachers, writers, and social workers. Professional men joined this black *bourgeoisie* and the Negro began to follow white American display and conspicuous expenditure.

This new leadership had no interest in Africa. It was aggressively American. The Pan-African movement lost almost all support. It was only by my hard efforts that the last Congress in Britain in 1945 got American Negro notice. After that all interest failed.

Today the American interest in Africa is almost confined to whites. African history is pursued in white institutions and white writers produce books on African while Negro authors and scholars have shied away from the subject which in the twenties and thirties was their preserve.

As big business gained in power and promoted war, what was ostensibly against Communism was really for colonial aggression in Asia and Africa.

In order to appease colored peoples, big business found it to its interest to yield ground on the color line in America. Race segregation in schools and travel was made illegal, although the law was not enforced in the former slave South. But this step toward the integration of Negroes into the American state greatly influenced American Negroes and led them to join in opposition to Communism, the Soviet Union, and socialism everywhere. While the right of the Negro to vote is still curtailed, yet it is growing in power and has to be courted. But big business dominates Negro business, including the Negro press. Negro soldiers form a considerable part of the military forces, and their integration into white units has further reconciled the American Negro to war even with colored peoples like the Koreans and Chinese.

But these fatal trends among us will not, must not, last. Leadership is arising which appreciates at its true value the great role which the Soviet Union and China are playing in the world and are destined to play. This leadership today is suffering persecution, but it will prevail.

As the world turns toward Africa as a great center of future activity and development and recognizes the ancient socialism of Africa, American Negroes, freed of their baseless fear of Communism, will again begin to turn their attention and aim their activity toward Africa. They will see how capitalistic exploitation, led by America, is exploiting and impoverishing Negroes of Africa and keeping them sick and ignorant, and thus indirectly encouraging the color line in America. They will realize how American Negroes are in position to help Africa; not only by their growing political power, but by their educational opportunities in the United States. They can, when they will, furnish technical guidance to Africa; they can give intellectual leadership working with and not for black Africa. When once the blacks of the United States, the West Indies, and Africa work and think together, the future of the black man in the modern world is safe.

NOTES

1. Du Bois examined the practicality of migration in 1904; see "The Future of the Negro Race in America," *The East and the West*, II (1904).—M.W.

2. In the preceding article, Du Bois gives a smaller figure.—M.W.

3. Du Bois's full-scale analysis of the Garvey movement can be found in "Back to Africa," *Century*, February, 1923.—M.W.

TRADITION AND INDUSTRIALIZATION

The Historic Meaning of the Plight of the Tragic Elite in Asia and Africa

RICHARD WRIGHT had a profound preoccupation with Africa and the Third World in the 1950s. As he Third World was beginning to throw off the yoke of European imperialism, it is not surprising that Wright and other black American intellectuals took African affairs under serious scrutiny. Three of his nonfiction works of that decade were devoted to that topic. "Tradition and Industrialization: The Historic Meaning of the Plight of the Tragic Elite in Asia and Africa" is the paper Wright reads at the African conference that Baldwin describes in his essay, "Princes and Powers." Wright's essay was published in his collection, *White Man Listen* (1957).

S o great a legion of ideological interests is choking the media of communication of the world today that I deem it advisable to define the terms in which I speak and for whom. In the heated, charged, and violently partisan atmosphere in which we live at this moment, all public utterances are dragged willy-nilly into the service of something or somebody. Even the most rigorously determined attitudes of objectivity and the most passionate avowals of good faith have come to be suspect. And especially is this true of the expressions of those of us who have been doomed to live and act in a tight web of racial and economic facts, facts viewed by many through eyes of political or religious interest, facts examined by millions with anxiety and even hysteria.

Knowing the suspicious, uneasy climate in which our twentieth-century lives are couched, I, as a Western man of color, strive to be as objective as I can when I seek to communicate. But, at once, you have the right to demand of me: What does being objective mean? Is it possible to speak at all today and not have the meaning of one's words construed in six different ways?

For example, he who advocates the use of mass educational techniques today can be, and usually is, accused of harboring secret Soviet sympathies, despite the fact that his advocacy of the means of mass education aims at a quick spreading of literacy so that Communism cannot take root, so that vast populations trapped in tribal or religious loyalties cannot be easily duped by self-seeking demagogues. He who urgently counsels the establishment of strong, central governments in the so-called underdeveloped countries, in the hope that those countries can quickly pull themselves out of the mire and become swiftly modernized and industrialized and thereby set upon the road to democracy, free speech, a secular state, universal suffrage, etc., can be and commonly is stigmatized as: "Well, he's no communist, *but* . . . ." He who would invoke, as sanction for experimental political action, a desire to seek the realization of the basic ideals of the Western world in terms of unorthodox and as yet untried institutional structures—instrumentalities for short-cutting long, drawn-out historical processes—as a means of constructing conditions for the creation of individual freedom, can be branded as being "emotionally unstable and having tendencies that *could* lead, therefore, to communism." He who would question, with all the good faith in the world, whether the philosophical ideas and assumptions of John Stuart Mill and John Locke are valid for all times, for all peoples, and for all countries with their vastly differing traditions and back-grounds, with the motive of psychologically freeing men's minds so that they can seek new conditions and instrumentalities for freedom, can be indicated as an enemy of democracy.

Confronted with a range of negative hostility of this sort, knowing that the society of the Western world is so frantically defensive that it would seek to impose conformity at any price, what is an honest man to do? Should he keep silent and thereby try to win a degree of dubious safety for himself? Should he endorse static defensiveness as the price of achieving his own personal security? The game isn't worth the candle, for, in doing so, he buttresses that which would eventually crush not only him, but that which would negate the very conditions of life out of which freedom can spring. In such a situation one's silence implies that one has surrendered one's intellectual faculties to fear, that one has voluntarily abdicated life itself, that one has gratuitously paralyzed one's possibilities of action. Since any and all events can be lifted by men of bad faith out of their normal contexts and projected into others and thus consequently condemned, since one's thoughts can be interpreted in terms of such extreme implications as to reduce them to absurdity or subversion, obviously a mere declaration of one's good intentions is not enough. In an all-pervading climate of intellectual evasion or dishonesty, everything becomes dishonest; suspicion subverts events and distorts their meaning; mental reservations alter the character of facts and rob them of validity and utility. In short, if good will is lacking, everything is lost and a dialogue between men becomes not only useless, but dangerous, and sometimes even incriminating.

To imagine that straight communication is no longer possible is to declare that the world we seek to defend is no longer worth defending, that the battle for human freedom is already lost. I'm assuming, however naively, that such is not quite yet the case. I cannot, of course, assume that universal good will reigns, but I have the elementary right, the bounden duty even, to assume that man, when he has the chance to speak and act without fear, still wishes to be man, that is, he harbors the dream of being a free and creative agent.

Then, first of all, let us honestly admit that there is no such thing as objectivity, no such objective fact as objectivity. Objectivity is a fabricated concept, a synthetic intellectual construction devised to enable others to know the general conditions under which one has done something, observed the world or an event in that world.

So, before proceeding to give my opinions concerning Tradition and Industrialization, I shall try to state as clearly as possible where I stand, the mental climate about me, the historic period in which I speak, and some of the elements in my environment and my own personality which propel me to communicate. The basic assumption behind all so-called objective attitudes is this: If others care to assume my mental stance and, through empathy, duplicate the atmosphere in which I speak, if they can imaginatively grasp the factors in my environment and a sense of the impulses motivating me, they will, if they are of a mind to, be able to see, more or less, what I've seen, will be capable of apprehending the same general aspects and tones of reality that comprise my world, that world that I share daily with all other men. By revealing the assumptions behind my statements, I'm striving to convert you to my outlook, to its essential humaneness, to the generality and reasonableness of my arguments.

Obviously no striving for an objective of attitude is ever complete. Tomorrow, or the day after, someone will discover some fact, some element, or a nuance that I've forgotten to take into account, and, accordingly, my attitude will have to be revised, discarded, or extended, as the case may be. Hence, there is no such thing as an absolute objectivity of attitude. The most rigorously determined attitude of objectivity is, at best, relative. We are human; we are the slaves of our assumptions, of time and circumstance; we are the victims of our passions and illusions; and the most that our critics can ask of us is this: Have you taken your passions, your illusions, your time, and your circumstances into account? That is what I am attempting to do. More than that no reasonable man of good will can demand.

First of all, my position is a split one. I'm black. I'm a man of the West. These hard facts are bound to condition, to some degree, my outlook. I see and understand the West; but I also see and understand the non- or anti-Western point of view. How is this possible? This double vision of mine stems from my being a product of Western civilization and from my racial identity, long and deeply conditioned, which is organically born of my being a product of that civilization. Being a Negro living in a white Western Christian society, I've never been allowed to blend, in a natural and healthy manner, with the culture and civilization of the West. This contradiction of being both Western and a man of color creates a psychological distance, so to speak, between me and my environment. I'm self-conscious. I admit it. Yet I feel no need to apologize for it. Hence, though Western, I'm inevitably critical of the West. Indeed, a vital element of my Westernness resides in this chronically skeptical, this irredeemably critical, outlook. I'm restless. I question not only myself, but my environment. I'm eager, urgent. And to be so seems natural, human, and good to me. Life without these qualities is inconceivable, less than human. In spite of myself, my imagination is constantly leaping ahead and trying to reshape the world I see (basing itself strictly on the materials of the world in which I live each day) toward a form in which all men could share my creative restlessness. Such an outlook breeds criticism. And my critical attitude and detachment are born of my position. I and my environment are one, but that oneness has in it, at its very core, an abiding schism. Yet I regard my position as natural, as normal, though others, that is, Western whites, anchored in tradition and habit, would have to make a most strenuous effort of imagination to grasp it.

Yet, I'm not non-Western. I'm no enemy of the West. Neither am I an Easterner. When I look out upon those vast stretches of this earth inhabited by brown, black, and yellow men—sections of the earth in which religion dominates, to the exclusion of almost everything else, the emotional and mental landscape— my reactions and attitudes are those of the West. I see both worlds from another and third point of view. (This outlook has nothing to do with any so-called third force; I'm speaking largely in historical and psychological terms).

I'm numbed and appalled when I know that millions of men in Asia and Africa assign more reality to their dead fathers than to the crying claims of their daily lives: poverty, political degradation, illness, ignorance, etc. I shiver when I learn that the infant mortality rate, say, in James Town (a slum section of Accra, the capital of the Gold Coast in British West Africa) is fifty percent in the first year of life; and, further, I'm speechless when I learn that this inhuman condition is explained by the statement, "The children did not wish to stay. Their ghost-mothers called them home." And when I hear that explanation I know that there can be no altering of social conditions in those areas until such religious rationalizations have been swept from men's minds, no matter how devoutly they are believed in or defended. Indeed, the teeming religions gripping the minds and consciousness of Asians and Africans offend me. I can conceive of no identification with such mystical visions of life that freeze millions in static degradation, no matter how emotionally satisfying such degradation seems to those who wallow in it. But, because the swarming populations in those continents are two-time victims—victims of their own religious projections and victims of western imperialism—my sympathies are unavoidably with, and unashamedly for, them. For this sympathy I offer no apology.

Yet, when I turn to face the environment that cradled and nurtured me, I experience a sense of dismaying shock, for that Western environment is soaked in and stained with the most blatant racism that the contemporary world knows. It is a racism that has almost become another kind of religion, a religion of the materially dispossessed, of the culturally disinherited. Rooted in my own disinheritedness, I know instinctively that this clinging to, and defense of, racism by Western whites are born of their psychological nakedness, of their having, through historical accident, partially thrown off the mystic cauls of Asia and Africa that once too blinded and dazed them. A deeply conscious victim of white racism could even be strangely moved to compassion for that white man who, having lost his mystic vision of a stern Father God, a dazzling Virgin, and a Dying Son who promises to succor him after death, settles upon racism! What a poor substitute! What a shabby, vile, and cheap home the white heart finds when it seeks shelter in racism! One would think that sheer pride would deter Western whites from such emotional debasement!

I stand, therefore, mentally and emotionally looking in both directions, being claimed by a negative identification on one side, and being excluded by a feeling of repulsion on the other.

Since I'm detached from, because of racial conditions, the West, why do I bother to call myself Western at all? What is it that prompts me to make an identification with the West despite the contradiction involved? The fact is that I really have no choice in the matter. Historical forces more powerful than I am have shaped me as a Westerner. I have not consciously elected to be a Westerner; I have been made into a Westerner. Long before I had the freedom to choose, I was molded a Westerner. It began in childhood. And the process continues.

Hence, standing shoulder to shoulder with the Western white man, speaking his tongue, sharing his culture, participating in the common efforts of the Western community, I say frankly to that white man: "I'm Western, just as Western as you are, maybe more; but I don't completely agree with you."

What do I mean, then, when I say that I'm Western? I shall try to define what the term means to me. I shan't here, now, try to define what being Western means to all Westerners. I shall confine my definition only to that aspect of the West with which I identify, that aspect that makes me feel, act, and live Western.

The content of my westernness resides fundamentally, I feel, in my secular outlook upon life. I believe in a separation of Church and State. I believe that the State possesses a value in and for itself. I feel that man—just sheer brute man, just as he is—has a meaning and value over and above all sanctions or mandates from mystical powers, either on high or from below. I am convinced that the humble, fragile dignity of man, buttressed by a tough-souled pragmatism, implemented by methods of trial and error, can sufficiently sustain and nourish human life, can endow it with ample and durable meaning. I believe that all ideas have a right to circulate in the marketplace without restriction. I believe that all men should have the right to have their say without fear of the political "powers that be," without having to dread the punitive measures or the threat of invisible forces which some castes of men claim as their special domain—men such as priests and churchmen. (My own position compels me to grant those priests and churchmen the right to have their say, but not at the expense of having my right to be heard annulled.) I believe that art has its own autonomy, a self-sufficiency that extends beyond, and independent of, the spheres of political or priestly power or sanction. I feel that science exists without any a priori or metaphysical assumptions. I feel that human personality is an end in and for itself. In short, I believe that man, for good or ill, is his own ruler, his own sovereign, his own keeper. I hold human freedom as a supreme right and good for all men, my conception of freedom being the right of all men to exercise their natural and acquired powers as long as the exercise of those powers does not hinder others from doing the same.

These are my assumptions, my values, my morality, if you insist upon that word. Yet I hold these values at a time in history when they are threatened. I stand in the middle of that most fateful of all the world's centuries: the twentieth century. Nuclear energy, the center of the sun, is in the hands of men. In most of the land mass of Asia and Africa the traditional and customary class relations of feudal, capitalistic societies have been altered, frequently brutally shattered, by murder and terror. Most of the governments of the earth today rule, by one pretext or another, by open or concealed pressure upon the individual, by black lists, intimidation, fiat, secret police, and machine guns. Among intellectual circles the globe over the desperate question has been raised: "What is man?" In the East as in the West, wealth and the means of production have been taken out of private hands, families, clans, and placed at the disposal of committees and state bureaucrats. The consciousness of most men on earth is filled with a sense of shame, of humiliation, of memories of past servitude and degradation—and a sense of fear that that condition of servitude and degradation will return. The future for most men is an apprehensive void which has created the feeling that it has to be impetuously, impulsively filled, given a new content at all costs. With the freeing of Asia and most of Africa from Western rule, more active and unbridled religion now foments and agitates the minds and emotions of men than at any time since 1455! Man's world today lies in the pythonlike coils of vast irrational forces which he cannot control. This is the mental climate out of which I speak, a climate that tones my being and pitches consciousness on a certain plane of tension. These are the conditions under which I speak, conditions that condition me.

Now, the above assumptions and facts would and do color my view of history, that record of the rise and fall of traditions and religions. All of those past historical forces which have, accidentally or intentionally, helped to create the basis of freedom in human life, I extol, revere and count as my fervent allies. Those conditions of life and of history which thwart, threaten and degrade the values and assumptions I've listed, I reject and consider harmful, something to be doggedly resisted.

Now, I'm aware that to some tender, sensitive minds such a decalogue of beliefs is chilling, arid, almost inhuman. And especially is this true of those multitudes inhabiting the dense, artistically cluttered Catholic countries of present-day Europe. To a richly endowed temperament such a declaration is akin to an invitation to empty out all the precious values of the past; indeed, to many millions such a declaration smacks of an attack upon what they have been taught to consider and venerate as civilization itself. The emotionally thin-skinned cannot imagine, even in the middle of our twentieth century, a world without external emotional props to keep them buttressed to a stance of constant meaning and justification, a world filled with overpowering mother and father and child images to anchor them in emotional security, to keep a sense of the warm, intimate, sustaining influence of the family alive. And I can readily conceive of such temperaments willing to condemn my attitude as being barbarian, willful, or perverse. What such temperaments do not realize is that my decalogue of beliefs does not imply that I've turned my back in scorn upon the past of mankind in so crude or abrupt a manner as they feel or think. Men who can slough off the beautiful mythologies, the enthralling configurations of external ceremonies, manners, and codes of the past are not necessarily unacquainted with, or unappreciative of, them; they have *interiorized* them, have reduced them to mental traits, psychological problems. I know, however, that such a fact is small comfort to those who love the past, who long to be caught up in rituals that induce blissful self-forgetfulness, and who would find the meaning of their lives in them. I confess frankly that I cannot solve this problem for everybody; I state further that it is my profound conviction that emotional independence is a clear and distinct human advance, a gain for all mankind and, if that gain and advance seem inhuman, there is nothing that can rationally be done about it. Freedom needs no apology.

Naturally, a man holding such values will view history in a rather novel light. How do these values compel me to regard the claims of Western imperialism? What virtue or evil do I assign to the overrunning of Asia and Africa by Western Christian white men? What about color prejudice? What about the undeniable technical and industrial power and superiority of the white West? How do I feel about the white man's vaunted claim—and I'm a product, reluctant, to be sure, of that white man's culture and civilization—that he has been called by his God to rule the world and to have all overriding considerations over the rest of mankind, that is, colored men?

And, since the Christian religion, by and large, has tacitly endorsed racism by the nature of its past historical spread and its present sway, how do I view that religion whose irrational core can propel it toward such ends, whether that religion be in Europe, Asia, or Africa? And, since tradition is generally but forms of frozen or congealed religion, how do I regard tradition?

I've tried to lead you to my angle of vision slowly, step by step, keeping nothing back. If I insist over and over again upon the personal perspective, it is because my weighing of external facts is bound organically with that personal perspective. My point of view is a Western one, but a Western one that conflicts at several vital points with the present, dominant outlook of the West. Am I ahead of or behind the West? My personal judgment is that I'm ahead. And I do not say that boastfully; such a judgment is implied by the very nature of those Western values that I hold dear.

Let me dig deeper into my personal position. I was born a black Protestant in that most racist of all the American states: Mississippi. I lived my childhood under a racial code, brutal and bloody, that white men proclaimed was ordained of God, said was made mandatory by the nature of their religion. Naturally, I rejected that religion and would reject any religion which prescribes for me an inferior position in life; I reject that tradition and any tradition which proscribes my humanity. And, since the very beginnings of my life on this earth were couched in this contradiction, I became passionately curious as to why Christians felt it imperative to practice such wholesale denials of humanity. My seeking carried me back to a crucial point in Western history where a clearly enunciated policy on the part of the Church spelt my and others' doom. In 1455 the Pope divided the world between Spain and Portugal and decreed that those two nations had not only the right, but the consecrated duty of converting or enslaving all infidels. Now, it just so happened that at that time all the infidels, from the white Western Christian point of view, were in Asia, Africa, the many islands of the Atlantic, the Pacific, and the then unknown Americas—and it just so happened that they were all people of color.

Further reading of history brought me abreast of a strong countercurrent of opposition to that Church that had imperialistically condemned all colored mankind. When I discovered that John Calvin and Martin Luther were stalwart rebels against the domination of a church that had condemned and damned the majority of the human race, I felt that the impulses, however confused, animating them were moving in the direction of a fuller concept of human dignity and freedom. But the Protestantism of Calvin and Luther did not go far enough; they underestimated the nature of the revolution they were trying to make. Their fight against the dead weight of tradition was partial, limited. Racism was historically and circumstantially embedded in their rejection of the claims of the Church that they sought to defeat. Calvin and Luther strove for freedom, but it was inevitably and inescapably only for their kind, that is, European whites. So, while recognizing the positive but limited nature of Calvin's and Luther's contribution, I had to look elsewhere for a concept of man that would not do violence to my own concept of, and feeling for, life.

What did magnetize me toward the emotional polarizations of Calvin and Luther was the curious psychological strength that they unknowingly possessed, a strength that propelled them, however clumsily, toward the goal of emotional independence. These two bold European insurgents had begun, though they called it by another name, a stupendous *introjection* of the religious symbols by which the men of their time lived. They were proponents of that tide that was moving from simple, naive credence toward self-skepticism, from a state of sensual slavery to the sights, sounds, and colors of the external world toward a stance of detachment. By some quirk of mental strength, they felt stronger than their contemporaries and could doubt and even doff the panoply of religious rituals and ceremonies and could either live without much of them or could, gropingly to be sure, stand psychologically alone to an amazing degree. In the lives of Calvin and Luther there had begun a dual process: on one hand, the emptying of human consciousness of its ancient, infantile, subjective accretions, and, on the other, a denuding of an anthropocentric world of the poetry that man had projected upon it. A two-way doubt of the world and of man's own self had set in, and this putting man and his world in question would not pause until it had enthroned itself in a new consciousness. Western man was taking that first step toward a new outlook that would not terminate until it had flowered in the bleak stretches of an undiscovered America which, ironically, was peopled by red-skinned "savages" who could not dream of doubting their own emotions or questioning the world that impinged upon their sensibilities. (The partially liberated Pilgrims slew those religiously captured "savages"!) Not understanding the implications of the needs prompting them, Calvin and Luther did not realize that what they were trying to do had already been neatly, clearly, and heroically done before by the brave and brooding Greeks who, overwhelmed by contradictory experiences and the antinomic currents of their own passions, had lifted their dazed eyes toward an empty heaven and uttered those bitterly tragic words that were to become the motto of abandoned Western man:

"What do we do now?"

The Protestant is a queer animal who has never fully understood himself, has never guessed that he is an abortive freeman, an issue of historical birth that never quite came to full life. It has been conveniently forgotten that the Protestant is a product and a result of *oppression*, which might well account for his inability to latch directly onto the Greek heritage and thereby save himself a lot of useless and stupid thrashing about in history. Stripped by the heavy, intolerant conditions of Catholic rule of much of his superfluous emotional baggage, the emerging Protestant rebel, harassed by his enemies and haunted by his own guilt, was doomed to *react* rather than *act*, to *protest* rather than *affirm*, never fully grasping what was motivating him until he had been swept by history so far beyond his original problem that he had forgotten its initial content of meaning. The Protestant was being called to a goal the terrifying nature of which he had neither the courage nor the strength to see or understand. The Protestant is the brave blind man cursed by destiny with a burden which he has not the inner grace to accept wholeheartedly.

The ultimate consequences of Calvin's and Luther's rebellious doctrines and seditious actions, hatched and bred in emotional confusion, unwittingly created the soil out of which grew something that Calvin and Luther did not dream of. (And this is not the last time that I shall call your attention to an odd characteristic of the Western world; the men of the West seem prone in their actions to achieve results that contradict their motives. They have a genius for calling things by wrong names; they seek to save souls and become involved in murder; they attempt to enthrone God as an absolute and they achieve the establishment of the prerequisites of science and atheistic thought; they seem wedded to a terribly naive and childlike outlook upon the world and themselves, and they are filled with consternation when their actions produce results that they did not foresee.) Determined to plant the religious impulse in each individual's heart, declaring that each man could stand face to face with God, Calvin and Luther blindly let loose mental and emotional forces which, in turn, caused a vast revolution in the social, cultural, governmental, and economic conditions under which Western man lived—a revolution that finally negated their own racial attitudes! The first and foremost of these conditions were the guaranteeing of individual conscience and judgment, an act which loosened, to a degree, the men of Europe from custom and tradition, from the dead hand of the past, evoking a sense of future expectation, infinitely widening man's entire horizon. And yet this was achieved by accident! That's the irony of it. Calvin and Luther, preoccupied with metaphysical notions, banished dread from men's minds and allowed them to develop that courageous emotional strength which sanctioned and spurred the amassing of a vast heap of positive fact relating to daily reality. As a result of Calvin's and Luther's heresy, man began to get a grip upon his external environment. Science and industry were born and, through their rapid growth, each enriched the other and nullified the past notions of social structures, negated norms of nobility, of tradition, of priestly values, and fostered new social classes, new occupations, new experiences, new structures of government, new pleasures, hungers, dreams, in short, a whole new and unheard of universe. A Church world was transformed into a worldly world, any man's world, a world in which even black, brown, and yellow men could have the possibility to live and breathe.

Yet, while living with these facts, Europeans still believed in and practiced a racism that the very logic of the world they were creating told them was irrational and insane!

Buttressed by their belief that their God had entrusted the earth into their

keeping, drunk with power and possibility, waxing rich through trade in commodi-
ties, human and nonhuman, with awesome naval and merchant marines at their
disposal, their countries filled with human debris anxious for any adventures,
psychologically armed with new facts, white Western Christian civilization, with a
long, slow, and bloody explosion, hurled itself upon the sprawling masses of human-
ity in Asia and Africa.[1]

Perhaps now you'll expect me to pause and begin a vehement and moral
denunciation of Europe. No. The facts are complex. In that process of Europe's
overrunning of the rest of mankind a most bewildering mixture of motives, means,
and ends took place. White men, spurred by religious and areligious motives—that
is, to save the souls of a billion or so heathens and to receive the material blessings
of God while doing so—entered areas of the earth where religion ruled with an
indigenous absoluteness that did not even obtain in Europe.

Are we here confronted with a simple picture of virtue triumphing over villainy,
of right over wrong, of the superior over the inferior, of the biologically fit blond
beast over biologically botched brown, yellow, and black men? That is what Europe
felt about it. But I do not think that that is a true picture of what really happened.
Again I call your attention to the proneness of white Europe, under the influence
of a strident, romantic individualism, to do one thing and call that thing by a name
that no one but itself could accept or recognize.

What, then, happened? Irrationalism met irrationalism. The irrationalism of
Europe met the irrationalism of Asia and Africa, and the resulting confusion has
yet to be unraveled and understood. Europe called her adventure imperialism, the
spread of civilization, missions of glory, of service, of destiny even. Asians and
Africans called it colonization, blood-sucking, murder, butchery, slavery. There is
no doubt that both sides had some measure of truth in their claims. But I state that
neither side quite knew what was happening and neither side was conscious of the
real process that was taking place. The truth lay beyond the blurred ken of both the
European and his Asian and African victim.

I have stated publicly, on more than one occasion, that the economic spoils
of European imperialism do not bulk so large or important to me. I know that today
it is the fashion to list the long and many economic advantages that Europe gained
from its brutal and bloody impact upon hundreds of millions of Asians and Africans.
The past fifty years have created a sprawling literature of the fact that the ownership
of colonies paid princely dividends. I have no doubt of it. Yet that fact does not
impress me as much as still another and more obscure and more important fact.
What rivets my attention in this clash of East and West is that an irrational western
world helped, unconsciously and unintentionally to be sure, to smash the irrational
ties of religion and custom and tradition in Asia and Africa. THIS, IN MY OPINION,
IS THE CENTRAL HISTORIC FACT! The European said that he was saving souls, yet he
kept himself at a distance from the brown, black, and yellow skins that housed the
souls that he claimed that he so loved and so badly wanted to save. Thank the white
man's God for that bit of racial and color stupidity! His liberating effect upon Asia
and Africa would not have been so thorough had he been more human.

Yes, there were a few shrewd Europeans who wanted the natives to remain untouched, who wished to see what they called the "nobility" of the black, brown, and yellow lives remain intact. The more backward and outlandish the native was, the more the European loved him. This attitude can be boiled down to one simple wish: The imperialist wanted the natives to sleep on in their beautifully poetic dreams so that the ruling of them could be more easily done. They devised systems of administration called "indirect rule," "assimilation," "gradual constitutional government," etc., but they all meant one simple thing; a white man's military peace, a white man's political order, and a white man's free trade, whether that trade involved human bodies or tin or oil.

Again, I say that I do not denounce this. Had even the white West known what it was really doing, it could not have done a better job of beginning to launch the liberation of the masses of Asia and Africa from their age-old traditions.

Being ignorant of what they were really doing, the men of Europe failed to fill the void that they were creating in the very heart of mankind, thereby compounding their strange historical felony.

There are Europeans today who look longingly and soulfully at the situation developing in the world and say: "But, really, we love 'em. We are friends of theirs!" To attitudes like that I can only say: "My friends, look again. Examine the heritage you left behind. Read the literature that your fathers and your fathers' fathers wrote about those natives. Your fathers were naive but honest men."

How many souls did Europe save? To ask that question is to make one laugh! Europe was tendering to the great body of mankind a precious gift which she, in her blindness and ignorance, in her historical shortsightedness, was not generous enough to give her own people! Today, a *knowing* black, brown, or yellow man can say:

"Thank you, Mr. White Man, for freeing me from the rot of my irrational traditions and customs, though you are still the victim of your own irrational customs and traditions!"

There was a boon wrapped in that gift of brutality that the white West showered upon Asia and Africa. Over the centuries, meticulously, the white men took the sons and daughters of the chiefs and of the noble houses of Asia and Africa and instilled in them the ideas of the West so the eventual Westernized Asian and African products could become their collaborators. Yet they had no thought of how those Westernized Asians and Africans would fare when cast, like fishes out of water, back into their poetic cultures. (These unemployed Asians and Africans eventually became national revolutionaries, of course!) Shorn of all deep-seated faiths, these westernized Asians and Africans had to sink or swim with no guides, no counsel. Over and above this, the Europeans launched vast industrial enterprises in almost all of the lands that they controlled, vast enterprises that wrought profound alterations in the Asian-African ways of life and thought. *In sum, white Europeans set off a more deep-going and sudden revolution in Asia and Africa than had ever obtained in all of the history of Europe.* And they did this with supreme confidence. On one occasion Christian English gentlemen chartered a royal company for one thousand years to buy and sell black slaves! Oh, what hope they had!

I declare that merely rational motives could not have sustained the white men who damaged and destroyed the ancient Asian-African cultures and social structures; they had perforce to believe that they were the tools of cosmic powers, that they were executing the will of God, or else they would not have had the cruel daring to try to harness the body of colored mankind into their personal service. The sheer magnitude of their depredations and subjugations ought to have given them pause, but it never did to any effective degree. Only a blind and ignorant militancy could have sustained such insane ventures, such outlandish dreams. Indeed, one could say that it was precisely because the white Westerner had partially lost his rooting in his own culture that he could remain so insensitive to the dangerous unleashing of human forces of so vast and catastrophic a sweep. Had he been more at home in his own world of values, sheer prudence would have made him quail before the earth-shaking human energies which he so rashly and diligently cut loose from their moorings.

Today the intelligent sons and daughters of the old-time European freebooters, despoilers, and imperial pirates tremble with moral consternation at what their forefathers did. Says Gunnar Myrdal, in his *An International Economy*, page 168 (Harper and Brothers: New York, 1956):

> The horrible vision often enters my mind of the ultimate results of our continuing and rapidly speeding up the practice, well established in some countries during the era of colonialism, of tossing together ever bigger crowds of illiterate proletarians—these new proletariats being even more uprooted than they were in the stagnant villages where they lived in the remnants of some culture and some established mores.

Who *took* here? Who *gave*? It is too complicated a process to admit of such simple questions. But the Europeans naively called it soul-saving, money-making, modern administration, missions of civilization, Pax Britannica, and a host of other equally quaint appellations. History is a strange story. Men enact history with one set of motives and the consequences that flow from such motivated actions often have nothing whatsoever to do with such motives. What irony will history reveal when those pages of Europe's domination of Asia and Africa are finally and honestly written! That history will depict a ghastly racial tragedy; it will expose a blind spot on the part of white Westerners that will make those who read that history laugh with a sob in their throats. The white Western world, until relatively recently the most secular and free part of the earth—with a secularity and freedom that was the secret of its power (science and industry)—labored unconsciously and tenaciously for five hundred years to make Asia and Africa (that is, the elite in those areas) more secular-minded than the West!

In the minds of hundreds of millions of Asians and Africans the traditions of their lives have been psychologically condemned beyond recall. Hundreds of millions live uneasily with beliefs of which they have been made ashamed. I say, "Bravo!" for that clumsy and cruel deed. Not to the motives, mind you, behind those deeds, motives which were all too often ignoble and base. But I do say "Bravo!" to the consequences of Western plundering, a plundering that created the conditions for the possible rise of rational societies for the greater majority of mankind.

But enough of ironic comparisons. Where do we stand today? That part of the heritage of the West that I value—man stripped of the past and free for the future—has now been established as lonely bridgeheads in Asia and Africa in the form of a Western-educated elite, an elite that is more Western, in most cases, than the West. Tragic and lonely and all too often misunderstood are these men of the Asian-African elite. The West hates and fears that elite, and I must, to be honest, say that the instincts of the West that prompt that hate and fear are, on the whole, correct. For this elite in Asia and Africa constitutes islands of free men, the FREEST MEN IN ALL THE WORLD TODAY. They stand poised, nervous, straining at the leash, ready to go, with no weight of the dead past clouding their minds, no fears of foolish customs benumbing their consciousness, eager to build industrial civilizations. What does this mean? It means that the spirit of the Enlightenment, of the Reformation, which made Europe great, now has a chance to be extended to all mankind! A part of the non-West is now akin to a part of the West. East and West have become compounded. The partial overcoming of the forces of tradition and oppressive religions in Europe resulted, in a round-about manner, in a partial overcoming of tradition and religion in decisive parts of Asia and Africa. The unspoken assumption in this history has been: WHAT IS GOOD FOR EUROPE IS GOOD FOR ALL MANKIND! I say: So be it.

I approve of what has happened. My only regret is that Europe could not have done what she did in a deliberate and intentional manner, could not have planned it as a global project. My wholehearted admiration would have gone out to the spirit of a Europe that had had the imagination to have launched this mighty revolution out of the generosity of its heart, out of a sense of lofty responsibility. Europe could then stand proudly before all the world and say: "Look at what we accomplished! We remade man in our image! Look at the new form of life that we brought into being!" And I'm sure that had that happened, the majority of mankind would have been Western in a sense that no atom or hydrogen bombs can make a man Western. But, alas, that chance, that rare and noble opportunity, is gone forever. Europe missed the boat.

How can the spirit of the Enlightenment and the Reformation be extended now to all men? How can this accidental boon be made global in effect? That is the task that history now imposes upon us. Can a way be found, purged of racism and profits, to melt the rational areas and rational personnel of Europe with those of Asia and Africa? How can the curtains of race, color, religion, and tradition—all of which hamper man's mastery of his environment—be collectively rolled back by free men of the West and non-West? Is this a utopian dream? Is this mere wishing? No. It is more drastic than that. The nations of Asia and Africa and Europe contain too much of the forces of the irrational for anyone to think that the future will take care of itself. The islands of the rational in the East are too tenuously held to permit of optimism. And the same is true of Europe. (We have but to recall reading of ideas to "burn up entire continents" to doff our illusions.) The truth is that our world—a world for all men, black, brown, yellow, and white—will either be all rational or totally irrational. For better or worse, it will eventually be one world.

How can these rational regions of the world be maintained? How can the pragmatically useful be made triumphant? Does this entail a surrender of the hard-bought national freedoms on the part of non-Western nations? I'm convinced that that will not happen, for these Asian and African nations, led by Western-educated leaders, love their freedom as much as the west loves its own. They have had to struggle and die for their freedom and they value it passionately. It is unthinkable that they, so recently freed from color and class domination of the West, would voluntarily surrender their sovereignty. Let me state the problem upside down. What Western nation would dream of abdicating its sovereignty and collaborating with powers that once so recently ruled them in the name of interests that were not their own—powers that created a vast literature of hate against them? Such an act would be irrational in the extreme. And the Western-educated leaders of non-Western nations are filled with too much distrust of an imperial-minded West to permit of any voluntary relinquishing of their control over their destinies.

Is there no alternative? *Must* there be a victorious East or a victorious West? If one or the other must win completely, then the fragile values won so blindly and accidentally and at so great a cost and sacrifice will be lost for us all. Where is the crux of this matter? Who is to act first? Who *should* act first? The burden of action rests, I say, with the West. For it was the West, however naively, that launched this vast historical process of the transformation of mankind. And of what must the action of the West consist? The West must aid and, yes, abet the delicate and tragic elite in Asia and Africa to establish rational areas of living. THE WEST, IN ORDER TO KEEP BEING WESTERN, FREE, AND SOMEWHAT RATIONAL, MUST BE PREPARED TO ACCORD TO THE ELITE OF ASIA AND AFRICA A FREEDOM WHICH IT ITSELF NEVER PERMITTED IN ITS OWN DOMAIN. THE ASIAN AND AFRICAN ELITE MUST BE GIVEN ITS HEAD! The West must perform an act of faith and do this. Such a mode of action has long been implied in the very nature of the ideas which the West has instilled into that Asian-African elite. The West must trust that part of itself that it has thrust, however blunderingly, into Asia and Africa. Nkrumah, Nasser, Sukarno, and Nehru, and the Western-educated heads of these newly created national states, must be given *carte blanche* to modernize their lands without overlordship of the West, and we must understand the methods that they will feel compelled to use.

Never, you will say. That is impossible, you will declare. Oh, I'm asking a hard thing and I know it. I'm Western, remember, and I know how horribly implausible my words sound to Westerners so used to issuing orders and having those orders obeyed at gun point. But what rational recourse does the West possess other than this? None.

If the West cannot do this, it means that the West does not believe in itself, does not trust the ideas which it has cast into the world. Yes, Sukarno, Nehru, Nasser and others will necessarily use quasi-dictatorial methods to hasten the process of social evolution and to establish order in their lands—lands which were left spiritual voids by a too-long Western occupation and domination. Why pretend to be shocked at this? You would do the same if you were in their place. You have done it in the West over and over again. You do it in every war you fight, in every crisis, political or economic, you have. And don't you feel and know that, as soon as order has been established by your Western-educated leaders, they will, in order to be powerful, surrender the personal power that they have had to wield?[2]

Let us recognize what our common problem really is. Let us rethink what the issue is. This problem is vast and complicated. Merely to grasp it takes an act of the imagination. This problem, though it has racial overtones, is not racial. Though it has religious aspects, it is not religious. Though it has strong economic motives, it is not wholly economic. And though political action will, no doubt, constitute the main means, the *modus operandi*, of its solution, the problem is not basically political.

The problem is freedom. How can Asians and Africans be free of their stultifying traditions and customs and become industrialized, and powerful, if you like, like the West?

I say that the West cannot ask the elite of Asia and Africa, even though educated in the West, to copy or ape what has happened in the West. Why? Because the West has never really been honest with itself about how it overcame its own traditions and blinding customs.

Let us look at some examples of Western interpretation of its own history. A Civil War was fought in America and American school children are taught that it was to free the black slaves. It was not. It was to establish a republic, to create conditions of economic freedom, to clear the ground for the launching of an industrial society. (Naturally, slavery had to go in such a situation. I'm emphasizing the positive historic aspects, not the negative and inevitable ones!) The French fought a long and bloody Revolution and French school children are taught that it was for Liberty, Equality, and Fraternity. Yet we know that it was for the right of a middle class to think, to buy and sell, to enable men with talent to rise in their careers, and to push back (which was inevitable and implied) the power of the Church and the nobility. The English, being more unintentionally forthright than others, never made much bones about the fact that the freedom that they fought for was a freedom of trade.

Do these misinterpretations of Western history by the West negate the power and net historical gains of the Western world? No. It is not what the West said it did, but what the results really were that count in the long run.

Why have I raised these points of western contradictions? Because, when non-Westerners, having the advantage of seeing more clearly—being psychologically *outside* of the West—what the West did, and when non-Westerners seek to travel that same road, the West raises strong objections, moral ones. I've had a white Westerner tell me: "You know, we must stay in Africa to protect the naked black natives. If we leave, the blacks we have educated will practice fascism against their own people." So this man was in a position to endorse the shooting down of a black elite because that black elite wanted to impose conditions relating to the control of imports and exports, something which his country practiced every day with hordes of armed policemen to enforce the laws regulating imports and exports!

The same objections are leveled against Nkrumah in the Gold Coast, against Sukarno in Indonesia, against Nasser in Egypt, against Nehru in India. Wise Westerners would insist that stern measures be taken by the elite of Asia and Africa to overcome the irrational forces of racism, superstition, etc. But if a selfish West hamstrings the elite of Asia and Africa, distrusts their motives, a spirit of absolutism will rise in Asia and Africa and will provoke a spirit of counterabsolutism in the West. In case that happens, all will be lost. We shall all, Asia and Africa as well as Europe, be thrown back into an age of racial and religious wars, and the precious heritage—the freedom of speech, the secular state, the independent personality, the autonomy of science—which is not Western or Eastern, but human, will be snuffed out of the minds of men.

The problem is freedom from a dead past. And freedom to build a rational future. How much are we willing to risk for freedom? I say let us risk everything. Freedom begets freedom. Europe, I say to you before it is too late: Let the Africans and Asians whom you have educated in Europe have their freedom, or you will lose your own in trying to keep freedom from them.

But how can this be done? Have we any recent precedent for such procedure? Is my suggestion outlandish? Unheard of? No. A ready answer and a vivid example are close at hand. A scant ten years ago we concluded a tragically desperate and costly war in Europe to beat back the engulfing tides of an irrational fascism. During those tense and eventful days I recall hearing Winston Churchill make this appeal to the Americans, when Britain was hard-pressed by hordes of German and Italian fascists:

"Give us the tools and we'll finish the job."

Today I say to the white men of Europe:

"You have, however misguidedly, trained and educated an elite in Africa and Asia. You have implanted in their hearts the hunger for freedom and rationality. Now this elite of yours—your children, one might say—is hard-pressed by hunger, disease, poverty, by stagnant economic conditions, by unbalanced class structures of their societies, by surging tides of racial shame, by oppressive and irrational tribal religions. You men of Europe made an abortive beginning to solve that problem. You failed. Now, I say to you: Men of Europe, give that elite the tools and let it finish that job!"

FREEDOM IS INDIVISIBLE.

NOTES

1. *See* The Psychological Reactions of Oppressed People.

2. Here is a paradox: Nehru is as powerful as an emperor; Nkrumah is a *de facto* dictator; yet both men are staunch democrats and are using their vast personal power to sponsor measures that will undermine their "cult of the personality"! The key to their motives is that they seek power not for themselves, but for their people!

SÉKOU TOURÉ

A New Kind of Leader

HOYT FULLER (1927–1981), a native of Detroit, was an editor, writer, teacher, and one of the leading lights of the Black Aesthetic Movement in the late sixties and early seventies. Among the magazines he edited were *Black World* and *First World*. This essay on Guinea president Sékou Touré appeared in Fuller's *Journey to Africa*, which was published in 1971 by Third World Press.

Thus the white European mind has worked, and worked the more feverishly because Africa is the Land of the Twentieth Century.

—W. E. B. Du Bois

Political power today is but the weapon to force economic power. Tomorrow, it may give us spiritual vision and artistic sensibility. Today, it gives us or tries to give us bread and butter, and those classes or nations or races who are without it starve, and starvation is the weapon of the white world to reduce them to slavery.

—W. E. B. Du Bois

The reception room, small and unassuming for a presidential palace, was also sticky hot. Somewhere behind a divan the motor of an air-conditioning unit whirred without wafting a breeze or dispelling the thickening odor of human sweat.

Across from me, the prim, dacron-suited emissary from the Israeli Embassy at Accra wiggled and gasped, flashing a miserable smile in a futile effort to disguise his utter misery. The sun-browned, shirt-sleeved Frenchmen in the room watched him squirm with malicious delight. They were old hands at the discomforts of Africa. They could take it.

Around the room, a waiting African occasionally glanced at the diplomat, sometimes with sympathy, sometimes with suspicion. A lean African in dandy-bright black and white shoes leaned forward and spoke. "Why don't you take your coat off?" he asked in French.

The diplomat knew only a few words of French and did not understand. He smiled dumbly at the African and appealed to me. I told him what the African had suggested. It was unthinkable. "No, I have an appointment at four o'clock with President Touré," he explained. "It's nearly four now."

But at four o'clock one of the uniformed palace guards who act as pages stepped in and read another name from a reception slip. A muscular young African in shorts jumped up and bounded to the door, following the guard into the verandah and up the stairs to the president's suite.

The diplomat frowned and, in an elaborate gesture that punctuated his outrage, raised his arm and regarded his watch.

Before the guard finally came in and read the diplomat's name more than a half hour later, two other Africans had been summoned from the room to interviews with their president. They had been waiting longer.

While the diplomat—perhaps not unduly—was raw with fury and probably gravely humiliated, no slight was intended. The incident served to point up some of the crippling inadequacies besetting the six-month-old Republic of Guinea.

The swaddling nation has only one ambassador-at-large (able and youthful Sorbonne graduate Diallo Telli) to receive and entertain visiting diplomats, and he is often representing the country elsewhere. The palace's two English-speaking aides, who could have assisted the diplomat, are usually neck-deep in interpretative work.

The Secretary of State, suave, granite-hard Fodé Cissé, must be as breathlessly busy—if not as widely traveled—as John Foster Dulles at the height of the American's world-girdling pursuit of his controversial foreign policy.

But more than anything else, the spectacle of a foreign diplomat taking his turn in line with ordinary citizens is indicative of the revolutionary personality in Guinea's presidential palace. For, even with adequate facilities and assistance, there remains the possibility that Sékou Touré would have received callers as they came.

In understanding Sékou Touré, it is better to realize at the offset that he is something absolutely new in world leaders and on the African scene. In the first place, at 37, he is perhaps the youngest chief of a non-monarchial member of the United Nations. He is also the only one of Africa's glittering galaxy of black leaders without a formal university education.

And, as president of the French West Africa–wide, 700,000-strong Union of Black African Workers (Union Générale des Travailleurs de l'Afrique Noire), he is the only national leader in the world who is also chief of a powerful international labor union.

American and European journalists like to compare Touré with Kwame Nkrumah, president of Guinea's sister-nation Ghana a few hundred miles down the Atlantic Coast. But, apart from their color and their mutual aim in asserting the black man's claim to a decisive voice in the destiny of Africa, there are few similarities between them.

Much is made of the legend that Touré is grandson of the mighty Almany

Samory Touré, the last of the Malinké warriors who waged valiant but futile war against the French conquerors of Guinea. Touré is noncommittal to the point of evasiveness about this illustrious chapter in his ancestry, but he readily admits the more pedestrian fact that he was born to peasant parents in the village of Faranah in 1922.

He studied at the École Coranique, the Moslem training school, and at primary and technical schools in Kankan and Conakry, the capital. Whatever other academic education he received was absorbed through independent reading and correspondence courses from Paris.

The practical education that catapulted Touré into the arena of politics began with his first important job as a postal and telegraph worker in 1941. He learned about union organizing and the politics of labor, the most bare-knuckled and savage of the breed.

But Sékou Touré is the hard-muscled, iron-nerved type who thrives on the difficult. With characteristic shrewdness and skill, he soon rose to the job of general secretary of the postal and telegraph union. After that, he never stopped rising. When he was voted to the top position in the French West African labor movement last January, he climaxed a steady advance of labor jobs that—in the past 15 years—covered virtually every important labor post in the French West African territories.

The American and European press has also made much of Touré's Marxist orientation. Inevitably, in his rise to power in conjunction with France's then Communist-dominated General Confederation of Labor, he was associated with Communists. He was even courted by them and packed off to a series of conferences in Warsaw and Prague. But, while asserting an adherence to Marxism, Touré denies he is a Communist.

"It seems to have become the custom to say that all governments that modify their economic conditions and the social and cultural systems imposed on them by colonialism are inspired by Marxism," Touré said. "The political unity of Guinea is no more the consequence of Marxism than is the independence of our country.

"It is possible that certain forms of Marxist organization respond best to the particular conditions of underdeveloped countries. It is even possible that certain structures of inspiration derived from Marxist conception respond better than all the others to the given realities of underdeveloped countries which are determined to overcome their enormous backwardness. But this is not the same as putting our people to the service of one philosophy or the other."

Dynamic is a puny word to describe the husky, handsome, hard-driving young head of Africa's newest independent nation, but it is more apt than any other. It is his extraordinary dynamism, cloaking boundless energy and passionate ambition, which enabled him to combine union activities with political interests and to scale both heights simultaneously.

At the same time that Touré was gaining his initial labor leader experience as general secretary of the postal and telegraph union, he was one of the founders of the R.D.A. (Rassemblement Démocratique Africain), French Africa's majority party. While climbing uninterruptedly up the labor ladder, he also held practically every important office in Guinea. He became, in turn, chief of the territorial assembly, mayor of Conakry (population 80,000; 5,000 Europeans), and deputy to the French National Assembly at Paris.

By the time he became vice president of the Guinea Council of Government in 1957, Touré had been for five years head of the P.D.G. (Parti Démocratique de Guinée), the Guinea arm of the R.D.A., and undisputed political chief of the territory.

When, in September 1958, Touré told France's de Gaulle that Guinea preferred "poverty in freedom to riches in slavery," he spoke for the nation. Guineans backed their leader with a staggering 98 percent vote for independence, and Sékou Touré rode into the presidency on a wave of acclamation.

Critics of former colonial countries frequently charge that the new African and Asian leaders play fast and fancy with democratic precepts. Touré dismisses such criticism with sharp, incisive observations.

"Africa is not Europe or America," he says. And to explain what he means, he cites the ancient tribal traditions of Africa which remain strong even among Africans with European or American educations. These traditions are many and varied, but an overriding characteristic of all African tribes is a deep respect for—and faith in—the established authority.

In the past, particularly in British-occupied Africa, this adherence to tradition was the instrument through which the colonialists ruled. To bring the people under their sway, the colonialists had only to bend the tribal chieftains to their will.

Now, as demonstrated in both Guinea and Ghana, the Africans' age-old custom of following a strong leader is part of the key to the phenomenal popularity and power of the new political chiefs.

Touré's second answer to his critics is this: "They say we are not democratic, but they had the chance to show us what democracy is, and they never did it."

He speaks from bitter experience. In his ascent to power, the French sought to silence him by exiling him to a job in another territory. Touré quit the job and returned to Conakry. He later led the strikes which won the first major pay raises and benefits for French West African workers.

In his cool, cunning manner, Sékou Touré exploits the natural tendency of the 2,500,000 inhabitants to almost deify their leader. By exhorting the population to extra effort in what he terms his "human investment" program, he succeeds in getting them to work long hours in the blistering heat or torrential rain building roads, bridges, clinics and schools.

By convincing the people that they will be performing a patriotic duty, he persuades them to merge land and labor in the experimental communal farming of rice, an important food staple.

To insure overwhelming turnouts at political rallies or to induce the populace of Conakry to clean the littered streets, Touré has only to tape a brief speech and have it broadcast intermittently over Radio Guinea (nine hours a day broadcasting time).

He is a gifted speaker who, with a minimum of words, can transform an audience of enraptured Guineans into an obedient chorus, breathlessly still or deafeningly loud, as he wants it.

He is a grand actor, a dramatic performer of the first rank, and many who have come to sneer have left murmuring grudging praise. He is aloof and imperious or warm and generous as the occasion seems to demand, or he can be all these things within a matter of minutes.

I met Touré first on the sun-parched suburban football field the day delegates to the U.G.T.A.N. elected him president. Dignitaries and guests sat on a natural earth mound in front of 30,000 milling, cheering Guineans, and Touré the people's idol was as serenely regal as an ebony god. His fine brown eyes flashed like a hot, searching flame in my face and he acknowledged our introduction with courtesy but no smile.

Two days later I met him again in his spacious office on the top floor of the three-story white-stone mansion built for French governors. He seemed, mis-leadingly, half his broad-shouldered, six-feet size behind the great desk. On the wall in back of him hung an enlarged photograph of himself and Nkrumah taken on the occasion of the Ghana-Guinea "union" at Accra last November. On the opposite wall were two giant portraits of Nkrumah and President Tubman of Liberia, who had gifted his new neighboring Head of State with a sleek, sky-blue 1959 De Soto sedan.

Touré did not rise to meet me. He shook hands from behind the desk, studying me with the dagger-sharp, fire-brown eyes. He was cautious, wary, like a man fighting a duel. Only toward the end of the interview did the eyes cease their probing and the strong jaw relax.

The next time I met Touré he came smiling from behind his desk, shook my hand warmly and threw a comradely arm around my shoulder. "And how is my American friend today?" he asked. We stood together at the window and looked through the spreading branches of the dinosaur-like fromager tree across the rolling palace grounds to the sea.

We talked casually of Guinea and of its problems and needs until Touré's secretary rushed in to announce the unexpected arrival of the American consul general from Dakar. Immediately Touré assumed another role. He became the gracious but serious Chief of State, the guarded fencer in the treacherous game of international politics.

Sékou Touré is a man of many moods and parts. And, perhaps above all, he is a man possessed with a sense of mission. That mission seems to be to lead his people forward into the modern industrial age in the shortest possible time. Beyond that, it is to raise the status of the African so that he stands on equal footing with any other man in any other place.

When I arrived in Conakry there were two imposing statues of former French governors of Guinea in different parts of the city, one of them in the small park (Place Ballay) opposite the presidential palace. One morning, on my way to the palace, I saw a band of workmen tearing down the statues. It was a graphically dramatic symbol of the mood of Touré—and perhaps of all black Africa.

That evening Touré told me that a new history of Guinea would be written for the nation's schools, and that black heroes would replace men like George Poiret and Noel Ballay, whom the French had immortalized with bronze monuments.

"They say that we are anti-white or anti-Western, but that is not the case," Touré said. "We are simply pro-Africa and pro-African. It certainly is time somebody was."

And it is that attitude which explains why Sékou Touré can let an elegant, educated diplomat cool his heels in a hot, airless room with simple, perhaps illiterate Africans. For a long, long while the African has been made to wait to the last. Now, at last, he can take his turn.

V

WASHINGTON'S COLORED ARISTOCRACY

Washington, D.C., was one of the most important black communities in America. There was and is a considerable black elite of college-educated men and women there who hold government jobs and who, in earlier days, were among the upper echelons of domestics. Musicians Duke Ellington and James Reese Europe came from Washington, D.C.'s, black elite. Numerous blacks, from Langston Hughes to Zora Neale Hurston to Amiri Baraka, passed through the city. Here are some essays about the black elite of Washington at the turn of the century and during the 1920s.

NEGRO LIFE IN WASHINGTON

PAUL LAURENCE DUNBAR (1872–1906) was a
short-story writer, an essayist, a novelist, songwriter, and, most notably, a
poet. Born in Dayton, Ohio, Dunbar showed a predisposition toward
literature and writing while in school. He published his first book of
poetry in 1892, *Oak and Ivy*. Dunbar received national attention when
William Dean Howells wrote an introduction to his third book of poetry,
Lyrics of Lowly Life (1896). Dunbar was largely known for his black
dialect poetry, an extremely popular mixed genre of local color,
humorous and sentimental writing which was invented and exploited by
white writers, some of them Southerners who found there was a
considerable market in the North for nostalgic ruminations about the
pre–Civil War South. As Dunbar became more famous, he found
himself able to move about in various strata of black social life. "Negro
Life in Washington" appeared in *Harper's Weekly*, January 13, 1900.
"Negro Society in Washington" appeared in the *Saturday Evening Post*
on December 14, 1901.

Washington is the city where the big men of little towns come to be
disillusioned. Whether black or white, the little great soon seek their
level here. It matters not whether it is Ezekiel Corncray of Podunk
Center, Vermont, or Isaac Johnson of the Alabama black belt—in Washington he
is apt to come to a realization of his true worth to the world.

In a city of such diverse characteristics it is natural that the life of any portion
of its people should be interesting. But when it is considered that here the experiment
of sudden freedom has been tried most earnestly, and, I may say, most successfully,
upon a large percentage of the population, it is to the lives of these people that one
instinctively turns for color, picturesqueness, and striking contrast.

It is the delicately blended or boldly differentiated light and shade effects of Washington negro life that are the despair of him who tries truthfully to picture it.

It is the middle-class negro who has imbibed enough of white civilization to make him work to be prosperous. But he has not partaken of civilization so deeply that he has become drunk and has forgotten his own identity. The church to him is still the center of his social life, and his preacher a great man. He has not—and I am not wholly sorry that he has not—learned the repression of his emotions, which is the mark of a high and dry civilization. He is impulsive, intense, fervid, and—himself. He has retained some of his primitive ingenuousness. When he goes to a party he goes to enjoy himself and not to pose. If there be onlookers outside his own circle, and he be tempted to pose, he does it with such childlike innocence and good-humor that no one is for a moment anything but amused, and he is forgiven his little deception.

Possibly in even the lower walks of life a warmer racial color is discoverable. For instance, no other race can quite show the counterpart of the old gentleman who passes me on Sunday on his way to church. An ancient silk hat adorns a head which I know instinctively is bald and black and shiny on top; but the edges are fringed with a growth of crisp white hair, like a frame around the mild old face. The broadcloth coat which is buttoned tightly around the spare form is threadbare, and has faded from black to gray-green; but although bent a little with the weight of his years, his glance is alert, and he moves briskly along, like a character suddenly dropped out of one of Page's stories. He waves his hand in salute, and I have a vision of Virginia of fifty years ago.

A real bit of the old South, though, as one sees it in Washington, is the old black mammy who trundles to and fro a little baby-carriage with its load of laundry-work, but who tells you, with manifest pride, "Yes, suh, I has nussed, off'n on, mo'n a dozen chillun of de X fambly, an' some of de men dat's ginuls now er in Cong'ess was jes nachully raised up off'n me." But she, like so many others, came to Washington when it was indeed the Mecca for colored people, where lay all their hopes of protection, of freedom, and of advancement. Perhaps in the old days, when labor brought better rewards, she saved something and laid it by in the ill-fated Freedman's Savings Bank. But the story of that is known; so the old woman walks the streets today, penniless, trundling her baby-carriage, an historic but pathetic figure.

Some such relic of the past, but more prosperous withal, is the old lady who leans over the counter of a tiny and dingy restaurant on Capitol Hill and dispenses coffee and rolls and fried pork to her colored customers. She wears upon her head the inevitable turban or handkerchief in which artists delight to paint the old mammies of the South. She keeps unwavering the deep religious instinct of her race, and is mighty in her activities on behalf of one or the other of the colored churches. Under her little counter she always has a contribution-book, and not a customer, white or black, high or low, who is not levied upon to "he'p de chu'ch outen hits 'stress." But one who has sat and listened to her, as, leaning chin on hand, she recounted one of her weird superstitious stories of the night-doctors and their doings, or the "awful jedgement on a sinnah man," is not unwilling to be put at some expense for his pleasure.

The old lady and her stories are of a different cast from that part of the Washington life which is the pride of her proudest people. It is a far cry from the smoky little restaurant on the Hill, with its genial and loquacious old owner, to the great business block on Fourteenth Street and its wealthy, shrewd, and cultivated proprietor.

Colored men have made money here, and some of them have known how to keep it. There are several of them on the Board of Trade—five, I think—and they are regarded by their fellows as solid, responsible, and capable business men. The present assessment law was drafted by a colored member of the board, and approved by them before it was submitted to Congress.

As for the professions, there are so many engaged in them that it would keep one busy counting or attempting to count the darkskinned lawyers and doctors one meets in a day.

The cause of this is not far to seek. Young men come here to work in the departments. Their evenings are to a certain extent free. It is the most natural thing in the world that they should improve their time by useful study. But why such a preponderance in favor of the professions, you say. Are there not other useful pursuits—arts and handicrafts? To be sure there are. But then your new people dearly love a title, and Lawyer Jones sounds well, Dr. Brown has an infinitely more dignified ring, and as for Professor—well, that is the acme of titular excellence, and there are more dark professors in Washington than one could find in a day's walk through a European college town.

However, it is well that these department clerks should carry something away with them when they leave Washington, for their condition is seldom financially improved by their sojourn here. This, though, is perhaps apart from the aim of the present article, for it is no more true of the negro clerks than of their white confrères. Both generally live up to the limit of their salaries.

The clerk has much leisure, and is in consequence a society man. He must dress well and smoke as good a cigar as an Eastern congressman. It all costs money, and it is not unnatural that at the end of the year he is a little long on unreceipted bills and short on gold. The tendency of the school-teachers, now, seems to be entirely different. There are a great many of them here, and on the average they receive less than the government employees. But perhaps the discipline which they are compelled to impart to their pupils has its salutary effect upon their own minds and impulses. However that may be, it is true that the banks and building associations receive each month a part of the salaries of a large proportion of these instructors.

The colored people themselves have a flourishing building association and a well-conducted bank, which do part—I am sorry I cannot say the major part—of their race's business.

The influence which the success of a few men will have upon a whole community is indicated in the spirit of venture which actuates the rising generation of this city. A few years ago, if a man secured a political position, he was never willing or fit to do anything else afterward. But now the younger men, with the example of some of their successful elders before them, are beginning to see that an easy berth in one of the departments is not the best thing in life, and they are getting brave enough to do other things. Some of these ventures have proven failures, even disasters, but it has not daunted the few, nor crushed the spirit of effort in them.

It has been said, and not without some foundation in fact, that a colored man who came to Washington never left the place. Indeed, the city has great powers of attracting and holding its colored population; for, belong to whatever class or condition they may, they are always sure to find enough of that same class or condition to make their residence pleasant and congenial. But this very spirit of enterprise of which I have spoken is destroying the force of this dictum, and men of color are even going so far as to resign government positions to go away and strike out for themselves. I have in mind now two young men who are Washingtonians of the Washingtonians, and who have been in office here for years. But the fever has taken them, and they have voluntarily given up their places to go and try their fortunes in the newer and less crowded West.

Such things as these are small in themselves, but they point to a condition of affairs in which the men who have received the training and polish which only Washington can give to a colored man can go forth among their fellows and act as leaveners to the crudity of their race far and wide.

That the pleasure and importance of negro life in Washington are overrated by the colored people themselves is as true as that it is underrated and misunderstood by the whites. To the former the social aspect of this life is a very dignified and serious drama. To the latter it is nothing but a most amusing and inconsequential farce. But both are wrong: it is neither the one thing nor the other. It is a comedy of the period played out by earnest actors, who have learned their parts well, but who on that very account are disposed to mouth and strut a little and watch the gallery.

Upon both races the truth and significance of the commercial life among the negroes have taken a firmer hold, because the sight of their banks, their offices, and places of business are evidences which cannot be overlooked or ignored.

As for the intellectual life, a university set on a hill cannot be hid, and the fact that about this university and about this excellent high-school clusters a community in which people, unlike many of the educational fakirs which abound, have taken their degrees from Cambridge, Oxford, Edinburgh, Harvard, Yale, Cornell, Welles-ley, and a score of minor colleges, demands the recognition of a higher standard of culture among people of color than obtains in any other city.

But, taking it all in all and after all, negro life in Washington is a promise rather than a fulfilment. But it is worthy of note for the really excellent things which are promised.

NEGRO SOCIETY IN WASHINGTON

Paul Laurence Dunbar

In spite of all the profound problems which the serious people of the world are propounding to us for solution, we must eventually come around to the idea that a good portion of humanity's time is taken up with enjoying itself. The wiser part of the world has calmly accepted the adage that "All work and no play makes Jack a dull boy," and has decided not to be dull. It seems to be the commonly accepted belief, though, that the colored people of the country have not fallen into this view of matters since emancipation, but have gone around being busy and looking serious. It may be heresy to say it, but it is not the truth.

The people who had the capacity for great and genuine enjoyment before emancipation have not suddenly grown into grave and reverend philosophers. There are some of us who believe that there are times in the life of a race when a dance is better than a convention, and a hearty laugh more effective than a philippic. Indeed, as a race, we have never been a people to let the pleasures of the moment pass. Anyone who believes that all of our time is taken up with dealing with knotty problems, or forever bearing around heavy missions, is doomed to disappointment. Even to many of those who think and feel most deeply the needs of their people is given the gift of joy without folly and gaiety without frivolity.

Nowhere is this more clearly exemplified than in the social doings of the negro in Washington, the city where this aspect of the colored man's life has reached its highest development. Here exists a society which is sufficient unto itself—a society which is satisfied with its own condition, and which is not asking for social intercourse with whites. Here are homes finely, beautifully and tastefully furnished. Here come together the flower of colored citizenship from all parts of the country. The breeziness of the West here meets the refinement of the East, the warmth and grace of the South, the culture and fine reserve of the North. Quite like all other people, the men who have made money come to the capital to spend it in those social diversions which are not open to them in the smaller and more provincial towns. With her sister city, Baltimore, just next door, the negro in Washington forms and carries on a social life which no longer can be laughed at or caricatured under the name "Colored Sassiety." The term is still funny, but now it has lost its pertinence.

A SOCIETY SUFFICIENT TO ITSELF

The opportunities for enjoyment are very numerous. Here we are at the very gate of the South, in fact we have begun to feel that we are about in the center of everything, and that nobody can go to any place or come from any place without passing among us. When the soldiers came home from the Philippines last summer, naturally they came here, and great were the times that Washington saw during their stay. At a dinner given in honor of the officers two Harvard graduates met, and after embracing each other, stood by the table and gave to their astonished hearers the Harvard yell at the top of their voices. One was a captain of volunteers, and the other, well, he is a very dignified personage, and now holds a high office.

And just here it might not be amiss to say that in the social life in Washington nearly every prominent college in the country is represented by its graduates. Harvard, Yale, Princeton, Cornell, Oberlin, and a number of others of less prominence.

The very fact of our being so in the way of traffic has brought about some very amusing complications. For instance, and this is a family secret, do any of you uninitiated know that there were three Inaugural balls? The whites could only afford one, but we, happy-go-lucky, pleasure-loving people, had to have two, and on the same night. There were people coming here from everywhere, and their friends in the city naturally wanted to show them certain courtesies, which was right and proper. But there are cliques, and more cliques, as everywhere else, and these cliques differed strenuously. Finally, they separated into factions: one secured the armory, and, the other securing another large hall, each gave its party. And just because each tried to outdo the other, both were tremendous successes, though the visitors, who like the dying man, had friends in both places, had to even up matters by going first to one and then the other, so that during the whole of that snowy March night there was a good-natured shifting of guests from one ballroom to the other. Sometimes the young man who happened to be on the reception committee at one place and the floor committee at the other got somewhat puzzled as to the boutonnière which was his insignia of office, and too often hapless ones found themselves standing in the midst of one association with the flower of the other like a badge upon his lapel.

Each faction had tried the other's mettle, and the whole incident closed amicably.

THE WAR OF THE SOCIAL CLIQUES

One of the beauties and one of the defects of Washington life among us is this very business of forming into cliques. It is beautiful in that one may draw about him just the circle of friends that he wants, who appeal to him, and from whom he can get what he wants, but on the other hand, when some large and more general affair is to be given which comprises Washington not as a home city, but rather as the capital of the nation, it is difficult to get these little coteries to disintegrate. The only man who is perfectly safe is the one who cries, "The world is my clique!" and plunges boldly into them all.

Of course, there are some sets which could never come together here. And we are, in this, perhaps imitators; or is it the natural evolution of human impulse that there should be placed over against each other a smart set?—yes, a smart set, don't smile—and a severe high and mighty, intellectual set, one which takes itself with eminent seriousness and looks down on all the people who are not studying something, or graduating, or reading papers, or delivering lectures as frivolous. But somehow, in spite of this attitude toward them, the smart young and even the smart old people go on having dances, teas and card parties, and talking small talk, quite oblivious of the fact that they are under the ban.

Washington has been card crazy this year, and for the first time on record the games did not end with the first coming of summer, but continued night after night as long as there was anybody in town to play them. For be it known that we also put up our shutters and go to the mountains or seashore, where we lie on the sands or in the open air and get tanned if our complexions are amenable to the process, and some of them are.

There are to my knowledge six very delightful card clubs, and I know one couple who for twenty-five years have had their friends in for cards on every Thursday night in the autumn and winter. If the charitable impulse overtakes us there is a run on the department stores of the city for bright new decks of cards and bisque ornaments, the latter to be used as prizes in the contests to which the outside world is invited to come and look on.

Even after the shutters are put up, when our Negro lawyers lay aside their documents, and our doctors put their summer practice on some later sojourner in town, the fever for the game follows the people to their summer resorts, and the old Chesapeake sees many a game of whist or euchre under the trees in the daytime or out on lantern-lighted porches at night.

But let no one think that this diversion has been able to shake from its popularity the dances. And how we dance and dance, summer and winter, upon all occasions, whenever and wherever we can. Even when, as this year, we have not been compelled by the inauguration of a president to give something "socially official," there is enough of this form of amusement to keep going the most earnest devotee. There are two leading dancing clubs formed of men, and one which occasionally gives a dance, but mostly holds itself to itself, formed of women. The two first vie with each other winter after winter in the brilliancy of their affairs, one giving its own especial welcome dance with four assemblies, the other confining itself to one or two balls each year.

NOT THE COMIC BALLS WE KNOW

Do not think that these are the affairs which the comic papers and cartoonists have made you familiar with; the waiters' and coachmen's balls of which you know. They are good enough in their way, just as are your butchers' picnics and your Red Men's dances, but *these* are not of the same ilk. It is no "You pays your money and you takes your choice" business. The invitations are not sent to those outside of one particular circle. One from beyond the city limits would be no more able to secure admission or recognition without a perfect knowledge of his social standing in his own community than would Mrs. Bradley-Martin's butler to come to an Astor ball. These two extremes are not so far apart, but the lines are as strictly drawn. The people who come here to dance together are people of similar education, training and habits of thought. But, says someone, the colored people have not yet either the time or the money for these diversions, and yet without a minute's thought there come to my mind four men, who are always foremost in these matters, whose fortunes easily aggregate a million dollars. All of them are educated men with college-bred children. Have these men not earned the right to their enjoyments, and the leisure for them? There are others too numerous to mention who are making five or six thousand a year out of their professions or investments. Surely these may have a little time to dance?

There is a long distance between the waiter at a summer hotel and the man who goes down to a summer resort to rest after a hard year as superintendent of an institution which pays him several thousand a year. In this connection it afforded me a great deal of amusement some time ago to read from the pen of a good friend of mine his solemn comments upon the negro's lack of dramatic ability. Why? Because he had seen the waiters and other servants at his summer hotel produce a play. Is it out of place for me to smile at the idea of any Harriet of any race doing *The Second Mrs. Tanqueray*?

View us at any time, but make sure that you view the right sort, and I believe you will not find any particular racial stamp upon our pleasure making. Last year one of the musical societies gave an opera here, not perhaps with distinction, but brightly, pleasantly, and as well as any amateur organization could expect to give it. Each year they also give an oratorio which is well done. And, believe me, it is an erroneous idea that all our musical organizations are bound up either in a scientific or any other sort of study of rag-time. Of course, rag-time is pleasant, and often there are moments when there are gathered together perhaps ten or twelve of us, and one who can hammer a catchy tune, rag-time or not, on the piano is a blessed aid to his companions who want to two-step. But there, this is dancing again, and we do not dance always.

Indeed, sometimes we grow strongly to feel our importance and to feel the weight of our own knowledge of art and art matters. We are going to be very much in this way this winter, and we shall possibly have some studio teas as well as some very delightful at-homes which will recall the reign, a few years ago, of a bright woman who had a wealth of social tact and grace, and at whose Fridays one met everyone worth meeting, resident here and from the outside. The brightest talkers met there and the best singers. You had tea and biscuits, talk and music. Mostly your tea got cold and you forgot to munch on your biscuit because better things were calling you. This woman is dead now. Her memory is not sad, but very sweet, and it will take several women to fill her place.

A SEASON OF LITERATURE, MUSIC, AND ART

There are going to be some pleasant times, though different in scope, in the studio of a clever little woman artist here. She is essentially a miniature painter, but has done some other charming and beautiful things; but above all that, and what the young people are possibly going to enjoy especially, she is a society woman with all that means, and will let them come, drink tea in her studio, flirt behind her canvases, and talk art as they know it, more or less. Her apartments are beautiful and inspiring. The gatherings here, though, will be decidedly for the few. These will be supplemented, however, later in the year by one of the musical clubs which is intending to entertain S. Coleridge Taylor, who is coming over from London to conduct his cantata, "Hiawatha." Mr. Taylor is a favorite here, and his works have been studied for some time by this musical club. It is expected that he will be shown a great many social courtesies.

An article on negro social life in Washington, perhaps, ought almost to be too light to speak of the numerous literary organizations here, the reading clubs which hold forth, but really, the getting together of congenial people, which is, after all, the fundamental idea of social life, has been so apparent in these that they must at least have this passing notice.

In the light of all this, it is hardly to be wondered at that some of us wince a wee bit when we are all thrown into the lump as the peasant or serving class. In aims and hopes for our race, it is true, we are all at one, but it must be understood, when we come to consider the social life, that the girls who cook in your kitchen and the men who serve in your dining-rooms do not dance in our parlors.

To illustrate how many there are of the best class of colored people who can be brought thus together a story is told of a newcomer who was invited to a big reception. A Washingtonian, one who was initiated into the mysteries of the life here, stood beside him and in an aside called off the names of the guests as they entered. "This is Doctor So-and-So," as someone entered the room, "Surgeon-in-Chief of Blank Hospital." The stranger looked on in silence. "The man coming in now is Judge Somebody Else, of the District." This time the stranger raised his eyebrows. "Those two men entering are consuls to Such-and-Such a place." The newcomer sniffed a little bit. "And ah!" his friend started forward, "that is the United States Minister to Any-Place-You-Please." The man who was being initiated into the titles of his fellow guests said nothing until another visitor entered the doorway; then he turned to his friend, and in a tone of disbelief and disgust remarked, "Well, now, who under the heavens is that? The Prime Minister of England or the King himself?"

Last summer was the gayest that Washington has seen in many a year. It is true that there are hotels and boardinghouses at many summer resorts and that some of our people gather there to enjoy themselves, but for the first time there was a general flocking to one place taken up entirely and almost owned by ourselves. The place, a stretch of beach nearly two miles long with good bathing facilities, and with a forest behind it, has been made and built up entirely by negro capital. Two men, at least, have made fortunes out of the sale and improvement of their property, and they, along with many others, are the owners of their own summer homes and cottages at Arundel-on-the-Bay, and Highland Beach, Maryland. Here the very best of three cities gathered this last summer. Annapolis and Baltimore sent their quota and our own capital city did the rest. It was such a gathering of this race as few outside of our own great family circle have ever seen.

There is, perhaps, an exaltation about any body of men and women who gather to enjoy the fruits of their own labor upon the very ground which their labors have secured to them. There was, at any rate, a special exaltation about these people, and whatever was done went off with éclat. There was a dance at least once a week at one or another of the cottages, and the beauty of it was that anyone who was spending the summer there needed to look for no invitation. He was sure of one by the very fact of his being there at all, a member of so close a corporation. The athletes did their turns for the delectation of their admirers, and there were some long-distance swimming contests that would have done credit to the boys in the best of our colleges. There were others who took their bathing more complacently, and still others who followed the injunction of the old rhyme, "Hang your clothes on a hickory limb, but don't go near the water." Cards, music and sailing parties helped to pass the time, which went all too swiftly, and the Isaak Waltons of the place were always up at five o'clock in the morning and away to some point where they strove for bluefish and rocks, and came home with spots. The talk was bright and the intercourse easy and pleasant. There was no straining, no pomposity, no posing for the gallery. When September came we began to hear the piping of the quail in the woods away from the beach, and our trigger-fingers tingled with anticipation. But the time was not yet ripe. And so the seal is to be set this winter upon our Maryland home by a house party, where the men will go to eat, smoke and shoot, and the women to read, dance and—well—women gossip everywhere.

This is but a passing glimpse of that intimate life among our own people which we dignify by the nature of society.

OUR WONDERFUL SOCIETY: WASHINGTON

LANGSTON HUGHES lived in Washington for a time with his mother when he returned from an overseas adventure. In fact, it was in Washington that Hughes was discovered by Vachel Lindsay as the busboy poet. Some of the incidents here are expanded in Hughes's first autobiography, *The Big Sea* (1940). "Our Wonderful Society: Washington" appeared in *Opportunity* in August 1927.

A s long as I have been colored I have heard of Washington society. Even as a little boy in Kansas vague ideas of the grandeur of Negro life in the capitol found their way into my head. A grand-uncle, John M. Langston, had lived there during and after the time of colored congressmen and of him I heard much from my grandmother. Later, when I went to Cleveland, some nice mulatto friends of ours spoke of the "wonderful society life" among Negroes in Washington. And some darker friends of ours hinted at "pink teas" and the color line that was drawn there. I wanted to see the town. "It must be rich and amusing and fine," I thought.

Four or five years passed. Then by way of Mexico and New York, Paris and Italy, through a season of teaching, a year at college, and a period of travel, I arrived at Washington. "Of course, you must meet the best people," were almost the first words I heard after greetings had been exchanged. "That is very important." And I was reminded of my noble family ties and connections. But a few days later I found myself a job in a laundry, carrying bags of wet-wash. The dignity of one's family background doesn't keep a fellow who's penniless from getting hungry.

It was not long, however, before I found a better place in the office of a national Negro organization. There I opened up in the morning, did clerical work, took care of the furnace, and scrubbed the floors. This was termed a "position," not a "job." And I began to meet some of the best people. The people themselves assured me that they were the best people—and they seemed to know. Never before, anywhere, had I seen persons of influence—men with some money, women with some beauty, teachers with some education—quite so audibly sure of their own importance and their high places in the community. So many pompous gentlemen never before did I meet. Nor so many ladies with chests swelled like pouter-pigeons whose mouths uttered formal sentences in frightfully correct English. I admit I was awed by these best people.

Negro society in Washington, they assured me, was the finest in the country, the richest, the most cultured, the most worthy. In no other city were there so many splendid homes, so many cars, so many A.B. degrees, or so many persons with "family background." Descendants of distinguished Negroes were numerous, but there were also those who could do better and trace their ancestry right on back to George Washington and his colored concubines: "How lucky I am to have a congressman for grand-uncle," I thought in the presence of these well-ancestored people.

She is a graduate of this . . . or, he is a graduate of that . . . frequently followed introductions. So I met many men and women who had been to colleges—and seemed not to have recovered from it. Almost all of them appeared to be deeply affected by education in one way or another, and they, too, had very grand manners. "Surely," I thought when I saw them, "I'll never be important unless I get a degree." So I began to spend ten cents for lunch instead of fifteen—putting the other nickle away for college.

Then I met some of the younger colored people, sons and daughters of the pompous gentlemen and pouter-pigeons ladies, some of them students at Northern colleges or at Howard. They were not unlike youth everywhere today—jazzy and loud. But, "They are the hope of the race," I was told. Yet I found that their ideals seemed most Nordic and un-Negro and that they appeared to be moving away from the masses of the race rather than holding an identity with them. Speaking of a fraternity dance, one in a group of five college men said proudly, "There was nothing but pinks there—looked just like 'fay women. Boy, you'd have thought it was an o'fay dance!" And several of the light young ladies I knew were not above passing a dark classmate or acquaintance with only the coolest of nods, and some- times not even that. "She's a dark girl but nice," or similar apologies were made by the young men for the less than coffee-and-cream ladies they happened to know. These best young people had, too, it seemed, an excessive admiration for fur coats and automobiles. Boasts like this were often to be heard! "There were more fur coats in our box at the Thanksgiving game than in anybody else's." Or concerning the social standing of a young lady: "Her father owns two cars." Or of a sporty new- comer in town: "He's got a racoon coat just like a 'fay boy." Or as the criterion of success: "He's one of our leading men. He has a Packard and a chauffeur."

But cars or fur coats or fine houses were not more talked about, however, than was culture. And the members of Washington society *were* cultured. They themselves assured me frequently that they were. Some of those who could pass for white even attended down-town theaters when *The Scandals* or Earl Carrol's *Vani ties* came to town. But when a concert series of Negro artists including Abbie

Mitchell and other excellent musicians, was put on at a colored theater, the audiences were very small and most of the members of cultured society were absent.

I knew that Jean Toomer's home was Washington and I had read his book *Cane* and talked about it with other readers in New York and Paris and Venice. I wanted to talk about it in Washington, too, because I had found it beautiful and real. But the cultured colored society of the capital, I mean those persons who always insisted that they were cultured, seemed to know little about the book and cared less. And when the stories of Rudolph Fisher (also a colored Washingtonian) appeared in *The Atlantic Monthly*, what I heard most was, "Why didn't he write about nice people like us? Why didn't he write about cultured folks?" I thought it amazing, too, that a young playwright of ability and three or four poets of promise were living in Washington unknown to the best society. At least, I saw nothing being done to encourage these young writers, for the leading women's clubs appeared to be founded solely for the purpose of playing cards, and the cultured doctors and lawyers and caterers and butlers and government messengers had little concern for poets or playwrights. In supposedly intellectual gatherings I listened to conversations as arid as the sides of the Washington monument.

There appeared, also, to be the same love of scandal among the best folks as among the lower classes. Sometimes I heard how such-and-such a pompous gentleman had struck his wife or how this or that refined couple had indulged in physical combat—all of which was very amusing but hardly compatible with a society which boasted of its gentility. Such consciously nice people ought never to let down the bars, I thought, but they did.

Washington is one of the most beautiful cities in the world. For that I remember it with pleasure. Georgia Douglass Johnson conversed with charm and poured tea on Saturday nights for young writers and artists and intellectuals. That, too, I remember with pleasure. Seventh Street was always teemingly alive with dark working people who hadn't yet acquired "culture" and the manners of stage ambassadors, and pinks and blacks and yellows were still friends without apologies. That street I remember with pleasure. And the few fine and outstanding men and women I met who had seemingly outgrown "society" as a boy outgrows his first long trousers—those men and women I remember with pleasure. But Washington society itself—perhaps I am prejudiced toward it. Perhaps I had heard too much about it beforehand and was disappointed. Or perhaps I didn't really meet the best society after all. Maybe I met only the snobs, and the high-yellows, and the lovers of fur coats and automobiles and fraternity pins and A.B. degrees. Maybe I'm all wrong about everything.—Maybe those who said they were the best people had me fooled.—Perhaps they weren't the best people—but they looked tremendously important. Or, perhaps they *were* the best people and it's my standard of values that's awry . . . Well, be that as it may, I have seen Washington, of which city I had heard much, and I have looked at something called "society" of which I had heard much, too. Now I can live in Harlem where people are not quite so ostentatiously proud of themselves, and where one's family background is not of such great concern. Now I can live contentedly in Harlem.

I, TOO, HAVE LIVED
IN WASHINGTON

BRENDA RAY MORYCK was a schoolteacher in
Washington who won prizes for her essays and short stories in
Opportunity and *The Crisis*. "I, Too, Have Lived in Washington" is a
response, a gentle if firm remonstrance, to Langston Hughes's harsh
criticism of the black bourgeoisie of Washington.

*"What went ye out into the wilderness to seek? A reed shaken with the
wind?—But what went ye out for to seek?"*

Fully aware that in quoting Biblical Scripture, I am exhibiting that behavior-
ism the learned Caucasian psychologists note as being peculiarly typical
of the Negro—"a naturally religious trend of thought sub-lying all material
consciousness," I nevertheless take delight in setting down the text by means of
which I begin my response to Mr. Langston Hughes, youthful and sometimes
charming poet, for the moment turned critic of the world in general (for all the
world lives in Washington—at least through some representative), while resting
from his opportunism. But since I am neither ashamed nor afraid of being a Negro,
I offer no apology for flaunting the badge of my race in turning to my use the
rhetorical phrases of Jesus Christ.

There is an ancient oriental saying, subtle and double-charged as were most
of the maxims born in the far east in early times, which has come down to us
through the ages until we fancy it but a common slogan of our own day, which
reads, "We seek what we find—we see what we look for."

We do.

I, too, have lived in Washington, and I have seen the sun setting over Virginia hills
across Potomac waters—the red sun, resplendent in immeasurable glory, sinking
behind green hills—reflected, until the last soft afterglow has melted into a purple-
dusk twilight, on the marble grandeur of the Lincoln Memorial Temple; I have
seen the miracle of America—the Japanese cherry blossoms in bloom around the

Tidal Basin, exquisite and delicate—divinely beautiful—fairyland on earth for a span; I have seen the sparkling waters of Rock Creek Park rushing over crags and stones between sun-spattered banks; I have seen children at play in the squares in Spring; I have seen from the enchanting great height of that granite shaft, the Washington Monument, all the beauty and the loveliness of design that is this nation's capital and all the open country and hills and rivers round about; I've viewed the Unknown Soldier's tomb and stood beside that dazzling, gleaming amphi-theatre which marks a people's tribute to their hero-dead. I have seen art in the Corcoran Galleries, and science at the Smithsonian Institute; I've seen, in the halls of Congress, law in the making—men rising to betray the sacred trusts borne by them, and not ashamed—scheming to shape some evil end for their own and not the people's good, and other stalwart champions arising to denounce and crush out the poison-weed ere it take root and flourish into treachery; I've seen the President and the First Lady, and their collies . . . and Paulina—; I've glimpsed some Swedish Royalty, and received a blinding flash of Roumanian Marie, her children and her retinue; I've seen ambassadors and their regalia; I've viewed the embassies and their elegance; I've seen the relics of the last war, maimed and wounded and blinded at Walter Reed; I've watched the crippled babies on their hospital porch in their pitiful attempts at play; I've seen the shops and buildings, the ceremonies and the people—and—I've seen the Negroes.

What went I out to see in Washington?

Yes—I've seen the Negroes. —I've seen the "best people"—those "persons of influence"—whom the young poet's trenchant pen has presented—"men with some money, women with some beauty, teachers with some education—pompous gentlemen, quite audibly sure of their own importance—ladies swelled like pouter-pigeons, whose mouths uttered formal sentences in frightfully correct English—persons who knew they were the best people," although they never assured me of the fact—no doubt respecting my riper years too much to presume to tease my credulity in the same manner that ensnared the gullible Langston. I've seen "the splendid homes, the many cars," read "the many A.B. degrees, and three of the five Ph.Ds belonging to colored women in this country, on programmes and pamphlets without number—though not with scorn (for is not the striving to attain the world's general standard of education a laudable endeavor?) The figures—125,000 college students in the United States in 1903, 438,000 in 1922 and today nearly 600,000 seem to argue that it seems a worthwhile pursuit to an ever increasing many; and I've talked with "the many persons with family background," legitimate and à main gauche.

Some of the younger colored people too, "sons and daughters of the pompous gentlemen and pouter-pigeon ladies," called "the hope of the race," says Mr. Hughes, although I did not know that they were, having heard quite the contrary from many of their despairing and disgusted parents, have come within my ken. And I heard a youth, dropped down from New York, speaking of a fraternity dance there, use those same "pink" and "o'fay" terms which Mr. Hughes gives as the language of his Washington character. (No doubt the New Yorker set the mode, since not to do as the Harlemite does is to place one's self beyond the pale of intelligent comprehension.) I've also passed "the several light young ladies" whose pseudo-Nordic ideal prohibited their public recognition of a swarthy-skinned friend—in New York, Boston, Philadelphia, Cleveland, Buffalo, and Baltimore, as well, but somehow or other the blind spot in my eye has always had a sudden simultaneous way of appearing to obscure my sight the instant my fair friends' vision begins to fail and I have not been able to recognize them either, thereby bringing down upon my own distinctly Negroid head, a similar charge of "passing," particularly if I happened to be in the company of genuine Caucasians when I so unfortunately went blind. (For four years while I was at college, I "passed"—so I am told now-a-days. For what, I haven't been able to ascertain, but I could not have been one Negro among fourteen hundred white girls—impossible!)

Dark girls, when they have lacked "charm" (to imitate Helen Hayes) 'tis true have sat against the walls of the dance hall all evening while the fair belles occupied the center of the floor, here as elsewhere, but at least they have been extended the courtesy of an invitation. New York has long since eliminated that problem by the surgeon's method.

Admiration for fur coats and automobiles among the younger generation of Washington I've likewise seen, although I cannot concede the adjective "excessive," deemed necessary by Mr. Hughes, since all young people everywhere in this age must have a fur coat or an automobile or both, and some of us older ones can't be happy without them either, but if this is a particularly silly Washington weakness why will not the New Yorkers attend the Thanksgiving game at all unless they can come gorgeously garbed in coats of the latest and most expensive furs to display in their Washington friends' boxes, and motor down in elegant and dazzling high-powered cars in which to park before these same friends' doors? And can it be that I read in a New York weekly in the society column only a month or so ago that Mr. and Mrs. So-and-So "were sporting a new Marmon on Seventh Avenue the other afternoon"; Dr. So Gross "was seen stepping on the gas of his new Pierce-Arrow, on 135th Street," and Miss Self-Important "departed for Atlantic City in her 1928 model Packard," while the Stay-at-Homes' "latest Lincoln sedan was seen parked in front of the Cotton Club"?

Absurd!—but true.

Again I have seen, but not heard, of Washington "culture," not at all unlike the "culture" of every city and every race the world-over—a cheap tinsel substitute for the realities of life—a sham blind to protect vacuity—the artificial barrier erected to deceive and dazzle the striving—and I have seen—Washington culture— "Georgia Douglas Johnson conversing with charm and pouring tea on Saturday nights for young writers and intellectuals"—a dark working man on Seventh Street, "who had not yet acquired 'culture' and the manners of stage ambassadors," tenderly herding his slightly less dark little family into an early evening film showing of Rin-Tin-Tin; "pinks and black and yellows," their heads bent together in "friendly fashion without apology" in a common attempt to solve a common problem at an interracial meeting; "the few fine outstanding men and women, who had seemingly out-grown 'society' as a boy outgrows his first long trousers."—I have seen the snobs and the strivers, the fools and the clowns, the simple and the weak, the frail and the evil—and then—I have seen Washington Society.

"Your actions speak so loudly, I cannot hear what you say," was the homely but pithy sentence by which one wise man damned up the explanatory flow of his companion's language ere it had clouded honest penetration, and if Mr. Hughes had uttered the same remark in time, he might have been the recipient of more wholesome and sane treatment at the hands of even the "elite" whom he mistook to represent Washington. In that fortunate event, he would have had the necessary leisure to discover who is who and why, as I did.

When I came to reside in Washington, less than three years ago, I was not totally unknown, having visited there two or three times during my childhood, and occasionally afterwards, but my acquaintanceship did not extend beyond a very few now facetiously termed "cave-dwellers" and their retiring daughters and sons, so my circle was very limited at the start. I had no ancestry, distinguished or otherwise, born, reared or careered in the capital, or even near it, so I had no preconceived notions of how things ought to be. I had heard, of course, as who has not?—of the grandeur of that earlier day when colored congressmen, orators, statesmen and eminent divines held splendid sway, and was duly impressed with what had been, in like manner as was Mr. Hughes, for despite his scorn and scoffing and skepticism, he is impressed. Else why does he call to notice his famous ancestor and bear with pride his honorable name if the sterling worth of those great men who placed the first bricks above the corner-stone laid by Abraham Lincoln for the civic, economic and political progress of the Negro is all a myth?

Unlike Mr. Hughes, however, being slightly older than he, I know that "the old order changeth" and I was quite prepared to meet the new, whatever it might be.

Instead of going forth in search of it, I remained at home and after many days, one symbol of it came to me in the form of an invitation from, to employ the parlance of the society editor, "one of the city's most prominent young matrons," a "pink" whom I had known long ago while summering in the mountains as a child, and who had paid me one fleeting call upon my arrival. It asked me to a supper party at her home.

I went—went into as exquisite a home as it has ever been my good fortune to enter, and since in my varied experience, it has been my privilege to cross the thresholds of the nouveau riche, time-worn aristocrats, and the mellow wealthy, I have seen some fine houses. But no one called my attention to the solid silver, the priceless linen, the Persian rugs or the old mahogany, nor the quantity and quality of the food.

There were, among the small group present, three well-known and successful lawyers, one of them on his way to the judge's bench, but nothing was said of the fact. I knew neither their profession nor their standing until afterwards, when I made personal inquiry concerning each. There was ease, there was fun, there was hospitality, and though I felt culture in the invitation, refinement and prosperity in the home, intelligence in the conversation, and knew my hostess to be a very charming modern edition of an old family with solid background, these things were not even whispered on the air. Yet the party lasted from eight in the evening until two the next morning—ample time to hear anything, especially in the loquacious precincts of fine drinks!

A guest whom I met at that supper, understanding me to be a stranger in town, next asked me to a dance. I went, I saw, I enjoyed—a gathering brilliant in its assemblage, gorgeous in its gowns and setting—rich in its jewels and furs and cars. Was it mere oversight that no one troubled to announce the figure of his bank account to me nor name his degree, nor point out his automobile, nor inform me of his importance in the community? Was I snubbed? Or were we all having too jolly and interesting a time to be bothered by such idiocy?

Next, followed a card party—a breathtaking revelation to me, for the stakes were high and the prizes purchased at prohibitive prices. Moreover, the women played with the tense seriousness of the seasoned gambler and played to win—those magnificent prizes, yet it was at this same party that I heard, as did several others— a Washingtonian, an elderly lady—gentle and elegant and formal rebuke another who had recently returned from the metropolis for bringing back the idle rumors rampant there.

Said the returned visitor in answer to a question put concerning the welfare of two prominent people: "Why they're about to separate. He's about to sue her for divorce."

General consternation and immediate interest on the part of everyone near.

"Why, did you expect anything else? This is the third time they've nearly broken up."

Still incredulity.

"Why that's common talk—in New York—the way she's behaved—everybody knows it."

Spoke the lady: "Yes, you are right, it *is* common talk—the talk of the common—cheap, common talk, and no self-respecting woman will repeat such rubbish."

And no one did thereafter. The card-playing was resumed.

Then followed other pleasures and privileges—never talked about—simply extended and granted and gradually intimacies sprang up—as charming and as sound as any ordinary friendships on earth can be, so that I came to know rather well a goodly number of people who lived well, dressed well, entertained elegantly and constituted society, if "the more cultivated portion of a community in its social relations and influences" constitutes society anywhere in the world.

Mr. Hughes claims that everywhere people were eager to impress him. My experience was quite the contrary. Everywhere, *I* was impressed. Born, bred and schooled among cultivated Caucasians, I had lost the last shred of illusion concerning the idealism and nobility of the majority belonging to the sophisticated classes, and I confess I was utterly unprepared for what I met. I went to dinner at the lovely home of a very prominent and able woman who occupies a high position in the educational world and is almost weekly feted and honored by some great college or university, and was altogether humbled at the simplicity of her reception and her constant and courteous attention to my every trivial need although the friend with whom she resides was my hostess rather than she.

In this same extraordinary charming retreat, I was again startled into humility by the long reticence concerning European residence of my friend, when after many visits, we fell into conversation about foreign books, the remark was casually made in passing comment. It is in this exquisite company too, that I learned that more was to be gleaned in five minutes concerning the worthwhile activities of the world, particularly literary pursuits, than could be heard in several hours in the New York that I know, yet the only sign of all this erudition is visible not audible—books in every crevice and cranny—books on every shelf and table—books, well-used.

Informal luncheon in the spacious homelike home of a man of world renown brought me face to face with the other side of a so-called society-mad family. The mother, a gracious, middle-aged lady is a great card-player, as are both her gay young daughters, and frequently the three capture all the prizes at party after party, yet on the warm summer afternoon that I made so delightful a visit among them, the mother had dismissed the maid that she might attend a picture show, and herself prepared the luncheon for fourteen people, herself, her distinguished husband, her five children, her son's wife, her two grandbabies, two nieces, and a nephew who were visiting there, and myself, and then sat down to preside charmingly over a family as jolly and happy, yet as loving and deferential as I can possibly conceive, and my imagination is most elastic when there is need.

After dinner, the great man took me into his garden which he himself finds recreation in keeping, and instead of discoursing to me upon the solar system or his vast importance or even his latest book, he pointed out the marvelous magnolia tree which Charles Sumner planted in a corner of the yard during the time that the distinguished ancestor of the present cynical Mr. Langston Hughes occupied the house, and then passed on—not to cabbages and kings, but cabbages and beets and carrots and lettuce and hollyhocks and nasturtiums and pansies.

Later in the day, the "society-mad matron" sat in the hammock and rocked a grand-baby to sleep (old-fashioned, isn't she?) while one flapper daughter lovingly embroidered a waist for her and the other cut the grass.

Now-a-days, I drop into that home often at any hour, any day, because I love it, and I find always the same happy, serene, well-ordered tone—a gracious mother as chataleine, the chum of her children, yet their respected authority and guide, and six joyous, wholesome young folks—for the married son and his wife and babies spend as much time with the mother and are as welcome there as in their own home.

Again, I formed an attachment for a very distinguished woman whose personality I admired as much as her great distinction and achievements. She graciously entertained my advances, and though tremendously busy at all times following her profession, and in much demand socially because her very presence dignifies any function, she yet found time to make me cordially welcome in her home whenever I chose to call, which was frequently. Everywhere, there was abundant evidence of refinement and cultivation and financial ease, yet mention of anything beyond the topics of the day, current literature, in which she is greatly interested, the decline of genuine scholarship, and trivialities (she is a great lover of fun and a good joke) was never made.

It was after more than a year of our fine acquaintanceship, though I had long known of the fact before, that she reluctantly talked of her trips abroad and sojourn in Europe, and it was not until I somewhat rather lately made the discovery for myself that she acknowledged her father to be the author of an eminent book I found reposing obscurely on a shelf in her library. She and her family entertain, quietly, without ostentation, but frequently and elegantly, and all the world is happy when he or she receives a bid to come.

The block in which I reside, where a representative group of society have their home, is known by the envious who can't find a house left to get into, as "Strivers' Row," but God forbid that it should derive its name from any similarity to certain other "Strivers' Rows" that I know of, which might with more exactitude be termed "Strifers' Rows." On it, there live an important Bishop of the Methodist Church— in the world, a towering, powerful and dominant figure—in his home, a simple, genial, kindly, cordial man, full of the love of his fellowmen and devoted to his family and his neighbors; a judge—pleasant, neighborly, quiet, minding his own business and nobody's else, who never yet has come and gone in his judicial robes and never will; the recorder of deeds—an able and efficient man in office, in "the row" the lover of little children and his dog—ever ready with a cheery greeting and hopeful comment for any and all who pass his way; a secretary-treasurer of a large university—smiling, thoughtful—a man invincible in the harness—after-hours, happy, strolling in the company of his youngest son; two physicians, whose offices in another section of town, make them glad to return to the beauty and serenity of their home ground—to be seen any evening cuddling a baby or their young children on the lawn as they relax before the night shift; four prominent lawyers—one, a very young man, whose scholastic record, academic honors, and subsequent achievements would have turned the head of any mortal with a less choice spirit than his, yet whose leisure hours are spent in earnest endeavor to bring about better educational facilities for young aspirants to the bar less fortunate than he, and in making more attractive for small boys' recreation at the Y.M.C.A.; two pharmacists, one with a flourishing drug-store which he is too modest to discuss; a young dentist, several business men, teachers, and an architect, all constituting Washington society. The "caterers, butlers and government messengers," I have not met, but then, unlike Mr. Hughes, I have not seen anything in Washington, nor even in my block, which by the way—I will tell on him—is the same in which he lived while here!

For solidarity and neighborliness, there is nothing like the charm of "Strivers' Row," of a spring or autumn twilight when between the children's going to bed and preparation for the evening's pleasure in or out of the home, there comes a pause in individual occupation and the residents meet casually in little informal groups before this or that one's fine home or stop to sit on the hospitable seats on the tiny lawns to chat for a moment of the day's history.

New York knows nothing of it—the human side of human life. It cannot even conceive it, cramped, jaded, restless, striving, sophisticated, cynical as it is. When it reads of pretty little Mrs. So and So, the wife of Dr. X, at this function tonight, that, tomorrow afternoon, the Country Club tomorrow night—a luncheon the next noon, it does not know how sweetly she has played with her adorable young children all day long, how carefully she is training them—how she tucks them in at noon and again at night before she goes forth to her own pleasure, and how tenderly she cares for her mother. How can it? How can anybody outside her intimate friends? Yet she is one of the younger matrons who form the society of Washington spelled with a capital S.

It is not hollow—Washington society—although its outer shell may be brittle, for I have touched and probed its mettle and not found it wanting: society—not "society" for I have neither the time nor the patience to be concerned with the latter, offered me, a stranger to many, entree to its pleasures. If I have seemed sometimes of late to cherish them little, it is not because they lack intrinsically something higher that I would have and so stand aloof in my condemnation, but merely because the woods and trees, sunlight and water, books, writing and the contemplative life make the greater appeal to me now, while for my kind, gay friends, constant indoor frivolity is more satisfying.

Like Mr. Hughes, I too, had heard of Washington ere I arrived—longer than he, because I am older, and much more because I am a woman, but fortunately for me I did not plunge from the sea-green perfection of a world tour or the sun-kissed vista of Mexican hills into a city as civilized and sophisticated as ultra-sophisticated New York. I came by way of Baltimore—but an hour's ride from the capital, where resides a group of cultured, not "cultured" (an eminent writer has recently drawn the fine distinction), colored people whose parallel is not easily to be found in any city—fine, intelligent, intellectual, home-loving, hospitable people with families—not large, but a child or two apiece as an earnest of their good intentions at wedlock, who, though they follow the daily round of worldly fashion—bridge, teas, luncheons, stags, poker and dances, yet find time for friendships and ideals, for kindness and sincerity, gentleness and consideration—for love, loyalty and beauty, and the permanent good of life, as well as for current events, scandal along with Lindbergh's flight and the threatened British-Russian War and the Chinese situation and *God's Trombones* (for like the rest of the great human family, they too share the common failings.)

Perhaps if Mr. Hughes had trod the training ground for a season as I did for several, he would have learned to skim off the froth from the cup which he would examine and look beneath for the essence to quaff. Diamonds and precious metals were never discovered on the crust of the earth. If one would seek for pearls, he must dive deep—and he who would have gold must not be satisfied with the first handful of dross which he scoops up when on his quest.

Mr. Hughes has been hasty—for I, too, have lived in Washington.

And though I long for the privilege of being near New York—hunger for the zest and stimulation, inspiration and freedom and life that is New York—for the shops, the theaters, the concerts, my club—go there at every possible opportunity, I still live contentedly here.

VI
AUTOBIOGRAPHY

The autobiographical type of personal essay remains the most attractive of all essay forms for the essay writer: it is the most free, yet conversely requires the most discipline to avoid self-indulgence; it can be the most far-ranging, yet is the most narrowly focused, upon the single ego. For blacks, this combination of confession and storytelling, of autobiography and polemical discourse, has been especially useful and has allowed for the production of several very fine pieces.

I —

BRENDA RAY MORYCK's "I—" was published in *Ebony* and *Topaz: A Collectanea* (1927).

When I was a very little girl, a strange and unaccountable idea persisted with me that I wanted to belong to the aristocrats of the earth. Psychologists would explain this complex by referring to the African kings and queens who loom so frequently on the horizon nowadays as the direct forbears of every Negro who achieves, and of many who aspire to achieve, but my mother offers a more physical and intimate reason. She spent the lovely Spring months preceding my birth in a serene and exclusive country seat on a tiny farm adjoining a magnificent estate, where the beautiful titled English woman for whom I was subsequently named, and who was graciously pleased to form an attachment for my mother and an interest in my approaching advent, was visiting.

Very early, I began to associate aristocracy with flat-heeled, square-toed shoes, in a day when most children's stubby feet were being sacrificed to the false grace of a pointed toe and ordinary shops refused to display even small children's boots without heels; with short white socks when a mistaken modesty bade mothers cover their small daughters' legs in long, black stockings; clean finger-nails when it was the vogue to cry "let children be children" (meaning let them be pigs); glistening teeth, free from food and film before the alarming days of "one in every five will have it"; loosely hanging, unberibboned locks when two or four tight braids, according to the texture of the hair, flamboyantly decorated with huge, bright-colored bows at the nape of the neck were the vogue; and severely tailored outer play garments, mostly dark blue, when little girls self-consciously appeared on sleds or skates bedecked in last year's finery, and bearskin, crushed plush and velvet betokened the style.

Looking at the children thus accoutred and then examining myself by careful scrutiny, I perceived a striking similarity. So elated was I by this discovery of homogeneity that I entirely forgot to note the difference in the color of our skins. I was so happy in just being a little girl of the sort I admired I neglected to remember that I was colored.

Something happened to me then—something so deeply satisfying, so limitless in its beneficence, so far-reaching in its results, that I set down details here cognizant of hazarding charges of snobbery. It was as if I had been slipped for all times into an impregnable suit of armor with which to shut in after years all subsequent buffetings of the world. No curious stares, no disapproving comments, nor the starkest criticism in my presence of my wise mother's extraordinary taste could shake my equanimity or self-satisfaction. The claim is made, I know, that we see life in retrospect through rose-colored glass, but the actual unembellished fact is that I— a Negro by birth—a very small girl by years—began my battle with a hostile, Caucasian-dominated life outside the home-nest, as a happy, self-assured, young being.

Later years soon dimmed the illusion that the symbol of aristocracy is outward dress and appearance—that it is even that soft-mannered or arrogant veneer which so often deceives—in fact that it is anything but the serenity and strength of mind which come from a consciousness of clear vision, straight thinking and a right evaluation of every detail of life's complexity—not blue-blood but a sterling heri- tage—a taste for the fine and the beautiful—courage and fineness; not wealth in dollars and cents, though to keep high our self-set standards today, we must have money and plenty of it or trail in the dust of unfulfillment a goodly portion of our splendid desires—not money—but riches—a keen and open mind—a fertile brain, a hungry intellect—a sane and wholesome outlook on life—joy in little things,— the gift to love and love abundantly;—not suavity—correct manners, soft-voiced covering of an empty or dishonest heart, nor yet hauteur—smug self-esteem through bending heads which might look up in competition—but gentility—that kindness, consideration, forbearance, tolerance, magnanimity and helpfulness to every living thing which betoken true refinement—but my firmly established belief that I could measure with earth's elite never vanished.

As a Negro, I came to learn that I belonged to a despised group—a group hailed everywhere by every ordinary white child as "niggers" or "darkies"—a practice much more common during my childhood even in the north than it is today slightly south of the Mason-Dixon line; that I must suffer impertinent and malicious stares at school every time "Old Black Joe" or "Swanee River" were sung unless I happened to be in the class of a child-lover—and thank God there were a number to whom I now offer gratitude, who smilingly chose the morning songs themselves and never seemed to remember the existence of those tunes; that I must hand over the set of tea-dishes fallen to my lot as an impartial or blind Santa Claus's gift from a Caucasian Baptist Sunday School Christmas tree because a white infant objected to "that little colored girl" having dishes while she had only a book; that I must play better basketball than any other member of the team to keep my place on it as representative of my high school; that I must always be in company with a certain lovely Caucasian in order to drink soda or eat luncheon in certain exclusive shops or bathe at certain

beaches; that the privilege of touring the beautiful southern part of "the land of
the free and home of the brave" must be foregone because of the insufferable
inconveniences maintained by discrimination; that colleges catered to prejudice,
and all learned people were not cultured; that some were cats and brutes and boors;
that men and women, too, of warped mind and narrow sympathies often dominated
the earth—at least a considerable portion of it, and bent to their evil wills their
brothers less fortunate because cursed with a black skin; that my people were burned
alive and seldom a voice raised in protest, yet gladly saluted the flag which refused
them protection, and in time of war, laid down their lives for a country in which
they had lived on sufferance; that "might is often right" so far as exploitation of
black men is concerned, and that justice is the white man's meed alone. I could
not help it. It was life.

Yet, for every ill, life offers compensation. Being a Negro is sweet at times. It
carries with it privileges which cannot but warm the heart of the most cynical and
callous. The bitter may denounce friendly overtures as patronage, asking only a fair
chance to make their mark according to their abilities, but this is a very partial old
world after all—a world in which the scales for reward and punishment are seldom
equal. We rise—too often, perhaps—on personal favor—not only Negroes, but all
people. Since we are of this world, if not with it, it seems sensible to rejoice in the
kind offices of our well-wishers. "Look not a gift horse in the mouth."

I soon learned that although a representative number of patched up and hungry-
looking little plebeians liked to call "Nigger, nigger, never die, black face and shiny
eye," and a few sturdy, rosy-cheeked ones, too, every time I passed by, the majority
of the children who came from big, comfortable-looking homes—even elegant
houses on quiet streets—(for I went to the public school in a day when intelligent
and far-sighted parents had not yet felt the "menace of socialization" or doubted
the efficacy of mass training for the individual, and the earlier popularity of the
private school and private tutor was on the wane)—were forever seeking me out to
make up their ring or complete their team or play their games, and were constantly
inviting me home to luncheon "because I want Mama to see you" (Mama being
one of those "wholesale-generalizationed" tongued ladies who had pronounced
sentence on all colored children as being rough, dirty, and foul-minded).

Remember, please, that I was very young and very human. I enjoyed it all.
Preening myself on my desirability as "such a *lovely* little colored girl," I soon let
it be known in certain "white trash" enemy groups that I was not allowed to associate
with common children! And when I went home at his invitation with my first
beau—an adorable eight-year-old named Leslie, who I might wish even now could
read these lines—and his family, all gathered on the large veranda of his home to
receive his fair lady, burst into laughter and gurgled, "Why she's *colored*," I thought
they were delighted to find me different!

Little prig—little fool! What does it matter—which or both—so I was happy.
Is it not every child's right to be happy? I was happy.

Again, the earmarks of my Negro blood won me a coveted position as alto in
a duet with a beautiful little Jewish soprano who has since become nationally
known. Nearly all the class entered the competition, but when, by elimination,

only three candidates were left, there was such bitterness and weeping and wailing between the two little white girls desirous of singing "The Miller of the Dee" with this exquisite, divine-voiced doll, that the teachers cut short all controversy with the naïve announcement, "If we let the little colored girl win, the others won't feel so badly." "Beauty and the Jacobin!" How times have changed!

My high school career was practically free of all race consciousness, due, I am now positive, to the absolute impartiality and unbiased principles of the head, a man of genial character but inflexible rule, and a corps of, for the most part, broad-minded, tolerant teachers who very adroitly never permitted the question of color and race superiority or inferiority to crop up. I was just one of the many, a single pupil in a classical school ministering to a heterogeneous group of hundreds of raw young people, making my mark and claiming notice according to my special talents, solely. Only when I made the basketball team was I conscious that my efforts alone had been superior to every other member's and yet I was last to be recognized. But who shall say the extra endeavor a Negro must always put forth in competition with white men does not rebound to his own benefit and credit? Was I not the better player on the court because of longer and more skillful practice before making the team?

Quite apart, however, from my school affiliations, there was another larger and more beautiful life opened to me, solely because I was a Negro. I may or may not have had an arresting personality, I may or may not have been well-bred, well-dressed, generally well-appearing. The fact remains that had I not been distinctly a member of my own racial group, I should never have become a quasi-protegée of an exquisite woman on whom the Gods had smiled in every way at her birth and on through life—who was graciously pleased to entertain me in her home, introduce me to her friends and take me about everywhere—not as her hired companion nor the daughter or granddaughter of some faithful retainer in her father's or mother's ménage, but as an interesting little colored girl who deserved to see the best that life offered, and who because of the barrier of a brown skin must otherwise be denied anything but occasional tempting glimpses.

Through her generosity, I tasted a life utterly beyond the reach of most Caucasians, tasted it under the pleasantest auspices, and therefore came to set store on being a Negro as something rare and precious.

The college years did not dispel this assumption. Rather, they tended to heighten it. The disappointments and heart-aches, which every normal teen-age girl away from home experiences, were not due to color prejudice. At my college, Wellesley, in my day—not so very long ago either—the authorities permitted no discrimination. The student body, consequently, taking their cue from their elders and betters as they always do, consciously or unconsciously even today, engaged in no wholesale active hostilities.

There were girls, of course, who tried to be mean and hateful—usually from small towns in the north and west—the southern girls, it is my joy to relate, with one lamentable exception—and that from the Nation's capital—were all ladies, and though their faces sometimes flamed with protest at the new order of relationships they were forced to endure, their good breeding never failed, and in time they came to be pleasantly civil outside the classroom as well as within, some of them even achieving a friendliness in senior year and a cordiality at reunions that was not to have been dreamed of in freshman days, but for the most part, everybody wanted to do something kind for the one little black girl—alien in a lively, callous, young world of fourteen hundred Caucasians, even the villagers to whom intimate contact with a Negro not a hairdresser or laundress was a privilege.

Again, it was always those choice spirits who roam the world and tread the high places of life unfettered by the bonds of public opinion—either the very, very wealthy or the very blue-blooded, or the jealous devotee of the true principles of democracy, eager to put into practice her newly-conned theories, who were most generous in their friendliness and delightful in their overtures. Sadly must I observe that it was seldom the orthodox Christian recognized by her piety in repeating the prayer for all sorts and conditions of men and her lip-service to "God created of one blood all nations for to dwell upon the face of the earth" who stepped aside from her own interests or widened her circle to include me, but then—she was not missed.

It was delightful—being a Negro at college. She who would decry the kind of satisfaction derived therefrom must indeed be a hypocrite or else abnormal. Let her consider the creature who walks alone through life, white or black—friendless, unnoticed, uncherished, and reflect that it is a normal human being's craving to be liked. If, for wholesome reasons, and certainly there is nothing unwholesome in being a Negro, except in the eyes of certain vicious Nordics who seek to make it appear so, a person is liked—what matters all the rest?

Even today, at a time when the entire attention of the white world at large is focused upon the Negro, with what intent or ultimate purpose it is difficult to forecast; when lynching is increasing, prejudice growing, the right to discriminate sustained on questions of civil right, north and west, as well as south, and unfair competition against the Negro threatening his economic existence except as a peon or pauper—there is a zest in being a Negro.

Read the recent editorial comment on a dainty brown-skinned, bird-throated comedienne, Florence Mills, and take thought of the homage an intelligent world pays to art irrespective of race or color. Sit in capacity-jammed Carnegie Hall and hear the delicate exquisite music made by Roland Hayes, and know him judged a supreme artist, not of his race but of the world. Then consider. Have I not cause for pride of race?

There is honey as well as hemlock in the cup of every Negro—sunlight as well as shadow.

But as a woman, what did I learn? That the sun shines on the just and the unjust—that the mountains clap their hands and the morning stars sing together? That the glory of the sunset fades into the exquisite dusk of twilight and the mid-darkness of night bursts into the glory of the dawn? That the green of the tree-leaf turns to a magic red and gold and when winter comes, spring is not far behind?

Did I learn this as a woman? Ah, yes, and more besides—that the peace and the beauty of earth—fulfillment—lie within the mind, embedded and enshrouded in an elusive quantity called soul—whose entity now men doubt. Bend the body to the rack, confine the intellect to the torture of eternal limitations, the soul is away and free—ranging the hills—roaming the fields, winging on the breeze to an elysium which only God can withdraw. The majesty of mountains, the loveliness of twilight, the ineffable beauty of sunsets, the rush of sparkling waters, the pure calm of the deep woods, the mystery of oceans—starlight, moonlight—sunlight— vast spaces under the infinite sky are mine—mine because I am a woman—a human being—one of God's great family for whom He created the world and all that therein is. Smiling eyes of children—blue eyes under golden curls as well as black eyes in tawny faces are turned toward me. Work, play, and that highest opportunity, the opportunity to help and to give, to mother and to heal—are mine. "Non ministrari sed ministrare" is the radiance of existence. And can I not keep company with the greatest minds of the earth for all times in my books?

Life is rich and beautiful to a woman.

I am a Negro—yes—but I am also a woman.

"Two men looked out from the prison bars,
One saw the mud, the other, the stars."

SO THE GIRL MARRIES

W. E. B. DU BOIS. The marriage of W. E. B. Du
Bois's daughter, Yolande, to poet Countee Cullen was probably the
grandest social moment in the history of the Harlem Renaissance. It was
certainly one of the biggest black weddings of the twenties. The marriage
was a disaster but Du Bois's musing immediately after the ceremony is
illuminating. "So the Girl Marries" was published in *The Crisis* in June
1928.

The problem of marriage among our present American Negroes is a difficult
one. On the one hand go conflicting philosophies: should we black folk
breed children or commit biological suicide? On the other, should we
seek larger sex freedom or closer conventional rules? Should we guide and mate
our children like the French or leave the whole matter of sex intermingling to the
chance of the street, like Americans? These are puzzling questions and all the more
so because we do not often honestly face them.

I was a little startled when I became father of a girl. I scented far-off difficulties.
But she became soon a round little bunch of joy: plump and jolly, full of smiles
and fun—a flash of twinkling legs and bubbling mischief. Always there on the
broad campus of Atlanta University she was in scrapes and escapades—how many
I never dreamed until years after: running away from her sleepy nurse; riding old
Billy, the sage and dignified draft horse; climbing walls; bullying the Matron;
cajoling the cooks and becoming the thoroughly spoiled and immeasurably loved
Baby of the Campus. How far the spoiling had gone I became suddenly aware one
summer, when we stopped a while to breathe the salt sea air at Atlantic City. This
tot of four years marched beside me down the Boardwalk amid the unmoved and
almost unnoticing crowd. She was puzzled. Never before in her memory had the
world treated her quite so indifferently.

"Papa," she exclaimed at last, impatiently, "I guess they don't know I'm here!"

* * *

As the girl grew so grew her problems: school; multiplication tables; playmates; Latin; clothes—boys! No sooner had we faced one than the other loomed, the last lingered—the next threatened. She went to kindergarten with her playmates of the campus—kids and half-grown-ups. The half-grown-ups, normal students, did me the special courtesy of letting the girl dawdle and play and cut up. So when she came at the age of ten to the Ethical Culture School in New York there loomed the unlearned multiplication table; and a time we had! For despite all proposals of "letting the child develop as it will!" she must learn to read and count; and the school taught her—but at a price!

Then came the days of gawky growth; the impossible children of the street; someone to play with; wild tears at going to bed; excursions, games—and far, far in the offing, the shadow of the fear of the color line.

I had a grand idea. Before the time loomed—before the hurt pierced and lingered and festered, off to England she would go for high school and come back armed with manners and knowledge, cap-a-pie, to fight American race hate and insult. Off the girl went to Bedale's, just as war thundered in the world. As a professor of economics and history, I knew the war would be short—a few months. So away went mother and girl. Two mighty years rolled turbulently by and back came both through the submarine zone. The girl had grown. She was a reticent stranger with whom soul-revealing converse was difficult. I found myself groping for continual introductions.

Then came Latin. The English teacher talked Latin and his class at Bedale's romped with Caesar through a living Gallia. The American teacher in the Brooklyn Girl's High did not even talk English and regarded Latin as a crossword puzzle with three inches of daily solution. "Decline Stella!"; "Conjugate Amo"; "What is the subject of 'Gallia est omnis divisa—'?" "Nonsense," said the girl (which was quite true) "I've dropped Latin!"

"But the colleges haven't," I moaned. "Why college?" countered the girl.

Why indeed? I tried Cicero "pro Archia Poeta." The girl was cold. Then I pleaded for my own spiritual integrity: "I have told 12 millions to go to college— what will they say if you don't go?" The girl admitted that that was reasonable but she said she was considering marriage and really thought she knew about all that schools could teach effectively. I, too, was reasonable and most considerate, despite the fact that I was internally aghast. This baby—married—My God!—but, of course, I said aloud: Honorable state and all that; and "Go ahead, if you like—but how about a year in college as a sort of, well, introduction to life in general and for furnishing topics of conversation in the long years to come? How about it? " "Fair enough," said the girl and she went to college.

Boys! queer animals. Hereditary enemies of fathers-with-daughters and mothers! Mother had chaperoned the girl relentlessly through high school. Most mothers didn't bother. It was a bore and one felt like the uninvited guest or the veritable death's head. The girl didn't mind much, only—"Well, really mother you don't need to go or even to sit up." But mother stuck to her job. I've always had the feeling that the real trick was turned in those years, by a very soft-voiced and persistent mother who was always hanging about unobtrusively. The boys liked her, the girls were good-naturedly condescending; the girl laughed. It was so funny. Father, of course, was busy with larger matters and weightier problems, including himself.

Clothes. In the midst of high school came sudden clothes. The problem of raiment. The astonishing transformation of the hoyden and hiker and basket ball expert into an amazing butterfly. We parents had expressed lofty distain for the new colored beauty parlors—straightening and bleaching, the very idea! But they didn't straighten, they cleaned and curled; they didn't whiten, they delicately darkened. They did for colored girls' style of beauty what two sophisticated centuries had been doing for blonde frights. When the finished product stood forth all silked and embroidered, briefly skirted and long-limbed with impudent lipstick and jaunty toque—well, thrift hung its diminished head and philosophy stammered. What shall we do about our daughter's extravagant dress? The beauty of colored girls has increased 100 percent in a decade because they give to it time and trouble. Can we stop it? Should we? Where shall we draw the line, with good silk stockings at $1.95 per pair?

"Girl! You take so long to dress! I can dress in fifteen minutes."

"Yes—Mamma and you look it!" came the frankly unfilial answer.

College. College was absence and premonition. Empty absence and occasional letters and abrupt pauses. One wondered uneasily what they were doing with the girl; *who* rather than what was educating her. Four years of vague uneasiness with flashes of hectic and puzzling vacations. Once with startling abruptness there arose the shadow of death—acute appendicitis; the hospital—the cold, sharp knife; the horror of waiting and the namelessly sweet thrill of recovery. Of course, all the spoiling began again and it literally rained silk and gold.

Absence, too, resulted in the unexpected increase in parent-valuation. Mother was enshrined and worshipped by the absent girl; no longer was she merely convenient and at times in the way. She was desperately adored. Even Father took on unaccustomed importance and dignity and found new place in the scheme of things. We both felt quite set up.

Then graduation and a woman appeared in the family. A sudden woman—sedate, self-contained, casual, grown; with a personality—with wants, expenses, plans. "There will be a caller tonight."—"Tomorrow night I'm going out."

It was a bit disconcerting, this transforming of a rubber ball of childish joy into a lady whose address was at your own house. I acquired the habit of discussing the world with this stranger—as impersonally and coolly as possible: teaching—travel—reading—art—marriage. I achieved quite a detached air, letting the domineering daddy burst through only at intervals, when it seemed impossible not to remark—"It's midnight, my dear," and "When is the gentleman going? You need sleep!"

My part in mate-selection was admittedly small but I flatter myself not altogether negligible. We talked the young men over—their fathers and grandfathers; their education; their ability to earn particular sorts of living; their dispositions. All this incidentally mind you—not didactically or systematically. Once or twice I went on long letter hunts for facts; usually facts were all too clear and only deductions necessary. What was the result? I really don't know. Sometimes I half suspect that the girl arranged it all and that I was the large and solemn fly on the wheel. At other times I flatter myself that I was astute, secret, wise and powerful. Truth doubtless lurks between. So the girl marries.

I remember the boy came to me somewhat breathlessly one Christmas eve with a ring in his pocket. I told him as I had told others. "Ask her—she'll settle the matter; not I." But he was a nice boy. A rather unusual boy with the promise of fine manhood. I wished him luck. But I did not dare plead his cause. I had learned—well, I had learned.

Thus the world grew and blossomed and changed and so the girl marries. It is the end of an era—a sudden break and beginning. I rub my eyes and readjust my soul. I plan frantically. It will be a simple, quiet ceremony—

"In a church, father!"

"Oh! in a church? Of course, in a church. Well, a church wedding would be a little larger, but—"

"With Countée's father and the Reverend Frazier Miller assisting."

"To be sure—well, that is possible and, indeed, probable."

"And there will be sixteen bridesmaids."

One has to be firm somewhere—"But my dear! who ever *heard* of sixteen bridesmaids!"

"But Papa, there are eleven Moies, and five indispensables and Margaret—"

Why argue? What has to be, must be; and this evidently had to be. I struggled faintly but succumbed. Now with sixteen bridesmaids and ten ushers must go at least as many invited guests.

You who in travail of soul have struggled with the devastating puzzle of selecting a small bridge party out of your total of twenty-five intimate friends, lend me your sympathy! For we faced the world-shattering problem of selecting for two only children, the friends of a pastor with twenty-five years service in one church; and the friends of a man who knows good people in forty-five states and three continents. I may recover from it but I shall never look quite the same. I shall always have a furtive feeling in my soul. I know that at the next corner I shall meet my best friend and remember that I forgot to invite him. Never in all eternity can I explain. How can I say: "Bill, I just forgot you!" Or "My *dear* Mrs. Blubenski., I didn't remember where on earth you were or indeed if you were at all or ever!" No, one can't say such things. I shall only stare at them pleadingly, in doubt and pain, and slink wordlessly away.

Thirteen hundred were bidden to the marriage and no human being has one thousand three hundred friends! Five hundred came down to greet the bride at a jolly reception which I had originally planned for twenty-five. Of course, I was glad they were there. I expanded and wished for a thousand. Three thousand saw the marriage and a thousand waited on the streets. It was a great pageant; a heart-swelling throng; birds sang and Melville Charlton let the organ roll and swell beneath his quivering hands. A sweet young voice sang of love; and then came the holy:

"Freudig geführt, Ziehet dahin!"

The symbolism of that procession was tremendous. It was not the mere marriage of a maiden. It was not simply the wedding of a fine young poet. It was the symbolic march of young and black America. America, because there was Harvard, Columbia, Smith, Brown, Howard, Chicago, Syracuse, Penn and Cornell. There were three Masters of Arts and fourteen Bachelors. There were poets and teachers, actors, artists and students. But it was not simply conventional America—it had a dark and shimmering beauty all its own; a calm and high restraint and sense of new power; it was a new race; a new thought; a new thing rejoicing in a ceremony as old as the world. (And after it all and before it, such a jolly, happy crowd; some of the girls even smoked cigarettes!)

Why should there have been so much of pomp and ceremony—flowers and carriages and silk hats; wedding cake and wedding music? After all, marriage in its essence is and should be very simple: a clasp of friendly hands; a walking away together of two who say: "Let us try to be one and face and fight a lonely world together!" What more? Is that not enough? Quite; and were I merely white I should have sought to make it end with this.

But it seems to me that I owe something extra to an idea, a tradition. We who are black and panting up hurried hills of hate and hindrance—we have got to establish new footholds on the slipping by-paths through which we come. They must at once be footholds of the free and the eternal, the new and the enthralled. With all of our just flouting of white convention and black religion, some things remain eternally so—birth, death, pain, mating, children, age, ever and anon we must point to these truths and if the pointing be beautiful with music and ceremony or bare with silence and darkness—what matter? The width or narrowness of the gesture is a matter of choice. That one will have it stripped to the essence. It is still good and true. This soul wants color with bursting cords and scores of smiling eyes in happy raiment. It must be as this soul wills. The girl wills this. So the girl marries.

GEORGIA SKETCHES

STERLING A. BROWN. In "Georgia Sketches,"
Sterling A. Brown wonderfully describes, among other things, attending a
dance concert among poor blacks, a not uncommon thing for Brown to
do. "Georgia Sketches" first appeared in *Phylon*, Third Quarter, 1945.

I. I VISIT WREN'S NEST

For a gentler reminiscence of Atlanta's past, I went out to see "Wren's Nest,"
along with Griff Davis, a young photographer. This modest old home in
West End, with many gables and gingerbread curlycues, is a mecca for
American school children and their teachers, who want to see where the kindly Joel
Chandler Harris created Uncle Remus, Brer Tortoise and Sister Cow.

Well, so did I: so I rang the front door bell. A little flaxenhaired girl answered.
In response to my request to go through the house, she stood there with her blue
eyes wide and, like Uncle Remus's Tar Baby, "she kept on saying' nothin'." Then
she skittered off. In a few minutes, her father, the caretaker, came to the door,
hurriedly putting on a shirt.

I told him that we would like to visit the shrine. He started to open the screen
door, and then noticed Griff. I had my hat on and he hadn't looked closely at me,
but Griff is brown.

"Who's this boy?" he asked, staccato.

"He is Mr. Davis, of Atlanta University," I answered slowly.

"No," the man said. "Sorry, but I can't let you all come in. The Association
has told me not to let in the colored."

I told him that I was writing a book, that at Harvard University in Massachusetts
I had written research papers on Joel Chandler Harris, that I had a scholar's interest

in Harris and his contribution to American literature, that Griff, Mr. Davis, was a serious student of photography, attempting to make camera studies of authentic Americans. I knew I wasn't going to get in, but I poured it on. I was thinking how the lonely lad Joel had hung around Negro cabins, none of them shut to him, listening to every wisp of talk, storing in his memory all the anecdotes and tricks of speech and song, piling up a rich compost as it were to produce those fine flowers that made his fame and fortune. So I poured it on. The caretaker's mouth was hanging open when I stopped, and Griff was grinning.

"I didn't make the rule," the caretaker complained. "Far as I'm concerned, it wouldn't make no difference. But the Association won't stand for it. They'd have my job."

He added that it would be all right to walk around the house, even to the gardens in the backyard. We declined the honor, but stopped at the pink-marble walk leading to the side. Upon each paving stone is printed the name of a Georgia author: Augustus Longstreet, Frank Stanton, Sidney Lanier, Thomas Holly Chivers.

"Now, take Chivers," I said pompously to Griff. The caretaker was on our heels, listening. "He was an unknown poet, of rare eccentric genius, much like, and quite influential upon Edgar Allan Poe. People in Georgia called him crazy, but I do not know that he was any crazier than the rest of them."

Griff turned to the caretaker, and asked, "I suppose it would be all right for me to take pictures?" The man thought it over, then, "I reckon so, " he grunted, and left. As rapidly as Griff focused the camera and worked those plates, he still could get only the front of Wren's Nest and the capacious rear of the caretaker, scrambling up the steps.

II. JITTERBUGS' JOY

Before the war ban on bus traveling, Atlanta was a good city for one-night stands. Several Negro businessmen formed an entertainment company to sponsor Negro name-bands at the municipal auditorium. Under all-Negro management the affairs had only a comparative sprinkling of whites. But they weren't missed; the Negroes came in droves. As Al Moron, the manager of the housing project, complained to me, "Atlanta Negroes will turn out in crowds for only two things; a free revival in church and a pay dance at the auditorium."

The crowds that I saw at those dances were composed largely of high school youngsters, of teen-age, or in the early twenties: the boys in polo shirts and full draped trousers; the girls in flowered print dresses, or snuggling sweaters, dark skirts, bright colored socks and low-heeled shoes. The place belonged to them those nights, and they took the lid off.

Between numbers they screamed and chased each other about, but when the music started, they either went silently into their pirouetting, stamping routine, or pressed around the footlights, staring hungrily at the famous jazzmen, anticipating time-honored riffs, applauding triumphantly at some startling improvisation, more often taut and concentrating, slaves to the harmony and the rhythm.

They knew some of the songs by heart—those the juke-boxes had plugged—

and they watched for the familiar breaks and solos. Often the bandleader had only to announce the number—as Louis Jordan did with "I'm Going to Move to the Outskirts of Town," and the wild welcome pealed. Jordan's sinuous alto sax could barely be heard over the roar of recognition. And so it was with Lionel Hampton's "Flying Home." Lionel had a band of youngsters, many from the West Coast who were on their first southern trip. The band and the crowd rivaled each other in fervor; the cheering and the brilliant brass section seemed to be on a "cutting contest," until finally the lanky young trumpeter went into a screaming spiral that shocked the noisy kids into quiet. Lionel, grinning widely, knocked the crowd out with his dexterous pommeling on the vibraphone, and nearly knocked himself out in that heat. Sweat was pouring off his face when he came backstage; the handkerchief he was mopping with was soaking. But it was worth it. "Man, that bunch out there is a killer!" And he rushed back to give them that perennial favorite "On the Sunny Side of the Street.":

"Rich as Rockefeller . . . Gold dust at my feet,
On the sunny side of the street . . ."

His hoarse engaging jive voice caught their mood and held it. They loved Lionel, no doubt of that. And he was solidly in the groove that night.

I heard Louis Armstrong on one of his infrequent trips back south. He wasn't as roly-poly as I had seen him in New York; he was reducing, he said, getting shed of some of that old avoirdupois, but he looked tired and drawn as well. As he delicately wrapped the large handkerchief around that famous trumpet and took a couple of brilliant solos, the crowd cheered him. But he wasn't a juke-box favorite, and only the elder generation of listeners recognized and honored him as king. His scat-singing was old stuff now, part of the idiom of the high school kids themselves. And a lot of Harry James had come to them over the air waves. Louis sang "When It's Sleepy Time Down South" in that gravelly voice that has so much warmth in it; then he and his sidemen joshed the words a bit, but it didn't quite click. "Folks down there live a life of ease": that wasn't the way these kids had heard it.

The night that Louis Armstrong played was a grand patriotic occasion. Attorney Walden urged the need for buying bonds; his clipped, dry speaking could barely be heard in the huge auditorium and was in contrast to the floridity and extravaganza that it interrupted. Graham Jackson, home-boy of Atlanta, a good pianist and accordion player, now recruiting officer for the Navy, appeared in the gleaming white uniform of a petty officer and gave a canned recruiting spiel. Then he turned and pumped old Satchmo's hand, exchanged a bit of jive talk, went over to the piano stool that Louis Russell gladly gave over to him, and showed his virtuosity on the keyboard. He was more enthusiastic here than while making his speech, and so was the crowd.

More whites were backstage to hear Louis Armstrong than on the other nights. There were soldiers and sailors with their girl friends, hep-cats all, some of them old friends of Louie's. You could hear his rasping voice all over the place: "What do you say, Gate!" "Well, if it ain't old so-and-so himself!" "Man, where you been all this time?" There was much shaking of hands and real camaraderie. Cliff McKay and I got to talking about how jazz tore down the walls. Some walls, anyway. We saw a white youngster stand back from the water fountain and say to a Negro, "You go ahead." Then he took his drink after the Negro. "You see that?" Cliff said. By themselves, or maybe in twos, they'll act O.K. When there are more than two they're scared of being called "nigger lovers."

I butted into an argument with two Negroes who were deciding who was the greatest clarinetist in the world. I learned later how foolish I was, as these were old cronies, one a garageman, the other an electrician, who enjoyed nothing more than making fools and liars out of each other. They both had a desire to play in jazz bands, and they both collected records. Their argument concerned Artie Shaw and Benny Goodman. I asked them about other clarinetists but they had never heard of Jimmy Noone and Sidney Bechet, and they knew little of Barney Bigard's solo work. Their argument ran that if these men I named were good, they would have been heard of, they would be in the big money, wouldn't they? When I admitted that Noone and Bechet, and even Bigard, were not in the big money as Shaw and Goodman were, they looked triumphant. "They just couldn't dig me, man."

A young white fellow eavesdropped on our talk, and followed me away. He was a real hep-cat from way back. He had played alto saxophone with a couple of the lesser-known bands. Yes, he knew Noone's and Bechet's work, very well. He was a native of Atlanta but had been all over the country. Now he was home, getting ready to go in the Coast Guard. He told over and over his experiences in the jazz world, naming with bushleaguer's wistfulness the top men he had met there. He stopped Louie and told him where and when he had heard him play. Louie was bluff and cordial, and gladly gave the boy an autograph. Then the boy asked him to play a number and dedicate it to him; he was going in the Coast Guard soon and it would be something to remember. Louie promised. "Sure thing, man," and rushed on-stage. He didn't get around to playing the number, though, and the white boy hovered in the wings, melancholy and lost, on the edge of a world that once he had had great hope of entering.

I heard the Earl Hines concert from out front up in the gallery. That night Earl was in good form, truly Father Hines, spanking the keys with all sorts of tricky rhythms and chord sequences. Finally, his white smile and his patent leather hair gleaming, he walked to the footlights, and held out his hand. The crowd knew what was coming before he announced it. It was "Skylark," their greatest juke-box favorite. Billy Eckstine, in his rich throaty voice, called "Skylark!" And hysteria broke loose.

I knew the words, straight out of the romantic books: I had wondered how they ever managed the voyage from England to Broadway, those phrases about "someone waiting to be kissed" in "some meadow in the mist," some "valley green with spring where my heart can go ajourneying;" "shadows in the rain," "blossom-covered lane," "wonderful music, vague as a will-o-the-wisp, crazy as a loon, sad as a gypsy serenading the moon." The skylark is told that the lover's heart is riding on its wings: if the skylark sees those beloved things anywhere—

"Won't you take me there?"

I knew that Eckstine's deep mellow singing, coupled with a fluent saxophone solo, did much to make the song popular. At first I wondered what these kids in their zoot-suit drapes, their jitterbugging costumes almost as uniform as athletic suits, had to do with valleys green with spring, or meadows in the mist, or with Keats and Shelley, even disguised in Tin-Pan Alley garb. What did these kids, lost in the cramped tenements of Atlanta's Darktown, have to do with Skylarks? I wondered what twist "crazy as a loon" could have for them. But as Eckstine repeated his chorus on demand, I caught what I felt to be the simple, deeper meaning. The will-of-the-wisp and "the gypsy serenading the moon" business might be foreign, but the "lonely flight," "the wonderful music in the night," those phrases were their language, and something deep in these young ones answered.

After the sentimental "Skylark," Earl Hines knocked out some jump numbers. The dancing was almost weird. The kids were seriously intent. Some of the girls were chewing gum, but all kept their faces expressionless. The wilder the gyrations, the more casual were the masks. The couples were perfect teams, apparently unconscious of anybody else on the floor. But there were no collisions, though the whirling and pirouetting were constant. A couple would embrace, swing off, the girl would be thrown away, then she would prance back, they would turn from each other, then without looking their hands would meet, clasp, and back their bodies would come into momentary embrace; all in perfect timing; a swift, clean-cut beautiful work of art. She was always there, he was always there; each anticipating the other, each knowing the other's improvising. It all seemed so effortless and easy, but I knew better. These perfectly coordinated pairs had mastered their skill, their sixth sense of each other, only after hours of practice at home to phonograph records, I knew. Many couples did not ever split up, the same boy continuing to dance with the same girl all evening long. Supple and strong, the boys still would have been awkward fielding a baseball; the girls surely had had little chance in Atlanta for swimming or tennis; this was a cheaper, more available sport, and they were winners at it. It was far from the hugging dances of the early jazz age; it was impersonal, a parade of coordinated rhythms. Each couple strove for perfection, but they seemed oblivious of attention, they seemed rather lost to the world. I saw little of the acrobatics for which entertainers are paid at New York's Savoy; it was a much simpler, but still accomplished routine that satisfied these kids. Many of the boys kept their caps on their heads; this was dancing too important for etiquette. I looked down on the dance floor from the gallery. It was a heaving sea of heads, shoulders, arms, bodies, legs and feet sweeping in irregular regular waves. I passed a white policeman who was fascinated at the spectacle; his face was a study. He was seeing frenzy, true enough, but it had discipline in it and strength. I wondered what he was thinking.

There were only a few exhibitionists. Two of these couples were pansies, with long hair and loud colored sateen shirts, wide open at the neck, and ringed with sweat. They wanted everybody to see them and they jitterbugged with grotesque exaggerations. But most of the kids were too busy to pay them attention. As long as the music lasted, they would swing their own time.

But when the music ended, the tense preoccupation snapped, the escape was done. Back the youngsters came to high-pitched talking and laughing and quarreling, or sullen walking about. There were some fights; knives were drawn in a few. At "Home, Sweet Home," some couples, exhausted from dancing, stupefied with drink, had to be routed out of their gallery seats. As we came down the long tunnel-like passages from the gallery, we saw liquor bottles everywhere. Drunks lurched against us. Leaving the hall, we drew in deep breaths of the cool morning air. We knew the spell was over for these kids. Just in front of us we heard raised voices, then a smack, and we saw a girl slide to the ground and a policeman forcing his way roughly in the crowd. Girl friends and boys friends rode in the Black Maria that night.

We got to Frank's car just a bit ahead of the pansies, who in their soprano voices were cursing each other and threatening knife play. Safe in the car, Frank wondered why I never got scared attending such affairs. "Anything could happen," he told me. "Some of these Negroes would cut you as quick as they'd look at you." Frank had been one of the most courageous athletes Morehouse had ever had, and I knew he didn't scare easily. He was right. Once the music ended, these crowds could be ugly and dangerous.

Frank was wrong in implying that I wasn't scared. I was, somewhat, but it was gloom rather than fear that I felt most deeply. I thought how often I had resented the charges against my people that they were merely happy, carefree dancers. This dancing had been skillful, certainly. But it wasn't free of care, the way I saw it; it was defiant of care instead. It was a potent drug, a reefersmoke, a pain-killer shot in the arm.

Tomorrow was coming for these kids with a sick thud. On their way back to their slum homes in Darktown, Ward 4, "Pittsburgh," some of them packed in jalopies, many more trudging the unlighted, unpaved streets, they knew what to look for tomorrow. The jazz and jitterbugging had warmed the damp and the darkness this night, but tomorrow had already set in: a tomorrow of crowded homes, poor food, dull work, little play and that snatched on the fly, and nothing to look forward to with any zest. Many of the boys would be in the army soon; what they had heard of that left them cold; and who knows what the hell comes next? The girls would grow up, they'd have their babies and bring them up in the same rickety shacks with the same worries about rent and food and clothing; and then they'd get to be like their mothers whose bitter scoldings and curses were soon to greet them. They were not alone: many white kids of America, depression's children too, knew the same hopelessness and uncertainty; they often sought the same escape. They swooned over Sinatra as these had raved over Billy Eckstine.

But these Atlanta kids weren't aware of that, and even if they had been, it wouldn't have altered their feelings. They had to grab their joy where they found it and hold on frenziedly, today. Tomorrow was another day, and from all they could see, was likely to be a hell.

HOW I TOLD MY CHILD
ABOUT RACE

GWENDOLYN BROOKS was born in 1917 in
Topeka, Kansas, and grew up in Chicago. She is a poet, novelist, and
autobiographer. Among her books are A *Street in Bronzeville* (1945),
Maud Martha (1953), and *Annie Allen* (1950), for which she won a
Pulitzer Prize. Her essay, "How I Told My Child About Race," was
published in *Negro Digest* in June 1951.

Before Negroes broke across Chicago's Cottage Grove Avenue, beginning
of necessity to eat their way east, it was a fascinating thing, only chilling,
to take a child out walking "beyond the borderline."

We never knew what our reception would be. Any one of three reactions on
the part of the pale population entrenched there was possible: one, indifference,
assumed or genuine; two, amusement; three, hostility, open or shut.

The false "indifferents" stalked past us with tight mouths. Their heads were
impatient and high. They wished we were in Africa, beating tom-toms. They wished
we had never been born. Although they would not look at us, were very careful to
"not see" us, they wondered at our brown, the quality of our features.

The genuine indifferents really did not know we were on the street at all.

Those who were amused either laughed outright at our approach, or took
delight in pretending to smother their merriment.

Those who were frankly hostile called us the usual assortment of irrelevant
names, or asked us why we did not stay on *our* side, or stared at us with enlarging
eyes.

A good deal of this was beyond my little boy at the time, for he was very small
when we began our series of walks, and since on all such occasions I merely marched
ahead looking as though only the pleasantest things in the world were happening,
or as though nothing at all was going on, he was, or seemed, deceived. (I have to

add "seemed" because we can never know, definitely, how or if or when a child is being affected subtly by subtle influences.) He went right on listening to birds and looking happily at clouds and trees and grass and buildings and whizzing cars. He went right on asking how the world got here, why stars closed their eyes, how the moon was broken.

By the time he was five, however, something had happened that certainly did command his attention. He knew without a doubt that something was wrong on this earth of God's, and that the sky, which held up that variable article, the moon, was not the only region where things were apt to get broken. For heaven's sake!

It was after eight o'clock on a lovely summer evening. We had been out walking in Washington Park enjoying the gentle air, and now were winding up our outing with the nicest part of it all, usually saved for last—a run down the "hills" of the Midway at 60th Street, and an exploration of some of the streets opposite, studded with the beautiful buildings of the university.

Presently, the darkness found us, on one of the little side streets, still admiring those really inspiring structures, and we decided to turn off for home at the next corner. About to do this, we were suddenly alarmed by a bevy of loud young voices, which came from a fast-moving car in the college road. "Ha ha! Look at the Niggers! Why, you black—" And the little group of six or seven young white men, piled helter-skelter in the car, began to throw handfuls of rocks at us. (*Why* did they have those rocks on hand?—in anticipation of the discovery of Nig-gers?) I covered my little boy's body with mine. It was all over in a minute. The pelting was done, the car was gone, and my decision was made never again to take evening walks east of Cottage Grove with my son.

Formerly I had felt that if any place at all was safe, the university district, mecca of basic enlightenment and progressive education, would be safe. The buildings, with their delicate and inspiring spires, seemed now to leer, to crowd us with mutterings—"Oh no, you black bodies!—no sanctuary here. You have found no sanctuary, you will find no sanctuary anywhere. This beauty is not for you, the architects, the builders, did not have the elongations of your filthy shadows in mind as they worked, as they shaped. Get out, get out; get out . . . "

As we obeyed, I saw that my little boy's face was strangely contorted. He was a "big boy" (of some past four) out escorting his mama, so it would be unseemly to cry. But he managed to ask why—why—why, would "those men" want to hurt us.

I said in effect, I cannot remember my exact words, that, had he not observed that the skins of "those men" were somewhat lighter than ours? He had seen such people before, had he not? Yes, but he had thought they were "just people," not really different from us. Yes, baby, and you were right: they are not different from us, but some of them—*not all*—do feel that, because their skins are lighter than ours, they are different, very different, from us, and even better than us, and that therefore they are entitled to rule others, and to give or take favors as they choose.

These people are wrong. Do not hate them for their wrongness, for hating them will not change them, but always remember why they feel the way they do, and when you are bigger you may be able to help them change the way they feel by teaching them, in many ways that you will learn about later, and by showing them that brown, black, yellow or red, you are a *person*, and good, wise, and helpful to the world. Even without *their* education in mind, you would want to be good, wise, and helpful anyhow. While you are little and helpless, you can do nothing but try to see trouble before it begins to hit you with stones, and get away from it as best you can.

On occasion, I have had recourse to the substance of this speech, with additions and activity suggestions as I felt they could be understood, but only when the subject was brought up by my son (which hasn't been often) or when there was a bombing, near race riot, or lynching about which he himself made a comment. I do not believe in dragging the subject of "race" down for frequent examination and hammering, because I think that children should be helped to view the samenesses among themselves and others, instead of forever having their attentions drawn to surface differences—which we ourselves, the adults, are convinced are, indeed, surface (or are some of us really in doubt, and in need of constant argument to give strength to our assumed "conviction"?).

My child has been fortunate—as many other modern Negro children are today—in being raised in an atmosphere that had room for friends of all colors. He has met and enjoyed (sometimes too much, due to his often over-enthusiastic assumption that our friends are just as much his as—and maybe more than—ours) Negroes, Gentiles, Jews, Japanese, so that unless something sudden and, in its way, violent, occurs, he appears to go along accepting without question the fact that people are people—all warm, all bathroomgoers—no matter what color they are.

I think that the question "What to tell my children about 'race'?" can pretty much be dropped, in the years ahead, if we will encourage freer association of our children with the children and adults of other races.

HOW I TOLD MY CHILD
ABOUT RACE

MARGARET WALKER is professor emerita of English at Jackson State University in Mississippi. She won the Yale University Younger Poets Award in 1942 for her book, *For My People*. She is also author of the Civil War novel *Jubilee* (1966) and *Richard Wright: Daemonic Genius* (1988). "How I Told My Child About Race" appeared in *Negro Digest* in August 1951.

A little over two years ago at Easter time our children received an album of records of nursery songs recorded by Frank Luther. Among the 37 songs is a group of lullabies. These songs have become household by-words. The two older children quickly memorized each one. The baby, less than two years old, is already cutting his musical teeth on one of these songs.

Among the lullabies is one particularly concerned with race. It is introduced in this fashion: "Do you know there are babies all over the world? Nice brown ones and pink ones and black ones and cute little yellow babies. Their mothers love them and sing to them just as your mother does, all over the world. Now here is what a Chinese mother sings to her little yellow baby to put him to sleep:

> Snail, snail, come out and be fed
> Put out your horns and then
>   your head
> And your papa and your mama
> Will give you Boy Martin.

I believe this was our children's first introduction to the subject of race. Before they grew old enough to ask the questions that inevitably face all Negroes who are parents and who live in America, we were trying to introduce them painlessly to a world of love and not hatred, of tolerance and not prejudice.

But there is no way to live without pain and sooner or later we have had to face the problem. I do not know whether we have faced it as honestly and courageously as we should, but there came the day when Marion asked, "Mama, are we colored?" and I said, "Yes." Imagine how I froze inside when she came to tell me how someone she loved and admired in our own race had called her the hated word.

"Mama, she called us a bad name!"

"What did she say?"

"She called us Niggers! She said, 'All right now, you Niggers get out of here.' Are we Niggers?"

I said, "No, you are Negroes, but not Niggers." And with that came the sneering retort: "What are they then? They are not white, so they must be Niggers."

This did not come from the white world. We have fought hard to protect them from any hostile attack upon their delicate and sensitive natures—avoiding the segregated bus for trips to town, carefully ignoring their requests for water from the Jim Crowed fountains in department stores and other public places; telling them they would not enjoy the pictures in the forbidden theaters or the exciting rides in the "white only" parks—but suddenly we faced the insensitive facts of life among our own.

Sooner than we hope we must stand up and face the issues honestly. Once the damage is done there is no way we can erase the emotional hurt, but we can strive to appeal to their growing understanding in an effort to buttress them with truth as well as love. We have their curiosity to satisfy as well as their feelings to consider.

Living as we do, deep in Dixie, facing every day not merely the question of race but the problems of Jim Crow or segregation, we have a tendency to build an unreal world of fantasy, to draw a charmed circle around us and within this circle to feel safe; to close our eyes to the bitter struggle, and to forget if possible all the ugliness of a world as near as our front door, and closer than the house across the street. We live on a college campus and here in a completely black world we often feel a certain kind of escape. We build a tower in which we rationalize our way of life. These become our protective coloring: the poker face, the masked eyes held straight ahead, the deaf ears, and the silent tongue.

Our children, however, do not allow us to remain cowards, complacent, nor withdrawn. They force us to face the bitterness and dare us to explain the pain. Much as it hurts, we owe them the truth.

There was the evening when we took a relative to the railway station and discovered that a chain prevented the Negroes from ascending the stairs to the Jim Crow train until the whites had all moved ahead. This had not happened to us before that night. I saw the bewildered look on Marion's face and the signs of nervousness gathering in James's eyes. Quickly I sought to explain that those people must walk farther to board the southbound train than we, and so they went first; in the morning we walk farther for the northbound train and we move ahead first. I do not think the children were convinced. They sensed something strange about the division of the people into two groups and this I did not discuss. I shall never forget the shock and puzzled look on their faces.

Children discuss race among themselves as much as their elders. They make their own rationalizations, and pin their own half-truths upon the web of lies that surrounds them. Marion and her playmates have had such a discussion. This past year she went to school as a first-grade pupil. At school she saw newsreels of the war in Korea as well as life on the domestic front at home in America. She came home bubbling with the excitement of any growing child slowly discovering a world constantly full of wonder. One day after school:

"Mama, guess what so and so said?"

"What did she say?"

"She said she would like to be white."

"Would you?"

"No."

"Why not?"

"Because white people try to destroy colored people." Then I knew it was time to stop for a long needed talk not merely about race and color, but in order to instill the kind of pride in race and in one's self that was part of my upbringing and of which I have never been ashamed. It was also time to stop the beginnings of prejudice against white people which we as Negroes acquire unconsciously and which I believe is just as egregious as that imposed against us. I told Marion that not all white people are bad, that every person is born with the capacity of loving as well as hating and that those who hate without a cause are blind and ignorant and do not understand why nor what they are hating. I told her that as long as people hate each other there will be wars such as we have now in Korea and that people must be taught to love just as they are taught to hate before the world can be what we want it to be. Then she asked me this:

"If a colored woman married a white man what would their baby be, and would that be all right?"

I confess this set me back on my heels. I looked at my husband and he was grinning. My bottom lip must have dropped because Alex kept egging me on: "Go on. Tell her. Do you believe in mixing the races?" I struggled to rise above evasion. This is what I told her: "If a colored woman married a white man their baby would be considered colored no matter how white the baby's skin would be. There are a lot of people in the world who think it would be all right, and there are a lot of people who think it would be all wrong. It depends on the people. They probably won't ever agree unless maybe someday anybody can marry whomever they choose without fear of what people will think or say or do because perhaps by that time race hatred will be forgotten."

Insofar as pride in race is concerned I began to question my child as a result of her questioning. I sought to know if she, only a few short weeks before her seventh birthday, thought of famous Negroes in terms of race and with pride. I knew she had heard boxing matches over the radio featuring Joe Louis and Ezzard Charles, only a few nights ago Marian Anderson on the Telephone Hour, a Sunday baseball game broadcast with Jackie Robinson playing for the Brooklyn Dodgers and I have read poems to her from *The Dreamkeeper* by Langston Hughes, so that I was not surprised when I asked her for names of famous people and she named these. What did surprise me, however, was to hear her name George Washington,

Abraham Lincoln, and Alexander Graham Bell in the same breath and coupled with these names. She did not distinguish people according to race and she did not know which of these was colored and which was white. Her father and I were pleased. We want her to be proud that she is a Negro, yes, but we also want her to think in terms of people as people and not only of race. We want her to think kindly of all people without malice, without bitterness, without hatred, and without prejudice.

So I have told my child about race, and in so doing I faced the same problem as that of answering such questions as Where do babies come from? How was I born? Where is God? and Why can't I see him?

Just as I had to tell Marion that babies live inside their mothers until they are large enough to be born and live alone. That God is all the Goodness in the world that is all around us but that we cannot see Him because He is a Spirit without face or hands or eyes or feet.

Even so I had to tell her that she is a Negro who can be proud that she is one of millions of colored people in the world and that she is a member of the human race.

TURNING THE BEAT AROUND

Lesbian Parenting 1986

AUDRE LORDE, born in 1934, is a black feminist lesbian poet and cancer sufferer who has written more than a dozen volumes of poetry and essays. She has lectured at various schools around the country and the world. "Turning the Beat Around: Lesbian Parenting 1986" is from her most recent book, *Burst of Light* (1988).

These days it seems like everywhere I turn somebody is either having a baby or talking about having a baby, and on one level that feels quite benign because I love babies. At the same time, I can't help asking myself what it means in terms of where we are as a country, as well as where we are as people of color within a white racist system. And when infants begin to appear with noticeable regularity within the gay and lesbian community, I find this occurrence even more worthy of close and unsentimental scrutiny.

We are lesbians and gays of color surviving in a country that defines human—when it concerns itself with the question at all—as straight and white. We are gays and lesbians of color at a time in that country's history when its domestic and international policies, as well as its posture toward those developing nations with which we share heritage, are so reactionary that self-preservation demands we involve ourselves actively in those policies and postures. And we must have some input and effect upon those policies if we are ever to take a responsible place within the international community of peoples of color, a human community which includes two-thirds of the world's population. It is a time when the increase in conservatism upon every front affecting our lives as people of color is oppressively obvious, from the recent appointment of a Supreme Court Chief Justice in flagrant disregard of his history of racial intolerance, to the largely unprotested rise in racial stereotypes and demeaning images saturating our popular media—radio, television, videos, movies, music.

We are gays and lesbians of color at a time when the advent of a new and uncontrolled disease has carved wrenching inroads into the ranks of our comrades, our lovers, our friends. And the connection between these two facts—the rise in social and political conservatism and the appearance of what has become known in the general public's mind as the *gay* disease, AIDS—has not been sufficiently scrutinized. But we certainly see their unholy wedding in the increase of sanctioned and self-righteous acts of heterosexism and homophobia, from queer-bashing in our streets to the legal invasion of our bedrooms. Should we miss these connections between racism and homophobia, we are also asked to believe that this monstrously convenient disease—and I use *convenient* here in the sense of *convenient for extermination*—originated spontaneously and mysteriously in Africa. Yet, for all the public hysteria surrounding AIDS, almost nothing is heard of the growing incidence of CAIDS—along the Mexican border, in the Near East and in the other areas of industrial imperialism. Chemically Acquired Immune Deficiency Syndrome is an industrial disease caused by prolonged exposure to trichloroethylene. TCE is a chemical in wholesale use in the electronic sweatshops of the world, where workers are primarily people of color, in Malaysia, Sri Lanka, the Philippines, and Mexico.

It is a time when we, lesbians and gays of color, cannot ignore our position as citizens of a country that stands on the wrong side of every liberation struggle on this globe; a country that publicly condones and connives with the most vicious and systematic program for genocide since Nazi Germany—apartheid South Africa.

How do we raise children to deal with these realities? For if we do not, we only disarm them, send them out into the jaws of the dragon unprepared. If we raise our children in the absence of an accurate picture of the world as we know it, then we blunt their most effective weapons for survival and growth, as well as their motivation for social change.

We are gays and lesbians of color in a time when race-war is being fought in a small Idaho town, Coeur D'Alene. It is a time when the lynching of two black people in California within twenty miles of each other is called nonracial and coincidental by the local media. One of the two victims was a black gay man, Timothy Lee; the other was a black woman reporter investigating his death, Jacqueline Peters.

It is a time when local and national funds for day care and other programs which offer help to poor and working-class families are being cut, a time when even the definition of family is growing more and more restrictive.

But we are having babies! And I say, thank the goddess. As members of ethnic and racial communities historically under siege, every gay and lesbian of color knows deep down inside that the question of children is not merely an academic one, nor do our children represent a theoretical hold upon some vague immortality. Our parents are examples of survival as a living pursuit, and no matter how different from them we may now find ourselves, we have built their example into our definitions of self—which is why we can be here, naming ourselves. We know that all our work upon this planet is not going to be done in our lifetimes, and maybe not even in our children's lifetimes. But if we do what we came to do, our children will carry it on through their own living. And if we can keep this earth spinning and remain upon it long enough, the future belongs to us and our children because we are fashioning it with a vision rooted in human possibility and growth, a vision that does not shrivel before adversity.

There are those who say the urge to have children is a reaction to encroaching despair, a last desperate outcry before the leap into the void. I disagree. I believe that raising children is one way of participating in the future, in social change. On the other hand, it would be dangerous as well as sentimental to think that childrearing alone is enough to bring about a livable future in the absence of any definition of that future. For unless we develop some cohesive vision of that world in which we hope these children will participate, and some sense of our own responsibilities in the shaping of that world, we will only raise new performers in the master's sorry drama.

So what does this all have to do with lesbian parenting? Well, when I talk about mothering, I do so with an urgency born of my consciousness as a lesbian and a black African Caribbean American woman staked out in white racist sexist homophobic America.

I gave birth to two children. I have a daughter and a son. The memory of their childhood years, storms and all, remains a joy to me. Those years were the most chaotic as well as the most creative of my life. Raising two children together with my lover, Frances, balancing the intricacies of relationship within that four-person interracial family, taught me invaluable measurements for my self, my capacities, my real agendas. It gave me tangible and sometimes painful lessons about difference, about power, and about purpose.

We were a black and a white lesbian in our forties, raising two black children. Making do was not going to be a safe way to live our lives, nor was pretense, nor euphemism. *lesbian* is a name for women who love each other. *Black* means of African ancestry. Our lives would never be simple. We had to learn and to teach what works while we lived, always, with a cautionary awareness of the social forces aligned against us—at the same time there was laundry to be done, dental appointments to be kept, and no you can't watch cartoons because we think they rot your feelings and we pay the electricity.

I knew, for example, that the rage I felt and kept carefully under lock and key would one day be matched by a similar rage in my children: the rage of black survival within the daily trivializations of white racism. I had to discover ways to own and use that rage if I was to teach them how to own and use theirs, so that we did not wind up torturing ourselves by turning our rage against each other. It was not restraint I had to learn, but ways to use my rage to fuel actions, actions that could alter the very circumstances of oppression feeding my rage.

Screaming at my daughter's childish banter instead of standing up to a racist bus driver was misplacing my anger, making her its innocent victim. Getting a migraine headache instead of injecting my black woman's voice into the smug whiteness of a Women's Studies meeting was swallowing that anger, turning it against myself. Neither one of these actions offered solutions I wanted to give my children for dealing with relationships or racism. Learning to recognize and label my angers, and to put them where they belonged in some effective way, became crucial—not only for my own survival, but also for my children's. So that when I was justifiably angry with one of them—and no one short of sainthood can live around growing children and not get angry at one time or another—I could express the anger appropriate to the situation and not have that anger magnified and distorted by all my other unexpressed and unused furies. I was not always successful in achieving that distinction, but trying kept me conscious of the difference.

If I could not learn to handle my anger, how could I expect the children to learn to handle theirs in some constructive way—not deny it or hide it or self-destruct upon it? As a black lesbian mother I came to realize I could not afford the energy drains of denial and still be open to my own growth. And if we do not grow with our children, they cannot learn.

That was a long and sometimes arduous journey toward self-possession. And that journey was sweetened by an increasing ability to stretch far beyond what I had previously thought possible—in understanding, in seeing common events in a new perspective, in trusting my own perceptions. It was an exciting journey, sweetened also by the sounds of their laughter in the street and the endearing beauty of the bodies of children sleeping. My daughter and my son made issues of survival daily questions, the answers to which had to be scrutinized as well as practiced. And what our children learned about using their own power and difference within our family, I hope they will someday use to save the world. I can hope for no less. I know that I am constantly learning from them. Still.

Like getting used to looking up instead of down. How looking up all the time gives you a slight ache in the back of the neck. Jonathan, at seventeen, asking, "Hey Ma, how come you never hit us until we were bigger'n you?" At that moment realizing I guess I never hit my kids when they were little for the same reason my father never hit me: because we were afraid that our rage at the world in which we lived might leak out to contaminate and destroy someone we loved. But my father never learned to express his anger beyond imaginary conversations behind closed doors. Instead, he stoppered it, denying me his image, and he died of inchoate rage at fifty-one. My mother, on the other hand, would beat me until she wept from weariness. But it was not me, the overly rambunctious child, who sold her rotting food and spat upon her and her children in the street.

Frances and I wanted the children to know who we were and who they were, and that we were proud of them and of ourselves, and we hoped they would be proud of themselves and of us, too. But I remember Beth's fifteen-year-old angry coolness: "You think just because you're lesbians you're so different from the rest of them, but you're not, you're just like all the other parents. . . ." Then she launched into a fairly accurate record of our disciplines, our demands, our errors.

What I remember most of all now is that we were not just like all the other parents. Our family was not just like all the other families. That did not keep us from being a family any more than our being lesbians kept Frances and me from being parents. But we did not have to be just like all the rest in order to be valid. We were an interracial lesbian family with radical parents in the most conservative borough of New York City. Exploring the meaning of those differences kept us all stretching and learning, and we used that exploration to get us from Friday to

Thursday, from toothache through homework to who was going to babysit when we both worked late and did Frances go to PTA meetings.

There are certain basic requirements of any child—food, clothing, shelter, love. So what makes our children different? We do. Gays and lesbians of color are different because we are embattled by reason of our sexuality and our color, and if there is any lesson we must teach our children, it is that difference is a creative force for change, that survival and struggle for the future is not a theoretical issue. It is the very texture of our lives, just as revolution is the texture of the lives of the children who stuff their pockets with stones in Soweto and quickstep all the way to Johannesburg to fall in the streets from tear gas and rubber bullets in front of Anglo-American Corporation. Those children did not choose to die little heroes. They did not ask their mothers and fathers for permission to run in the streets and die. They do it because somewhere their parents gave them an example of what can be paid for survival, and these children carry on the same work by redefining their roles in an inhuman environment.

The children of lesbians of color did not choose their color nor their mamas. But these are the facts of their lives, and the power as well as the peril of these realities must not be hidden from them as they seek self-definition.

And yes, sometimes our daughter and son did pay a price for our insisting upon the articulation of our differences—political, racial, sexual. That is difficult for me to say, because it hurts to raise your children knowing they may be sacrificed to your vision, your beliefs. But as children of color, lesbian parents or no, our children are programmed to be sacrifices to the vision of white racist profit-oriented sexist homophobic America, and that we cannot allow. So if we must raise our children to be warriors rather than cannon fodder, at least let us be very clear in what war we are fighting and what inevitable shape victory will wear. Then our children will choose their own battles.

Lesbians and gays of color and the children of lesbians and gays of color are in the forefront of every struggle for human dignity in this country today, and that is not by accident. At the same time, we must remember when they are children that they are children, and need love, protection, and direction. From the beginning, Frances and I tried to teach the children that they each had a right to define herself and himself and to feel his own and her own feelings. They also had to take responsibility for the actions which arose out of those feelings. In order to do this teaching, we had to make sure that Beth and Jonathan had access to information from which to form those definitions—true information, no matter how uncomfortable it might be for us. We also had to provide them with sufficient space within which to feel anger, fear, rebellion, joy.

We were very lucky to have the love and support of other lesbians, most of whom did not have children of their own, but who loved us and our son and daughter. That support was particularly important at those times when some apparently insurmountable breach left us feeling isolated and alone as lesbian parents. Another source of support and connection came from other black women who were raising children alone. Even so, there were times when it seemed to Frances and me that we would not survive neighborhood disapproval, a double case of chicken pox, or escalating teenage rebellion. It is really scary when your children take what they have learned about self-assertion and nonviolent power and decide to test it in confrontations with you. But that is a necessary part of learning themselves, and the primary question is, have they learned to use it well?

Our daughter and son are in their twenties now. They are both warriors, and the battlefields shift: the war is the same. It stretches from the brothels of Southeast Asia to the blood-ridden alleys of Capetown to the incinerated lesbian in Berlin to Michael Stewart's purloined eyes and grandmother Eleanor Bumpurs shot dead in the projects of New York. It stretches from the classroom where our daughter teaches black and Latino third graders to chant, "I am somebody beautiful," to the college campus where our son replaced the Stars and Stripes with the flag of South Africa to protest his school's refusal to divest. They are in the process of choosing their own weapons, and no doubt some of those weapons will feel completely alien to me. Yet I trust them, deeply, because they were raised to be their own woman, their own man, in struggle, and in the service of all of our futures.

THE IVY LEAGUE
NEGRO

WILLIAM MELVIN KELLY was born in 1937 and teaches at Sarah Lawrence College. His most famous novel is *A Different Drummer* (1962). "The Ivy League Negro," about Kelly's education, was published in *Esquire* in August 1963.

f I have seen one, I have seen at least ten movies about an immigrant father (named Mendelberg, MacNabb, Martinez or Mazzoni—take your pick) who saves his pennies to send his boy, John, to college. There is usually a scene in which the father stands before a group of well-wishers and, in broken English, toasts his son: "I didn't mind working hard because I know it is for my son, Johnny, that I am breaking my back—for Johnny to take and go to the college and come back a great man."

The next important scene is John's homecoming. He looks at the cheap furniture, the doilies covering everything, and feels shame and disgust for it all. His world is bigger and newer now and he is uncomfortable in the old house. He sees his father (it is his father because the Oedipal conflict has to appear sooner or later) as an antiquated old tyrant. He and his father argue and John walks out, slamming the door.

Finally, after he has amassed a fortune in some business of which his father does not approve, John gets an urgent three-in-the-morning phone call from Mama: "Johnny, come quick. Papa's had a stroke." John, turning to his blonde, blue-eyed wife, who is in the other twin bed, says, "It's Papa. He's going fast. I must get to him."

John jumps into his Ferrari (a concession to the Old World) and drives to the local slum. He and his father have a deathbed reunion. His father gasps that he knows in some ways John was right; the world is moving forward. John reciprocates by saying he now realizes that some of the old ways are better; Madison Avenue is not all they say it is. The old man dies happy. John drives back to his mansion and his wife meets him at the door with a plate of bacon and eggs and a Martini.

I must admit in all fairness that this movie has been made so many times probably because it contains good doses of truth. The cultural differences between the immigrant father and his American son are vast. Ironically, the father brought his son to America just to secure for him an education and better opportunities.

It has been different for the American Negro. Here at least is one stereotype with which, until recently, he has not been connected. The reasons are well-known: the Negro did not come here looking for broader opportunities; he was brought by force. Even after slavery was abolished, horizons did not widen. It took the European immigrant one generation to be accepted in America's mainstream; after six or more generations, the African "immigrant" remains one.

Now, finally, the brown Johnny is beginning to march home from college to argue with his father. But when he denounces the old man and stomps out, slamming the door, he finds that in most cases there is no place for him to go.

The last is perhaps an oversimplification, as are most statements about The Problem. But there is some truth in it. A lot depends on the individual Negro and what his life has been, on what he wants and why. Even to understand such a simple statement you will have to know what it is like for a Negro to grow up in America, whether it be in Mississippi, in Harlem, or as I did, in the north Bronx.

There is a time in the childhood of every Negro when he realizes he is different. I am not talking now about his awareness that prejudice and inequality exist in America, nor about the bitterness, resentment and hatred that may or may not grow in his heart with the awareness of his being different; I am talking merely of the realization he is different.

As I said, I was raised not in a ghetto, but in the north Bronx, the only Negro boy on a predominantly Italian-American block. Knowing this, you must not immediately assume I was always unhappy; you must not assume I was always fighting my way to school; this was not at all the case. On the contrary, being the only Negro gave me a wonderful advantage; I was always a very important part of the games my white friends and I played. When we played the Lone Ranger, I was always Tonto. When we fought the Japs, I was always the Friendly Native. This is because I was not so much "colored" as brown, and too good a friend to be one of the outlaws or Japanese.

Being the Friendly Native is perhaps more important than you may realize for the way we played it, the Friendly Native was second only to General MacArthur, and since the good general was continually being captured, drugged, wounded, beaten, or shot, it was the Friendly Native who took over command of Allied Operations in the Pacific Theater.

If it is important for a child to be part of the group of boys his age in his neighborhood, then I was content and secure. I remained so until the day I took my first good look at my grandmother.

My grandmother was white; at least she looked white, like an old Italian woman who sat, on spring and summer afternoons, in a red beach chair on the sidewalk across the street. My grandmother had long, soft, straight white hair, which she bunned at the back of her head. Her nose was not flat like mine and her lips were thin. This did not bother me at all, but it was certainly interesting, and so one day I asked her about it. Why did she look white when I looked Negro?

She told me it was a long story. And it was too. I cannot remember how much of it she told me at the time, for later she told it all, but she did say, in passing, that her grandfather had been a general in the Confederate Army. (Actually he was a colonel, but to me any soldier who was not a private, sergeant or captain was a general.) I was not even interested in which war he fought; being related to a general was all I needed to know.

At this time, around 1944, everybody on the block under ten was actively engaged in fighting the Japanese in the vacant lot next to my house, and so I ran outside that day, bursting with news of the general in my family. I expected my friends to be impressed to their very sneakers. Instead, they did not at all believe me. "That's a lie. And besides, who ever heard of a colored general?"

"But he wasn't colored. He was white."

"Then how can he be your relative? You're colored."

I am sure that no unkindness was meant; theirs was simply the viewpoint of our age. Negroes were Negroes; whites were whites. But still I could not answer the question. I only knew something had happened a long time before that had returned to make me seem a ridiculous liar to my friends. For me, it never really went any further than that and I must consider myself lucky. To other Negro children, growing up in other places, the awareness of difference grows into bitterness and hatred—or resignation and despair.

Not too long after he learns he is different, the Negro child discovers how ambiguous is his position in this country. He learns that being colored is not a matter of actual color, not a fact of description—dandelions are yellow, Negroes are gold ochre— but something else and he does not know what.

The plight of the Negro in America is not that he is different, rather that he spends so much time in painful contemplation on the meaning of the difference. He realizes the white man, and most other Negroes, have attached a value to the difference, and that the value is usually a negative one. He can discover no basis in fact for the negative value, but since everyone else seems to accept it, he becomes convinced that his own judgment is faulty. At this point he is close to convincing himself or has already convinced himself of his own inferiority. Further, since his belief in his own inferiority is an irrational one, it does not help him to define himself, to gain self-knowledge. He is not better off than when he started, in fact, a good deal worse.

This is not true of any other minority in this country, or perhaps in the world. A Chinese in America has a language, a food, a way of life. As a child, his father can tell him all manner of things about the meaning of being Chinese. He may later decide the Chinese way of doing things is inferior to the American way. In this case, however, it will be a real decision, based on real alternatives. This is true, in varying degrees, of all religious, racial and national groups in America. But the

Negro was so completely cut loose from Africa that next to nothing is left of it in his culture. He is more completely American than anyone else in this country, not because, as some say, he has been here so long, but because the American culture is the only culture he knows.

You may say the Negro developed the spirituals and jazz. And perhaps because Negroes did these things, the entire race can be proud. But being Italian is not only knowing that Leonardo da Vinci was Italian. It is knowing too an Italian way of doing everything from cooking food to raising children. And in these terms, the Negro way is the American way. To a Negro, a beautiful Negro girl is one who looks most white, because the standards of beauty of white America are the only ones a Negro knows. If this girl is almost white, if she has light skin, straight hair, thin lips, blue eyes, and a sharp nose—what is the meaning of the adjective *Negro*?

The Negro does not know, but still it is his name.

To be a Negro is to be a man waking up in a hospital bed with amnesia. He asks the doctor who he is, what is his name. The doctor tells him, but the name means nothing to the man. He will take the name anyway, simply because it is better to have a name, even one which holds no meaning, than to have no name at all.

In the same way the Negro takes his name, trying to find personal value in the value others give it. By the time any Negro reaches his late teens, no matter what his life may have been, whether he grew up in the South, in Harlem, or in private school, as I did, he has seen a bewildering number of reactions to his "name," to his skin color. More mystical Negroes will tell him he is a "brother," that his skin knows innately things the white man will never know, that it has natural rhythm, the natural talents of dancing, singing, and athletics, that he is innately "soulful" and in the next breath will condemn the white man for believing in the stereotypes of natural athletic and show-business talent. White bigots will tell him that he is lazy, shiftless, dull-witted and jovial, and that he is also sullen, conniving, and has enough energy to pursue, catch and rape any white woman within a hundred miles. Professional liberals will treat him as a cause, will tell him he should get the same treatment as any other human being, but will forgive him the most vulgar behavior as if he were some big, dumb animal. He will have been told all manner of things about himself, and chances are he will be able to see none of these things in himself.

And so he comes to an Ivy League school—to Harvard (for Harvard is the Ivy League school I know best), and whether or not he knows it, he will be hoping to find himself, not only in the same way that all young men hope to find themselves in exotic places—in Paris, Tahiti, or Cambridge, Massachusetts—but also as a Negro; he will want to discover finally and forever the importance to him of the one-sixteenth of an inch of brown skin which covers his body.

I first entered Harvard Yard one afternoon in late September. I walked through the gate leading past Lehman Hall. On my left was Matthews Hall, built in the Victorian era, and covered with the black spidery fire escapes and grotesque stonework of that period. On my right was Grays Hall, built a few years earlier and somewhat plainer. I stopped between them, as the empty Yard opened up in front of me. The leaves on the trees were dark green; the grass too was green and I remember thinking that it looked like the view in an Easter egg. A lone student, pale from a summer in Widener Library, appeared and walked along one of the crisscrossing black asphalt paths. "This is the place," I whispered to myself. "This is the place I've been looking for."

It was, but not exactly in the way I thought it would be.

An academic community, especially one like Harvard, which attaches so much importance to intellectuality that it sometimes seems the ideal situation would be one in which only disembodied ideas and minds went to class, is a place where a Negro can forget almost entirely about his skin, his Negro consciousness. Negro consciousness has been discussed fully by others; I need not go into it except to say, for those who have never heard of it, the Negro consciousness is the part of a Negro's mind that functions not for him as an individual human being, but for him as a Negro, for his race. It is the part of his conscience which asks him, before he commits any act, "Is it good for the Negro race?"

At Harvard, this part of his mind is soon lulled to sleep. He does not need it. He only has time enough to think of himself as an individual student, going to class, studying for examinations, waiting for his marks. Furthermore, among Harvard Negroes, race pride, as it would be known in Harlem ("If a Negro does it, it's good") is something like patriotism, in a flag-waving sense—antiquated, shallow-minded and conformist. Everything at Harvard is geared to make a man think for himself, to formulate his own ideas. Blind devotion to race does not stand up against analysis, as so often for college students a belief in God does not. To believe in God, Old Glory, or the Marines, and finally the mystical power of a sixteenth of an inch of brown skin takes faith. Harvard is a pragmatic and empirical place.

So at Harvard, a Negro will gain an awareness of himself as a single human being, an awareness of his apartness from any group of human beings, and further, if he has never had one before, chances are he will make one good white friend. They may even room together. They will go to movies, get drunk, study and eat together; across the darkness, they will listen to each other snore.

He will then have found something in common with a white man, on a human level. This takes away a big piece of his Negro consciousness. In order to be a Negro, truly and completely, to believe in a mystical racial unity, a Negro must hate all whites. But having formed an attachment to a white man, a Negro can never again believe in the single and complete attachment of race, can never again believe, if he did before, that all white men are the devil incarnate.

Some do keep their Negro consciousness intact. They are in a minority, and are usually from the South; their wounds are too deep; their scar tissue is too tough. A fellow in my class believed without reservation that the white man was born hating Negroes. Nothing could shake his belief in this principle. He finally became a Socialist, deciding that capitalism bred racial prejudice. Nothing short of a Socialist revolution in this country would change the situation.

For most, constant awareness of their skin color fell away. They did remember from time to time, but remembered it as a nightmare they had dreamed once outside the walls of Harvard Yard.

At Harvard, and at any other Ivy League school, the Negro not only loses his Negro consciousness or at least the sore edge of it, but perhaps will acquire something else: the opportunity to develop a certain aristocratic attitude even toward the white man. Not that he is boorish and goes around telling non-Harvard people they are beneath him. It is rather that he comes to believe, in a quiet way, that Harvard is the best school in the country and therefore that he is one of the select. Yale Negroes feel the same about Yale; Dartmouth Negroes the same about Dartmouth and so on.

One summer, I worked as a plasterer's helper, and having only my lunch hour to do it, I ventured into a bank to open a savings account. I was wearing my work clothes, plaster-covered dungarees and a dirt-encrusted sweatshirt. I asked the teller to instruct me. He eyed me up and down—wondering, I suppose, if I had stolen the money I was about to deposit.

"Step this way." I could hear distaste in his voice.

We walked across the marble floor to a desk, behind which sat a man of forty or so, who had the distinguished look which can only be acquired by working in close proximity to huge sums of money. He, too, looked at me with distaste, but coolly gracious, gave me the forms to fill out. He deposited my money for me, and returned with the cashier's receipt.

I got up to leave, moving just fast enough to cover his glass-top desk with a film of plaster dust. Then I remembered I would be returning to school in a few weeks and decided to register the change of address with him now. I came back to his desk. He looked up, annoyed: "Yes?"

"I'll be going back to school the last week in September and I want to give you that address."

"All right." He rattled through some things on his desk, and came up with a blank slip of paper. "What's the address?"

By this time I was self-conscious at having come into a bank dressed as I was and stammered, "Adams House A-24, Harvard Coll—"

I stopped as he looked up surprised. There was a new expression on his face, something close to stunned respect. "Harvard?"

I nodded.

"Well." His tone changed immediately, became more friendly. "Harvard. Why don't you sit down, Mr. Kelly."

I did. We discussed Ivy League sports. He knew far more about them than I did. He asked me what my major was; I told him. His had been the same. "But," he was timid and almost ashamed, "I only went to Columbia myself."

Graciously I replied: "I'm sure you got a good education at Columbia." (As they used to say in nineteenth-century novels, I blush to admit I actually said that.)

His reply was as self-depreciating as mine had been condescending: "But, Mr. Kelly, not as good as at Harvard."

From time to time at Harvard, I had conversations with both Negroes and whites which centered around the magical power of the name—Harvard. And I feel sure the power applies to the names Brown, Columbia, Cornell, Dartmouth, Princeton and Yale, along with Williams, Amherst and a good many other Eastern colleges. But as his self-esteem grows, the Ivy League Negro sometimes fails to realize that in order for the spell to be invoked, the magic word must be said aloud. In other words, to my bank executive, I would have remained a dirty, irreverent Negro if I had not told him my college address. There have been times when, because I said nothing of my education, I was guest to the same scorn and discrimination that any Negro faces. I have also run across people who have considered me no more than an educated savage, thus leaving their racial prejudice wholly intact. At such times, I was treated ambiguously, with respect for the school I attended, but with none for me as a human being.

I have not meant to give the impression that Harvard is an oasis for the Negro; as free from prejudice as the academic community can be, in that a Negro can gain respect and stature because of intellectual achievement—and even though, to an instructor, grader or professor, a Negro is an albino, without color—when it comes to socializing and dating, his sixteenth of an inch of brown skin still serves to inhibit and exclude him.

Very few white girls at Radcliffe and fewer at Wellesley would date a Negro. If a white boy and a Negro boy roomed together, they might go on double dates, but probably this would be the exception.

Because of the shortage of Negro girls at Radcliffe—in my class, I think there were two out of three hundred—the Negro at Harvard goes for his social life across the river to Boston, and especially to Boston University, which is called jokingly, "the Howard University of the North," because so many Negroes attend and because, in comparison to Harvard, they seem to party so much. The city of Boston also has chapters of the three major Negro fraternities: Alpha Phi Alpha, Kappa Alpha Psi and Omega Psi Phi. Most Negroes at Harvard join one of these, and get their cans fanned and heads shaved before initiation finishes. The fraternities give parties and dances, and each has a traditional connection with one or another Negro sorority.

In my class at Harvard, out of a thousand boys, there were ten Negroes. By the end of the first three weeks of the term, I had met them all. A Negro in a new situation will look, either consciously or unconsciously, for the other Negroes. He will not feel really at home until he knows how many there are, their names, and where they came from. I always compare it to two spies in enemy territory dropping notes scribbled on matchbook covers as they pass one another in the street.

If you had taken the ten in my class and the two girls at Radcliffe and added to these twelve all the Negroes in the entire Ivy League and the women's colleges of similar stature (Smith, Vassar, Wellesley and so on) and tossed all of us into one room, each of us would know at least ten others.

This is because, among other reasons, richer people send their children to better schools. There are few enough rich Negroes for all of them to have met at least once, and thus their children know one another. Also the names of these rich Negroes appear quite often in the social columns of the Negro press and magazines and are well-known. Further, college boys are always looking for attractive, datable girls.

By the end of October, a Negro at Harvard who really cares will know at least the names of all the attractive Negro girls at all the women's Ivy League colleges. An example: my wife went to Sarah Lawrence. I had heard of her at least three years before I finally met her.

Although these students do not make up a tightly knit social group, they will often turn up at the same parties in New York, Boston, Washington, and Philadelphia where, in April each year, are held the Penn Relays. For more than one obvious reason, when spring vacation arrives, Negro students cannot go to Florida or Bermuda. It has become traditional for not only Ivy League but most Negro college students (from as far west as Chicago, as far south as Tennessee or Louisiana) to go to Philadelphia in the spring, to view the Relays through a drunken haze, to party throughout a sleepless weekend.

The Ivy League Negro, and in general, most educated or upper-class Negroes, have an ambiguous attitude toward the uneducated, lower-class Negro. There is, at the same time, disdain and deep love for the "diddy-bop" and the "jungle-bunny"— that is, the lower-class Negro man and woman. With one breath, the Ivy League Negro will ridicule him for his lack of taste, the flashy and revealing clothes of his women, his "dese, deys, dems and doses," and with his next breath he will envy him for his apparent love of life, his women's Africanesque or exotic beauty, and, believe it or not, his rough-and-ready sexuality.

In short, I am saying that in an unconscious effort to become completely integrated into American life, the Ivy League Negro sometimes adopts and accepts the stereotypes and the prejudices of mainstream America—including color prejudice.

Well, not completely. As the Ivy League Negro becomes more learned, more refined, he develops certain feelings of superiority toward all uneducated people, white and Negro. By his new standards, or perhaps by those he brought with him to college, the diddy-bop's tastes are crude and gaudy, his language is crude.

It is not so much real prejudice as it is that he has come to feel himself closer to the educated white man than to the uneducated Negro. This has nothing to do with pomposity or snobbishness. It is that his interests are different.

The upper-class and educated white man can view, without guilt, the lower-class white man with a certain distaste and contempt. But an educated Negro who holds the same attitude toward uneducated Negroes carries on his back huge bundles of guilt. His Negro consciousness begins to work. He feels he has betrayed his race. It is hard for him to separate acceptance of the prejudices of the American mainstream from justified feelings of apartness from the uneducated Negro, from justified pride in his accomplishments.

This ambiguity of feelings is more or less general to every Negro. It is one ramification of the conflict between the Negro consciousness and the individual personality. If a drunken white man boards a subway, stretches out on a seat and goes to sleep, the other whites on the subway will react to him only in individual ways, but they will not feel he has brought shame on the entire white race.

However, should a drunken Negro board a subway, each Negro present will be attacked by a confusing variety of emotions, all descending on him at about the same instant. He will feel his individual attitude toward drunks, ranging from sympathy to disgust, depending on who and what he is. He will hate and be ashamed of the drunk because he is undermining the image of dignity the race is trying to present in its struggle for equal rights (as if a human being must be dignified to be treated as a human being). He will hate the white man because he is sometimes so shallow as to see the entire composition of a race in one drunken member, and also because given the choice between a drunken Negro and a sober Negro, he will choose to think the worst. And finally, he will feel love and sympathy for the drunk because he knows it is the white man's shallow and prejudiced attitude which has helped to drive this Negro, not only to the bar or the bottle, but also to the dope pusher, the phony religious leader, the fortune-teller and palm reader, and more recently, to the Black Muslims, who have not only supplied escape, as do the others, but also the taste of victory and power; who teach that rather than feeling downcast because of his rejection and exclusion from American life, the Negro should not desire to enter in the first place to contaminate his divine blood by mixing it with the blood of the white devil: who have turned the American nightmare of irrational prejudice on its head and made it a faith.

An ambiguity of feeling then is not confined to the educated Negro, but it probably takes a greater toll on him, simply because education has never seemed to make things clearer and more absolute, but more shadowy and many-sided. They say usually that the more questions a person asks, the more answers he receives. It is also quite true that the more questions a person asks, the more questions that are left unanswered.

The uneducated Negro growing up in a ghetto learns different things. As far as he is concerned, his experience boils down to one absolute principle: the white man hates him. He is certain without doubt the white man will hire him last, fire him first, that the white man will exploit him in his own neighborhood in any way he can, that the white man will send his police to brutalize him. He knows all this and carries his defenses high. He finally reaches the point when he believes that even a genuinely kind act hides a savage blow. The white man has always, and will always hate him. For his own good, he must always hate the white man.

It is in the nature of man, I think, to search constantly for an absolute truth in which he can believe, be it God, Jesus, the Blessed Virgin, Allah, Art, Country, Home, Mother or Race. It does not seem to matter that his search turns up chaos under apparent order; man searches for his absolute anyway. If you can accept this, you can see that the uneducated Negro comes closer to having found his Truth— the white man hates him—and the educated Negro, the Ivy League Negro is far from finding his.

At the very beginning, I said that when the brown Johnny denounces his father and storms out of the house, he finds he has no place to go. That may not only be an oversimplification, but an exaggeration. It is rather that if the entire Negro race is caught between an Africa to which it can never return and an America in which it has so far been denied the right to participate completely, then the educated Negro is further caught between a race he feels he has grown away from and a class which will not fully accept him. The only way out is for an educated Negro to work for the betterment of his race. Since very few human beings have the reformer's zeal, very few educated Negroes find fulfillment in the cause for Negro rights. Those who do have found a way to resolve the conflict between Negro consciousness and individual personality.

A friend of mine, a recent graduate from quite a good Eastern college, decided not to take a safe, well-paying job in New York, but went to Georgia to help in registering Negroes to vote.

Recently, I met a mutual friend of ours, an Ivy League Negro. He was working in some not very important job in some not very important agency. I asked him if he had heard about our friend in Georgia.

He said he had. "I got a letter from him. He said he'd been spit at a couple of times. Someone told me he'd been shot at. I don't know if that's true."

"That takes guts," I said.

"Yeah, but you have to be a little nuts too. Going down there, getting spit on by those ignorant bastards, maybe even shot at, and working with a lot of dumb colored people." He looked a trifle sad. Then he chuckled. "I guess I'm just too . . . refined for that kind of crap."

That about sums it up.

DON'T HAVE A BABY
TILL YOU READ THIS

NIKKI GIOVANNI, born in 1943, is the author of several volumes of poetry, including *Cotton Candy on a Rainy Day* (1978), *Black Feeling, Black Talk* (1968), and *Black Judgment* (1969). She has also written several volumes of prose including *Gemini* (1971), from which the essay "Don't Have a Baby Till You Read This" is taken.

Well, you see, I hadn't talked with you, that is, you weren't born and I wasn't expecting you to be. So I decided to spend Labor Day with my parents in Cincinnati. Now, when I told my doctor, because you didn't have a doctor yet, that I was going, he thought that I was going to fly, he told me later, though he couldn't have really thought that because airlines won't let you fly in the last month. But anyway he wasn't thinking and neither to tell the truth was I. So I started out in Auntie Barb's new convertible Volkswagen and we all know how comfortable they are when you plan to drive 800 miles. But that's really not important.

We actually got started about 7:00 A.M. so that we could beat the morning traffic. When we hit the Pennsylvania Turnpike, I thought that was the turning point. We had stopped for lunch before the long stretch into West Virginia when this big black car went zoooooming past us and this thing fell out. I thought, how awful that those white people in the *passing lane* would be throwing out garbage. Then it became obvious that it wasn't and I said, God, I'm gonna hit that dog that fell out of that car, and just as I was adjusting to that Barb said, "IT'S A CHILD!" and I hit the brakes and luckily so did the truck driver in the middle lane and I hopped out of the car while the truck stopped. And the father ran back saying, "Oh, my God! Oh, my God!" but the mother just sat in the car and didn't even turn around and the other small child, another little girl, just looked back to see and maybe there was a glint in her eye, but it's hard to tell under excited circumstances. And

Barb said, "What cha doing getting out of the car? What if that truck hit you?" And I thought it would be a terrible thing for an evil militant like me to be hit on the turnpike because some white people threw their child out the window the way they throw their cats in the lake and I vowed it would never happen to me again. But you were inside and you stirred and I said, "Emma," because I called you Emma, thinking that you were going to be a girl, and I was naming you after your great-grandmother, "I'll never throw you out the car 'cause we don't treat our children that way."

And Barb was so upset by the whole thing that she asked me if I wanted her to drive. Barb was always that way. She figures if she's upset then everybody is more upset than she is because she thinks she's so cool and all. But knowing that about her I drove until we hit Athens, Ohio, and she brought us into Cincy.

When we walked into the house my mother—since you weren't born she was still just my mother—said, "When you gonna have that thing? You look like you're gonna have it any minute!" And being modern and efficient and knowing she doesn't know anything about having children, I said, "Oh, Mother, the baby isn't due until the middle of September. And I don't look like that." She was walking around the house all bent over backwards with her flat tummy poking out and laughing at me. Your Aunt Gary laughed at me also but I reminded her she hadn't had a baby in ten years and things had changed since then. Plus I was tired so I said I was going to bed and Gary said, "Why not spend the night with us since we'll have to go to the store tomorrow for the weekend?" And I said the way Mommy was treating me I should go somewhere because it was obvious she wasn't going to let up, so I said, "Emma and I will spend the night with Gary."

At which Gary said, "You're having a boy and we ought to decide on a name for him." You know how group-oriented Gary is. So she called everyone and said, "We have to name Nikki's baby." I said, "Her name is Emma. But I don't have a middle name for her." And we kicked that around. Then Gus came upstairs—he always goes downstairs when all his women come home for some reason—and said, "You know, my father's name was Thomas." And I said, "Well, if it's a boy we'll name him Thomas." And the reason I could be so easy about saying I'd name a Black child in 1969 Thomas was that I knew you'd be a girl. So we settled the name thing and I went and had an extended B.M., and I thought, that junk on the turnpike really shaped my constipation up. And really, which you may remember, I thought you were constipation all through the first four months, so it wasn't unusual that I still thought that. Your very first foods were milk of magnesia and Epsom salts because I kept thinking I was a little stopped up. And when I didn't get regular I started the sitting-up exercises because I thought I was in bad shape and getting too fat for the laxatives to work. And to tell the truth I didn't think of being pregnant until we were in Barbados and the bikini suit stretched under my tummy and I told Barb, "I think I'm going to have a baby, Barb." And she said she had suspected as much.

So we went out to Gary's to spend the night and Barb went to Grandma Kate's and Mommy and Gus had to stay all by themselves. And the next morning I was tired but I had been tired so long I hopped out of bed with Chris, who offered to fix me one of those good cheese, dried ham and turkey sandwiches that he fixes for breakfast, and I had to turn the little guy down and settle for tea. Chris asked, "Are you really gonna have a baby?" and I said, "It looks like that." And he said, "Is it hard?" And I said, "I don't know much about it but Emma probably knows what to do." And he said, "Well, I'm glad to have my own first cousin 'cause everybody else has first cousins. But I wish you'd have a boy." And I said, "It's really out of my hands, Chris." And he smiled that Chris smile that says you-really-could-do-it-if-you-wanted-to-but-you-don't and said, "If you have a boy I can give him all my old clothes and teach him how to swim and give him my football helmet." And I said, "I think it's going to be a girl. But we don't have to worry about that now." So he went to wake his mother up so we could go to the grocery store. Gary came to breakfast saying, "Chris really wants you to have a boy 'cause most of his friends have brothers and since he doesn't he's got nobody to fight with him." And I said, "Gary, why don't you have a baby or talk to Barb or Mommy? Because I'm going to have a girl." And she gave me that Gary smile that says you-really-could-do-it-if-you-wanted-to-but-you-don't and said, "Well, I don't see why Chris never gets anything he wants from this family. He's part of it like anyone else." And we went to the store.

You know Gary's sense of organization, so all her friends and Mommy and Gus came over that night to fix the food for Labor Day. And we were up late playing bid whist because I love bid whist and since most of my friends are ideologists we rarely have time for fun. But I was winning when I told A.J., my brother-in-law, "I think I'll call it a day." And I went to lie down. Gary came back and said, "Are you in labor?" And I said, "Of course not. The baby isn't coming until the middle of September." And I stretched out. Then Barb came back and said, "Are you having pains?" And I said, "No, I'm not, 'cause the baby isn't coming until the middle of September and that's two weeks away and I'm just tired and a little constipated. Maybe I should take a laxative." And she said, "Just stretch out." Then I heard Gus tell Mommy, "You better go see about Nikki. Those children don't know anything about babies." And Mommy, who usually prefers not to be involved, said, "They know what they're doing." But he prodded her with "*What kind of mother are you?* The baby's back there in pain and all *you* care about is your bid!" So she came back and tenderly said, "Your father thinks you're going to have the baby. Are you all right?" And I said, "Of course, I'm just a little constipated." And she asked if I wanted a beer. "When I was pregnant with Gary I drank beer a lot and it helped." So I said yes to pacify her and I heard Gus say, "You're giving the baby a *BEER*? Lord, Yolande! You're gonna *kill* the child!" And she said something real soft and everybody laughed and Mommy didn't come back.

Then the house was quiet and I still didn't feel well and I kept thinking if I could just use the bathroom it would all be OK, but I couldn't use the bathroom. So I was pacing back and forth and Chris came out and said, "Are you having the baby?" and I said no. And Gary came out and said, "It may have been ten years but I think you're having the baby." And I said, "Don't be ridiculous. I paid my hospital bill in New York and I'm not having the baby here." And she said, "OK, but I'm going to call Barb 'cause you've been up all night." And I said, "It's only

3:00 A.M. and don't wake anybody up. I'm not having the baby. It's the junk I ate on the turnpike." But she called Barb, who said, "Maybe we better call Dr. Burch in New York because he would know." And I said, "Don't call him and wake him up. I'm not having any baby." But she did. Dr. Burch said I wasn't having the baby until the first of October according to his calculations but to take me to the hospital anyway to be sure and to let him know no matter what time. And that was when I first realized that he actually cared and he said to tell me not to worry because it's a simple thing and I thought, uh-huh. And poor A.J. was awakened to take me. They said I wouldn't be in labor until the water broke but to keep an eye on it. So everybody went back home to bed and Barb slept on the couch.

Around six I noticed I was still up and I was really tired and I started crying and saying, "If I just understood what's wrong I would feel better!" And Barb said, "You're probably going to have the baby." And I said, "No, Barb. You know I'm not until the middle of September." And she said, "Burch says the first of October so you both may be off." "Emma," I said, "you wouldn't do this to me." But you didn't move. I had started to the toilet for the umpteenth time when I wet on myself and I was so embarrassed that I felt like a fudgecicle on a hot day or a leaf in autumn. I just wanted to get it over with. So Barb whispered something to Gary who told A.J. and the next thing I knew I was on my way to the hospital again. This time they said, "Take her right on in." And the doctor came to check me and said, "Take her right on upstairs." Then he smiled at me: "You're going to have a baby."

"A BABY? BUT I DONT KNOW ANYTHING ABOUT HAVING A BABY! I'VE NEVER HAD A BABY BEFORE." And I started crying and crying and crying. What if I messed up? You were probably counting on me to do the right thing and what did I know? I was an intellectual. I thought things through. I didn't know shit about action. I mean, I could follow through in group activities, I could maybe even motivate people, but this was something I had to do all by myself and you were counting on me to do it right. Damn, damn, damn. Why me?

When in doubt, I've always told myself, be cool and positive. Like when they said God was dead and Forman asked for his money back, I said, "God was a good fellow when he was around." You know what I mean—the moderate statement. When L.B.J. decided not to run for president again I said, "That's good." You know? There's something positive in everything. We've got to keep things balanced. So when they wheeled us upstairs and I immediately understood it was you and me and I wasn't going to be much good crying, I stopped and went to sleep.

"SHE WENT TO SLEEP? IN THE MIDDLE OF LABOR?" my mother said. And she came right out to the hospital. But there wasn't anything she could do so she just sat down and had a beer with one of the ambulatory patients. The nurse woke me up and asked how I felt and I said fine because I didn't want to upset her with my troubles. And I tried to go to sleep again. I had been up all night and was quite tired. Then the doctor came and said, "Bear down when you have pain." So I grunted. And he said, "Are you in pain now?" And I said I didn't want him to think I was being negative but I wasn't in pain until he stuck his hand up there. And he told the nurse, "Maybe we better take the baby. Get her doctor on the phone." So they called Burch and he said, "You better take the baby if she's sleeping because that is a bad sign." And they told me what he'd said. Then this cherubic woman came in and said, "I'm your anaesthesiologist and I'm going to give you a spinal." Then she began explaining all the various things about it and I said, "Under more normal circumstances I'm sure this would be very interesting. But right now if you'd just like to go ahead and do it it would be fine with me. I mean, I really trust the hospital a lot right now and I'm sure you're more than qualified." She looked at me rather perplexedly and I was going to suggest we meet in the cafeteria the next day when I don't remember anything more. Then there was this blinding light and the doctor said, "We'll have to give you a Caesarean," and I said I knew that when I realized I was pregnant or at least I wanted to. And he said, "We'll give you a bikini cut," and I tried to explain that I didn't GIVE A DAMN what they gave me, just get the baby. And the bikini cut didn't work because then I heard, "Nurse, he won't come out this way. We'll have to give her. . . ." I decided: when in doubt. . . . Then he said, "I think we've got him," and I opened my eyes because I wanted to know what you looked like in case they misplaced you or something and there you were, butt naked and really quite messy, and they said, "Mother"—why do they call people that?—"you've got a boy." And I thought, but I was having a girl. Then I went to sleep for a good rest.

When I woke up I thought it was the next day, only it was the day after that. And people kept coming around saying, "She looks much better." I thought, God, I must be really fine, so I asked the floor nurse for a mirror and she said, "Be right back," but she wasn't. Then I noticed a line running into my arm and one out of my leg and it dawned on me I must look like hell on a stick. And I thought it behooved me to ask about my condition. The nurses all said, "You're fine now, Mother," and I said, "My name is Nikki," and they said, "Yes, Mother." So when Gary came I was interested in how I had done. And she, typical of hospital personnel, said, "You're much better now." So I said, "How was I then?" "A good patient." And I said, "Gary, when I get up I'm gonna kill you if you don't tell me." "Well, you would have come through with flying colors if your heart hadn't stopped. That gave the doctors some concern for a while. Then the baby—he's cute; did you know he was sucking his thumb in the incubator? The smartest little guy back there. Well, he was lying on your bladder and a piece of it came out. But other than that you're fine. Mommy and Gus and Barb and I were with you all the time." And I thought, uh-huh. "And Chris is really glad you had a boy. He said he knew you could do it if you wanted." And I thought, uh-huh.

Then she had to leave the floor because the babies were coming. I pulled my gown straight and worked my way into a sitting position and smiled warmly like mothers are supposed to do. And the girl next to me got her baby. Then all the people on my side. Then all the people on the other side. And I started to cry. The floor nurse said, "What's the matter, Mother?" and I cried, "Something has happened to my baby and nobody will tell me about it." And she said, "No. Nursery didn't know you were well. I'll go get it for you." And I said, "Him. It's a boy." So she brought you to me and Gary was right. Undoubtedly the most beautiful, intelligent, everything baby in the world. You had just finished eating so we sat, you in your bassinet and me in my bed, side by side. Then the nurse said, "Don't you want to hold him?" And I started to say, bitch, holding is to mothers what sucking is to babies what corners are to prostitutes what evasion is to politicians. But I just looked at her and she looked at the lines into and out of me so she put you in the bed, and you were very quiet because you knew I didn't feel too swell and if you did anything I wouldn't be able to help you.

The next morning my doctor came by and said his usual and I said, "I guess so I'm alive," and he said, "If you'll eat I'll take the tube out of your arm." Remembering what hospital food had been like when I'd had my hemorrhoidectomy a couple of years back, I hesitated, but he reminded me that I could feed you so I was suckered. And I was glad because I met the dietician, who was really a wonderful woman. But I made the mistake of saying I liked oatmeal and she made the mistake of giving me a lot and I didn't eat it, and they said, "Mother, if you don't eat we'll have to put the tube back in." So I had to tell her to keep my diet thing together. Institutions make it hard for you to make friends. Then someone asked if I wanted you circumcised and I said yes and they brought you back and you were maaaad. And I loved it because you showed a lot of spirit. And I snuck you under the covers and we went to sleep because we'd both had a long, hard day. They said you wouldn't let the nurse in white touch you for a good long time after that, which is what I dig about you—you carry grudges. And that was a turning point. I decided to get you out of there before they got your heart.

It's a funny thing about hospitals. The first day I was really up and around they were having demonstrations on how to avoid unwanted pregnancies, and I really was quite interested but since I was from New York and in their opinion didn't belong on the ward they called everyone who was ambulatory together and left me in the bed. Then they privately visited the catheterized patients, of whom I was still one, and they passed me by with one of those smiles nurses give you. And the aides came over and one said, "I understand you teach school. What are you doing on the ward?" And I said, "I teach school and I'm here to have the baby." "But you're from New York." And failing to see the connection I said, "I'm Gary's little sister," and they said, "Oh." But since they never thought of me as being a poor black unwed mother I didn't get any birth control lessons. Hospitals carry the same inclinations as the other institutions.

That Wednesday they brought you to me for the morning feeding and you, being impatient and hungry, were crying all the way. When I heard the wail, I knew it was you and it was. You cried and cried and I was struggling to get you up in the bed and you didn't care anything at all about the problems Mommy was having. Finally I got you in and fed you and you smiled. I swear you did, just before I put the bottle in. Well, I had pulled the curtain so we could be alone and I guess they forgot about us because when they came to get the babies they left you. And I sat and watched you sleeping. Then I started crying and crying and Gary came in and caught me. "What's the matter with you?" she sympathetically asked and I said, "He's so beautiful," and I cried a little longer and she said, "You sure are silly," looked at you and then said, "He really is beautiful, almost as pretty as Chris," and I thought, uh-huh.

She left to get me some cigarettes and I decided to sit all the way up so I could cuddle you, and for some reason I started feeling real full but I knew I didn't have to use the bathroom because I was catheterized, so I paid it no mind. Gary brought the cigs back and I lit up my first cigarette since coming to the hospital. Then it happened. The bed was flooded with urine. And I with great exactitude said, "NURRRSE," and she came running. "What's the matter, Mother? What are you doing with the baby still here?" "Never mind that! I've wet the bed." And she laughed and laughed. "You're the only catheterized patient in my knowledge who ever wet the bed." Then she called someone to change it. The aide laughed too and said, "What's the baby doing still in here?" And I made up my mind to ask the doctor as soon as he came.

"What do I have to do to get out of here?" "What's the rush? You can take your time." "I wanna go home." "To New York? That'll be a long time." "To my mother's." "Well, if you can walk and use the bathroom, we'll let you out Sunday. But I don't think you should worry about that." "I'll be ready."

So the first thing I had to do was get out of bed. I hadn't been out of bed since I got in because I had peeped a couple of days before that the position I was in was the critical position. The woman on the other side in number 1 had been moved but I had stayed. People had moved into number 2 but I was still in 1. And I guess if they had told me how sick I was when I was that sick, I would have died. So in the interest of not upsetting God I just lay back and did what they told me to. Now I had to get up so I could get you home.

First I got the bag and flung my legs over the side. Then I smoked a cigarette to congratulate myself. Then I stood up. And I must say the world had changed considerably since I had lain. Everything was spinning. But you know me. If there's a challenge, I'll overcome. So I moved on to the chair. I was huffing and puffing like I had just felled a tree or climbed a mountain, and I was scared. What if I fell and they decided to keep me there for another week or so? But I made it into the chair and sat up. My timing was perfect. The nurse who messed with stitches came by and smiled. "Oh, you're sitting up?" And I said sure with a smile, hoping she wouldn't see the sweat I was working up. "Maybe I'd better get back in bed so you can examine me" (rather hopefully put out), and she said it would be better. Well, at least I had done the first thing.

That evening I sat up for a delicious dinner of warm milk (just to room temperature), gray goo and green goo. They smiled and said, "It'll make you strong," and I thought about my mother saying the same thing about Father John's medicine and I thought, uh-huh.

You can tell a lot about a woman from the way she masturbates. Some go at it for a need thing, some because their hand just happened to hit it, some to remember their childhood. Some women turn on their backs, some their stomachs, some their sides. You can peep a whole game from that one set. So in the interest of finding what was left and what wasn't I reached down to this skinned chicken and said to myself, yeah, it's still there but good and tired. And it wasn't in the mood for any games. I felt the necessity to check since every stranger in the world it seemed had looked up my legs. Institutions still haven't found a way to give service and leave the ego intact. Realizing for one that I hadn't needed to be shaved and for two never having been very hairy, I got nervous and wanted my mother. "Will it grow back?" I asked and she said sure, it always does. But it had taken me a good nineteen years of brushing and combing and high-protein diet to get the little I had and maybe it'd take that long to grow back. "Certainly not. It'll be there before you know it," but I still worried. I wanted to get out of there before they shaved my head and took my kidney.

The next thing, since I had so easily mastered sitting up, was walking down to the nursery and back. I made that my goal since I would have you as a reward at the end and the bed at the return. As I stepped lightly from my bed and grabbed my bag, flung my pink robe in grand style over my shoulders and started from position 1 to the nursery, I heard a collective gasp go up in the ward—"Ooooooo"— and I smiled, waved my hand a little and then proceeded. Visions of the old house flew before my face. We lived now in an all-black city called Lincoln Heights. It wasn't our first real home but it was our first house. When we'd gotten that house we'd all been very excited because I would have a yard to play kickball in, Gary would have a basement to give parties in, Mommy would have a real living room and Gus would have peace and quiet. It was ideal. And we all could make all the noise we wanted to. I have always thought it's very important for people to have their own piece of land so that they can argue in peace and quiet. Like when we had rented an apartment, we hadn't really been able to have arguments and Mommy and Daddy had had to curse each other out on Saturday afternoons so that the landlady wouldn't complain. But now they could fight all day long and well into the night without disturbing anyone. And Gus could throw things and Mommy could call him a motherfucker without appearing to be crude. People need something all to themselves.

I was halfway down the aisle. I passed the fifteen-year-old who had cried, "Help me," because she hadn't known how to feed her baby. I was quickly approaching the thirty-five-year-old who had had the twelve-pound baby. I was going past the girl who listened to "I Can't Get Next to You" all day long on her godawful radio.

We had lived in the old house until I was seventeen; Mommy and I had decided that she and Gus made enough money to have a new house. "I ain't moving" was Gus's reply to our loving suggestion. "I'm happy where I am. A man gets comfortable in his house and the next thing you know they want him to move." And we began looking for houses in Lincoln Heights because we didn't want to lay too much on him at one time. I mean, my father is an old man and it's been proved that old people die earlier when they are uprooted. Like my grandmother would probably have lived another ten or twenty years, but urban renewal took her home that she had lived in for forty-three years, and she was disjointed and lost her will to live. Like a lot of other old folks. I guess nobody likes to see memories paved over into a parking lot. It just doesn't show respect.

So we found a nice little home on the other side of Lincoln Heights and mentioned to my father how we were closing the deal and would be moving in a month. "Nikki, you and your mother can do what you want. She never did listen to me anyway. But I'm staying here." "But you'll be all alone." "Nope. I'll have my radio and I can listen to the ball games. I don't need any of you." "But we need you, Gus. What's a family without you? Who will fuss at us and curse and make us get off the grass? Who will say we can't take the car? Who will promise to build a barbecue pit if you don't come?" "Well, that's different. If you all really need me, I guess I'll go. I thought you didn't want me to." "God, we'd have a dull damn house without you."

So we all prepared to move.

Now, my mother is a very efficient woman, in her mind. And she has a lot to do. So moving day when the movers came we had only packed up the bathroom. But typical of the communal spirit, they all just packed us up and we moved.

The new house was a dream from the git. We were the first and only people to live in it. Gus planted a garden and began to fix up a den and library in the basement. Mommy had a big kitchen and a real living room. We all had a separate bedroom. It was going to be great.

I moved on down to the nursery. You were asleep so I couldn't see you and I headed back.

Yep, I would be good and glad to get home.

The nurse wheeled me down to Gary's waiting car. The nurse carried you and I carried your things. It was the first time you had on clothes and you looked really funny all dolled up and I thought: no doubt about it, the most beautiful baby in the world.

We hightailed it, though I didn't want to go quite that fast, out to Mom and Gus's. I asked Gary to slow down a couple of times but she said the air was polluted and she didn't want you exposed any more than was absolutely necessary. And I thought, that's good logic, so we hit a cruising altitude and before we knew it we were breaking like crazy for exit 19. Your sweet little hand gripped my sweaty big one and we went to sleep for the last half-mile.

When we drove up Gus ran out to grab you but Flora, Mommy's friend, was there and when he set foot in the house she grabbed you. Gary and Chris had run ahead to see if they could hold you and I struggled with your things and my things to get out of the car. Then I had to knock on the door because my hands were full and Gus said, "Come on in, Nikki. Can't I hold the baby? After all, I did name him." And I said, "Can somebody open the door?" and Chris came since he knew he was on the tail end of holding you. Then Flora, who is definitely noted for being proper and Christian and ladylike, said, "I have the baby, Gus, so you may as well go sit down because I'm going to hold him," and she put a double clutch on you and I knew there was nothing I could say. I sat down to smile benevolently at you and then Mommy said, "Why don't you go lie down?" and Gary said, "Yeah, go lie down," and Flora, who is almost always reticent, said, "You may as well go lie down because I'm holding the baby till I leave," and she drew you closer, and I decided there was nothing I could say so I went to lie down.

They had fixed up my old room and had very bright colors on the bed and all kinds of jingle toys for you. They had bought a bassinet, which was of course blue with white lace, and three pairs of jeans. Chris later told me that was his idea since he knew little boys preferred jeans to most other clothes. I felt relatively secure when I lay down because your bassinet and diapers were in my room.

Then I noticed that it was dark and no one had been back in my room for anything. Dogs! I said to myself. They have diapers out front, I'll bet cha. So I struggled into a robe and hobbled outside. "Hi, lady," Gary said. "What cha doing outa bed?" "Yeah, Nikki, go on back to bed," Gus said. "We got everything under control." "Nik, can I hold the baby?" Chris asked and Mommy said, "Would you like a beer? I drank a lot of beer when I had Gary." So I decided to go back to bed.

The next couple of days I spent just getting oriented to being in someone else's home after having had my own for so long. Then I made the grand discovery. THE GRAND DISCOVERY. *Finnegan's Wake* is true. You have got to overthrow your parents but good or you'll live to regret it. Which is not that some parents aren't hip. Or nice. Or loving. But no matter how old you are or what you do you're a baby to your parents. I'll bet you even when Candy Stripe, the famous strip-tease dancer, goes home she's a baby to her mother. My grandmother wouldn't give my mother a key to the house when we visited her and I was old enough to remember that! Even Agnew's mother probably thinks he's still a child. If he ever was. Parents are just like that. So I decided I would have to take complete control of you if I was ever going to get back to my own house again.

First the bath. "Mommy, I think I'll bathe the baby today." "I can do it. I took off from work so I could look after you two." "Yeah, but they taught me a new way to bathe him in the hospital. And you probably aren't familiar with that."

She ambled rather hysterically over to the phone to call Gary. "I think she's still under the anaesthesia because she said I don't know how to wash the baby," and Gary said something and she hung up and called Gus. "I don't know who she thinks bathed her all that time," and Gus said something and she hung up and said, "Why don't you bathe the baby and I'll just watch?" I smiled a sly, sly smile and thought, hurrah for me! But it wore me out so I went back to bed while Gram got to play with a clean baby.

Tuesday after the bath, I sat down with my mother, whom we should hereafter refer to as Gram, for a cup of coffee. "Nikki," she said slowly, like she always does when she has true information to impart, "I don't want you to think I'm meddling in your business. I know you're grown and able to take care of yourself. But don't you think it's time you learned to bake? I didn't learn to bake until after you were born and it's a terrible burden on your child when everyone else has cakes and cookies homemade and your child is the only one with sweets from the bakery."

I immediately understood the importance of what she was saying. It's true, I thought, only I remembered what it was like having her make lumpy cakes with soggy icing. Maybe she, being a grandmother and all, could help out now. I didn't know a single grandmother who couldn't bake. And after all, who was I to scorn her offer? We younger people should recognize that the older generation didn't survive all these years without some knowledge. So I got up to face the blackberries. Then I understood her sneaky grandmother psychology. If I baked the cobbler I would be too tired to feed the baby. The hurrieder I went the behinder I got and I accepted my defeat for the day.

By Wednesday I was worn out. She had won. They—because Gus was definitely a part of it all—started coming in in the morning to get you and I would see you at lunch; then I had to go back to bed and wouldn't see you until it was your bedtime. I somehow felt neglected. Now, it's true that I was tired and it's true that they loved me but I sat all day in my old bedroom and I couldn't play with you and I failed to see going through all that mothers go through to have grandparents take over. I decided I would have to go against my history and my ancestors' way of doing things: "I WANT MY BABY NOW, DO YOU HEAR ME? NOW!" And Gus came in to say I'd wake you up if I kept up that noise. "IF I DON'T GET MY BABY RIGHT AWAY I WILL ROUSE THIS WHOLE NEIGHBORHOOD AGAINST YOU TWO GRANDPARENTS, DO YOU HEAR ME?" And Gus told Mommy maybe they'd better bring you to me and Mommy said real low, "Or put Nikki in the basement," and I sprang at her: "AHA! I KNOW YOUR SNEAKY PLANS. ALL YOU CARE ABOUT IS TOMMY AND I WON'T STAND FOR THAT. I'M YOUR BABY AND DON'T YOU FORGET IT." Then she cuddled me on her lap and said real soothing things and walked me back to my room. I had almost gotten you and I would be more successful at dinner, I vowed. Then I had to admit that they still loved me and that did make it a lot better. Or harder. But anyway, I needed a lot of love and that's what I knew.

Friday I went back to the hospital. I was doing fine. I could go home next week and you could too. They gave me a prescription for something and I asked Gus if he'd stop on the way home and get it filled. "Gary can do it. We'd better get the boy home," he said, and I said all right. Then I realized Gary didn't know what it was and I couldn't get it until she and Chris and A.J. came out, but I thought that'll be all right, so we went on home. Then when Gary came out she took pictures of you and I took pictures of you and Gary and I forgot about it. The next morning I asked again and Gus said, "What's the rush? You'll be here another week or so." And I said, "I'll be here longer than that if I don't get it filled." And he said, "Well, there's always plenty to eat in this house and you know you're welcome to stay," and I dug it. So I said, "Tommy needs alcohol, and while you're there get this filled," and he said, "Why didn't you tell me the boy needed something?" and he flew. I called New York and said Sunday I'd be home. Because I had to come to grips with a very important thing—as I said, *Finnegan's Wake* is true.

So everyone began adjusting to the fact that we were leaving. Mommy said, "I'll be glad because I have things to do and I haven't been doing them. Besides, I'm a busy woman and I work and I have a lot to do and won't hardly miss you at all. You know I'm a supervisor and I'm. . . ." And I said, "We'll be back Christmas," and she felt better. Gus said, "Well, it's good that you're going, Nikki, 'cause the boy cries in the middle of the night and sometimes when the ball game is on I can't even hear it, and your mother and I kinda like the peace and quiet when nobody is around," and I said, "We'll be coming in on the twenty-first so you'll have to meet us." And Gary just cried and cried and Chris said, "You shouldn't leave— you should stay and Mommy will go get your things and I'll teach Tommy how to swim," and I said, "You can come visit us, Chris, as soon as school is out and we'll be home for Christmas." And we began packing and piling into the car and Gus said he wanted to go to the airport but it was going to be frost tomorrow so he had better look after the tomato plants and everybody else just openly cried all the way to the airport but you just peacefully slept while the plane took off and we came home.

BOB'S HOUSE . . .
AN OASIS OF CIVILITY

WILLIAM DEMBY's "Bob's House . . . An Oasis of
Civility," about visits to the home of poet Robert Hayden
(1913–1980), was published in *Obsidian*, Spring 1981. Demby, born
in 1922 in Pittsburgh, has worked as a jazz musician and a
screenwriter in Rome. He is currently an associate professor at the
Staten Island College of the City University of New York. His most
famous and celebrated novel is *Beetlecreek*, published in 1950.

Last week a dinky package came to my house in Sag Harbor. It was from my
oldest sister Juanita who lives in Washington, D.C. Her house burned
down and the clumsy package contained some of my papers from Fisk
University: notes from my classes, old versions of *Beetlecreek*, aborted short stories
written when I was a G.I. in Italy. There was also a worn copy of the *Fisk Herald*.
This issue, April 1947, contained stories by Alvin Cooper and Ben Johnson and a
poem by Bettie D. Latimer. The masthead includes Ann E. Allen and Jean Stewart
as staff members. Robert E. Hayden is listed as the adviser.

I think it was every Tuesday night (or maybe it was some other day of the week,
but I'm sure it wasn't a weekend night because I don't remember any conflicts with
my dating arrangements) all of us would go over to Bob and Erma's house for wine
and culture. This was 1946 and 1947, so there wasn't all that much culture around
the country let alone a nice elitist campus like Fisk. In those days if you said "social
conscience" it very well might have meant having something to do with the color
of someone's skin.

But Bob's house was an oasis of civility. There was Danish furniture, mod-
ernist prints on the wall, a bright electric atmosphere of urbane sophistication.
You could forget Willshoot, the campus guard, whose specialty was zeroing in
on necking couples and freezing them with a flashlight and, rumor had it,

occasionally a gun. Seated on cushions and sipping wine we would discourse about Existentialism or whatever was being discussed nationally in the Sunday newspapers. We would listen to string quartets (Bartok) from the vast collection of albums on the bookshelf. We would leaf through the mint fresh editions Bob used to get through the mail.

Ben Johnson and I (we both beat it to Europe after graduation) were veterans from the Italian campaign. I had written short stories all during the war, had absorbed as much Italian culture as I could during my leaves in Rome and Naples; I had come to Fisk by chance. I meant to go to Yale to study drama, but one week my brother Frank and I decided to visit my sister Gloria who was already attending Fisk. I had grown up in a white neighborhood in Pittsburgh and had had little experience with "colored" (not black, yet) women and Fisk that spring was ripe and gorgeous with beautiful women and I succumbed. I hastily enrolled. Even today Fisk means beautiful women to me, and my years there were lyrically the happiest days of my youth. I must have been president of everything. My juices flowed and overflowed and I felt on top of the world.

Bob would glide across the campus following his thick glasses, and inevitably he would be dressed in a Harris tweed jacket of a heather color, a yellow oxford button-down shirt with stripes, and a bright ruby bowtie, handtied. I was freakish about clothes myself and I really appreciated Bob's style—a Michigan version of ivy-league. Bob would walk into the classroom with the book he would be reading from stuck with bookmarks. We would secretly count the bookmarks in the book and groan inwardly if there were more than five sections he was going to read from. Classes with Bob were so-so: we preferred the wine and cheese nights at Bob's house. Bob would laugh like a moose at something and it was all right to poke fun at the campus fogies and traditionalists. Nothing truly revolutionary, no overthrowing of any institutions, just sprucing them up a bit, New-York-a-fying our outlook. John Brinnin came, Henri Cartier-Bresson came (he told me that he never cropped a picture, that it had to be composed in the mind, that the relationship between life and reality and art was exactly like that—it had to be looked at and shaped in the mind).

Bob read his poems and we felt adult and artists ourselves. We felt that we were on the same level as Bob because of the war we had just come home from. We liked everything Bob wrote. I would read from my own manuscripts and Bob's praise could quicken my pulse more than the girls could do on those weekend dates. Gradually Bob turned me into an artist by just allowing me to talk to him on the same level, letting me join in that braying moose laugh at the others, the philistines.

I was writing *Beetlecreek* in Bob's creative writing class. I couldn't figure out what the novel was really about. I kept submitting the first chapter over and over again. I would go up to the *Herald* office in the tower of the Library and type away, hour after hour. But still the novel wouldn't come into focus. I am looking at one of those yellowing pages now: ". . . now the air had been infused with the morning sweetness—a sweetness that embraced all the smells of the village and took from each some quality that would give to the spring perfume its great capacity for gladdening the soul. . . ." Spring and sex at Fisk could really heat up your prose. There are two notes on the sheet written in pencil in Bob's handwriting.

On the righthand margin is the note: "comma before participial phrase . . ." At the top of the page is written: "Very good, but I think the scene with Bobby is too short to have the desired effect . . ."

A DEATH
IN THE FAMILY

KENNETH A. MCCLANE is an associate professor of English at Cornell University. He has written numerous volumes of poetry and has received wide acclaim for his work. "A Death in the Family," a moving portrait of his dying brother, was mentioned as a notable essay in *The Best American Essays of 1986*. The essay was published by *The Antioch Review* (1985).

He was a kid of about the same age as Rufus, from some insane place like Jersey City or Syracuse, but somewhere along the line he had discovered that he could say it with a saxophone. He had a lot to say. He stood there, wide-legged, humping the air, filling his barrel chest, shivering in the rags of his twenty-odd years, and screaming through the horn *Do you love me? Do you love me? Do you love me?* And, again, *Do you love me? Do you love me? Do you love me?*

—JAMES BALDWIN, *Another Country*

I recall how difficult it was for me to realize that my brother loved me. He was always in the streets, doing this and that, proverbially in trouble, in a place, Harlem, where trouble indeed was great. At times we would even come to blows, when, for example, drunk as he could be, he wished to borrow my car and I had visions of his entrails splayed over the city. I remember one incident as if it were yesterday: Paul, my younger brother, physically larger than me, his hand holding a screwdriver, poised to stab me, his anger so great that his brother, the college professor, wouldn't let him drive his "lady" home, even though he could barely walk. I can still see him chiding me about how I had always done the right thing, how I was not his father, how I was just a poor excuse for a white man, the last statement jeweled with venom. And from his place, this was certainly true: I had done what I was expected to do; and the world, in its dubious logic, had paid me well. I was a college teacher; I had published a few collections of poems; I had a wonderful girlfriend; and what suffering I bore, at least to my brother's eyes, centered around my inability to leave him alone. Luckily, this confrontation ended when my father rushed in on us, our distress exceeded only by the distress in his eyes. Later, my brother would forget the events of that evening, but not the fact that I had not lent him the car. For my part I would never forget how we were both so angry, so hate-filled. I, too, that night, might have killed my brother.

As children we were often at each other's throats. The difference in our ages, just two years, was probably a greater bridge than either of us welcomed. And so we often went for each other's pressure points: the greater discomfort enacted, the more skillful our thrust. But this was child's play, in a child's world. On that November night when my brother and I confronted each other with hate and murder in our eyes, I realized I had mined a new intensity, full of terror and, though I didn't know it then, of love.

Though he was incredibly angry (bitter some might say), I always admired my brother's honesty and self-love. It seemed that everything he thrust into his body was a denial of self—alcohol, smoke, cocaine—yet his mind and his quick tongue demanded that he be heard. In a world full of weakness, he was outspoken, never letting anyone diminish him. When he was at the wheel in that torturous abandon euphemistically called "city driving," he invariably would maneuver abreast of a driver who had somehow slighted him, and tell him, in no uncertain language, where he could go and with utmost dispatch. Paul never cared how big, crazy, or dangerous this other driver might be. When I cautioned him, reliving again and again the thousand headlines of MANIAC KILLS TWO OVER WORDS, he would just shrug. "He's a bastard, needs to know it." I remember how scared I became when he would roll down the window—scared and yet proud.

My brother was unable to ride within the subway, moving immediately to the small catwalk between the cars, where the air might reach him. He complained that he was always too hot, that the people were too close; indeed, as soon as he entered the train, sweat began to cascade off him, as if he had just completed a marathon. Later this image would remain with me: my brother, feet apart, sweat pouring from his body, trying to keep his delicate balance between the two radically shifting platforms, while always maintaining that he was fine. "Bro, I'm just hot." I would later learn that these manifestations were the effects of acute alcoholism; I would later learn much about my brother.

Like the day's punctuation, Paul would make his numerous runs to the *bodega*, bringing in his small brown paper bags, then quickly returning to his room, where he would remain for hours. Some days you would barely see him; my father could never coax him out. Paul saw my father as the establishment, "fat man" he would call him, though this too was somewhat playful. With Paul play and truth were so intermeshed that they leased the same root. One had to be forever careful of traveling with a joke only to find that no joke was intended. Or, just as often, finding sympathy with something Paul said, one was startled to see him break out in the most wondrous smile, amusement everywhere. In this spectacle, one thing was enormously clear: Paul was a difficult dancer. And like all artists, his mastery was also, for the rest of us, cause for contempt. We enjoyed his flights; but we also sensed, and poignantly, that they were had at our expense. Clearly we had failed as listeners, for Paul had not sought to befuddle us; but we, as the majority, were in the position of power and could always depend on it as our last defense. And power, arguments to the contrary, is rarely generous.

My brother would stay in his room for hours, watching the box, playing his drums, talking to his endless friends who, until he was just about to die, came to sit and talk and smoke. Paul inevitably would be holding court: he knew where the parties were, could get anyone near anything, had entrée with the most beautiful girls, who sensed something in his eyes that would not betray them. Many of his friends would later become doctors, a few entertainers, all of them by the most incomprehensible and tortuous of routes. The black middle class—if it can really be termed that—is a class made up of those who are either just too doggedly persistent or too stupid to realize that, like Fitzgerald's America, their long sought-after future remains forever beckoning and endlessly retreating. And Paul's friends, who sensed his demise well before we did, as only the doomed or the near-doomed can, were as oddly grafted to class—or even the promise of respectability—as it is humanly possible to imagine. Like Paul, they sat waiting for the warden, knowing only that the walls exist, that the sentence is real. Indeed, if the crime were lack of understandable passion, they were guilty a hundredfold. But it is not understanding, alas, that the world is interested in. And the world—they rightfully sensed—was certainly not interested in them.

Paul was no saint. Like most of us, he exhibited the confusions and the possibilities that intermittently set us on our knees or loose with joy. He wasn't political in the established way; his body, in its remoteness, was political. It said that the state of the world was nothing he cared to be involved with. Fuck it, he'd say.

In the language of the street, Paul was a "lover." And like all lovers he believed that the pounding of the bed frame testified to something that "his woman" best understood. And in the logic of his bed and of those who shared it, women's lib to the contrary, there seemed to be no complaints. Often I wondered about his use of the term "my woman," the possessiveness of it, the language that brought to mind the auction block and a brutal history that had profited neither of us. But Paul's woman was like his life: if I had my job and my poems, he had his woman. Feminists might complain of this uneasy pairing—I certainly share their concern—but within the brutal reward structure of the ghetto, where one's life is often one's only triumph, such a notion is understandable. My brother's woman was his only bouquet, the one thing that testified that he was not only a man, but a man whom someone wanted. Arguments notwithstanding, no manner of philosophy or word play can alter the truth. My brother loved his "woman" in the most profound sense of the word, since his love centered on the greatest offering he could give, the sharing of himself. And I do not mean to be coy here. For when you are, in

Gwendolyn Brooks's terms, "all your value and all your art," the gift of yourself is an unprecedented one.

But this is a brother's testimony; it is a way of a brother living with a brother dead. It doesn't have the violence of unknowing—the great violence that kept me for so long feeling guilty, which still makes the early morning the most difficult time. I remember how Paul volunteered to watch our cats when Rochelle and I, living for a three-month exile in Hartsdale, New York, had to be away. Max, the large white one, hell-bent on intercourse with the hardly possible, hid within the wall and Paul went nearly crazy, looking here and there, wondering if he should call, afraid that disaster had no shores. Strange how I recall this; it certainly isn't important. But Paul was scared—scared more so because he loved animals, saw in their pain more than he saw in ours, in his.

In July, my father called to say that I had best come to New York. Paul was ill. Very ill. He would probably die. The whole thing was incredible. My father has the nagging desire to protect those he loves from the worrisome. What this tends to create, however, is the strangest presentiment: when he does finally communicate something, it is always at the most dire stage, and the onlooker can barely understand how something has become so involved, so horrible, so quickly; or is thrown, similarly, into the uncomfortable position of confronting the possibility that one failed to acknowledge something so momentous occurring. In either case, one is completely unprepared for revelation, and no matter what my father's heroic designs (and they were that), one's horror at not being allowed to participate in the inexorable, outdistances any possible feeling of gratitude. Although pain cannot be prepared for, neither can it be denied. But on this day, my father's voice was that of cold disbelief—the doctor without any possible placebo. And I was in the air in a few hours.

At that time I was involved in teaching summer school, and the day before one of my students had suggested that we read Baldwin's "Sonny's Blues." I had read the story some years before and had been favorably impressed, though I couldn't remember any of its particulars. Well, at 6:15 I got on the airplane, armed with a few clothes and Baldwin. Little did I know that that story would save my life, or at least make it possible to live with it.

"Sonny's Blues" is about an older brother's relationship with his younger brother, Sonny, who happens to be a wonderful jazz pianist and a heroin addict. The story, obviously, is about much more: it involves love, denial, and the interesting paradox by which those of us who persist in the world may in fact survive not because we understand anything, but because we consciously exclude things. Sonny's older brother teaches algebra in a Harlem high school, where algebra is certainly not the only education the students are receiving. There are drugs, dangers, people as hell-bent on living as they are fervent on dying. But most importantly, "Sonny's Blues" is about the ways in which we all fail; the truth that love itself cannot save someone; the realization that there are unreconcilable crises in the world; and, most importantly, the verity that there are people amongst us, loved ones, who, no matter what one may do, will perish.

Now, I read this story on the plane, conscious, as one is only when truly present at one's distress, of the millions of things going on about me. The plane was headed to Rochester, a course only capitalism can explain, for Rochester is west of Ithaca; and New York, my destination, is east of Ithaca, my place of origin. Clearly this makes no sense, but neither does serving gin and tonic at 6:15 A.M. And I was thankful for that.

The hospital was located in central Manhattan, some five blocks from my father's newly acquired office. My father had just moved from his long-held office at 145th Street, because he had routinely been robbed; the most recent robbery had taken on a particularly brutal nature, when the intruders placed a huge, eight-hundred-pound EKG machine atop him to pin him to the floor. Robberies in this neighborhood were not unusual: my father had been robbed some eight times within the previous four years. But with the escalation of the dope traffic, and the sense that every doctor must have a wonderful stash, doctors, whether, like my father, they had no narcotics at all, became prime targets. My father loved his office; he had been there since he first came to New York in 1941. Although he could have made much more money in midtown, he remained by choice in Harlem. As a child I could not understand this. I wanted him to be amongst the skyscrapers, with the Ben Caseys. Little did I know then that his forsaking of these things was the highest act of selflessness. As he once quietly stated, probably after a bout of my pestering, "Black people need good doctors, too." I imagine my father would have remained in his office until a bullet found his head had not my mother finally put her foot down and declared, "Honey, I know thirty-five years is a long time, but you've got to move."

I walked past my father's new office and headed into the Intensive Care Unit of Roosevelt Hospital. There I met my father and the attending physician—two doctors, one with a son—and listened to the prognosis. Medicine, as you know, has wonderful nomenclature for things: the most horrible things and something as slight as hiccups have names that imply the morgue. But the litany of my brother— septicemia, pneumonia—had the weight, rehearsed in my father's face, of the irreconcilable. My brother was *going* to die. The doctor said my brother was *going to die*. They would try like hell, but the parameters (the word parameters had never before been so important to me) left little in the way of hope.

It is difficult enough to be a parent and have a thirty-one-year-old child dying of alcoholism, his gut enlarged, his eyes red, lying in a coma. It is even more difficult, however, when you are a parent and also a doctor. For you have a dual obligation, one to a profession, a way of seeing, and one to nature, a rite of loving. As a doctor, my father knew what was medically possible—as surely as did any well-trained specialist—in my brother's precarious situation; he certainly knew what the parameters dictated. But as a parent, hoping like any parent that his child might live, he knew nothing, hope being a flight from what is known to the fanciful. And so these two extremes placed my father in a country rarely encountered, a predicament where I could sense, even then, his distress, but a place from which no one could save him.

In the two weeks that would follow, my mother, in grief, would ask my father what were Paul's chances. And he—doctor, parent, and husband—would be placed in that country again and again. As a parent every slight twitching of Paul, a slight movement of the lips, a small spasm of the hand, would move him to joy, to speculation—was that an attempt at words, was Paul reaching out? But as a doctor, he knew the terrible weight of parameters—how a word, no matter how strange its sound or source, does involve meaning. So, often he was placed in the terrible paradox of stating what he least wanted to hear. That yes, it was possible that Paul was reaching for us; but the parameters, the this test and the that test, suggested that Paul was still critical, very critical. And we never pressed him further, probably sensing that he would have to announce that these small skirmishes with the inevitable, like water pools just before turning to ice, could not remove the fact, no matter how much we or he would wish it so, that Paul was going to die. Moreover, for us, this dalliance with hope was a temporary waystation so that we could harden our own tools for the coming onslaught. My father did not have this privilege; he was, like all the greatest heroes, the angel without the hope of heaven.

In many ways the third factor in my father's difficult situation now came most into play, that of husband. My mother, like all of us, clung to hope; but more, she clung to her son. There is no way to detail the sense of a mother's love. In substance, a mother protects her son from the world, which, she rightly senses, is unceasingly bent on his destruction. Yet in my house, since Paul was an artist, so remote, my mother, in a sense, defended a phantom, defending him in much the way one supports the constitutional right of due process. For my mother, Paul was to be protected in theory: he was an artist; he was sensitive; he was silent. This identification with him and with those of his facets the world was bound not to respect— and indeed never did—made her involvement with Paul all the more intense, for he was not only the issue of her womb but the wellspring of her imagination.

My father certainly understood some of this, yet his way of reacting to any ostensible conundrum was conditioned by his medical school training. If there is a problem, he maintained, it can be reasonably addressed. And so he hoped that Paul would descend from his room and tell him what the problem was, why he wasn't finishing college, why he continued to drink so heavily, what, in God's name, did he do up in that room? And as it became obvious that the Socratic method demanded an interchange between two consenting mentors, my father became increasingly concerned and distressed. (The problem with any axiom is that it is valuable only as long as it works: my father's belief in reason had served him happily heretofore; yet now he was encountering an unforeseen circumstance. And he, like all of us when confronting Paul, had little in the bank.)

In any event, my father, in the hospital, was forced continually to grapple with three very difficult responsibilities all somehow connected. My mother, as Paul, miraculously, showed slight signs of rallying (the doctors had originally stated that he had a 10 percent chance of surviving), continued to find reasons, as all of us did, for hope. I recall how my wife and I visited one day and Paul actually extended his wobbling hand—and I, relating this later to my father, actually did press him, asking him if he thought Paul could possibly make it. My father, caught between a brother's hope and the sense that miracles do happen, and possibly even to him, said: "Yes, I think he could; but the parameters (*again that word*) are inconclusive."

(Now I know that he didn't believe that Paul could live—the doctor in him didn't believe it, that is.)

But the most difficult moments for my father came, I think, when he had to explain to my mother, his wife, what he saw, trying always to remember that she was a grieving mother and a hopeful one; and no matter what was happening, might happen, he had to remain a source of strength for her, as she had so often been for him. In this difficult barter, my father also had to worry about my mother's natural inclination to believe the impossible, for hope would make us all immortal, while at the same time protecting that part of her which would permit her to bear this thing, no matter what the outcome. My father continued to caution my mother about the dire state of my brother. The word *parameter* became as palpable to my family as my brother's breath. And the boundaries, no matter what my brother's outward appearance, remained the same. It was enough to drive one crazy. With the weather, when the sun rises and the skin feels warm, the thermometer registers one's sense of new heat. Yet with my brother it seemed that our senses were at war with the medical reality. What, then, in this place, were cause and effect?

During the last week of my brother's life, my mother became increasingly angry with my father, blurting out, "You sound as if you want your son to die." Clearly this was an outburst culled out of anguish, frustration, and grief. And yet it adequately gave language to my father's paradox. Never have I seen the mind and the heart so irrefutably at odds.

My brother died after five coronaries at two A.M. thirteen nights after he was admitted to intensive care. His funeral took place some 250 miles from New York, on lovely Martha's Vineyard, where Paul and the family had spent our happiest years. The funeral was a thrown-together affair: 90 percent grief and the rest dogged persistence that something had to be done. The service was a plain one, with an Episcopal minister reading from the dreary *Book of Common Prayer*. My mother had hoped that someone could better eulogize my brother, someone who might get beyond the ashes-to-ashes bit and talk about the stuff of him, possibly so that we, his family, might finally get to know the person who had slowly drained away from us. The one reverend who knew my brother begged off, with the excuse that Paul had traveled a great distance from when he knew him. And that, to say the least, was the profoundest ministry that man had ever preached.

Although the funeral was a hasty affair, with little notice—and though we hardly knew many of Paul's friends—somehow a large contingent gathered, coming from Vermont, New York, and elsewhere, many of them for the first time at a funeral of one of their peers. I can't adequately describe the motley assemblage. Suffice it to say that these were the Lord's children, the ones who had tasted the bread of this world and waited, still, for manna. One young woman said a few words, choked them out, and then the sobbing began.

I think this meditation aptly ends with his friends, for they knew him and loved him as we did. In Baldwin's *Another Country*, one of the characters, Vivaldo, is described as feeling that "love is a country he knew nothing about." With the death of my brother, I learned about love: my love for him; my love for my parents; their love for one another; my love for those thin-shelled children who gathered on that small hillside to pay witness to one of theirs who didn't make it, who evidenced in his falling that death indeed is a possibility, no matter how young one is or how vigorous. I can't say that I know who my brother was, but I know that I miss him, more now than ever. And love, yes, is a country I know something about.

BODY AND SOUL

STANLEY CROUCH's lyrical essay "Body and Soul" is
from his collection *Notes of a Hanging Judge* (1990). Crouch, a noted
essayist and jazz critic, is a recent recipient of the Whiting Writer's
Prize.

I. THE LAST DAY

During the day, Rome has the feeling of rot and revelation one experiences
when in the private domain of a handsome old woman, where sweat,
stale cologne, rouge, yellowed notes and papers, bottled remedies with
indecipherable labels, crumbling flowers, photographs that seem to have been taken
in a brownish gray mist, clothes stained with experience but never worn anymore,
and the smells of countless meals have formed a heavy collective presence in the
air. Its ruins are like the sagging and corded throatline of a beauty once too sensuous
to be believed and now too soulful to be perfectly understood. Of course, nothing
we worry about is old in the halls where the laws of nature were written, but in our
human effort, with everything over so fast, a city like Rome seems very, very old.

On the last morning there, I decided to beat the summer sun to the punch.
All of the notes, timbres, rhythms, and harmonies of the festival called Umbria
Jazz, the feelings of awe and mystery, blood sacrifice and integrity that resonate
from the cathedrals and museums of Perugia, Assisi, and Florence were moving
from my memory to my spirit, and it was fully an hour and a half before dawn.
The forthcoming heat of the day was presaged by the quality of subtly repressed
steam given to the morning air by the slight humidity. Two stars shone in apparent
sympathy with the slow and gooey low notes of a brood of pigeons clustered some-
where up on the roof of our hotel, and outside in the street men were loading a
white newspaper truck. From the distance of perhaps 70 feet, they seemed to be
singing as they spoke in the sleep-laden, grumbling, dictatorial—even celebratory—

Italian that makes so much of vowels that the most mundane order or response can sound like kindling for an aria. I thought again of how the flares and loops of Italian speech remind me of the sound and feeling of jazz, where the sensual weight, inflection, and rhythm of notes count for so much.

Within an hour I was on the street, intent on an early morning walk. After seven or eight blocks I turned, and nearly a mile away stood the Coliseum. As I walked toward it, part of the pleasure was watching the structure grow even larger and more distinctive as I grew closer. There had been a light rain sometime in the night and the wetness gave the Roman oval an evaporating sheen that seemed to fuse past and present, since the droplets that fell from one place or another made it appear freshly excavated and washed down. But mostly the Coliseum looked like a huge crown of chipped and perforated stone. Its circumference and height were less breathtaking than hypnotic, giving off an imagined hum of history much like that of a movie projector as my mind computed the emotion accumulated through a montage of associations, from Hollywood to the history book; decadents and gladiators, religious fanatics and lions. Of course, the greatest gladiator of our age came from Kentucky and attempted to immortalize his Olympic victory in 1960 with some pool hall doggerel—"How Cassius Took Rome"—at a press conference held on the newly painted red-white-and-blue steps of his home in Louisville, where his father broke out with a patriotic song in his best Russ Columbo imitation.

II. ON THE WAY

In the winter of 1982, I had been invited to Umbria Jazz by Alberto Alberti, an alternately melancholy and exuberant ex-soccer player who books the bands. He described Perugia as a charming medieval town in the hills, and guaranteed me that I would love it and the music and the people. I thought he might be right, but I also figured that there would be much more to write about than fine jazz playing, since I could do that in New York. That section of the world, stretching from the Greco-Roman era to the Renaissance, had inspired in me a repository of images: Poseidon hanging out down Africa way, enjoying fast women of river hips who baptized him nightly; the tugs of literal war between the Greeks and the Carthaginians for control of Sicily; Hannibal; the genetic footprints of boots in the boudoir that left an olive complexion and a twisted wooliness to the hair of certain Italians; and the Renaissance paintings in which the solemn black king is right there in the manger at the beginning of Christianity. No doubt about it: I would go.

The flight itself was quite swinging, given its complement of Negro jazz musicians. For all their ego and sometimes crippling pursuit of hipness, they bring with them a downhome quality that personifies the best the race has yet produced. Among them I know again the barbershops and the pool halls, the big family dinners and the counterpoint of whist and domino games, the back porches and the locker rooms, the street corners and the church parking lots where I had learned so much while tested against the gruff friendship and gallows wit that have come, sometimes as slowly as the proverbial molasses in January, all the way from those slave cabins where the partying and the singing went on late into the night, puzzling old Thomas Jefferson, who knew his human property had to meet their mules and their labors in the dawn morning, to grunt and sweat until dusk. Standing at the back of the plane, swapping tales and jokes as the jet's windows opened to darkness on the left side and light on the right, I thought of how the old people had always said, "Justice may not have delivered our mail yet, but we still had a lot of goddam fun along the way—and raised as much sand as the alligator did when the pond went dry! You can believe *that*."

III. PERUGIA

We arrived in Rome and took a bus to Perugia, the headquarters of Umbria Jazz, traveling north on roads that passed between hills that supported both simple tiled houses and, now and again, castles embodying the will to security and civilization that resulted in armaments as well as the quarrying and dragging of the stone up that terrain. From those heights, the citizenry fought for sovereignty from invaders and rival provinces or, much later, against the control of the church. Perugia, whose history stretches back to the Etruscan age, is at the pinnacle of an especially steep group of hills, now partially surrounded by walls that provided the Romans with models of unscalable protection. Because of its very long past, Perugia, like all of Italy, is so steeped in a complex range of human time that it pulls together the superficial incongruity of the historical periods that create its atmosphere—the ancient walls, the misty and green and faded-orange landscapes already familiar from Renaissance paintings, the churches, the town squares, the sloping stone streets, the small cars designed to get through them, the motorcycles, the buses whose wide turns barely miss the walls and pedestrians, the opera house, the sidewalk cafés in which the culture of the city slowly sizzles, and the clothes that look a season or two ahead in elegance and verve of style.

IV. HANNIBAL AD PORTAS

Later, on the train to Florence: Out that window, where Italians are presently sunbathing, had come Hannibal, fighting at Lake Trasimene in 217 B.C., utilizing the beginnings of tank warfare, his Negro mahouts on elephants, the pachyderms girded for battle, their voluminous bellowing in the Alpine air behind them, their tusks and tonnage ready for the Roman legions that would be whipped to their knees and crushed. The survivors of slain Flaminius's decimated army fled throughout Etruria and Umbria, some hiding within the walls of Perugia, Perugia that was to send doomed volunteers to the terrifying Roman defeat at Cannae, where Empire seemed at end, and Perugia that was to furnish wood and grain for Scipio's fleet, helping to bang the gong on the big Punic dream of victory within the bastion of the boot, since Hannibal—great, wily, eloquent, and treacherous Hannibal—after 17 years of fighting, would return to an invaded Carthage, sue for peace, be refused by a bitter Scipio, and face his multitongued army's destruction at Zama, elephants and all.

V. UMBRIA JAZZ

Umbria Jazz wasn't like any other festival I had attended because it included jazz clinics, films, and concerts for audiences that sometimes had better ears than I expect even in New York. Those ears were also evident in the Italian tenor players I heard in the clinic, many of whom startled me with more soulful sounds than the canned Coltrane you hear so often in New York. Somewhere down the steep stone streets and around this corner and that, passing through the cool shadows of buildings that date back to the Middle Ages, the classes were held in an edifice that bore the inscription CHARLIE PARKER SCHOOL OF JAZZ, an insignia that bespoke a conquest much different than the Roman seal of AUGUSTA PERUGIA. Dan Morgenstern of Rutgers University was brought over to lecture on jazz history, while tenor saxophonist Paul Jeffrey headed a faculty of musicians who ranged from their early twenties to their fifties—trumpeter Terence Blanchard, alto saxophonist Frank Strozier, pianist Harold Mabern, guitarist Kevin Eubanks, bassist David Eubanks, and drummer Jimmy Cobb. Jeffrey, a repository of jazz fact and lore and a model of patience and inspiration, said of the students, "They want to know about the soul part, about phrasing, time, and sound. Soul. They come looking for that." Mabern taught with the fervor of a deacon assigned a recalcitrant Sunday school class and had similar observations. "The reason cats come over here and have a good time is that they hear the truth. These people want the best they can get. They don't let this skin scare them into some other stuff. They want the real deal."

Carlo Pagnotta's plan for the festival included David Chertok's jazz films, music in the piazzas, in the tent—Teatro Tenda—20 minutes away, and a concluding performance in Narni, an hour from Perugia. Other than the excessive treble from the sound crew, who botched the first few concerts in the tent, there were no problems, unless one considered some well-deserved booing and cat-calling problems. But it had not always been that way. When Pagnotta began producing concerts with the cooperation and financing of local government in 1973, many of the young people who came treated the performances like rock and roll happenings polluted with radical stances. Music with melody, harmony, and instrumental control was considered the art of repression and the symbol of the enslavement of black people, while the opportunists of the "avant-garde" were celebrated as the voices of freedom. The concerts moved from town to town with the unruly young people following them, and things became so bad that the owners of local shops began to board up their windows and doors when the festival arrived. But in 1978, Pagnotta pared down the traveling aspects of the festival, adding a resident American group every night at Il Panino, a club at the end of a twisting street that descends and descends, testing the mettle of those who drink too much and try to walk home. Professor Germano Marri, an old friend of Pagnotta, was elected president of Umbria that same year. With his handsome seriousness and idiomatic wit, Marri appears to represent a communism as distinct from that of Russia and its totalitarian satellites as his superb suits are from their bad tailoring. Perhaps because aesthetic quality is so thick in the air and ambience of Perugia, Marri and his staff appreciate the human complexity that has eluded almost all socialist creation. The communist organization ARCI puts together the concerts in conjunction with Perugina Chocolate and Alitalia Airlines, and allows the music to exist free of avant-garde fashion. Perhaps they know it makes more sense for the new order to spread public joy than to risk the bitterness and stoic paranoia that pervade *The Book of Laughter and*

Forgetting and *Man of Iron*. But this is in keeping with the history of Italian art, which provides strong proof that variety and divergence of taste are what have made the country and the culture what it is.

VI. DEAR OLD SOUTHLAND

In the warm afternoon light of the courtyard of the Hotel La Rosetta, over meals served under big umbrellas by waiters in white coats, Italy, as unfamiliar and foreign as it was, recalled the best in the American South. But in the streets, people seemed to float or sit in a meditative silence, or fashion their own angles on an effortless aristocracy shaped equally of confidence, curiosity, and sympathy, all of which could explode into lucid laughter or the metallic chatter of argument. The disdain for excessive activity during the hottest part of the day meant that Perugia's streets were nearly empty from one in the afternoon until four, when the shops opened up and the people filled the outdoor cafés, drinking mineral water or coffee or beer or wine, often mulling over ice cream, then strolling or stretching. I was convinced of the parallels when I found out that what we call hanging out is known there as *dolce fa niente*—sweet time for nothing. As Albert Murray was to say when I asked him about Italy later, "Long before there were Southerners in the U.S.A., there were Southerners in Italy, and it also meant a certain climate, a certain hospitality, a certain musicality in the language, and sometimes even a certain kind of violence and tendency to vendetta. In the more learned circles, the European vision of the Southerner is much like that of anyone who understands our South: the feeling created is that of an easeful relationship to culture and a spontaneity that says, deep down—the point of learning how to cook all this food and talk this way and wear these fine clothes is to have a good goddam time, man!"

In that atmosphere, usually in the courtyard or the hotel's bar, the moody and attractive George Coleman, who has the demeanor of a powerful Memphis deacon, would move from mournful aloofness to earthly humor, from impassive sullenness to buoyancy, carrying his ex-fullback bulk in a relaxed march, his arms swinging almost straight up and down, his long elegant fingers ever ready to throttle from the tenor saxophone virtuoso passages that manifested the loneliness of many years of discipline. In residence at Il Panino with the wonderful Ronnie Mathews Trio, Coleman was to play every night as he always does, giving everything he had, working mightily for his money and not backing up until he'd forced roars and loud applause from the audience. He is clearly one of the lords of his instrument, but, above all, he is a house-rocker.

VII. TUNES IN A TENT

Rocking a house is not the same as rocking a tent, and that is what was expected of the players the first few nights. The procession of events began at lunch, after which many of the musicians, observers, and listeners would go to see Chertok's films in Teatro Pavone, the opera house with painted ceilings, gold-leaf railings, five tiers of boxes, and an atmosphere reminiscent of the finest American movie palaces. The splendidly photogenic faces and forms of artists like Louis Armstrong and Duke

Ellington, Lester Young and Charlie Parker, Jo Jones and Thelonious Monk, recalled Kenneth Clarke's description of the men in a Masaccio: "They have the air of contained vitality and confidence that one often sees in the founding fathers of a civilization." After Chertok's films, an American band would play in the opera house, followed later on by an Italian group heard in the open air of a piazza. Then there was dinner and the choice of a bus ride to the tent concert or an American group in a piazza. I always went to the tent.

The bus ride was brief and there was an excitement to riding downhill, passing the foreign signs and shops while lolling back in the pleasant air of Umbrian summer as it flowed in through the windows, and seeing the lights thicken on the right as we neared the blue striped tent patterned with Union Jacks. We leaned to the left as the bus wheeled around the tent in a big arc and let us all out at a gate near the artists' trailers. There was also a small tent where you could buy beer and snacks. Given the history of Umbria Jazz, if one bought a beer in a can or a bottle, it had to be transferred to a paper cup in case the buyer got riled during the performance and decided to throw the container at the stage. Everywhere were fans, including families with small children in tow, all surveyed by a number of good-looking young Italian men in splendid khaki uniforms, carabinieri serving the years of their mandatory military terms. There is something attractively civilized about young policemen who can represent authority with neatness, confidence, pleasant manners, and a physical strength reserved for lawbreakers, not the victims of their own boredom or problems with aggression. I thought that if the law ever became important again in America, the draft could supply an antidote to the fatigue and cynicism of the understaffed and overworked police, who would be provided with a constant influx of young fresh blood. There would be enough police to have them strolling beats again. If the uniform were as fine as those in Italy, the cop might even become a heartthrob for the ladies, a role young men have always found attractive.

In the tent there was playing both excellent and deplorable, while in the late-night jam sessions in the sweatbox of Il Panino, the music was alternately blistering and romantic. This was made clear on the first evening, when the Italian audience showed its taste by booing the grotesque flute playing of Herbie Mann, though they applauded Freddie Hubbard, whose mixture of Clifford Brown and Clark Terry has resulted in a sound now as golden and streaked with red as a ripe peach. Hubbard was inventive with Mann's terrible rock band, but he got what he needed later that evening when he sat in with the group at Il Panino, building motives from the line of "Rhythm-a-Ning," shaping harmonic charges prickling with dissonance, and firing staccato punctuations that now and again gave way to smears which arced through the air like big, bright fish. George Coleman sustained the excitement with his style of perpetual substitutions—note-laden arpeggios as slippery as beaded curtains of polished stone dipped in boiling oil—while the rhythm section of pianist Ronnie Mathews, bassist Walter Booker, and drummer Hugh Walker coalesced into a mighty engine of harmony and percussion. It had been a long night, but I left Il Panino rekindled and ready for the next day, greatly satisfied by the dragon blasts of inspired artistry I had heard in that boiling club down that long and winding street.

VIII. WERE YOU THERE?

Italy is a land of many masters, and it would have been provincial not to take advantage of what was available on walks or at the National Gallery of Umbria right there in Perugia, or at the Cathedral of St. Francis in Assisi, less than an hour away by bus. On a morning when I had decided to explore the city or travel someplace near, I would be out on foot, feeling the uneven stone of many of the streets as the people seeped from their homes and the sounds of footfalls, rustling clothes, and voices replaced the silence. As I made my way to the Assisi bus past the farmers wheeling their produce into Perugia, I saw a Gypsy boy with a concertina and a frazzled cat on a chain. For some reason, he reminded me less of a kid imitating an Italian organ grinder than of the street preachers of my youth who used to stand at the bus stops, chanting the promises of damnation for most and salvation for the rest each time one of the big yellow and green vehicles would stop and release passengers.

After taking a bus down from Perugia into a valley, then through flat lands backdropped by low hills, where little farms were pressed together as closely as possible, going on through small towns with their second-story windows covered by wooden shutters that kept out the day's early heat, ascending again on roads that rolled and weaved until arriving in Assisi, only to see the Cathedral of St. Francis at the highest part of the city, I experienced the calm such places must have provided for their congregations as soon as I entered the huge church, felt its easy coolness, and began to concentrate on the craft and the emotional radiation of its painted walls. And though there are still those who think that the Negro, like Caliban or the gigantic Moor in Bernini's "Fountain of the Four Rivers" in Rome, should recoil in bitterness, disgust, and alienation at the abundance of those works that document a star-bumping plateau of Western civilization, I felt that the painted walls were as familiar in feeling and function as the religious and secular music I had heard as a child in church and at home. People are exalted by a great religious painting hung in a gallery in much the same way they are by a superb recording of Mahalia Jackson.

Whether in biblical tales or annals of the suffering of the saints, perhaps the most important religious vision projected through the Italian plastic arts is its sense of moral responsibility. It can cost your life, or tear your heart, but it can also separate you from savages. They understood the costs in blood and also, as one sees in Donatello's "The Sacrifice of Isaac" in Florence, the costs in overwhelming anguish. Oh, yes, I had encountered that sense of life in those Negro churches, where the deacons stood before us, big men humming and singing in their soaked white shirts and dark suits, where the choir would enter from the rear in their swishing robes and so fill the room with mighty song that the roof seemed in danger of loosening and blowing away, where the tales and dreams of the Bible became almost three-dimensional as the worshipers rose to an impersonal oneness with what they expressed, preaching or crying or singing of the rumblings and the ruthlessness—and the *rightness!*—in the bosom of this old world.

Just as biblical lore had provided a comprehensive range of human situations for the painter, the sculptor, and the architect, Christianity had proven a perfect conduit for the movement from the vital though superstition-ridden world of Africa into the accumulated complexity of theme and ethics inherent in the biblical stories, an accumulated complexity that stood them well in the society of successive riddles that is America. Not only did the body of reinterpreted Old Testament beliefs born in rebellion against the Roman Empire speak to the slaves, but they sometimes fought to give voice themselves, reenacting the sedition of their forebears in Rome. I recalled how I had been told in Texas that, since old evil master didn't want his chattel property practicing religion, the slaves would wet down the walls of the cabins at night and gather many buckets and bowls and basins of water to also absorb the sound so that they could preach and pray in secret, separating themselves from the savages who owned the big house and the beasts of the fields.

In much the same way the Italian painters made their religious figures look Italian rather than Middle Eastern or even Negroid in features, facial expression, and dress as they personalized the lessons of Alexandria and Constantinople, the Negro slaves modified the stiff hymns to fit sensibilities that demanded richer conceptions of melody, percussion, and call-and-response. By adding an African-American dimension to religious material that remained Protestant, they made music that would provide an essential model for secular Negro musicians in the same way the mastery of perspective is essential to secular Renaissance painting. And eventually the sermons of the most imaginative ministers evolved into a poetry that functioned as an oral equivalent of Dante, who brought to the vernacular literature of Italian Christianity what Homer had to the mythology of Greece. A perfect example is this selection from a sermon Zora Neale Hurston took down in Florida in 1929:

> I heard the whistle of the damnation train
> Dat pulled out from the Garden of Eden loaded wid cargo goin to hell
> Ran at break-neck speed all de way thru de law
> All de way thru de prophetic age
> All de way thru de reign of kings and judges
> Plowed her way thru de Jordan
> And on her way to Calvary when she blew for de switch
> Jesus stood out on her track like a rough-backed mountain
> And she threw her cow-catcher in
> His side and His blood ditched de train.
> He died for our sins.
> Wounded in the house of his friends.

In short, a metaphoric and epic sense developed that proved perfectly compatible with how Vincent Sheean described the sweep of the spirituals Marian Anderson selected after sailing through Bach and Schubert in Salzburg in 1935; "At the end . . . there was no applause at all—a silence instinctive, natural, and intense, so that you were afraid to breathe. What Anderson had done was something outside the limits of classical or romantic music: she frightened us with the conception, in musical terms, of course, but outside the normal limits, of a mighty suffering." Had Sheean heard Anderson in the Cathedral of St. Francis, I believe he would have found himself surrounded by visual expression of the same sort.

IX. UPLIFT AND FRUSTRATION

The feelings left after the last notes on the second and third nights fused uplift and frustration. V.S.O.P. II, under the leadership of pianist Herbie Hancock, also featured bassist Ron Carter, drummer Tony Williams, trumpeter Wynton Marsalis, and saxophonist Branford Marsalis. Except for Williams, who proved a great drummer can sound as insensitive as a four-year-old, the group performed with invention, fire, and dazzling taste. Wynton Marsalis played shocking pedal notes at fast tempos; Branford Marsalis was never less than a split second behind Hancock's often complex chords, spelling them out as he twisted and bent them; Hancock pulled his unique timbre out of the instrument and spaced his ideas with dramatic effectiveness; while Carter inspired and supported as he crafted bass parts and rhythms of such drive that they almost made up for the drummer's incessant banging. On the third night, the Rutgers University Saxophone Ensemble under the direction of Paul Jeffrey was a casualty of the sound crew: guest soloist George Coleman was either distorted or inaudible, Jeffrey's orchestrations of Coltrane improvisations were so muddily amplified that they might as well have been written in unison, and only the extraordinary piano and drums of Harold Mabern and Jimmy Cobb could be heard throughout, with the good bass beat of David Eubanks appearing and disappearing. Protests resulted in vast improvements the next evening and, after Richie Cole's aggressively mediocre set, Sphere—tenor saxophonist Charlie Rouse, pianist Kenny Barron, bassist Buster Williams, and drummer Ben Riley—displayed distinct arrangements that primed the ear for their improvised command of the subtleties of inflection, color, and rhythm. From the first note, the chill on the patina of the evening air lifted and the huge tent felt intimate. It was one of the best performances I have heard all year.

X. THE RELIGION OF GLORY: CAKEWALKING BABIES

> The new religion as I have called the love of glory . . . a thing of this world, founded as it is on human esteem.
>
> —BERNARD BERENSON, *The Italian Painters of the Renaissance*

When I considered how the development of African-American music telescoped the evolution of Italian art, I had no difficulty seeing slavery and segregation as American versions of the Dark Ages, or recognizing how the soaring self-assertion and mocking false faces of the parades and social clubs of New Orleans provided the local musicians with a Renaissance sense of carnival. After all, Berenson says, "The moment people stopped looking fixedly toward heaven, their eyes fell upon earth, and they began to see much on its surface that was pleasant. Their own faces and figures must have struck them as surprisingly interesting. . . . The more people were imbued with the new spirit, the more they loved pageants. The pageant was an outlet for many of the dominant passions of the time . . . above all [the] love of feeling . . . alive." Given the attempts to depersonalize human beings on the plantation, or reduce them to the simplicity of animals, it is understandable that a belief in the dignity of the Negro and the joyous importance of the individual resulted in what is probably the century's most radical assault on Western musical convention. Jazzmen supplied a new perspective on time, a sense of how freedom and discipline could coexist within the demands of ensemble improvisation, where the moment was bulldogged, tied, and given shape. As with the Italian artists of the Renaissance, their art was collective and focused by a common body of themes, but for jazzmen, the human imagination in motion was the measure of all things.

As I thought of turn-of-the-century New Orleans, the Crescent City with its street songs and its opera houses, with the visual stretch of African-Americans from bone to beige to brown to black, with its Negroes dressed as Indians or parodying the Mardi Gras in their own Zulu Ball, with the bands riding on wagons and battling for the affection of the listeners, with the grief of the music on the way to the bone orchard and the zest of its celebration on the way back, the frescoes reminded me of the aural palimpsests of the old 78-rpm recordings with the red or blue-black labels that my mother had saved, those fragile discs that carried the hissing documentation of blues divas and jazzmen on their worn surfaces, from which the music struggled through the haze of primitive engineering. Just as Kenneth Clarke observed that the Italian Renaissance contributed its ideas in visual terms rather than reasoned argument or speculation, the same can be said about jazz, since its thoughts about American life arrived not in the philosophical text but in the well-picked note on moment's notice and the physical response of dance. You can tell that those people believed in an African-derived sense of infinite plasticity that lent to the bending and drastic rearranging of songs, just as they believed in the molten democracy of the *groove*, when a band catches its stride and every decision made by every individual not only carries his stamp but makes for a collective statement that transcends the particular. You can hear their frothing exuberance as they recognize that they can control the formless rush of the present and paint their faces on its canvas.

XI. DIZZY ATMOSPHERE

It was the next night and the last night of tunes in the tent, and Dizzy Gillespie looked less handsome than angry. He had been loudly booed after kicking off his performance with two dull would-be funk numbers. I was told later, "In Italy, we feel if a musician is great, he should be great. In America, it may be necessary for Miles Davis or Sonny Rollins to play rock and roll—or perhaps it is less painful to act young than wise. Here we feel sad or angry when a great man will abandon wisdom for ignorance. The more polite would say innocence. Why should they travel this far to put on a silly mask?"

The booing was to the good: Gillespie, who had been sulking on the piano bench, rose and roared forth with a succession of improvisations of such savage invention it must have been somewhat difficult to be Jon Faddis standing there next to him, knowing the only thing you could add that night was higher notes. The old master feinted, ducked, and worked out phenomenal accents that italicized the abstractions within his long phrases, proving that when angered, a sore-headed bear will rise to beat the band. Trombonist Curtis Fuller was exquisite and guitarist Ed Cherry worked some pulsive variations on the voicings of McCoy Tyner. Everyone left that evening aware that they had witnessed a master in matchless form.

XII. RENAISSANCE IN RED BEANS AND RICE

You cannot have a Renaissance without a Giotto. He stripped away what Clarke calls the "decorative jumble" of images that made the medieval school both highly stylized and emblematic, offering in its place the weight and the sacrifice, the disappointment and the exaltation of human beings concurring and conflicting. In a sense, he discovered the individual in the pageant and, sometimes with the aid of bas-relief halos, pushed the force and substance of experience right at us, settling for neither mush nor surrender. Berenson points out that all of his lines are functional, that they are defined by movement, that he charged trivial objects with a power that not only transformed them but ignited the consciousness of the viewer.

In his own way, Louis Armstrong did the same. He discovered that his powers of imagination could stand alone, with the clarinet and the trombone of the conventional New Orleans band silenced, no longer needed to express the intricate and subtle musicality provided by the multilinear antiphonal style. His monumental ideas swelled a fresh world above his accompanying improvisers. In Armstrong's work there is a new kind of confidence that had never existed in Western music, an aural proof that man can master time through improvisation, that contemplation and action needn't be at odds. A quantum leap of control heralded a new relationship between the artistic consciousness and the body that has yet to inspire what could be a new school of brain research. Armstrong found that he could hear a chord, digest it, decide what to play, tell his lips, lungs, and fingers what to do, and express his individuality within the mobile ensemble as rhythms, harmonies, timbres, and phrases flew forward around him. He had mastered what A. E. Hotchner calls "the ability to assimilate simultaneous occurrences."

Unlike Giotto, Armstrong had immediate impact. He became a hero of epic proportions to fellow musicians. One remembers first hearing him sound like an archangel from a riverboat, another touching him just as he was going on stage and feeling an electric shock. Yet another recalls him taking the measure of a challenge at a cornet supper in Harlem and standing the listeners on their chairs, tables, and plates as he played notes that were like hot, silver solder splashing across the roof that supports the heavens. In his sexuality and the daredevil displacements of his abstractions, Armstrong is more in spirit with Picasso, but his position in an African-American Renaissance is unarguable. He delivered a virtuosity fresh from the frontier of his imagination, giving the trumpet an expressive power it never had. Armstrong brought a purer sound to the instrument's upper register, playing high notes that were functional rather than decorative, and his strings of eighth notes lifted the horn from a vocal, shouting riff style to a standard-bearer of melody interwoven with virtuoso rhythms. And it is clear that in the spirit of Giotto, Armstrong ignited the consciousness of his listeners by charging often uninteresting songs with artistic power, spontaneously transforming them through both an editing and embellishing process. When you hear Armstrong at his finest, he is like the Negro acrobat in the Roman sculpture, calmly balanced on the head of the crocodile of the moment. Berenson says that what a major artist does is show that human beings can cope with the complexities of life—and who could deny that in the face of Armstrong's greatest improvisations?

XIII. BLUES FOR JULIUS III

The final night of Umbria Jazz in Perugia, before the festival's actual conclusion in the mountain town of Narni, took place at Piazza IV. A bandstand had been set up next to the Great Fountain, which dates from 1275, and in front of the Cathedral of St. Lawrence, where a bronze statue of Julius III sat facing the back of the stage and the eyes of the assembled masses. In a way, the feeling of festival that had been building all week was now swelling in the streets with the people. There were African students in small clusters, Americans who were there studying Italian, Europeans on vacation, but, most of all, Italians, from the very young to the older women with calf muscles built from walking the inclines of the stone streets. There were no costumes and no streamers, yet the air felt full of colors and thick with the moisture of dance.

Before joining the dinner group, I listened to some of Ray Mantilla's Space Station, as it started the people near the bandstand dancing to the rushes and thumps of its Afro-Hispanic rhythms. Especially entrancing was the orchestral use of the traps by Joe Chambers, whose spare musicality gave the impression of a pianist playing timbres and multiple rhythms instead of lines and chords. Next, in the summer air, Jackie McLean played with a passion as scarlet as a fall maple and notes as bright and golden as an October birch. In the spirit of the Pagliacci lyricism of Charlie Parker, McLean's sound was as brutish in timbre as it was plaintive and prideful. But his tone could also glow when he swung on the hard New York blues, or floated his ballad notes on the stream of flesh and memory. Yes, he was in fine form, skittering his lines across the chords set by vibist Bobby Hutcherson, whose music rushed forth or lulled in the air like hankty and piss-elegant chimes. Billy Higgins balanced both instruments on his ride cymbal and buffed them with his stripped-down snare accents, now and again using his toms and bass drum like nearly inaudible thunder. Bassist Herbie Lewis had the heavy and dark effect of a tonal percussionist. A very hot stage was set for the Umbria Jazz All-Stars.

It was late when the All-Stars took the stand, bringing with them the lore of many a dancehall, night club, jam session, and party rich with fine women, handsome men, whiskey, whist, coon can, dominoes, and the smells of downhome food steaming in the pots. On the front line were the Texas tenors: Arnett Cobb, who stands on his metal crutches and shapes each saxophone note like an individual bellows crafted to build heroic fire; Illinois Jacquet, a barrelhouse bull on wheels roaring into red capes; and Buddy Tate, who can rattle the pulpit of the bandstand with his sensuous renditions of blue-toned scripture. There was Al Grey, a master of the plunger who sometimes plays as though coaxing bulbous notes into his trombone rather, than pushing them out. The rhythm section of pianist John Lewis, bassist Eddie Jones, and drummer Gus Johnson strung and loosened the bow of the bat with wit and encouragement. Then there was Scott Hamilton, less a seasoned star than a young man still in search of himself, wavering back and forth between recitations of Lester Young and Tate. But on song after song, with the rhythm section simmering and steaming under them, the veterans tore away everything that stood in the path of celebration, creating a pulsation that could be answered only with dance. And dance they did engender, especially with the inevitable encore—"Flying Home"—lifting the crowd with the bells of their horns into a massive articulation of unsentimental happiness. As green Julius III gave his blessing and the medieval Great Fountain bubbled over a democratic series of reliefs spanning local politicians, Christianity, astrology, history, education, Roman origins, and the most popular fables of Aesop, I heard the sound of American democracy become an international phenomenon and thought that if Hannibal had these kinds of troops, he would have easily taken the Roman Empire. With a song.

XIV. BIRD OF PARADISE

The next day I went to the National Gallery of Umbria, again watching the figures slowly change from dark-eyed and dark-skinned to northern Italian. When I got to Piero della Francesca's polytych, it was like an explosion. Even though he was working with the new level of virtuosity that full-blown control of perspective allowed, della Francesca carried everything with him—the gold leaf and steepled frame and the sacrificial themes. There was an arrogance to his lyricism, especially in the perfectly measured distances and details of the section depicting the annunciation, but there was also the aloof idealism most confident virtuosi have in common. He used "no specialized expression of feeling," as Berenson observed, and the effect at first is one of coldness. Thomas Craven describes his figures as "masked in sullen gravity . . . their attitudes majestic and defiant." But what actually is taking place is a protest against the limitations of painting and an expression of unruffled confidence in the command of detail, a mastery that can concentrate on subtlety and overall effect rather than a conventional display of emotional states. That may account for the absolute stillness another writer sees in his figures.

In two cases, della Francesca's version of what Clarke calls "the new pessimism" rivals—or exceeds—Giorgione's "Col Tempo," where a whithered beauty stares with the remorse of age at the viewer. In della Francesca's "The Flagellation of Christ," we see a whipping in the background while a group of well-dressed men converse about other business in the foreground, presaging the modern theme of public indifference to personal pain and degradation. On the right side of "The Death of Adam," he comments on the loss of Eden. An old man who had once been vibrant and handsome now sits feebly on the ground as his wife stands behind him, equally aged and with her flaccid dugs drooping and uncovered, a deadpan comment on the Renaissance ideal of physical beauty that no paintings of fine faces and figures—or prayer—will diminish.

As I examined della Francesca's work, his absolute stillness and his rejection of conventional expression reminded me of Charlie Parker. Parker brought a fierce and fresh virtuosity to the saxophone, protesting its limitations, and discarded the vibrato many considered necessary for the expression of deep feeling in the work of his predecessors. He depended on the voluminous details of his loquacious melody notes, his high-handed harmonic sophistication, and the seemingly impossible gradations of attack he brought to rhythms that themselves seemed beyond enunciation. Like that of the Italian painter, Parker's work brims with sullen gravity, majesty, and defiance, it is an art possessed by an idealism which says that only in the transcendence of the difficult can we know the intricate riches and terrors of the human soul. Both the painter and the saxophonist created continuity and contrast through echoing and near-echoing. The painter used figures and faces as motifs while varying features and skin tones, hair color and texture, dress and body position; the result is a series of geometrical calls and responses from one end of a painting to the other. In Parker's best work, he constantly reshapes phrases and rhythms, extending them, leaving something out here, adding something there, or compressing what he has previously played into a swinging board from which he bounces into more elaborate linear variations. Parker also left nothing behind, revolutionizing every detail of the jazz tradition. Parker became a colossus of human consciousness who could process and act upon material with a meticulous lyricism at any tempo. In his finest improvisations, you hear an imagination given the wide dimension of genius, running up a hill potted and mined with obstacles, but delivering its melodies with a sometimes strident confidence in their imperishability.

XV. NOT UNTIL NARNI

Traveling from Perugia, we crossed frightening gorges and saw the terrain become steeper until we arrived at a gas station and had to switch to buses small enough to get through a gate and up the narrow road to our destination. Narni is made almost completely of stone, with arches that cast shadows and lead into the descending side streets or into buildings that crest the city on the other side of the square where the concert was held. A big bandstand had been set up in front of a large fountain and though the music was more than an hour away because of a power failure, Italians of all ages had begun to gather around the stage and were staring at us with overt curiosity and pleasure as we made for the bars or the little stand beyond an imposing Roman arch where sandwiches and beer were sold.

I found myself wandering through the city and its back streets, imagining the time when the clop of shod hooves and the rattling of wagons had filled the air, when word of Garibaldi's triumphs arrived, when the problems of putting in telephone service and electric lights and plumbing had been met with wires and fenced-in generators and the sewers full of turning pipes. Then I wondered if the first jazz notes had arrived by phonograph or radio. Narni had the look and feel of a place where modern life was but another loop on a very long tape of time. As I had been told by an Italian named Maurice Cohen: "In Italy, you can stand in the middle of your past and feel the present and dream about the future. You know that what is adaptive is what is lasting and that the key to Italian civilization, what some mistake for exceptional friendliness, is a confidence in the fact that though you might be influenced, you won't be consumed. You will merely take what is good and make it Italian. After all, the spaghetti first came from China with Marco Polo, but the Chinese did not make *pasta*. Italians did. Merchants came from all over the world to Florence, but Italians invented *banking*. And so it goes. That is our way and that is our safety." (I later found out that Cohen had been born in France.)

By the time I returned, the klieg lights were on, an Italian television crew was at work documenting the event, the square was filled with many people either standing or sitting on the ground, and in the houses that surrounded the square were families seated and crowded in their second-floor windows or old women leaning on sills with their elbows. A big band from Rome had finished their set and I was soon to wish they would kidnap American tenor saxophonist Bob Berg and teach him to cook. Even with the same rhythm section that had so perfectly supported George Coleman and Freddie Hubbard, Berg managed to never swing a note, only bluster through the tunes with the aimless intensity of a fly caught between a closed window and a screen. The staff Paul Jeffrey put together played quite well until monitor problems led to tempo waverings even stable swingers like Harold Mabern and Jimmy Cobb couldn't set right. There were also early conflicts between Mabern's thick voicings and the obbligatos of Kevin Eubanks until the guitarist let Mabern have it and made his statements with good lines in his features. Frank Strozier invented bittersweet alto saxophone melodies, built tension with circular breathing, and delivered his ideas with rhythms both fluid and bumptious. Terence Blanchard, always a poignant player, surged through the trumpet with big intervallic leaps and an almost impersonal sense of heartbreak interwoven with desire that stung the audience, while Jeffrey, caught in the memory of the Umbria All-Stars, reached in the bucket and swung the bell off the tenor. I admire Woody Herman's refusal to sit down and moulder away, but his Young Herd concluded the concert with more precision than passion and swung about as hard as a buried log of teakwood, while the leader's singing was an unpleasant memento of minstrelsy.

It was after two in the morning and the streets were still filled with listeners who seemed reluctant to turn in, especially the old women in the second-floor windows, who were apparently determined to watch everything dismantled and packed before they called it a night. As for us, we were all taken to a banquet on the elevated patio of a hotel in Turni, where the staff showered Pagnatta with champagne and I stared at some of the most beautiful women I had ever seen in my life. By the time we returned to Perugia, it was almost dawn but I was still lit up and ready for the train ride to Florence, all the jazz notes behind me but the memory of an extraordinary people and their thirst for festival still in the front of my mind.

XVI. FIRENZE

One of the first things that impressed me in Florence was the army of well-dressed men and women on motor scooters shooting down the streets, their double-breasted summer suits, their striped dresses and sheer stockings, their briefcases and purses in place as they rounded corners or deftly moved between cars. There was also the sunlight that would smooth itself across the sky and loom in its seemingly imperishable weight just beyond the city's many shaded spaces, the cypress trees and the hills where Michelangelo designed the snaking fortifications, the huge cathedrals that maintain their grandeur in an almost ancient skyline dominated by tile the color of dried red mud, the infinity of shops with everything available from custom-made shoes to the most remarkable suits and dresses, wallets, purses, and scarves; the street market near the Duomo that the sellers would build each morning from poles and rectangles of plywood or formica, the horse-drawn carriages in which you could travel near the Ufizzi, the squadrons of pigeons that would light near the Fountain of Neptune, hustle a few bread scraps, and march in place behind the platoons of Japanese tourists, who faced the labor of lugging around their many cameras, packages, and guide books with determination and explosive smiles. The smallest sandwich stand might provide a simple but delicious snack, a glass of mineral water, and the parting choice of 42 imported beers. It was hard not to be impressed.

But I met a small, dark man from a town in Calabria who had been living in Florence for 20 years. He gave an impression of the city that was less hostile than sarcastic and indicative of the hometown pride you consistently encounter in Italy. He felt that the Florentines were very closed and unfriendly because they thought they were "too civilized." Yet they made more grammatical mistakes than anybody, he went on to say, and suggested that when Frederick II conquered Sicily and opened schools in which Italian was taught, he may have inspired Dante to write in the language. "The Florentines cannot say it is not so. Like all of us, they do not know. But I will bet you they have *never heard* of Frederick II."

I mentioned that I had been surprised by how softly people spoke during dinner the previous night—when I joined some Americans and we began laughing and joking, the people at the other tables kept staring at us.

"On the bus," he smirked, "where people should be talking and enjoying themselves, you would think they are whispering inside themselves in church. They do not like the loud."

It would be silly to come to Florence, where they do not like the loud, and not join those who line up in the morning outside the Gallery of the Tribune to see "Prisoners" and "David," standing huge and lighted by the sun beneath the cupola at the end of the room, its musculature and the stare of the eyes familiar as the remembered images of the greatest boxers. Kenneth Clarke says that the look of the head "involves a contempt for convenience and a sacrifice of all those pleasures that contribute to what we call civilized life. It is the enemy of happiness." Looking at it, I could not help but think of Muhammad Ali, fresh from the attrition and the tuning of the training camp, coming up the aisle to face Sonny Liston, the Goliath of the boxing ring; or Ali standing in his sullen poignance as he recited with charming bravado one of his rhymed predictions of how he would fell the big ugly bear from Philadelphia or going to his locker room after his victory and suffering through the ice-covered and blackening cummerbund of bruises left by the bear's body punches.

There is also an air of gloom surrounding "David" because we know, as

Michelangelo must have, how he was torn down by temptation and megalomania. There is perhaps no story of forbidden love quite so great and heartbreaking as the tragedy David enters when struck by the wonders of Bathsheba's lush body bathed in the morning light. Though he knows from firsthand experience the power and wrath of his God, David will still commit adultery, thus spitting upon the laws he is bound to uphold, then further corrupt his powers as king by eventually using them to design what was perhaps the first example of bureaucratic murder as he moved to rid himself of Bathsheba's husband, Uriah the Hittite. Next he must face the whirlwind of incest and fratricide among his children that culminates when Absalom, groomed in princely privilege as favorite son, rises to try and smite down his father. When I think of David moaning the name of his slain and seditious son, finally aware that even the chosen and the most gifted have no guarantees against the wages of obsession, I also think of Ali: his ego and addiction to celebration, his victory over the second Goliath of George Foreman in the humid bush of Zaire and the almost mythological grandeur of his third fight with Joe Frazier in Manila, then his desire for one last dance in the light of international praise and awe shaping in him a belief in magic that helped result in the once-quick tongue now battling ruefully—at the pace of a child reading his first schoolbook—to enunciate a simple sentence. Even so, just as we know that "David" is at the edge of a journey to a pinnacle from which he will fall, dragged in the dirt by his lust, we will always also know that there were moments when Ali, expanding our expectations of a heavyweight's grace, courage, and cunning, won and made it New Year's Eve all over the world.

The Duomo nearly overcomes the visitor through the grandeur of its collective art and design. I was most surprised by the black, gray, white, salmon, brown, and plum patterns of its marble floor. In an apparent attempt to simultaneously prove the glory of mathematic precision and illustrate the perfect construction of the universe, a series of rhyming geometrical images on either side of the huge church reveals the contemporary painting that begins with Mondrian's "Broadway Boogie Woogie" as little more than contrived decoration.

But the Florentine sensibility also encompasses the Medici chapels, where the gargoyle narcissism of the room honoring the Medici princes makes technical mastery revolting. Its overdone green, gray, plumb, red, and apricot marble has the garishness associated with drag balls and expresses not the resonance of a culture but its hollowness. By contrast, there is the consonant poetry of the white and green marble Michelangelo used to design the New Sacristy under the same roof, diminished only by the predictive science fiction of the female figures who are dangerously close to transsexuals, with their male thighs, muscular bodies, and tacked-on breasts.

I will never forget how many times I circled Michelangelo's unfinished "Pietà" in the museum behind the Duomo, fascinated by the possibilities for style it suggested. Its mix of the finished and the unfinished gives the impression of an intersection between realism and expressionism, between living flesh, dead flesh, and the spirit. For me, the big figure that hovers over the expired Christ seems to be death lifting his body beyond the equally spiritual figure of Mary, who is lost in lamentation for her son. I floated back much faster than I could have by plane and much further all the way to a street not far from my old home in Los Angeles and into the living room where a wake was being held, with food and liquor everywhere, with men and women in dark clothes, and was memory-listening to a mother talking about how she had been with her dead son in the chapel for the last time as he lay in state, his body waiting for the ritual next morning that would take him to the burying ground. "I took Oran's hand and put it in mine, just like I did when he would get sick and ask me to rub his arms. The hand was cold but it wasn't stiff and it felt like it always did. The only difference was the fingertips had turned blue." She looked up, her face the color of mustard with a subtle undertone of beige, worn with grief and surely knowing what Mary had known.

XVII. ROMA

On that last morning in Rome, I stood before the Coliseum, relaxing into the thought of how much of my own experience had been clarified by exposure to foreign forms. It had been a steaming afternoon the day before when I arrived, bedding down in a hotel near the train station, in a section popular with the vacationing Arab middle class. A cab ride had taken me around the ancient city, which combined past and present even more startlingly than the others. Rome is both sad with the knowledge of the mystery of fate and vital with the awareness of how clearly human passions can speak through the ages, whether from the Egyptian obelisks that shoot up toward the sun or the ruins and fountains that detail the carcasses of empire and the glory of invention.

Because it was summer, many of the residents were vacationing and avoiding tourists, but there were still plenty of Italians at work who never gave the impression of oppressive boredom you become accustomed to in New York. One feels the presence of time with a special intensity here because the drive that brought those obelisks back from Egypt and pushed up the Pantheon or the Vatican or the Coliseum or the many fountains seems almost tangible. There is also a glow of confidence that comes from having survived monsters from antiquity to Mussolini, who used to speak from that balcony there. At the same time, there is the silt and the brown dust that has accumulated from the exhaust of automobiles and mutes the surfaces of streets and buildings with the gloom of the modern age. But perhaps that gloom has been overstated by pessimists who ignore the modes of redress and the reduction of degradation and squalor that have come in the wake of the Magna Carta and the Continental Congress. After all is said and done the world has a richer human image of itself now despite its problems, but the way those Italians carry themselves is not so much an assertion of hope as of the ironic continuity that a long history provides.

On my only evening there, I saw a tall and darkly attractive group of African women walking in line as the Italians covered the streets on the way to shop or eat. One was especially striking, with brilliant black eyes, a long neck circled by the lines that are often seen by Africans as marks of beauty, and a long red dress that billowed and stopped just short of her ankles. She reminded me of the bas-reliefs at the Tazza D'Oro coffee shop where an African woman is depicted showering Rome with coffee beans, but not of a brace of Brooklyn ersatz Africans I had met in Florence, with their hair looking like sooted mops, their noses run through by rings, their bodies reeking the overwrought oils sold with incense in New York, and their attire the tacky and misbegotten emulation of an Africa that exists only in the minds of romantic primitivists rather than the continent which may someday rise to shake the world with its natural resources as Hannibal shook Rome with his elephants.

As I looked at those African women, I wondered if the descendants of slaves owned by fellow Africans would ever influence the world in the way those who were brought to America had. I knew then that slavery in America was as much ironic luck as it was enormous misfortune, since what U.S. slaves had endured made for a culture in which celebration was a form of protest that remade social, aesthetic, and athletic conventions. We are indeed fortunate to live in a period when we can see changes that began when the first slaves ran away from the plantation or learned to play the fiddle or sing hymns or read. Of course, that was only the beginning. E. Franklin Frazier once observed that certain field slaves, never having seen the master and the mistress work, thought freedom meant preening and kicking back behind mint juleps. It is pretty clear that too many African regimes haven't understood that a well-oiled and functioning infrastructure that marshals and markets all resources must precede the underhanded luxuries of success. The attempts to leap-frog directly to corruption have cost their economies dearly but, given the history of France since the Revolution, there is no need to count them out prematurely. Africans will probably learn their lessons the hard way, as others have, and then push more chairs to the big table of world power.

XVIII. PRECIOUS LORD

On the returning flight, I struck up conversation with a group of Negro pilgrims from Florida who had just been to the holy land, where they had walked in Jerusalem just like John. I had noticed them almost as soon as the plane took off, for they sat together and exuded a familiar combination of sobriety, wit, and warmth as they listened to one another, joked, or mused. The men all wore dark or gray suits with vests and the women either pantsuits or straight and simple dresses, their occasional diamond rings shining below knuckles and above their liver-colored nail polish. As I had first looked at them, recalling the heat of the churches and the steam of the sermons, I was reminded of the old saying, "Our race is like a flower garden, everything from lily-white to blue-black." When an African-American painter masters mixing all the colors necessary to capture such a range of skin tones, the painting of figures might be revitalized.

The pilgrims were still excited by what they had seen in Jerusalem and were comparing emotional reactions to the religious art of Rome. One woman said that there was a lot wrong with the way Catholics practiced the religion, but that their paintings and the sculpture told the truth. "They knew how a mother feels when her child is in pain and she can't do nothing about it," she observed. Their pastor said, "If I had somebody like that Michelangelo to paint my church, a man that inspired, we couldn't stay in there. We would need a bigger place. They would feel the truth vibrating through that paint. Yes, sir, when you stand in that Vatican, you can't help but feel the glory behind everything."

The preacher's words brought me back to the Coliseum, where I'd remembered how the Christians who had been meat for the lions began the protests that led to the fall of the Roman Empire after it converted to Christianity and could no longer justify chattel labor. I then recalled the Civil Rights Movement, when an empire of segregation and lynch-law had been torn asunder by those radicalized pastors and their nonviolent troops cracking the pillars of a temple to injustice with their bodies while singing reworked old spirituals that stung with political messages and threats to the redneck kingdom of violence. Then I saw again Mahalia Jackson painting an aural portrait of the suffering of the Southern saints as she sang "Precious Lord, Take My Hand" at Martin Luther King's funeral, her image projected by a television set, a wet handkerchief in her hand, her hair thick and dark above her head, the dress frilled and white, and her body trembling with the passage of each note. For some strange reason as I walked near the ruins of the Senate, it came to me how radio waves and phonograph recordings had beamed the disembodied songbird of jazz into the ears of many virgins, giving birth to an international body of listeners who had been transformed in some vital way by that annunciation. At that moment, it was easy to see that the melancholy I have often felt when staring at the sealed-up palace of bebop innovation that was Minton's Playhouse in Harlem, or the stripped-away testaments to the night life of Kansas City, is a melancholy unfounded. The human point is not that something has decayed, but that when the times and the spirits were right, men and women met their challenges, and their efforts rose as brightly as the sun did on that last Roman morning.

LOOKING FOR
MR. RIGHT

TERRY MCMILLAN's "Looking for Mr. Right" is from
the February 1990 issue of *Essence* magazine and touches upon a
sensitive subject: the successful late-30s black female's inability to find
a mate or to have an enduring relationship. McMillan is the author of
Disappearing Acts, and the best-selling *Waiting to Exhale,* and the
editor of a book of black short fiction, *Breaking Ice.*

Maybe it's just me, but I'm finding it harder and harder to meet men. And when I do the atmosphere often feels strained, as if they're thinking, "She's probably another woman over 30 looking for a husband." They're right.

Times sure have changed. When I was in my twenties, I don't remember it being all that hard to meet a man and get familiar, even though we may have ended up only being friends. But these days, if you're "serious," men look at your interest in them as entrapment. They don't like being "pursued" and as a result tend to back away. Lately my girlfriends and I, who are all over 30, are spending more time looking for or trying to develop some kind of strategy that will result in landing a lifetime companion. What it boils down to is a guessing game: How should we act? What should we say or do that won't seem threatening? It's sad to think that we've gotten to this—that we actually have to *think* about how to go about finding a man. But what's even sadder is that some men make you feel guilty for looking. I don't feel guilty.

I grew up and became what my mama prayed out loud I'd become: educated, strong, smart, independent and reliable. "I don't want you growing up having to depend on no man for everything," she always said. But she didn't suggest for a minute that upon gaining a certain kind of professional recognition I'd not need or want one. Now it seems as if carving a place for myself in the world is backfiring.

Never in a million years would I have dreamed that I'd be 38 years old and still single. I am not embarrassed about it, just tired of it. I had planned on being married by the time I was 24, but instead I went to graduate school. Ended up loving and living with a number of men who, for whatever reasons, didn't take life as seriously as I did. At 32 I had a baby, and not long afterward I split from my son's father.

I haven't had a steady man in my life for so long that I'm beginning to wonder if I'll ever find one. I spend more time thinking about sex than actually doing it, and sex was something I never imagined I'd have to get used to doing without. I keep asking myself, *What am I doing wrong?* I've done what I consider to be all the "right things": I still look good, I'm honest and I have a lot to offer someone. So why over the last few years have I had only two powerful but short-lived relationships, in which both men just stopped calling one day with no explanation? "They're probably just scared," my friends said. Scared of what?

Sometimes I think that even though a lot of "professional" men claim to want a smart, independent woman, they're kidding themselves. Some of them seem to feel secure only as long as you're passive, don't take much initiative and let them call the shots. But as soon as they realize you're not willing to sit in the backseat because you also know how to drive, they feel so threatened they try to figure out ways to get you to back down, back off or just acquiesce until you appear to be tamed. I'm not tamable.

In the good old days, men seemed more aggressive. They would walk up to you in a minute, strike up a conversation, ask you for your phone number and then follow it up. I can't count the times recently when I've walked into a social gathering where there were plenty of men, but for some reason they either didn't acknowledge me at all, or if on a lucky day I happened to be noticed and contact was made, there was this businesslike quality in their voices, as if I were a prospective client. The warmth is missing.

I remember when folks used to have house parties—not brunches—on Saturday nights, when all you had to do was call up someone and ask where the party was and you went, and other folks came and brought their friends, and we *all* talked and laughed and danced. Lots of times you spotted him or he spotted you, and he probably asked you to dance, and if you felt something special being in his arms or liked the tone of his voice or what he had to say after the song was over, then the night became much too short. There was a genuine, organic level of excitement and curiosity that has been replaced by a slew of superficialities: what you do for a living; how much you make; how you dress; if you'll make pretty babies. I miss the casual intimacy we used to have.

The other day I was driving with all the windows rolled down, blasting Anita Baker and Tracy Chapman back to back and I became grief-stricken. Every time I hear their songs I end up remembering the men I've loved, how good it was then, and just how empty my life often feels without a man in it now. I turned off the music because I got sick of feeling sorry for myself, and then I wondered, *Just when did things start to change?* By the time I pressed the garage-door opener and pulled inside, it was clear: I didn't have these problems when my life didn't have any real definition, when I wasn't making much money, when I hadn't published much of anything.

Last summer, an ex of mine said with some glee, "It's lonely at the top, isn't it, baby?" Although I'm certainly not at the "top," as he put it, I got his point. It is lonely "out here." But I wouldn't for a minute give up all that I've earned just to have a man. I just wish it were easier to meet men and get to know them.

Just last night, as I sat on the top step of this big beautiful house I bought in the desert and looked out at the mountains, the phone rang. It was my mama. "You sitting at home again?" she asked. I didn't feel like explaining how tired I was of going out just in hopes of meeting someone and how it always failed. I'm tired of the search and want someone to find *me*. I hung up and heard a woman on the radio singing something about "I thought we'd be happy ever after." I cried a little and then cried some more. I felt entitled. Then "Keep On Movin' " played. I felt a boost. I looked at all the space I have in my house and started laughing out loud. Hell, maybe I'll throw a party, invite all my friends from all over the country, get some of those blue lights and play some Smokey or Aretha or The O'Jays, and maybe, just maybe, I'll even spike the punch.

ACKNOWLEDGMENTS

Every effort has been made to contact copyright holders; in the event of an inadvertent omission or error, the editor should be notified.

"Beauty is Just Care . . . Like Ugly is Carelessness" by Toni Cade Bambara first appeared in *Essence*. Reprinted by permission of the author.

"The Negro Artist and Modern Art" by Romare Bearden is reprinted by permission of the Estate of Romare Bearden.

"The Ebony Flute" by Gwendolyn Bennett used with the permission of the National Urban League, Inc.

"How I Told My Child About Race" by Gwendolyn Brooks copyright © Gwendolyn Brooks. Reprinted by permission of the author.

"Our Literary Audience" by Sterling Brown used with the permission of the National Urban League, Inc.

"Georgia Sketches" by Sterling Brown first appeared in *Phylon*, third quarter, 1947. Reprinted by permission.

"Body and Soul" by Stanley Crouch is reprinted from *Notes of a Hanging Judge* by Stanley Crouch, published by Oxford University Press in 1990. Reprinted by permission of the author.

"The Dark Tower" by Countee Cullen used with the permission of the National Urban League, Inc.

"Billie Holiday's Strange Fruit" by Angela Davis first appeared in *Political Affairs*. Reprinted by permission.

"Bob's House . . . An Oasis of Civility" by William Demby first appeared in *Obsidian*.

"Africa and the American Negro Intelligentsia" by W. E. B. DuBois is from the *W. E. B. DuBois Reader*, edited by Meyer Weinberg. Reprinted by permission of HarperCollins Publishers, Inc.

"So the Girl Marries" by W. E. B. DuBois originally appeared in *Crisis Magazine*. Reprinted by permission.

"Impressions of the Second Pan-African Congress" by Jessie Fauset originally appeared in *Crisis Magazine*. Reprinted by permission.

"The Mind of the American Negro" by E. Franklin Frazier used with the permission of the National Urban League.

"Sékou Touré: A New Kind of Leader" by Hoyt Fuller is reprinted from *Journey to Africa*, published by Third World Press in 1971. Reprinted by permission.

"Cultural Strangulation: Black Literature and the White Aesthetic" by Addison Gayle is reprinted from *The Black Aesthetic* edited by Addison Gayle, published by Doubleday in 1971.

"Don't Have a Baby Til You Read This" by Nikki Giovanni is reprinted by permission of the author.

"The Negro Writer and His Roots: Toward a New Romanticism" by Lorraine Hansberry. Copyright © 1969, 1981 by Robert Nemeroff. All rights reserved.

"Negro Martyrs are Needed" by Chester Himes is reprinted by permission of Roslyn Targ Literary Agency, Inc., New York, New York 10011. Copyright © 1943, 1944, 1973 by Chester Himes.

"Where Are the Films About Real Black Men and Women?" by Ellen Holly first appeared in *The New York Times*. Reprinted by permission of the author.

"The Virgin Islands," "Senator Willis (Ohio) and the Virgin Islands," and "Congress and the Virgin Islands" by Casper Holstein used with the permission of the National Urban League, Inc.

"The Negro Artist and the Racial Mountain" by Langston Hughes first appeared in *The Nation* magazine, June 23, 1926. Reprinted by permission.

"Our Wonderful Society: Washington" by Langston Hughes used with the permission of the National Urban League, Inc.

"Negroes Without Self-Pity" and "The Rise of the Begging Joints" by Zora Neale Hurston first appeared in *American Mercury* in November 1943 and March 1945, respectively. Reprinted with permission of HarperCollins Publishers, Inc.

"Philosophy and Black Fiction" by Charles Johnson first appeared in *Obsidian*. Reprinted by permission.

"Self-Determining Haiti" by James Weldon Johnson first appeared in *The Nation* on August 28, 1920, September 4, 1920, September 11, 1920, and September 25, 1920. Reprinted by permission.

"The Ivy League Negro" by William Melvin Kelly first appeared in *Esquire*. Reprinted by permission.

"Inside These Walls" by Etheridge Knight is reprinted by permission of the author.

"The American Negro's New Comedy Act" by Louis Lomax first appeared in *Harper's Magazine*, June 1961. Reprinted with permission.

"Turning the Beat Around: Lesbian Parenting 1986" by Audre Lorde is reprinted from *A Burst of Light* by Audre Lorde, published by Firebrand Books, Ithaca, New York.

"Black Critic" by Haki R. Madhubuti is reprinted from *Jump Bad: A New Chicago Anthology* edited by Gwendolyn Brooks, published by Third World Press in 1971.

"The Redevelopment of the Dead Black Mind: The Building of Black Extended Family Institutions" by Haki R. Madhubuti is reprinted from *Enemies: The Clash of Races* published by Third World Press in 1978.

"Necessary Distance: Afterthoughts on Becoming a Writer" by Clarence Major is reprinted by permission of the author.

"Challenge to Negro Leadership: The Case of Robert Williams" by Julian Mayfield first appeared in *Commentary*. Copyright © 1961 by Julian Mayfield. Reprinted by arrangement with the estate of Julian Mayfield.

"A Death in the Family" by Kenneth A. McClane copyright © 1985 by The Antioch Review, Inc. First appeared in the *Antioch Review*, Vol. 43 No. 2 (Spring, 1985). Reprinted by permission of the editors.

"Once More the Germans Face Black Troops" by Claude McKay used with the permission of the National Urban League, Inc.

"Looking for Mr. Right," by Terry McMillan, is reprinted by permission of the author.

"On Becoming an American Writer" by James Alan McPherson is from *The Atlantic Monthly*, December 1978. Copyright © by James Alan McPherson. Reprinted by permission of Brandt & Brandt Literary Agents, Inc.

"Nordic Education and the Negro: A Curse or a Boon?" by E. Frederick Morrow used by permission of the National Urban League, Inc.

"I, Too, Have Lived in Washington" by Brenda Ray Moryck used by permission of the National Urban League, Inc.

"Identity, Diversity, and the Mainstream" by Albert Murray © 1970 by Albert Murray. Reprinted with the permission of Wylie, Aitken & Stone, Inc.

"Inside the Sit-Ins and Freedom Rides" by Diane Nash from Alain Locke, ed., *The New Negro* (New York: Atheneum, 1992).

"The Ethos of the Blues" by Larry Neal is reprinted with permission from *The Black Scholar*.

"What Their Cry Means" by Gordon Parks is reprinted with permission of the author.

"Art and Life" by Elizabeth Prophet is reprinted from *Phylon*, fourth quarter, 1940. Reprinted by permission.

"The Black Youth Movement" by J. Saunders Redding is reprinted from *The American Scholar*, Volume 38, Number 4, Autumn, 1969. Copyright © 1969 by The Phi Beta Kappa Society. Reprinted by permission of the publisher.

"What Jazz Means to Me" by Max Roach is reprinted with permission from *The Black Scholar*.